Seco Edition

SOCIOLO 2

for OCR

Stephen Moore   Dave Aiken   Steve Chapman

Approved publication

OCR

RECOGNISING ACHIEVEMENT

Collins

An imprint of HarperCollinsPublishers

William Collins' dream of knowledge for all began with the publication of his first book in 1819. A self-educated mill worker, he not only enriched millions of lives, but also founded a flourishing publishing house. Today, staying true to this spirit, Collins books are packed with inspiration, innovation and practical expertise. They place you at the centre of a world of possibility and give you exactly what you need to explore it.

Collins. Do more.

Published by Collins
An imprint of HarperCollins*Publishers* Limited
77–85 Fulham Palace Road
Hammersmith
London W6 8JB

Browse the complete Collins catalogue
at **www.collinseducation.com**

Reprint 10 9 8 7 6 5 4 3 2 1

ISBN 13: 978 0 00 720065 8
ISBN 10: 0 00 720065 X

British Cataloguing in Publication Data.
A cataloguing record for this publication is available from the British Library.

Commissioned by Thomas Allain-Chapman
Consultant editor Peter Langley
Project managed by Hugh Hillyard-Parker
Production by Sarah Robinson
Edited by Ros Connelly, Carol Schaessens
Cover design by Blue Pig Design
Internal design by Patricia Briggs
Typesetting by Hugh Hillyard-Parker
Figures typeset by Liz Gordon
Cartoons by Oxford Designers and Illustrators
Photo research by Suzanne Williams
Index by Indexing Specialists (UK) Ltd, Hove, UK
Printed and bound by Imago

Author dedications

Dave Aiken: As always, thanks especially to Maggie for her generosity of spirit, capacity for hiding resentment and seemingly limitless practical and emotional support and love. Thank you to the lovely Leo for reminding me that there is life beyond work. Thanks to the grown-up kids, Laurie and Amelia, for getting on with their own lives (congratulations to both for their excellent degree grades), to Steve Chapman and Pete Langley for their professional support, and to the Collins team for their patience.

In loving memory of Audrey Aiken (1930–2002)

Steve Chapman: For Fiona

CONTENTS

Sociology A2 for OCR

ACKNOWLEDGEMENTS

The publishers would like to thank the following for permission to reproduce photographs. The page number is followed, where necessary, by T (top), B (bottom), L (left), R (right) or C (centre).

Getty Images (1/AFP); Alamy (2/Janine Wiedel); Alamy (4/Robert Llewellyn); Still Pictures (19/Still Pictures); www.JohnBirdsall.co.uk (20/www.JohnBirdsall.co.uk); Photofusion (26L/Bob Watkins); Photofusion (26TR/Mo Wilson); Empics (26BR/Tony Harris/PA); Impact Photos (28/Steve Parry); Still Pictures (32L/Still Pictures); Getty Images (32R/Nicolas Russell); Rex Features (34/Image Source); Alamy (38TL/Septemberlegs); Corbis (38TR/Bernard Annebicque/Sygma); Alamy (38B); Corbis (39/Bassouls Sophie/SYGMA); Sally & Richard Greenhill (43); Rex Features (44/Dennis Stone); OnAsia Images (46/Gerhard Jörén); Punchstock (50/Digital Vision); Alamy (52R/David Sanger); Alamy (52L/Peter Usbeck); Getty Images (52B/Stephen Mallon); Punchstock (53/ image100); Alamy (60L/Profimedia.CZ s.r.o.); Corbis (60R/Reuters); Alamy (67/Barbara Ludman); Punchstock (68/Digital Vision); Getty Images (69R/Jon Gray); Rex Features (69); Courtesy of The Police Federation (74); Photofusion (75/Paula Solloway); Alamy (80/Crispin Hughes); John Walmsley Education photos (87); Sally & Richard Greenhill (88L); Sally & Richard Greenhill (88B); Sally & Richard Greenhill (88T); Mary Evans Picture Library (89); Still Pictures (95/Edward Parker); Punchstock (98/SW Productions); Photofusion (102TL/Stan Gamester); Sally & Richard Greenhill (102TR); Network Photographers (102B); Rex Features (106); Sally & Richard Greenhill (110); John Walmsley Education photos (113); Rex Features (116BL); Bubbles (116BR); Bubbles (116TR); Sally & Richard Greenhill (116TL); Corbis (117/Gabe Palmer); Sally & Richard Greenhill (118); Alamy (122L); Alamy (122R); Corbis (124/Jose Luis Pelaez, Inc.); Rex Features (128TL); Rex Features (128BL); Sally & Richard Greenhill (128TR); Sally & Richard Greenhill (128BR); Photofusion (129/Crispin Hughes); Sally & Richard Greenhill (133); Rex Features (135/Sipa Press (SIPA)); Photofusion (140CT); Sally & Richard Greenhill (140L); Rex Features (140CB); Rex Features (140R); Still Pictures (142); Empics (151); Sally & Richard Greenhill (157); Alamy (160); Rex Features (162); Science Photo Library (166/Oullette & Theroux/Publiphoto Diffision); Photofusion (169/P Solloway); Alamy (170L/Libby Welsh); Network Photographers (170R/Barry Lewis); Alamy (178/Peter Titmuss); London Aerial Photo Library (184/London Aerial); Rex Features (188); Alamy (190R/Paul Ridsdale); Corbis (190L/Poppy Berry); Science Photo Library (193); Empics (198/PA); Corbis (205/Joe Mahoney); Rex Features (206L/Consolidated News Pictures Inc); Rex Features (206CL); Getty Images (206CR/Peter Dazeley); Rex Features (206R/Richard Young); Corbis (207/Bettmann); Rex Features (208/Ray Tang); Getty Images (210T/David Teuma); Empics (210B/Sean Dempsey/PA); Science Photo Library (214/Chris Knapton); Rex Features (220L/Julian Makey); Rex Features (220TR/Dave Penman); Alamy (220BR/Janine Wiedel);

Getty Images (224/AFP); Alamy (231/Homer Sykes); Corbis (233/Bernard Bisson); Rex Features (234/ALF); Corbis (238L/Jeff J Mitchell); Empics (238R/Owen Humphreys); Getty Images (245); Getty Images (248/AFP); Punchstock (249/Flying Colours Ltd); Alamy (252/Janine Wiedel); Getty Images (253/Mark Renders); Alamy (254/The Photolibrary Wales); Redferns Music Picture Library (256/Jim Steele); Punchstock (257/Keith Brofsky); Photofusion (260/Mike Hoyle); Corbis (262/Helen King); Getty Images (267/Henry Guttmann); Alamy (270); Anti-Slavery International (274); Rex Features (276); Punchstock (283/Stockdisc); www.JohnBirdsall.co.uk (284TR/www.JohnBirdsall.co.uk); Alamy (284BL/Sam Appleby); Alamy (284BR/Robert Judges); Alamy (289/John Phillips); Alamy (292/geogphotos); Getty Images (297/Getty Images); Getty Images (300L/AFP); Rex Features (300R/Sipa Press); Punchstock (305/Ron Chapple); Alamy (308TL/Tim Graham); Getty Images (308TR/Getty Images); Punchstock (308BL/Flying Colours Ltd); Alamy (308BR/David Levenson); Alamy (313/profimedia); Rex Features (316); Photofusion (319/Paul Doyle); Photofusion (324/Maggie Murray); Photofusion (326/Jacky Chapman); Redferns Music Picture Library (332/Tony Russell); Punchstock (337/ImageState); Alamy (341/Sally and Richard Greenhill); Corbis (342).

Every effort has been made to contact copyright holders, but if any have been inadvertently overlooked, the publishers will be pleased to make the necessary arrangements at the first opportunity.

The organization of the book

The book is divided into a series of units, each linking into OCR A2-level modules. Each unit consists of a number of topics, which divide the unit into manageable parts. Each topic starts by building on your prior knowledge; it then goes on to provide all the knowledge you need, before giving you the chance to check your understanding and reinforce key concepts. There is then an opportunity to apply the knowledge by practising an exam-style question. Finally, there are research- and internet-based extension activities, creating opportunities to explore issues further.

Features of the textbook

Each topic contains a number of features designed to help you with learning, revision and exam-preparation. These are illustrated and described on the following two pages.

Sociology at A2-level: A guide for OCR candidates

The table below shows how the units in this book relate to the OCR A2-level specification. Turn to Unit 9: *Preparing for the A2 exam* (pp. 340–6) for more detail and an explanation of the courses and their assessment.

How this textbook covers the OCR A2 specification

Textbook unit	OCR A2
Unit 1 Sociological theories	Knowledge and understanding of sociological theories are essential for every A2 module, although they are not a separate part of the specification.
Unit 2 Crime and deviance	**A2 Module 2536** Power and control: Crime and deviance option
Unit 3 Education	**A2 Module 2536** Power and control: Education option
Unit 4 Health	**A2 Module 2536** Power and control: Health option
Unit 5 Social policy and welfare	**A2 Module 2536** Power and control: Social policy and welfare option
Unit 6 Protest and social movements	**A2 Module 2536** Power and control: Protest and social movements option
Unit 7 Applied sociological research skills	**A2 Module 2537** Applied sociological research skills. Also provides the content for **A2 Module 2538**: Personal study
Unit 8 Social inequality and difference	**A2 Module 2539** Social inequality and difference

Getting you thinking

The opening activity draws on your existing knowledge and experiences to lead in to some of the main issues of the topic. The questions are usually open and, although suitable for individual work, may be more effectively used in discussion in pairs or small groups, where experiences and ideas can be shared.

Main text

The important sociological concepts, debates and the latest research are all covered. A careful balance between depth and accessibility is maintained in every unit.

Defining power

gettingyouthinking

All of the people shown above exercise some sort of power.

1. What type of power do you think they exercise?
2. How do these types of power differ from each other?
3. Rank these individuals in hierarchical order on the basis of how much power they exert over your life.
4. How might Madonna's success have equipped young females today with more power than their mothers?

The above exercise should have shown you that power can take several different forms and can be exercised in a number of direct and indirect ways. For example, you are unlikely to meet George Bush or Osama Bin Laden, but they still exercise considerable power over your life. For example, terrorism on the streets of Britain in 2005 is seen by some as a result of the policies of these two individuals. In 2005, the power of the police to stop and search you, and even use violence on you, considerably increased as a result of these terrorist attacks. Similarly, it can be argued that if you are a female, Madonna's success impacts directly on your capacity to exercise power. You exercise more power than your mother because Madonna's career over the years has contributed to an acceptance of a wide range of activities for women that were once considered deviant.

Max Weber and power

In the most general sense, power refers to any kind of influence exercised by individuals or groups on others. For example, Max Weber defined power as the chance or probability of an individual or group of people imposing their will on others despite resistance, i.e. where A has power over B to the extent that A can get B to do something that B would not otherwise do. This conception of power – the **zero-sum view of power** – implies that the exercise of power involves negative consequences for some individuals and groups because it involves repression, force and constraint. Weber believed that such power could be exercised in a range of social situations.

---

focusonresearch

Simon Charlesworth (2002)
A phenomenology of working-class experience

Simon Charlesworth's study focuses on working-class people in Rotherham in Yorkshire, the town where he grew up. Charlesworth based his study on 43 unstructured, conversational interviews, though he clearly spoke to large numbers of people whom he knew socially. Many of the people to whom he spoke were male, but at least a third were female. Charlesworth finds class seeping into all aspects of life in Rotherham and the lives of the people are ones of suffering. The loss of a man's job, for instance, has a physical consequence because it can lead to fear and panic consequent on loss of earnings. Older people are faced with the difficulties of learning to cope with a changing world, and even his younger respondents are often surprised by the behaviour of those even younger than themselves. One of the main points is that miserable economic conditions seem to cause people to feel both physically and psychologically unhealthy.

Many of the workers experience a lack of identity and a sense of being devalued because of the loss of status accompanying the lack of paid work. Others see no point in education or qualifications because even if they acquire them, they are not able to obtain decent work. There are further problems for those who do go to university or college in that they feel out of place and excluded from the culture because they are not fully part of it. The culture of the working-class lad demands that he be respected.

Changes in the social climate have left people without a sense of belonging to each other or of understanding how the world is developing. They have little sense of hope in the future and worry for their children. This has been one of the direst results of the years of Thatcherism and recent government policies that have not fully challenged the views of the New Right. He claims people feel rage and suffering; unemployment is destructive to people because it forces them into poverty. The culture that develops is one of having to make do, or to buy only what is necessary. It is marked by social and spiritual decay. Language is marked by heavy use of swearing and often friendship is displayed through a form of public insult.

Adapted from Blundell, J. and Griffiths, J. (2002) *Sociology since 1995*, Vol 2, Lewes: Connect Publications

1. Identify two criticisms that might be made of Charlesworth's methods as described in the passage above.
2. What factors have caused working-class culture in Rotherham to be marked by a 'social and spiritual decay'?

Focus on research activities

A recent piece of interesting and relevant research is summarized, followed by questions that encourage you to evaluate the methods used as well as the conclusions drawn.

synoptic link

social inequality and difference

Trade unionism: an example of an OSM

It is useful when looking at the evidence for inequality in all its shapes and forms to consider the role of both old and new social movements.

OSMs such as socialism and trade unionism were very focused on social-class inequalities. They played a major role in the introduction of social policies that tackled poverty and class-based inequality in the UK, such as pensions, welfare benefits, the comprehensive education system and the National Health Service.

NSMs, on the other hand, are more likely to focus on single issues, such as human rights, animal rights, the environment and antiglobalization, as well as identity politics focused on women's rights, disability or sexuality – for example, gay rights have been promoted by groups such as Outrage and Stonewall. Interestingly, NSMs have tended to attract a very middle-class membership. Some sociologists suggest that NSMs are now more influential than OSMs because social class has declined as a source of identity in people's lives. However, survey evidence suggests that social class is still perceived by manual

workers as the major cause of their low socioeconomic position. Groups representing the poorest groups continue to play a key role in encouraging the government to see the eradication of poverty as a priority.

Synoptic links

Synopticity refers to the linking of each module in the course to the final synoptic module, *Social inequality and difference*.

Check your understanding

These comprise a set of basic comprehension questions – all answers can be found in the preceding text.

Check your understanding

1. Identify Giddens' four links between sociology and policy.
2. Give an example from the text which shows how sociology has influenced policy.
3. How can an awareness of disability issues influence policy?
4. Explain what evidence-based policymaking is.
5. Explain what is meant by sociology having been 'colonized' by government.
6. How do postmodernists view the relationship between sociology and policy?
7. If sociologists provide the 'facts' why don't governments always base their policies upon these facts?

Key terms

There are simple definitions of important terms and concepts used in each topic, linked to the context in which the word or phrase occurs. Most key terms are sociological, but some of the more difficult but essential vocabulary is also included. Each key term is printed **in bold type** the first time it appears in the main text.

KEY TERMS

Edgework – derives from Lyng. Refers to activities of young males which provide them with thrills, derived from the real possibility of physical or emotional harm (e.g. stealing and racing cars; drug abuse).

Ethnographic – form of observational research, in which researcher lives amongst, and describes activities of, particular group being studied.

Focal concerns – term used by Miller to describe key values.

Illegitimate opportunity structure – an alternative, illegal way of life that certain groups in society have access to.

Status frustration – according to Cohen, when young men feel that they are looked down upon by society.

Strain – term used by Merton and other functionalists to describe a lack of balance and adjustment in society.

Subculture – a distinctive set of values that provides an alternative to those of the mainstream culture.

Subcultural theories – explanations of crime and deviance focusing on the idea that those who deviate hold different values to the majority.

Techniques of neutralization – justifications for our deviant actions.

web.tasks

1. Find out about government policies on training at the Department for Education and Skills website at **www.dfes.gov.uk**

   Do you think that these will be successful? Do they represent real opportunities for young people, or might there be other motives behind the policies?

2. Look into the proposed reforms of 14 to 19 education at **www.dfes.gov.uk/14-19**

   Do you think these would have had more success in bridging the vocational academic divide than have past initiatives?

Web tasks

Activities using the worldwide web to develop your understanding and analysis skills. This feature also serves to identify some of the key websites for each topic.

Research ideas

Suggestions for small-scale research that could be used as class or homework activities. Many are suitable to use as the basis for Personal Studies.

research idea

- Your local police force will have an ethnic minority liaison officer (or similar title). Ask them to come to your institution to talk about their work and, in particular, stop and search. Before they come, get into small groups and sort out a list of questions – ideally, you should then e-mail them to the officer to base their talk on.

exploring changes in the class structure

Item A

Employment by gender and industry (UK)

Social class	MALES (%) 1981	MALES (%) 2001	FEMALES (%) 1981	FEMALES (%) 2001
Manufacturing	32	22	17	8
Distribution, hotels, catering and repairs	17	22	26	27
Financial and business services	11	19	12	18
Transport and communication	9	9	3	4
Construction	9	5	2	1
Agriculture	2	2	1	1
Energy and water supply	4	1	1	–
Other services	17	18	38	41
All employee jobs (millions)	13.2m	12.8m	10.0m	12.7m

Source: Short-term Turnover and Employment Survey, Office for National Statistics

Item B

<< Middle-class occupations are no longer as secure as they used to be. The drive to cut costs, boost labour productivity and reduce staffing levels which began in factories has spread through offices and has infected the management and professional grades. Mergers and takeovers have also sometimes led to site closures, rationalizations and redundancies, and sometimes to new businesses taking on new functions. For example, most banks and building societies have become multipurpose financial service providers. An outcome has been the creation of new management and professional specialisms, which have required staff to adapt. Many of these changes have been enforced rather than voluntary. Also, more of the moves have been sideways or downwards rather than upwards. As a result, we see less satisfaction and fulfilment in these jobs because the the 'onward and upward' view of management careers is now outdated.>>

Source: Roberts, K. (2001) *Class in Modern Britain*, Basingstoke: Palgrave

(a) Using only the information in **Item A**, identify two trends in employment in the UK between 1981 and 2001. (6 marks)

(b) Identify **two** factors that may have led to managers and professionals being less secure and satisfied in their work (**Item B**). (6 marks)

(c) Identify and explain **two** reasons why researching the upper class might be more difficult than researching the middle and working classes. (12 marks)

(d) Using your wider sociological knowledge, outline the evidence for the view that all social classes enjoy a similar standard of living. (22 marks)

(e) Outline and assess the usefulness of sociological explanations for the view that changes in the workplace mean that there are no longer distinct differences between non-manual and manual workers in the UK today. (44 marks)

Exploring ...

Data-response activities that follow the format of OCR A2-level exam papers wherever possible. They can be used to assess your progress at the end of each topic, as well as providing regular exam practice.

AT THE START OF EACH UNIT IN THIS BOOK, there is a table that matches the contents of the topics with the OCR A2 specification. If you look below, you will see that no table exists for this first unit on Sociological theories or perspectives. Is that a mistake or do these theories not appear in the specification? If they don't, then why are they included?

There is no separate section for sociological theory in the OCR A2 specifications. Yet it underpins much of the work you will do during your A2 Sociology course. Terms such as 'functionalist', 'Marxist', 'feminist', 'social action' and 'postmodern' appear in the specifications for the different units you will study and often in examiners' questions. So knowing something of the background to these theories is essential.

It is likely that you were introduced to the main sociological perspectives during your AS-level course and many of the theories discussed in this unit will be familiar to you. However, at A2 the examiners expect more depth in your knowledge as well as an awareness that there are divisions within theories as well as between them. For example, the writings of Karl Marx have been adapted by a series of sociologists during the 20th century to update them in the light of social changes. These writers are often described as 'neo-Marxists' because they have created 'new' versions of traditional Marxism.

The two topics in this unit are divided according to the times in which different sociological theories emerged. The first topic covers the perspectives that developed during the period of modernity – roughly between the beginnings of sociology after the industrial revolution and the 1960s and 70s. Some of these, such as Marxism and functionalism, offered overall explanations for the ways in which societies worked and saw them progressing through a series of stages.

The second topic focuses on contemporary sociological theories – those that have developed over the last 25 years. Perspectives such as postmodernism reject previous attempts to develop theories that cover all societies at all times; instead, they place at their centre the endless complexity and uncertainty of societies today. Whether these newer perspectives represent an accurate picture of the social world today or are taking sociology away from the big questions of social order and change that inspired the creation of the subject originally is something about which you will have to make up your own mind.

Sociological theories

Modernist sociological theories

gettingyouthinking

Use your knowledge from your AS-level studies to match each of the sentences below with the sociological theories they are most closely associated with. Explain your decisions.

1 Society is like a human body – every part of it helps to keep society going.

2 The ruling class benefits in every way from the operation of society while the workers get far less than they deserve.

3 Britain is a patriarchal society. Men generally have more power and prestige than women across a range of social institutions.

4 People have an active role in shaping social life. People do not feel themselves to be the puppets of society.

5 Society has experienced such major upheavals that the old ways of explaining it just won't work any more. We are entering a new sort of society.

6 Social behaviour is determined and made predictable by the organization of society.

If you are not sure, the possible answers are given below (upside down). The actual answers to the questions are provided at the end of the topic on p. 9.

Social structure theory – functionalism – feminism – Marxism – social action theory or interactionism – postmodernism

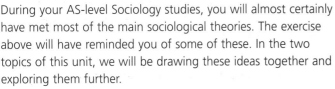
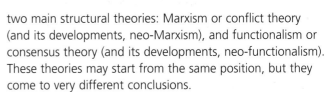

During your AS-level Sociology studies, you will almost certainly have met most of the main sociological theories. The exercise above will have reminded you of some of these. In the two topics of this unit, we will be drawing these ideas together and exploring them further.

This topic explores what are known as modernist theories. **'Modernism'** or 'modernity' refers to a period of history in 19th- and 20th-century Western societies that was characterized by major technological, social and political advances. It was within this period and driven by these ideas of rational, progressive thought that sociology was born. The main modernist approaches are Marxism, functionalism and **social action theory** (**interactionism**), and these have dominated sociology for much of the subject's existence.

Modernist theories are divided into two main perspectives – structural approaches and social action approaches:

- *Structural approaches* attempt to provide a complete theory of society. They begin their analyses from the 'top', by looking first at society as a whole and then working down to the individual parts, and finally to individuals. There are two main structural theories: Marxism or conflict theory (and its developments, neo-Marxism), and functionalism or consensus theory (and its developments, neo-functionalism). These theories may start from the same position, but they come to very different conclusions.

- *Social action theories* do not seek to provide complete explanations for society; instead they start by looking at how society is 'built up' from people interacting with each other. Quite how far 'up' they arrive is a matter of debate – though one version of social action theory, known as **labelling** theory, does seek to explain the construction of social rules.

Functionalism

Functionalism is closely associated with the work of Talcott Parsons. His work dominated US sociology and vied with Marxist-based approaches in Europe from the 1940s until the 1970s. Today, it still provides us with a useful and relatively simple framework for approaching the study of society.

Parsons' aim was to provide a theoretical framework that combined the ideas of Weber, who stressed the importance of understanding people's actions, and those of Durkheim, who emphasized the necessity of focusing on the structures of societies and how they function.

Parsons' starting point, taken from Durkheim, was the organic analogy – that is, he imagined society as similar to a living being that adapts to its environments and is made up of component parts, each performing some action that helps the living being to continue to exist. In the case of human beings, for example, our organs provide functions to keep us alive – for example, the heart pumps blood. It exists for that purpose and we would not have it if there was no need to pump blood. Other creatures have developed alternative methods of survival – for instance, reptiles do not have hearts as they do not pump blood around the body. Similarly, institutions exist, or don't, because of their functions for the maintenance of society.

Just as our bodies need to resolve certain basic needs in order to survive, so do societies. Parsons (1952) suggests that there are four needs (or **functional prerequisites**) that all societies have to overcome:

- *Adaptation* (the economic function) – Every society has to provide an adequate standard of life for the survival of its members. Human societies vary from hunters and gatherers to complex industrial societies.
- *Goal attainment* (the political function) – Societies must develop ways of making decisions. Human societies vary from dictatorships to democracies.
- *Integration* (social harmony) – Each institution in society develops in response to particular functions. There is no guarantee that the different institutions will not develop elements that may conflict. For example, in **capitalism** the economic inequalities may lead to possible resentment between groups. Specialist institutions therefore develop that seek to limit the potential conflict. These could include religion, notions of charity and voluntary organizations.
- *Latency* (individual beliefs and values) – The previous three functional prerequisites all deal with the structure of society. This final prerequisite deals instead with individuals and how they cope. Parsons divides latency into two areas:
  - *Pattern maintenance*: this refers to the problems faced by people when conflicting demands are made of them, such as being a member of a minority religious group and a member of a largely Christian-based society. In contemporary sociological terms, we would call this the issue of identity.
  - *Tension management*: if a society is going to continue to exist, then it needs to motivate people to continue to belong to society and not to leave or oppose it.

Pattern variables

For a society to exist, it must fulfil the functional prerequisites listed above. However, 'society' is a concept that does not exist in itself, but is rather a term for a collection of people. When Parsons says that a 'society' must resolve certain problems, what he actually means is that *people* must act in certain ways

that enable society to fulfil its needs and ensure its continuation. This is the role of culture, which emphasizes that members of society ought to act in particular ways and, in doing so, ensure that the functional prerequisites are met.

Parsons claims that in all societies there are five possible cultural choices of action. The different answers the cultures provide lead to different forms of social behaviour and thus different ways of responding to the functional prerequisites. It is within these five sets of options that all cultural differences in human societies can be found.

Parsons calls these cultural choices of action **pattern variables**. They are:

- *Affectivity or affective neutrality* – Societies can be characterized either by close interpersonal relationships between people, or by relationships where the majority of interactions are value-free. For example, a small rural society may well be based upon personal knowledge of others, whilst in a large, urban society people hardly know each other.
- *Specificity or diffuseness* – The relationships people have can be based on only one link or on many. We may know others simply as a teacher or a colleague, whereas in simpler societies, they may be cousin, healer, ceremonial leader and so on.
- *Universalism or particularism* – In contemporary societies, we believe that rules should apply equally to everyone (even if they don't), yet in many societies rules are not regarded as necessarily being applicable to all. Royalty, ethnic groups, religious leaders may all be able to behave differently.
- *Quality or performance* – This is linked to the previous pattern variable. Should people be treated according to their abilities or by their social position at birth?
- *Self-orientation or collectivity orientation* – Do societies stress the importance of individual lives and happiness or that of the group?

The answers that the culture of a society provides for these five pattern variables determines the way that people behave, which Parsons describes as social roles.

Criticisms within the functionalist approach

Robert Merton (1957) belonged to the same functionalist approach as Parsons. However, Merton was critical of some of Parsons' arguments and proposed two amendments to functionalist theory:

- Parsons assumed if an institution was functional for one part of society, then it was functional for all parts. But Merton points out that this ignored the fact that some institutions can be both **dysfunctional** (or harmful) for society, as well as functional. In particular, he cites the example of religion, which can both bring people together and drive them apart.
- Merton suggests that Parsons failed to realize the distinction between manifest (or intended) functions and latent (or unintended consequences) of these actions. Merton says that this makes any analysis of society much more complex than Parsons' simple model.

synopticlink

The functionalist analysis of inequality is most closely associated with the view of Davis and Moore (1955). Their work built on the ideas of Durkheim and Parsons to provide an explanation of why inequality exists in societies. They argue that inequality is actually functional because it provides a mechanism for ensuring that the most important positions in society are filled by the most talented and motivated people. Important positions require years of

social inequality and difference

education and training – and considerable sacrifice. Individuals are motivated to compete with each other and to make these sacrifices by the promise of high rewards of income and/or status when they finally take up their position.

Davis and Moores's work has provoked much criticism from both within and outside the functionalist perspective. A fuller account of these debates is provided on p. 293.

Criticisms outside the functionalist approach

Sharrock *et al.* (2003) argue that there are several main criticisms of functionalism, listed in the next column.

focus on research

Pete Saunders (1996)
Do the best reach the top?

Functionalist theory suggests that society is formed as it is because that is functionally the best way of maintaining its existence. This includes inequalities in class and status. Many critics argue it is not true that the most gifted achieve the top positions, but that success has more to do with inheritance and parental support. Saunders wished to demonstrate that in fact the best do achieve. He used evidence from the *National Child Development Study*, a longitudinal study of 17 000 children born in 1958 to see what their chances of social mobility were. In 1991, he had access to information on 6800 individuals from the study in full-time employment and concluded that occupational status was closely related to ability and effort. His results, therefore, support the functionalist argument.

Saunders, P. (1996) *Unequal but Fair? A study of class barriers in Britain*, London: IEA

1 In what ways do Saunders' results 'support the functionalist argument'?

- Functionalism overemphasizes the level of consensus in society. Apart from the simplest of societies, people have different values and attitudes within the same society.
- Parsons suggests that society is like an organism, yet this is not true. Organisms actually exist as biological entities, have a natural form and a natural life cycle. Society, on the other hand, is a concept, consisting of the activities of possibly millions of people. There is no natural cycle or natural form.
- Functionalists have real problems explaining social change. If, as Parsons claims, institutions exist to fulfil social needs, then once these needs are fulfilled, there is no reason to change them. Unless, therefore, there are some external changes which impact on the four functional prerequisites, societies should never change in form.
- Parsons seems to ignore differences in power. Yet differences in power can have strong impacts upon the form that society takes and whose interests it reflects.
- Finally, as interactionists point out, human beings in the Parsonian model of society seem rather like puppets having their strings pulled by all-powerful societies via pattern variables. Interactionists, postmodernists and late-modernists all combine to argue that people are much more 'reflexive', making choices and constructing their lives.

Neo-functionalism

Other writers following in the functionalist tradition include Mouzelis (1995) and Alexander (1985). Both these writers argue strongly for the overall systemic approach provided by Parsons. They dispute criticisms of Parsons that suggest he is not interested in how people act, and argue that with some modification Parsonian theory can allow for people to be 'reflexive', making decisions for themselves. These modifications to the theory also help explain social change.

Marxism

The second major sociological perspective that, like functionalism, aims to create a total theory of society by linking individual motivations and wider structural context is the tradition that has developed from Marxism. Marxism derives from the 19th-century writings of Karl Marx (1867/1973), who sought to create a scientific explanation of societies. His starting point was that the economic system of any society largely determined the social structure. The owners of the economic structure are able to control that society, and construct values and social relationships that reflect their own interests. Other groups in society, being less powerful, generally accept these values and social relationships, even though they are not in their interests.

Marx began by suggesting that all history can be divided into five periods or epochs, which are distinguished by ever more complex economic arrangements. The history of all societies begins with what he entitled 'primitive **communism**' – simple societies, such as hunters and gatherers, where there is no concept of private property and everything is shared. From that point it passes through the ancient societies such as that of Asia and Rome, through feudalism until it reaches the crucial stage of capitalism. According to Marx, capitalism would inevitably give way to the final stage of history, that of communism.

The Marxist model

Marx developed a theoretical model to describe the development of societies through these epochs. In each of the five epochs there is a particular economic structure (the economic base or **means of production**), which, except in primitive communism, is always controlled by a ruling class. This ruling class then constructs a whole set of social relationships (the **relations of production**) that benefit them and allow them to exploit all others who do not share in the ownership of the means of production. According to Marxist economic theory, the means of production are always advancing, becoming more complex and capable of producing greater wealth – nothing can stop this onward march of technology. However, the values that the ruling group create to benefit themselves tend to move much more slowly. Within each epoch, at the beginning, the values of the ruling class help technology move forward, but over time, because the values do not move as fast, they begin to get in the way of the move forward of technology – in fact, they actually impede it. At this point, a new, challenging group arises with values and ideas that would help the means of production advance, and, after a degree of conflict, they gain control of society and begin to

construct their own relations of production. A new epoch has started and the process begins again.

Criticisms of Marx

Marx's work has probably been subjected to more critical discussion and straight criticism that any other sociological theory. This is mainly because it is as much a political programme as a sociological theory. However, specific sociological criticisms of Marx's work include the following:

- The description of capitalism and its inevitable move towards a crisis has simply not occurred. Indeed, capitalism has grown stronger and, through globalization, has spread across the world.
- The polarization of people into a tiny rich minority and an extremely poor majority has also not occurred. There is huge inequality, but at the same time there has been a massive growth in the middle classes in society – the very group that Marx predicted would disappear.
- Capitalism changed significantly after Marx's death with the introduction of a range of health, pension, housing and welfare benefits, which were missing from Marx's analysis.

Neo-Marxism

The basic model of Marxist theory has provided the platform for an entire tradition of writing in sociology. His ideas have been taken up and developed by a wide range of sociologists, keen to show that the model, suitably amended, is still accurate. Neo-Marxists seek to overcome the criticisms listed above.

The extent of writings within the Marxist tradition is too great to cover in any detail, but three versions of neo-Marxism provide us with a fairly representative sample of developments.

The Frankfurt School

The Frankfurt School is associated with the works of three major neo-Marxists: Marcuse, Adorno and Horkheimer, all of whom were originally at Frankfurt University. In separate books,

s y n o p t i c link

The majority of Marx's work concerned inequality in capitalist society and the factors that would, in his opinion, lead on to a communist society. Within capitalism, there is a ruling class, or 'bourgeoisie', that owns the industry and commerce. All other people who work for a wage, no matter how prestigious or well paid, are members of the working class or proletariat. The bourgeoisie construct relations of production to their own benefit, including concepts of private property, wage labour and the justification of wide inequalities of wealth.

The majority of the population accept the inequalities of the system because of the way that dominant institutions, such as religion and education, justify the prevailing economic and social situation. Marx describes them as suffering from **'false consciousness'**. However, there always

s o c i a l i n e q u a l i t y and d i f f e r e n c e

is a degree of conflict between some groups in society who are aware of their exploitation and the bourgeoisie – Marx saw these people as being 'class conscious'. **Class consciousness** manifests itself in terms of strikes and political protest, all examples of **class conflict**.

Over time, capitalism will enter a period of crisis, caused by ever-increasing competition amongst industries, leading to fewer and fewer large employers – who are able to lower the wages on offer to such an extent that the majority of the population live in poverty. At such a point, with a tiny minority of very rich capitalists and a huge majority of relatively poor people, radical social change is inevitable. This change will usher in the final epoch of communism. Marx's views of social inequality are discussed further on pp. 293–4.

Marcuse (1964/1991), Adorno (1991) and Horkheimer (1974) criticized Marx for being an **economic determinist** – that is for believing society is mainly determined by the economic system. They argued that people's ideas and motivations are far more important than Marx ever acknowledged. Their critique contained three important elements:

● *Instrumental reason* – According to Adorno, Marx failed to explore the motivations as to why people accepted capitalism and the consumer goods it offers. Adorno suggests that it was wrong of Marx to dismiss this as simply 'false consciousness'. So people work hard to have a career and earn money, but quite why their aim should be to do this is never explored. Thinking in capitalism is therefore rational in terms of achieving goals themselves as long as the actual reasons for having those goals are not thought about rationally.
● *Mass culture* – Marcuse argued that Marx had ignored the importance of the media in his analysis. Marcuse suggested that the media play a key part in helping to control the population by teaching people to accept their lot and to concentrate on trivial entertainment.
● *The oppression of personality* – The third element of their critique of Marx focused on the ways that individuals' personality and desires are controlled and directed to the benefit of capitalism. Before capitalism, there was no concept of 'the work ethic'; people did the work that was required and then stopped. Capitalism, and particularly industrial production, needed people who accepted going to work for the majority of their lives and having little leisure. In the early stages of capitalism, therefore, pleasure and desire as concepts were heavily disapproved of – hence the puritan values of Victorian England. But in later capitalism, when it was possible to make money out of desires (and in particular sex), the desires were emphasized. Sex is now used, for example, to sell a wide range of products. According to the Frankfurt School, therefore, even our wants and desires are manipulated by capitalism in its own interests.

Althusser and the concept of relative autonomy

One of the most sociologically influential neo-Marxist approaches was provided by Althusser (1969), who argued that Marx had overemphasized how much the economic system drove society. Althusser suggested that capitalist society was made up of three interlocking elements:

● the economic system – producing all material goods
● the political system – organizing society
● the ideological system – providing all ideas and beliefs.

According to Althusser, the economic system has ultimate control, but the political and ideological have significant degrees of independence or autonomy. In reality, this means that politics and culture develop and change in response to many different forces, not just economic ones. Althusser used the term **relative autonomy** to describe this degree of freedom of politics and values. This may not at first seem very important, but what it suggests is that society is much more complex and apparently contradictory than in traditional Marxist analysis. So, the march towards a communist state is not clear, but is confusing and erratic.

Althusser also used this argument in his analysis of politics and the state. For Marx, the role of politics was simply to represent the interests of the ruling class, but for Althusser, the state was composed of two elements:

● **repressive state apparatuses** – organizations such as the police and the army
● **ideological state apparatuses** – the more subtle organizations including education, the media and religious organizations.

Both sets of apparatuses ultimately work for the benefit of capitalism, but there is a huge variation in the way the perform this task, with some contradictions between them.

Althusser's work provided a huge leap forward in neo-Marxist thinking, as it moved away from a naive form of Marxism (rather similar to functionalism), which simply said that everything that existed did so to perform a task for capitalism. Instead, while recognizing this ultimate purpose, Althusser highlighted the massive contradictions and differences between the various institutions of society.

Harvey: a late-modernist approach to Marxism

Some of the most recent and interesting sociological theorizing within neo-Marxism comes from the contemporary work of Harvey (1990). Harvey is extremely unusual for a neo-Marxist in that he develops Marxism within a postmodernist framework. As we see in the next topic, postmodernism is a movement that sees a fragmentation of society and a move toward image and superficiality in culture. Harvey argues that this move to postmodernity has been the result of economic changes occurring in the 1970s leading to the move away from manufacturing to commerce, media and retail as the main employers. Coupled with the development of globalization, these changes have presented massive challenges to capitalism.

According to Harvey, capitalism has, however, been clever in its responses to these economic changes, developing new sources of profit through the creation of whole new areas of commerce – what he calls **flexible accumulation** – in particular, through the manipulation of identity, with developments in fashion, travel and new forms of music. Globalization, too, has been utilized to produce cheap goods, which are given added value by being marketed in the more affluent nations.

At the same time, Harvey points out that there have been many real changes that have affected capitalism quite drastically. For example:

● National governments are less powerful than ever before in modernity, and so change now lies at the global, rather than national, level.
● Real political discourse within the traditional frameworks of government and political parties has been replaced by image politics, where what *appears* to happen is more important than what *actually* happens.

social inequality and difference

The work of the German sociologist Max Weber (1864–1920) accepted some of Marx's ideas but rejected others. Like Marx, he believed that social inequality resulted from a struggle for scarce resources in society. Although he agreed with Marx that this struggle was primarily concerned with economic resources, he also felt it could involve competing for status and political power.

Weber saw class in economic terms and agreed with Marx that the major class division is between those who own the forces of production and those who do not. However, he saw more differences in the middle and working classes than Marx, and did not agree that class conflict was inevitable.

Weber believed that economic class was not the only basis for the formation of groups keen to compete for scarce resources. Groups may form because their members share similar status in society. These may include occupational, ethnic and religious groups as well as those who share a particular lifestyle. There may be different status groups within one economic class.

Finally, Weber focused on political power. He identified groups which he called 'parties', whose members were concerned with influencing government policies to be more in line with the interests of their members. These groups might include trade unions, professional associations, the Automobile Association and the RSPCA.

Weber believed that it was important to understand the links between class, status and party to achieve a full understanding of social inequality. His ideas are discussed further on pp. 296–7.

Adapted from Haralambos and Holborn (2004)

- Social class as the dominant form of division between members of societies has been partly replaced by a range of divisions linked to gender, ethnicity, religion and even alternative political movements, such as the green movement.

Social action theories

According to social action theories, the way to understand society is not to start analysis at the top (analysing the structure of society, as Marxism and functionalism do), but to begin from the 'bottom' – analysing the way people interact with each other. Social action theorists do not set out to construct a grand theory along the lines of Marxism or functionalism, but are much more content to sketch out the rules of social interaction. These approaches (which are sometimes referred to as 'phenomenological approaches') explore the day-to-day, routine actions that most people perform. Interactionists (social action theorists/phenomenologists) set out to see how individuals actually *create* society through these routine actions.

Symbolic interactionism

Symbolic interactionism – the full name for interactionism – derives from the writings of Mead (1934) and then Blumer (1962) at the University of Chicago. Both Marxism and functionalism seemed to suggest that people were like marionettes controlled by the 'relations of production' or the 'pattern variables'. Instead, symbolic interactionism sees people as actively working at relationships, creating and responding to symbols and ideas. It is this dynamic that forms the basis of interactionists' studies.

The theory of symbolic interactionism has three core ideas: the symbol, the self, the interaction.

- *The symbol* – The world around us consists of millions of unique objects and people. Life would be impossible if we treated every separate thing as unique. Instead, we group things together into categories which we then classify.

Usually, we then give each group a name (which is a symbol). Examples of symbols include 'trees', 'women', 'gay men', 'terrorists'. You will immediately see that the symbol may evoke some feelings in us; they are not necessarily neutral terms. So, the world is composed of many symbols, all of which have some meaning for us and suggest a possible response or possible course of action. But the course of action we feel may be appropriate may not be shared by everybody.

- *The self* – In order for people to respond to and act upon the meanings that symbols have for them, they have to know who they are within this world of symbols and meaning. I cannot decide how I ought to behave until I know who I am and therefore what is appropriate for me to do in certain circumstances. This crucially involves us being able to see ourselves through the eyes of others. Blumer suggests that we develop this notion of the self in childhood and in particular in games playing. When engaging in a game with others, we learn various social roles and also learn how these interact with the roles of others. This brings us to the third element of interactionism, the importance of the interaction itself.

- *The interaction* – For sociology, the most important element of symbolic interactionism is actually the point at which the symbol and the self come together with others in an interaction. Each person in society must learn (again through games) to take the viewpoint of other people into account whenever they set out on any course of action. Only by having an idea of what the other person is thinking about the situation is it possible to interact with them. This is an extremely complex business – it involves reading the meaning of the situation correctly from the viewpoint of the other (What sort of person are they? How do they see me? What do they expect me to do?) and then responding in terms of how you see your own personality (Who am I? How do I want to behave?). There is clearly great scope for confusion, error and misunderstanding, so all people in an interaction must actively engage in constructing the situation, reading the rules and symbols correctly.

Goffman and the dramaturgical approach

Erving Goffman (1968) was heavily influenced by symbolic interactionism in his studies of people's interaction in a number of settings. Goffman's work, which has been called the **dramaturgical** approach, is based on similar ideas to symbolic interactionism in that he explores how people perceive themselves and then set out to present an image of themselves to others. Goffman suggests that people work out strategies in dealing with others and are constantly altering and manipulating these strategies. The basis of his ideas is that social interaction can best be understood as a form of loosely scripted play in which people ('actors') interpret their roles.

Evaluation of symbolic interactionism

Interactionism provides a rich insight into how people interact in small-scale situations. However, as a theory it is rather limited in scope and is as much psychological as sociological. Its main weakness lies in its failure to explore the wider social factors that create the context in which symbol, self and interaction all exist and the social implications of this. This means that it has no explanation of where the symbolic meanings originate from. It also completely fails to explore power differences between groups and individuals, and why these might occur.

web.task

Add to your notes and depth of knowledge on sociological theory by looking at sections of the following excellent website from Hewett School. Go to:

www.hewett.norfolk.sch.uk/CURRIC/soc/Theory1.htm

Some of these criticisms were answered by Becker (1963) and other writers within the labelling perspective. Labelling theory is explored on pp. 38–45 of Unit 2 (*Crime and deviance*), so we will deal with it only very briefly here. An offshoot of symbolic interactionism, labelling theory focuses on explaining why some people are 'labelled' as deviant and how this impacts on both their treatment by others and their perception of themselves. Becker specifically introduces the notion of power into his version of symbolic interactionism and demonstrates how more powerful groups are able to brand certain activities or individuals as deviant, with consequences that are likely to benefit themselves and harm those labelled deviant. One particular study which combines these is his analysis of the imposition and repeal of the laws on prohibition (making alcohol manufacture and sales illegal) in the USA in the early 20th century. He showed how powerful groups came together,

Check your understanding

1. What is the 'organic analogy'?
2. In your own words identify and briefly explain 'functional prerequisites'.
3. What are the 'means of production' and how do they relate to the 'relations of production'?
4. What does Harvey mean by 'flexible accumulation'?
5. Explain in your own words what the key difference is between social action theories and structural theories.
6. Explain any one criticism of interactionism.

KEY TERMS

Capitalism – term used originally by Marx to describe industrial society based on private ownership of property and businesses.

Class conflict – in Marxist analysis, the inevitable conflict arising between social classes based on their differing economic interests.

Class consciousness – in Marxist analysis, the awareness of belonging to a social class.

Communism – term used originally by Marx to describe societies where ownership of land, businesses and so on is shared and not privately owned.

Dramaturgical – refers to Goffman's version of interactionism, in which he sees people rather like actors in a play, with some of the script written and some ad-libbed.

Dysfunctional – in functionalist theory, activities or institutions which do not appear to benefit society.

Economic determinism – belief that the form of society is mainly determined by the economic system.

False consciousness – in Marxist analysis, the lack of awareness of being exploited.

Flexible accumulation – a term used by the neo-Marxist writer Harvey to explain how capitalism has continued to find new ways of profiting from people.

Functional prerequisites – in functionalist theory, societal needs.

Ideological state apparatuses – a term used by the neo-Marxist writer Althusser for those institutions which he claims exist to control the population

through manipulating values, such as the media.

Interactionism – shorthand term for symbolic interactionism.

Labelling – a theory developed from symbolic interactionism which was adapted for use in studies of deviance.

Means of production – in Marxist analysis, the economic structure of a society.

Modernism (modernity) – a period in history characterized by the belief that rational thought can be used to understand and explain the world.

Pattern variables – in functionalist theory, cultural choices as 'suggested' by the society.

Relations of production – in Marxist analysis, the social relationships in a society.

Relative autonomy – a term used by the neo-Marxist writer

Althusser to suggest that society is not determined as much as Marx suggested by the economic base.

Repressive state apparatuses – a term used by the neo-Marxist writer Althusser for those institutions which he claims exist to control the population through aggressive means, such as the police.

Social action theory – another name for symbolic interactionism; social action theories focus on how society is built up from people interacting with each other.

Symbolic interactionism – a theory associated with G.H. Mead that argues that people constantly work via symbols (language, writing, and so on) to construct society through the process of social interaction.

based on a mixture of genuine zeal and self-interest, to introduce the prohibition laws and he explores the consequences for society. It is, therefore, possible to apply symbolic interactionism to broader social situations and also to include power in the analysis.

Conclusion

In this topic, we have explored a variety of modernist theories, which provide two approaches to understanding society. The first is the structural approach utilized by Marxism and functionalism. This approach starts from the 'top' and works downwards and claims to provide a total theory of society. The second approach starts its analysis from the bottom and works upwards. This is the social action approach utilized by symbolic interactionism. Both approaches have strengths and weaknesses, which has led sociologists to take sides in a debate lasting more than 20 years. However, changes in society during the 1980s led many sociologists to be dissatisfied with both approaches. We move on to see the results of this dissatisfaction in the next topic.

researchideas

1 Conduct a small study of your own in which you explore the nature of symbolic interaction. How do people respond to symbols? Do they respond differently?

2 Choose a selection of 10 pictures and words. Ask a group of students what each picture or word means to them and what actions each one might suggest they do. You could include photos of almost anything, from an ashtray to a xylophone – the point is to explore what thoughts and actions everyday objects imply for people.

Answers to 'Getting you thinking'

1 Functionalism
2 Marxism
3 Feminism
4 Social action theory or interactionism
5 Postmodernism
6 Social structure theory

exploring modernist theories

Item A

The functionalist method sees any system as having needs or requirements. If the system is to survive, and to continue in more or less its current form, then these needs must be met in some way. The idea of need is quite simple. A human body needs food if it is to survive; it will die without this food. How then can functional analysis be used in the study of societies? The first step is to identify the needs of society. A society is assumed to be a relatively self-contained unit. As such it has many internal needs. These include the biological and psychological needs of its members and the needs to maintain boundaries and identity. However, many needs can only be met if the society draws on resources from the external environment, for example by producing food – the economic need. These theories see social systems as characterized by harmony and consensus. Marx's view, on the other hand, viewed conflict and division as normal features of all societies. Social systems develop over time as a result of contradictions that arise as a result of their economic systems.

Adapted from Fulcher, J. and Scott, J. (2003) *Sociology* (2nd edn), Oxford: Oxford University Press

Item B

The difference between society and nature is that nature is not man-made, but society is. While not made by any single person, society is created and recreated afresh, by participants in every encounter. It is indeed only made possible because every member of society is a practical social theorist who draws upon their knowledge and resources, normally in an unforced and routine way.

Giddens, A. (1993) *The New Rules of Sociological Methods,* London: Hutchinson

1 (a) **Identify whether the approaches to sociology discussed in Item A are structural or social action theories.** (2 marks)

(b) **Identify the two theories referred to in Item A.** (4 marks)

(c) **Identify and briefly explain two of the societal needs identified in Item A.** (4 marks)

(d) **With reference to Item A and elsewhere, briefly examine the reasons why some sociologists suggest that a structural perspective is the best way to understand society.** (10 marks)

2 **Assess the contribution of functionalism to an understanding of society.** (40 marks)

Feminist, late-modern and postmodern sociological theories

gettingyouthinking

Kate Rainbow, the 31 year old owner of a communications company, says ... 'It's only now becoming obvious, but the market in accessorizing is huge _ Swarovski crystal covers for Blackberries, laptop bags, phone fascias and phone charms. The potential to customize phones and gadgets will grow immensely. People, women in particular, want to make their gadgets individual in some way. Lee agrees: 'Increasingly the lines between jewellery or accessory and gadget are being blurred. You can literally wear your phone or your digital camera around your neck on necklaces designed for that purpose.'

Extract from Polly Vernon 'She's gotta have it', *The Independent Technology Magazine*, Issue 1, 31 July 2005

PRETTY IN PINK
The ultimate accessory for the swankiest fashionista, the Motorola Pink Razr oozes style and sophistication. Mirroring the design of the Motorola Razr, this limited-edition Pink Razr will be on every woman's wish list. Plus, its digital camera is ideal for capturing those festive moments, while its two-speaker sound system means you can party to your favourite Christmas tune.

Source: *Eve* magazine, December 2005 issue

1 **Look at the photograph and the text in the top right-hand corner. What do you think it and the main text below tell you about:**
   (a) **women today**
   (b) **modern technology?**

2 **Is this photograph illustrating fashion or technology? Explain your answer.**

3 **Does it matter if modern technology (mobile phones/MP3 players, etc.) is stylish or is what it looks like irrelevant?**

4 **Do you think that young people now live in a world transformed by technology?**

As we explored in Topic 1, sociology emerged during the period of modernity and the subject was shaped by the dominant ways of thinking of that time. Reflecting the natural sciences, sociology searched for a theoretical perspective that could explain how society was structured, how it functioned and how it changed over time. The theoretical approaches of Marxism and functionalism both claimed to do this, but by the 1970s, sociologists began to accept the fact that these major theoretical approaches simply failed to provide an adequate explanation for the existence of society. It was during this period that social action perspectives became popular, but for most sociologists these had limited value as they never claimed to provide the overarching theoretical frameworks that functionalism and Marxism had claimed. By the 1980s (and ten years earlier for feminists), sociologists were aware, through their studies of culture, gender, social class and the economy,

that enormous changes were taking place. The traditional 'modern' social characteristics of strong social classes, clear gender roles and party-based politics, all linked to an economic system based on industrial production, were no longer an accurate reflection of British (and most other Western) societies. Sociological theory was simply unable to explain these changes. It was in this vacuum that a new breed of theorizing emerged.

One group of writers believed that modernity had moved towards what is now commonly known as '**late modernity**' (or '**high modernity**' according to Giddens (1984)). A separate, much more radical group of theorists argued that society really had totally changed and had moved into a **postmodern** era – hence the term 'postmodernists'.

A third group of sociologists are feminists, who provide the bridge in sociological theorizing from structural and interactionist theories through to postmodern approaches.

Feminism

Gender roles and the issue of patriarchy are explored in a number of units in this book. Feminism as a social and political movement has been concerned to expose the inequalities that exist in the treatment of women in society. However, linked to this movement has been a development in theoretical approaches to explain the situation of women in society.

In many ways, feminism could be seen to be the battering ram that smashed down the closed doors of sociological thinking. Feminism initially emerged from a Marxist theoretical framework, but many feminist writers soon found this approach too constricting and moved beyond this towards more radical theories. Eventually, as we shall see later, feminism and one of its offshoots, 'queer theory', began to question some of the very basic concepts upon which sociology was built – in fact, the very notion of male and female came under attack.

Marxist feminism

The first writers in modern feminist sociology were heavily influenced by Marxist or critical sociological theories. **Marxist feminists** argued that the subordination of women to men was directly linked to their position within a capitalist society. Women benefited capitalism in two important ways:

- Women provided free domestic labour to capitalism. With the exclusion of women from paid employment in the early to mid-19th century, women remained at home to undertake 'housework'. By undertaking household tasks at no cost to the employers, women enabled men to work longer hours. By providing support, comfort and meals to the male, the workers were in a better state to work harder and more effectively.
- Women provided the means by which the next generation of workers (the children of the working class) were born and brought up – again, at no cost to the employers. Marxist feminists called this second function the '**reproduction of labour power**'.

Marxist feminists then simply adapted traditional Marxist theory to account for the situation of women. However, a number of criticisms of this approach emerged. One major criticism was that this approach was 'teleological', a way of saying that the

starting point of the argument was also the conclusion. Marxist feminists believed that there had to be a reason why women were excluded from the workforce and then undertook domestic labour for men. The answer had to be (given Marxist theory) linked to it benefiting capitalism. They therefore looked for the benefits to capitalism of women working at home and came to the conclusions we have just seen. Walby (1986) points out, for example, that one could just as easily have argued that women staying at home harmed capitalism. If women were employed, they would provide competition to men for work and wages could be lowered, for example. Also, as we now know, increased income from employment for women actually increases profits for capitalism through the improved spending power of women.

Radical feminism

However, perhaps the most important criticism provided by **radical feminists** such as Millett (1970) and Firestone (1971) was that patriarchy was to be found in most societies and was not necessarily linked to capitalism. According to these writers, men and women form 'sex classes', which have very different interests and levels of power. Men are the dominant class and use their power to exploit women in any way possible, not just economically. In a famous phrase, Millett argued that the 'personal is political', by which she meant that men exploit women through and in their personal, particularly sexual, relationships. These radical feminists focused on the issues of male/female emotional relationships, their sexual activities and the routine use of violence by men against women. It was within this tradition that claims were made that 'all men are rapists' – meaning that heterosexual sexual relationships were based upon imbalances of power in which women were effectively coerced into seeing sexual intercourse within male terms. Also, as we shall see later, the radical feminists argued that same-sex relationships between women were defined as being deviant, rather than a normal alternative.

Delphy (1977) takes a slightly different approach, emphasizing, like the radical feminists, the key role of the family. Like Marxists, however, she argues that the household is an important and underrated place of work. Indeed, she refers to 'housework' as 'the domestic mode of production' and argues that the work performed by women is highly productive, and yet men dominate within the household as

synoptic link

social inequality and difference

Sylvia Walby (1986, 1990) suggested that the radical feminist and Marxist approaches could be combined. In the **dual systems approach**, women were seen as being exploited both by capital and by men. Walby sees capitalism and patriarchy working together to exploit women.

She argues that there are two main forms of patriarchy – private and public – that have switched in importance over time. In the 19th century, patriarchy took a largely private form, with women isolated in the home and having no place in public affairs. Women were under the control of men within the family, subject to male views on sexual

relations and possible domestic violence. By the mid-20th century, women had begun to force their way into public life once again. However, a different form of patriarchy now developed, in which women were segregated into lower-paid and less prestigious employment. They were also heavily underrepresented in the more powerful positions in business and politics. Walby also pointed to the role played by cultural institutions, such as the media, in maintaining public patriarchy.

Walby's ideas are discussed further on pp. 329–30.

they have the economic power. Within the family, the views and wishes of men prevail. Some support for this position comes from studies of family poverty (Joseph Rowntree Foundation 1995) which indicate that even rates of poverty are much higher for women and children in families than for men, as men are more likely than women to spend money on themselves rather than the family.

Criticisms of feminist theory

Feminist theory has not gone uncriticized. A huge amount of debate has been generated by the approaches just explored.

First, some feminist writers, notably radical feminists seem to suggest that patriarchy occurs everywhere, though in different forms. Other feminists, such as the Marxist feminists, argue instead that patriarchy is located within capitalism. Clearly, the two positions are contradictory. Furthermore, if patriarchy is universal, then this might suggest that there is some biological basis for it. This is because one of the key tests used by sociologists to prove some form of behaviour derives from 'the social' is that the behaviour either varies across societies or simply does not exist in some. However, where some behaviour is universal, then sociologists usually accept that this is biological in origin. So, if patriarchy exists across all societies, as radical feminists believe, then it could be argued that the basis lies in biology. This has led some feminist sociologists to argue that whilst women are in the stages of advanced pregnancy, childbirth and child-rearing, they are more likely to be dependent on men. Patriarchy can therefore be linked to reproduction. However, other writers, such as Walby, strongly reject this biological basis.

More recently, Delamont (2001) amongst others, has pointed out that feminist writers seem to assume that women share a common position of exploitation. She points out instead that there are many divisions between women on grounds of income and social class, ethnicity and religion.

A further development of this argument, which leads us into contemporary theory on gender and patriarchy, is that the categories 'male' and 'female' are closed and oppositional. That is the theoretical position of early feminism: that men and women are *essentially* different. However, Robert Connell (1995) has developed a rather different approach to this and suggests that the traditional notion of two sexes with one sex dominating another is too simple.

Masculinities

Once pointed out, it could seem strange that feminism spent little or no time exploring the notion of masculinity. Indeed, ideas about men in much feminist writing fail to question any of the stereotypes about men, their behaviour and attitudes. Connell has made this exploration the heart of his work on patriarchy and theory. He points out that most feminist theorizing on patriarchy has been based on exploring what *structures* constrain women. Feminist theory then debates whether it is 'the family' or 'the economic system', or possibly both together. Connell suggests that it is more useful to look at how people actually behave – what he calls their 'practices' (behaviour). Connell's work bears a resemblance to Giddens'

theoretical approach, in that he sees the social world as consisting of how people behave. If they behave differently, then the supposed structures will no longer exist. The relevance to gender and patriarchy is that both men and women engage in practices that result in us believing in and actually having two sexes, male and female. The roles of women and the structure of patriarchy only exist within a framework of the practices of both men and women. Connell then sets out to disentangle what these practices are and how they maintain the roles of men and women.

According to Connell, society has a gender order: a hierarchy of different sorts of masculinities and femininities. At the top of the hierarchy is what he calls '**hegemonic masculinity**'. (The term 'hegemonic' refers to a dominant way of thinking and acting.) Heterosexuality is the foundation of hegemonic masculinity, but this also involves toughness, a degree of authority and the ability to unleash aggression. Idealized versions of this hegemonic masculinity as portrayed in the media often include sports and film stars. Most men cannot achieve this level of masculinity, but because it benefits men overall, they nevertheless support this ideal, engaging in what he calls '**complicit masculinity**'. There are other forms of 'subordinated masculinity', particularly that of 'homosexual masculinity', which is stigmatized and excluded by those who subscribe to hegemonic masculinity.

It is not just masculinity that is variable and hierarchical in form; a ladder of femininities exists too. Top of this ladder is 'emphasized femininity', which consists of 'sociability, compliance, desire for titillation and acceptance of marriage and child-rearing'.

The key point about Connell's work for feminism is that he brings a complexity to bear on the subject and an awareness that any analysis of gender has to realize that there are numerous different sorts of male and female behaviour. To speak about 'male' and 'female' as if they were two coherent and clearly distinguishable groups is mistaken. Instead, he emphasizes the importance of seeing a range of behaviours.

Late modernity and postmodernity

The distinction between late-modern and postmodern theory

Most students of sociology are understandably confused over the distinction sociologists make between late modernity (or 'high modernity') and postmodernity.

Perhaps the simplest way of dividing the two is that late modernity sees society as having changed and developed new aspects. The task of the late-modernist theory is to adapt more traditional theories of sociology.

Postmodern theorists argue that the whole 'sociological project' was part of a period of history – modernity – in which a particular way of viewing society developed that was closely related to a set of economic and social circumstances. We have now moved into a new set of economic and social circumstances based largely on communication and image, and therefore traditional sociological models have no value at all.

Late or high modernity

In the previous topic on modernism, we saw that the major split between theoretical approaches concerned which 'end' of human society sociologists emphasized. On one side of the argument were 'structural' theorists, such as Marx and Parsons, who, no matter what their differences, stressed that the only way to understand human behaviour was to locate it firmly within a dominant, controlling structural framework. Their theories suggested that people were manipulated by their cultures. On the other side, however, writers from the social action tradition, such as the interactionists, argued equally passionately that the only way to see society was as an abstract concept consisting of the interaction of individuals and groups. People were actively engaged in defining the world around them and then responding to these definitions.

By the 1980s, most sociologists began to tire of this argument and looked for ways out of it – there had to be a way to combine the two perspectives.

Giddens' structuration theory

The best known and currently highly influential attempt to resolve the argument can be found in the work of Giddens (1984). Giddens calls his theory **structuration theory**, which, as you can tell from the name, combines the concepts of structure and action.

Structure in Giddens' writings

The starting point for Giddens is that there is such a thing as structure, but only as a way to describe patterns of behaviour of people in society. Structure has no existence beyond this. He therefore rejects the traditional modernist notion of something 'out there' that determines how we behave.

> « Society only has form, and that form only has effects on people, in so far as structure is produced and reproduced in what people do. » (Giddens and Pierson 1998)

The simple way that Giddens himself explains this is by using the example of a language. We all use a series of words and grammatical rules to communicate. We may not know all the words and we may not be aware of what the rules actually are – we just use them. The language therefore exists, but it only does so because we make it exist through our use of it. Giddens calls this 'situation'. Bearing this in mind, structure consists of two key elements: *rules* and *resources*. Both of these combine to influence how we act:

- Rules are procedures we generally follow in everyday life. They can be formal or informal depending upon the situation and their perceived seriousness. Rules are not fixed and may be changed over time. (Again, think of his analogy with language.)
- People have differing resources – by which he is referring to access to different levels of power. These resources consist of material resources (such as wealth and income), symbolic resources (such as personal or job-related prestige), biological resources (such as physical attractiveness) and cognitive resources (such as intelligence or skills).

The structure of society, then, consists of people following rules, but different people have different resources to deploy in order to use or amend these rules.

Agency and the duality of structure

If structure is actually only people (or **agents** as Giddens calls them) behaving in certain ways, then why is it important? Because, Giddens argues, people draw from society the shared stock of knowledge that they use to guide their actions (that is, 'the rules' above). People therefore make society, but in doing so give themselves the rules and structure to guide them in their actions. This intimate two-way relationship is described by Giddens as the '**duality of structure**'.

Ontological security

Ontology refers to the issues to do with the reality of the world. According to Giddens, humans have a need for a sense of security, provided by rules and resources. As he puts it, people wish to believe that the 'natural and social worlds are as they appear to be'. He describes this situation as '**ontological security**'.

The desire for security and the existence of shared understanding helps people engage in regular patterns of social life. This regularity then helps society to remain stable.

Reflexivity and transformative capacity

In seeking ontological security, people are clearly seeking stability. However, we know that people also seek to bring about social change. You may also recall from your study of functionalism (see Topic 1, pp. 3–4) that there was a real problem with the theory in explaining social change. Giddens

synoptic link

social inequality and difference

Giddens suggests that in high modernity, social class, though still existing, has changed. He accepts that differences in power and resources exist, but he rejects the notion of social class as consisting of traditional cohesive groups (as suggested by Marxists) and argues that a much more complex pattern of stratification has replaced it. Social classes are no longer clearly hierarchical, but now overlap considerably. Social classes are also highly fragmented within themselves, with different groups existing within each class. Finally, people within classes are aware of the meaning and implication of their claims to belong to a class and are able to amend or change their self-image.

says that this change takes place because people are constantly monitoring their situation and their place in society, and assessing whether they match their idea of self-personality – this process is known as 'reflexive monitoring'. If people are unhappy or have an ideal of what they want, then they will actively seek change. Unlike in the Marxist or functionalist view, people are not puppets controlled by others. By engaging in reflexivity, people have a '**transformative capacity**' to change society.

As a way of illustrating his theory, Giddens points to Willis' *Learning to Labour* (Willis 1977) as an example of structuration, where the young lads' choices of action and the wider structure of society interact to provide an outcome that reflects both. Willis studied a group of 12 working-class boys for 18 months at the end of their schooldays, and then briefly into their first employment. The 'lads' showed little interest in studying, as they knew that their future lay elsewhere in unskilled physical labour. At school, they passed their time by 'having a laff' in lessons and making fun of teachers and the harder-working pupils ('ear 'oles'). Their choice of behaviour in school guaranteed their school failure, thus ensuring that the future that they knew would come about for them actually did come about. When they later entered these unskilled jobs, the skills of 'having a laff' and passing time enabled them to cope with the work. To summarize, the boys made choices based on their awareness of the wider society and their place in it. It is possible that they could have made other choices, but did not do so. The interaction of their choices and the 'reality' of society resulted in the outcome they predicted.

Criticisms of Giddens

Although Giddens' work is very influential and has attracted much attention, Cuff *et al.* (1990) question how original his ideas actually are. They suggest that these are really just a collection of ideas drawn from a variety of sources. Much of Giddens' work, they suggest, goes little further than the work of some of the founders of sociology. Many would argue that Giddens is merely updating Weber. Despite Giddens claiming the originality of ideas such as 'transformative capacity', sociologists such as Craib (1992) suggest that similar ideas can also be found in Marx, who once wrote 'men make their own history albeit not in circumstances of their own choosing' or even in Parsons' concept of pattern variables. Cuff and colleagues also suggest that Giddens' theory has rarely been successfully applied, least of all by Giddens himself. Giddens has used the example of Willis' work, yet Willis himself was working from a Marxist perspective.

Beck and the sociology of risk

Another sociologist pushing forward the boundaries of sociology within the 'late modernity' framework is the German sociologist Ulrich Beck. Beck (1992/1999) argues that a central concern for all societies today is that of risk and this concept has permeated the everyday life of all of us. There are three elements to Beck's thesis: **risk society**, **reflexive modernization** and **individualization**.

Risk society

According to Beck, modernity introduced a range of 'risks' that no other historical period has ever had to face. Note that Beck uses the term 'risk' in a very specific way. Throughout history, societies have had to face a wide range of 'hazards', including famine, plague and natural disasters. However, these were always seen as beyond the control of people, being caused by such things as God or nature. Yet the risks faced by modern societies were considered to be solvable by human beings. The belief was that industrialization, public services, private insurance and a range of other supports would minimize the possibility of risk. Indeed, the very project of sociology began with a desire to control society and minimize social problems.

However, in late modernity (which Beck calls 'advanced or reflective modernization'), the risks are seen as spiralling away from human control. No longer can risks be adequately addressed to the same standards as they were in modernity. Problems such as global warming and nuclear disaster are potentially too complex for societies to deal with.

Reflexive modernization

Late modernity, in which people are reflexive (as outlined in the work of Giddens), leads to their questioning how these risks became uncontrollable – that is, they begin to question the political and technological assumptions of modernity. People begin to be aware of risk and how they as individuals are in danger. They also seek ways of minimizing risk in all spheres of their lives. Risk and risk avoidance become central to the culture of society. This helps explain the growth in control of young children by parents trying to minimize any possible risk to them from cars, paedophiles and the material they watch on television. At the level of politics, there is a huge demand for governments to seek to identify and control every possible risk.

Beck argues that although it is the global political and technological 'system' itself that is the cause of the risk, there has been little attempt to confront the problems at this level; rather, risk avoidance operates at the personal and lower political levels.

Individualization

Beck links the move towards individualization with the move away from 'tradition' as an organizing principle of society. In modern societies, most aspects of people's lives were taken for granted. Social position, family membership and gender roles, for example, were all regarded as 'given'. In late modernity, however, there has been the move towards individualization, whereby all of these are now more open to decision-making. So, the background is of risk and risk awareness, and the foreground is of people making individual choices regarding identity and lifestyle as they plan their lives.

Criticisms of Beck

Beck has been criticized by a number of writers. Turner (1994) argues that Beck's distinction between 'hazard' and 'risk' is dubious. People have always faced 'risk' and have always sought to minimize this in whatever ways were available at the time, such as religion or some other means that we might now consider of little value. Nevertheless, there was an awareness that something could be done to combat the 'hazard'.

A second criticism derives from Beck's argument that the response to risk was largely individual. Yet a range of political movements have been formed to combat global warming, eradicate poverty in Africa and stop the spread of HIV/AIDS. These are all political movements which are international in scope and which indicate that people do believe that it is possible to control the risks that Beck identifies. In July 2005, a G8 summit took place at which the richest countries in the world committed themselves to seek to resolve poverty in Africa and global warming. A series of rock concerts was also put on across the world to draw attention to the need for the G8 leaders to tackle these issues. However, in defence of Beck, his writings have been so influential that one could equally reply that it is his work that has led people to believe it is possible to challenge global threats.

Elliot (2002) argues that Beck's work fails to recognize differences in power. Beck has suggested that the risk is spread across all groups in society and that differences in power are relatively unimportant. Elliot disputes this, suggesting instead that rich and powerful groups are able to limit risk and to have greater influence on the context in which the risk occurs.

Postmodernism

Postmodernist approaches to sociology emerged in the 1980s, providing a powerful challenge to traditional 'modernist' theories that sought to create an all-encompassing theory to explain society.

Two key postmodernist writers are Baudrillard (1980, 1994) and Lyotard (1984). Although Baudrillard had originally been a Marxist academic and his early works supported a neo-Marxist perspective, he later attacked the 'grand theories' such as Marxism and functionalism. Lyotard and Baudrillard dismissed these as merely **meta-narratives**, or elaborate stories, that effectively gave comfort to people by helping them believe there was some rational, existing basis to society. According to the postmodernists, sociological theory, like science and most other academic subjects, was simply a set of stories or narratives belonging to a specific period in history – the period of modernity, whose root lie in the 18th-century historical movement known as the Enlightenment. This was the term used by those at the time for an academic movement which applied rational thought to solving scientific, economic, political and social questions. It is difficult for us today to accept that it was really not until then that academics began to believe that the natural and social worlds were governed by forces or laws that could be uncovered through scientific endeavour. The more the laws of economics and science could be uncovered, it was argued, the greater would be the progress in ridding the world of hunger, disease, war and all other problems.

The Enlightenment gave birth, in turn to modernity, the period of 19th- and 20th-century history characterized by significant technological, social and political advances in Western societies. It was within this period that sociology was born. All of the founders of sociology were very strongly influenced by the idea that societies were progressing from traditional or premodern societies through to modern ones based on science, technology and the industrial process. This belief in scientific and social progress based on the application

KEY TERMS

Agents – Giddens' term for people.

Complicit masculinity – the idea that, although most men cannot achieve an 'ideal-type' of hegemonic masculinity, they still support it, since subscribing to this model benefits them.

Dual systems approach – a feminist approach which combined elements of radical feminism and Marxist feminism.

Duality of structure – the notion that people both make society and are strongly influenced by it.

Hegemonic masculinity – a term used by Connell to describe a dominant idea of how men ought to behave.

High modernity – Giddens' term for late modernity.

Hyperreality – the idea that we live in a world that is increasingly perceived and experienced via the media.

Individualization – a decline in accepting socially approved roles and an increasing stress on personal choices.

Late modernity – a term to describe contemporary society, in which the traditional social groupings, economic organization and culture have all changed so profoundly that traditional sociological explanations no longer hold true.

Marxist feminism – feminist theorists who base their theory on an adapted version of Marxism.

Meta-narratives – a postmodernist term used to refer to the structural theories of Marxism and functionalism.

Ontological security – the idea that people want to believe there is some reality beyond them in society, giving them the psychological confidence to engage in interaction.

Postmodern – a different perspective on contemporary society that rejects modernism and its attempts to explain the world through overarching theories. Instead, it suggests that there is no single, shared reality and focuses attention on the significance of the media in helping to construct numerous realities.

Radical feminism – feminist theorists (and usually political activists) who see men and male behaviour as the main cause of women's position in society.

Reflexive modernization – the idea that risk avoidance becomes a major factor in social organization.

Reflexivity – Giddens' term for the ability to perceive yourself as others see you and to create your own identity.

Reproduction of labour power – term used by Marxist

feminists to explain the role of women in helping capitalism to renew itself by producing new children and socializing them.

Risk society – Beck suggests that contemporary societies are best characterized as ones where people are aware that they face complex risks that are not open to individual control.

Sign-objects – Baudrillard's term for the notion that we buy items to express ourselves, not for their function.

Simulacrum (plural 'simulacra') – media images that have no basis in reality, but which people increasingly model their behaviour upon.

Structuration theory – the term used for Giddens' theory, which seeks to combine both structural and social action theories.

Transformative capacity – the ability of people to change society.

of rational thought was taken for granted until the 1970s when the postmodernist movement began to emerge.

At their simplest, postmodern theories argue that there cannot be any overarching theoretical explanation of society. This is because society exists only as a reassuring 'narrative'. In order to understand society as it is today, we need to have a deep awareness of the role of the media in creating an image of society that we seek to live out.

Lyotard

Lyotard argues that economic expansion and growth, and the scientific knowledge upon which they are based, have no aim but to continue expanding. This expansion is outside the control of human beings as it is too complex and simply beyond our scope. In order to make sense of this, to give ourselves a sense of control over it and to justify the ever-expanding economic system, grand narratives have been developed. These are political and social theories and explanations that try to make sense of society, which in reality is out of control. Marxism and functionalism and all other sociological theories fall into this category. The role of sociology, therefore, has been to justify and explain, while the reality of life for most people has simply not accorded with the sociological explanations. Lyotard sees contemporary society not as described in sociological theories, but as one that consists of isolated individuals linked by few social bonds.

Baudrillard

Baudrillard is also a critic of contemporary society. Like Lyotard, he sees people as isolated and dehumanized. Lyotard was particularly interested in the notion of knowledge as serving to justify the narratives of postmodern society. He argued that knowledge was a commodity that was bought and sold, and this buying was usually undertaken by big business and government. The result was that what people know about the world (knowledge) was that filtered through business and government. Baudrillard was also interested in the way that knowledge and understanding of the world are created, but his main emphasis was on the media.

The death of the social

Baudrillard notes that, in contemporary societies, the mass of the population expresses a lack of interest in social solidarity and in politics. The hallmark of this postmodern society is the consumption of superficial culture, driven by marketing and advertising. People live isolated lives sharing common consumption of the media, through which they experience the world. According to Baudrillard this can best be described as the 'death of the social'.

Media and the experience of the world

The media play a central role in the death of the social. Baudrillard argues that people now have limited direct experience of the world and so rely on the media for the vast majority of their knowledge. As well as gaining their ideas of the world from the media, the bulk of the population are also influenced in how they behave by the same media. Rather than the media reflecting how people behave, Baudrillard argues that people increasingly reflect the media images of how people behave. Of course, at some point, the two move so close together that the media do start once again to mirror actual behaviour, as actual behaviour 'catches up' with the media images.

Sign-objects and the consumer society

In the 21st century, a significant proportion of Western societies are affluent. Members of those societies are able to consume a large number of commodities and enjoy a range of leisure activities. However, Baudrillard argues that this consumption moves people ever further away from social relationships and ever closer to relationships with their consumer lifestyles. Yet the importance of objects in our lives has little to do with their use to us, but much more to do with what meaning they have for us. We purchase items not just because they are functionally useful, but because they signify that we are successful or fashionable. Consumer goods and leisure activities are, in Baudrillard's terms, '**sign-objects**', as we are consuming the image they provide rather than the article or service itself.

Hyperreality and the simulacrum

Baudrillard argues that, in modern society, it is generally believed that real things or concepts exist and then are given names or 'signs'. Signs, therefore, reflect reality. In postmodern society, however, signs exist that have no reality but themselves. The media have constructed a world that exists simply because it exists – for example, take the term 'celebrity'. A celebrity is someone who is defined as a celebrity, they do not have to have done anything or have any particular talent. It is not clear how one becomes a celebrity nor how one stays a celebrity. Being a celebrity occurs as long as one is regarded as a celebrity. Where a signs exists without any underlying reality, Baudrillard terms it a '**simulacrum**'. He believes that the society in which we live is now increasingly based upon simulacra. The fact that so much of our lives are based upon signs that have no basis or reality has led Baudrillard to suggest that we now live in a world of '**hyperreality**' – a world of image.

Check your understanding

1. **Explain the differences between Marxist feminists and radical feminists.**

2. **What does Connell mean by 'hegemonic masculinity'?**

3. **Why is social structure like a language, according to Giddens?**

4. **What is the difference between late-modern and postmodern theory?**

5. **What is a 'risk society'?**

6. **Explain in your own words the term 'hyperreality'.**

Criticisms of postmodernism

Postmodernism has been very influential in sociology and can probably claim to have generated the huge growth in the academic subject of media studies. However, its success has been more in pointing to the failure of grand theories rather than in putting anything positive in its place. Of course, postmodernists in reply would argue that that is precisely their point! Baudrillard or Lyotard, though they reject any idea of value-free sociology, do appear to be more critics of society than sociological theorists. Their work is shot through with value-judgements about what is real and what is worthwhile – so their dismissal of contemporary media-based society is less a sociological statement than a political one. Postmodernists have also been criticized for their failure to accept that not everything is hyperreal. People do live in reality, and some people have much greater access to goods and services than others.

exploring feminist, late-modern & postmodern theories

Item A

In modern societies self-identity becomes an inescapable issue. Even those who would say that they have never given any thought to questions or anxieties about their own identity will inevitably have been compelled to make significant choices throughout their lives, from everyday questions about clothing, appearance and leisure to high-impact decisions about relationships, beliefs and occupations. Whilst earlier societies with a social order based firmly in tradition would provide individuals with (more or less) clearly defined roles, in post-traditional societies we have to work out our roles for ourselves.

The mass media is also likely to influence individuals' perceptions of their relationships. Whether in serious drama, or celebrity gossip, the need for 'good stories' would always support an emphasis on change in relationships. Since almost nobody on TV remains happily married for a lifetime – whether we're talking about fictional characters or real-life public figures – we inevitably receive a message that monogamous heterosexual stability is, at best, a rare 'ideal', which few can expect to achieve. We are encouraged to reflect on our relationships in magazines and self-help books (explicitly), and in movies, comedy and drama (implicitly). This knowledge is then 'reappropriated' by ordinary people, often lending support to non-traditional models of living. Information and ideas from the media do not merely *reflect* the social world, then, but contribute to its shape, and are central to modern reflexivity.

Adapted from Gauntlett, D. (2002) *Media, Gender and Identity*, London: Routledge

Item B

The aspect of Madonna that strikes one most is her use of image. Martin Amis has said: 'She is the self-sufficient postmodern phenomenon ... A masterpiece of controlled illusion.'

In many ways Madonna is a victim of her own image. She lives totally within the artificially constructed reality of the image. She has become one with her Image. But she is not alone in that. This is central, not just to Madonna, but also to our culture. Think of the tremendous developments of our technological age and the impact of the media that has come with it; image is dominating more and more of our lives. And increasingly we see the blurring of image and reality, the fusing of the public and private persona, the dissolving of the differences, so that everything becomes image, and reality disappears. In politics, style replaces substance, in commerce packaging and promotion replace quality, in society how you look replaces who you are, form replaces content, the outer presentation replaces the inner reality.

Adapted from the website of 'Facing the Challenge' (www.facingthechallenge.org/madonna.htm)

1 (a) Identify **two** examples of significant choices people now have to make about their lives (**Item A**). (2 marks)

(b) Identify the **two** theoretical approaches associated with **Items A and B**. (4 marks)

(c) Identify and briefly explain the terms 'self-identity' and 'reflexive' (**Item A**). (4 marks)

(d) With reference to **Items A and B** and and elsewhere, briefly examine how late-modern and postmodern approaches argue that the media can affect identity. (10 marks)

2 Assess the contribution of feminism to our understanding of society. (40 marks)

THIS UNIT BEGINS by considering the social nature of crime and deviance. It then goes on to explore a simple but quite frightening idea – that everyone is essentially self-seeking and that we are all quite capable of breaking the law. The only reason why we do not is that early in our lives we learn a variety of values and beliefs that prevent us breaking the law. The idea is frightening because it presents society as a very fragile thing, with the potential to collapse at any time if social control fails.

If the first topic illustrates the significance of learning how to behave, then the second one discusses the more formal mechanisms of control and punishment that exist.

Topic 3 explores what are often called 'strain' theories. It examines the way that people strive to make a success of their lives, but how if various hurdles are put in their way by society, then they may turn to crime or deviance.

Labelling theory is covered in Topic 4. This explores how certain groups create deviance by defining particular activities as deviant and what the consequences are for those who engage in these activities. Labelling theory focuses on the power of groups such as the police to label others as deviant. However, Marxists – the subject of Topic 5 – argue that it is the structure of capitalist society itself that creates deviance by blocking off the chances of the majority of the population. Crime arises from this unfairness.

At this point we pause to draw breath, in Topic 6, by exploring the patterns of crime and how we measure

these, before moving on to slightly more applied sociological theories.

One of the key issues that Marxism (and to some extent labelling theory) raised was the way in which the crimes of the powerful tend to be ignored. We return to these issues in Topic 7, where we explore white-collar and corporate crimes to see why they occur and what explanations there are for the criminal justice system's relative lack of interest in this area.

Topic 8 explores the ways in which gender is related to crime. As well as looking at the explanations put forward for low levels of female crime, we also examine the growth in interest in the notion of 'masculinity' – this has become a particularly important concept in recent years in understanding youth offending.

Topic 9 takes us into a very controversial area: the relationship – if any – between ethnicity and crime. In this topic, we try to clarify the facts and provide explanations drawn from our earlier theoretical studies for these facts.

Topic 10 brings us up to date with the latest criminological ideas. The impact of postmodernism has been powerful in criminology and, above all else, there has been an attack on the idea that one can explain offending in rational, logical terms. Postmodernists have turned to emotions and impulses in their search for an explanation, and we examine these exciting ideas here.

OCRspecification	topics	pages
Social nature of crime and deviance		
Defining crime and deviance, their social construction and relativity.	Topic 1 examines definitions of key terms, along with the social construction and relativity of crime and deviance. Topic 4 on labelling theory is also highly relevant, and the theme recurs in a range of contexts throughout the unit.	20–25 38–45
Social reactions to crime and deviance and their consequences, including the role of the mass media.	Social control issues are the focus of Topics 1 and 2 and social reaction is a key factor in the discussion of labelling theory in Topic 4. The role of the mass media in the creation of 'moral panics' is also covered in this topic.	20–31 38–45
Patterns of crime and victimization		
Measuring crime and the fear of crime; criminal statistics, self-report and victim surveys.	Covered in Topic 6.	52–59
Patterns of crime and victimization by social profile; social class, ethnicity, gender, age and region.	The broad patterns are explained in Topic 6. Social class is covered primarily in Topics 5 and 7, ethnicity in Topic 9, gender in Topic 8, and region in Topic 6.	46–79
Theories and explanations of crime and deviance, e.g. structuralist, interactionist, feminist and realist approaches.	Structuralist approaches include Marxism (Topic 5) and strain theory (Topic 3). The interactionist approach is represented by labelling theory in Topic 4. Feminist views are covered in Topic 8, and left and right realism in Topic 10.	32–51 66–73 80–85
Power, control & the problem of crime		
Agents of social control and the role of law, the police, the criminal justice system, penal systems, the mass media and the state, criminalization and control.	Social control is covered at length in Topics 1 and 2. The criminal justice system, the police and so on are discussed in the context of labelling (Topic 4), Marxism (Topic 5) gender (Topic 8), ethnicity (Topic 9) and realism (Topic 10).	20–31 38–51 66–85
Solutions to the problem of crime, the relationship between sociology and social policy.	Each theory has its own implications for solving the problem of crime and these are covered in the appropriate topics. Particular social policies and their relationship to sociological thinking are discussed in separate sections throughout the unit. The discussion of realism in Topic 10 is particularly relevant.	80–85

Crime and deviance

Deviance and control theories

gettingyouthinking

The 'Social Responsibility' Quiz

1 You see someone chucking a used McDonald's burger carton on the pavement. Do you:

 a tell them to pick it up?
 b ignore it?
 c pick it up yourself and put it in the nearest bin?

2 You pass a homeless person begging in the street. Do you:

 a give them some money (at least 20p)?
 b pretend you haven't seen them?
 c tell them to 'get a job'?
 d say to them that you won't give them money, but you will buy/give them a cup of coffee and a sandwich if they want it?

3 A particular student is always being made fun of by other students in your year. Do you:

 a join in bullying them?
 b feel sorry for the person, but do nothing?
 c confront the bullies?
 d tell a tutor or person in authority?

4 You see a purse on the dance floor of a club. You pick it up and it contains just under £50. Do you:

 a hand it in to the manager of the club?
 b take the money?
 c leave the purse and the money on the floor?

Scoring

Q1	a 5	b 1	c 2	
Q2	a 2	b 1	c 0	d 5
Q3	a 0	b 1	c 5	d 3
Q4	a 5	b 0	c 1	

Results

7 or less: You are a horrible person, aren't you! Change to Business Studies immediately!

8–12: You are someone who cares about other people – shame you don't actually do anything about it!

13–19: Caring, helpful and, perhaps, a little bit smug!

20: Very impressive, but a bit dangerous. Learn to keep your mouth shut and not to confront people, if you wish to live to an old age.

1 Why do you think people don't commit more crimes and deviant acts?

2 Do you think people are 'naturally' greedy and selfish, or do you believe that they are essentially generous and good? Explain why.

3 What do you think would happen if we had fewer police and fewer laws? Would chaos be the result or would people control themselves?

The activity above should have encouraged you to think about the reasons why most of us do or don't conform to the laws of society. What exactly is controlling us and how successful is it? You will probably remember from your AS course that all societies attempt to control the behaviour of their members. Modern societies use both **informal social control** (through agencies such as the family) and **formal social control** through organizations such as the police and military.

However, before we look at **control theories**, we need to be clear about the key terms in the unit.

The topic begins by looking at the problems sociologists experience when trying to define '**deviance**' and '**crime**'.

After that, there is a discussion of functionalist approaches to crime and social control, and Marxist views of social control. Marxist perspectives on crime and deviance are the subject of Topic 5.

Defining deviance

Most people accept that deviance can take many forms, but exactly what sorts of behaviour are deviant is far less clear. Some people may see using animals for the testing of medical treatments as a normal and accepted part of life, while others may condemn it. What is more, some discussions of what is deviant – for example, the debate about 'assisted suicide' – bring out strong moral and political views, and groups will call on the government or the police or the courts to 'do something about it'.

So how can we identify what exactly constitutes deviance? Clinard and Meier (2001) identify four types of definition: statistical, absolutist, reactivist and normative.

Statistical definitions

According to **statistical definitions**, deviance occurs when behaviour is very different from the average. What most people do is normal and what a minority do is deviant. The problem here is that a small minority of people have never drunk alcohol, never broken the law or never had premarital sex, but few of us would describe these actions as deviant. This definition fails to take into account the actual meaning of deviance.

Absolutist definitions

Absolutist definitions focus on values. As you learnt during your study of *The Individual and Society* at AS-level, values are the guiding principles through which we live our lives, such as the importance of protecting human life. If everyone in a society agrees on these basic and fixed principles, then clear guidelines for behaviour are created. In certain societies, for example, there is almost universal acceptance of a set of guiding values provided by the teaching of religious leaders or by sacred texts such as the Bible or the Koran. Deviance occurs when people move away from these established guidelines.

This kind of definition has some links with the functionalist perspective, which sees societies as based on shared values (see the section on 'Functionalist approaches' on pp. 22–23).

Absolutist definitions can be criticized for the following reasons:

- They fail to take into account variations in values between different subcultures in complex modern societies.
- They ignore power relations in society, which mean that some groups are able to impose their values and standards of behaviour on others. This point of view has connections with Marxist and other critical views, which are discussed in Topic 5.

Reactivist definitions

From a **reactivist** viewpoint, deviance is simply a label applied to some acts and the people responsible for them. If there is no social reaction, then there is no deviance. So deviance is not about an act itself, it is about the way others judge that act. As Becker puts it:

<< *The deviant is one to whom that label has successfully been applied; deviant behaviour is behaviour that people so label.* >> (Becker 1963)

This definition of deviance provides the basis for what has become known as 'labelling theory'. Labelling theory focuses on the ways in which agents of social control, such as the police, label certain activities and groups, and the effect that labelling has on the individuals and groups labelled as 'deviant'. In many cases, it actually increases the likelihood of future deviance. Labelling theory is discussed at length in Topic 4.

The problem with reactivist definitions is that they fail to provide any explanation of what it is about certain acts that cause others to view them as deviant. Surely some acts such as violent assault and theft do violate agreed standards of behaviour?

Normative definitions

Normative definitions are based on the idea of deviance as behaviour that contradicts social norms. You will have learnt during the AS course that a norm is an accepted way of behaving or thinking in a particular situation, and that norms are learnt during the process of socialization. Norms can vary over time, between societies, and between groups within a society – for example, swearing is accepted as normal in some groups but would be thoroughly disapproved of in a church service. When norms are not followed, social disapproval will often occur and negative sanctions may result. Deviance can be defined as the violation of a norm, which causes social disapproval and may provoke negative sanctions.

This definition reflects modern societies more effectively than absolutist definitions. It takes into account the constantly changing nature of deviance and can be combined with a reactivist definition to provide a fuller picture of the process of creating deviance. However, it doesn't tell us why some norms are considered more serious than others and fails to locate the origin of norms in power relations. For example, feminists would argue that many norms about the behaviour of women and men are based on patriarchal power relations.

Defining crime

Crime can be defined simply as activities that break the law in any particular society. All modern societies have laws and social institutions, such as the police and courts, to enforce those laws.

However, the relationship between crime and deviance is not so simple. Some crimes, such as speeding, are seen as acceptable by many people, while some acts are considered deviant but are not crimes – attempted suicide, for example.

Hagan (1994) identifies three factors that affect the way in which acts of crime and deviance are perceived.

- *Social agreement* – This refers to the extent to which the public believe that a law or norm benefits society. If people cannot agree on how strongly a norm or law should be enforced, then it is likely to be weak. Laws and norms regarding animal rights may fall into this category.

- *Social response* – The seriousness of a crime or act of deviance can be determined by the strength of the sanctions it provokes. The use of cocaine as pain relief for upper-class women was seen as acceptable in the early 20th century but is now treated much more seriously. It has a higher level of social response.
- *Social harm* – This refers to the level of harm that a particular act causes. Some crimes, such as burglary, harm people in a very direct way, whereas the use of illegal drugs is seen by many as a 'victimless' crime.

These three factors are all high in the case of serious crimes but are not always linked. For example, corporate crimes (those committed by businesses in the pursuit of profits) cause huge monetary and other forms of damage, but the social response is often minimal. (This is discussed further in Topic 7.)

The academic study of crime is known as **criminology**.

The relativity of deviance

Norms are **relative**: they change over time, and they vary between different societies and different groups. This means that deviance, too, is relative and culturally determined. The following points demonstrate the relativity of deviance using the example of cocaine.

Definitions of deviance vary in the following ways.

- *Historically* – Ideas about acceptable behaviour change over time. Cocaine was widely prescribed by doctors in the USA up until the 1880s and the example of its use by upper-class women shows how it was still acceptable in some circles in the early 20th century.
- *Between different societies* – The Peruvian government allows limited cultivation of coca, the plant from which cocaine is derived. Coca is an accepted part of life in the Andes for many inhabitants, where it is often taken as a traditional remedy to stave off hunger and altitude sickness.
- *Between different groups within a society* – Modern societies are characterized by the existence of a range of social groups known as 'subcultures'. These can be ethnic groups, religious groups, age groups, regional groups and so on. Each subculture – whilst probably sharing a majority of norms and values with others – may develop some of its own. For example, the illegal use of drugs such as cocaine is a norm among the members of some subcultures.

Deviance as a social construction

Something is socially constructed if it is the result of the culture and/or structure of a society. It should be clear to you already that deviance is socially constructed; the rest of the unit explores this process in detail. The following points summarize some of the key ways in which deviance is socially constructed.

Social creation of norms and laws

Norms change over time as a result of social activity. Particular groups may argue for change, whilst others want to maintain things as they are. Troyer and Markle (1983) illustrate this process using the example of cigarette-smoking. At the end of the 19th century, smoking was widely condemned as it was associated with heavy alcohol consumption amongst working-class immigrants and prostitution amongst women. It became acceptable – even desirable – after the First World War as increasing numbers of people took up the practice. However, attitudes changed again during the 1960s, as the link between tobacco and various illnesses was covered in the media. By the 1990s, smoking bans were restricting the use of cigarettes in public places – it was becoming increasingly deviant again.

Powerful groups are the most likely to be able to define what is normal and deviant. Further discussion of these processes occurs throughout the unit, but particularly in Topics 4, 5 and 7.

Social causes of deviance

There are also approaches to understanding the causes of deviance that are not sociological. Some explanations may focus on biological factors, emphasizing the genetic make-up of some individuals. Psychological explanations may look to early childhood experiences or inadequate personality development. These approaches tend to see deviance as a form of illness that can be treated. However, the evidence to support them is, at best, sketchy.

Sociological accounts of the causes of deviant behaviour focus on the learning of deviant roles and behaviour through the values and norms of particular groups in particular societies. Some values and norms support conformity whilst others support deviance. In other words, deviant roles and behaviour are socially constructed. Many of the topics in this unit provide explanations of this process.

Social reactions to deviance

Deviance can actually be created by the reactions of others to particular behaviour. As we have seen, labelling theory is based on the view that deviance only exists because certain acts are viewed by some people as deviant. The social process of labelling may involve agents of social control, such as the police, social workers and teachers, as well as the mass media (who play an important role in the labelling process), drawing attention to particular issues, defining particular people and acts as deviant and creating 'moral panics' (see pp. 42–3).

Functionalist approaches to crime

Durkheim

For Durkheim, crime and deviance were central to understanding how society functions. He identified two different sides of crime and deviance for the functioning of society:

- a *positive* side that helped society change and remain dynamic
- a *negative* side that saw too much crime leading to social disruption.

The move towards late-modernity and the linked stress on the importance of the individual as opposed to the family or community, have had a significant impact on a wide variety of social issues. Some sociologists suggest that this has led to a decline of informal social control from the family and community, which has helped contribute to the increase in offending rates. Others have pointed to the way that the decline of traditional working-class communities has impacted on voting patterns. The Labour Party, which once could rely on the solid support of equally

solid working-class inner-city communities, is now aware that voting is based on a much wider range of issues, in which the interests of the individual are important. However, if the decline in community has occurred for the majority White population, for many ethnic-minority groups the sense of community has not shown similar levels of decline and remains strong, possibly as a defence mechanism in the face of racism and social exclusion.

Positive aspects of crime

According to Durkheim (1982, originally 1895), crime – or at least a certain, limited amount of crime – was necessary for any society. He argued that the basis of society was a set of shared values that guide our actions, which he called the **collective conscience**. The collective conscience provides a framework with boundaries, which distinguishes between actions that are acceptable and those that are not. The problem for any society is that these boundaries are unclear, and also that they change over time. It is in clarifying the boundaries and the changes that a limited amount of crime has its place. Specifically, Durkheim discussed three elements of this positive aspect:

- *Reaffirming the boundaries* – Every time a person breaks a law and is taken to court, the resulting court ceremony and the publicity in the newspapers, publicly reaffirms the existing values. This is particularly clear in societies where public punishments take place – for example, where a murderer is taken out to be executed in public or an adulterer is stoned to death.
- *Changing values* – Every so often when a person is taken to court and charged with a crime, a degree of sympathy occurs for the person prosecuted. The resulting public outcry signals a change in values and, in time, this can lead to a change in law in order to reflect changing values. An example of this is the change in attitude towards cannabis use.
- *Social cohesion* – Durkheim points out that when particularly horrific crimes have been committed, the entire community draws together in shared outrage, and the sense of belonging to a community is thereby strengthened. This was noticeable, for example, in the USA following the September 2001 attacks on the World Trade Center.

The negative aspects of crime: anomie

While a certain, limited amount of crime may perform positive functions for society, according to Durkheim, too much crime has negative consequences. Perhaps his most famous concept was that of '**anomie**', which has been widely used and adapted in sociology. According to Durkheim, society is based on people sharing common values (the collective conscience), which form the basis for actions. However, in periods of great social change or stress, the collective conscience may be weakened. In this situation, people may be freed from the social control imposed

by the collective conscience and may start to look after their own selfish interests rather than adhering to social values. Durkheim called this situation anomie. Where a collapse of the collective conscience has occurred and anomie exists, crime rates rocket. Only by reimposing collective values can the situation be brought back under control.

Durkheim's concept of anomie was later developed and adapted by Merton, who suggested Durkheim's original idea was too vague. Merton (1938) argued that anomie was a situation where the socially approved goals of society were not available to a substantial proportion of the population if they followed socially approved means of obtaining these goals. According to Merton, people turned to crime and deviance in this situation. Turn to Topic 3, p. 33 for more details on Merton's theory.

Hirschi: bonds of attachment

Hirschi (1969) was also heavily influenced by Durkheim's ideas. Durkheim's concept of anomie suggests that if people are not 'controlled' by shared social values, then they look after their own short-term interests without concern for others. This led Hirschi to turn around the normal sociologist's question of 'Why do people commit crime?' to another, equally intriguing one: 'Why *don't* people commit crime?'

By asking this question, Hirschi focuses sociologists' attention on what forces hold people's behaviour in check, rather than what propels them into crime. Hirschi argued that criminal activity occurs when people's attachment to society is weakened in some way. This attachment depends upon the strength of the **social bonds** that hold people to society. According to Hirschi, there are four crucial bonds that bind us together:

- *Attachment* – To what extent do we care about other people's opinions and wishes?
- *Commitment* – This refers to the personal investments that each of us makes in our lives. What have we got to lose if we commit a crime?
- *Involvement* – How busy are we? Is there time and space for law-breaking and deviant behaviour?
- *Belief* – How strong is a person's sense that they should obey the rules of society?

The greater a person's attachment to society, the lower their level of crime.

Crime and control: a Marxist perspective

Marxist writers such as Scraton (1997) argue that crime is an indication of class conflict and that as most social control benefits capitalism, the decline of control might be bad for capitalism, but good for radical social change. On the other hand, left realists such as Matthews and Young (1992) see the decline of community controls and the resulting increase in crime and antisocial behaviour as directly harmful for the working class.

Box (1983) has suggested another way of looking at social control and crime. He agrees with the more right-wing writers in that it is release from social control that propels people into committing crime. However, his starting point is not that people are basically bad, but that capitalist society controls and exploits workers for its own ends – or, rather, for the benefit of the ruling class. When people are released in some way from direct control, then they are much more likely to commit crime because they see the unfairness of the system. Box argues there are five elements that can weaken the bonds of capitalist society and propel individuals into committing crime:

1 *Secrecy* – If people are able to get away with a crime, especially by not having it noticed in the first place, then they are more likely to attempt to commit crime. According to Box, this is one key factor that helps explain why white-collar crime (such as fraud) takes place. The majority of white-collar crime simply goes undiscovered.
2 *Skills* – Most people are simply unable to commit serious crime. Minor offending and antisocial behaviour generally occurs on the spur of the moment. Serious crime, however, requires planning and knowledge, plus the skill to carry it out.
3 *Supply* – Even knowledge and skill are not enough by themselves. The potential offender must also be able to obtain the equipment and support to be able to carry out most serious crimes. For example, a burglar needs a 'fence' to whom to sell his (burglary is an overwhelmingly male activity!) stolen goods.
4 *Symbolic support* – All offenders must have some justification for their activities. An excellent example of this are the techniques of neutralization suggested by Matza (Sykes and Matza 1962) (see Topic 3).
5 *Social support* – Coupled with the idea of symbolic support is the need for others who share similar values to support and confirm the values that justify crime. (Social support is another way of describing a subculture – see Topic 3.)

Box is therefore suggesting that control theory can be applied from a left-wing perspective and is not necessarily conservative in its approach. For Marxists, social control operates for the benefit of the ruling class and once this is weakened, it is possible that people will turn to crime to express their disillusionment with capitalism. **Critical criminologists** still take this position and argue that criminals are engaging in a form of political act in their crimes; if they were made more aware of the circumstances that propelled them into crime, they might well act in a more politically conventional way.

Conclusion: control theories

Control theories all share the belief that crime is the result of the restraints imposed by society being weakened. The overall approach is a very conservative one which stresses that were it not for forces of social control such as the family then people would resort to their natural greedy and unpleasant selves.

The only, rather maverick, exception to this argument is Box's version of critical criminology, which agrees that crime results from the weakening of social control – but sees social control as a bad thing, operating for the benefit of the ruling class.

Check your understanding

1 **What are the differences between reactivist and absolutist definitions of deviance?**
2 **Explain how deviance is relative, using your own example.**
3 **In what ways can deviance said to be socially constructed?**
4 **Give two examples of the positive aspects of crime according to Durkheim.**
5 **Explain how crime could be negative for society.**
6 **Explain the terms: 'attachment', 'commitment', 'involvement', 'investment' and 'belief'. Use an example of your own to illustrate each term.**
7 **What five elements can weaken the bonds of society, according to Box?**
8 **What theoretical approach influences Box's writing? How?**

research idea

Conduct your own social-responsibility survey, as described in the 'Getting you thinking' at the start of this topic (on p. 20). Compare your findings with the ideas in this topic.

web.task

Your local authority will have a Community Safety Partnership detailing the activities your area is engaging in to tackle crime.
Visit it and see what initiatives are being carried out. You can find the address at www.homeoffice.gov.uk/crime-victims/
A typical example of a Community Safety Partnership site is www.safercambs.org/
Try that first for ideas if you wish.

Absolutist definitions – the view that deviance occurs when people move away from universally agreed guidelines.

Anomie – term, first used by Durkheim, to describe a breakdown of social expectations and behaviour. Later used differently by Merton to explain reactions to situations where socially approved goals were impossible for the majority of the population to reach by legitimate means.

Collective conscience – term used by Durkheim to describe the core, shared values of society.

Control theories (of crime) – competing explanations of the way in which social control operates in society.

Crime – activities that break the law of the land and are subject to official punishment

Criminologists – social scientists who study crime.

Critical criminology – work of criminologists influenced by Marxist thinking.

Deviance – the violation of a norm, which causes social disapproval and may provoke negative sanctions.

Formal social control – the regulation of social behaviour through groups and organizations set up for that purpose, such as the police.

Informal social control – the regulation of social behaviour by agencies of socialization, such as the family.

Normative definitions – the view of deviance as behaviour that contradicts social norms, causing social disapproval and possibly provoking sanctions.

Reactivist definitions – view of deviance as a label applied by other people to some acts and the people who commit them; if there is no social reaction, there is no deviance.

Relativity – the idea that such things as norms and ideas about what constitutes deviance change over time, and vary between different societies and between different groups

Social bond – in control theories, the forms of social control that prevent people acting in a deviant way.

Statistical definitions – the view that deviance occurs when behaviour is very different from the average.

exploring deviance and control theories

Item A

For those on the right politically, the family is the key institution in generating law-abiding behaviour. Here discipline is learnt, impulse curbed, respect instilled and the grounding of civilized behaviour laid down in childhood to inform the adult throughout the future trials of life. But for those on the left, the focus on the family is seen as a 'red herring'. Thus it is argued that the type of family is irrelevant to the causes of crime and delinquency. Instead, the causes lie in the wider forms of social injustice, such as economic deprivation and racism.

Adapted from Young, J. (1999) *The Exclusive Society*, London: Sage

Item B

Control theory has been most often used to explain 'ordinary' youth offending, rather than other forms of crime. Nelken, for example, suggests that it is a 'weak candidate for explaining white-collar crime', because such individuals appear to have substantial commitments. However, the theory has been used extensively in attempting to account for the low rates of crime by women compared to men, with the argument presented that women have a much stricter socialization pattern and are much more heavily controlled in society in terms of acceptable actions. Control theory relies very heavily upon family-based explanations of crime, where people are, or are not, adequately socialized into the conformity. However, this raises questions about what values families ought to bring their children up to believe. In fact, the whole approach (apart from its Marxist version) can be criticized for ignoring wider factors beyond the media and the family in creating the conditions for crime.

Adapted from Coleman, C. and Norris, C. (2000) *Introducing Criminology*, Cullompton: Willan, pp. 67–9

(a) Using **Item A**, identify what those 'on the left' see as the basic cause of crime. (1 mark)

(b) Identify and briefly explain **two** ways in which control theory might explain the low rates of crime by women as opposed to men **(Item B)**. (8 marks)

(c) Identify **three** ways in which deviance might be linked to the family. (9 marks)

(d) Identify and explain **two** reasons why crime might be beneficial to society. (12 marks)

Exam practice

(e) Outline and assess control theories of crime. (60 marks)

Power, control and the problem of crime

gettingyouthinking

1 How does each of the photographs illustrate an example of the way people are controlled?

2 What different types of control are being used?

3 Who is responsible for the control?

Social control

Societies can only exist if there is a degree of order and predictability, otherwise there would simply be chaos. This order is unlikely to arise spontaneously and so societies (or the more powerful members of society) develop methods to control those who fail to stick to the rules. They do so by a mixture of:

- **informal social control** based upon a range of **sanctions** such as negative comments, looks and exclusion
- **formal social control** based upon organizations that exist solely or partly to enforce 'order'.

The exact mixture between informal and formal control mechanisms used depends upon the type of society. For example, smaller and less complex groups with strongly shared

values might rely more upon informal methods, whilst large, complex and multicultural societies generally have to use specific organizations.

Approaches to understanding social control

Sociologists agree that all societies need to impose control on their members, in order to ensure predictability of behaviour and stability. Beyond this, however, there is considerable dispute as to who benefits from this control and about how to explain the form that state control takes.

- Functionalist writers see the criminal justice system as operating to look after the interests of society as a whole. Without control and punishment, society would collapse into a state of anomie.

- At the other extreme, Marxist writers argue that the criminal justice system operates for the benefit of the ruling class. The law and the police are the agents of the ruling class and exist to eliminate opposition.
- Foucault (1977) put the issue of social control at the centre of his writings, and argued that any society is a battleground between competing interests. A key to gaining power is to control what is considered to be knowledge, and the methods of gaining knowledge. Those who succeed in having their definition of knowledge accepted gain power, and in turn will use it to enforce their view of the world. The criminal justice system and, particularly, the forms of punishment used play a crucial role in this by imposing the values of the powerful.

Changes in social control

Stan Cohen (1985) has suggested a number of key themes in the changing nature of the formal control in Western societies.

Penetration

Historically, societies had fairly simple forms of control – with the state passing a law which was then haphazardly enforced by whatever authorities existed at the time. However, Cohen argues that increasingly the law is expected to penetrate right through society, and that conformity and control are part of the job that schools, the media and even private companies are supposed to engage in.

Size and density

Cohen points out the sheer scale of the control apparatuses in modern society, with literally millions of people working for the state and other organizations involved in imposing control – and over a period of time, millions having that control imposed upon them. For example, approximately one-third of all males under 30 have been arrested for a criminal offence. Cohen points out that the range of control agencies is increasing and as they do so, they 'process' ever larger numbers of people.

Identity and visibility

Cohen argues that control and punishment used to be public and obvious, but more recently there has been a growth in subtle forms of control and punishment. Closed-circuit TV (CCTV), tagging, legally enforceable drug routines for the 'mentally-ill' and curfews are all part of an ever-growing and invisible net of control. He also notes that the state has handed over part of its monopoly of controlling people to private organizations. So there has been a growth in private security companies, doorstaff at nightclubs and even private prisons.

Feeley and Simon: actuarialism

Feeley and Simon (1992) have suggested another element of contemporary social control, which they term **actuarialism**. The term derives from the insurance industry, where the people who work out the chances of a particular event happening (and therefore the price to charge for insurance) are known as actuaries (see Topic 10, p. 83) for further material on actuarial approaches). Feeley and Simon argue that in contemporary society, the stress of social control has changed from controlling deviant behaviour, to controlling potentially deviant people. Therefore, agencies of social control work out just who is likely to pose the greatest risk of deviance and then act against them. The police patrol working-class and ethnic-minority areas, whilst the private security companies police the shopping developments, monitor people who enter and exclude the potential troublemakers – defined as the poor, the young and the homeless.

They extend Cohen's argument that other agencies as well as the state are involved in social control and argue that there is a process of **privatization** of social control agencies, with increasingly large amounts of surveillance and control of the population by for-profit companies.

Finally, Feeley and Simon argue that there has been a growth in new, more subtle forms of social control which they call **disciplining**, where people are helped in a non-coercive way to do what the organization wants. For example, Disney controls tens of thousands of people each day in its parks in subtle ways, but this still results in people behaving as Disney wishes.

Davis: Control of space

Davis, in the very influential book *City of Quartz* (1990), studied Los Angeles and pointed out that there is an increasing division between the affluent, living in segregated and (privately) protected areas, and the areas lived in by the poorer majority. The role of the police is to contain the poor, segregating them in their ghettos.

Punishment

A key component of social control is punishment. This has therefore been an area of interest to sociologists, as it helps us to resolve in whose interests social control operates and also to tell us about the extent and nature of formal social control.

Durkheim

As discussed in Topic 1, Durkheim (1960) believed that societies could only exist if the members shared certain common, core values, which he called the collective conscience. These common values dictate acceptable behaviour. However, many other values exist too which have rather less general acceptance (ranging from ones generally accepted to those that are openly in dispute). Thus a system of law exists that places a boundary line, clearly marking where actions go beyond the boundary of acceptance into behaviour generally regarded as so deviant as to be illegal.

According to Durkheim, when people act against societal values, then generally a system of informal control operates to coerce them back into conformity. However, if their behaviour crosses the boundary into illegal behaviour, then the formal system of punishment is generally used. Durkheim argued that both the basis and the form of punishment changes over time. In less complex, **mechanistic societies**, punishment is based on **retribution** – by which savage penalties are imposed upon the wrongdoer in order to demonstrate society's abhorrence at the breaking of the commonly shared values. The punishment will be both public and physical in nature – so people are executed, mutilated and branded.

As societies develop and become more complex (**organic societies**), then the punishment shifts away from public punishment to imprisonment, and the aim of the punishment is more to force the person to make amends for their wrongdoing. He called this '**restitutive** law'.

Marxist approaches

Early Marxist writers such as Rusche and Kircheimer (1939) agree with the general Marxist argument that laws reflect the interests of the ruling class. However, they go further and argue that the forms of punishment also reflect their interests. As these interests change, so do the forms of punishment. Rusche and Kircheimer claim, for example, that slavery was an early form of punishment because of the need for manual labour, and that in feudalism the state used physical punishment as there was slightly less need for labour, but the peasants still needed to be repressed. With the arrival of capitalism, the prisons served the useful purposes of, first, training workers in the disciplines of long hours of meaningless work (for example, the treadmill) in poor conditions, and, second, of mopping up the unemployed.

To support this argument, they pointed out that in times of high unemployment the prison population expands and then contracts in periods of high employment.

Foucault

Foucault's claims (1977) that punishment has changed over time – from being physical and public to **internalized** and intense – echo the work of Durkheim. In pre-industrial societies, offenders were seen as having offended against God or the rulers and were savagely punished for this. Punishment was conducted in public in order to warn others. However, over time – as crime came to be seen as deviance from accepted codes of behaviour – the aim of punishment was to bring the person back into society and under control. This is achieved by having 'experts' whose job it is to make sure that the person fully internalizes the need to conform. The punishment has shifted then from the body to the mind of the offender.

focusonresearch

Hough and Roberts (2004)

Perceptions of youth crime

Mike Hough and Julian Roberts conducted research on the public's attitudes to youth offending and the punishment of young people. They inserted additional questions into the Office of National Statistics Omnibus Survey (the ONS is a government department) which takes place every month (on a variety of subjects). Researchers have to buy a block of questions and Hough and Roberts bought a block of 30 questions. Government trained interviewers then conducted interviews with 1692 people aged over 16. The block of questions took about 15 minutes to complete. The response rate was 67 per cent.

Hough and Roberts found that people have negative perceptions about youth and the youth justice system. People believe that offending rates are higher than they are in reality and than young people are unlikely to be punished.

Hough, M. and Roberts J.V (2004) *Youth Crime and Youth Justice Public Opinion in England and Wales*, Oxford: Blackwell

1 Suggest reasons why respondents believed that offending rates are higher than they really are.

The police

The main agency responsible for the enforcement of social control is the police force. They are the arm of the state whose role it is to maintain public order and to enforce the law. There are two main positions in understanding the relationship of the police to society: the consensual approach and conflict policing.

The consensual approach

A consensual approach sees the police as having a close relationship with the local area being policed, and the role of the police force being to represent the interests of the majority of law-abiding people, defending them against the minority of offenders. Police officers are drawn from the community and reflect its characteristics. Individual offenders are caught as a result of complaints made by the community.

Policing and forms of social control have been examined closely by neo-Marxist sociologists, who are interested in finding out the ways that capitalist society controls the proletariat. Althusser (1971) argues that the police are part of the 'state apparatus' that seeks to control the population by repressive methods. However, he also argues that there are other agencies involved in social control that perform the same task, but using a more positive approach; these include education, religion and the media. Therefore, rather than seeing the police as being a distinctive control group, they should be seen as part of a broad spread of 'repressive state apparatuses'.

In a similar manner, Hall *et al.* (1978) argue that most people provide little trouble to capitalism as they are sucked into it through employment, mortgages and consumption. The role of the police is to deal with those on the margins of society – young people, ethnic minorities, street-life people and such like – who pose a threat because they are not bonded into capitalism.

Conflict policing

This model of policing has been suggested by Scraton (1985), who argues that the police can best be seen as an occupying force, imposed upon working-class and ethnic-minority communities. Police officers largely patrol working-class and ethnic-minority areas where they impose the law and order that reflects the interests of the more powerful groups. Lea and Young (1984) describe this as **'military-style' policing**, which is characterized by the use of large numbers of police officers patrolling an area in vehicles, using advanced technology for intelligence gathering.

According to Reiner (1997), those who are stopped and searched, or questioned in the street, arrested, detained in the police station, charged and prosecuted, are disproportionately young men who are unemployed or casually employed, and from discriminated-against minority ethnic groups. The police themselves recognize that their main business involves such groups, and their mental social maps delineate them by a variety of derogatory epithets: 'assholes', 'pukes', 'scum', 'slag', 'prigs'.

Discretion, policing and the law

As we have noted, it is the job of the police to enforce the law. However, there are so many laws that could be applied in so many different circumstances that police officers need to use their **discretion** in deciding exactly which laws to apply and in what circumstances. Sociologists have been particularly interested in studying the nature of such discretion, and in seeing the implications for different groups in society. Discretion can also provide evidence to support one or other of the (consensual or conflict) styles of policing we have just discussed.

Reiner (1992) has suggested three ways of explaining the basis of police discretion: individualistic, cultural and structural.

Individualistic

The explanation for police discretion is that a particular police officer has specific concerns and interests and thus interprets and applies the law according to them. Colman and Gorman (1982) found some evidence for this in their study of police officers in inner London. In particular, they noted individual racist police officers who would apply the law more harshly on certain ethnic minorities.

Cultural

New recruits enter a world that has a highly developed culture – evolved from the particular type of job that police officers must do. Police officers are overwhelmingly White and male. They work long hours in each other's company and are largely isolated from the public. The result of this is the development of a very specific occupational culture – sometimes referred to as a **'canteen culture'**. According to Skolnick (1966) this has three main components – and we can add a fourth suggested by Graef (1989): that of masculinity.

- *Suspiciousness* – As part of their job, police officers spend much of their time dealing with people who may have committed a criminal offence. As part of their training, therefore, they are taught to discriminate between 'decent people' and 'potential trouble-makers'. According to Reiner (1992), they categorize and stereotype certain people as 'police property'. This involves regarding young males, and particularly youths from ethnic minorities, as potential troublemakers.
- *Internal solidarity and social isolation* – We have just noted how police officers spend large amounts of time in the company of their peers, isolated from the public. They also rely upon each other in terms of support in times of physical threat and when denying accusations from the public.
- *Conservatism* – Those who join the police in the first place are rarely politically radical, and while the actual job of policing emphasizes a non-political attitude – police officers must uphold the law – it also upholds traditional values and the very nature of the state. Added to the factors of social isolation and the majority recruitment from White males, this generates a strong sense of conservative values.
- *Masculinity* – The majority of police officers are male and drawn from the working class. The culture of police officers very much reflects traditional working-class values of heavy drinking, physical prowess and heterosexuality. Racial stereotyping is also heavily emphasized and linked with assuming the role of a police officer.

Structural

A third approach, derived from Marxist theory, stresses that the very definition of law is biased in favour of the powerful groups in society and against the working class. Therefore, any upholding of the law involves upholding the values of capitalist society. Police officers' definition of crime in terms of street crimes and burglary (as opposed to white-collar or corporate crime and their repression of the working class) derives from their role as agents of control of a capitalist society. Their internal values simply reflect the job they have been given to do.

Evidence for this view can be found in Tarling's study (1988) which showed that over 65 per cent of police resources are devoted to the uniformed patrolling of public space – particularly poorer neighbourhoods and central city areas. The result is that, as Morgan found out, about 55 per cent of prisoners in police custody were unemployed, and of the rest, 30 per cent were in manual, working-class jobs. Most detainees were young, with 60 per cent being under 25, and 87 per cent of all of those arrested being male. Finally, over 12 per cent were from African or African-Caribbean backgrounds – despite these groups forming less than 3 per cent of the population.

Check your understanding

1. **What three key changes in social control did Cohen identify?**

2. **What factors influence the way punishment has changed, according to Durkheim?**

3. **What explanation do Marxists provide for the development of prisons?**

4. **Identify and explain the two models of policing that have been identified.**

5. **Identify the components of the police occupational culture.**

6. **Why is an understanding of police discretion important?**

Criminal justice, ethnicity and gender

The treatment of different social groups within the criminal justice system has been the focus of heated debate among sociologists. Particular attention has been paid to the possibility that the criminal justice system discriminates against people from ethnic-minority backgrounds and against women. These are discussed in Topics 8 (gender) and 9 (ethnicity).

Having looked at the issue of social control, Topics 3 to 5 examine alternative sociological theories of the causes of crime and deviance. Later in the unit, Topic 10 explores realist and postmodern approaches to crime and deviance, which often focus on the issue of social control.

research ideas

1. CCTV cameras are an extremely popular means of social control. How many of these are in your town centre? Identify a couple of roads which are covered by CCTV and then ask a small sample of the people in that street if they are aware of the cameras. What are their views? Is Cohen's view true that there is an ever-growing web of hidden control?

2. Arrange to interview a local police officer about how they use their discretion. Are sociological explanations justified by the answers?

web.task

Search the following sites about the death penalty and attitudes to it. Can sociology throw any light on the debate?

- www.amnesty.org.uk/action/camp/dp/index.shtml
- www.deathpenaltyinfo.org/

KEY TERMS

Actuarialism – refers to the division of people into potentially deviant groups and controlling them on this basis.

Canteen culture – a term which refers to the occupational culture developed by the police.

Disciplining – the process of control through non-coercive methods.

Discretion – the fact that the police have to use their judgement about when to use the force of the law.

Formal social control – see Key terms p. 25.

Informal social control – see Key terms p. 25.

Internalize – when people come to accept, and possibly believe, some value or rule.

Mechanistic societies – technologically and socially simple societies, as identified by Durkheim, in which people are culturally very similar.

Military model of policing – policing which is imposed upon the population.

Offending rates – statistics referring to how many crimes are committed, and by which groups of people.

Organic societies – culturally and technologically complex societies, as identified by Durkheim, in which people are culturally different from each other.

Privatization – giving control from the state to private companies.

Restitutive – a model of law based upon trying to repair the damage done to society.

Retributive – a model of law based upon revenge.

Sanctions – measures taken to control a person or group.

Item A

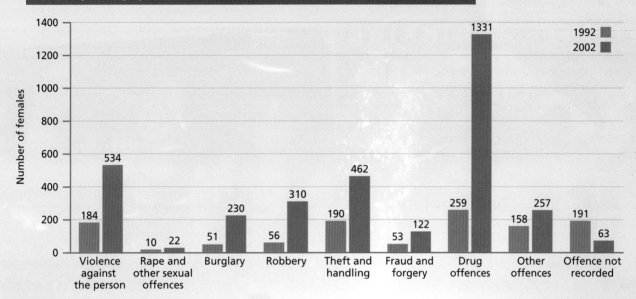

Female prison population under an immediate sentence 1992 and 2002

Number of females

Offence	1992	2002
Violence against the person	184	534
Rape and other sexual offences	10	22
Burglary	51	230
Robbery	56	310
Theft and handling	190	462
Fraud and forgery	53	122
Drug offences	259	1331
Other offences	158	257
Offence not recorded	191	63

Source: Councell, R. (2003) *The prison population in 2002: a statistical review*, Findings 228, Home Office RDS www.homeoffice.gov.uk/rds/pdfs2/r228.pdf

Item B

Police discretion is inevitable and sometimes desirable, given the nature and circumstances of everyday police work: the need to make choices at every level about priorities, the need to interpret general legal rules in specific enforcement situations, and so on. However, the problem is that police discretion is often exercised in discriminatory ways. The social functions and focus of police work remain remarkably stable over time, as some social groups were and still are more likely to be subject to police attention than others. A series of biases, involving not only the stereotypes used by the occupational culture, but also elements of policing routines and practices, produce patterns of bias on lines of class, gender and ethnicity. The occupational culture may also have resulted in discrimination against Black police officers and female officers.

Adapted from Carrabine, E., Iganski, P., Lee, M., Plummer, K. and South, N. (2004) *Criminology*, London: Routledge, pp. 278–9

(a) Using **Item A**, identify the single biggest offence for which women were imprisoned in 2002. (1 mark)

(b) Identify and briefly explain **two** reasons why the police use discretion in their work (**Item B**). (8 marks)

(c) Identify **three** trends or patterns in **Item A**. (9 marks)

(d) Identify and explain **two** ways in which 'police discretion is often exercised in discriminatory ways'. (12 marks)

Exam practice

(e) Outline and assess the role of the police in the social construction of crime and deviance. (60 marks)

Strain and subcultural theories

gettingyouthinking

1 **What do you think of the people in the photos: are they having a good time or just acting stupidly – or both?**

2 **In your opinion, why do some young males start fights?**

3 **Who do you think are more important in influencing your day-to-day behaviour, your family or your friends?**

4 **If your friends wanted you to do something that you considered acceptable behaviour, but your parents expressly forbade it, what would you do?**

You may well feel that your friends exert a considerable influence on your life. Sometimes, groups of friends develop norms and values that are unconventional and may encourage deviant acts. **Subcultural theories** share the common belief that people who commit crime usually share different values from the mass of law-abiding members of society. However, crime-committing people do not live in complete opposition to mainstream values, rather they have 'amended' certain values so that this justifies criminal behaviour – hence the term '**subculture**'.

Strain is a term that is used to refer to explanations of criminal behaviour that argue that crime is the result of certain groups of people being placed in a position where they are unable, for whatever reason, to conform to the values and beliefs of society. Many sociologists use the term interchangeably with 'subculture'. Although, strictly speaking, they are not the same thing (for example, Merton is a 'strain' theorist and does not really discuss subculture), we have put them together here because of the degree of overlap between the two approaches.

The origins of subculture

Subcultural theories derive from two different schools of sociology – and if you think carefully about each of the later approaches we discuss, you will probably be able to tell which school of thought they derive from.

Appreciative sociology

The first parent-school is that of the University of Chicago, which developed in the early part of the 20th century in response to the dramatic social change that was taking place in US cities at that time. Chicago sociologists were determined to appreciate the wide variety of different cultures and lifestyles in Chicago that existed as a result of the huge influx of migrants arriving from all over Europe and southern USA. Chicago sociologists pioneered the use of participant observation in their research. They simply wanted to observe and note down the sheer variety and dynamism of urban life. Integral to this was

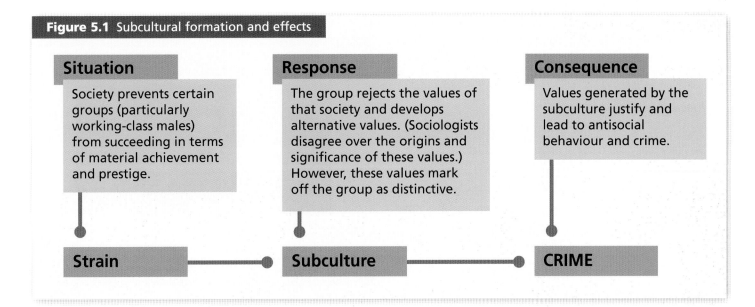

Figure 5.1 Subcultural formation and effects

Situation	Response	Consequence
Society prevents certain groups (particularly working-class males) from succeeding in terms of material achievement and prestige.	The group rejects the values of that society and develops alternative values. (Sociologists disagree over the origins and significance of these values.) However, these values mark off the group as distinctive.	Values generated by the subculture justify and lead to antisocial behaviour and crime.

Strain ———→ **Subculture** ———→ **CRIME**

the study of deviant groups, with Frederic Thrasher's *The Gang* (1927) and Whyte's *Street Corner Society* (1943) demonstrating that deviant groups in society had clear norms and values of their own that justified their different behaviour.

Strain theory

In the 1930s, Robert Merton (1938), tried to locate deviance within a functionalist framework. For Merton, crime and deviance were evidence of a poor fit (or a strain) between the socially accepted goals of society and the socially approved means of obtaining those desired goals. The resulting strain led to deviance.

Merton argued that all societies set their members certain goals and, at the same time, provide socially approved ways of achieving these goals. Merton was aware that not everyone shared the same goals; he pointed out that in a stratified society the goals were linked to a person's position in the social structure. Those lower down had restricted goals. The system worked well as long as there was a reasonable chance that a majority of people were able to achieve their goals. However, if the majority of the population were unable to achieve the socially set goals, then they became disenchanted with society and sought out alternative (often deviant) ways of behaving. Merton used Durkheim's term anomie, to describe this situation.

The following different forms of behaviour then could be understood as a strain between goals and means:

- *Conformity* – The individual continues to adhere to both goals and means, despite the limited likelihood of success.
- *Innovation* – The person accepts the goals of society but uses different ways to achieve those goals. Criminal behaviour is included in this response.
- *Ritualism* – The means are used by the individual, but sight of the actual goal is lost, e.g. the bureaucrat or the police officer blindly enforcing the letter of the law without looking at the nature of justice.
- *Retreatism* – The individual rejects both goals and means. The person dependent upon drugs or alcohol is included in this form of behaviour.

- *Rebellion* – Both the socially sanctioned goals and means are rejected and different ones substituted. This is the political activist or the religious fundamentalist.

Criticism of Merton

Merton has been criticized by Valier (2001) amongst others for his stress on the existence of common goals in society. Valier argues that there are, in fact, a variety of goals that people strive to attain at any one time.

Illegitimate opportunity structure

The idea of strain between goals and means had a very significant impact on the writings of Cloward and Ohlin (1960), who owed much to the ideas of Merton.

They argued that Merton had failed to appreciate that there was a parallel opportunity structure to the legal one, called the **illegitimate opportunity structure**. By this they meant that for some subcultures in society a regular illegal career was available, with recognized illegal means of obtaining society's goals. A good example of this is given in Dick Hobbs' book *Bad Business* (1998). Hobbs interviewed successful professional criminals and demonstrated how it is possible to have a career in crime, given the right connections and 'qualities'.

According to Cloward and Ohlin, the illegal opportunity structure had three possible adaptations or subcultures:

- *Criminal* – There is a thriving local criminal subculture, with successful role models. Young offenders can 'work their way up the ladder' in the criminal hierarchy.
- *Conflict* – There is no local criminal subculture to provide a career opportunity. Groups brought up in this sort of environment are likely to turn to violence, usually against other similar groups. Cloward and Ohlin give the example of violent gang 'warfare'.

- *Retreatist* – This tends to be a more individual response and occurs where the individual has no opportunity or ability to engage in either of the other two subcultures. The result is a retreat into alcohol or drugs.

Evaluation of Cloward and Ohlin

This explanation is useful and, as Hobbs' work shows, for some people there really is a criminal opportunity structure. But the approach shares some of the weaknesses of Merton's original theory:

- It is difficult to accept that such a neat distinction into three clear categories occurs in real life.
- There is no discussion whatsoever about female deviancy.

Status frustration

Writing in the mid 1950s, Albert Cohen (1955) drew upon both Merton's ideas of strain and also on the **ethnographic** ideas of the Chicago school of sociology. Cohen was particularly interested in the fact that much offending behaviour was not economically motivated, but simply done for the thrill of the act. (This is as true today as it was in the 1950s, for vandalism typically accounts for about 18 per cent of current crime recorded by the British Crime Survey.)

According to Cohen, 'lower-class' boys strove to emulate middle-class values and aspirations, but lacked the means to attain success. This led to **status frustration** – that is, a sense of personal failure and inadequacy. The result was that they rejected those very values and patterns of 'acceptable' behaviour that they could not be successful within. He suggests that school is the key area for the playing out of this drama. Lower-class children are much more likely to fail and consequently feel humiliated. In an attempt to gain status, they 'invert' traditional middle-class values – behaving badly and engaging in a variety of antisocial behaviours.

Criticisms of Albert Cohen

- There is no discussion of females. His research is solely about males.
- The young 'delinquents' need to be brilliant sociologists to work out what are middle-class values and then invert them!
- Cohen fails to prove that school really is the key place where success and failure are demonstrated.

Focal concerns

In the late 1950s, Walter Miller developed a rather different approach to explaining the values of crime when he suggested that deviancy was linked to the culture of lower-class males. Miller (1962) suggested that working-class males have six '**focal concerns**' that are likely to lead to delinquency:

- *Smartness* – A person should both look good and also be witty with a 'sharp repartee'.

focus on research

Philippe Bourgois (2002)
In search of respect

≪ *I want to place drug dealers and street level criminals into their rightful positions with the mainstream of US society. They are not 'exotic others' operating in an irrational netherworld. On the contrary, they are 'made in America'. Highly motivated, ambitious inner-city youths have been attracted to the rapidly expanding, multi-billion dollar drug economy precisely because they believe ... [in] the American Dream.*

In fact, in their pursuit of success, they are even following the minute details of the classical yankee model for upward mobility. They are aggressively pursuing careers as private entrepreneurs: they take risks, work hard and pray for good luck. ≫

Bourgois, P. (2002) *In Search of Respect* (2nd edn), Cambridge: Cambridge University Press

1 **How does Bourgois' quotation above illustrate both the ideas of Merton, and of Cloward and Ohlin?**

- *Trouble* – 'I don't go looking for trouble, but ...'.
- *Excitement* – It is important to search out thrills (see Katz, Topic 8, p. 71).
- *Toughness* – Being physically stronger than others is good. It's also important to be able to demonstrate this.
- *Autonomy* – It is important not to be pushed around by others.
- *Fate* – Individuals have little chance to overcome the wider fate that awaits them.

According to Miller, then, young lower-class males are pushed towards crime by the implicit values of their subculture.

Evaluation of Miller

Miller provides little evidence to show that these are specifically lower-class values. Indeed, as Box (1981) pointed out, they could equally apply to males right across the class structure.

Applying subcultural theory: the British experience

The studies we have looked at so far have mainly been American ones. However, subcultural studies were being undertaken in Britain too – though with a variety of results. Howard Parker (1974) successfully applied Miller's focal concerns in his study of working-class 'lads' in inner-city Liverpool (although, as we have already noted, he could probably have applied these equally successfully to rugby-playing students at Liverpool University).

On the other hand, studies by David Downes (1966) of young working-class males in London could find no evidence of distinctive values. Instead, Downes suggested that young working-class males were 'dissociated' from mainstream values, by which he meant that they were concerned more about leisure than their long-term future or employment, and were more likely to engage in petty crime. So, in the UK, evidence of distinctive subcultures has been fairly difficult to obtain.

Subterranean values

One consistent criticism of subcultural theories was that there was little evidence to demonstrate a distinct set of antisocial values. Even if there were subcultures, were they a response to middle-class values or to a distinctive set of working-class values? Matza put these criticisms together to make a strong attack upon subcultural theory (Sykes and Matza 1962). Matza argued that there were no distinctive subcultural values, rather that all groups in society used a shared set of **subterranean values**. The key thing was that most of the time, most people control these deviant desires. They only rarely emerge – for example, at the annual office party, or the holiday in Agia Napa. But when they do emerge, we use **techniques of neutralization** to provide justification for our deviant actions (see Fig. 5.2). As we said earlier, the difference between a persistent offender and a law-abiding citizen is simply how often and in what circumstances the subterranean values emerge and are then justified by the techniques of neutralization.

Matza's critique of subculture is quite devastating. He is saying that all of us share deviant, 'subcultural values', and that it is not true that there are distinctive groups with their own values, different from the rest of us.

Subculture: the paradox of inclusion

In his book *On the Edge*, Carl Nightingale (1993) studied young Black youth in an inner-city area of Philadelphia. For Nightingale, subculture emerges from a desire to be part of the mainstream US culture – that is, subculture emerges from being rejected and marginalized by the mainstream society. Nightingale notes the way that Black children avidly consume US culture by watching television with its emphasis on consumerism and the success of violence – yet at the same time they are excluded economically, racially and politically from participating in that mainstream US culture. The response is to overcompensate by identifying themselves with the wider culture by acquiring articles with high-status trade names or logos. Once again, drawing upon Merton's ideas, the subculture reflects the belief that it is not so much how these high-status goods are obtained rather the fact of possessing them. In the USA, these are often obtained through violence, expressed in violent gangs and high crime rates.

Similarly, Philip Bourgois' study of El Barrio (2002), looks at the lives of drug dealers and criminals in this deprived area of New York and finds that they, too, believe in the American Dream of financial success. The values of their 'subculture' are really little different from mainstream values, the only difference being that they deal drugs in order to get the money to pursue an all-American lifestyle.

So, both Nightingale's and Bourgois' versions of subculture take us back to the strain theory of Merton, and Cloward and Ohlin, emphasizing that the desire to be included leads to the actions that ensure that they are excluded from society.

Contemporary alternatives to subculture

Postmodernism

Most of the approaches we have looked at here, as well as the Marxist subcultural approaches described in Topic 5, seek to explain deviant behaviour by looking for some rational reason why the subculture might have developed. Recent postmodern approaches reject this explanation for behaviour. Katz (1988),

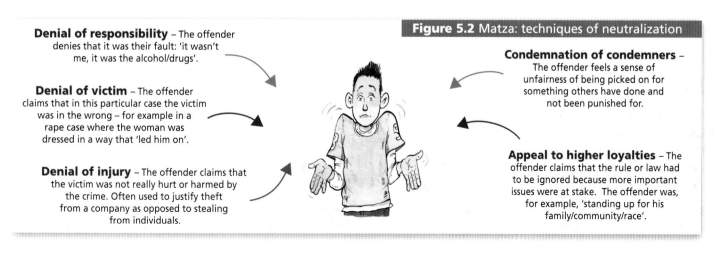

Denial of responsibility – The offender denies that it was their fault: 'it wasn't me, it was the alcohol/drugs'.

Denial of victim – The offender claims that in this particular case the victim was in the wrong – for example in a rape case where the woman was dressed in a way that 'led him on'.

Denial of injury – The offender claims that the victim was not really hurt or harmed by the crime. Often used to justify theft from a company as opposed to stealing from individuals.

Figure 5.2 Matza: techniques of neutralization

Condemnation of condemners – The offender feels a sense of unfairness of being picked on for something others have done and not been punished for.

Appeal to higher loyalties – The offender claims that the rule or law had to be ignored because more important issues were at stake. The offender was, for example, 'standing up for his family/community/race'.

Subculture as a concept is not solely related to crime and deviance; it is widely used throughout sociology to explain just why particular groups behave in ways that are different from the rest of society. These applications of the idea of subcultural theory are also often shot through with value judgements on the part of sociologists. In schools, for example, numerous sociologists, notably Willis, have uncovered antischool subcultures where the students oppose the values of the school and get pleasure from being disruptive. In Willis' study there seems a degree of admiration for the lads.

Murray (1990) has used the term in a much broader and more negative sense to claim the existence of an 'underclass' of people who prefer to live off state benefits and petty crime. The females are likely to have early pregnancies and are single parents, while the males will father a number of children by different partners, but are unlikely to support their children financially. Murray's arguments are strongly contested by other sociologists however. Whereas, Murray writes disapprovingly about the underclass, Stacey writes supportively about the development of gay and lesbian families. Stacey identifies a new subculture emerging of gays and lesbians rejecting the dominant values regarding the importance of heterosexuals as the only people able to have a family with children.

for example, argues that crime is seductive – young males get drawn into it, not because of any process of rejection but because it is thrilling. In a similar manner, Lyng (1990) argues that young males like taking risks and engaging in '**edgework**' as he puts it. By edgework, he means going right to the edge of acceptable behaviour and flirting with danger.

Neo-Tribes

Maffesoli (1996) introduced a postmodernist innovation in understanding subcultures with his argument for the existence of neo-tribes. Maffesoli was unhappy with the idea that the idea of subculture had been transformed from a concept based on values more into one of a group sharing a set of values. He suggested that it was much better to think of subcultures in terms of 'fluidity, occasional gatherings and dispersal'. Neo-tribes then referred more to states of mind and lifestyles that were very flexible, open and changing. Deviant values are less important than a stress on consumption, suitably fashionable behaviour and individual identity that can change rapidly.

Masculinity

Subcultural theory is overwhelmingly male subcultural theory. The assumptions underlying the vast bulk of the writings we have looked at within this tradition have been discussing masculine behaviour. However, as Collison (1996) points out, they may well have missed the significance of this. In order to explain male offending behaviour, it is important to explain the nature of being male in our society and the links masculinity itself has to crime. The work of Connell (1995) is particularly interesting here in that he sees the existence of a hegemonic masculinity which males both conspire with and aspire to. The emphasis of this hegemonic masculinity is very similar in values to Miller's early work on 'lower-class values'. However, Winlow (2004) argues that the values are best seen within the context of a changing economic social structure. Winlow suggests that the traditional (working-class) male values fitted physical work undertaken by men in industrial settings. These have now gone and the values are inappropriate for

contemporary employment. He suggests too that the problem may be even greater for those young men excluded completely from employment.

Policy issues

Subcultural theories themselves have had relatively little influence on government policies, although there has been much concern about problem youth engaging in antisocial behaviour. Since 1998, two major pieces of legislation have defined a series of actions deemed antisocial and these can now be punished by a range of orders including Anti-Social Behaviour Orders (ASBOs). Underpinning these is the idea that the behaviour and values of certain groups of young people conflict so greatly with those of the majority that they are beyond any other form of social control.

KEY TERMS

Edgework – derives from Lyng. Refers to activities of young males which provide them with thrills, derived from the real possibility of physical or emotional harm (e.g. stealing and racing cars; drug abuse).

Ethnographic – form of observational research, in which researcher lives amongst, and describes activities of, particular group being studied.

Focal concerns – term used by Miller to describe key values.

Illegitimate opportunity structure – an alternative, illegal way of life that certain groups in society have access to.

Status frustration – according to Cohen, this occurs when young men feel that they are looked down upon by society.

Strain – term used by Merton and other functionalists to describe a lack of balance and adjustment in society.

Subculture – a distinctive set of values that provides an alternative to those of the mainstream culture.

Subcultural theories – explanations of crime and deviance focusing on the idea that those who deviate hold different values to the majority.

Techniques of neutralization – justifications for our deviant actions.

Check your understanding

1. What is meant by 'appreciative sociology'?
2. How does Merton use the idea of anomie to explain deviance?
3. How, according to A. Cohen, does school failure lead to the formation of subcultures?
4. How does the idea of 'techniques of neutralization' undermine some subcultural arguments?
5. What do we mean by the 'paradox of inclusion'?
6. Why is the idea of 'masculinity' relevant to understanding criminal behaviour?

web.task

Go to the Home Office Website. At **www.homeoffice.gov.uk/rds/ pdfs/hors209.pdf** **you will find the Research Study 209 on Findings from the 1998/99 Youth Lifestyles Leisure Survey. Look at pp. 34–35 on family and friends and offending. Does this provide any evidence to support or undermine subcultural theory?**

exploring strain and subcultural theories

Item A

Strain and subcultural theories have, in the main, been concerned with explaining high rates of delinquency within the lower classes. They take the criminal law and statistical representations of offending rates as given. They propose that both the origins and developments of juvenile delinquency are structurally determined, and as such also offer a general framework for understanding all crime by contending that the denial of legitimate opportunity acts as the major cause of crime. However, subsequent studies, based in particular upon self-report research, have found that most people from all social classes commit deviant acts. Strain and subcultural theories have been criticized therefore for being both class and gender biased. In ignoring both how commonplace crime is and how much is committed my middle-class people, it conveys the impression that lawlesnesss is exclusively a working-class and male phenomenon.

Adapted from Muncie, J. (2004) *Youth and Crime*, London: Sage, p 107

Item B

<<We did not say that participant observation is the best method for gathering data for all sociological problems under all circumstances. We did not say this and, in fact, we fully subscribe to his view 'that different kinds of information about people and society are gathered most fully and economically in different ways, and that the problem under investigation properly dictates the methods of investigation'. We did say, and now reiterate, that participant observation gives us the most complete information about social events and can thus be used as a yardstick to suggest what kinds of data escape us when we use other methods. This means simply, that, if we see an event occur, see the events preceding and following it, and talk to various participants about it, we have more information than if we only have the description which one or more persons give us through questionnaires or interviews. We intended to refer only to specific and limited events which are observable, not to large and complex events.>>

Source: Becker, H. and Geer, B. (1969) 'Participant observation and Interviewing: a rejoinder', in G. McCall and J.L. Simmons (eds) *Issues in Participant Observation*, New York: Addison-Wesley

(a) Using **Item A**, identify what strain and subcultural theories have been largely concerned to explain. (1 mark)

(b) Identify and briefly explain **two** features of strain theory. (8 marks)

(c) Identify **three** possible reasons for the formation of ethnic subcultures. (9 marks)

(d) Identify and explain **two** reasons why sociologists might use participant observation in the study of **(Item B).** (12 marks)

Exam practice

(e) Outline and assess subcultural theories of crime and deviance. (60 marks)

Labelling theory

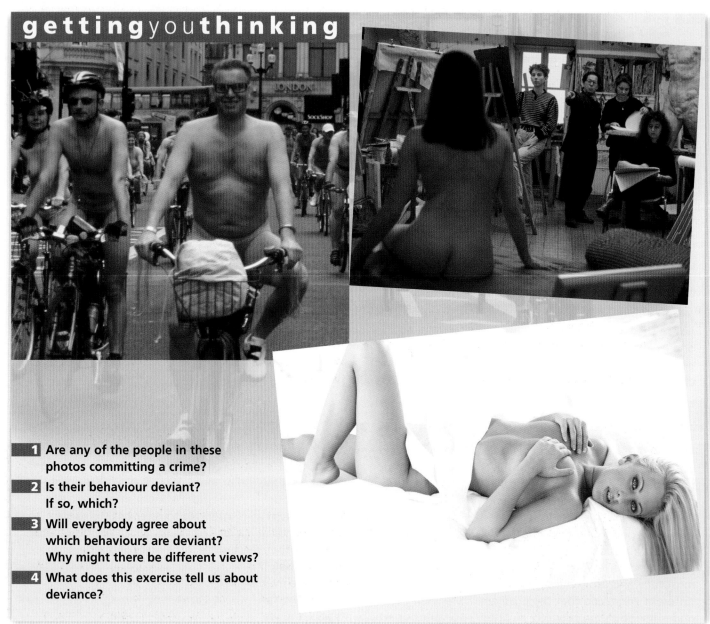

gettingyouthinking

1. Are any of the people in these photos committing a crime?
2. Is their behaviour deviant? If so, which?
3. Will everybody agree about which behaviours are deviant? Why might there be different views?
4. What does this exercise tell us about deviance?

Understanding deviance: reaction not cause

Most approaches to understanding crime and deviance (with the exception of Marxist approaches) accept that there is a difference between those who offend and those who do not. On the basis of this assumption, they then search for the key factors that lead the person to offend.

However, since the early 1950s, one group of sociologists influenced by **symbolic interactionism** have questioned this approach. They argue that this approach makes a mistake in its fundamental assumption that lawbreakers are somehow different from the law-abiding. Labelling theory suggests instead that most people commit deviant and criminal acts, but only some people are caught and stigmatized for it. So, if most people commit deviant acts of some kind, it is pointless trying to search for the differences between deviants and non-deviants

– instead the stress should be upon understanding the reaction to and definition of deviance rather than on the causes of the initial act. As Howard Becker (1963) puts it:

≪ *Deviancy is not a quality of the act a person commits but rather a consequence of the application by others of rules and sanctions to an 'offender'. Deviant behaviour is behaviour that people so label.* ≫

This is a radically different way of exploring crime; in fact, it extends beyond crime and helps us to understand any deviant or **stigmatized** behaviour. Labelling theory has gradually been adopted and incorporated into many other sociological approaches – for example, Taylor, Walton and Young (1973) have used it in their updating of Marxist criminology, while postmodernist approaches also owe much to it.

The best-known exponent of 'labelling theory' is Howard Becker. In the book *The Outsiders*, Becker gives a very clear and simple illustration of the labelling argument, drawing upon an anthropological study by Malinowski (1948/1982) of a traditional culture on a Pacific Island.

Malinowski describes how a youth killed himself because he had been publicly accused of **incest**. When Malinowski had first inquired about the case, the islanders expressed their horror and disgust. But, on further investigation, it turned out that incest was not uncommon on the island, nor was it really frowned upon provided those involved were discreet. However, if an incestuous affair became too obvious and public, the islanders reacted with abuse, the offenders were ostracized and often driven to suicide.

Becker, therefore, argues the following:

1 Just because someone breaks a rule, it does not necessarily follow that others will define it as deviant.
2 Someone has to enforce the rules or, at least, draw attention to them – these people usually have a vested interest in the issue. (In the example of the incestuous islanders, the rule was enforced by the rejected ex-lover of the girl involved in incest.)
3 If the person is successfully labelled, then consequences follow. (Once publicly labelled as deviant, the offender in Malinowski's example was faced with limited choices, one of which was suicide.)

Responding to and enforcing rules

Most sociological theories take for granted that once a person has committed a deviant or criminal act, then the response will be uniform. This is not true. People respond differently to deviance or rule-breaking. In the early 1960s, when gay people were more likely to be stigmatized than now, John Kitsuse (1962) interviewed 75 heterosexual students to elicit their responses to (presumed) sexual advances from people of the same sex. What he found was a very wide range of responses from complete tolerance to bizarre and extreme hatred. One told how he had 'known' that a man he was talking to in a bar was homosexual because he had wanted to talk about psychology! The point of Kitsuse's work is that there was no agreed definition of what constituted a homosexual 'advance' – it was open to negotiation.

Howard Becker

Labelling theory and symbolic interactionism provide similar analyses of individual behaviour. Symbolic interactionism argues that the social world consists of 'symbols' that have a culturally defined meaning to people and suggest appropriate ways of acting. These

Labelling theory and symbolic interactionism

symbols are not fixed and may change over time. Every time two or more people interact with each other, they amend their behaviour on the basis of how they interpret the behaviour of the other people. A second element of symbolic interactionism is the way that people develop images of themselves and how they should 'present' themselves to other people, which is known as the 'self'.

The ideas of labelling theory are very similar, with some changes in language, so instead of symbol, the word 'label' is used. Instead of using the term 'the self', the term 'master status' is used.

There is one great difference between symbolic interactionism and the form of labelling developed by such writers as Becker: symbolic interactionism is not interested in power differences, whereas labelling theory focuses on the way that differences in power can lead to some people imposing labels on others (and the consequences of this).

In Britain today, British Crime Survey statistics show that young Black males are more likely to be stopped for questioning and searching than any other group. This is a result of the police officers' belief that this particular social group is more likely to offend than any other; for this reason, they are the subjects of 'routine suspicion'.

Criticism

Akers (1967) criticized labelling theorists for presenting deviants as perfectly normal people who are no different from anyone else until someone comes along and slaps a label on them. Akers argues that there must be some reason why the label is applied to certain groups/individuals and not others. As long as labelling fails to explain this, then it is an incomplete theory.

The consequences of rule enforcement

As we have just seen, being labelled as a deviant and having laws enforced against you is the result of a number of different factors. However, once labelled as a deviant, various consequences occur for the individual.

The clearest example of this is provided by Edwin Lemert, who distinguished between '**primary**' and '**secondary**' **deviance** (Lemert 1972). Primary deviance is rule-breaking, which is of little importance in itself, while secondary deviance is the consequence of the responses of others, which is significant.

To illustrate this, Lemert studied the coastal **Inuits** of Canada, who had a long-rooted problem of chronic stuttering or stammering. Lemert suggested that the problem was 'caused' by the great importance attached to ceremonial speech-making. Failure to speak well was a great humiliation. Children with the slightest speech difficulty were so conscious of their parents' desire to have well-speaking children that they became overanxious about their own abilities. It was this very anxiety, according to Lemert, that led to chronic stuttering. In this example, chronic stuttering (secondary deviance) is a response to parents' reaction to initial minor speech defects (primary deviance).

The person labelled as 'deviant' will eventually come to see themselves as being bad (or mad). Becker used the term '**master status**' to describe this process. He points out that once a label has successfully been applied to a person, then all other qualities become unimportant – they are responded to solely in terms of this master status.

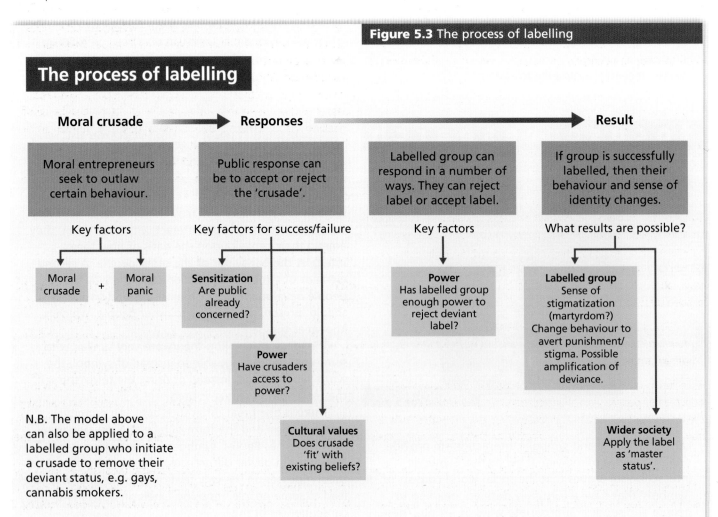

Figure 5.3 The process of labelling

Labelling theory and social policy

Labelling theory has not directly influenced government policies towards law and order as such, but there are elements of it mixed in with other policies. In the previous topic, we discussed the use of Anti-Social Behaviour Orders to combat youth offending in particular. People who have these orders imposed upon them can be publicly identified with posters of them being put up in local shops, posted through letter boxes and put in the newspapers. The aim of this is to humiliate the individual and to inform the community that something is being done against antisocial behaviour. However, it is possible that by doing this, a self identity or master status of being a troublemaker is actually being created.

Rejecting labels: negotiability

The process of being labelled is, however, open to 'negotiation', in that some groups or individuals are able to reject the label. An example of this is Reiss's (1961) study of young male prostitutes. Although they had sex with other men, they regarded what they did as work and maintained an image of themselves as being 'straight'.

Deviant career

These ideas of master status and negotiability led Becker to devise the idea of a **'deviant career'**. He meant by this all the processes that are involved in a label being applied (or not) and then the person taking on (or not) the self-image of the deviant.

Creating rules

Once labelling theorists began the process of looking at how social life was open to negotiation and that rule enforcement was no different than other social activities, then attention shifted to the creation of rules and laws. Why were they made? Traditionally, sociologists had taken either a Marxist perspective (that they were made in the interests of the ruling class) or a functionalist/pluralist perspective (which argued that laws in a democracy reflected the views of the majority of the population). Becker (1963) doubted both these accounts and argued instead that:

> << *Rules are the products of someone's initiative and we can think of the people who exhibit such enterprises as '***moral entrepreneurs***'.* >>

So, labelling theorists argue that laws are a reflection of the activities of people (moral entrepreneurs) who actively seek to create and enforce laws. The reasons for this are either that the new laws benefit the activists directly, or these activists believe that the laws are truly to the benefit of society.

Becker's most famous example is his study of the outlawing of cannabis use in the USA in 1937. Cannabis had been widely used in the southern states of the USA. Its outlawing was the result of a successful campaign waged by the Federal Bureau of Narcotics which, after the repeal of the prohibition laws (that had banned alcohol), saw cannabis as a growing menace in society. Through a press campaign and lobbying of senior politicians, the Bureau was successful in outlawing the growing and use of the drug. However, Becker points out that the campaign was only successful because it 'plugged in' to values commonly held in the USA which included:

1 the belief that people ought to be in control of their actions and decisions
2 that pleasure for its own sake was wrong
3 that drugs were seen as addictive and, as such, 'enslaved' people.

The term Becker used to describe the campaign was of a '**moral crusade**', and it is this terminology (along with the concept of moral entrepreneurs) which sociologists use to describe movements to pass laws.

Criticisms

The idea that there are those who seek to pass laws or to impose rules upon others has been accepted by most sociologists. However, Marxist writers in particular have pointed out that there is a wider framework within which this is placed. Are all laws just the product of a particular group of moral entrepreneurs? If so, then what are the conditions under which some groups succeed and others fail? Labelling theory does not really answer this issue very well; in fact, labelling theory does not have a coherent theory of power, as it argues that more powerful groups are able to impose their 'definition of the situation' on others, yet does not explain why some groups have more power than others and are more able to get laws passed and enforced that are beneficial to them. In defence of labelling theory, Becker (1970) does suggest in a famous article ('Whose side are we on?') that there are differences in power and that it is the role of the sociologist to side with the underdog. (We explore this in more detail below.) However, no overall theory of differences in power is given.

Labelling and values

We have just mentioned a famous article by Becker, in which he argues that labelling theory has a clear value position – that is, it speaks up for the powerless and the underdog. Labelling theorists claim to provide a voice for those who are labelled as deviant and 'outsiders'.

However, Liazos (1972) criticizes labelling theorists for simply exploring marginally deviant activities, as by doing so, they are reinforcing the idea of pimps, prostitutes and mentally ill people as being deviant. Even by claiming to speak for the underdog, labelling theorists hardly present any challenge to the status quo.

Gouldner (1968) also criticizes labelling theorists for their failure to provide any real challenge to the status quo. He argued that all they did in their studies was to criticize doctors, psychiatrists and police officers for their role in labelling – and they failed ever to look beyond this at more powerful groups who benefit from this focus on marginal groups. Gouldner is putting forward a Marxist argument, by claiming that labelling theorists draw attention away from the 'real crime'.

Crime, labelling and the media

Labelling theory alerts us to the way in which the whole area of crime depends upon social constructions of reality – law creation, law enforcement and the identities of rule breakers are all thrown into question. The media play a key role in all three of these processes, as most people's perceptions of crime are actually created – or at least informed – by the media.

Labelling theory has contributed two particularly important concepts to our understanding of the relationship between the media and crime:

● deviancy amplification
● moral panics.

Deviancy amplification

The term '**deviancy amplification**' was coined by the British sociologist Leslie Wilkins to show how the response to deviance, by agencies such as police and media, can actually generate an increase in deviance. According to Wilkins (1964), when acts are defined as deviant, the deviants become stigmatized and cut off from mainstream society. They become aware that they are regarded as deviants and, as a result of this awareness, they begin to develop their own subculture. This leads to more intense pressure on them and further isolation, which further confirms and strengthens them in their deviance.

Jock Young (1971) used this concept in his study of drug use in North London. He showed that increased police activity led to drug use being 'driven underground'. This had the effect of isolating users into a drug subculture, with 'a distinctive style of dress, lack of workaday sense of time, money, rationality and rewards', thus making reentry to regular employment increasingly difficult – which, of course, made it difficult for them to afford the drugs. The scarcity of drugs drove the price up and this drew in professional criminals who regarded it as worthwhile entering the illicit drug business; criminal rings developed and the competition between them led to violence. It also led to the use of dangerous substitutes and adulterants in drugs by suppliers, interested only in maximizing profits, thus creating a situation where users no longer knew the strength of drugs and were consequently more likely to overdose. The process described here caused wide public concern which spurred the police to intensify their clampdown even further, which only served to accelerate the spiral of this 'amplification' process.

Figure 5.4 Crime and the media

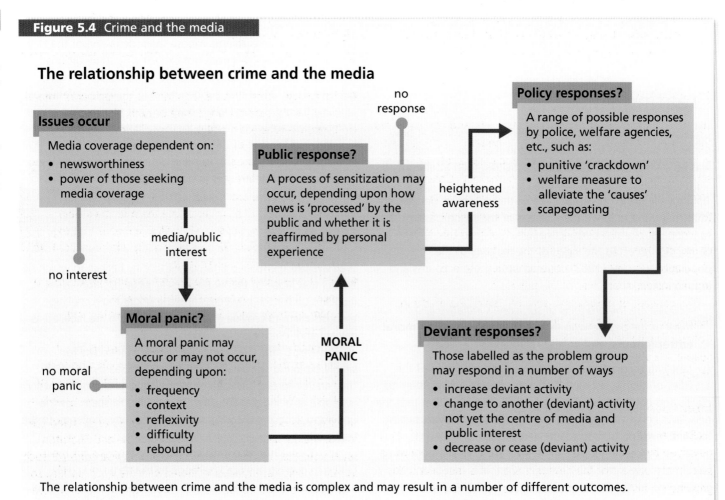

The relationship between crime and the media is complex and may result in a number of different outcomes.

Labelling theory has been widely used outside crime and deviance – in particular in education and health. It is of particular use wherever professionals, or at least people in power begin to treat people differently on the basis of stereotypes and labels. This can have very great significance on people's lives.

Within the area of criminal justice, police officers are most likely to act against young people and people with a street lifestyle (beggars, street drinkers and so on), whom they regard as a nuisance.

In education, boys of African-Caribbean origin are often viewed as potential troublemakers and sociologists argue that teachers will reinterpret their actions in such a way as to strengthen this belief. The teachers themselves are not being deliberately racist, as they may well also hold the belief that Asian girls are all hardworking. As a result, teachers may encourage the girls and discourage the boys. This labelling can have important consequences for their academic success and for their chances in the job market.

In many ways, social differentiation is closely bound up with labels and stereotypes – for example:

- People with regional accents are seen as less intelligent than those who use BBC English.
- Males ought to behave in 'masculine' ways, otherwise it may be evidence that they are gay.

Labelling in the classroom

- Women are naturally mothers and if they do not exhibit 'motherly' behaviour there must be something wrong with them.

Labelling as a concept moves far outside criminology right across sociology.

Moral panics

The idea of **moral panics** both overlaps with and complements the concept of deviancy amplification. The term was first used in Britain by Stan Cohen in a classic study (1972) of two youth subcultures of the 1960s – 'mods' and 'rockers'. Cohen showed how the media, for lack of other stories, built up these two groups into **folk devils**. The effect of the media coverage was to make the young people categorize themselves as either mods or rockers. This actually helped to create the violence that took place between them, which also confirmed them as troublemakers in the eyes of the public.

The concept of moral panic and the role of the media in helping to create them, has been widely used in sociology since Cohen's original British work – though perhaps the best adaptation of this is the study by Hall and colleagues of 'mugging' (see Topic 5).

Moral panics: an outdated idea?

McRobbie and Thornton (1995) argue that 'moral panics', as described by Cohen in the 1960s, are outdated and have to be seen in the context of the development of the media and the growing sophistication of the audiences. McRobbie and Thornton make the following points:

- *Frequency* – There has been an increasing number of 'moral panics' – they are no longer rare or particularly noteworthy.
- *Context* – Whereas moral panics would scapegoat a group and create 'folk devils' in the 1960s, today there is no single, unambiguous response to a panic as there are many different viewpoints and values in society.
- *Reflexivity* – As moral panics as a concept are so well known, many groups try to create them for their own benefit. However, the same knowledge means that the media know this and do not necessarily wish uncritically to start a moral panic over an issue.
- *Difficulty* – Moral panics are much more unlikely to start in society because it is far less clear today what is unambiguously 'bad'. Society is too fragmented and culturally pluralistic.
- *Rebound* – People are more wary about starting moral panics as there is the possibility of it rebounding on them. So politicians who start a campaign about family values or drugs have to be very careful about their own backgrounds.

Labelling has been very important in helping to understand the role of the media. However, if what McRobbie and Thornton say is true, then by their very success, sociological concepts such as moral panic have gradually filtered into the wider society, so that journalists and politicians are now aware of them and use them in their decisions about what actions to take.

Heckert and Best (1997)

The stigmatization of red hair

Heckert and Best conducted a study into the impact of having ginger hair. For some years there has been a negative image promoted about ginger-haired people and the researchers argued that people with ginger hair are negatively labelled and are treated as deviants. They interviewed 20 ginger-haired people in all, nine males and eleven females, using open questions. They found that ginger-haired people were viewed as having all or some of the following characteristics – hot tempered, clownish, weird, wild (women) or wimpy (men). They were typically treated more negatively in childhood and as a result had low levels of self-esteem. Interestingly, both researchers were ginger-haired!

Heckert, D.N. and Best, A. (1997) 'Ugly Duckling to Swan: Labeling Theory and the Stigmatization of Red Hair', *Symbolic Interaction*, 20(4), pp. 365–84

1 How might the researchers' own ginger hair have influenced respondents?

2 Evaluate the reliability and representativeness of this research.

KEY TERMS

Deviancy amplification – when the action of the rule enforcers or media in response to deviance brings about an increase in the deviance.

Deviant career – the various stages that a person passes through on their way to being seen as, and seeing themselves as, deviant.

Folk devils – groups associated with moral panics who are seen as troublemakers by the media.

Incest – sex between close members of a family (other than man and wife).

Inuits – previously known as 'eskimos'.

Master status – when people are looked at by others solely on the basis of one type of act (good or bad) which they have committed; all other aspects of that person are ignored.

Moral crusade – the process of creating or enforcing a rule.

Moral entrepreneur – person or group which tries to create or enforce a rule.

Moral panic – outrage stirred up by the media about a particular group or issue.

Primary deviance – the act of breaking a rule.

Secondary deviance – the response to rule breaking, which usually has greater social consequences than initial rule-breaking.

Stigmatized – labelled in a negative way.

Symbolic interactionism – a theory derived from social psychology which argues that people exist in a social world based on symbols that people interpret and respond to. Labelling theorists tend to substitute the term 'label' for 'symbol'.

Check your understanding

1 Instead of looking at the cause of crime, what does labelling theory focus on?

2 What theoretical approach does labelling theory derive from? How?

3 Explain and give one example of what labelling theorists mean when they say that the response to law-breaking is variable.

4 Explain the importance of the term 'master status' in understanding deviance.

5 In what way does the labelling approach to the introduction of laws differ from the Marxist approach?

6 How has labelling theory been criticized?

7 Explain the importance of the idea of 'deviancy amplification'.

8 What criticisms have been made of the term 'moral panic'?

research idea

- Conduct a survey to discover young people's perceptions of the elderly. Do their views represent particular labels and stereotypes?

  Then interview a small number of elderly people. Are they aware of stereotypes and labels? How do they feel about these labels? Do they affect them?

  Be sensitive in your interviewing technique, following the usual ethical guidelines.

web.tasks

1 Becker studied the way in which cannabis was made illegal (see above). Search the worldwide web for information about the campaign to make cannabis legal (or at least 'decriminalized') in Britain. Are there any parallels, in your opinion?

2 Search the worldwide web for newspaper and other information about any moral panic of your choice (e.g. concern over film violence, drugs such as ecstasy, underage sex). To what extent can you identify the key features of a moral panic, such as media exaggeration, the creation of 'folk devils', the activities of moral entrepreneurs, and so on?

exploring labelling theory

Item A

Becker believed that labels such as 'deviant' and 'criminal' were so stigmatizing that they came to constitute what he called the 'master status' of the deviant, overriding any other role, position or self-conception that the individual might exercise or hold. The fact of the assigned label, once it is known, becomes much more important to people than any other known characteristics or activities of the individual. The master status of deviant becomes a defining one both for self-identity and social identity. The labelled individual begins to be excluded from conventional relationships and is caught up in the criminal role. The labelled person, Becker argues, moves into a deviant group, which provides them with rationalizations, motives and attitudes which support deviant behaviour.

Adapted from: Valier, C. (2002) *Theories of Crime and Punishment*, Harlow: Longman

Item B

Labelling theory – with its rejection of so-called positivistic criminology – was closely allied to the development of the sociology of deviance. This sociology not only changed the theoretical base for the study of criminals, but also brought in its wake a dramatic restructuring of empirical concerns. Sociologists turned their interests to the world of expressive deviance; to the twilight marginal worlds of tramps, alcoholics, strippers, dwarfs, prostitutes, drug addicts, nudists; to taxi-drivers, the blind, the dying, the physically ill, the handicapped and even to a motley array of problems of everyday life. It opened up the field of inquiry so that it was possible to discuss a range of areas hitherto neglected – thereby enabling the foundations for a formal theory of deviance and a method for understanding the routine and the regular through the eyes of the powerless.

Adapted from Carrabine, E., Iganski, P. , Lee, M., Plummer, K. and South, N. (2004) *Criminology: A Sociological Introduction*, London: Routledge, p. 74

(a) Identify the term Becker used to describe the status which resulted from the labelling process (**Item A**). (1 mark)

(b) Identify and briefly explain **two** consequences of being labelled deviant (**Item A**). (8 marks)

(c) Identify **three** features of 'positivistic criminology'. (9 marks)

(d) Identify and explain **two** ways in which labelling theory changed the sociological approach to understanding crime and deviance (**Item B**). (12 marks)

Exam practice

(e) **Outline and assess interactionist explanations of deviance.** (60 marks)

Marxist approaches

gettingyouthinking

In the 1990s, Russia moved from a communist-based economy to a capitalist one. Part of this process was to create a stock exchange where people could buy and sell shares in companies. Experts from Harvard University advised them and were, according to this article, accused of illegally obtaining up to $34m by using this knowledge.

'Harvard University and one of its star economists will pay almost $30m to settle civil charges* brought by the US government. It is alleged that the professor illegally made a personal fortune from work in the 1990s helping Russia privatize hundreds of companies. Andrei Shleifer was found guilty by a federal judge last year of inappropriately investing in the same financial markets he was responsible for creating in Russia.

In 2000 the government filed a suit against Harvard for up to $102. If the case had gone to court, Harvard would have been liable for up to $34m and Mr Shleifer could have owed three times that figure.'

Griffiths, K. (2005) 'Harvard to pay $30m to settle with US government', *The Independent*, 5 August, p. 58

* Civil actions in court consist of private disputes in which one side asks for financial compensation from the other side. Criminal actions are where people are charged with criminal offences and can be punished, including being sent to prison.

1 What are your immediate reactions to the newspaper article – surprise, anger, shrug of shoulders? Do you think that having to pay back a proportion of the money 'obtained' was an adequate punishment?

2 Do you think that the police and criminal justice system treat people equally? What reasons can you suggest for your answer?

3 Look at the photo of the children working in a factory in south-east Asia – they work up to 12 hours a day and earn a very low wage. It is legal. Do you think it is wrong? Do you think it should be made illegal (as it is in Britain)?

4 On what basis do you think that something should be made a crime?

5 Using your own ideas, can you find any examples of activities that you think ought to be crimes, but are not? Can you suggest why they are not crimes?

The activity above should have alerted you to the possibility that laws, and the way they are applied, may favour certain groups – in most cases the rich and powerful. This is the starting point for Marxist and neo-Marxist approaches – often referred to as critical criminology.

The traditional Marxist approach

Karl Marx himself wrote very little about crime, but a Marxist theory of crime was first developed by Bonger as early as 1916 and then developed by writers such as Chambliss (1975). The overall background to this approach was based on the Marxist analysis of society, which argues that society is best understood by examining the process whereby the majority of the population are exploited by the owners and controllers of commerce and industry. Marxists argue that this simple, fundamental fact of exploitation provides the key to unlock the explanations for the workings of society.

The key elements of the Marxist or critical criminological approach include:

- the basis of criminal law
- the dominant **hegemony** of the ruling class
- law enforcement
- individual motivation
- crime and control.

The basis of the criminal law

The starting point for Marxist analysis is that all laws are essentially for the benefit of the ruling class, and that criminal law reflects their interests. For example, concern with the laws of property ownership largely benefit those with significant amounts of property. For those who are poor, there is little to steal. Personal violence is dangerous, and the ruling class wish to control the right to use violence in society through their agents – the police and the army. Criminal law therefore operates to protect the rich and powerful.

Law creation and the dominant hegemony

In capitalist societies, the ruling class impose their values – that is, values that are beneficial to themselves – upon the mass of the population. They do this through a number of agencies, such as the education system, religion and the mass media. (This concept of ruling-class values being imposed upon the population is commonly known as 'hegemony'.)

This dominant set of values forms the framework on which laws are based in a democracy. However, we have just seen that, according to Marxists, the set of values is actually 'forced' on the people. Thus, what they believe they are agreeing to as a result of their own beliefs is, in reality, in the interests of the ruling class.

Law enforcement

Despite the fact that the law-making process reflects the interests of the ruling class, many of these laws could provide benefits for the majority of the population if they were applied fairly. However, even the interpretation and enforcement of the law is biased in favour of the ruling class, so that the police and the judicial system will arrest and punish the working class, but tend not to enforce the law against the ruling class.

Individual motivation

Marxist theory also provides an explanation for the individual motivation underlying crime. Bonger (1916), the very first Marxist writer on crime, pointed this out. He argued that capitalism is based upon competition, selfishness and greed, and this formed people's attitudes to life. Therefore, crime was a perfectly normal outcome of these values, which stressed looking after oneself at the expense of others. However, Bonger also said that in many cases, poor people were driven to crime by their desperate conditions

Crime and control

As we saw earlier, the ruling class in capitalism constantly seeks to divert the attention of the vast majority of the population away from an understanding of the true causes of their situation, and to impose their values through the mass media, religious organizations and the education system. These institutions provide alternative accounts of reality justifying the capitalist system as the natural and best economic system. Crime plays a significant part in supporting the ideology of capitalism, as it diverts attention away from the exploitative nature of capitalism and focuses attention instead on the evil and frightening nature of certain criminal groups in society, from whom we are only protected by the police. This justifies heavy policing of working-class areas, 'stop and searches' by the police of young people, and the arrests of any sections of the population who oppose capitalism.

An example of the traditional Marxist approach

William Chambliss' study of British vagrancy laws provides an illustration of the ways in which laws may be directly related to the interests of the ruling class. The first English vagrancy laws appeared in 1349, one year after the outbreak of the Black Death plague that was to kill more than one-third of the country's entire population. One result of the catastrophe was to decimate the labour force, so that those who were left could ask for high wages – and many people did this, moving from village to village in search of high pay. To combat this, the vagrancy laws were introduced, requiring every able-bodied man on the road to accept work at a low, fixed wage. The law was strictly enforced and did produce a supply of low-paid labour to help the workforce shortage. For almost 200 years the laws remained unchanged, but in 1530, changes were introduced which altered the emphasis of the laws to protect the concerns of an increasingly powerful merchant class from the many highway robbers who were preying on the traffic of goods along major highways. The vagrancy laws were amended so that they could be used to punish anyone on the road without a job, who was presumed to be a highwayman.

In both cases, the law was introduced and imposed in such a way as to benefit the ruling class – whilst apparently being concerned with stopping vagrants from travelling around England.

Criticisms of the traditional Marxist approach

1. The victims of crime are simply ignored in this analysis. The harm done by offenders is not taken into account. This is particularly important, as the victims are usually drawn from the less well-off sections of the population.
2. The explanation for law creation and enforcement tends to be one dimensional, in that all laws are seen as the outcome of the interests of the ruling class – no allowance is made for the complexity of influences on law-making behaviour.

The New Criminology

Partly as a result of these criticisms of what was a fairly crude Marxist explanation of crime, and partly as a result of the influence of interactionism (see Topic 4), Taylor, Walton and Young attempted to produce a fully social theory of deviance in *The New Criminology* (1973). This became an extremely influential book – possibly because it was a fairly successful fusing of Marxism and interactionism, the two most prominent theories of that time.

The new criminologists argued that in order to understand why a particular crime took place, it was no use just looking at the individual's motivation (e.g. alcohol or jealousy) and obvious influences (e.g. family background), which is what traditional positivist sociology might do. A Marxist perspective must be taken which looks at the wider capitalist society that helps generate the circumstances of the crime and police response to it. It is also important to use interactionist ideas to see how the behaviour of victim, offender, media and criminal justice system all interact to influence how the situation develops.

Ideology and the New Criminology

A further element of the New Criminology was that apart from the actual analysis that is suggested, it also argued that any sociology of crime and deviance had to be critical of the established capitalist order. This meant that instead of accepting the capitalist definition of crime and seeking to explain this, its role ought to be to uncover and explain the crimes of the rich. There was no attempt to be unbiased, rather the approach looked critically at the role of the police, the media and the criminal justice system in general – pointing out how they serve the needs of the ruling class.

Part of this critical approach to crime and criminal justice was to look in a fresh way at the ordinary criminal, who should best be seen as someone who is angry at capitalism and mistakenly expresses this anger through crime, rather than politics.

As we shall see in Topic 10, this later led to debates between **'left realists'**, who seek to work within the current system, and those who remained true to the ideas of critical criminology.

A good example of critical criminology is the work of Stuart Hall *et al.* (1978) in *Policing the Crisis: The State and Law and Order*. In the 1970s, London witnessed a growth in 'muggings', i.e. assault and robbery of people in the streets. The media focused on this crime and a wave of publicity forced the problem to the top of the political and policing agenda. Although Hall did not exactly follow the model put forward in *The New Criminology*, the general critical criminological framework was used – see Table 5.1 below.

Table 5.1 The new criminology

What a fully social theory of deviance must cover, according to Taylor *et al.* (1973)	Application of these ideas in Hall *et al.* (1978)
The wider origins of the deviant act	The 1970s was a period of considerable social crisis in Britain, the result of an international downturn in capitalist economies.
The immediate origins of the deviant act	This turmoil was shown in a number of inner-city riots, conflict in Northern Ireland and a high level of strikes. The government was searching for a group that could be scapegoated, to draw attention onto them and away from the crisis.
The actual act	Mugging – which according to the police was more likely to be carried out by those from African-Caribbean backgrounds.
The immediate origins of social reaction	Media outrage at the extent of muggings, linked to racism amongst the Metropolitan Police.
The wider origins of social reaction	The need to find scapegoats and the ease with which young men from African-Caribbean backgrounds could be blamed.
The outcome of social reaction on the deviants' further action	A sense of injustice amongst ethnic minorities and a loss of confidence by ethnic minority communities in the criminal justice system.
The nature of the deviant process as a whole	The real causes of crime were not addressed and were effectively hidden by the criminal justice system.

Criticisms of the New Criminology

Traditional Marxists such as Hirst (1975) argued that the New Criminology strayed too far from the Marxist tradition. Others, such as Rock (1988), who were concerned directly in combating crime, argued that it gave far too romantic a view of criminals (in later writings, Young echoed this criticism and suggested it was one of the reasons for his development of left realism – see Topic 10). Feminist criminologists, such as Pat Carlen (1988), pointed out that there was absolutely no specific discussion of the power of patriarchy in the analysis, which simply continued the omission of women from criminological discussion.

Methodologically, it has always been extremely difficult to apply this perspective, as it is so complicated. In fact, no sociologist has actually managed to use this approach and so it remains more as an interesting model than an approach which guides research.

Marxist subcultural theory

A second strand of thought that developed from Marxism, was a specific explanation for the existence of subcultures amongst the working class. According to The Centre for Contemporary Cultural Studies (a group of writers at Birmingham University), capitalism maintains control over the majority of the population in two ways:

- ideological dominance through the media
- economic pressures – people want to keep their jobs and pay their mortgages.

Only those groups on the margins of society are not 'locked in' by ideology and finance, and thus are able to provide some form of resistance to capitalism. The single largest group offering this resistance is working-class youth.

According to Brake (1980) amongst others, this resistance is expressed through working-class youth subcultures. The clothes they wear and the language they use show their disdain of capitalism and their awareness of their position in it. Brake argues that this resistance, however, is best seen as '**magical**'. By magical, he means that it is a form of illusion that appears to solve their problems, but in reality does no such thing. According to him, each generation of working-class youth face similar problems (dead-end jobs, unemployment, and so on), but in different circumstances – that is, society changes

constantly so that every generation experiences a very different world, with the one constant being that the majority will be exploited by the ruling class.

Each generation expresses its resistance through different choice of clothes, argot (slang and patterns of speech), music, and so on. But each will eventually be trapped like their parents before them.

Criticism of the Marxist subcultural approach

Methodological Problems

Stan Cohen (1980) pointed out that these writers were simply biased in their analysis. They wanted to prove that working-class youth cultures were an attack on capitalism, and therefore made sure that they fixed the evidence to find this. He pointed out, for example, that there were many different ways to interpret the subcultural style of the groups, and that the interpretation that the Marxist writers had imposed was just one of many possibilities. The researches using this method knew what they wanted (signs of subcultural resistance) when

synopticlink

Marxist approaches to crime link closely to the wider sociological debates about social class. The arguments discussed in Unit 8, Topic 4 regarding the decline in class and the growth of alternative bases for identity, also provide a criticism of Marxist explanations of crime, which rely heavily on the argument that there is ongoing class conflict between the working class and the bourgeoisie.

social inequality and difference

A particularly strong criticism has been provided by the postmodernist theorist Sarah Thornton (1997), who argues that Marxist subcultural theory is 'empirically unworkable', as social class no longer exists in its traditional form, but has been replaced by divisions based on gender and status. These, in turn, are based on media and on genuine cultural innovations by young people.

they started looking at youth culture and so they extracted what they wanted to prove their theory and ignored what did not fit it.

Theoretical Problems

Blackman (1995) points out that the stress on the working-class basis of subcultural resistance ignores the huge variation of subcultures based on variations in sexual identity, locality, age, 'intellectual capacity' and a range of other social factors. Thornton (1995) argues that there is simply no 'real' social-class basis to youth subcultures at all; these are, in fact, creations of the media.

An overview of Marxist or critical criminological approaches

Critical criminology has provided a very powerful counterbalance to explanations of crime and deviance that focus on the individual, their family or the community in which they live. Critical criminology has forced sociologists to explore the wider social, economic and political factors which shape society. Perhaps most of all, they point out that crimes can only happen when people break the law, but that the law itself reflects differences in power between groups. Powerful groups, they claim, can ensure that the law, and the enforcement of the law, reflects their interests.

However, Marxism as a significant theoretical perspective in sociology has been on the wane for a number of years. The questions it raises remain as important, but the answers provided by critical criminologists have been less influential in the subject.

Brake (1985)
Comparing youth subcultures

Brake undertook a comparative study of youth culture across the USA, Canada and Great Britain from the 1930s. Brake argues that all the variations in youth cultures across these countries can be traced back to young people's responses to particular social, economic and political events over the period. According to Brake, subcultures provide young people with both a collective and, within that, an individual identity. The actual basis of youth subculture, he argues, is one of resolving the specific social problems that young people face at any particular time. Brake suggests that the dominant influence on the form of youth culture varies according to social class, ethnicity or gender, depending upon how the young people experience their particular problems.

In order to gather material for his study, Brake undertook secondary analysis of the published research by other sociologists within each country on youth subcultures, and also reinterpreted some of his own earlier work. Brake supplemented this with reading and exploring non-sociological descriptions of youth activities over the period.

One major criticism of Brake's work is that he began with the theoretical idea that youth culture was a collective response to resolving young people's problems and then sought out support for this position. It is reasonable to argue that Brake was, therefore, selective in his choice of material.

Brake, M. (1985) *Comparative Youth Culture: The sociology of youth cultures and youth subcultures in America, Britain and Canada*, London: Routledge

1 **What do we mean by a 'comparative approach'?**

2 **What did Brake use to obtain the evidence for his theoretical approach?**

3 **What problems are there with this approach?**

Check your understanding

1 **How does the ruling class impose their values on others?**

2 **According to Marxists, how neutral is the law?**

3 **What is Bonger's explanation of individual motivation for crime?**

4 **How does Chambliss's research on vagrancy support a Marxist view of crime?**

5 **In what ways does the New Criminology utilize both Marxism and interactionism?**

6 **Why is it convenient for capitalism to find scapegoats?**

7 **How do Marxists explain the development of working-class subcultures?'**

8 **How do working-class subcultures resist capitalism?**

9 **In what way is their resistance 'magical'?**

10 **How have different Marxist approaches to crime and deviance been criticized?**

KEY TERMS

Hegemony – the ideas and values of the ruling class that dominate thinking in society.

Left realist – a development from Marxist criminology which argues that it is better to work within capitalism to improve people's lives, than to attempt wholesale social change.

'Magical' – illusory; in this context, something that appears to solve problems, but in reality does not.

Scapegoats – groups in society (usually relatively powerless) who are blamed by the powerful for the problems of society, thus drawing attention away from the real causes of crime.

web.tasks

1 Look up the website
www.socialistparty.org.uk
To what extent do you think the Marxist analysis contained in it accurately explains today's problems?

2 **Using the worldwide web, look up newspaper reports and background information about any recent terrorist or criminal event. See if you can apply the 'New Criminology' framework of Taylor, Walton and Young to interpret the event.**

research idea

Choose any one contemporary subcultural style. What are the favoured clothes, argot, style of music and other distinguishing features (e.g. skateboard)? What explanations can you offer for the origins of these? Interview members of the group to find the meaning they give to their dress, language, and so on.

exploring Marxist approaches

Item A

The criminal law is thus not a reflection of custom but a set of rules laid down by the state in the interests of the ruling class, and resulting from the conflicts built into class-structured societies; criminal behaviour is, then, the inevitable expression of class conflict resulting from the exploitative nature of economic relations.

Criminality is simply not something that people have or don't have; crime is not something some people do and others don't. Crime is a matter of who can pin the label on whom, and underlying this sociopolitical process is the structure of social relations determined by the political economy.

Adapted from Chambliss, W. (1975) 'Towards a Political Economy of Crime', *Theory and Society*, Vol. 2 (abridged)

Item B

Marxist explanations for crime have been heavily criticized for their 'Robin Hood' approach to crime, presenting the criminal as a class warrior redistributing property from rich to poor and its victims as deserving little sympathy. Little account was taken of the real harm caused to these victims, who are for the most part poorer people themselves. Furthermore, criticisms of Marxist approaches were reinforced by the collapse of Marxist-inspired political systems in Eastern Europe in the 1990s. Feminist writers began to argue that it was gender not social class that divided people, whilst late-modernist writers suggested that the division of society into enormous class 'blocs' was no longer accurate – if it ever had been.

Adapted from Coleman, C. and Norris, C. (2000) *Introducing Criminology*, Cullompton: Willan, pp. 75–6

(a) Using **Item A**, identify the 'inevitable expression of class conflict'. (1 mark)

(b) Identify and briefly explain **two** elements of the Marxist explanation for crime (Item A). (8 marks)

(c) Identify **three** criticisms of Marxist subcultural theory. (9 marks)

(d) Identify and explain **two** ways in which the Marxist approach may be described as a 'Robin Hood' approach to crime (**Item B**). (12 marks)

Exam practice

(e) **Outline and assess the usefulness of Marxist approaches to an understanding of crime and deviance.** (60 marks)

Patterns of crime

gettingyouthinking

1 **Have you had any crime (no matter how minor) committed against you in the last year? What was it? Did you report it to the police? Explain the reasons for you reporting/not reporting it.**

2 **Which of the three people in the photographs is most likely to be the victim of an attack at night on the streets? Explain the reasons for your answer.***

3 **Which car is more likely to be stolen: a smart new BMW or a 15-year-old Vauxhall Astra? Explain your answer.***

4 **Is bullying a crime? Please explain the reasons for your answer.***

5 **At school/college, how does the institution deal with bullying, cannabis use and 'minor' thefts? What implications does this have for official statistics?**

Answers to these questions are given on p. 59.

Our commonsense ideas about crime do not always match the picture revealed by statistics. Many of us believe that crime is something committed by the less wealthy against the more wealthy and more vulnerable sections of the community. This view may well have influenced your answers to the questions above. However, police figures indicate that poorer areas have higher crime rates than wealthy areas, that young men are more likely to be the victims of crime than old ladies, and that battered Ford Fiestas are more likely to be stolen than the latest executive BMW. But are these figures accurate, and how can we use statistics about crime to help us understand why some people commit crimes?

In order to understand why people commit crime, we need first to find out who commits crime and what sorts of crimes are committed. Sociologists use three different ways to build up this picture of crime. Each method provides us with particular information, but also has a number of weaknesses that need to be identified if our picture is to be accurate. The three methods of collecting information are:

- police-recorded statistics
- victim surveys
- self-report studies.

Police-recorded statistics

Police-recorded statistics are drawn from the records kept by the police and other official agencies, and are published every six months by the **Home Office**.

The **official statistics** are particularly useful in that they have been collected since 1857 and so provide us with an excellent historical overview of changing trends over time. They also give us a completely accurate view of the way that the criminal justice system processes offenders through arrests, trials, punishments, and so on.

Police-recorded statistics as social constructions

Police-recorded statistics are **social constructions** – they cannot be taken simply at their face value because they only show crimes that are reported to and recorded by the police. When we dig a little deeper, a lot of hidden issues are uncovered.

Reporting crime

Police-recorded statistics are based on the information that the criminal justice agencies collect. But crimes cannot be recorded by them if they are not reported in the first place, and the simple fact is that a high proportion of 'crimes' are not reported to the police at all. According to the **British Crime Survey** (Home Office 1998), we know that individuals are less likely to report a 'crime' to the police if they regard it as:

- too trivial to bother the police with
- a private matter between friends and family – in this case they will seek redress directly (get revenge themselves) – or one where they wish no harm to come to the offender
- too embarrassing (e.g. male rape).

Other reasons for non-reporting of crimes are that:

- the victim may not be in a position to give information (e.g. a child suffering abuse)
- they may fear reprisals.

On the other hand, people are more likely to report a crime if:

- they see some benefit to themselves (e.g. an insurance claim)
- they have faith in the police ability to achieve a positive result.

Recording of crimes

When people do actively report an offence to the police, you would think that these statistics at least would enter the official reports. Yet in any one year, approximately 57 per cent of all crimes reported to the police fail to appear in the official statistics. Figure 5.6 on the next page shows the proportion of the crimes committed that are reported to the police and the proportion recorded by the police.

The role of the police

Clearly the police are filtering the information supplied to them by the public, according to factors that are important to them. These factors have been identified as follows:

British Crime Survey

The British Crime Survey (BCS) was first introduced in 1982, heavily influenced by a similar type of survey which had been undertaken in the USA since 1972 (funded by the US Department of Justice). Originally, the UK studies were every two years, but since 2000, they have been carried out every year. The sample size is enormous, with almost 40 000 people being interviewed. The idea behind the study is that by asking people directly what crimes have been committed against them, the problems of crime reporting and police recording are avoided. Supporters of the survey suggest that it is more 'valid' than the police statistics.

The sampling technique is based on (a) all households in England and Wales and then (b) anyone over 16 living in these households. The households are selected using the Postcode Address File, developed by the Post Office to recognize all households in Britain. Interviews last 50 minutes and each person is asked if they have been the victim of a list of selected crimes. There is then a smaller 'sweep' (a subsample), who are asked to answer questions on a selected (sometimes sensitive) issues directly into a laptop computer.

Is the BCS more accurate than the police-recorded statistics? The answer provided by Maguire (2002) is that the BCS is neither better nor worse, but simply provides an alternative, overall picture of crime which helps fill in some gaps in the police-recorded statistics.

1 What steps does the BCS take to maximize the representativeness of the survey?

2 Can you identify any groups who may still be left out of the survey?

3 Why do you think respondents in the smaller subsample are asked to input their answers directly into a laptop computer?

Figure 5.6 Reporting and recording of crime

Proportions of BCS estimate of all crime reported to the police and recorded by them (comparable subset of crimes), year to September 2004

All incidences of crime

- Not reported to the police 57%
- Reported and recorded 32%
- Reported to the police, but not recorded 11%

Source: Nicholas, S. *et al.* (2005) *Crime in England and Wales 2004/5*, Home Office Statistical Bulletin

British courts work on the assumption that many people will plead guilty – and about 75 per cent of all those charged actually do so. This is often the result of an informal and largely unspoken agreement whereby the defence will try to get the charges with the lightest possible punishment put forward by the prosecution. (In the USA, this bargaining is far more open than in Britain, and is known as **plea-bargaining**.) The result is an overwhelming majority of pleas of guilty, yet these pleas are for less serious crimes than might 'really' have been committed. The statistics will reflect this downgrading of seriousness.

The role of the government

What is considered to be a crime changes over time, as a result of governments changing the law in response to cultural changes and the influence of powerful groups. Any exploration of crime over a period is therefore fraught with difficulty, because any rise or fall in the levels of crime may reflect changes in the law as much as actual changes in crime. A good example of this is the way that attitudes to cannabis use have shifted – while there has been an increase in the numbers of people possessing and using cannabis (both of which are a crime), the number of arrests for its possession has actually declined, as the police respond to public opinion. The police statistics might make it look as if cannabis use is actually declining, when it is not.

Sociology A2 for OCR

- *Seriousness* – They may regard the offence as too trivial or simply not a criminal matter.
- *Social status* – More worryingly, they may view the social status of the person reporting the matter as not high enough to regard the issue as worth pursuing.
- *Classifying* – When a person makes a complaint, police crimes officers must decide what category of offence it is. How they classify the offence will determine its seriousness. So, the police officer's opinion determines the category and seriousness of crime (from assault, to aggravated assault for example).
- *Discretion* – Only about 10 per cent of offences are actually uncovered by the police. However, the chances of being arrested for an offence increase markedly depending upon the 'demeanour' of the person being challenged by a police officer (that is, their appearance, attitude and manner). Anderson *et al.* (1994) show that youths who cooperate and are polite to police officers are less likely to be arrested than those regarded as disrespectful.
- *Promotion* – Police officers, like everyone else, have concerns about career and promotion. This involves relationships trying to impress senior officers. However, at work they also need to get on with other colleagues, who do not like officers who are too keen (as this makes more work for everyone). Arrests reflect a balance between comradeship and a desire for promotion (Collinson 1995).

The role of the courts

Official statistics of crimes committed and punished also reflect the decisions and sentences of the courts. However, these statistics, too, are a reflection of social processes.

Victim surveys

A second way of estimating the extent and patterns of crime is by using **victimization** (or **victim**) **surveys**. In these, a sample of the population, either locally or nationally, are asked which offences have been committed against them over a certain period of time.

Strengths of victim surveys

This approach overcomes the fact that a significant proportion of offences are never recorded by the police. It also gives an excellent picture of the extent and patterns of victimization – something completely missing from official accounts. The best known victimization study is the British Crime Survey which is now collected every year and has been in operation since 1982 (see Focus on research, p. 53).

Weaknesses of victim surveys

- The problem of basing statistics on victims' memories is that recollections are often faulty or biased.
- The categorization of the crimes that has been committed against them is left to the person filling in the questionnaire – this leads to considerable inaccuracy in the categories.
- Victim surveys also omit a range of crimes, such as fraud and corporate crime, and any crime where the victim is unaware of or unable to report a crime.
- Despite victim surveys being anonymous, people appear to underreport sexual offences.

Figure 5.7 Perspectives on criminal statistics

Different sociological perspectives take a range of positions on the usefulness of criminal statistics.

Positivist

Early sociological theories of crime and deviance, particularly those influenced by functionalism such as Merton's, were based on an uncritical acceptance of the accuracy of official criminal statistics.

Interpretive

The 'labelling' view rejects the accuracy of crime statistics. Instead, it concentrates on understanding the way they are socially constructed. Labelling views are covered in detail in **Topic 4**.

Marxist

Marxists believe that law and its enforcement reflects the interests of the ruling class. The crimes of the poor are strictly enforced and the immoral activities of the rich either ignored or not defined as criminal. Statistics will reflect these inequalities and scapegoating. Critical criminology is the subject of **Topic 5**.

Perspectives on criminal statistics

Feminist

Feminists believe that crime statistics do not reflect the amount of crime against women, such as sexual attacks and domestic violence. These often occur in a 'private' domestic setting where the police are reluctant to get involved. Also, many women do not feel they can report these offences. The issue of gender and crime is explored in **Topic 8**.

Late modern

See the section on 'The data explosion and the risk society' (p. 56)

Left realist

These sociologists accept that crime is a genuine problem, especially for poorer groups in society. Crime statistics cannot simply be rejected as inaccurate. Left realists favour detailed victim surveys in local areas. These can reveal the basis for many people's genuine fear of crime. More detail on this perspective can be found in **Topic 10**.

- The BCS itself suffers from the problem of not collecting information from those under 16, although this is not necessarily a problem of victim surveys as such. The British Youth Lifestyles Survey (2000), for example, was carried out specifically to obtain detailed information on crimes against younger people.

Local victim surveys

The BCS is a typical cross-sectional survey, and as such may contain some errors – certainly, it does not provide detailed information about particular places. This has led to a number of detailed studies of crime focusing on particular areas. These provide specific information about local problems.

The most famous of these surveys were the **Islington Crime Surveys** (Harper et al. 1986 and Jones et al. 1995). These showed that the BCS underreported the higher levels of victimization of minority ethnic groups and domestic violence.

The media and sensitization

Victim surveys are dependent upon people being aware that they are victims. This may seem obvious, but in fact this depends very much on the 'victim' perceiving what happens to them as being a crime. The media play a key role in this as they provide illustrations of 'crimes' and generally heighten sensitivity towards certain forms of behaviour. This is known as **sensitizing** the public towards (certain types of) activity that can be seen as a crime worth reporting. A positive

example of this has been the change in portrayal of domestic violence from a family matter to being a criminal activity.

Self-report studies

The third method for collecting data is that of **self-report studies**. These are surveys in which a selected group or cross-section of the population are asked what offences they have committed. Self-report studies are extremely useful as they reveal much about the kind of offenders who are not caught or processed by the police. In particular, it is possible to find out about the ages, gender, social class and even location of 'hidden offenders'. It is also the most useful way to find out about victimless crimes such as illegal drug use.

Weaknesses of self-report studies

- The problem of validity – The biggest problem is that respondents may lie or exaggerate, and even if they do not deliberately seek to mislead, they may simply be mistaken.
- The problem of representativeness – Because it is easy to study them, most self-report surveys are on young people and students. There are no such surveys on professional criminals or drug traffickers, for example!
- The problem of relevance – Because of the problem of representativeness, the majority of the crimes uncovered tend to be trivial.

Nevertheless, the only information that we have available of who offends, other than from the official statistics of people who have been arrested, comes from self-report studies, and they have been very widely used to explore such issues as crime and drug use.

Figure 5.8 summarises the processes and problems involved in different methods of finding out about patterns of crime.

The data explosion and the risk society

Maguire (2002) has pointed out that since the 1970s there has been a huge increase in the amount of statistics gathered on crime and 'antisocial behaviour'. Before then, the main source of information was the government publication *Criminal Statistics*, which relied solely upon criminal justice agencies for the figures. Since the 1970s, information has come to be gathered on wider aspects of crime:

- Unreported and unrecorded offences – Information is collected through the BCS.
- Specialist subcategories of crime – There are now literally hundreds of crime categories that official statistics record.
- Hidden crime – Information on sexual offences, domestic violence, white-collar crime and, most recently, corporate crime has started to be gathered.
- Victim perspectives – Possibly the most recent innovation has been the collection of information from the victims of crime.

Garland (2001) suggests that it is not just an expansion of knowledge for its own sake that has driven the explosion of statistical information. He suggests instead that the answer can be found within the concerns of late modernity. During modernity, governments took upon themselves the task of controlling crime and punishing criminals. According to Garland, most people believed that the government had crime control in

hand. Garland suggests that in late modernity, there is a much greater sense of uncertainty and risk, and governments are no longer believed to catch and punish all criminals. Instead, the government engages in **risk management** – it gathers statistics on crime so that it can better assess and manage this risk. Garland has also introduced the notion of '**responsibilization**' – part of risk management is to push responsibility for avoiding becoming victims of crime back onto individuals. The statistics are part of this process of informing individuals how best to avoid becoming victims of crime.

Patterns of offending

Using the three methods of gathering information, sociologists have managed to construct an interesting picture of offending and victimization patterns.

Types of offences

Property crime

According to the British Crime Survey, 62 per cent of crime in 2000 was accounted for by some form of property theft, with burglary and vehicle theft forming the bulk of these.

Violent crime

All forms of violence account for approximately 20 per cent of BCS-reported crime, but the huge majority of these acts of violence – about 68 per cent – consisted only of very minor physical hurt (at most slight bruising). In fact, only about 5 per cent of violent crimes reported involved more than trivial injury.

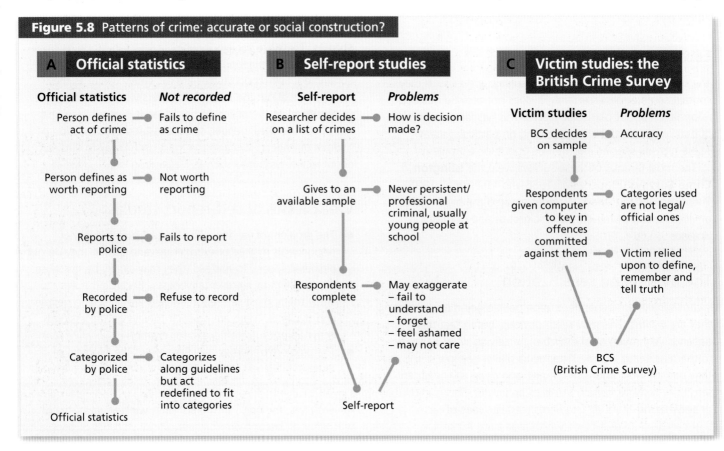

Figure 5.8 Patterns of crime: accurate or social construction?

social inequality and difference

People from Black and ethnic-minority backgrounds were at greater risk of being victims of crime than the White population, according to the 2002/3 British Crime Survey. However, this can largely be explained by the fact that the age profile of ethnic minorities in Britain has a much higher proportion of younger people. Younger people (of any ethnic background) are more likely to be victims of crime than any other age group. However, there are some differences in the types of crime that ethnic minorities are more likely to be victims of – particularly mugging and other forms of 'street crime'. Also, they were much more likely to be victims of 'hate' crime.

Types of victims

Victims of violence

Young males, who form the majority of the unemployed or low-waged, have a particularly high chance of being victims. Interestingly, in about 88 per cent of cases of violence, the victim and perpetrator know each other.

Victims of property crime

Victims of property crime are most likely to be low-income households living in poorer areas.

Repeat victimization

Victim surveys demonstrate not only that some people are more likely than others to be victims in the first place, but that a proportion of the victims are likely to be targeted more than once (**repeat victimization**). Twenty per cent of all households burgled experienced repeat burglaries and one tiny group has a disproportionately high chance of being victimized: 0.4 per cent of householders accounted for 22 per cent of all burglaries.

The statistics suggest that crime does not happen to everyone: it targets the poorer and less powerful groups in society more than the affluent, and those who live in more deprived urban areas more than those who live in the suburbs or countryside (see below). The statistics also tell us that violent crime tends to happen between people who know each other, even live together.

Fear of Crime

Ethnicity

People from Black and ethnic-minority backgrounds are more likely to be worried that they will be victims of most forms of crime compared to the majority White population. As the Synoptic link above outlines, the greater risk of victimization for people from ethnic-minority backgrounds simply reflects the high proportion of young people in those groups.

Gender

Women are nearly three times as likely as men in England and Wales to be very worried about physical attack (17 per cent compared with 6 per cent), yet, in fact, men are slightly more likely than women to be a victim of violent crime (5 per cent compared with 3 per cent).

Age

Both males and females under the age of 25 reported the highest levels of worry for nearly all crimes – in particular, 25 per cent of women aged 16 to 29 were very worried about rape. This worry about crime was lower among men and women aged 60 and over. This does reflect the higher chances of people in younger age groups being victims. However, the number of sexual offences against women by strangers is very small.

focus on...

Regional variations in crime

The figures on the right show your chances of being a victim of crime in different regions of England and Wales. As the figures are 'rates', the number of people living in the different areas is taken into account.

Source: Dodd et al. (2004)

1 Identify and suggest explanations for the regional differences in crime shown.

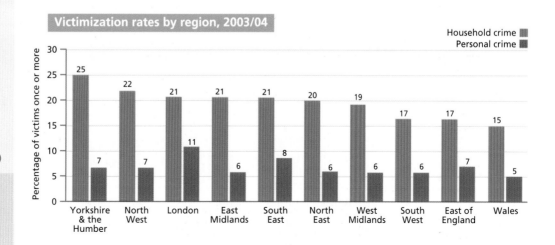

Victimization rates by region, 2003/04

Household crime ■
Personal crime ■

Percentage of victims once or more

Region	Household crime	Personal crime
Yorkshire & the Humber	25	7
North West	22	7
London	21	11
East Midlands	21	6
South East	21	8
North East	20	6
West Midlands	19	6
South West	17	6
East of England	17	7
Wales	15	5

Types of offenders

According to both official statistics and self-report studies, offenders are most likely to be young and male. The peak age of offending for males is about 18, and for females about 14.

The next three topics attempt to explain why some of the patterns identified here exist. They focus on crime and class, gender and ethnicity respectively.

Check your understanding

1 Explain why official statistics give a completely accurate picture of the workings of the criminal justice system.

2 Explain why official statistics do not give an accurate picture of the number and types of crimes committed.

3 Why might official statistics give a more accurate picture of the amount of car theft than the amount of domestic violence?

4 How might a person's 'demeanour' affect their likelihood of arrest?

5 Explain why so many people plead guilty in court.

6 Do reductions in arrests for possession of cannabis reflect a decrease in the use of the drug? Explain your answer.

7 Suggest three crimes that you think people might be willing to admit to being victims of when questioned in a victimization study.

8 Why might some people exaggerate the amount of crime that they have committed in a self-report study?

9 Suggest two reasons why young males might make up the majority of victims of violence.

10 Explain why repeat victimization may occur.

researchideas

1 The table below is based on a national sample of people aged 16 and over, who were asked to indicate what the greatest problem in their area was.

	Very/fairly big problem (%)	Very/fairly common (%)
Teenagers hanging around	32	51
Rubbish and litter	31	42
Vandalism	32	34
Drug use/dealing	33	31
Run-down homes	13	15
Noisy neighbours	9	14
Abandoned cars	13	14
Racial attacks	7	5
People sleeping rough	4	3

Conduct a small pilot survey of 14 to 16 year olds using the categories in the table. Do your results reflect the results here? Why do you think there may be differences?.

2 Carry out interviews with a small sample of people of different ages and genders to discover the factors that influence public reporting of crime. Does it depend on seriousness, whether the crime has a victim or other factors? Does likelihood of reporting correlate with variables such as age or gender?

web.task

Find the site of the Home Office at
www.homeoffice.gov.uk

Go to the section on Research Development Statistics. Try to find figures about the amount and type of crime using official statistics, self-report studies and victim studies. What similarities and differences can you find? Try to explain the patterns you find.

KEY TERMS

British Crime Survey – annual victimization survey carried out by the Home Office.

Home Office – government department responsible for criminal justice matters.

Islington Crime Surveys – famous local victimization studies focusing on one area of North London.

Official statistics – statistics released by government agencies.

Plea-bargaining – where there is an informal (sometimes unspoken) agreement that if an accused person pleads guilty to a lesser crime than that of which he or she is accused, the prosecution will agree.

Repeat victimization – where people are victims of the same crime more than once.

Responsibilization – Garland suggests this is the shift towards blaming people for becoming victims of crime, by suggesting

they have not taken adequate precautions.

Risk management – the process whereby governments stop trying to prevent all crime and instead see it as their job to limit the risk of crime for the population.

Self-report studies – where people are asked to note down the crimes they have committed over a particular period.

Sensitizing – refers to the extent of disorder or minor criminal activity that people will accept.

Social construction – in this case, refers to the fact that statistics represent the activities of the people constructing the statistics rather than some objective reality.

Victimization (or victim) surveys – where people are asked what crimes have happened to them over a particular period.

Item A

Worry about crime*: by sex and age, 2003/4, England and Wales

	Theft from a car**	Theft of a car**	Burglary	Mugging	Physical attack	Rape	Insulted or pestered
Males							
16–29	16	18	10	9	8	7	4
30–59	14	14	11	6	5	3	4
60 and over	9	11	10	7	5	2	2
All aged 16 and over	13	14	10	7	6	4	4
Females							
16–29	16	20	16	17	22	24	10
30–59	11	15	15	14	17	19	10
60 and over	8	12	14	15	13	12	7
All aged 16 and over	11	15	15	15	17	18	9

* Percentages of people who were 'very worried' about selected types of crime
** Based on respondents residing in households owning, or with regular use of, a vehicle

Source: Dodd et al. (2004)

Item B

The 'true facts' of offending have been, and will remain, unknowable. There are three main means by which crime rates have been estimated – recorded crime statistics, victim surveys and self-report studies – but none can claim to provide an objective and incontrovertible picture. The problem arises because all quantitative data depend not only on which behaviours are perceived and defined as crime, but also on the validity of the various statistical measures and on the range of interpretations that can legitimately be made up of any figures, no matter how they are produced. Most obviously, changes in policing priorities, or changes in what the law counts as crime, or shifts in public tolerance will all affect statistical representations of the crime problem.

Munice, J. (2004) *Youth and Crime*, London: Sage

(a) Using **Item A**, identify the percentage of women, aged 16 to 29 questioned who were 'very worried' about being 'physically attacked'. (1 mark)

(b) Identify and briefly explain **two** methods of collecting crime statistics. (8 marks)

(c) Identify **three** trends and/or patterns in the table in **Item A**. (9 marks)

(d) Identify and explain two criticisms of victim studies as a method of obtaining accurate information about crime. (12 marks)

Exam practice

(e) Outline and assess the usefulness of official statistics of crime to sociologists. (60 marks)

Answers to Getting you thinking (p. 52)

2 The young man is more likely to be a victim of an attack.

3 The older car is more likely to be stolen.

4 Yes, generally, bullying is a crime as it involves threats and/or actual violence.

Occupational and corporate crime

- In 1998, in Lanarkshire a local butcher failed to comply with hygiene regulations and to cooperate with local authority enforcement officials. As a result 450 people became ill, some very seriously, and 21 died.
- In 1999, in Glasgow, two students died in a fire in a house converted to small flats. The fire was started accidentally. The flats were not registered with the local authority and had not been inspected.

1 What, in your view, is the difference between an 'accident' which results in someone being harmed and a 'crime' which results in someone being harmed?

2 Should smoking be made illegal? Justify your view.

3 In your view, were the two incidents described above unfortunate 'accidents' or crimes?

4 Each year, small children die in Britain because of accidents resulting from playing with unsafe, cheap imitations of more expensive toys. Who is to blame? The children? The parents? The manufacturers? Or are these just unfortunate accidents?

What is meant by 'occupational crime' and 'corporate crime'?

The study of **occupational crime** and **corporate crime** developed from the original work of Sutherland (1940) in the 1940s. Sutherland used the term '**white-collar**' **crime** to refer to crime committed by people who worked in offices. However, Sutherland's work overlaps with the interests of Marxist writers who were interested in the 'crimes of the powerful'. Both approaches share the concern that traditional research into crime centres on such things as robbery and burglary, and in doing so focuses on working-class offenders. People committing offences such as fraud, who tend to be at the other end of the class structure, tend to be ignored.

Although there has been general agreement with Sutherland's argument that crime committed by the powerful needed studying, there remains considerable debate between sociologists about exactly what should be studied under this term. Sutherland (1940) originally defined white-collar crime as 'crime committed by a person of respectability and high social status in the course of his occupation'.

The definition is unfortunately very vague and includes within it two, quite different activities: on the one hand, it means crimes against the organization for which the person works, and on the other, crimes for the benefit of the organization for which the person works or which they own.

Occcupational and corporate offending: the problem of law

There is one more problem in the debate about what occupational/corporate crime actually is. Very often, when sociologists talk about white-collar or corporate crime, they may actually not be discussing actions that are illegal – that is, if the company or person is 'caught', no one is likely to go in front of a judge and face the possible personal risk of going to jail. Instead, the crime studied may actually be the breaking of supervisory codes (as in financial services) or technical standards (chemical content of consumer goods), or may refer to a whole range of actions that are, it could be argued, harmful and may even lead to death, but are not strictly speaking illegal – low safety standards at work, but that meet minimum legal criteria, for example. In fact, as Nelken (2002) points out, the debate about corporate crime is as much about corporate practices and sociologists' biases about what is morally wrong, as it is about breaking the law.

Some writers, such as Pearce and Tombs (1998), argue that corporate crime ought to extend to the manufacture of cigarettes or alcohol – both of which are linked to illness and death. Others point out that transnational companies that manufacture in poorer nations where safety standards are negligible, are engaging in human-rights violations and are therefore committing crime – even if they are acting in a perfectly legal way according to the laws of the country where they are manufacturing.

So, much of the debate about occupational or corporate 'crime' goes beyond the limits of the law and looks at actions that have harmful consequences – and, in doing so, takes us beyond the limits of conventional criminology, opening up debates about what the sociology of crime and deviance ought to study.

The distinctions between occupational and corporate crime

This has led to two confusing and overlapping traditions:

- Studies of *occupational crime* – How and why people steal from companies and the public in activities associated with their jobs; for example, the employee who claims false expenses from the company or who overcharges customers and keeps the additional amount.
- The study of *corporate crime* – Much more important as a field of study in sociology, this is crime by corporations or businesses that has a serious physical or economic impact on employees, consumers or the general public. Corporate crime is motivated by the desire to increase profits.

Corporate crime

The impact of corporate crime

Many sociological approaches – particularly that of the left realists – have pointed out the enormous costs of conventional crime to society, as well as the damage it does to the quality of people's lives. Those interested in studying corporate crime argue, however, that the costs of conventional crime are actually dwarfed by corporate crime. There are no contemporary calculations of the cost of corporate crime, but the figures used by Conklin (1977) 30 years ago in his study in the USA are still staggering today.

<< *The direct cost of business crime surpasses the cost of such conventional crimes as larceny, burglary, and auto-theft. (In 1977) the estimated loss from these three crimes was about $3 billion to $4 billion a year. This figure pales in significance when compared with an estimated annual loss of $40 billion from various white-collar crimes. Half that results from consumer fraud, illegal competition and deceptive practices.* >>

An example of this was the collapse of the US stock market (in particular, property and banking corporations) at the end of the 1980s in the USA. This was the result of financial mismanagement and sometimes downright fraud and has cost in the region of a trillion dollars. Yet, interestingly, this was largely covered by a US government 'loan' that has covered the deficit. In 1998, Enron, a huge US company, went bankrupt with debts of $31 billion. According to Reiman (2003):

<< *Enron hid the degree of indebtedness from investors by treating loans as revenue, hiding losses by creating new companies and then attributing losses to them and not Enron and of encouraging company employees to buy Enron shares while the executives apparently knew of its shaky condition and were busy selling off their own shares.* >>

The 'costs' of corporate crime are not just economic. Carson (1970) studied the loss of life in the exploration for oil in the North Sea resulting from the lack of concern by exploration companies about the safety issues of the workers. This was later tragically illustrated in 1988 by the loss of 168 lives when the Piper Alpha oil rig exploded. Similarly, corporate negligence and management failings have also been pointed to more recently in a series of rail crashes involving loss of life at Paddington, Potters Bar and Hatfield.

We pointed out earlier the way that corporate 'crime' can **transgress** the boundaries of crime through acts that may not actually be illegal, but are regarded by sociologists as morally reprehensible and often a violation of certain human rights.

According to Michalowski and Kramer (1987), modern transnational corporations can practise a policy of **law evasion**, for example setting up factories in countries that do not have pollution controls or adequate safety legislation, rather than producing in countries with stricter standards. They may sell goods to poorer countries when the goods have been declared unsafe in the more affluent countries (a fairly common procedure with pharmaceuticals). Box (1983) has claimed that multinationals dump products, plants and practices illegal in industrialized countries on to undeveloped or underdeveloped countries. They are able to do this because the poorer countries do not have the resources to control the large companies and also because officials are likely to accept bribes.

Corporate crime is, therefore, a major problem for society and actually cost economies more than conventional crimes. What is particularly interesting is just how little attention is paid to them and how sanctions against those engaged in this form of crime are relatively minor.

Obstacles organizations need to overcome to make profit, according to Box

Box suggests that there are a number of potential obstacles that organizations may have to overcome in order to achieve their goals:

- *The government* – This will impose laws to regulate production and commerce, for example on insider trading in investments, or pollution as a result of productive practices in manufacturing.
- *Employees* – They may not wish to work as hard or perform the sorts of tasks/run the risks the organization wants.
- *Consumers* – They might not wish to purchase certain products if they knew the full facts concerning their production, or might not be willing to pay the additional costs to make the product of good quality/safe. An example of this is the food industry that uses a wide range of food-adulterating practices and poor animal-husbandry to produce cheap food.
- *The public* – Pressure groups may want to influence consumers and the government to change or enforce legislation. The proposed regulations might harm the profits of the companies.

Box argues that all of these groups represent potential barriers to companies achieving their goals, and these barriers may have to be overcome, possibly in illegal ways.

Occupational crime

The impact of occupational crime

Theft by employees is a major source of crime in Britain – though whether the action of depriving an employer of goods, services or money is actually defined as theft is a real issue. Ditton (1977) and Mars (1982) have both studied theft by employees and found that in the range of industries they studied – from workers in the tourist industry to bakery delivery drivers – minor theft was regarded as a legitimate part of the job and redefined into a 'perk' or a 'fiddle'. Indeed, according to Mars, fiddling was part of the rewards of the job. For their part, according to Clarke (1990), management generally turned a blind eye to fiddles, accepting them as part of the total remuneration of the job and taking these into account in determining wage structures.

Fraud is a criminal offence covering a wide range of situations, but if we focus only on fraud by employees on employers, Levi (1987) found that in the late 1980s, 75 per cent of all frauds on financial institutions such as banks and building societies were by their own employees. Of 56 companies he surveyed, over 40 per cent had experienced fraud of over £50 000 by employees that year. However, employers were very reluctant to prosecute as they feared that by doing so, they could attract negative publicity.

Practices of occupational crime extend into the professions too. Functionalist writings on the reason for the existence of the professions (Parsons 1964) stress that the key difference between professionals and most other workers is the degree of trust placed in them by their clients/patients. According to Nelken (2002), however, there is a considerable body of evidence pointing to fraudulent claims made by doctors and dentists against insurance companies in the USA and, to a smaller extent, against the NHS in Britain.

Explaining occupational and corporate crime

Sociologists have sought to incorporate occupational and corporate crime into existing theories – though with varying degrees of success. The approaches include:

● personality-based explanations
● differential association and subcultural theory
● emotion-based approaches
● labelling theory
● anomie
● Marxist explanations.

Personality-based explanations

Gross (1978) studied a range of individuals who had been successful in large companies. He found that they shared similar personality traits. They tended to be ambitious, to see their own success in terms of the company's success and, most relevant, that they had an 'undemanding moral code' (that we might term 'being unscrupulous'). According to Gross, the more successful they were, the less their sense of obligation to conform to wider social obligations. They accepted that personal and company success was more important than legal constraints. The difficulty with this kind of 'explanation', however, is then explaining why they are like this in the first place – it is rather like saying that criminals offend because they have an 'undemanding moral code'!

Differential association and subcultural theory

Sutherland (1940), who initiated the sociological discussion of white-collar crime, argued that his theory of **differential association** helped account for why business executives committed such enormous amounts of crime that benefited themselves and their organizations. Sutherland claimed that the culture of the organization might well justify committing illegal or dubious acts in order to achieve the organization's goals. Geis (1967), for example, examined the evidence given to congressional hearings into illegal price-fixing agreements of companies in the USA. He found that people taking up posts in organizations tended to find that price-fixing was an established practice and they would routinely become involved as part of the learning process of their jobs.

As early as 1952, Aubert studied how rationing procedures had been subverted during World War II by officials and members of food organizations, so that favouritism was shown to some groups and individuals (including themselves). Aubert (1952) found that these 'white-collar criminals' had an 'elaborate and widely accepted ideological rationalization for the offences'. In fact, criminal practices were quite normal. Evidence that such practices continue to this day comes from Braithwaite's (1984) study of the pharmaceutical industry, where bribing health inspectors was regarded as a perfectly normal part of business practice.

Emotion-based approaches

More recently, the interest in emotions and the meaning of masculinity has spilled over into explaining occupational and organizational crime. Often, when studying these forms of crime, the researcher is puzzled that people who earn huge incomes or who have enormous power, put themselves at risk either by seeking further personal gain, or more surprisingly perhaps, leading the company into illegal activity with limited personal benefits. According to Portnoy (1997), the answer could lie in the search for thrills and excitement. This is no different from the explanations offered for other forms of crime by writers such as Lyng and Katz (see Topic 8, p. 71). Portnoy describes a world of excitement and thrill-seeking in the world of high finance where the excitement is as valued by the executives as are the financial benefits. In a similar manner, Punch (1996) argues that high finance is a world of 'power struggles, ideological debate, intense political rivalry, manipulation of information buffeted by moral ambiguity'. For these writers, then, crimes by companies and by individuals are explicable by thrill-seeking. Interestingly, this also links to ideas of masculinity, as the majority of people in senior positions are male, with high-risk 'macho' attitudes regarded positively by the culture of big business.

Labelling theory

According to Mars (1982), this approach provides the most appropriate avenue for understanding occupational crime and how employers respond to it. Employees build up expectations about what they deserve and what is an appropriate or 'fair' payment for the job; if they do not receive this, will engage in illegal practices to reach the 'fair' salary.

Mars, in his study of the catering industry (1982), explains theft by employees and sharp practice by restaurant owners by referring to the conflicting values of capitalism:

>> *There is only a blurred line between **entrepreneuriality** and flair on the one hand and sharp practice and fraud on the other.* >>

How this is labelled by the person and the company employing them will determine the outcome of the label – criminal, 'overstepping the mark' or simply 'sharp practice'. Nelken (2002) examined the workings of the English Family Practitioner Panels which examine the cases of NHS professionals accused of not having complied with their NHS contracts – in other words, accused of defrauding the NHS by overclaiming. His conclusion was that 'everything possible was done to avoid the impression that potentially criminal behaviour is at issue' – thus where 'misconduct' (theft) was proved, the NHS professional had income withheld, but nothing else. Nelken notes that on one occasion where the dentist involved admitted to 'fraud', the Panel 'pleaded with him to retract his admission' so that it would not pass on for criminal prosecution. Nelken therefore argues that crime committed by professionals is rarely defined as such.

On a broader scale, labelling theory can help explain corporate crime in a rather different way. Labelling theory argues that negative labels are applied to certain groups or organizations when other, more powerful groups are able to impose that label. According to Nelken (2002), much of corporate crime can be explained by this. Legislation making some forms of activity legal or illegal is 'fought over' by various interest groups and the resulting law will reflect the views and interests of the more powerful.

Anomie

Merton's anomie approach has also been applied to explain both occupational and corporate crime. Anomie theory states that every society has culturally approved goals and means to achieve these goals; if people are unable to obtain the goals by the culturally approved means, then they will develop alternatives. Box, who straddles a number of theoretical perspectives, used the idea of Merton's version of anomie (Topic 3) to help explain why organizations break the law. Box (1983) argues that if an organization is unable to achieve its goals using socially approved methods, then it may turn to other, possibly illegal, methods of achieving its goal of maximizing profit.

The idea of anomie was also developed in a wider way by Braithwaite (1984), who argued that corporate crime could be seen as: 'an illegitimate means of achieving any one of a wider range of organizational and personal goals when legitimate means are blocked.' In his study of the pharmaceutical industry, he found that scientists were willing to fabricate their results in order to have their products adopted by their companies. The motivation for this was often not solely financial greed, but as often as not the desire for scientific prestige.

Similarly, in the high-pressure world of business, individuals who perceive themselves as failing may turn to various alternative modes of behaving, including occupational crime, according to Punch (1996).

However, Nelken (2002) is sceptical about the worth of anomie theory. He points out that anomie theory fails to explain why some individuals and companies choose illegal responses and others legal. Nelken suggests that until this is made clear, then the explanation is just too vague.

Marxist explanations

Perhaps the theoretical approach that has most enthusiastically adopted the study of corporate crime is the Marxist tradition. Corporate crime fits the critical criminological view that the real criminals are the rich and powerful. Critical criminologists argue that despite the fact that the powerful are able to use their dominance of society to avoid having the majority of their activities defined as illegal, they will still break the law where it conflicts with their interests. Furthermore, if they are actually caught, then they are less likely to be punished.

Swartz (1975) argues that as capitalism involves the maximization of corporate profits, then 'its normal functioning produces deaths and illnesses'. So, business crime is based upon the very values and legitimate practices of capitalism. Box (1983) has pointed out the success that the powerful have had in promoting the idea that corporate crime is less serious and less harmful than the range of normal street crimes, violence and burglary. Box describes this as a deliberate process of 'mystification' that has helped keep corporate crime as a minor object of study in criminology.

This theme was taken up by Frank Pearce (1976) who was interested in why there were so few prosecutions against corporations and senior business people. He concluded that they were so rare because otherwise there would be an undermining of the belief that the vast majority of crime is carried out by the working class. If the true pattern of crime came to be known by the bulk of the population, then it would create a crisis of legitimacy for the ruling class.

Slapper and Tombs (1999) claim that their research into the behaviour of large transnational companies in developing countries demonstrates the Marxist case that illegal and immoral practices are normal under capitalism. These companies routinely sell unsafe products, pay low wages and provide dangerous working conditions.

However, Carrabine et al. (2004) have criticized the Marxist position on corporate crime, by pointing out that the provision of poor working conditions, pollution of the environment and low pay are not restricted to capitalist societies. Until the collapse of the Soviet Union, some of the most dangerous and lowest paid work was under a communist regime. They point as well to the Chernobyl nuclear plant in the Ukraine which overheated, causing a large area of the country to be irradiated and caused a range of radiation-based diseases for generations to come. Nelken (2002) also points out that there are numerous laws controlling businesses in capitalist societies, when a simple Marxist perspective would suggest that the power available to the ruling class would limit such legislation to a minimum.

Check your understanding

1. Explain the difference between corporate and occupational crime.
2. Which costs society more, white-collar crime or 'conventional' crime? Illustrate your answer with figures.
3. What three obstacles do companies have to overcome, according to Box?
4. How does this lead to corporate crime?
5. Explain how corporations can engage in law evasion.
6. Why are Marxists particularly interested in studying corporate crime?
7. Give two examples of occupational crime from the text.

research ideas

- Interview some friends about their part-time work. Do petty pilfering and other minor fraud occur? How is it justified? Are they aware of any examples of illegal or irresponsible business practice in the organization itself? Emphasize the confidentiality of their responses.

KEY TERMS

Corporate crime – crimes committed by companies against employees or the public.

Differential association – the theory that deviant behaviour is learnt from, and justified by, family and friends; if people interact with others who support lawbreaking, then they are likely to do so themselves.

Entrepreneuriality – qualities of people with original ideas for making money.

Law evasion – acting in such a way as to break the spirit of laws while technically conforming to them.

Occupational crime – crimes committed against a company by an employee.

Transgress – to cross over (conventional) boundaries; in criminology, it refers to legal acts that are harmful to others, but are not normally included in legal ideas of 'crime'.

White-collar crime – a term originally used by Sutherland for both occupational and corporate crime.

web.tasks

1 **Visit the Serious Fraud Squad website at** www.sfo.gov.uk/publications

Go to the annual review for last year. What does this tell you about the number of cases of fraud under investigation and how many were actually prosecuted? In your view, what proportion of government resources is devoted to combating serious fraud?

2 **Corporate Watch is a website packed with examples of corporate irresponsibility:** www.corporatewatch.org

Prepare a report on one or two examples.

exploring occupational and corporate crime

Item A

Reiman (2003) shows how the poor are arrested and charged out of all proportion to their numbers for the kinds of crimes poor people generally commit: burglary, robbery, assault and so forth. Yet when we look at the kinds of crimes poor people almost never have the opportunity to commit, such as antitrust violations (stock market fraud), industrial safety violations, embezzlement and serious tax evasion, the criminal justice system shows an increasingly benign and merciful state. The more likely it is for a particular form of crime to be committed by middle- and upper-class people, the less likely it is that it will be treated as a criminal offence.

Carrabine, E., Iganski, P., Lee, M., Plummer, K. and South, N. (2004) *Criminology: A Sociological Introduction*, London: Routledge

Item B

Underlying the above are serious tensions of how cyberspace is to be policed in future. The definitions of acceptable and unacceptable internet behaviour are being shaped by powerful groups who see other risk groups as a threat to their interests. In some ways, the development of rules on the internet reflects that of the wider society where powerful groups impose their version of law and order on others.

Adapted from Wall, D. (1999) 'Getting to grips with cybercrime', *Criminal Justice Matters*, 36, pp.17–18

(a) According to Reiman (**Item A**), which group is charged with crimes out of all proportion to their numbers? (1 mark)

(b) Identify and briefly explain **two** reasons why the criminal justice system may be 'merciful' to the middle and upper classes (**Item A**). (8 marks)

(c) Identify three ways in which the internet may provide opportunities for harmful and criminal activity (**Item B**). (9 marks)

(d) Identify and explain **two** ways in which labelling theory can contribute to an understanding of occupational and corporate crime. (12 marks)

Exam practice

(e) Outline and assess the view that occupational and corporate crime are underrepresented in criminal statistics. (60 marks)

Gender and crime

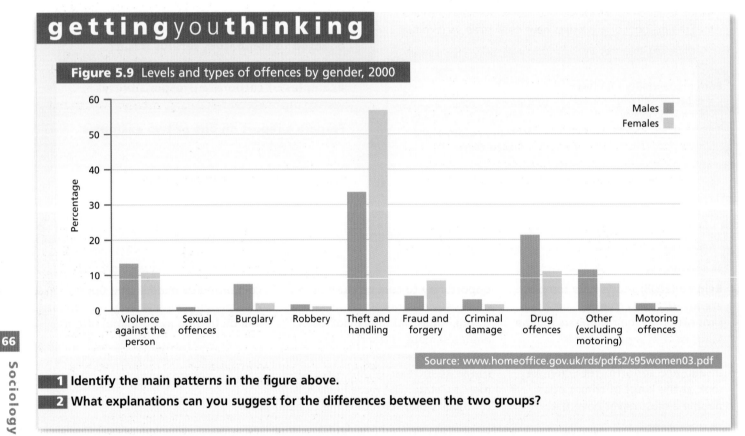

Figure 5.9 Levels and types of offences by gender, 2000

Source: www.homeoffice.gov.uk/rds/pdfs2/s95women03.pdf

1 Identify the main patterns in the figure above.

2 What explanations can you suggest for the differences between the two groups?

In this topic, we want to explore the relationship that gender has to offending. Official records show an overwhelming predominance of males compared with females committing crime. Self-report studies, too, show a noticeable, if less marked, difference between the offending levels of males and females. Given this, there has to be something in the different construction of femininity and masculinity that can help us to explain these differences. In this topic, we will try to unravel some of the strands of explanation offered.

Before we do so, however, we need to explain why, surprisingly perhaps, there has been relatively little research that explicitly sets out to explain the links between gender and offending. It seems that most sociologists have started off with the assumption that males commit more crime, and have then moved on to explore why it is that only some males commit crime. Explanations offered by sociologists have, therefore, concentrated mainly on comparing offending males with non-offending males, without explaining why males are more likely to offend in the first instance.

The topic falls into two main areas of discussion:

- the issue of women and crime
- male gender roles and crime.

First, we ask why women have been ignored in the sociology of crime and delinquency, before turning to examine the explanations for lower rates of female offending. In the second part of the topic, we turn things on their head and ask what lessons the exploration of gender roles might have for male offending. The answers we arrive at may be rather surprising, for it seems that the opening-up of criminology by feminists provides us with clues as to why males have such high rates of offending. Indeed, so significant are these insights that much contemporary criminology is heavily influenced by them (see Topic 10 for more detail).

Invisible female offenders

Anyone studying the sociology of crime and deviance will notice after a while that it is mainly about male offending. In fact, it would not be unfair to call it the sociology of male crime and deviance. Although it is true that the majority of offenders are male – comprising about 80 per cent of all official statistics on offenders – it is surprising that 20 per cent of all offenders are simply ignored.

Frances Heidensohn (1989) has criticized the male dominance of the subject (known as **malestream** criminology) and has suggested that there are four reasons why it is so:

- *Male dominance of offenders* – As the majority of offenders are male, for many sociologists it was therefore most appropriate to study them, rather than the minority of female offenders.
- *Male domination of sociology* – Although the majority of sociology students are women, it has always been the case that the majority of academics have been male. According to Heidensohn, sociological topics of investigation reflect a male view and male interests.
- *Vicarious identification* – This follows from the previous point. Men study what interests them, and, applied to crime, this is most often the lives of the marginal and the exciting, i.e. **vicarious identification**.
- *Sociological theorizing* – Male sociologists constructed their theories without ever thinking about how they could be applied to females. Most traditional theories are 'gender blind'; in effect, that means they ignore the specific viewpoint of women.

Explaining female crime: women's roles

Most theories that explain crime, as we saw earlier, implicitly accept that males are more likely than females to commit crime. In the process, criminologists have omitted to explain what it is that makes males more likely than females to commit crime. There have, however, been a number of exceptions to this and we explore these approaches in this section. Three major approaches to explaining the relationship between women and offending are:

- biological explanations
- sex-role theory
- changing role or 'liberationist' perspective.

focus on research

Positivistic approaches apply traditional scientific methods to the study of human behaviour. In criminology, the best-known study has been the longitudinal research associated with Farrington (2002). This research is based on a sample of 411 males who were first studied as children in 1961/2 and who have been followed throughout their lives to explore the differences between those who offended and those who did not. In methodological language, the offending is the independent variable and the social factors are the dependent variables. The results of the study have suggested that low income, large families

Farrington and Painter (2004)
Gender differences in offending

and erratic discipline are key factors in predicting offending amongst boys. However, in 2004, Farrington and Painter made contact with the families of the original 411 males and studied the offending patterns of the females. This involved interviewing 519 sisters. They found that, overall, females were far less likely to commit offences, but when they did, they were different from the ones committed by the males. Whereas males were more likely to commit burglary and vehicle theft, girls were more likely to shoplift and engage in 'deception' offences. Females also had a shorter 'lifespan' of offending, so they started earlier and finished earlier. Female offenders were also more likely to be concentrated in fewer families than male offenders, so that male offending is much more widespread. However, the most important conclusion that Farrington and Painter reached was that the crucial factors influencing females to commit crime were low family income and 'poor parenting', which included erratic discipline, lack of praise, limited supervision and low interest in school attainment.

Farrington, D.P. and Painter, K.A. (2004) *Gender Differences in Offending: implications for risk-focussed prevention*, Home Office Online Report 09/04, www.homeoffice.gov.uk/rds/onlinepubs1.html

1 **What methodological problems are associated with longitudinal studies?**

2 **Compare and contrast the patterns and factors associated with male and female offending identified by Farrington and Painter.**

Gender and murder

Studies have shown that women tend to murder husbands and lovers, while men tend to murder friends and strangers. Women also tend to use less violence than men. They tend to murder in their own homes and use kitchen implements.

1 Suggest how the differences in men's and women's patterns of murder might be related to the role of women in society.

Biological explanations

This approach has been used by different writers to explain why the overwhelming bulk of women do not offend and conversely why a small minority do. It starts from the belief that women are innately different from men, with a natural desire to be caring and nurturing – both of which tend not to be values that support crime. 'Normal' women are therefore less likely to commit crime. On the other hand, some women writers such as Dalton (1964) have claimed that hormonal or menstrual factors can influence a minority of women to commit crime in certain circumstances.

Sex-role theory

Sex-role theory argues that women are less likely to commit crime than men because there are core elements of the female role that limit their ability and opportunity to do so. There are a number of different versions of this theory, all of which can fit quite comfortably together.

Socialization

According to this approach, girls are socialized differently to boys. The values that girls are brought up to hold are those that simply do not lead to crime. Talcott Parsons (1937) argues for instance, that as most child-rearing is carried out by mothers, girls have a clear role model to follow that emphasizes caring and support. Evidence to support this differential socialization was provided by Farrington and Painter (2004) in their longitudinal study of female offenders. They uncovered different patterns of socialization between offenders and non-offenders. In particular, they found that female offenders were much more likely to have had harsh or erratic parenting, and to have had little support or praise from their parents for their achievements at school and in their community.

Social control

Females are less likely to commit crime because of the closer levels of supervision that they are subjected to at home in childhood. This control carries on throughout life, with the role of women being more constrained that that of males. Heidensohn (1996), for example, says:

> ≪ An examination of female criminality and unofficial deviance suggests that we need to move away from studying infractions and look at conformity instead, because the most striking thing about female behaviour is how notably conformist to social mores women are. ≫

Heidensohn points to the wide range of informal sanctions to discourage women from straying from 'proper' behaviour, including gossip, ill repute and the comments of male companions. Hagan (1987) studied child-raising patterns in Canada and argued that there was significantly greater informal control of daughters' activities in families compared to sons.

Marginalization

In order to commit crime, a person needs to have the opportunity to do so. The narrower range of roles that women are allowed to have consequently limits their opportunities to commit crime, as they are more confined by their socialization and social control than men.

The result of these three influences on the lives of females, is to deflect them away from offending and towards conformity.

The changing role or 'liberationist' perspective

So far in this topic, we have characterized female sex-roles as being more passive and less aggressive than those of males. However, a number of writers including Adler (1975) have suggested that the increasing rates of female crime are linked to their freedom from the traditional forms of social control, discussed above, and their acceptance into more 'masculine' roles. More recently, Denscombe (2001) has argued that changing female roles over the last ten years mean that increasingly, females are as likely as males to engage in risk-taking behaviour. In his research into self-

Laidler and Hunt (2001)
The girls in the gang

Laidler and Hunt studied girl members of US gangs in the San Francisco Bay area. The research consisted of interviews with 141 gang members and ethnographic research over a period of 10 years. The researchers argue that gang membership is fragmented along gender lines, with female members of the gang having clear roles and responsibilities, as do the males. The 'homegirls' in the study face dilemmas similar to those faced by respectable girls, having to walk a narrow line between being attractive to males and valued for that, but also not engaging in sexual relationships with too many boys. Both males and females in the gang use informal methods of social control to ensure conformity.

Laidler and Hunt are suggesting therefore that, despite appearing deviant to the wider society, the majority of homegirls actually conform to gender roles.

Laidler, K.J. and Hunt, G. (2001) 'Accomplishing femininity among the girls in the gang', *British Journal of Criminology*, 41(4)

1 Identify the research method most closely associated with ethnographic research.

2 Explain how the findings of the study led the authors to the conclusion that 'the majority of homegirls actually conform to gender roles.'

images of 15 to 16 year olds in the East Midlands, in which he undertook in-depth interviews as well as focus groups, he found that females were rapidly adopting what had traditionally been male attitudes. This included such things as 'looking hard', 'being in control' and being someone who

can cope with risk-taking. This provides theoretical support for the fact that female crime levels are rising much more quickly than male ones, not just in terms of numbers but also in terms of seriousness of crimes committed.

Westwood (1999) develops similar ideas when she argues that identities are constantly being reconstructed and reframed. The concept of a fixed female identity has limited our understanding of crime, and so we need to understand how women are reconfiguring their identity in a more confident, forceful way, and the possible link to the growth of female crime. However, Heidensohn (2002) disputes this argument, citing evidence from a number of other studies which show that convicted offenders tend to score highly on psychological tests of 'femininity', indicating, according to her, that they have not taken on male roles.

Transgression: A postmodernist critique

The various explanations of female crime put forward were not popular with feminist sociologists as they felt that they were not really adequate explanations for the differences between male and female causes for offending. Pat Carlen (1992) argued, for example, that these were theoretically weak and represented a sort of 'bolt-on' to existing male criminology.

It was in response to the need for a feminist version of criminology, i.e. one that answered the concerns of women, that Carol Smart (1990) introduced the idea of a **transgressive criminology**. By this, Smart was suggesting that criminology itself as a discipline was tied to male questions and concerns and that it could never offer answers to feminist questions. Instead of trying to produce a feminist criminology by asking the question, 'What can feminism offer criminology?', feminists should be arguing, 'What can criminology offer feminists?' The answer to this question lay in looking at a whole range of activities (both legal and illegal) that actually harm women, and asking how these came about and how they could be changed. The term 'transgression', in this context then, meant to go beyond the boundaries of criminology. This did lead to feminists (and sympathetic male sociologists) looking more closely at things such as:

- the way women stayed in at night for fear of becoming victims
- domestic violence
- how women were treated by the law in issues of rape and harassment (where they form the overwhelming bulk of the victims).

Transgression is a good example of the postmodern influence in sociology, when the traditional boundaries of sociology and the categories used to classify issues are abandoned, and new, fresher ways of thinking are introduced.

Figure 5.10 Feminist perspectives on crime and deviance

Although male sociologists have largely ignored female offending, feminist writers from the various strands within feminism have all sought to include criminological analyses within their approaches.

Liberal feminism

This approach to feminism is based on the idea that by bringing women onto the agenda and by demonstrating how women have been ignored in research, there will be greater understanding of female deviance. In particular, new theories can be developed that will cover both males and females.

Radical feminism

Radical feminists argue that the only way to understand crime is to see it through a female perspective – and research should be based on the assumption that all men are prepared to commit crimes against women if given the chance. Women should construct their own unique approaches to explaining crime and deviance, and this should incorporate the threat from men.

Feminist perspectives on crime and deviance

Socialist feminism

This approach stresses that the position of men and women in general – and with reference to crime in particular – can only be understood by locating males and females within the context of societies divided by both sexism and by capitalism.

Postmodern feminism

The work of Smart (1990) and Cain (1986) is particularly important since they argue that the very concerns of criminology (burglary/street crime, etc.) are actually a reflection of male concerns, and that women should be looking beyond these to study how harm comes to women in the widest sense possible. Feminist criminology should not accept the (male) boundaries of criminology, but should look at the way women are harmed by a whole range of processes.

Women and sentencing

Despite committing less crime overall, the number of women who receive prison sentences has always been high compared to the numbers prosecuted, with about 34 per cent of women receiving jail sentences for their first offence, compared to approximately 10 per cent of men. This seems to suggest that women are sentenced more harshly than men. But a study by Hedderman and Hough (1994) showed that when women with similar backgrounds were charged with similar crimes to men, they received more lenient sentences. Heidensohn (2002) also found that women are more likely to receive shorter sentences than men. This has been described as a process of 'chivalry', by which we mean that the male-based legal system treats women differently, seeking to explain away their offending, as males find it difficult to accept that women can be 'bad' – merely 'led astray'. Farrington and Morris (1983), argue that magistrates and judges distinguish between 'types' of women and that certain 'types' are more likely to receive harsher sentences than men, whilst others receive more lenient sentences. So, when sentencing, judges are more likely to take into account issues of family responsibility, marital status and 'moral background'.

All in all, the evidence to support gender bias in the criminal justice system is complex and contradictory, and no clear conclusions can be drawn – this is primarily because there are too many variables to take into account. Until a definitive study can be done, the arguments will continue.

Explaining male crime: male roles and masculinity

Smart's idea of transgression, linked to the growing importance of postmodern analysis, began to feed back into mainstream criminology. Some sociologists began to go beyond the traditional confines and to revisit the issue of why most crime is male crime.

Normative masculinity

The analysis of masculinity began with the Australian sociologist, Bob Connell (1995). He argued that there were a number of different forms of masculinity, which change over time – in particular, he identified the concept of hegemonic masculinity (see Topic 3, p. 36). Although crime was not central to his analysis, the idea of multiple, constructed masculinities was taken up by Messerschmidt (1993).

Connell argues that a '**normative masculinity**' exists in society, highly valued by most men. Normative masculinity refers to the socially approved idea of what a 'real male' is. According to Messerschmidt, it 'defines masculinity through difference from and desire for women'. Normative masculinity is so prized that men struggle to live up to its expectations. Messerschmidt suggests then that masculinity is not something natural, but rather a state that males only achieve as 'an accomplishment', which involves being constantly worked at.

However, the construction of this masculinity takes place in different contexts and through different methods depending upon the particular male's access to power and resources. So, more powerful males will accomplish their masculinity in different ways and contexts from less powerful males. Messerschmidt gives examples of businessmen who can express their power over women through their control in the workplace, while those with no power at work may express their masculinity by using violence in the home or street. However, whichever way is used, both types of men are achieving their normative masculinity.

So, it is achieving masculinity that leads some men to commit crime – and in particular crime is committed by those less powerful in an attempt to be successful at masculinity (which involves material, social and sexual success).

The idea that masculinity is the actual basis of crime is reflected in the writings of a number of writers.

Katz: seductions of crime

A postmodern twist on the idea of masculinity is the work of Katz (1988), who argues that what most criminology has failed to do is to understand the role of pleasure in committing crime. This search for pleasure has to be placed within the context of masculinity, which stresses the importance of status, control over others and success.

Katz claims that crime is always explained with reference to background causes, but rarely attempts to look at the pleasure that is derived from the actual act of offending or 'transgression', as he calls it. Doing evil, he argues, is motivated by the quest for a 'moral self-transcendence' in the face of boredom. Different crimes provide different thrills, that can vary from the 'sneaky thrills' of shoplifting, to the 'righteous slaughter' of murder.

Katz argues that by understanding the emotional thrills that transgression provides, we can understand why males commit crime. Katz gives the example of robbery, which is largely undertaken, he claims, for the chaos, thrill and potential danger inherent in the act. Furthermore, in virtually all robberies 'the offender discovers, fantasizes or manufactures an angle of moral superiority over the intended victim', such that the robber has 'succeeded in making a fool of his victim'. This idea of the thrill of crime has been used to explain the apparent irrational violence of football 'hooligans', and also the use of drugs and alcohol.

Katz's work is clearly influenced by the earlier work of Matza (1964) (see Topic 3), who has argued that constructing a male identity in contemporary society is difficult. Most youths are in a state of **drift** where they are unsure exactly who they are and what their place in society is. For most young males, this is a period of boredom and crisis. It is in this period of life that any event that unambiguously gives them a clear identity is welcomed, and it could equally be an identity of offender as much as employee. Committing offences provides a break from boredom, pleasure and a sense of being someone – for example, a gang member or a 'hard man'.

Lyng: edgework

A linked argument can be found in the work of Lyng (1990), who argues that young males search for pleasure through risk-taking. According to Lyng, the risk-taking can best be seen as 'edgework', by which he means that there is a thrill to be gained from acting in ways that are on the edge between security and danger.

This helps explain the attractiveness of car theft and 'joy riding', and of searching for violent confrontations with other groups of males. By engaging in this form of risk-taking, young men are in Messerschmidt's terms 'accomplishing masculinity', and also proving that they have control over their lives.

Masculinities in context

The work of Connell (via Messerschmidt) and the arguments of Katz and Lyng have been very influential in contemporary criminology. However, they have all been criticized for not slotting the notion of masculinities into a context. So, Winlow (2004) has asked questions about the conditions in

synoptic link

One of the most obvious points about crime is that the overwhelming majority of offenders are male. However, it wasn't really until the rise of feminist writings in the 1970s that sociologists began to look at the possible relationship with the values of being a 'real' male. Ideas about subculture began to be replaced with notions of how masculinity was created and the impact this had on how men, and particularly young men, behaved. Once the idea of masculinity emerged, sociologists realized that it could explain a lot about the behaviour of young men in general. One especially fruitful area of study was of the educational experiences of young males. Over the past 20 years, there has been a huge shift in the

social inequality and difference

comparative success rates of males and females at school, with girls having significantly better exam success than boys, and also exhibiting far less poor behaviour in the classroom. The reason for these differences in behaviour appears to be that the accepted notion of what a young male ought to be in society (or dominant hegemonic model of masculinity) contradicts the role required in the school of an obedient, hard-working pupil. Masculinity, as portrayed in the media, means being tough, possibly aggressive, sexually active and a person of action. None of this fits easily with the role of a school student.

which men demonstrate their aggressiveness, and why is that young, working-class males are more likely to be violent? The answer, he argues, lies in the changing nature of the economy in late modernity. For generations, working-class masculinity has been linked to manual employment in manufacturing industry. With the huge changes in the economy, most notably the decline in manual work and the increase in low-level, white-collar employment, a significant proportion of the male working-class population has been excluded from the possibilities of regular employment. According to Wilson (1996), this has resulted in the development of an urban underclass who manifest a range of violent and antisocial behaviours. The masculinity they exude, therefore, can only be understood within the context of the changing economic structure of Britain.

KEY TERMS

Drift – term used by Matza to describe a state where young men are unsure exactly who they are and what their place in society is.

Malestream – a term used to describe the fact that male ways of thinking have dominated criminology.

Normative masculinity – the socially approved idea of what a real male is. According to Messerschmidt, it 'defines masculinity through difference from and desire for women'.

Sex-role theory – explanations based on the restricted roles women are claimed to have in society.

Transgression – feminist theorists use this term to suggest a need to 'break out' of the confines of traditional criminology.

Vicarious identification – when people obtain a thrill by putting themselves in the place of another person.

Check your understanding

1 Why was it that criminology traditionally ignored female crime?

2 Give three examples of sex-role theory.

3 How is the idea of 'transgression' relevant to the debate about gender and crime?

4 In your own words, explain the term 'normative masculinity'. How does it help us to understand crime?

5 What is 'moral transcendence'?

6 Suggest three examples of 'edgework'.

7 What implication for the level of female crime is there as a result of the changing role of women in recent years?

Gender and crime: policy issues

Feminist theories have had a very significant impact on social life in terms of rejection of traditional socialization patterns in the family and legislation to ensure equal treatment in employment. Many of the traditional explanations for female crime are therefore being challenged by legislation which has been passed over a period of 30 years. In terms of female victimization, the main concern is continuing high levels of domestic violence. To combat this, strict new guidelines are provided for police officers attending cases of alleged domestic violence and all forces have experts in the area. Similar policy initiatives have been introduced in regard to rape. In terms of committing crime, the issue of masculinity and in particular its link to alcohol and violence is emerging as a concern of policymakers. New licensing laws that impose strict conditions on licensees who allow underage or excessive drinking have been introduced and licensing hours have been made more flexible to avoid confrontation at any one, standard pub-closing time. However, the key issue of dominant or hegemonic masculinity and its links to violence and crime has not been tackled.

research ideas

1 Devise a simple 'self-report' questionnaire (see Topic 6) with a maximum of ten questions. The offending behaviour or deviant acts should be fairly minor, but common (e.g. starting a fight, drinking alcohol under age).

2 Either working in groups or individually, divide your questionnaires into two sets. Give out one set of questionnaires to be completed anonymously. Use the other set with interview techniques to complete the questionnaire directly.

● Are there different results between the two methods?
● Are there any differences between males and females?

web.task
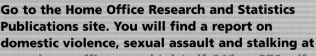

Go to the Home Office Research and Statistics Publications site. You will find a report on domestic violence, sexual assault and stalking at www.homeoffice.gov.uk/rds/pdfs04/hors276.pdf

What does this report tell you about the relationship between gender and these crimes?

Item A

Offenders as a percentage of the population: by age, 2000, England & Wales

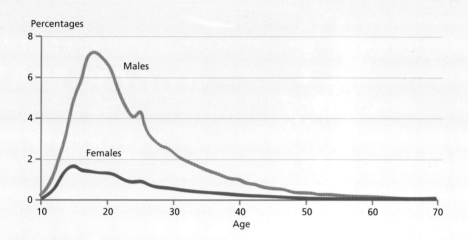

Source: National Statistics on Line http://www.statistics.gov.uk/cci/nugget.asp?id=442

Item B

Graham and Wells placed posters in three launderettes near their university in Ontario, Canada, offering $10 to young males who had been involved in bar fights to participate in a telephone interview. People who called were given an explanation of the study and assured that their responses would be confidential. All interviews were recorded. A total of 35 interviews were conducted in total – most were university students, with a small proportion of unemployed, and only 10% were actually in employment. The authors wanted to find out the role of alcohol in aggression. What they discovered was that alcohol was not particularly important in leading to aggression in bars. They suggest that 'male honour, face-saving, group loyalty and fighting for fun' were the key motivators. What emerged most strongly was the general acceptance, 'even positive endorsement' of aggression in bars as a normal part of male values. So it is not alcohol that causes the violence, but how 'masculinity' as a set of values determines how alcohol is understood and used. When policymakers stress that it is alcohol that is the cause of violence, they are simply wrong – it is masculinity which is the ultimate cause.

Adapted from Graham, K. and Wells, S. (2003) '"Somebody's gonna get their head kicked in tonight!" Aggression among young males in bars: a question of values?', *British Journal of Criminology*, 43(3), p. 546

(a) Using **Item A**, identify the peak age of offending for women. (1 mark)

(b) Identify and briefly explain **two** causes of aggression in bars (**Item B**). (8 marks)

(c) Identify **three** disadvantages of the method of telephone interviewing used in the research described in **Item B**. (9 marks)

(d) Identify and explain **two** patterns shown in the graph in **Item A**. (12 marks)

Exam practice

(e) Outline and assess sociological explanations of gender differences in crime rates. (60 marks)

Ethnicity and crime

Racism 'rife in justice system'

One of the Home Office's own studies, published today, found that people from ethnic-minority communities were put off joining the police because they anticipated that they would be isolated and subjected to racism. Many also expected to face a level of hostility from their own communities if they joined the police. Members of Black and Asian groups sometimes themselves had negative attitudes towards ethnic-minority officers, the study found.

Vikram Dodd, *The Guardian*, Monday 20 March 2000

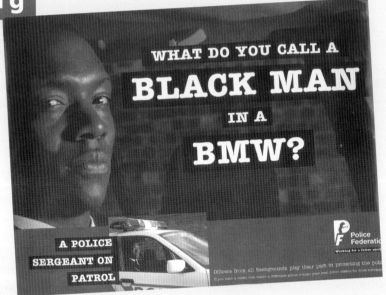

WHAT DO YOU CALL A **BLACK MAN** IN A **BMW?**

A POLICE SERGEANT ON PATROL

Police Federation
Working for a fairer service

1 What point is being made by the Police Federation poster above?

2 Why do you think this poster was thought necessary?

3 Why do you think that some members of ethnic-minority groups are 'put off' joining the police?

4 Why do you think that 'Black and Asian groups ... had negative attitudes towards ethnic minority officers'?

A recurring theme in media reporting of street crime since the mid-1970s has been the disproportionate involvement of young males of African-Caribbean origin. It has partly been on this crime–race linkage that the police has justified the much greater levels of **stop and search** of young, Black males, than of White males.

Images of Asian criminality have, until recently, portrayed the Asian communities as generally more law-abiding than the majority population. However, after the attack on the World Trade Center in New York in 2001 and, more significantly, the bombings in 2005 on the London Underground, a new discourse has emerged regarding Muslim youths. The newer image is of them as being potentially dangerous – a threat to British culture.

Just discussing the relationship between criminality and race is itself a difficult task, and some sociologists argue that making the subject part of the A-level specifications actually helps perpetuate the link. After all, there are no discussions on 'White people and crime'!

Despite these reservations, sociologists have set out to examine the argument that there is a higher rate of crime by certain ethnic minorities, and the counterclaim that the criminal justice system is racist.

Offending, sentencing and punishment

Offending

There are three ways of gathering statistics on ethnicity and crime:

- official statistics
- victimization studies
- self-report studies.

Official statistics

According to Home Office statistics (Home Office 2005), about 9 per cent of people arrested were recorded as 'Black' and 5 per cent as 'Asian'. This means that relative to the arrest rates of the population as a whole, Black people were over three times more likely to be arrested than White people were. Asian people's rates were similar to those for White people.

Official statistics tell us the numbers of people arrested by the police. However, they are not necessarily a reflection of offending rates, but can be seen just as much as a comment on the actions of the police. If, as some sociologists argue, the

Waddington *et al.* (2004)
Race, the police, and stop & search

Waddington, Stenson and Don were concerned at the way it has become accepted that members of minority ethnic groups are unfairly stopped by the police. They therefore undertook research in Reading and Slough, two towns to the west of London. The researchers used a variety of methods. These included:

- direct non-participant observation of police officers, including watching CCTV footage
- detailed analysis of the official records of stop and search
- interviews with police officers about their stop and search activities.

The researchers argue that the evidence suggests that police officers do stop a proportionately high number of young members of ethnic minority groups (and of White groups), but that these figures are in direct proportion to their presence in the central city areas and their likelihood to be out at night. Those groups who are most likely to be out in the evening in high crime areas are most likely to be stopped and in these areas young people, and particularly young members of ethnic minority groups, are most likely to be out. They conclude that police stop and searches in the area they researched reflected the composition of people out on the streets, rather than any ethnic bias.

Waddington, P.A.J., Stenson, K. and Don, D. (2004) 'In proportion – race, and police stop and search', *British Journal of Criminology*, 44(6)

1 Comment on the range of methods used by the researchers. Are there any other groups that might have been interviewed?

2 Explain how the researchers reached their conclusion that 'police stop and searches in the area they researched reflected the composition of people out on the streets, rather than any ethnic bias'.

actions of some police officers are partly motivated by racism, then the arrest rates reflect this, rather than offending rates by ethnic-minority groups.

Victimization studies

Victim-based studies (such as the British Crime Survey) are gathered by asking victims of crime for their recollection of the ethnic identity of the offender. According to the British Crime Survey, the majority of crime is **intraracial**, with 88 per cent of White victims stating that White offenders were involved, 3 per cent claiming the offenders were Black, 1 per cent Asian and 5 per cent 'mixed'.

About 42 per cent of crimes against Black victims were identified as being committed by Black offenders and 19 per cent of crimes against Asians were by Asian offenders. The figures for White crimes against ethnic minorities are much higher – about 50 per cent, though this figure needs to be seen against the backdrop of 90 per cent of the population being classified as White.

Like official statistics, asking victims for a description of who committed the crimes is shot through with problems. For a start, only about 20 per cent of survey-recorded crimes are personal crimes (such as theft from the person), where the victims might actually see the offender. Bowling and Phillips (2002) argue that victims are influenced by (racial) stereotypes and 'culturally determined expectations' as to who commits crime. Certainly, research by Bowling (1999) indicates that where the offender is not known, White people are more likely to ascribe the crime to those of African-Caribbean origin.

Self-report studies

Self-report studies use an anonymous questionnaire to ask people what offences they have committed. Graham and Bowling's study (1995) of 14 to 25 year olds for the Home Office found that the self-reported offending rates were more or less the same for the White, Black and Asian respondents.

Sentencing

After arrest, those of African-Caribbean backgrounds are slightly more likely to be held in custody and to be charged with more serious offences than Whites. But they are more likely than average to plead, and to be found, not guilty. However, if found guilty, they are more likely to receive harsher sentences – in fact, those of African-Caribbean backgrounds have a 17 per cent higher chance of imprisonment than Whites.

Those of Asian origin are also more likely than average to plead not guilty, but more likely than average to be found guilty, but have an 18 per cent lesser chance of being imprisoned.

Sociologists are divided as to whether these statistics mean that members of ethnic minority groups are discriminated against. Bowling and Phillips (2002) summarize the 'patchy' knowledge of sociologists, by saying that the research indicates that both direct and indirect discrimination (types of charges laid, access to bail, etc.) against members of ethnic minority groups does exist.

Punishment

In British prisons, the numbers of African and African-Caribbean prisoners is proportionately (that is, in terms of their proportion of the population as a whole) 7.8 times higher than would be expected, and is 0.77 times higher for those of Asian origin. In 1998, the rate of imprisonment per 100 000 of the general population was 1245 for Black people, 185 for Whites and 168 for Asians.

Policing and ethnic minority groups

We have already seen that there are considerable differences between the arrest rates for members of ethnic minority groups and those for Whites, with those of African-Caribbean origins having a four times higher rate of arrest than Whites. Sociologists are split between those who argue that this reflects real differences in levels of offending and those who argue that the higher arrest rates are due to the practices of the police.

A reflection of reality?

Sociologists all reject the idea that there is an association between 'race' and crime, in the sense that being a member of a particular ethnic group in itself has any importance in explaining crime. However, a number of writers (Mayhew *et al.* 1993) argue that most crime is performed by young males who come from poorer backgrounds. This being so, then there would be an overrepresentation of offenders from minority ethnic groups, quite simply because there is a higher proportion of young males in the ethnic-minority population than in the population as a whole. It is also a well-researched fact that minority ethnic groups overall are likely to have lower incomes and poorer housing conditions. These sociologists would accept that there is evidence of racist practices by certain police officers, but that the arrest rates largely reflect the true patterns of crime.

Phillips and Brown's (1998) study of ten police stations across Britain found that those of African-Caribbean origin accounted for a disproportionately high number of arrests. However, they found no evidence that they were treated any differently during the arrest process, with about 60 per cent of both Blacks and Whites and about 55 per cent of Asians eventually being charged.

Racist police practices?

A second group of sociologists see the higher arrest rates as evidence of police racism. Within this broad approach there are a number of different explanations.

Reflection of society approach

This approach, often adopted by the police, is that there are some individuals in the police who are racist, and once these 'bad apples' are rooted out, the police force will not exhibit racism. This approach was suggested by **Lord Scarman** (1981)

in his inquiry into the inner-city riots of 1981. According to Scarman, the police reflect the wider society and therefore some racist recruits may join.

Canteen culture

The 'canteen (or working) culture' approach (see p. 29 and Key terms p. 30) argues that police officers have developed distinctive working values as a result of their job. Police officers have to face enormous pressures in dealing with the public: working long hours, facing potential danger, hostility from significant sections of the public and social isolation. The result is that they have developed a culture in response that helps them to deal with the pressures and gives them a sense of identity. The 'core characteristics' of the culture, according to Reiner (1992), include a thirst for action, cynicism, conservatism, suspicion, isolation from the public, macho values and racism.

Studies by Smith and Gray (1985), Holdaway (1983) who was himself a serving police officer at the time, and Graef (1989), all demonstrated racist views amongst police officers who, for example, held stereotypical views on the criminality of youths of African-Caribbean origin. Most importantly, it led them to stop and search these youths to a far greater extent than any other group. In fact, African-Caribbean people are six times more likely than Whites to be stopped and searched by the police.

Institutional racism

After the racist murder of a Black youth, Stephen Lawrence in 1993, and after very considerable pressure from his parents, the **Macpherson Inquiry** was set up to look at the circumstances of his death and the handling of the situation by the police. Sir William Macpherson concluded that the police were characterized by **institutional racism**. By this he meant that the police have 'procedures, practices and a culture that tend to exclude or to disadvantage non-White people' (cited in Bowling and Phillips 2002).

The key point about institutional racism is that it is not necessarily intentional on the part of any particular person in the organization, but that the normal, day-to-day activities of the organization are based upon racist ideas and practice. This means that police officers might not have to be racist in their personal values, but that in the course of their work they might make assumptions about young Black males and the likelihood of their offending that influence their (the police officers') attitudes and behaviour.

Theorizing race and criminality

Left realist approach

Lea and Young, leading writers in the left realist tradition, accept that there are racist practices by the police (1993). However, they argue that, despite this the statistics do bear out a higher crime rate for street robberies and associated 'personal' crimes by youths of African-Caribbean origin. They explain this by suggesting that British society is racist and that young ethnic-minority males are economically and socially **marginalized**, with

The use of the term 'moral panic' has moved from the confines of sociology into general use, so that every time there is media interest in a particular topic, it is described as a 'moral panic'. Even within sociology, the idea of moral panic has spread from its original use by labelling theorists, who were interested in the effects of the media in labelling groups as deviant and troublemakers, to Marxist-influenced writers such as Stuart Hall, who successfully integrated the concept into his analysis of how young Black youths come to be

social inequality and difference

associated with high levels of crime. Weiner has taken a rather more cynical view of a moral panic and has suggested that there has been an antifeminist moral panic regarding the lower success rates of males in education. She argues that instead of there being a celebration of women finally overtaking males in the education system, the male-dominated media has changed the message to a moral panic about the problem of male failure.

---

lesser chances of success than the majority population. Running alongside this is their sense of relative deprivation. According to Lea and Young, the result is the creation of subcultures, which can lead to higher levels of personal crime as a way of coping with marginalization and relative deprivation (see Topic 10 for a discussion of Realist criminologies).

Capitalism in crisis

A study by Hall et al. (1978) of street crime ('**mugging**') illustrates a particular kind of Marxist approach. According to Hall, the late 1970s were a period of crisis for British capitalism. The country was undergoing industrial unrest, there was a collapse in the economy and the political unrest in Northern Ireland was particularly intense. When capitalism is in crisis the normal methods of control of the population may be inadequate, and it is sometimes necessary to use force. However, using obvious repression needs some form of justification. It was in these circumstances that the newspapers, basing their reports on police briefings, highlighted a huge increase in 'mugging' (street robberies).

According to Hall, the focus on a relatively minor problem, caused by a group who were already viewed negatively, served the purpose of drawing attention away from the crisis and focusing blame on a scapegoat – young African-Caribbean males. This 'moral panic' (see Synoptic link above) then justified increased numbers of police on the streets, acting in a more repressive manner.

Hall's analysis has been criticized for not making any effort actually to research the motivations and thinking of young African-Caribbean males. What is more, the association between 'criminality and Black youth', made by the police and the media, has continued for over 25 years, and so it seems unlikely that this can be explained simply by a 'crisis of capitalism'.

Cultures of resistance

A third approach overlaps with the Marxist approach just outlined. According to this approach, linked with Scraton (1987) and Gordon (1988), policing, media coverage and political debates all centre around the issue of 'race' being a problem. Minority ethnic groups have been on the receiving end of discrimination since the first migrants arrived, leaving them in a much worse socioeconomic position than the White majority.

In response to this, **cultures of resistance** have emerged, in which crime is a form of organized resistance that has its origins in the **anticolonial** struggles. When young members of minority ethnic groups commit crimes, they are doing so as a political act, rather than as a criminal act.

There are a number of criticisms of this approach. Lea and Young (1993) have been particularly scathing, pointing out that the majority of crimes are actually 'intraracial', that is 'Black on Black'. This cannot therefore reflect a political struggle against the White majority. Second, they accuse writers such as Scraton of 'romanticizing' crime and criminals, and in doing so ignoring the very real harm that crime does to its victims.

Exclusion and alternative economies

This approach integrates the previous approaches and relates quite closely to the work of Cloward and Ohlin (1960) (see Topic 3). A good example of this sort of argument is provided by Philippe Bourgois' study (2002) of El Barrio, a deprived area in East Harlem, New York. Bourgois spent seven years living and researching the street life and economy of El Barrio, whose inhabitants were overwhelmingly Puerto Ricans, illegal Mexican immigrants and African-Americans.

Bourgois argues that the economic exclusion of these minority ethnic groups, combined with negative social attitudes towards them, has forced them to develop an 'alternative economy'. This involves a wide range of both marginally legal and clearly illegal activities, ranging from kerbside car-repair businesses to selling crack cocaine. Drug sales are by far the most lucrative employment: 'Cocaine and crack … have been the fastest growing – if not the only – equal-opportunity employers of men in Harlem'.

Running alongside this informal economy has developed a distinctive (sub)culture, which Bourgois calls 'inner-city street culture' – as he puts it:

<< this 'street culture of resistance' is not a coherent, conscious universe of political opposition, but rather a spontaneous set of rebellious practices that in the long term have emerged as an oppositional style. >>

This subculture causes great damage because the illegal trade in drugs eventually involves its participants in lifestyles of violence, substance abuse and '**internalized rage**'. Many of the small-scale dealers become addicted and drawn into violence to support their habit. Furthermore, their behaviour destroys families and the community. The result is a chaotic and violent 'community' where the search for dignity in a distinctive culture leads to a worsening of the situation.

Although this is an extreme lifestyle, even for the USA, elements of it can help us to understand issues of race and criminality in the UK. Exclusion and racism lead to both cultural and economic developments that involve illegal activities and the development of a culture that helps resolve the issues of lack of dignity in a racist society. But both the illegal activities and the resulting culture may lead to an involvement in crime.

Statistical artefact approach

The **statistical artefact** approach suggests that the higher levels of involvement of young males from an African-Caribbean background in crime is more a reflection of how the statistics are interpreted than of a genuinely higher level. Fitzgerald *et al.* (2003) researched ethnic-minority street crime in London, comparing crime rates against a wide range of socioeconomic and demographic data. They also interviewed a cross section of young, ethnic-minority offenders and their mothers, as well as running focus groups of 14 to 16 year olds in schools. The outcomes of the study were complex, but they throw light upon a number of the other explanations we have discussed so far:

- FitzGerald and colleagues found that street crime is related to levels of deprivation in an area, as well as to a lack of community cohesion, as measured by a rapid population turnover. This reflects crime levels in Britain as a whole, as we know amongst all ethnic groups that the higher the levels of deprivation in an area, the higher the levels of crime.
- They found that the high rates of ethnic-minority offending were directly linked to the numbers of young, ethnic-minority males. Once again, all statistics point to young males as the highest offending group in the population, whatever their ethnic background. As there are higher proportions of young, ethnic-minority males in the population as a whole, and in London in particular, then we would expect there to be higher rates of crime committed by ethnic-minority males – if only as a reflection of the high percentage they form of all young males.
- They found that there was a statistical link between higher crime levels and lone-parent families. African-Caribbean households are more likely to be headed by a lone parent, so there would be a statistical link here too.

- They found that there was a subculture which had developed amongst certain ethnic-minority children that provided justification for crime. This was very closely linked with school failure and alienation from school. However, similar views were held by White school-age students who were doing poorly at school or who were no longer attending. A disproportionate amount of all crime is performed by young, educationally disaffected children of all backgrounds.

In conclusion, therefore, Fitzgerald and colleagues suggest that there is no specific set of factors which motivate young, ethnic-minority offenders – they are exactly the same ones as motivate White offenders. However, the overrepresentation of young males from African-Caribbean backgrounds is partly the result of their sheer numbers in the age band in which most offending takes place.

Check your understanding

1. What different interpretations are there concerning the arrest rates of members of ethnic minority groups?

2. What do we mean when we say that the majority of crime is 'intraracial'?

3. Identify any two problems with the statistics derived from 'victimization studies'.

4. What are self-report studies? Do they confirm the statistics derived from the arrest rates?

5. What two general explanations have sociologists put forward for the higher arrest rates of members of minority ethnic groups?

6. Explain the significance of the terms 'canteen culture' and 'institutional racism' in explaining the attitudes and behaviour of the police towards minority ethnic groups.

7. How do 'left realist sociologists' explain the relationship between ethnicity and crime?

8. What is the relationship between crises in capitalism and police action against 'muggers'?

9. What does the term 'culture of resistance' mean?

research idea

Your local police force will have an ethnic minority liaison officer (or similar title). Ask them to come to your institution to talk about their work and, in particular, stop and search. Before they come, get into small groups and sort out a list of questions – ideally, you should then e-mail them to the officer to base their talk on.

web.task

The Home Office produce an online publication Race and the Criminal Justice System, which contains a wide range of up-to-date statistics. Explore the site and make your own mind up about the way that ethnic minorities interact with the criminal justice system.
www.homeoffice.gov.uk/rds/pdfs/s95race00.pdf

Anticolonial struggles – historically, Black resistance to Western attempts to control and exploit Black people.

Cultures of resistance – the term used to suggest that ethnic-minority groups in Britain have developed a culture that resists the racist oppression of the majority society.

Institutional racism – racism that is built into the normal practices of an organization.

Internalized rage – term used by Bourgois to describe the anger and hurt caused by economic and social marginalization.

Intraracial – within a particular ethnic group.

Lord Scarman – in 1981 there were serious inner-city disturbances, particularly in Brixton in London. Lord Scarman led a government inquiry into the causes of these 'riots'.

Macpherson Inquiry – Sir William Macpherson led an inquiry into the events surrounding the murder of Stephen Lawrence (allegedly) by White racists, and the subsequent police investigation.

Marginalized – a sociological term referring to those who are pushed to the edge of society in cultural, status or economic terms.

Mugging – a term used to describe street robbery. It has no status as a specific crime in England and Wales.

Statistical artefact – the 'problem' emerges from the way that the statistics are collected and understood.

Stop and search – police officers have powers to stop and search those they 'reasonably' think may be about to, or have committed, a crime; this power has been used much more against ethnic-minority youths than White youths.

exploring ethnicity and crime

Item A

The notion that increasing youth unemployment, coupled with a high young population in the Black community, and the effects of massive, well-documented, racial discrimination and the denial of legitimate opportunity, did not result in a rising rate of real offences is hardly credible... [This] real increase in crime is amplified as a result of police action and police prejudice.

Adapted from Lea, J. and Young, J. (1993) *What is to be Done about Law and Order?*, London: Pluto

Item B

Jacobs and colleagues studied car theft in St Louis in the USA. Their research methods were particularly interesting. The sociologists conducted interviews with young people who were actively engaged in 'carjacking'. They were found by a 'field recruiter' who was himself a member of the 'city's criminal underworld'. This man (who was African-American) offered prospective interviewees $50 to participate.

The researchers eventually interviewed 28 people, 25 males and three females. All of these were of African-American background. The interviews lasted for one and a half hours and the researchers claimed that there were no significant discrepancies in what the interviewees told them.

They conclude: 'We are not so naive to think that the offenders never embellished their stories to impress us. And a few may have lied to protect themselves. Nevertheless we believe that undetected cases of distortion were sufficiently rare that they do not undermine the overall quality of the data.'

The research indicates the problems faced in studying deviant groups, particularly from ethnic minorities by middle-class researchers. Although the researchers claimed that their research was accurate, the fact that they paid offenders and then had no way of confirming the truth of what they said, throws doubt upon the validity of their findings.

Adapted from Jacobs, B.A., Topalli, V. and Wright, R. (2003) 'Carjacking, streetlife and offender motivation', *British Journal of Criminology*, 43(4)

(a) According to the writers of **Item A**, what amplifies the real increase in crime among the 'Black community'? (1 mark)

(b) Identify and briefly explain **two** reasons why some groups are more likely to be stopped by the police than others. (8 marks)

(c) Identify **three** reasons why there might be high crime rates among African-Caribbean minority ethnic groups **(Item A)**. (9 marks)

(d) Identify and briefly explain **two** disadvantages of the methodological approach used in the research described in **Item B**. (12 marks)

Exam practice

(e) Outline and assess the view that ethnic minorities are overrepresented in official crime statistics. (60 marks)

Contemporary criminology: from realism to postmodernism

gettingyouthinking

People on large social-housing estates and in the inner cities are having their lives blighted by crime. Imagine you have just formed a new government and you have a choice. You are not sure, but you think the real causes of crime are probably poverty and deprivation. You can spend all your money tackling poverty and hope that it has an effect on crime in, say, 20 years or you can spend the money on more police officers, CCTV, better street lighting, and a whole range of other anticrime measures. You are aware that these may lower the crime rate today, but do nothing to address the 'real' causes.

1 Do you think it is ever possible to eliminate crime? Explain your answer.

2 What would you do? (No, you cannot do both!) Give the reasons for your choice.

3 Are there problems with crime in the area where you live? What sorts of crime? What would be your ideal solution if you could do something about it today?

4 Do you feel 'at risk' of crime? If you do, what precautions do you routinely take?

5 Are there particular individuals or types of people you avoid? Why?

This topic brings us up to date with sociological theorizing on crime. Rather than seeing it as a topic completely isolated from other, earlier topics, it might be better to regard it as a topic of unfinished business! Throughout the book, we stress the importance of late-modern and postmodern ideas in contemporary sociology. These ideas are still working their way through sociology and are leading to new divisions and debates. In this topic, we refer back to earlier ideas and arguments from late-modernist and postmodernist thinkers and you should take the opportunity to go back and check on these earlier arguments.

The aim of this topic is to show the very different directions that contemporary sociology is taking in its approach to understanding crime. At the one extreme, we find the realist criminologies that have emerged from functionalism and Marxism. These have been 'tamed' in such a way that both are now very influential in government policy-making. The two approaches contain within them many of the themes and arguments we have examined during the course of this unit and have provided coherent explanations for crime and suggestions for tackling it.

At the other extreme, are the ideas drawn from late modernity and postmodernity which are critical of the way that criminology has been drawn into the policy-making process. Indeed, much of the late-modernity perspective is an extended criticism of current policies.

Postmodern theorists go further in their criticisms of most sociological theorizing on crime. They suggest instead that the definitions of crime are simply social constructions in which criminologists have been very much involved in creating false notions of what crime is. They also suggest that the careful theorizing of crime promoted by most criminologists is based on the false belief that crime can be explained rationally; instead, they point to emotion and the irrational.

Realist criminology

In an earlier topic, we looked at criminal statistics. We learned that the victims of crime are, perhaps surprisingly, more likely to be the poor and the disadvantaged than the rich. Furthermore, the majority of crime occurs in inner-city areas and in large social-housing developments, where there is real concern over the amount of crime – a concern which sociologists had previously simply missed. It was within this context of uncovering the true extent, victims and location of crime that two very different approaches developed:

- **right realism** – deriving from the **right-wing** theories of James Q. Wilson and emphasizing **'zero tolerance'**.
- **left realism** – deriving from the writings of Lea, Young and Matthews who emphasize the importance of tackling deprivation and of getting policing to respond to the needs of the local population.

Right realism

Right realism originated in the USA with the writings of James Q. Wilson. In 'Broken Windows' (Wilson and Kelling 1982), Wilson argued that crime flourishes in situations where social control breaks down. According to his analysis, in any community, a proportion of the population are likely to engage in 'incivilities', which might consist of such things as dropping litter, vandalism or rowdy behaviour. In most communities, this behaviour is prevented from going further by the comments and actions of other members of the local community. Effectively, the amount and extent of incivilities are held in check by the response of others. However, if the incivilities go unchecked, then the entire social order of the area breaks down and gradually there is a move to more frequent and more serious crime. The parallel which Wilson drew was with abandoned buildings; he asks whether anyone had ever seen just one window broken? The answer was, of course, that once one window was broken, then they all were.

Once crime is allowed to happen, it flourishes. Wilson was strongly influenced by the work of the American theorist Amitai Etzioni, and his theory of **communitarianism** (1993) – which stresses the fact that only local communities by their own efforts and local face-to-face relationships can solve social problems.

The conclusion that Wilson drew was that the police should have a crucial role to play in restoring the balance of incivilities and helping to recreate community. He argued that most police officers engage in law enforcement – that is ensuring that the law is not broken and apprehending offenders if they have committed an offence. He argued that this did relatively little to reconstruct communities and prevent crime (after all only about 3 per cent of offences result in successful prosecutions). Police should instead be concentrating on order maintenance. By this he means using the law to ensure that the smaller incivilities – groups of rowdy youths, noisy parties, public drug use – are all crushed. According to him, this would help to create a different view of what was acceptable behaviour, and would make public areas feel safe again for the majority of people.

After a version of his ideas was adopted in New York, under the slogan 'zero tolerance', and there appeared to be a decline in crime, the term was adopted throughout America and to some extent in the UK as a description of a much harsher form of street policing.

Platt and Takagi (1977) criticize this approach for concentrating exclusively on working-class crimes and ignoring the crimes of the powerful. Furthermore, it ignores ideas of justice and law enforcement and advocates instead the maintenance of social order – even if it is at the expense of justice.

Left realism

Left realism developed primarily as a response to the increasing influence of right realism over the policymakers in Britain and America. In the USA, the main writer has been Elliot Currie, while in Britain, left realism is associated with Jock Young, John Lea and Roger Matthews.

Young was one of the founders of 'critical criminology' (see Topic 5) that introduced elements of interactionist theory into Marxism in order to provide a 'complete' theory of crime. However, Young became increasingly disenchanted with the Marxist approach that stressed that criminals should be seen as the victims of the capitalist system and that sociological analyses of crime should stress the criminality of the rich and powerful. This disillusionment was fuelled by a series of local victimization surveys, e.g. in Islington and Merseyside, that showed that the real victims of crime were the poor and the powerless, and that these people viewed street crime and burglary as one of the main social problems they faced.

Young (1986) argued that it was the role of criminology to provide relevant and credible solutions for policymakers to limit the harm that crime was doing to the lives of the poorer sections of the community. This approach led to a bitter debate in sociology, with many influential left-wing criminologists attacking Young for selling out. (The implication of Young's new argument is that the role of sociologists is to help the government to combat crime. For Marxists, crime exists because of capitalism, and the government represents capitalism.) Young responded by labelling Marxist criminology as 'left idealism', meaning that it was great in theory, but had no practical solutions.

The left realist explanation of crime has three elements: relative deprivation, marginalization and subculture.

Relative deprivation

The concept of **relative deprivation** derives from the writings of Runciman (1966), who argued that political revolutions only occurred when the poor became aware of the sheer scale of the differences between themselves and the rich. Without this knowledge, they generally accepted their poverty and powerlessness. It is not, therefore, poverty that leads to revolution, but awareness of their relative poverty.

Applying this concept to crime, Lea and Young (1984) pointed out that poverty or unemployment do not directly cause crime, as, despite the high unemployment experienced in the economic depression in Britain from the late 1920s to the 1930s, crime rates were considerably lower than they were in the boom years of the 1980s. According to Lea and Young, the expectations of 1930s' youth were much lower than those of contemporary young people, who feel resentful at what they could actually earn compared with their aspirations.

Marginalization

Marginalization refers to the situation where certain groups in the population are more likely than others to suffer economic, social, and political deprivation. The first two of these elements of deprivation are fairly well known – young people living in inner cities and social-housing estates are likely to suffer from higher levels of deprivation than those from more affluent areas. The third element – political marginalization – refers to the fact that there is no way for them to influence decision-makers, and thus they feel powerless.

Subculture

This draws partially upon the Marxist subcultural approach (see Topic 5), but more heavily from the ideas of Robert Merton (see Topic 3). Subcultures develop amongst groups who suffer relative deprivation and marginalization. Specific sets of values, forms of dress and modes of behaviour develop that reflect the problems that their members face. However, whereas the Marxist subcultural writers seek to explain the styles of dress, and forms of language and behaviour as forms of 'resistance' to capitalism, Lea and Young do not see a direct, 'decodable' link.

For Lea and Young (1984), one crucial element of subcultures is that they are still located in the values of the wider society. Subcultures develop precisely because their members subscribe to the dominant values of society, but are blocked off (because of marginalization) from success. The outcome of subculture, marginalization and relative deprivation is street crime and burglary, committed largely by young males.

Criticisms of left realism

Marxist or 'critical criminologist' writers have attacked realism for ignoring the 'real' causes of crime that lie in the wider capitalist system and of ignoring the crimes of more powerful groups in society by simply concentrating on street crime.

Feminist and postmodernist criminologists, such as Pat Carlen (1992) and Henry and Milovanovich (1996), have argued that left realist criminology accepts the establishment's view of what crime is and so concentrates its attention on issues to do with street crime and burglary. They argue, instead, that one role of criminology ought to be exploring the way that society harms less powerful groups.

Overview of realism

Realist approaches to crime have actually been put into practice, in a modified form, by New Labour governments since the late 1990s. However, just as these were being accepted by decision-makers, a rather different view of society and the place of crime within it were emerging. Interestingly, the realist approaches are perfect examples of what the late-modern approaches argue is the main concern of modern society – risk. Both left and right realism emerged from the concerns about the high crime rates in the inner cities and large housing estates, where risk of crime was much higher. The theories and the policy options which emerged were directly informed by risk models. As we shall see in the next section, these ideas of risk are a construction of late-modern and postmodern societies.

Late modernity and crime

All sociology has been affected by the insights provided by the late-modernist and postmodernist perspectives, and criminology is no different. As outlined in Unit 1, Topic 2, late modernity refers to a number of changes in society which include:

- changes in the economy from production to service industry
- the growth of a global as opposed to national economies
- the decline in traditional social institutions such as social class and the family, and their replacement with greater emphasis on individual identity and aspirations
- the growth in importance of the mass media.

synoptic link

social inequality and difference

Left Realism's use of relative deprivation to help explain subculture is not a new idea, but was developed by Runciman in the 1950s to help explain political stability. Runciman argued that the actual amount of poverty and deprivation in a society is less important in bringing about radical social change than an *awareness* of being poor and deprived. Right-wing politicians often point out that people today are actually much better off than ever before in history, yet there is probably a greater sense of deprivation than ever before. This sense of relative deprivation has been explored by sociologists in a number of areas. A sense of relative deprivation fuels the motivation to commit crime: the media construct images of what success actually is and those who are excluded from this feel that this exclusion is unfair. A similar idea was developed by Merton in the 1930s with his idea of 'anomie'. Relative deprivation has also been used by sociologists to explore the growth of religious communities. Where people feel unfairly excluded and relatively deprived, they may turn to religion both to explain their position and to gain solace and prestige. The growth in Pentecostal churches in Britain, attended largely by people of African and Caribbean origins, is one example of responses to relative deprivation. More recently, there has been a suggestion that interest in Islam by young British people of Pakistani origin is a response to their marginal and (relatively) deprived position in British society.

These changes provide the backdrop for a range of new theories and explanations for crime.

Actuarial approaches to crime

In earlier topics, we explored the development of notions of 'risk' as devised by Giddens (1999) and Beck, who suggested that late-modern society is characterized by the development in both personal and governmental spheres of a 'calculative attitude' towards risk. In criminology, too, writers such as O'Malley (1992) have developed similar ideas about the significance of ideas of risk to an understanding of crime. These writers suggest that in late-modern society, individuals and governments are less concerned about justice being done than they are about limiting risk to themselves. Although the difference between risk and justice does not seem very great, in fact, according to O'Malley, it is enormous. In societies where the concern is with justice, then when a crime is committed, the government will seek the person who is guilty, try and punish them.

In late modernity, where governments are concerned about risk, then an '**actuarial**' approach is taken. The term 'actuarial' is taken from insurance companies, who work out what the risks are for a particular problem and then base their charges on that – thus young males pay higher motor insurance premiums because they are the drivers most likely to be involved in accidents, even if individual young males are very good, careful drivers. Therefore, in late modernity, governments are not concerned with individual guilt or innocence, but with controlling the behaviour of potentially deviant groups. Through such reasoning, young people are now seen as a problem group, and a range of legal measures, such as Anti-Social Behaviour Orders (ASBOs), are brought in to control everyone – *before* any offence might be committed. Feeley and Simon (1992) called this the new penology, which they argue is 'less concerned with responsibility, fault, ... or diagnosis ... but with techniques to identify, manage and sort (people) by dangerousness'.

Actuarial theories do not explain crime, but they do provide a different way of understanding how societies respond to very high levels of crime. They suggest that as crime levels are so high, it is simply impossible to sustain the fiction (upon which criminology itself is based) that criminals are different from the mass of the population.

The criminology of the other

This idea of the lack of difference between the criminal and 'law-abiding', has been further explored by Garland (1996), who argues that in late modernity, crime levels are so high that there has been a cultural response. This response is to divide criminals into two types – the **criminology of the self** and the **criminology of the other**:

● The *criminology of the self* is based on the idea that these criminals are similar to the majority of the population – rational and self-seeking. Therefore, ordinary people must

engage in sensible activities to limit the risk of violence or theft. Do not go in poorly lit streets, lock up your possessions and avoid confrontations.

● *Criminology of the other* refers to those on the borders of our understanding – child molesters, rapists and terrorists. These people are outsiders by whom we feel truly threatened and who should be excluded from normal standards of justice and punishment.

Young (1999), in his later writings, has taken up this theme and has moved away from left realism to explore the way in which societies in late modernity systematically exclude significant sectors of the population, labelling them as outsiders of whom we ought to be afraid. Referring in particular to US society, Young points out that there are currently almost 1.6 million people imprisoned, with a further 5.1 million under some form of judicial control – with the overwhelming majority coming from minority ethnic groups. Young also points out that Britain is steadily increasing its use of imprisonment, with more people in prison and on probation than ever before. Much of the writings of late-modernist writers on the subject of the role of crime and punishment shows similarities to the early work of Durkheim (see Topic 1).

Postmodernity and crime

Like late-modernist theorists, postmodernists have provided an entirely different way of looking at crime and, in some ways, these do not sit easily with more traditional explanations.

Postmodernism is based upon a rejection of the so-called grand narratives of science and structural sociological theories; postmodernists are particularly dismissive of Marxism and functionalism. Postmodern theorists agree with the analysis of social change which late-modernists describe, but provide a rather different analysis, one based upon the idea of fragmentation, difference and incoherence. One key element of this rejection of coherence involves resurrecting the importance of the irrational. This is very important, for most other forms of sociological theorizing have sought to explain the factors that could reasonably make someone offend, and so answers such as family upbringing, subcultural values, anomie and so on, were provided. Postmodernism breaks with this and takes us back to a whole range of emotions as precursors to crime.

Thrills

In Topic 8, we explored the work of Lyng and Katz, both of whom lie within this tradition, as well as the ideas of Connell and Messerschmidt. Lyng suggests that crime can be seen as a form of edgework, giving thrills by placing oneself on the edge of safety, but not stepping over. Katz wrote about the seductiveness of crime, whereby people are drawn into expressing their true feelings of rage and humiliation through what he calls 'righteous' acts, which can include violence and murder. Messerschmidt's work emphasizes the importance of maintaining the imagined role of masculinity.

However, a whole range of other emotion-based theories also exist. Levin and McDevitt (2002) have argued that much crime can be explained by thrill-seeking. Their reward for violence or theft is as much psychological as social, providing 'the joy of exhilaration and the thrill of making someone suffer'. However, Levin and McDevitt's argument fails to explain why this should provide thrills for some and not for the majority of people. Fenwick and Hayward (2000) provide this answer by suggesting that this thrill provides an escape from the dullness of everyday routines. According to them, when a person commits a crime, they then have 'feelings of self-realization and self-expression', which 'bring them alive'.

Shame and self-esteem

Scheff et al. (1989) argue that notions of shame and self-esteem are very important, yet these emotions are rarely acknowledged in contemporary society. High self-esteem means that people usually feel proud of themselves, while low self-esteem reflects a feeling of shame about themselves. Scheff argues that shame is a fundamental concept that we are constantly monitoring by looking at ourselves as we imagine others see us. Scheff argues that when somebody who has low self-esteem (that is, feelings of shame) experiences what they consider to be a humbling situation, then they may explode into a 'rage', which is a defence against the threat to what little self-esteem they have. Anger and rage are, therefore, self-defence mechanisms. According to Scheff, this is why ideas of 'respect' and 'dissing' (disrespecting) people are so important for young males, particularly from minority ethnic groups. Two ethnographic studies of US life in urban ghettos in the USA powerfully illustrate Scheff's argument. Bourgois (2002) and Anderson (1999) both point out that a key feature of life in these deprived urban areas is the amount of respect that people seek to gain for themselves. Being respected has positive outcomes in terms of status in the eyes of others, which in turn provides social and economic benefits. However, respect has to

be won, and in both studies this is generally obtained through the use of extreme violence when required, as well as appropriate dress and demeanour.

Constitutive criminology

Perhaps the single most coherent attempt at a postmodern criminology has been provided by Henry and Milovanovic (1996), who argue that it is mistaken to seek causes of crime, as crime is just one way of thinking about certain acts – in other words, crime is a socially constructed concept. This argument may seem to take us back to the ideas of labelling theorists (Topic 4) and critical criminologists (Topic 5), but the crucial difference between the **constitutive criminology** and these approaches is that, while labelling and Marxist theories see the basis of law in differences in power, constitutive criminology sees instead 'drift, seduction, chaos, discourse' as reasons for law. Because of this, they argue that it is almost impossible to find a rational basis for criminal law and suggest instead that the basis of any future criminal law should be harm to others in any sense at all. They argue that two key groups who work to co-produce definitions of crime are criminologists and journalists:

- Criminologists are part of that process which separates one form of harm from others and calls it 'crime', by accepting the socially constructed notion of crime rather than challenging it.
- The media are interested in only certain types and images of crime and thus their presentation of crime has become that which we regard as important crime.

Check your understanding

1 Make a list of key similarities and differences between right and left realism.

2 How has the idea of communitarianism been applied to the fight against crime?

3 What do left realists believe are the causes of crime?

4 Explain the term 'relative deprivation'.

5 What do late-modern criminologists mean by 'risk'?

6 Explain the importance of shame and self-esteem for crime, according to postmodern theorists?

7 How do constitutive criminologists argue that crime is socially constructed?

Actuarial – refers to the process of working out risk.

Communitarianism – an approach associated with the US writer Amitai Etzioni. He argues that government should encourage the rekindling of a sense of community. Local communities can then take over responsibilities for local problems.

Constitutive criminology – a postmodern term referring to the way that the idea of crime has been socially constructed.

Criminology of the other – the view that those who commit certain types of crime are non-human and evil.

Criminology of the self – the view that those who commit crime are essentially (flawed) people like ourselves.

Left realism – a Marxist-derived approach to criminology that argues that crime hurts the most vulnerable in society rather than the rich and powerful, and so more resources need to be spent on helping and protecting these poorer victims of crime.

Marginalization – refers to people living on the margins of society, in particular lacking any say over decision-making.

Relative deprivation – when the most deprived are put in a situation where they can compare their situation with others who are affluent, they become aware of their own relatively disadvantaged state and become discontented.

Right realism – approach to crime deriving from the right-wing theories of James Q.

Wilson and emphasizing 'zero tolerance'.

Right-wing – approaches that reject the idea of state intervention in health, welfare and educational services, regarding private companies as more effective in providing services than the government.

Zero-tolerance – using the law to ensure that smaller incivilities (groups of rowdy youths, noisy parties, public drug use) are all crushed.

exploring contemporary criminology

Item A

The period of history after the Second World War until the 1980s was one where there was there was a consensus stretching across a large section of informed opinion that the major cause of crime was impoverished social conditions. It was clear that poverty, poor housing and a low quality of life led to antisocial behaviour. In order to combat this, slums were demolished, educational standards improved, full employment advanced, and welfare spending increased. By the 1970s, the highest affluence in the history of humanity was achieved, yet still crime increased.

It is in this context that we argue there is no simple relationship between disadvantage and crime.

Adapted from Young, J. (1997) 'Left Realist Criminology: Radical in its Analysis, Realist in its Policy', in *The Oxford Handbook of Criminology* (2nd edn), Oxford: Oxford University Press

Item B

Postmodernists argue for respecting the existence of a plurality of perspectives as against the notion that there is one single truth from a privileged perspective; local contextual studies in place of grand narratives; an emphasis on disorder, flux and openness, as opposed to order, continuity and restraint. Therefore, the belief that offenders act rationally in deciding and planning their crimes is inadequate for a full understanding of the majority of acts of crime which are committed.

Adapted from Stones, R. (1996) *Sociological Reasoning*, Basingstoke: Macmillan (quoted in Carrabine, E., Iganski, P., Lee, M., Plummer, K. and South N. (2004) *Criminology: A Sociological Introduction*, London: Routledge)

(a) According to **Item A**, until the 1980s, what did most people believe was the main cause of crime? (1 mark)

(b) Identify and briefly explain **two** ways in which antisocial behaviour has been tackled in the past (**Item A**). (8 marks)

(c) Identify **three** causes of crime according to left realists. (9 marks)

(d) Identify and explain **two** ways in which postmodernism aids an understanding of crime and deviance (**Item B**). (12 marks)

Exam practice

(e) Outline and assess the usefulness of realist approaches to an understanding of crime and deviance. (60 marks)

EDUCATION IN THE UK IS A FASCINATING AREA FOR STUDY: on the one hand, it provides a fertile ground for applying sociological theories in practical and tangible ways; on the other, it gives a real insight into the way political decisions impact on society. The way in which different educational sectors have been changed over the last 60 years also provides insights into the impact of social class, gender and ethnicity on UK society.

Schools for which parents pay fees are known as 'private' or 'independent' schools. The top independent schools (e.g. Eton, Harrow, Roedean) are also called 'public schools' (233 out of the 2000 private schools that belong to an organization called the Headmasters Conference). About 7.5 per cent of the school population attend such schools, yet about 75 per cent of the top jobs in the UK (such as top politicians, senior army officers, judges and senior civil servants) are held by ex-independent-school pupils.

A wide variety of schools and educational institutions exist today, following the policies of various governments, which have enabled different areas to continue to offer different provision. Parents choosing secondary schools for their children often face a bewildering range of options from single sex or co-educational comprehensive schools, City academies, specialist schools, Foundation schools (which are not controlled by the local authority but by central government and which may select on the basis of ability) and perhaps even a voluntary school (a school which emphasizes a particular faith) to – for those who can afford it – the various private schools.

The first two topics ask important questions about the complexity of the education system in Britain. The starting point for this unit is the question: why does education exist? Topic 1 covers the views of the key sociological perspectives on this important question. The second important question is: how did our education system develop? Topic 2 traces the main changes since the Second World War.

The next three topics look at educational success and failure. If the education system is effective, then it might be hoped that every pupil would have a fair chance of success. However, there are pretty clear relationships between social differences such as class, gender and ethnicity and educational achievement. In Topic 3, the focus is on social class, while Topic 4 covers ethnicity and Topic 5 gender. Finally, the last topic looks at the links between education, work and the economy.

OCR specification	topics	pages
Education, socialization and identity		
Education and socialization; the relationship between primary and secondary socialization, cultural transmission and reproduction; values, skills, knowledge and roles.	The role of education in socialization is discussed in Topic 1.	88–93
Institutional processes; classroom knowledge, the hidden curriculum, streaming and labelling.	These are explored in Topic 1 and also in the context of class, ethnicity and gender in Topics 3, 4 and 5.	88–93 102–121
Patterns and trends in educational achievement		
Patterns of inequality of educational achievement according to social class, gender and ethnicity.	Discussed in Topics 3 (social class), 4 (ethnicity) and 5 (gender).	102–121
Theories and explanations of differential educational achievement, e.g. macro and micro approaches, including materialist, culturalist, structuralist and social action theories.	These theories and explanations are covered in Topic 3 in particular. However, there is further discussion in Topics 4 and 5.	102–121
Trends in achievement and participation and the implications for policy and provision.	Covered in Topics 3, 4 and 5. Parts of Topics 2 and 6 are also relevant.	94–127
Power, control and the relationship between education and the economy		
Education and training; the relationship between the vocational and the academic curriculum, the role of educational professionals and the relationship between schooling, employment and the economy.	These issues are covered in Topic 6.	122–127
Theories of the transition from school to work, e.g. functionalist, Marxist, feminist and new right theories.	The main theories are covered in Topic 1 while Topic 6 is also relevant here. Feminist views are discussed in Topic 5.	88–93 116–127

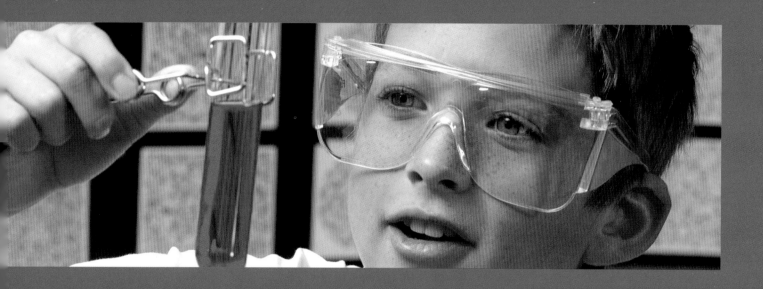

UNIT **3**
Education

The role of education in society

gettingyouthinking

1 Look at the photographs above. Using these and any other ideas you may have, make a list of the purposes of school for:

   (a) individuals
   (b) society as a whole.

2 Is there anything that occurs in schools that you feel has no purpose? If so, what?

3 What have you really learned at school/college this week? Who will gain from your acquiring this knowledge, set of attitudes or skills?

4 Could you learn effectively without school?

5 Would society suffer if schools did not exist? Explain your answer.

The education system is one of the most influential institutions in society. It takes individuals from the age of 4 or 5, for six or so hours per day, over a period of at least 11 years. It bombards them with a vast amount of knowledge, attitudes and skills. These are acquired either formally through set lessons or informally through what is known as the **hidden curriculum** – the processes involved in being 'schooled' and the various interactions that take place while in school. By the time they finish compulsory education, most pupils will have spent over 15 000 hours in lessons.

So why do modern societies invest so much in **schooling** the next generation? Some of the answers can be found by looking at the introduction of compulsory education over 100 years ago.

The introduction of compulsory education

Children of the upper and middle classes have always had the option of private schooling, but **state education** for all has only been available in Britain since 1880, when it was made compulsory for children up to the age of 10. There were a number of possible reasons for the introduction of compulsory education:

- *To create a more skilled workforce* – Britain had been 'the workshop of the world' through the 19th century, but other countries were catching up. Many employers believed that, in order to remain competitive, the new industrial society required a numerate, literate workforce able to cope with the complexities of modern industrial production.

- *To improve the effectiveness of our armies* – The high casualties of the Crimean War (1854–6) were seen as partly due to inexperience and poor tactics. Better-trained, fitter soldiers (who could read, write and count) might have given Britain a better showing.

- *To resocialize the feckless (aimless or wasteful) poor* – Many Victorians felt that the working classes were poor through their own fault – spending unwisely, drinking too much and living immorally. They needed to be taught to lead a more responsible and respectable life.

- *To reduce the level of street crime* – Remember Oliver Twist? Many felt that compulsory schooling would get young pickpockets 'off the streets', thus reducing the high levels of petty theft.

- *To ward off the threat of revolution* – The upper classes feared the 'tide of socialism' that was 'sweeping' through Europe. (After all, Marx himself was writing throughout the period leading up to the introduction of compulsory education.) Free education, on the one hand, could make the ruling classes appear generous, while on the other, giving them **ideological control** over the masses. The working class would learn to respect authority, follow instructions and conform to rules.

- *To provide a 'human right'* – Many **liberal** thinkers felt that education could improve the life experience of all citizens, including the working class.

Many of the above influences are still shaping the modern education system. The introduction of **Key Skills**, numeracy and literacy in primary schools, and all the developments in **vocational education** (discussed in Topic 6), reflect continuing concern about the skills levels of the workforce. Similarly, the importance of discipline and rules in schools indicates that the social control of young people is still a priority.

Most sociologists agree that education is important, both in teaching skills and in encouraging certain attitudes and values, but they disagree about why this occurs and who benefits from it.

Functionalist approach

Functionalists argue that education has three broad functions:

1 *Socialization* – Education helps to maintain society by socializing young people into key cultural values, such as achievement, individualism, competition, **equality of opportunity**, social solidarity, democracy and religious morality. Durkheim was particularly concerned that education should emphasize the moral responsibilities that members of society had towards each other and the wider society. In his view, the increasing tendency towards individualism in modern society could lead to too little social solidarity and possibly anomie (a state of normlessness or lack of shared norms). This emphasis can be seen today in the introduction of citizenship and the maintaining of religious education as a compulsory subject. Parsons, too, recognized the social significance of education. He suggested that it forms a bridge between the family and the wider society by socializing children to adapt to a **meritocratic** view of achievement. In the family, **particularistic standards** apply – a child's social status is accorded by its parents and other family members. However, in wider society, **universalistic standards** apply – the individual is judged by criteria that apply to all of society's members. Education helps ease this transition and instil the major value of achievement through merit. Both Durkheim and Parsons are criticized for failing to recognize the diversity of values in modern society and the extent to which the main beliefs of some groups, notably the powerful, are promoted through the education system.

What does the picture left tell us about the reasons for the introduction of compulsory education during the 19th century?

The functionalist theory of stratification links very closely to functionalist views on the role of education in society. It was developed by Davis and Moore (1955) in an important paper called 'Some Principles of Stratification'. Their basic premise was that some roles in society are more functionally important than others and need the people with the most talent (i.e. skill and intelligence) to fulfil them. In their view, this talent is relatively rare. In order to attract those with talent and to compensate them for the sacrifices they have to make while they hone their talent through appropriate education and training, they have to be better rewarded than the rest and, ultimately, deserve better pay, higher status and more attractive working conditions. These inevitably bring with them higher social standing. Social stratification is functional and necessary, therefore, because it ensures that the most talented fulfil the most functionally important roles in society. Education identifies and nurtures that talent, and accredits those who possess it. Critics point out that the relationship between talent and reward is questionable, e.g. as in the relatively low status and rewards given to nurses compared with doctors. Credentialism (the increasing need to possess qualifications) is said to be more about keeping people out than training them up. Finally, the disproportionate number of upper- and middle-class children identified as 'talented' calls into question the process of selection. (For more detailed criticisms of Davis and Moore's theory see Unit 8, p. 293.)

2 *Skills provision* – Education teaches the skills required by a modern industrial society. These may be general skills that everyone needs, such as literacy and numeracy, or the specific skills needed for particular occupations. As the division of labour increases in complexity and occupational roles become more specialized, longer periods in education become ever more necessary.

3 *Role allocation* – Education allocates people to the most appropriate job for their talents, using examinations and qualifications. This ensures that the most talented are allocated to the occupations that are the most functionally important for society. This is seen to be fair because there is equality of opportunity – everyone has the chance to achieve success in society on the basis of their ability. Critics consider the ideas of equality of opportunity and meritocracy to be a myth and question the correspondence between occupational status and talent (see Synoptic link above).

Marxist approach

Marxists challenge the functionalist approach. Althusser (1971) disagrees that the main function of education is the transmission of common values. Rather, he argues that education is an ideological state apparatus (see Unit 1, p. 6). Its main function is to maintain, legitimate (justify) and reproduce, generation by generation, class inequalities in wealth and power, by transmitting ruling-class or capitalist values disguised as common values. Althusser argues that this is done through the hidden curriculum: the way that schools are organized and the way that knowledge is taught means that working-class people are encouraged to conform to the capitalist system, and accept failure and inequality.

Bowles and Gintis (1976) argue that education serves to reproduce directly the **capitalist relations of production** – the hierarchy of workers from the boss down – with the appropriate skills and attitudes. Education ensures that workers will unquestioningly adapt to the needs of the system, without criticism.

Bowles and Gintis's '**correspondence theory**' suggests that what goes on in school corresponds directly to the world of work. Teachers are like the bosses, and pupils are like the workers, who work for rewards (wages or exam success). The higher up the system the individual progresses, however, the more personal freedom they have to control their own educational or working experiences, and the more responsibility they have for the outcomes.

Bowles and Gintis point out, however, that success is not entirely related to intellectual ability. Those pupils who fit in and conform rise above those who express attitudes or display behaviour that challenge the system. Bowles and Gintis go as far as to say that this is irrespective of ability, as some of the most creative and talented are among the latter group. Schools, therefore, reproduce sets of workers with the appropriate behaviour and values for the positions that they come to occupy. This explains why White middle-class pupils tend to do better whatever their ability. The education system disguises this injustice through the myth of meritocracy, so that those denied success blame themselves rather than the system. The hidden curriculum of the school not only reproduces the relations of production, it makes inequality in society appear legitimate and fair. Many employers, however, point out that schools are failing to produce workers who fully meet their needs, and the formal rather than the hidden curriculum has become more explicitly designed to match the requirements of industry through developments in vocational qualifications, for example.

Functionalists see education as turning pupils into model citizens, while Marxists argue that it merely turns working-class kids into conformist workers. However, despite their differences, functionalist and Marxist accounts of education do share some similarities – for example, they are both structural theories (see Unit 1, p. 2) in that they see social institutions as more important than individuals. Consequently, they do not pay much attention to what actually goes on in classrooms or to the views and feelings of teachers and pupils.

An alternative view: Paul Willis

A further criticism of Bowles and Gintis's view that schools have a simple correspondence with the world of work is provided by Paul Willis (1977). He presents a major critique of both perspectives when he points out that both theories are **deterministic**. This means that they both see pupils as passive products of the educational system. Both theories, argues Willis, fail to take into account the tendency of many pupils to resist these processes. (After all, are most kids in your experience docile 'teacher's pets'?)

Willis used a wide variety of research methods in his study of 12 educationally disaffected boys during their last year at a Midlands school and first few months in work. Through the use of observation and participant observation in class around the school and during leisure activities, he identified proschool and antischool subcultures, which were nicknamed the 'earoles' and the 'lads' respectively. 'Earoles' did what teachers expected of them, whereas the 'lads' took little notice of school rules, teachers and work – they substituted their own definitions of what school was about, based on 'having a laff'. When Willis

followed the 'lads' into their first jobs, he found significant similarities between the school counterculture and shopfloor culture – in particular, disdain for authority and the tendency to minimize work while maximizing 'having a laff'. Willis concluded that the lads recognized that the manual jobs to which they aspired – 'real masculine work' – did not require educational success in traditional terms, and in developing strategies to cope with the boredom of school, the 'lads' were also developing a way of coping with the boring and routine type of job that they would ultimately end up in. Even rebellion, says Willis, is reproducing the right type of workforce needed for the capitalist system – a workforce who are uncritical and 'just get on with it'. The lads are not simply suffering from false consciousness; they partly understand the reality of their situation, yet actively choose destinations that ultimately serve to trap and exploit them.

Willis's study is a good example of an **eclectic** approach to sociology. He uses an ethnographic, interactionist approach to understand the meanings pupils give to their schooling, and then applies a Marxist perspective to explain them. Recent writers have applied some of Willis's ideas to present-day

How do these cartoons illustrate Willis's view of education?

antischool subcultures, seeking to address a common criticism of Willis's work (now a quarter of a century old) – that is, that he concentrated solely on White working-class males, neglecting 'the potential of female, Black and disabled students as significant agents of resistance' (Rikowski 2001).

Approaches such as Marxism and functionalism, which relate educational experiences to wider society, as well as interactionism, which focuses more on the actual workings of the school, feature throughout the sociology of education, so it is important to have a good grasp of these theories. Postmodern ideas, which explore the range of experience of the increasingly diverse groups within the contemporary UK, are also becoming more important.

Check your understanding

1 Give three of the main reasons why education was made compulsory in 1880.

2 According to functionalists, what are the main functions of schools?

3 How, according to Parsons, does the education system form a bridge between the family and the wider society ?

4 What appears to be the relationship between educational achievement and the levels of social mobility in society?

5 What does Althusser consider to be the main purpose of education, and how is it achieved?

6 Why do you think the theory of Bowles and Gintis is sometimes called 'correspondence' theory? Give examples.

7 Why, according to Bowles and Gintis, do White middle-class pupils do better?

8 Who were the 'earoles' and the 'lads'?

9 What examples of proschool and antischool subcultures exist in your school or college, and by what names are they known?

10 How does Paul Willis challenge the traditional functionalist and Marxist accounts?

research ideas

1 Interview a range of your teachers. Ask them to explain the values which they consider are encouraged by the following aspects of school organization and routine: assemblies, speech days, sports days, school uniform, registration, house competitions, school rules, prefects, detention.

Evaluate the extent to which their responses subscribe to functionalist, Marxist or liberal views of education.

2 Organize a small research project to discover what people consider to be the primary purpose of education. Compare class, gender and age patterns in terms of the extent to which the wider social purposes are recognized. Which groups see school as most individually beneficial – for example, as helping someone to get a better job?

web.task

Search for government educational policy documents and statements at www.dfes.gov.uk. What are the government's stated aims? How do these aims relate to the sociological views you have been introduced to in this unit?

KEY TERMS

Capitalist relations of production – how members of the workforce are organized in relation to each other under capitalism. (In capitalist industrial societies, this is usually hierarchical, with a few at the top making all the decisions and giving out orders, while the majority do what they are told.)

Correspondence theory – a Marxist idea that the structures and processes in schools correspond with those in the workplace.

Deterministic – the view that a particular outcome is inevitable.

Eclectic borrowing freely from various sources; in this context, mixing a range of explanatory approaches.

Equality of opportunity – every person having the same chances.

Hidden curriculum – the informal learning of particular values and attitudes in schools.

Ideological control – getting people to behave in a desired way by convincing them that it is in their interests to behave in that way.

Interactionism – a sociological perspective that takes a small-scale approach to the study of society, focusing particularly on how individuals react to each other in specific social situations.

Key Skills – competence in communication, application of number and information technology as applied to post-16 study, assessed through portfolio evidence and external written tests.

Liberals – open-minded people who believe in personal freedom, democracy (the involvement of everyone in decision-making) and the rights of others.

Meritocracy – a society in which people are rewarded on the basis of merit, i.e. intelligence

and ability, usually via examinations and qualifications.

Particularistic standards – judgements pertaining to specific circumstances, e.g. within a family situation.

Schooling – the process of compulsory education.

State education – education provided by local and central governments.

Universalistic standards – widely held, shared judgements.

Vocational education – education designed to teach the skills needed for particular occupations.

Item A

Extract 1

The space won from the school and its rules by the 'lads' is used for the shaping and development of particular cultural skills principally devoted to 'having a laff'. The 'laff' is of particular importance to the 'lads' – 'We can make them laff, they can't make us laff.' It is used in many contexts – to defeat boredom and fear, to overcome hardship and problems – as a way out of almost anything. The school is generally a fertile ground for the 'laff'. Specific themes of authority are explored, played with and used in their humour ... When a teacher comes into the classroom he is told 'It's alright, Sir, the deputy's taking us, you can go. He said you can have the period off.' The 'lads' stop second and third years around the school and say 'Mr Argyle wants to see you.' Argyle's room is soon choked with worried kids.

Extract 2

Joey: On a Monday afternoon, we'd have nothing right? Nothing hardly relating to schoolwork, Tuesday afternoon we have swimming and they stick you in a classroom for the rest of the afternoon, Wednesday afternoon you have games and there's only Thursday and Friday afternoon that you work, if you call that work. The last lesson Friday afternoon we used to go and doss, half of us wagged out of lessons and the other half go into the classroom, sit down and just go to sleep ...

Paul Willis: What's the last time you did some writing?

Fuzz: Last time was in careers, 'cos I writ 'yes' on a piece of paper, that broke me heart 'cos I was going to try and go through the term without writing anything. 'Cos since we've come back, I ain't dun nothing [it was halfway through term].

Willis, P. (1977) *Learning to Labour*, Aldershot: Ashgate

Item B

If Britain is ever to achieve industrial and economic prosperity again, schools should encourage competition, discipline, decency, self-reliance and eventually prosperity, through a return to hard work, selection, higher standards and biblical morality. We must make it clear to children that there is a distinction between work and play. The playground is the playground, available in short doses for the release of high spirits and horseplay. The classroom, where such are still to be found, is a place where the dominant value is work, labelled as such, and not disguised as anything else. It should be a place where results are expected against a certain time schedule; a place where children should learn, as early and as frequently as possible, the satisfaction, joy and legitimate pride of being stretched to the very limit of their capacity and thereby turning in as faultless a piece of work as they can manage; a place where the teacher gets it across that our second best is not good enough; a place where the shortcomings of even the worst homes are to some extent rectified and not used as a constant excuse for inaction. Schools should get a hard grip on the surly, deceptive and uncooperative, at the earliest possible moment. It is imperative to support the hard-working, the inventive and the original. This means selection, ideally as sophisticated and even-handed as possible. We must toughen up the educational process so that everything else – learning, creativity, technical skills, wealth-creating potential – can flourish properly.

Adapted from a speech made in 1984 by Tom Howarth, Senior Tutor, Cambridge University, quoted in R. Burgess (ed.) (1986) *Education, Schools and Schooling*, Walton-on-Thames: Thomas Nelson

---

(a) Using **Item A**, explain the purpose to the 'lads' of 'having a laff'. (1 mark)

(b) Identify and briefly explain **two** reasons why the 'lads' (**Item A**) may have rejected the values of the school. (8 marks)

(c) Suggest **three** ways in which the writer in **Item B** would like to revise schooling to return Britain to 'industrial and economic prosperity'. (9 marks)

(d) Identify and explain **two** ways in which schools serve the interests of society. (12 marks)

Exam practice

(e) Outline and assess the view that education benefits the ruling class. (60 marks)

How has education changed?

gettingyouthinking

SECONDARY SCHOOL PERFORMAN...

BOLTON	KEY STAGE 3 RESULTS				GCSE/GNVQ RESULTS		
	PUPILS AGED 14	(% achieving level 5 or above in test)			PUPILS AGED 15	5 or more Grades A*-C	5 or more Grades...
		ENGLISH	MATHS	SCIENCE			
Al Jamiah Al Islamiyyah	22	55%	59%	36%	23	0%	22%
Bolton Muslim Girls' School	65	95%	71%	54%	61	54%	97%
Bolton School Boys' Division	-	-	-	-	139	96%	96%
Bolton School Girls' Division	-	-	-	-	120	99%	99%
Canon Slade CofE School	270	90%	90%	88%	246	81%	98%
The Deane School	154	46%	53%	47%	175	27%	80%
George Tomlinson School	123	41%	42%	42%	85	22%	91%
Harper Green School	288	68%	59%	59%	258	36%	92%
Hayward School	260	63%	58%	56%	232	31%	91%
Little Lever School Specialist Language College	210	64%	70%	63%	231	47%	97%
Lord's College	-	-	-	-	9	44%	89%
Mount St Joseph RC High School, Bolton	183	63%	67%	69%	205	42%	92%
Rivington and Blackrod High School	310	70%	71%	69%	303	52%	94%
St James's Church of England Secondary School	200	80%	83%	84%	178	56%	98%
St Joseph's RC High School and Sports College	174	73%	85%	78%	154	69%	98%
Sharples School	214	48%	56%	66%	203	42%	90%
Smithills School	328	65%	58%	62%	278	45%	95%
Thornleigh Salesian College	256	75%	71%	71%	235	58%	97%
Turton High School Media Arts College	246	80%	83%	83%	239	57%	97%
Westhoughton High School	229	63%	72%	65%	211	53%	91%
Withins School	223	34%	42%	31%	203	18%	81%
LEA average for schools in Bolton area		65%	66%	65%		46.7%	
National average		67%	67%	67%		51.5%	

A world of opportunity

Our languages staff also visit our partner primary schools, both to teach and support their colleagues in those schools.

We work to develop an international ethos throughout the school. Language and international links pervade the whole curriculum.

Events such as our international days (below) see students take part in a wide range of workshops and activities including international cuisine, samba music, caribbean poetry and weather forecasting.

In an increasingly cosmopolitan society – and with so many opportunities for living and working abroad – it is the job of all educators to prepare young people for that exciting world.

As East Sussex's first Specialist Language College we offer students the chance to learn a variety of modern foreign languages. Our excellent teaching rooms and facilities include a purpose-built ICT suite, recently opened by Dr Lid King, the National Director of Languages (above).

As well as giving students the chance to communicate directly with their counterparts overseas, ICT gives access to a wealth of online learning materials and help.

The teaching of languages isn't confined to normal curriculum time: courses such as Business German and Holiday Spanish are open to members of the school and local community.

We achieved Specialist Language College status with the help of many supporters and sponsors, including BAA Gatwick, Aspect Beauty and Bodyshop. We continue to value and nurture all our links with the local and wider communities.

"Being able to say a few words in a local language makes faces light up and doors ope..."

Chailey School
A Specialist Language College

1. **Why do so many schools produce glossy brochures? Where does the money to produce these come from? What else could it be spent on?**

2. **Why have recent governments been keen to produce education 'league tables'?**

3. **Apart from improving quality, what can schools do to improve their position in league tables?**

4. **Why do you think the developments discussed here are sometimes referred to as the 'marketization' of education?**

5. **What arguments can be put forward:**
   (a) **in favour of marketization?**
   (b) **against marketization?**

This topic will examine some of the major changes in the organization of the education system in England and Wales, and, in particular, the role played by central government.

1944 to 1965

Until the Second World War (1939–45), children of the working classes attended elementary school up to the age of 14. The school-leaving age was then raised to 15 in 1947. Since its introduction in 1880, compulsory state education had been a fairly haphazard affair, controlled by local administrators who oversaw the provision of basic skills plus religious and moral instruction, with boys and girls often taught separately – girls were usually trained in domestic competence, and boys in technical skills. A small proportion of bright working-class children won scholarships to continue with free education in otherwise fee-paying schools that were mainly attended by the middle classes.

The tripartite system

As part of the aim to create a 'land fit for heroes' after the Second World War, Butler's Education Act of 1944 introduced '**secondary education** for all'. The upper classes continued to be educated in the **public schools** and top universities. The Act had no effect upon their education, but it did aim to abolish class-based inequalities within education. A tripartite system was to be introduced, providing three types of school, each suited to one of three types of ability:

- grammar schools for the academic
- secondary technical schools for the artistic/creative
- secondary modern schools for everyone else.

The basic principle underlying this system was 'equality of opportunity for all'. All children would take an **IQ test** at 11 in order to allocate them to a school suited to their abilities. Only those who 'passed' the **11+** test went to grammar or technical schools. However, schools were supposed to have similar standards of provision, and **parity of esteem**, as each school aimed to provide the most suitable education for the development of each type of learner.

Problems of the tripartite system

- Middle-class children were disproportionately 'selected' for grammar schools, and working-class children for the secondary moderns. Many middle-class children who failed the 11+ were sent into private education by their parents.
- Working-class self-esteem was further damaged by the poor image secondary moderns had. 'Parity of esteem' did not happen, and employers, parents and children themselves generally viewed secondary moderns as inferior to grammar schools, which were also able to recruit better-qualified teachers and had better resources.
- The impact that labels have upon pupils' self-concept and motivation was becoming more widely recognized. Sociological research indicated that being labelled a failure created a self-fulfilling prophecy, as secondary modern pupils were not expected to achieve by their teachers and did not bother trying (see 'Focus on research' on the right).
- It was felt by some that the IQ tests were culturally biased against working-class children.
- Very few technical schools were built, due to the greater cost of equipping them.
- Many people were critical of the system because of the unfair way in which it operated. Girls were often sent to secondary moderns even though they had passed the 11+, because schools then were more commonly single-sex and there were fewer girls' grammar schools. Girls' marks were also adjusted downwards because it was assumed that boys matured later.
- There were also regional variations. It was twice as easy to get into a grammar school in some parts of the country, compared with others, because the percentage of available places varied.

By the mid-1950s, it was generally agreed that the tripartite system had failed in its aims. Educational attainment was overwhelmingly class based – most working-class children left school at 15 and entered work, while middle-class children continued into further and higher education. Twenty per cent of the school population went to grammar schools, 5 per cent to technical schools and 75 per cent to secondary moderns. A system that failed three-quarters of all schoolchildren was seen

Rosenthal and Jacobson
'Pygmalion in the classroom'

Much research in the 1960s focused on the way school organization affected achievement. Low teacher expectation as a result of streaming or selective schooling became a particular focus of attention. One particularly influential study was conducted in the USA by Robert Rosenthal and Lenore Jacobson. They noted that Mexican children, a traditionally low-achieving group, also suffered from low teacher expectations. They devised an experiment to test the hypothesis that teachers' expectations in themselves affected their pupils' educational attainment.

They were able involve a suitable sample of teachers in their research by posing as educational psychologists. They claimed that a sophisticated IQ test, which they had devised, could identify children who could be predicted to display 'dramatic intellectual growth' in the future. They administered the test to pupils and told the teachers which pupils had scored highly and which had not. However, no real testing took place. 'High-flying' and 'non-achieving' pupils had, in fact, simply been labelled at random.

A few months later, they administered a real intelligence test and found that the so-called 'high flyers' achieved significantly higher scores than the so-called 'underachievers'. The teachers also perceived the former to be happier, better-adjusted and more interesting than the rest. Fascinatingly, those pupils who were not labelled as high flyers, but who performed well, against expectations, were described as showing 'undesirable' behaviour.

As pupils were not told of their initial 'assessment' outcome, Rosenthal and Jacobson concluded that their research demonstrated that the expectations held by teachers about their pupils' ability were a significant influence upon pupils' intellectual development.

Rosenthal, R., and Jacobson, L. (1968) *Pygmalion in the Classroom*, New York: Holt, Rinehart & Winston

1 **How might this research be criticized as unethical?**

2 **How did research such as this help to justify serve to justify the phasing out of the tripartite system?**

3 **Several attempts to replicate this research have failed to find a similar correlation between teachers' expectations and pupil achievement. How else might pupils in this subsequent research have responded to low teacher expectations?**

as a great waste of talent – although many middle-class parents wanted to retain it. Other middle-class parents whose children were in danger of failing the 11+ were keen for selection to be abolished; as Benn and Chitty (1996) have since pointed out, while the middle class was expanding, the grammar schools were not.

1965 to 1979

Comprehensive schools

In 1965, the Labour government instructed all local authorities to submit plans for comprehensive reorganization. Comprehensive schools educated all children – regardless of class, gender, ethnicity and ability – under one roof. The aim was to promote both social justice and tolerance. A great deal of money was spent on upgrading facilities and on teacher training, so that these schools could not only maintain the standards of the grammar schools, but also provide a broader curriculum and greater sporting and recreational opportunities.

The Labour government also embarked on a rapid expansion of higher education, creating more universities, the polytechnics and the **Open University**. All of these innovations were aimed at increasing working-class access to higher education. However, the public school system and its disproportionate access to **Oxbridge** remained intact.

In 1967, the Labour government set up six Educational Priority Areas (EPAs) in poverty-stricken areas of the UK, which received more cash and more teachers for primary schools. This was known as **compensatory education** (see Topic 3, pp. 103–4). The scheme was eventually abandoned in the 1970s having shown little sign of success.

Successive changes of government delayed the progress towards full comprehensivization and it was not until the middle of this period that comprehensive schools finally outnumbered selective schools. Rather than replacing the tripartite system, both systems continued to co-exist. By the beginning of the 1970s, the Conservative government would only allow schools to apply to go comprehensive on a school-by-school basis rather than within an entire local authority. This clearly affected the capacity of comprehensives to live up to the ideal, as in many areas, the more able middle-class pupils were creamed off by the local grammar school. In any case, comprehensivization could not overcome the fact that catchment areas in the inner cities tended to be socially divided and homogeneous, so the schools in each catchment area tended to have the same type of pupils rather than the comprehensive mix intended.

'Progressive education' and mixed-ability teaching

In 1972, the school-leaving age was raised to 16, forcing all pupils to sit exams. Teachers had to find new ways of engaging this sometimes reluctant extra year-group. More significantly, many teachers had seen the damage caused by the labelling of

pupils according to ability (both in the tripartite system and by **streaming** in comprehensive schools). Where LEAs had gone comprehensive, the abolition of the 11+ freed up the curriculum of the junior schools. Oxfordshire was one of the first counties to scrap the exam, along with Leicestershire, the West Riding of Yorkshire, Bristol and London. It was in these areas, also, that the system of streaming, which reinforced the methodology of whole-class teaching and perpetuated the damaging influences of labelling, was replaced by other approaches to teaching and learning. Sociologists such as Hargreaves (1967) had shown that middle-class children tended to occupy the upper streams, while working-class children were located in the lower streams, even when the children were of similar measured ability. The opportunities began to open up for teachers to address the needs of the full ability range, rather than focus on just the more able, as had previously been the case.

Informed by new ideas about pedagogy that had initially influenced teaching in the primary schools freed by the abolition of the 11+ in their area, secondary-school teachers also wanted to enable all pupils to achieve their maximum potential; rather than teach all of the class the same thing at the same time, they believed that learning should be child-centred and a process of guided discovery. Teachers in comprehensives, therefore, also began to experiment with mixed-ability teaching.

By the late 1960s, critics were claiming that **progressive education** was neglecting the '3 Rs' (**R**eading, w**R**iting, a**R**ithmetic), and that standards had fallen. Comprehensives, especially in the inner cities, were frequently attacked for lack of discipline, poor results, truancy and large class sizes. The opposition education minister, Margaret Thatcher, eventually became prime minister in 1979, and teachers were never to have the freedom to exercise their professional autonomy again.

1979 to 1988

Conservative education policy in the 1980s was characterized by the following initiatives:

- *An emphasis on preparing young people for work and industry* – A number of measures such as the introduction of Youth Training Schemes and work experience in schools became known as the '**new vocationalism**' (see Topic 6 for more details).
- *A renewed focus on selection* – In 1980, the **Assisted Places Scheme** was introduced, giving bright working-class pupils free places in public schools if they passed the school's entrance exam.
- *Centralization and a rejection of localized policy and provision* – Local funding that reflected social deprivation was felt to have been excessive and wasteful, especially where Labour-controlled local authorities were involved. Other ways of funding schools were introduced, invariably at the expense of poorer areas, but good for the government in terms of middle-class votes.

Many of the policies introduced by the 1988 Education Reform Act, such as SATs, league tables, a National Curriculum and an educational marketplace, are still in place today.

League tables have created 'sink schools' that no one wants to go to, filled with pupils from the working class and disadvantaged groups. On the other hand, schools at the top have disproportionate numbers of middle-class pupils whose parents can afford to live in or move to the area, or use their cultural capital (see p. 104) to influence the admissions process (Ball *et al.* 1994). Pressure on schools to achieve good league-table positions, has led to the reintroduction of setting and streaming (Sukhnandan and Lee 1998). Working-class pupils, being more likely to occupy lower sets, are therefore less likely to be entered for exams than before. The vocational/academic divide is as wide as ever, with mainly working-class pupils being steered

towards vocational subjects, and girls and boys into gendered vocational areas (DfES 2002a). A growing proportion of comprehensives that become foundation and specialist schools will be able to select 10 per cent of their intake according to ability. Accusations that the National Curriculum is culturally biased, emphasizing White, middle-class culture, history and experience at the expense of others (McNeill 1988, Ball 1995) remain. Black boys are four times more likely to be expelled than White pupils (Connolly 1998). Even perceptions of school are more gendered than ever, boys rejecting the goal of school success as 'feminine' or 'girly' (Francis 2000), while for most girls, subject choices lead to a much narrower range of career options than for boys (EOC 2005).

The organization of schooling, it seems, is as likely to reproduce social inequalities as it ever was.

1988 to 1997

The most influential legislation since 1944 was introduced with the 1988 Education Reform Act. This brought with it a new emphasis on competition and choice, and a move away from **egalitarianism**:

- The Assisted Places Scheme was expanded.
- All pupils would study the **National Curriculum** – This would involve the same subject content at various key stages from the age of 7 to 16, in Maths, English, Science, History, Geography, Technology, Music, Art, physical education (PE) and a modern language. It would include only 10 to 20 per cent of optional subjects, with more options allowed at GCSE (the new exam standard to replace CSE and O-level).
- Pupils would sit national tests (**SATs**) at 7, 11 and 14. These would be used to draw up **league tables** which would inform parents of each school's performance.
- Schools could decide how to manage their budgets or, if they wished, opt out of local-authority control altogether, and become **grant-maintained** (GM) schools, which could make their own decisions about how to recruit pupils. Funding was also directly proportional to the numbers of pupils enrolled. From 1994, they could select on the basis of ability if they wished.
- **Marketization** – Parents would be allowed to choose which school to send their children to. The restrictions on entry were removed, allowing popular schools to expand, while unpopular schools might be closed. Increased competition between schools for pupils would, it was hoped, drive standards up further.
- A new inspection system was proposed (introduced in 1992) for all schools, to be overseen by a new body called

Ofsted. Inspections were to be more rigorous and inspection reports published, providing a further source of information about schools for prospective parents.
- **City Technology Colleges** were to be introduced, co-funded by industry, to provide special opportunities for pupils in inner-city areas.
- The Act also established a Polytechnic and a University Funding Council with strong representation from commerce and industry.

Critics felt that the Act was actually concerned with reducing the power of the Labour-controlled local authorities that had become centres of opposition to the Thatcherite 'reforms'.

Concerns were also expressed over the damaging, stressful effects of testing on pupils. **Parental choice** was largely a myth, as few extra places were available in the most popular schools. League tables were felt to be counterproductive by many, as low achievers and difficult pupils were less likely to be entered for examinations than before, because schools did not want their results affected. The National Curriculum has since been slimmed down, while the extent of testing was reduced after protests from overburdened teachers.

Throughout this period, it became increasingly clear that many Conservatives favoured the reintroduction of selection at the age of 11. In 1994, the then Education Secretary John Patten encouraged the setting up of new grammar schools and allowed GM schools to select some of their intake.

During the 1997 general election campaign, Conservative leader John Major (who had succeeded Margaret Thatcher as Prime Minister in 1990) declared that he would like to see 'a grammar school in every town'.

Ball, Bowe and Gerwitz (1994)
Market forces and parental choice

Ball, Bowe and Gerwitz conducted research between 1991 and 1994 into the impact of the 1988 ERA and in particular parental choice. They studied 15 schools in three neighbouring LEAs. The overall effect of parental choice, they argue, is to have increased the advantages of middle-class families in securing better education for their children.

Middle-class parents were able to exploit their advantages in the market and bring social and cultural advantages to bear. As a consequence, their children were more likely to go to the schools of their choice. In contrast, working-class families, who were no less interested in the education of their children, lacked material and cultural resources. Ball and his colleagues concluded, not surprisingly, that the reforms had made education less egalitarian. In summary, they drew the following conclusions:

1 Publication of league tables forces schools to be more interested in attracting academically able pupils and to target more resources to children who are likely to be successful in examinations.
2 Schools have been forced to spend more money on marketing, with the result that resources are often diverted from special needs in order to do this.
3 Middle-class parents are more able to manipulate the system to their advantage. They have 'cultural capital' (see p. 104): they know how to impress a headteacher, mount successful appeals and make multiple applications.
4 Middle-class parents can use their money to gain other advantages:
   (a) pay for transport to more distant schools
   (b) move to areas where there are successful schools
   (c) afford extra coaching and childcare.

Adapted from Ball, S.J., Bowe, R. and Gerwitz, S. (1994) 'Market forces and parental choice', in S. Tomlinson (ed.) *Education Reform and its Consequences*, London: IPPR/Rivers Oram Press

1 **What impact has the ERA had in schools which may have affected the educational opportunities of the less able?**

2 **What strategies outside school can middle-class parents adopt to improve the chances of their children gaining access to better schools?**

For sale:
within catchment area of
sinking comprehensive
school – £200,000

For sale:
within catchment area of
desirable specialist school
– £300,000

New Labour: 1997 onwards

The Conservatives, who had been in office since 1979, were swept from power in 1997 by New Labour. However, the new Labour Prime Minister, Tony Blair, faced strong condemnation by sending his children to the London Oratory School, a selective Roman Catholic school. 'Choice,' he argued, 'would not be sacrificed to political correctness.'

New Labour inherited the Conservatives' new initiatives and took most of them forward to introduce **Curriculum 2000**. Post-16 students had long been criticized for being too narrowly specialized in their studies and lacking essential skills for higher education and employment. Also, the vocational/academic divide (the lack of parity of esteem between vocational students studying on BTEC, GNVQ and NVQ courses and students studying A-levels) was seen to be depriving industry of the brightest students.

With the introduction of Curriculum 2000, more mixing of academic and vocational studies became possible, and the number of courses increased. Rather than just three A-levels, students could now study four or five courses including AS-levels (a level between GCSE and A-level), or vocational subjects (BTECs, GNVQs), plus a Key Skills qualification. In the second year, they would then continue either with the vocational subjects they wished to specialize in or with the full A-level (A2). However, integrated vocational and academic programmes have largely failed to materialize, proving unpopular with both pupils and their parents.

New Labour also introduced many initiatives of their own, including the abolition of higher education grants and the extension of student loans. They tried to tackle **social exclusion** by improving educational opportunities for the long-term unemployed and single mothers. Grant-maintained schools were renamed '**foundation schools**'. They no longer receive grants from central government, but still retain special status and therefore have a great deal of control over how they recruit pupils. Extra funding has been poured into the inner cities, and pupils in lower-income families can now apply for

Educational Maintenance Allowances. Across the age ranges, Labour have tried to improve standards. A literacy hour and a numeracy hour have been introduced to primary schools; more emphasis has been put on inspection, while Learning and Skills Councils have been set up to improve standards in post-16 education and training.

Diversity and parity of esteem revisited

Under the Conservatives, the general thrust of change had been towards a system that was standardized, measurable, accountable and cost-effective. However, recent developments are emphasizing more diversity.

- **Specialist schools** have been encouraged and 10 per cent of their pupils can be selected according to ability. By 2003, over 1000 comprehensive schools nationally (23 per cent) had top-up funding to help them develop their specialism. The government intends to extend the specialist school programme to at least half of all comprehensives by 2006.
- In 2001, it was proposed that **City academies** should be established to provide high-quality education for all age groups in deprived areas of the inner city. **Academies** are now being extended to deprived rural areas.
- New Labour have also encouraged differentiation within the system to develop the potential of the most able. There is a growing tendency to teach pupils according to their individual needs and aptitudes. This has led to abler primary school children being taught alongside older age-groups, increased use of banding and setting, and the introduction of more tiers within GCSE specifications. In 2002, the government set up the Gifted and Talented Educational programme in order to identify the brightest 5 per cent of pupils aged between 11 and 16 who might benefit from programmes run by the new National Academy for Gifted and Talented Youth. It was argued that these children had 'special needs' that were just as important as those of the children who had difficulty with the basics. However, research by the National Foundation for Educational Studies (2002) found that pupils who mainly benefited from the Gifted and Talented scheme were disproportionately female, of White UK origin and middle-class.
- A re-emphasis on the world of work was apparent in the Increased Flexibility Programme. This involved schools in developing links with employers and local colleges to provide vocationally related courses. A number of vocational GCSEs have also been developed to assist with this process. Work-related learning became a compulsory part of the National Curriculum in 2005.
- As part of the 'New Deal' initiative, socially excluded groups, such as the long-term unemployed and single mothers, were identified in order to give them opportunities through 'individual learning accounts'. This scheme aimed to provide people aged 19 or over with up to 80 per cent of the costs of a training scheme of their choosing so that they could return to work with new or enhanced skills. The government also set up the University for Industry, under the brand name of Learn Direct in order to bring new opportunities to adults seeking to develop their potential.

There has been an emphasis for some time on the notion of a coherent system of 14-to-19 education and a unified qualifications framework that finally removes the barriers between vocational and academic courses. At the time of writing, this initiative appears to have stalled in the wake of Labour's third election victory in 2005, the general view being that the recommendations of the Tomlinson Enquiry into 14-to-19 education (see below) are perhaps too radical just yet.

Despite greater variety of provision since the introduction of the National Curriculum, the overall emphasis remains on measurement, accountability and cost-effectiveness. However, there is a growing recognition that the education system needs to deliver success for all, whatever their background. The buzz words of diversity and choice may either reflect a more postmodern perspective in educational thinking or simply provide a smokescreen for the reintroduction of selective practices within the British education system.

Sociological thinking has either informed change or been critical of it at various points in the process. This is especially apparent in sociological explanations of differential educational attainment – that is, why some social groups do better or worse than others – as the following topics will show.

focus on . . .
Education for 14 to 19 year olds

Some young people haven't been doing as well at school as they could be, and leave education without the basic skills needed to enter work. The latest research shows that around half of all students who take their GCSEs get fewer than five at grade C or above. Under the new system, all young people will be offered the opportunity of having education that meets their particular needs. There will be more opportunities to learn in a different, more adult environment – including the potential for significant experience in the workplace.

Students will be able to follow a course in one of 14 specialized Diplomas, which means they can focus sooner on the subjects that matter to them. The first five of the specialized Diplomas will be introduced from 2008. These will cover: ICT (information communication technology), engineering, health and social care, creative and media industries and construction and the built environment.

Under the changes, GCSE English, maths and ICT will include 'functional' skills that young people will find useful for their adult life and the world of work. A new General Diploma will be awarded to those young people achieving the equivalent of five GCSEs at grade A* to C including English and maths.

Subjects are also going to be more challenging, to make sure that students reach their full potential and are stretched while they're at school. For example, students taking A-levels will have the option to tackle more demanding questions, an extended project and higher-education modules. Achievements in these options will be recognized by universities and colleges.

Adapted from the Department for Education and Skills website (www.dfes.gov.uk)

1 **To what extent do you agree with the government's proposals for 14–19 education?**

Check your understanding

1. How was the education system organized prior to 1944?

2. Why was Butler's Education Act introduced?

3. Why did the idea of 'parity of esteem' not work?

4. What were the aims of progressive education?

5. Why did the abolition of the 11+ in some areas help bring about more progressive approaches to teaching and learning?

6. How did the 1988 Education Reform Act seek to create a uniform and more efficient system?

7. Why would critics argue that the Act was more concerned with curbing the influence of Labour-controlled local authorities?

8. Why was post-16 education reformed?

9. How has secondary educational provision become more diverse in recent years?

research ideas

1. Conduct a survey on a sample of adults over the age of 45, including ex-grammar and ex-secondary modern school pupils. Compare their experiences in terms of teacher expectations, personal feelings, attitudes to school, the curriculum, examination success, age at leaving education, final job/career.

2. Interview an experienced member of your school or college staff. Ask them to describe the impact that the following changes had upon their educational career and experiences:

   (a) the introduction of the National Curriculum, school/college inspections, league tables, competition between schools/colleges, parental choice

   (b) the introduction of Curriculum 2000, including new AS-levels and Key Skills

   (c) the introduction of Citizenship and work-related learning.

KEY TERMS

11+ – IQ test taken at the age of 11 to determine what sort of school you would attend under the tripartite system.

Academies (previously called **City academies** but now being opened in deprived rural areas) – all-ability schools established by sponsors from business, faith or voluntary groups working in partnerships with central government and local education.

Assisted Places Scheme – a scheme whereby the government funds bright students from the state sector to attend public schools.

City academies see **Academies**

City Technology Colleges – schools funded partly by industry, aimed at giving extra opportunities to inner-city pupils.

Compensatory education – making more resources available to schools in poorer areas in order to compensate (make up) for deprivation.

Curriculum 2000 – a complete revision of post-16 education, whereby students in their first year take more subjects at a level between GCSE and A-level. They then specialize in fewer subjects at full A-level in the second year.

Egalitarianism – the practice of not recognizing, or even eliminating, differences in social status and wealth.

Foundation schools – schools funded directly by central government rather than local authority. They do not have to conform to local authority guidelines, e.g. on selection (known as 'grant-maintained schools' before 1998).

Grant-maintained schools see **Foundation schools**

IQ tests – supposedly objective tests that establish a person's 'intelligence quotient' (how clever they are).

League tables – rank ordering of schools according to their test and examination results.

Marketization – the move towards educational provision

being determined by market forces.

Mixed-ability teaching – teaching pupils together, regardless of their ability.

National Curriculum – what every pupil in every state school must learn, decided by the government.

New vocationalism – a series of measures in the 1980s that re-emphasized the importance of work-related education.

Open University – university set up to provide a means of acquiring degree-level education by distance learning, via correspondence, video and TV.

Oxbridge – the collection of colleges forming Oxford and Cambridge universities.

Parental choice – ability of parents to choose which schools to send their children to.

Parity of esteem – equal status, equally valued.

Progressive education – child-centred approaches to teaching and learning.

Public schools – the top private fee-paying schools, e.g. Eton, Harrow, Roedean.

SATs (Standard Attainment Tests) – tests for 7, 11 and 14 year olds in English, maths and science. Used to compare school performance.

Secondary education – education between ages 11 and 16.

Social exclusion – the situation where people are unable to achieve a quality of life that would be regarded as acceptable by most people.

Specialist schools – schools which have a particular focus within their curriculum and links to specialist areas of work, e.g. arts and media, business, languages, healthcare and medicine; they can select 10 per cent of their intake on the basis of ability.

Streaming – where pupils are taught all of their lessons in groups according to their perceived ability.

Vocational – work-related.

Item A

Those who get Grade C at GCSE boost their school's league table position. Those who get a D or less don't score at all. Gillborn and Youdell in their research *Rationing Education* (Open University Press, Buckingham 1999) have noted that a new ethos has emerged in schools which they call the 'A-to-C economy'. They found schools were having to prioritize particular groups in order to survive and that everything in the three schools they studied (two in London, one in the Midlands) was being judged in proportion to the percentage of A to Cs the school was likely to get. They were constantly promoting any innovation that would make their league table figures look good, such as a move away from mixed-ability teaching towards setting, as in some subjects the syllabus is different for the different tiers. Other strategies include encouraging lower-ability pupils to opt for non-examined subjects, entering pupils for the lower tier (grades C to G) because there is more chance of them achieving a C grade than risking them taking the higher-tier papers even though they may have the chance to achieve an A or B grade. Their research showed that the students who were disadvantaged by the system were mainly Black, White working-class, or had special needs.

Adapted from Smithers, R. and Berliner, W. *The Guardian*, 19 March 2002; Ahmed, K. *The Observer*, 24 February 2002

Item B

Ex-private [fee-paying] school students hold upwards of 75 per cent of the top jobs in British institutions, including the government, the civil service, the church, the legal system, the armed forces and the financial system in the City. Yet, they make up only about 7 per cent of the school population. Furthermore, those who control these institutions come overwhelmingly from a few exclusive schools – for example, Eton, Harrow, Winchester and Westminster – and have attended Oxford or Cambridge universities (the so-called 'Oxbridge connection'). Those who occupy the top jobs perpetuate these inequalities in two ways:

- by sending their own sons and daughters to these same schools
- by appointing new recruits to top jobs from these schools.

This restrictive elite self-recruitment is known as the 'old boy' (or 'school tie') network. (Public schools don't have to follow the National Curriculum, nor are their teachers inspected by central government officers.)

Adapted from Denscombe, M. (1993) *Sociology Update*, Leicester: Olympus Books

(a) Using **Item A** explain what is meant by 'league tables'. (1 mark)

(b) Identify and briefly explain **two** reasons why many schools have moved away from mixed-ability teaching (**Item A**). (8 marks)

(c) Suggest **three** ways in which someone in a 'top job' can attempt to ensure that their sons and daughters attain a position of similar status (**Item B**). (9 marks)

(d) Identify and explain **two** ways in which educational reform has increased the control of education by those outside the education system. (12 marks)

Exam practice

(e) Using material from the Items and elsewhere, assess the view that changes to the education system have resulted in greater equality of opportunity for all pupils. (60 marks)

web.tasks

1 **Visit the site www.eng.umu.se/education/ which provides an excellent history of British education in words, pictures and contemporary documents.**

2 **Visit the Standards site www.standards.dfes.gov.uk and find information on different types of schools and key educational initiatives.**

Class and educational achievement

gettingyouthinking

● Of the 43 051 pupils who were eligible to take GCSE or equivalent exams in 2003/04, 6.7 per cent left school without a GCSE grade A to G. These children were overwhelmingly from unskilled and semiskilled social backgrounds (see chart below).

Social-class grouping	% with higher education	% attended private school	% with no qualifications	% with literacy and numeracy below level 1
1 Professional	78	26	3	6
2 Employers/Managers	35	12	17	8
3a Intermediate non-manual	30	6	19	12
3b Skilled manual	9	1	40	21
4 Semiskilled manual	5	1	56	31
5 Unskilled manual	1	1	74	37

Note: Level 1 means foundation level GCSE grade D to G equivalent; 'below level 1' therefore means below the level of a GCSE pass.

Adapted from DFES *Skills for Life Survey*, October 2003, HMSO, and HEFCE Survey 2004

● In the most deprived 10 per cent of areas, 38.8 per cent of pupils attending maintained schools achieved 5 or more A* to C grades at GCSE and equivalent in 2004, compared to 65.2 per cent of pupils attending maintained schools in the least deprived 10 per cent of areas.

In addition, children from working-class backgrounds:

● are less likely to be found in nursery schools or preschool playgroups
● are more likely to start school unable to read
● are more likely to fall behind in reading, writing and number skills
● are more likely to be placed in lower sets or streams
● are more likely to leave school at the age of 16
● are less likely to go on into the sixth form and on to university.

1 Make a list of possible explanations for the points in the list on the right. Use the photographs to help you.

2 Compare your list with those of others. Rank the explanations you have identified in order, with the most important first.

3 Explain why you have ranked some explanations higher than others.

It seems obvious: our educational success or failure is simply the result of our ability and motivation. When sociologists look at educational achievement, however, they find that there are distinct patterns. It seems that ability and motivation are closely linked to membership of certain social groups.

Class: patterns of achievement

Differential educational attainment refers to the tendency for some groups to do better or worse than others in terms of educational success. The issue was initially considered by sociologists solely in terms of class as they attempted to explain the huge class differences that existed between schools within the tripartite system (see p. 94). Differences between boys and girls and between different ethnic groups are a more recent focus, which will be explored in Topics 4 and 5.

While many of the policy changes since 1998 have been about raising the standards of teaching and learning in schools, and many reports suggest that school quality does have an impact on achievement across all social classes, such research needs to be put into context. According to research by the DfES (2004), differences between schools in terms of performance have little to do with the effectiveness of teaching (which contributes to an 8 per cent difference). The SATs scores on entry to secondary school (73 per cent impact) and the proportion of pupils receiving free school meals (19 per cent impact) highlight the significance of factors outside the school, such as class differences.

Explanations of class differences in educational attainment

Differential educational attainment has been explained in a number of ways:

- **material deprivation**
- **cultural disadvantages**
- **cultural capital**.

Material deprivation

Certain groups have less money than others and so are not able to make the most of their educational opportunities.
For example:

- They may not have the time and space at home to do schoolwork.
- They may not be able to raise money for educational trips.
- They may not have access to educational materials such as books, computers and the internet.
- They may experience ill health, have to work part-time to support their studies, or have to care for younger siblings.

Governments have attempted to reduce the material disadvantages faced by working-class pupils through **positive discrimination**. This takes the form of programmes of

Excellence in Cities (EiC)

This government programme to develop new strategies to raise performance was set up in March 1999 to improve the education of inner-city children; the aim was to drive up standards to match those found in the best schools. The following five items comprise the main policy strands.

- **Specialist Schools** (see p. 99)
- **Learning Mentors** – 800 were appointed in July 2000; the plan is to recruit 3000, in an attempt to reduce the numbers of pupils excluded each year, currently 12 000.
- **Learning Support Units** – 450 have been established to tackle problems of disruptive pupils without excluding them; the target is 1000 including 360 outside the EiC programme.
- **Gifted and Talented Children** – part of a national strategy for educationally gifted and talented pupils, including summer schools at universities for those pupils whose families have not themselves been to university.
- **Beacon Schools** – one of the main strands of the EiC initiative, established to help raise standards in schools through the sharing and spreading of good practice through mentoring, work shadowing, in-service training and consultancy.

compensatory education (see previous topic) which plough more resources into poorer areas. The Conservative government in the 1990s allocated up to 25 per cent more money to local authorities in poor areas, while the introduction of Education Action Zones by the Labour government in the late 1990s was also an attempt to raise standards by compensating for deprivation. Schools in deprived areas were given extra funding and allowed more independence than other state schools. However, the scheme was not extended beyond its initial five-year term. Excellence in Cities is a recent initiative which aims to improve the education of children in the inner cities (see panel above).

An Ofsted report (2004) into EiC noted that standards in primary schools had risen in most areas. It also noted that the proportion of pupils achieving at least five grade Cs at GCSE has also risen faster than the national average within a minority of schools supported by the EiC initiative. In addition, learning mentors, introduced under the scheme, are having a significant effect on the attendance, behaviour, self-esteem and progress of the students they support. The same Ofsted report was critical of Education Action Zones, which were described as poorly organized and wasteful of money. They noted that educational standards had actually fallen in some areas and truancy by secondary pupils was generally high.

This notion of compensatory education has also been extended to include post-16 students. The recent introduction of **Educational Maintenance Allowances** for post-16 students has two main aims:

1 to offset the need for older students to work part time, often for long hours, to support their studies
2 to support parents by removing the need for them to pay for their child's travel, equipment and food costs while they remain in schooling.

Many New Right thinkers are highly sceptical about the value of compensatory education, seeing it as an initiative of the 'nanny state'. Underclass theorists, such as Marsland (1996) and Murray (1994), have long argued that the unstable family life, inferior socialization and lack of discipline experienced by the poor, result in increased levels of crime, educational underachievement and higher levels of single parenthood. The journalist Melanie Phillips in her critique of the comprehensive system, *All Must Have Prizes* (1997), further argues that working-class educational underachievement arises as a result of teachers being too willing to blame poverty for underachievement when the real reason is the poverty of teaching and parenting. Phillips goes on to argue that educational underachievement has been made worse by liberal social policy, which has given too many rights and powers to children. This increase in children's rights, according to Phillips (2001), has led to parents taking less responsibility for the parenting process and pupils taking less responsibility for themselves.

While the intention of government may have been to foster greater social inclusion, recent changes have been less favourable to poorer groups in terms of university education. Forsyth and Furlong (2003) found that the costs of higher education and the prospect of debt were putting bright working-class students off higher education, despite higher achievement post-16 for pupils of lower social classes. At the same time, those working-class students who did enter higher education often had to juggle academic commitments with part-time work. The decision to introduce £3000 top-up fees in 2003 has also been controversial. Research by the Centre for the Economics of Education (Forsyth and Furlong 2003) suggests that the expansion of university places planned for 2010 will lead to a sharp rise in less-able children from wealthy families going to university and a decline in working-class students of all abilities.

Cultural disadvantages

The education system is mostly controlled by middle-class people, many of whom are White. Those who share these characteristics may well be viewed more positively and be more likely to succeed in the tests and exams created to assess their abilities. The 11+ test (see Topic 2) was criticized for middle-class bias. Being able to unscramble an anagram (a jumbled-up word) such as 'ZOMRAT' to form the name of a famous composer (MOZART) is much easier for a child familiar with anagrams (because their parents do crosswords) and classical composers (because they have seen their names on CD covers in their parents' music collection).

Language and social class

Research into language use and social class by Bernstein (1971) has been very influential in the sociology of education. He identified class differences in spoken and written language which, he argued, disadvantage working-class children. The middle classes succeed not because of greater intelligence but merely because they use the preferred way of communicating.

In examining the link between language and learning, Bernstein distinguished between two codes:

1 The **restricted code** – in which the sentences are short, vocabulary is limited and few adjectives are used. As a result, such language is context bound, i.e. has to be interpreted in the context in which it is used and assumes the listener shares the same set of experiences.
2 The **elaborated code** – characterized by long sentences, a rich vocabulary and a complicated structure of phrases that depend upon and link with each other. This form of language use is context free and so is better suited to the more formal, impersonal communication required by the education system.

Bernstein argued that the restricted code is the language form most commonly adopted by working-class children, while the elaborated code is typically used by the middle class and therefore is the form generally accepted in school by teachers and in examinations.

This has obvious implications for the learning experience of working-class children who, when attending school, are entering into a world where they have less experience of the language used. Not only are they less able to express themselves in ways deemed acceptable, but they are also less likely to feel as at home in the kind of environment that the middle-class child has become already used to, through their preschool socialization. In this way, the school system plays a part in reproducing social inequality. By having to become familiar with and use the language of the middle class, working-class children are inevitably disadvantaged.

Cultural capital

Bourdieu and Passeron (1977) provided a more explicitly Marxist emphasis, taking Bernstein's ideas further. They developed the idea of 'cultural capital' to explain cultural influences on educational success, suggesting that middle-class culture (cultural capital) is as valuable in educational terms as material wealth (economic capital). The children of the dominant classes come to school equipped with cultural capital, in that they subscribe to values, norms, experiences, linguistic skills and forms of knowledge, which fit into the middle-class ethos of the school. This cultural capital is the product of their '**habitus**', i.e. their home environment. Their daily experience in their habitus results in them internalizing particular ways of thinking that come to be taken for granted, such as going to university one day. Such children normally achieve their educational goals, especially as their parents can also offer other material support, e.g. paying for extras such as books, courses, trips and private education.

The children of the working classes, on the other hand, experience a 'cultural deficit' – they soon realize that the school and teachers attach little value to their experiences and values. In order to succeed, such children rapidly have to acquire the sorts of skills associated with cultural capital. Most fail to do this and are alienated by the middle-class nature of schooling. Such pupils often come into conflict with the school and end up either losing interest and withdrawing themselves or they are eliminated by public examinations.

Furthermore, the ruling classes are able to define the knowledge and culture of subordinate groups as less worthy of attention and study. The result is that *all* classes come to accept failure to demonstrate proficiency in the application of middle-class cultural capital as just and legitimate. Bourdieu refers to this as '**symbolic violence**'.

The home and the school

Early studies of the relationship between the home and the school, such as that of Douglas (1964), suggested that a significant influence on pupil's attainment was parental interest in their child's education, as evidenced by the extent to which they visited the school and discussed progress with teachers. Douglas concluded that this was much higher among middle-class parents and hence helped explain differences in achievement. More recent studies have cast doubt on the claim that working-class parents are somehow less interested in their child's education. When researchers actually interviewed parents, they uncovered a very different picture. Sharpe and Green (1975) argued that parents who had been defined by the teachers in the school they studied as being uninterested in their child's education were very ready to talk about their children's education, very articulate about their reasons for holding their views, and fully able to justify and support their views with appropriate evidence. Lareau (1997) also noted the extent of working-class parental interest but highlighted the impact of the cultural advantages of the middle class on teacher perceptions. He pointed out that teachers saw the home and the school operating ideally as a partnership in which parents backed up the school by encouraging their children to reinforce schoolwork at home. For example, a parent reading to children was seen to have particular importance. Parents who agreed with and who had the resources to conform to the ideal, appeared to advantage their children, while those who relied on the schools alone to educate their children (the working class) could negatively affect their child's progress. Teachers were likely to assume from this apparent lack of support that working-class pupils could not be expected to make similar levels of progress, thus initiating a self-fulfilling prophecy.

In addition, the likelihood of developing an effective partnership was further hampered by the lack of cultural correspondence between working-class parents and teachers. Lareau noted that 'interactions between (working-class) parents and teachers were stiff and awkward', whereas meetings between school staff and middle-class parents were more relaxed. Indeed, an open-house meeting was described by one teacher as being like a 'cocktail party without the cocktails'.

Ball *et al.* (1994) showed how middle-class parents are able to use their cultural capital to play the system so as to ensure that their children are accepted into the schools of their choice. The strategies they use include attempting to make an impression with the headteacher on open day, and knowing how to mount an appeal if their child is unsuccessful in their application to a particular school. West and Hind (2003) found that interviews were also often used to exclude certain types of families, particularly working-class and poor families, whereas middle-class parents often had the cultural capital to negotiate such interviews successfully. The government plans to ban such interviews in 2005.

In *Education and the Middle Class* (2003), Power *et al.* note that once middle-class parents had secured a place in the school of their choice, 'travelling time, homework and the schools' perceived exclusiveness made it difficult for children to maintain an 'external' social life, thus focusing peer-group activity within

Cultural capital in action

I did badly in my Maths test

We'll complain to the headmaster – he's a personal friend

We'll buy you a revision guide

We'll hire a private tutor

Let's go through every question together – I was good at Maths

We'll write to the school and ask to change groups, so you get the best teacher

Leech and Campos
Selection by mortgage

Research at Warwick University in 2001 found that middle-class parents were willing to pay a premium of almost 20 per cent on house prices in order to get their children places at good comprehensives. Their study of two areas of Coventry found that house prices within the catchment areas of two popular schools were between 15 per cent and 19 per cent higher than similar homes lying just outside these areas. Top of the league for higher house prices near desirable schools is Ashover school in Derbyshire, which has an average house price in its catchment area of £275 000. That's £200 000 higher than the norm for houses in the area.

The research found that middle-class parents are very adept at playing the system which allows parents to state a school preference and which permits popular schools to expand. This 'selection or admission by mortgage' reinforces social-class disparities in education, because suburban schools which serve affluent areas cannot expand sufficiently to include all who want to go there. This has resulted in the shrinking of catchment areas and consequently the social-class make-up of schools. League tables distort these trends further as middle-class parents consult them and make financial decisions about home-buying which benefit their children.

Leech, D. and Campos, E. (2000) *Is Comprehensive Education Really Free? A study of the effects of secondary school admissions policies on house prices*, University of Warwick Economic Research Paper 581

1 **What stops working-class children from gaining access to schools in 'good areas'?**

2 **Why is this phenomenon called 'selection by mortgage'?**

the school territories and in the company of academically able and often ambitious students like themselves'. They conclude that an important aspect of cultural capital is the pursuit of 'conspicuous academic achievement' by both middle-class parents and children.

The influence of the school: interactionist explanations

Interactionist explanations of differential educational achievement – based on 'labelling theory' (see Topic 4, pp. 112–13) – look at what goes on in schools themselves, and, in particular, teacher–pupil relationships. These theories had a major impact on the development of both the comprehensive system and the idea of 'progressive' education. Labelling theories suggest that teachers judge pupils not by their ability or intelligence, but by characteristics that relate to class, gender and ethnicity, such as attitude, appearance and behaviour. Becker (1971) showed how teachers perceive the 'ideal pupil' to be one who conforms to middle-class standards of behaviour.

Rosenthal and Jacobson (1968) devised an experiment to test the hypothesis that teachers' expectations in themselves affected their pupils' educational attainment (see 'Focus on research', p. 95). They randomly selected 20 per cent of the new intake of an elementary school in the USA and told the teachers that these children had scored highly on intelligence tests. This was untrue as no testing had taken place. However, when they returned to the school some months later, Rosenthal and Jacobson found that their sample had forged ahead of the other 80 per cent of pupils. They concluded that their research demonstrated that the expectations held by teachers about their pupils' ability were a significant influence upon pupils' intellectual development.

The teachers also perceived the fortunate 20 per cent to be happier, better adjusted and more interesting than the rest. Fascinatingly, those pupils who were not labelled as high flyers, but who performed well, against expectations, were described as showing 'undesirable' behaviour.

One of the main ways in which pupils are 'labelled' is by setting and streaming.

Setting and streaming

Middle-class teachers are more likely to perceive middle-class behaviour as evidence of commitment to study, and working-class cultural demeanour as evidence of indiscipline, lower ability or motivation. They may hold different expectations of eventual achievement, which in turn can affect pupils' progress according to the ways in which they are labelled and sorted into ability groups.

With regard to streaming, there is evidence that teachers expect less of those in bottom streams and this undermines the quality of their teaching. Keddie (1971) found that streaming had a profound effect upon teacher attitudes and practices. For example, 'A' streamers were trusted to work with the minimum of supervision and to make a contribution to class discussion, while teachers believed that 'C' streamers were in need of constant social control and rarely left them on their own.

A range of studies, such as Hargreaves (1967) and Ball (1981), suggest that those in the bottom streams – typically from working-class backgrounds – may react to their perceived inferior status by forming delinquent or antischool subcultures which award status to their members on the basis of antischool activity by being disruptive and avoiding work. Such behaviour, of course, confirms the teachers' labelling.

Woods (1979) however has argued that pro- and antischool subcultures are only two possible responses among many. Adapting Merton's typology of deviance, he includes ingratiation (conformity, being 'teachers pet'), ritualism (going through the motions/steering clear of confrontation), retreatism (daydreaming, truancy) and rebellion (rejection of the school's values and causing confrontation). Furthermore, as Furlong (1984) has noted, pupils do not necessarily adopt one form of consistent response and may switch between a range of responses at different times within particular lessons and with certain teachers. Most research confirms that setting and streaming more commonly produce subcultural responses in working-class pupils that ultimately lead to lower educational achievement.

More recent research by Campbell (2001) shows how subject setting and streaming by ability advantages those at the top, whose attainment increases, while those in the bottom sets do not increase their attainment at the same rate or to the same level. The overall effect is to depress attainment and therefore contribute to increasing social inequality. Numerous writers have suggested that the influence of league tables has increased the tendency for schools to separate pupils on the basis of ability. Hallam (2002) studied the literature on ability grouping from the first studies in 1949 to 2001 and examined research evidence from the UK, USA, Europe and the Far East. She notes that such grouping is not always based on attainment within specific subjects – it has also been based on behaviour and used as a means of socially controlling particular groups of pupils. Hallam's research survey indicates that setting tends to be beneficial for the more-able pupils in the top groups, while those in bottom sets generally receive little challenge or stimulation, and consequently can easily become demoralized, disruptive and disaffected. Stephen and Cope (2003) carried out a small-scale but in-depth study of 27 children transferring from nursery school to primary, and found that most 5 year olds in their study appeared to know that they were in a particular mathematics or reading group because of their abilities.

Stephen Ball (2002) goes so far as to suggest that setting is 'social barbarism', because it allows well-off children to be separated from 'others' whom their parents may consider socially and intellectually inferior. He points out that research evidence shows that grouping by ability leads to greater social-class inequalities between children. Studies show that pupils in bottom sets are often taught by the youngest and least experienced teachers with the highest rates of staff turnover. Also, there is less interaction between pupils in lower sets compared with higher sets. Pupils in lower sets experience lower self-esteem because they are both dispirited and demeaned by the experience. They are more likely to be alienated from school, apathetic about education and consequently disruptive.

The curriculum

Some sociologists have argued that what is taught in schools – the curriculum – actually disadvantages the working class. The knowledge that they encounter at school does not connect with their own cultural experience. Working-class experience is almost invisible in the school curriculum. History, for example, tends to deal with the ruling classes – such as kings, queens and politicians – rather than with the vast majority of ordinary people.

Recent government policies have emphasized the importance of differentiating between pupils. One the one hand, this promotes the idea that pupils need to be taught in different ways depending upon factors such as their ability and their

synoptic link

Public schools in Britain are actually not public but private, fee-paying institutions. Their independence from the rest of the education system distinguishes them from systems in other countries. While there is a minimal degree of state supervision, few pieces of educational legislation have had any effect upon them. They were left untouched by the 1944 Education Act as well as by comprehensivization and they have no obligation to test children at 7, 11 and 14 or to follow the National Curriculum. Studies of private education (e.g. Roker 1994) also suggest that these schools transmit a hidden curriculum which is geared to hierarchy, elitism and future leadership roles. Better-off parents among the middle and upper classes may pay over £20,000 per year for the top public schools such as Eton, Harrow, Rugby or

social inequality and difference

Charterhouse. Such schools belong to a body known as the Headmasters Conference along with over 200 of the top private schools. Class sizes tend to be half those in state schools, 88 per cent of their pupils go on to University compared with 29 per cent from State schools (DfES 2002a), and almost half the students at Oxbridge Colleges are from private schools. The figures are more alarming when you consider that only 7 per cent of school pupils attend fee-paying schools.

Individuals who attend public schools dominate the higher positions in British society. A study by Reid (1998) showed that 84 per cent of judges, 70 per cent of bank directors and 49 per cent of top civil servants went to public schools.

learning styles. On the other hand, differentiation between pupils also now takes place through the creation of different types of school – some of these emphasize an academic curriculum, some specialize in particular subject areas that have currency in the local job market and some emphasize work-related learning and vocational studies. The encouragement of differing curriculum models in schools means that, increasingly, a less comprehensive intake will be attracted. Academically focused schools, high in the league tables, are more populated by middle-class, able pupils. Specialist and foundation schools are allowed to continue to select 10 per cent of their pupils on the basis of aptitude. The remaining comprehensive schools will have an ability range skewed towards the lower end and populated by a higher proportion of working-class pupils. Research by the Education Network (2002) found that specialist and foundation schools (see Topic 2) have an advantaged intake compared with their comprehensive school neighbours, and less than half the number of deprived children, as measured by the number of free school meals.

Class is still considered by far the most significant factor influencing educational attainment – thought to have three times the effect on educational achievement of ethnicity and five times the impact of gender (Drew 1995). However, these other dimensions are still important and will be explored in the following two topics.

Check your understanding

1 How has recent government policy attempted to address material deprivation?

2 Why are New Right thinkers critical of compensatory education?

3 How do material factors influence working-class students' experience of higher education?

4 Give three examples of ways in which differences in class culture might affect achievement in education.

5 What does Bourdieu mean by the concept 'habitus'?

6 How does Ball argue that cultural capital helps middle-class children to gain a place in the school of their choice?

7 How do recent studies criticize the view that working-class parents are less interested in their child's education than middle-class parents?

8 Using examples, explain how labelling can affect educational success.

9 What does Ball mean by the term 'social barbarism' in relation to setting?

10 How does the recent development of differentiation within and between schools impact on class and educational achievement?

KEY TERMS

Cultural capital – cultural skills, such as knowing how to behave, speak and learn, passed on by middle-class parents to their children.

Cultural disadvantage – term used in two ways: 'cultural deprivation' theory suggests that the backgrounds of some pupils are in some way deficient or inferior (e.g. in not placing sufficient emphasis on the importance of education); 'cultural difference' explanations suggest that pupils' backgrounds are simply different, and that the mismatch with the culture of the school places them at a disadvantage.

Differential educational attainment – the extent to which educational achievement differs between social groups.

Educational Maintenance Allowance (EMA) – a means-tested sum of up to £30 per week given to post-16 students to support them in meeting the daily costs of coming to school. The payments are paid only if the student proves they are attending regularly.

Elaborated code – style of communication identified by Bernstein and associated with the middle classes; it uses detailed and grammatically correct sentences with varied vocabulary.

Habitus – the aspects of an individual's norms and values that are rooted in their day-to-day experiences and routines.

Material deprivation – lack of money leading to disadvantages such as an unhealthy diet and unsatisfactory housing.

Positive discrimination – treating certain groups more favourably than others, usually to help overcome disadvantages.

Restricted code – style of communication identified by Bernstein and associated with working-class communities; sentences are short, grammar not always correct, vocabulary limited and meaning relies on context.

Symbolic violence – in this context, the ways in which the ruling class are able to define their own culture as superior and other classes accept this as legitimate; no actual violence is used, but the effect is violent in its effect in terms of condemning working-class pupils to educational failure.

web.task

Use the UCAS website at **www.ucas.ac.uk** to investigate class differences in higher education applications. What patterns can you find and how do they appear to be changing? Has the reduction in government financial support for students in the last few years had any effect on applications?

research idea

- Interview other people in your class to find out their experiences of setting and banding. Compare their experiences with Ball's views on p. 107.

Item A

Despite the fact that state school intake at the top universities has increased by 35 per cent, or almost 6000 students annually, there are still some 3000 students from the maintained sector 'missing' from these top universities each year. These are students who achieve A-level grades high enough to attend our leading universities, but who – for one reason or another – are not admitted. The table on the right compares actual numbers from each sector with 'benchmark' numbers (that is, what the expected numbers would be, based on entry qualifications gained by students and the subjects those students are studying).

Students from the independent sector are as likely to go to a leading university as students from the state sector who achieved two grades higher at A-level.

Benchmark and actual state school intakes, 1998/9 to 2001/2

	1998/9		2001/2	
	Benchmark (%)	Actual (%)	Benchmark (%)	Actual (%)
Birmingham	78	73	80	76
Bristol	73	57	74	60
Cambridge	66	53	68	55
Durham	77	63	78	67
Edinburgh	78	66	78	63
Imperial	73	62	74	59
LSE	74	62	74	64
Nottingham	75	72	76	69
Oxford	68	50	69	55
St Andrews	80	59	76	62
UCL	75	57	76	58
Warwick	76	77	76	76
York	77	79	77	79
Totals	74	64	75	65

Note: brown shading indicates universities with deficits of 10 per cent or more between actual and benchmark intakes.

Adapted from The Sutton Trust (2005) *State School Admissions to our Leading Universities An update to 'The Missing 3000'*, London: The Sutton Trust

Item B

A study conducted by the Sutton Trust in 2004 found that the overall rate of Free School Meal eligibility at the top-achieving schools is 3.0 per cent, compared to a national secondary school average of 14.3 per cent. Only 6 schools – or 3 per cent within the top 200 – have FSM rates which are equal to or above the national average. The intake of the top 200 is significantly more affluent than the school population as a whole. The findings also suggest that the top-achieving schools do not reflect the social make-up of their immediate areas: the average rate of FSM eligibility in the postcode sectors of the top 200 schools is 12.3 per cent – almost 10 percentage points and more than four times higher than the schools' average rate. In only 11 of the top 200 schools does the FSM eligibility rate reflect that of their local area.

Adapted from The Sutton Trust (2005) *Rates of Eligibility for Free School Meals at the Top State Schools,* London: The Sutton Trust

(a) Using **Item A**, explain what is meant by the term 'maintained sector'. (1 mark)

(b) Suggest **two** possible reasons why students from the independent sector are as likely to go to a leading university as students from the state sector who achieved two grades higher at A-level **(Item A)**. (8 marks)

(c) Identify **three** reasons why working-class students may be less likely to go to university than middle-class students. (9 marks)

(d) Identify and briefly explain why there is greater achievement in schools with low numbers of pupils receiving FSM **(Item B)** (12 marks)

Exam practice

(e) Assess the view that factors within schools are the greatest influence on social-class differences in educational achievement. (60 marks)

Ethnicity and educational achievement

gettingyouthinking

Read the information below and then answer the questions that follow.

Drawing on the best evidence ever assembled on race and achievement in England, David Gillborn and Heidi Safia Mirza found that, while all the principal minority groups now achieve higher results than ever, White pupils have improved more than most (Gillborn and Mirza 2000). As a result, some minorities are even further behind the majority than they were a decade ago. The situation is especially serious for Black, Pakistani and Bangladeshi pupils. These are some of the report's key findings:

- Black pupils often enter school better prepared than any other group but fall behind as they move through the system.
- The achievement gap between 16-year-old White pupils and their classmates of Pakistani and African-Caribbean origin has roughly doubled since the late 1980s.
- The gender gap is now present in every ethnic group. Girls are more likely to achieve five higher grade GCSEs in all the principal minority groups.
- The gender gap is beginning to make good some ethnic inequalities. Girls of Bangladeshi, Pakistani and African origin now outstrip White boys, but girls of African-Caribbean origin (38 per cent) are less likely to achieve five higher grade passes than White boys (45 per cent), Bangladeshi boys (40 per cent) and Indian boys (58 per cent).
- Too few local education authorities (LEAs) take race seriously. Around one in three do not monitor exam results for differences between ethnic groups.

Furthermore, according to a DfES research paper (2005):

- Black male pupils are twice as likely to have been categorized as having behavioural, emotional or social difficulties as White British boys.
- Within the Excellence in Cities initiative, Black Caribbean and Black African pupils were more likely than other groups to have reported seeing a learning mentor. Ethnic-minority pupils were less likely than White pupils to be identified for the 'Gifted and Talented' strand of the programme.

1 What evidence is there that the educational achievement of some ethnic groups has shown less improvement than that of others?

2 What do you understand by the phrase 'The gender gap is beginning to make good some ethnic inequalities'?

3 What do you think may be the cause of the underachievement of some ethnic groups?

4 What do you think needs to be done to address the underachievement of some ethnic groups?

Material and cultural explanations of educational disadvantage referred to in the previous topic also apply to the experience of ethnic minorities, because many tend also to be working class. In every ethnic group, middle-class pupils achieve higher average results than working-class pupils from the same ethnic group. However, middle-class Black pupils are the lowest attaining middle-class group. Their chances of five higher-grade GCSEs (38 per cent in the most recent figures) are less than working-class Indians (43 per cent), and only a little better than working-class Whites (34 per cent) (DfES 2002b).

Bangladeshi, Pakistani and Black children are more likely to be brought up in low-income families and subsequently suffer educational disadvantages in line with or worse than those of working-class Whites.

Drew (1995) examined the relative impact of class, gender and ethnicity on educational attainment. While class was clearly the most important factor, African-Caribbean males were still at the bottom of each class group in terms of attainment. However, African-Caribbean females, although they suffer from initial disadvantages in school, tend to do significantly better than working-class White pupils by the time they take their GCSEs. Fuller (1984) suggests that they may appear 'cool' in order to present a positive self-image to boys and teachers, but that they recognize the importance of getting good qualifications.

Children of Indian, Chinese and African-Asian origin also do very well within the education system. There is a strong emphasis on self-improvement through education in these cultures, and many of the children come from professional backgrounds, providing support, appropriate role models and material advantages. Their culture is perceived more positively by teachers than that of African-Caribbean males. In addition to all of the points listed in the previous topic (for children from working-class backgrounds), African-Caribbean males:

- tend to get fewer GCSEs and poorer grades than any other group (in 2005, only 25 per cent gained five A* to C grades, compared with a national average of over 50 per cent)
- are much more likely to be classified as having Special Educational Needs (8 per cent of the ethnic group as opposed to 5 per cent for Whites in 2004)
- are between four and 15 times more likely to be excluded than White boys, depending on locality (Sewell 1996, DfEE 2000).

While some Pakistani and Bangladeshi children do relatively badly in school, recent research has shown these groups to be catching up. The length of time Asian immigrant groups have lived in Britain varies. Those who have been here longer achieve more highly in the education system, because older siblings educated here are able to help their younger brothers and sisters. Also, reflecting changes within the White community, females generally tend to perform better than males within each ethnic group.

Material and cultural factors

While Black and Asian minorities are relatively overrepresented in the lower social classes, Indian families are an exception. According to the Trades Union Congress (2005), Bangladeshi and Pakistani families are four times more likely to be poor than a White family, whereas Indian families generally have incomes that are comparable with White families. The fact that Indian pupils' performance far exceeds that of the other Asian groups would suggest that material factors are a significant influence on the underachievement of some of the other minority groups.

Children of Indian, Chinese and African-Asian origin also do very well within the education system because of cultural factors. There is a strong emphasis on self-improvement through education in these cultures, and many of the children come from professional backgrounds, providing support, appropriate role models and material advantages. Their culture is perceived more positively by teachers than that of African-Caribbean males.

African-Caribbean underachievement has been blamed on the high numbers of one-parent families in African-Caribbean communities. While 22 per cent of White families were headed by a single parent, the figure for all Asian families is just 11 per cent, while the figure for African-Caribbean families is 48 per cent (*Social Trends* 2004). Some politicians have suggested that, because many of these families are female-headed, African-Caribbean boys, in particular, lack the discipline of a father-figure, and this, they suggest, may account for the high percentage of African-Caribbeans in special schools. For girls, on the other hand, the role model provided by a strong, independent single mother is a motivating influence, which helps to explain their relative success in education.

focus on research

National Statistics
Ethnicity, gender and achievement

Look at the table below, and then answer the question that follows.

Achievements at GCSE/GNVQ in 2003, by ethnicity, free school-meal provision and gender

GCSE or GNVQ 5 or more A* to C	Non-free school meals						Free school meals					
	15 year olds			% achieving			15 year olds			% achieving		
	Boys	Girls	Total	Boys	Girls	Total	Boys	Girls	Total	Boys	Girls	Total
White	210,995	204,442	415,437	50.2	61.1	55.6	28,036	27,507	55,543	17.1	24.2	20.6
Mixed	3,680	4,013	7,693	49.3	62.6	56.3	1,160	1,295	2,455	22.7	33.4	28.4
Asian	12,631	11,779	24,410	53.9	65.5	59.5	5,949	5,607	11,556	32.9	45.5	39.0
Black	6,154	6,543	12,697	33.1	48.7	41.1	3,003	3,175	6,178	21.5	31.7	26.8
Chinese	953	850	1,803	72.1	79.8	75.7	128	116	244	62.5	75.9	68.9

Source: DfES 2003

1 The entitlement to free school meals is often used as an indicator of low income. What do the figures above tell us about:

(a) educational achievement (as measured by GCSE performance) and gender
(b) educational achievement and ethnicity
(c) educational achievement and social class (as measured by entitlement or not to free school meals)
(c) the relationship between class, gender and ethnicity in relation to GCSE attainment?

Many working-class and ethnic-minority pupils may also feel undervalued and demotivated by an educational system that does not recognize their qualities, which are based on their class and ethnic culture. Furthermore, as Blair *et al.* (2003) suggest, it may also be the case that this schooling involves teaching practices and expectations based on cultural norms, histories and general cultural references unfamiliar to many ethnic-minority pupils.

A recent study showed that recent arrival into UK had a significant negative effect on performance (by the equivalent of more than one level in each core subject). Like social class and recent arrival, the level of mother's education was also a significant factor (Haque and Bell 2001).

Language has also been seen as a problem for children of African-Caribbean origin, who may speak different dialects of English, and for children from other ethnic groups who come from homes where a language other than English is spoken. This language difference may cause problems in doing schoolwork and communicating with teachers, leading to disadvantage at school.

Ball (2002) shows how ethnic-minority parents are at a disadvantage when trying to get their children into the better schools. The parents, especially if born abroad, may not have much experience of the British education system and may not be able to negotiate the system. This may be compounded by a lack of confidence in their English-language skills.

Issues such as uniform (which markets a school well and fosters an impression of discipline) may disrupt teacher–pupil relationships, particularly between teachers and ethnic-minority pupils whose cultural influences may exert more pressure on them to subvert the formal dress codes of the school, e.g. by refusing to remove baseball caps. This may provoke more antischool behaviour, truancy and the constructive exclusion of 'problem children'. Gewirtz (2002) identifies further socially excluding practices, such as the creation of complex application forms requiring high levels of literacy and often available only in English.

Labelling and racism in schools

Boys of African-Caribbean origin often have the label 'unruly', 'disrespectful' and 'difficult to control' applied to them. Gillborn (1990) found that African-Caribbean pupils were more likely to be given detentions than other pupils. The teachers interpreted (or misinterpreted) the dress and manner of speech of African-Caribbean pupils as representing a challenge to their authority. In perceiving their treatment to be unfair, the pupils responded, understandably, in accordance with their labels. Tony Sewell (1996) claimed that many teachers were fearful of Black boys in school, the result of socialization into stereotypical assumptions. Jasper (2002) goes further to suggest that the expectations that White female teachers have of Black boys' behaviour dictate the form and style of the teaching that they offer them, a style less conducive to learning than they offer to other groups. However, Sewell has recently been attacked by many in the Black community for suggesting that Black culture and peer pressure are as detrimental to the achievement of Black children as racism. Sewell argues that an antiintellectual culture and knowledge of sport and popular music give Black children status in the eyes of White students, but harm their own chances of success in education.

While few would argue that teachers display overt racism, Wright (1992) found considerable discrimination in the classroom. She observed Asian and African-Caribbean children in primary schools and found that teachers paid Asian pupils, especially girls, less attention. They involved them less in discussion and used simplistic language, assuming that they had a poor command of English. Teachers also lacked sensitivity towards aspects of their culture and displayed open disapproval of their customs and traditions. This had the effect of making the girls feel less positive towards the school. It also attracted hostility from other pupils, who picked up on the teachers' comments and attitude towards the Asian pupils. Despite this, teachers did have high expectations of Asian pupils with regard to academic success. Connolly (1998) has conducted similar research and confirmed her findings.

The same was not true of African-Caribbean pupils, who were expected to misbehave and who were more harshly treated than White pupils who exhibited similar 'bad' behaviour. Teachers also made little effort to ensure that they pronounced names correctly, causing embarrassment and unnecessary ridicule. Finally, pupils of both Asian and African-Caribbean origin were victims of racism from White pupils.

Gillborn (2002) argues that schools are institutionally racist through the way that teachers interpret policy in a way that disadvantages Black pupils. For example, the practice of setting, schemes for gifted and talented pupils, and vocational schemes for the less academic all underrate the abilities of Black children, relegating them to low-ability groups, a restricted curriculum and entry for lower-level exams. Hatcher (1996) examined the role of school governing bodies and found that they gave low priority to race issues, failing to deal adequately with pupil racism. Furthermore, formal links with ethnic-minority parents tended not to exist, which meant that little was done to address their concerns, and ethnic-minority pupils' needs therefore tended to be low priority or disregarded.

Pupil subcultures

Sociologists have identified a number of ways ethnic-minority pupils respond to the racism, prejudice and discrimination that they may face and have analysed the subsequent impact that these responses may have on their educational performance.

In responding to teachers' labels, racism and poor economic prospects, Black males construct a form of masculinity which earns respect from peers and females. According to both Sewell (2000), and O'Donnell and Sharpe (2000), the subcultures that arise are antieducational, prioritizing conspicuous consumption above academic success, the latter being seen as 'feminine'. This macho response may no longer be as necessary for White youths as it had been in earlier studies by Willis (1977) and Hargreaves (1967), owing to improved employment and training opportunities for White boys. For young Black men, however, opposition to schooling still has some relevance. A similar response has been identified among some Asian youths – in particular, Bangladeshi boys, whose economic prospects are generally bleaker than those of other Asian groups. According to Sharpe and O'Donnell, this macho 'warrior' perception by peers exists alongside perceptions of other Asian youths as 'weaklings' conforming to demands of the school or 'patriarchs', whose loyalty lies with the prescriptions of the male-dominated Asian family.

Some evidence indicates that Black females are antischool, but pro-education. They resent low teacher expectations and labelling, but are more determined to succeed than many other groups, especially Black boys. Both Fuller (1984) and Mirza (1992) have noted how Black girls respond to the failure of the

focus on research

David Gillborn & Deborah Youdell
Rationing education

Gillborn and Youdell (1999) studied two London comprehensive schools over a two-year period using lesson observation, analysis of documents, and interviews with pupils and teachers. In both schools, approximately twice as many White as Black pupils were achieving five or more higher grade GCSE passes.

Although Gillborn and Youdell found that 'openly racist teachers and consciously discriminatory practices were rare', they did find that 'widespread inequalities of opportunity are endured by Black children'. Teachers had an expectation that 'Black pupils will generally present disciplinary problems and they therefore tended to feel that 'control and punishment' had to be given higher priority than 'academic concerns'. They also expected Black pupils, on average, to do less well than their White peers.

In their turn, most Black pupils felt they were disadvantaged. By and large, the Black pupils expected to be blamed for disciplinary problems and they expected that teachers would underestimate their future achievements. In these circumstances, it was hardly surprising that they ended up doing, on average, less well than the White pupils attending the same schools.

Adapted from Haralambos, H. and Holborn, M. (2004) *Sociology: Themes and Perspectives* (6th edn), London: Collins Education

1 **What problems are there in researching racism among teachers?**

2 **Why might teachers have expected Black pupils to present discipline problems?**

school to address their needs by rejecting the help of teachers, which they regard as patronizing and, though sometimes well-meaning, misguided. The girls respond outwardly by appearing to reject the values of the school through their dress, attitudes and behaviour. In terms of academic achievement, however, Fuller is more optimistic than Mirza about the outcomes and suggests that the strategies they adopt in working with and helping each other enable them to succeed academically. In Mirza's study, on the other hand, rejection of teachers' help and limited involvement in lessons were seen to place them at a disadvantage academically, even though they preserved high self-esteem. According to Connolly (1998), South Asian girls are generally successful in the education system, where they enjoy high teacher expectations, but they may be overlooked because of their relative passivity, or they may feel marginalized and left out of discourses relating to intimacy, love and marriage because of stereotypical assumptions about Asian family life.

The curriculum

Some sociologists have argued that the curriculum – what is taught in schools – actually disadvantages ethnic minorities. The knowledge that they encounter at school may not connect with their own cultural experience, while **ethnocentrism**, resulting from the use of out-of-date material, could be potentially offensive by reflecting old colonial values and racial stereotypes. Coard (1971) showed how the content of education also ignored Black people. The people who are acclaimed tend to be White, while Black culture, music and art are largely ignored. Coard argued that this led to low self-esteem among Black pupils. However, this assertion was refuted by both the Swann Report (1985) and Stone (1981), who noted that, despite feeling discriminated against by some teachers, African-Caribbean children had been able to maintain an extremely positive self-image.

Since the 1970s, some effort has been made to address the neglect of other cultures in the curriculum. **Multicultural education**, which acknowledges the contribution of all of the world's cultures, has become more common, although it has been criticized for focusing only on external factors ('saris and samosas') and failing to address the real problem of racism. Ethnic-minority languages still do not have the same status as European languages, and schools are still required to hold Christian assemblies. The National Curriculum itself has also been criticized for being ethnocentric – especially in its focus on British history and literature. Geography also emphasizes Britain's positive contribution to the rest of the world, rather that the negative consequences of unfair trade and employment practices. Ball (1995) suggests that the National Curriculum promotes an attitude of 'little Englandism', which harks back to a golden age of empire and past glory while ignoring the history of Black and Asian people.

However, while the curriculum may be ethnocentric, it is unlikely that this, in isolation, is a major factor in the underachievement of ethnic minorities, as it is not the case that all pupils from ethnic-minority backgrounds underachieve to similar degrees. Indian and Chinese pupils' achievement, for example, is above the national average.

Problems of categorization

Classifying according to ethnic origin is by no means simple. The term 'ethnic minorities', for example, includes many different groups and does not take account of class and gender differences within those groups. Gillborn and Gipps (1996) argue that terms such as 'White', 'Black', 'Asian' and 'other'

actually prevent any real understanding of differences in achievement. Postmodernists go further: they argue that the increasingly diverse nature of contemporary societies makes it impossible to explain educational achievement (or anything else) in terms of broad categories such as class or ethnicity, and that the generalizations that are made actually do more harm than good. They suggest that a conscious attempt needs to be made to understand the complexities of cultural difference and identity in modern society.

Check your understanding

1 Briefly describe some of the material disadvantages that might be faced by ethnic minorities from working-class backgrounds (see also previous topic).

2 What are the possible reasons for differences in educational achievement between Asian groups?

3 Suggest two reasons why some ethnic minorities do well within the education system.

4 Give three examples of ways in which cultural differences may affect ethnic achievement in education.

5 What aspects of school organization may lead to the social exclusion of ethnic-minority pupils?

6 How may the labelling of Black boys and girls have a negative impact upon their achievement?

7 How, despite generally high expectations, does the behaviour of teachers towards Asian children impede their success?

8 What evidence is there that schools are institutionally racist?

9 How might the curriculum itself disadvantage ethnic-minority pupils?

10 What barriers to understanding underachievement are caused by placing pupils into broad ethnic categories?

KEY TERMS

Ethnocentric – emphasizing White middle-class culture at the expense of other cultures.

Multicultural education – education that recognizes cultural diversity.

research idea

Analyse the content of a sample of textbooks at your school or college. Focus on visual images, examples and case studies. To what extent do they recognize the variety of ethnic groups in contemporary Britain?

1 Search for statistics about ethnic groups and education at the Standards Site, an online service for teachers in England, which has been set up to help raise standards of achievement in schools. It is managed by the Standards and Effectiveness Unit (SEU) of the DfES:

www.standards.dfes.gov.uk/ethnicminorities/

What statistics and reports are available?

Do they tell us anything about the government's priorities?

2 Use the UCAS website at www.ucas.ac.uk to investigate class and ethnic differences in higher education applications. Select 'Statistics' and then choose from the menu.

What patterns can you find and how do they appear to be changing? Has the reduction in government financial support for students in the last few years had any effect on applications?

exploring ethnicity and educational achievement

Item A

Permanent exclusion rates[1]: by ethnic group, 2001/02

England
Rate per 10 000 pupils

[1] The number of permanent exclusions per 10 000 pupils (headcount) in each ethnic group in primary, secondary and special schools (excluding dually registered pupils in special schools) for compulsory school age.

Source: Department of Education and Skills

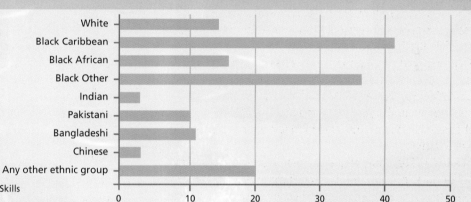

Item B

Source: Adapted from Trowler, P. (1995) *Investigating Education and Training*, London: Collins Educational, p. 113; and Haralambos, M. and Holborn, M. (2000) *Sociology: Themes and Perspectives* (5th edn), London: Collins Educational, pp. 869–70

Percentage of those reaching A-level/vocational equivalent standard, by ethnic group	1988	1997
● All ethnic minorities	31%	39%
● White	38%	46%
16 to 19 year olds in full-time education		
● All ethnic minorities	56%	63%
● White	37%	50%

(a) Using **Item A**, outline differences in exclusion rates between Black African and the other Black groups. (1 mark)

(b) Identify and briefly explain two reasons why permanent exclusion rates are higher for Black pupils **(Item A)**. (8 marks)

(c) Suggest **three** possible reasons why, despite greater staying-on rates than Whites, ethnic minorities still achieve fewer post-16 qualifications than Whites **(Item B)**. (9 marks)

(d) Identify and explain **two** ways in which pupils' cultural background may influence their achievement in school. (12 marks)

Exam practice

(e) Outline and assess the view that it is schools themselves that are the cause of differences in achievement amongst ethnic groups. (60 marks)

Gender and educational achievement

getting you thinking

1 What do the pictures suggest are the key differences in the socialization of boys and girls?

2 What features of schooling might seem more in line with girls' experiences outside school?

3 What features of schooling might seem to conflict with boys' experiences outside school?

4 What, according to Ray O'Neil, has increased the mismatch between boys' socialization and schooling?

≪ It is my view that boys are simply not socialized in a way that suits the process of being educated. The overstimulating, action-packed and exciting world they are now able to choose to belong to outside, more than ever conflicts with the relatively confined and passive nature of the classroom environment. ≫

Ray O'Neil, deputy headteacher of a primary school in Gravesend, Kent

Until the late 1980s, there was much concern about the underachievement of girls. They did not do quite as well as boys in exams, and were also less likely to take A-levels and enter higher education. However, since the early 1990s, girls have begun to outperform boys at most levels of the education system. For example, they do better at every stage of the National Curriculum SAT results in English, Maths and Science, and in all subjects at GCSE and A-level. However, there are still concerns about the subject choices made by girls. For example, they are still less likely than boys to apply for degree courses in the 'hard' sciences (chemistry and physics) and information technology. This may impact negatively on their post-educational opportunities in terms of training and jobs.

Why has girls' achievement improved?

The job market

About half of all women of working age were in employment in 1960; in 2005, the proportion had risen to just under three-quarters. There are increasing job opportunities for women in the **service sector** of the economy, while the availability of traditional male manual work has reduced considerably. Many girls have mothers in paid employment providing positive role models and contributing, often equally, to the household economy. As a result, girls recognize that the future offers them more choices – they are provided with the incentive to seek economic independence, and careers are now a real possibility.

Female expectations

Many women are now looking well beyond the mother–housewife role. In a 1976 survey, Sue Sharpe discovered that girls' priorities were 'love, marriage, husbands, children, jobs and careers, more or less in that order'. When the research was repeated in 1994, she found that the priorities had changed to 'job, career and being able to support themselves' above all other priorities. The greater visibility of women in popular culture in assertive and independent roles may also have promoted female ambition. From Miss Dynamite and Madonna, through films such as *Erin Brockovich* and *Tomb Raider*, to TV shows such as *Sex in the City* and *Friends*, female strength and independence are celebrated.

Feminism

The work of feminist sociologists in the 1970s and 1980s led to a greater emphasis on equal opportunities in schools. Teaching approaches and resources were monitored for sex bias to ensure more 'girl-friendly schooling', especially in the sciences. Consequently, teachers are now more sensitive about avoiding gender stereotyping in the classroom. Various antisexist initiatives have raised both teachers' and girls' consciousness. Single-sex classes in some subjects, projects such as **Girls into Science and Technology**, and the exploration of sexism through **PSE** and citizenship classes have all made a difference.

Sexism in school texts

Some 30 years ago, Glenys Lobban (1974) carried out research into gender stereotyping within children's reading schemes. She demonstrated how the early years of schooling can reinforce traditional ideas about gender. Reading-books at that time had twice as many heroes as heroines, females were predominantly portrayed in domestic situations, and males invariably took the lead in most joint activities. You might think that, since then, feminist influence and antisexist initiatives would have eradicated such blatant disparity.

However, in the 1990s, Best (1993) conducted similar research. She found that an even lower proportion of books contained heroines, three-quarters of the female characters were shown in domestic situations compared with 15 per cent of males, and men had 69 different occupations compared with women who only had 18. While some non-traditional characters were now evident, e.g. two female sailors, a female jockey and a male babysitter, they were the exception.

Abraham (1996) conducted further research into secondary-school textbooks and found that maths texts were extremely male dominated and, where women did appear, they were involved in domestic activity such as shopping for food, while men were much more active, running businesses or investing. Such stereotyping was less evident in French GCSE texts, which did show women in work situations. However, such roles tended to be stereotypical women's work, such as air hostess, secretary or model.

1 What effects might the gender stereotyping have on female subject choice at school and university?

2 What method of research is commonly used to analyse gender stereotyping in books? Why?

Weiner (1995) has argued that teachers have more forcefully challenged stereotypes since the 1980s and many sexist images have been removed from learning materials. However, recent analysis of primary- and secondary-school textbooks show that there is still a long way to go in the quest to eradicate sexist material from the school curriculum and to represent more equally the experience of both males and females in society (see 'Focus on research', p. 117). Weiner has even described the secondary school history curriculum as a 'women-free zone'.

Behaviour

There is mounting evidence that girls work harder and are more motivated than boys. On average, girls put more effort into their work and spend more time on homework. They take more care with presentation of their work, are better organized and, consequently, meet deadlines more successfully than boys. Research shows that:

- on average, girls read three times as much as boys
- while the average Year 7 girl will spend 40 minutes on a homework task, the average boy will spend 12 minutes
- the concentration span of girls is four times greater than that of boys.

Many boys believe school work should be done at school, and are not prepared to draft and redraft assignments (Burns and Bracey 2001).

Furthermore, some research shows that boys' behaviour causes them to be seen to be less cooperative than girls, and teachers are, therefore, more likely to engage in successful interactions with girls, thus raising the girls' sense of self-esteem and achievement levels. Swann and Graddol (1994) found that boys are able to attract the teacher's glance more easily than girls and so get more opportunity to speak in lessons. However, the teacher's energy is expended in confronting male boisterousness rather than focusing on schoolwork as is the case in interactions with female pupils. Swann (1992) also found that boys dominated class discussion, often interrupting, but that girls preferred paired work which involved listening and cooperating. This capacity to take turns added to the positive perception teachers had of girls, helping to create the self-fulfilling prophecy of girls' greater achievement levels.

Changes in the organization of education

The National Curriculum emphasis on science means that girls cannot avoid doing some 'hard' science. Also, according to many writers, such as Mitsos and Browne (1998), coursework at GCSE and in some A-levels, as well as the portfolio-building required by some vocational courses, requires organizational skills and sustained motivation – skills that girls seem to be better at than boys. However, Debra Myhill (1999) points out that recent shifts to increase the proportion of unseen examinations in English have actually been paralleled by an increase in the outperformance of boys by girls in that subject. The New Right thinker Pirie (2001) has argued that the old O-

Ann Phoenix

Proper men?

Ann Phoenix of Birkbeck College said, 'We found 11 to 14 year olds believed you could not be masculine and be seen to be working hard at school. It is the same whether the boys are White, Black, Asian, working-class or middle-class. They think that to be properly masculine, you have to be good at sport, particularly football … you need to be seen not to work. Those who are clever – swots, stiffs, boffs or whatever you want to call them – are unpopular and seen as not male.'

Daily Telegraph, 10 November 1998

1 **What evidence is there that gender differences cut across class and ethnic differences?**

2 **How does Phoenix suggest boys' peer groups control the ways boys display their masculinity?**

level (replaced by GCSE in 1988) was a boy's exam with its 'high risk, swot it all up for the final throw' approach to assessment. By contrast, GCSE, AS and A-level now favour the more systematic and consistent approach of girls.

Better socialization for schooling

Research shows that girls spend their leisure time differently from boys. Whereas boys relate to their peers by *doing* (i.e. being active in a range of ways), girls relate to one another by talking. This puts girls at an advantage, because school is essentially a language experience – most subjects require good levels of comprehension and writing skills.

<< *The replacement of organized social games with TV and DVD and the decline in occasions such as mealtimes, with the rules of social interaction impressed into them, have largely deprived the modern boy of opportunities to catch up with the girls in terms of language development. Modern computer games in particular exercise those already advanced spatial and visual abilities, but hardly address language deficiency.>>* Rupert Kirby of practicalparent.org, (Discovery Home and Health 2000)

Among boys, peer-group pressure is often very strong. It is noticeable from research that boys who do well at school are often helped at home, away from the view of the peer group. Boys often consider it weak to request help from a teacher and it is also especially difficult for a boy to accept help from another boy. Girls, on the other hand, are happy to help each other. It is an acceptable part of being female.

What are the concerns about boys' achievement?

● Boys are behind girls by the age of 6. Patterns of underachievement of reading and writing are set very early.

● The average girl is outperforming the average boy by 10 per cent across Key Stages 3 and 4 and A-level.

● At age 11, the average boy is nine months behind the average girl in development of speaking skills, 12 months behind in literacy and six months behind in numeracy.

● In English at GCSE, 64.4 per cent of girls achieve a high grade, compared with 46.9 per cent of boys. Traditionally, boys have matured later than girls, who have always been ahead in language at primary level.

● Less-able boys are virtually unemployable because they lack interest, drive, enthusiasm and social skills (Burns and Bracey 2001).

● Young men are much more likely than young women to be excluded from school (DfES 2003).

● 'Many boys talk of being bored and said that education has little relevance to them ... Boys and young men want a varied curriculum to combat boredom for those who are less academic' (*Listen Up*, Home Office, consultation with young people carried out by National Youth Agency and Youth Net 1999).

Why are boys underachieving?

Changes in the job market/status frustration

Some commentators, notably Mac an Ghaill (1994), suggest that working-class boys are experiencing a 'crisis of masculinity'. They are socialized into seeing their future male identity and role in terms of having a job and being a 'breadwinner'. However, the decline of **manufacturing industry** and the rise in long-term unemployment make it increasingly unlikely that males will occupy these roles.

Moreover, new jobs in the service sector are often part-time, desk-based, and suited to the skills and lifestyles of women. In some families, females may be the primary breadwinners. Consequently, traditional masculine roles are under threat. Working-class boys' perception of this may influence their motivation and ambition. They may feel that qualifications are a waste of time because there are only limited opportunities in the job market. They may see their future as bleak and without purpose, and, as a result, they don't see any point in working hard at school.

Peer-group status

Some boys may gain 'street cred' and **peer-group status** from not working. These boys may create subcultures in some schools, which are both anti-education and anti-learning. Their members may well see schoolwork as 'uncool' and unmasculine. In particular, reading may be regarded as boring, feminine and to be avoided at all costs. This may explain why boys are less conscientious and lack the application for coursework skills. The following quote from a headteacher illustrates this well:

> << *It is better to be famous for being a clown or a toughie than working hard and being a failure.*>>
> Bob Perris, headteacher, Hedworthfield Primary School, Jarrow

synoptic link

Recent research (Kenway 1997, Arnot *et al*. 1999 and Myers 2000) has shown that equal-opportunities strategies relating to gender have largely fallen off the educational agenda in recent years (unless they relate specifically to improving boys' achievement). Extensive social and economic changes and the impact of 'second-wave' feminism in the second half of the 20th century have led to shifts in gender roles in Western society, most easily evidenced in the ever-increasing numbers of women now engaging in paid work. Such changes, coupled with concerns at boys' underachievement at GCSE level, have lead to anxieties about men's future roles, and even to suggestions that equal opportunities promoting girls' achievement and opportunity have 'gone too far'.

Yet, despite the recent educational success of girls, and women's increased representation in the workplace,

social inequality and difference

gender continues to influence our behaviour, choices and life outcomes (Rees 1999, Francis 2000a). Gender roles in the family remain largely unchanged, and the most powerful jobs continue to be overwhelmingly dominated by men. Within education, male and female pupils continue to construct their gender identities differently, with consequences for their learning and school experiences. Research continues to demonstrate that a 'hidden curriculum' helps to perpetuate, rather than to deconstruct, gender difference. Further, these gender constructions impact on the subject choices made by students as soon as an element of educational choice is introduced (Francis 2000b), and such choices hold implications for their future career paths and quality of life (Rees 1999).

Social control differences

According to Mitsos and Browne (1998), there is also some evidence that teachers are not as critical with boys as they are with girls. They may have lower expectations of boys, expecting them to be disruptive and their work to be late, rushed and untidy. Some research suggests that boys are less positively influenced than girls, or even turned off, by primary-school environments which are female dominated and may have an emphasis on neatness and tidiness.

Unrealistic attitudes

There are signs that boys' overconfidence may blind them to what is actually required for educational success. Research indicates that they are surprised when they fail exams and tend to put their failure down to bad luck rather than lack of effort. On the other hand, girls are more realistic, even self-doubting, and try that much harder in order to ensure success. However, according to Francis (2000b), boys are no longer likely to consider themselves more able than girls, as was the case in the 1970s and 1980s. Also, Francis notes that boys are more likely to have career aspirations that are not only unrealistic, but less likely to require academic success, e.g. professional footballer, whereas girls' career ambitions more often require academic success, e.g. doctor.

What about the future?

Some feminist researchers are concerned that girls are still underachieving because of disruptive boys. Teachers may be so tied up with controlling boys that girls don't get the attention they deserve. Recent research shows that girls' educational achievement has improved despite continuing male dominance of the classroom, curriculum content (for example, the focus in history on the lives of men) and greater demands on teacher time (Francis 1998).

Feminists are also still concerned about the narrow subject choices that females are making at further and higher education level. Females are still more likely to take arts subjects, and males are more likely to take scientific and technological subjects. Such gender stereotyping may be the result of gender socialization in early childhood (e.g. different toys and activities around the home), teacher advice on subject choice, and a continuing perception that the sciences are masculine subjects.

The debate may be influenced by social class and gender. Although middle-class girls outperform all other groups, working-class girls constitute a significant number of underachievers in the school system, and should not be neglected. Moreover, girls from some ethnic backgrounds perform significantly worse than many other groups.

Many feminists believe that the current concern about boys and achievement is simply a 'moral panic'. Weiner et al. (1997) argue that the media see the underachievement of Black and working-class boys as a problem because it may lead to the creation of a potentially dangerous underclass. They also see failure to celebrate girls' achievement as part of a backlash against female success.

Check your understanding

1. What have been the overall trends in male and female achievement in the last 20 years?

2. How might changes in the economy affect both female and male attitudes towards education?

3. How may changes in both the organization of the education system and classroom practices have benefited the education of females?

4. How may aspects of boys' socialization explain why they underachieve at school?

5. What characteristics do male antischool cultures possess that undermine educational success for boys?

6. How do the allegedly unrealistic attitudes of boys impact upon their motivation towards schoolwork?

7. What concerns do feminists still have over the influence of boys on girls' educational experiences?

8. Explain how class and ethnicity may be just as important as gender in explaining the current achievement patterns of boys.

research ideas

1. Conduct a content analysis of two science and technology textbooks used at your school or college. One should be significantly older than the other, if possible. Count the number of times that males and females appear in diagrams, photographs, etc., and record how they are shown. Find examples that are gender specific. What roles do they suggest as typical for each gender? Is there a change over time?

2. Interview a sample of boys and girls. Try to find out if they have different expectations about future success. Are there differences in the amount of time they spend on homework?

web.task

The government's concern about gender and achievement is demonstrated by their creation of a website devoted to the issue. Visit it at www.standards.dfee.gov.uk/genderandachievement for statistical data and summaries of research.

KEY TERMS

Girls into Science and Technology – a pre-National Curriculum initiative designed to encourage females to opt for science and technology.

Manufacturing industry – industries that actually make goods. Most of the work in such industries is manual and based in factories.

Peer-group status – being seen as 'big' or important in the eyes of friends and other people around you.

PSE – Personal and Social Education; sometimes known as PSHE (including Health Education) or PSME (including Moral Education).

Service sector – a group of economic activities loosely organized around finance, retail and personal care.

exploring gender & educational achievement

Item A

Debates about boys and schooling take three main forms. There are stories about 'poor boys', who are victims of feminism or teachers, about schools which fail them and about their 'laddishness'. 'Poor boys' stories call for alterations to the curriculum and teaching to favour boys. 'Failing schools' stories lead to punitive inspection processes, hit squads and action zones. Like 'poor boys', the 'boys will be boys' (laddishness) stories call for alterations to teaching to favour boys and, in addition, seek to use girls to police, teach, control and civilize boys. But these responses are based on oversimplified explanations of what is happening in schools. Not all boys are doing worse than girls. The picture is far from simple. Rather than spending our time in handwringing, we must try to understand the complexity of the situation. If we ask 'Which boys, in which areas, are doing badly?', we find that the impact of class and ethnicity on achievement is greater than that of gender.

Adapted from Epstein, D. *et al.* (eds) (1999) *Gender and Achievement*, Milton Keynes: Open University Press

Item B

'Reports of girls' GCSE success obscure the true picture,' says Gillian Plummer. Yet another simplistic, statistical interpretation of gender differences in examination results makes the national news: 'Boys are outperformed by girls in GCSEs.' As a result, the government wants all education authorities to take action in raising the academic performance of boys.

But beware: simplistic statistical analyses are dangerously misleading. We do not have a hierarchy in which girls are positioned in the top 50 per cent and boys in the bottom 50 per cent at GCSE. It is social class, not gender or race differences, which continues to have the single most important influence on educational attainment in Britain.

The majority of boys and girls from socially advantaged families do much better in all subjects at GCSE than the majority of girls from socially disadvantaged families.

While, overall, girls do outperform boys at GCSE, working-class girls do only marginally better than working-class boys in public examinations.

The desperate need for detailed research on the educational failure of the majority of working-class girls has been hidden by:

- statistics recording the admirable rise in the achievements of middle-class girls, who are taken to represent 'all girls'
- serious concerns about the deviant behaviour and particularly poor exam performance of working-class boys.

It is dangerous and inaccurate to imply that all boys underperform and that all girls do well.

The real question is: what action is being taken to raise the academic performance of working-class girls (as well as other underachievers)?

Adapted from *Times Educational Supplement*, 23 January 1998

(a) Using **Item A**, explain what is meant by the term 'laddishness'. (1 mark)

(b) Identify and briefly explain **two** reasons for the underachievement of boys (**Item A**). (8 marks)

(c) Suggest **three** reasons why the writer of **Item B** believes that 'simplistic statistical analyses are ... misleading' with regard to gender differences in educational achievement. (9 marks)

(d) Identify and explain **two** ways in which features of school life may help to shape pupils' gender identities. (12 marks)

Exam practice

(e) Outline and assess the view that initiatives promoting girls' achievement and opportunity have 'gone too far'. (20 marks)

Education, work and the economy

gettingyouthinking

1 Which of your experiences, both in school and out of school, have been helpful in developing knowledge and skills that may prove useful in your working life?

2 Which of the individuals in the photographs do you most admire? Why?

3 Do you think that vocational education is perceived less positively than academic education? Why do you think this might be the case?

4 Do you think that this may have had a bearing on Britain's lack of economic success relative to other countries?

5 Might the 'Oxbridge' (i.e. academic) route – as the perceived height of success – be in any way to blame for the lower status of other routes to jobs in British society? If so, how?

The 'new vocationalism'

Ever since the introduction of compulsory education, successive governments have recognized that the low status of work-related (or vocational) education is a problem. In Topic 1, we saw how these concerns helped to justify the introduction of compulsory state education in the first place; the concern then was that an uneducated workforce would diminish the nation's economic efficiency, and so, in order to restore the UK to its place of prominence as 'the workshop of the world', we would have to educate our workforce, as had our competitors. These arguments – linked to a functionalist position – reappeared in the 1980s. It was claimed that the British workforce lacked appropriate technical skills because schools had lost touch with the needs of industry. Individuals who left school at 16 or 18 were ill equipped for work. Even those with higher qualifications tended to enter professions such as law or medicine rather than engineering or manufacturing. Consequently, Britain was viewed as being at a disadvantage in relation to international competition, and it was suggested that this 'skills crisis' was a significant factor in Britain's industrial decline.

It was felt that education had been dominated for too long by the liberal humanist tradition and the academic concerns of the universities, which emphasized a critical appreciation of subject knowledge for its own sake. This was fine for developing a nation of critics, but no help in developing the economy – in fact, it was a barrier, according to the New Right.

Although people interested in industry have for a long time studied vocational courses – such as City and Guilds qualifications or BTECs (provided by the Business and Technology Education Council) in colleges of further education – these were mostly post-school courses. It was felt that school pupils had not got enough experience of industry to make proper decisions about what jobs they wanted to do. While the more able school leavers may have been denied an industrial future due to lack of awareness, the less able needed the proper knowledge and skills to make them more employable. So a number of schemes were developed, which were grouped together under the title the 'new vocationalism'.

These training and education schemes aimed to make young people more familiar with the world of work. They included schemes such as General National Vocational Qualifications (GNVQs – which developed skills and knowledge related to broad occupational areas) and National Vocational Qualifications (NVQs – job-specific qualifications which demonstrate 'on the job' competencies such as 'production machine sewing'), which are often studied part time in college in the evening, or on day release, alongside full-time work.

Vocational education involves industry-related studies, mainly based in school or college. TVEI was an example of this: aimed at 14 to 19 year olds, it involved devolving a sum of money to schools and colleges for them to spend on work-related curriculum development, trips to workplaces and visits by expert speakers, or work-related resources and equipment such as computers. Vocational GCSEs are a modern, accredited example. **Vocational training**, on the other hand, is designed to develop job-specific knowledge and skills in mainly work-like situations. NVQs and Apprenticeships are modern examples. Key developments in vocational training are outlined in Table 3.1 below.

Criticisms of the 'new vocationalism'

Vocational education and training have had many critics, particularly from neo-Marxist writers. Finn (1987) argues that

Table 3.1 Developments in vocational education and training since 1997

Date	Development	Issues
1997 to the present day	The **New Deal** (part of the government's 'welfare to work' programme) was introduced to those under 25 in receipt of benefits. They are required to accept a subsidized job, do voluntary work, clean up the environment or take up full-time education or training. The scheme was extended in 2000 to over-25s who had been out of work for more than two years, including single parents and the disabled.	Figures showed that by March 1999, of the 250 000 who started the scheme, almost half had left or finished with about 40 per cent gaining 'real' jobs. The percentage who stay in jobs longer than three months is now less than 30 per cent. A common feature of programmes such as New Deal is that they help to get people into work in areas where jobs are plentiful, but are much less effective in areas where fewer jobs are available.
2001	The **Learning and Skills Council (LSC)** was set up to organize post-16 and vocational education and training in April 2001, bringing together all the previous learning providers under a single funding regime.	The LSC has five key objectives – to: 1 extend participation in education, learning and training 2 increase engagement of employers in workforce development 3 raise achievement of young people 4 raise achievement of adults 5 raise quality and effectiveness of education and training and user satisfaction. The LSC is now also responsible for the funding of sixth forms in community, voluntary, foundation and special schools.
2002	The **Increased Flexibilities Programme** provided funding for vocational courses for 14 to 16 year olds.	Vocational GCSEs are available in eight subjects: applied art and design, applied business, engineering, health and social care, applied information and communications technology (ICT), leisure and tourism, manufacturing, and applied science. They include a practical approach to learning and are equivalent in size to two general GCSEs.
2004–5	**Modern Apprenticeships** (re-named **Apprenticeships** in 2005) allow young people to learn on the job, building their skills and gaining qualifications as they earn money.	Demand for Apprenticeships from young people is three times the level of supply from employers. There is now a campaign designed to create thousands more high-quality Apprenticeships. Achievement rates in many sectors are worryingly low.
	Statutory work-based learning at Key Stage 4 – Work-based learning became compulsory as part of the National Curriculum at Key Stage 4. Schools are required to develop a framework for planning, managing and keeping under review their programme of work-related learning.	Whilst work-related learning within colleges may continue for some pupils, work-related provision will now have to be incorporated into schools.

there is a hidden political agenda to vocational training. It provides cheap labour for employers, keeps the pay rates of young workers low, undermines the bargaining power of the unions (because only permanent workers can be members) and reduces politically embarrassing unemployment statistics. It may also be intended to reduce crime by removing young people from the streets.

Critics such as Phil Cohen (1984) argue that the real purpose of vocational training is to create 'good' attitudes and work discipline rather than actual job skills. In this way, young people come to accept a likely future of low-paid and unskilled work. Those young unemployed who view training schemes as cheap labour, and refuse to join them, are defined as irresponsible and idle, and are 'punished' by the withdrawal of benefits.

It is not proven that young people lack job skills. Many have already gained a lot of work experience from part-time jobs. Youth unemployment is the result not of a shortage of skills, but of a shortage of jobs.

Critics also point out that the sorts of skills taught to YTS trainees are only appropriate for jobs in the secondary labour market. This consists of jobs that are unskilled, insecure, and pay low wages – such jobs offer little chance of training or promotion, employer investment is very low, and labour turnover is consequently very high.

In practice, it is lower-ability students who tend to be channelled into vocational courses. The new vocationalism thus introduces another form of selection, with working-class and ethnic-minority students being disproportionately represented on these courses.

f o c u s o n **r e s e a r c h**

Equal Opportunities Commission
Free to choose?

Free to Choose is the final report from the Equal Opportunities Commission investigation into sex segregation in training and work.

The EOC has found real evidence of support for change among young people:

- 80 per cent of girls and 55 per cent of boys said that they would or might be interested in learning to do a non-traditional job.
- 25 per cent of boys said caring work sounded interesting or very interesting and 12 per cent of

girls were interested in construction; in reality, fewer than 3 per cent of childcare Apprenticeships are male and fewer than 2 per cent of construction Apprenticeships are female.
- 92 per cent of women and men said that they would want any children about to enter the workforce to be able to make job choices without worrying about traditional stereotypes of women's and men's working roles.

Despite this, the EOC found that:

- Only a sixth (15 per cent) of young people received any advice or information on work experience in a sector with a workforce currently dominated by the opposite sex.
- In one survey, of the 45 childcare work experience placements undertaken, only two were filled by boys, whereas only 29 of the girls had listed it as first choice.
- Some young people reported being actively discouraged to pursue a career outside the norm for their sex. One female trainee plumber said: 'Schools careers – it would have been good if they had just not discouraged us.'
- 67 per cent of women didn't know, when they chose their career, about the often lower pay for work mostly done by women and, of these, two-thirds of young women said they would have considered a wider range of career options had they known.
- Apprenticeships are perpetuating gender segregation or even making it worse.

Adapted from Equal Opportunities Commission (2005) *Free to Choose: Tackling Gender Barriers to Better Jobs*, EOC

1 Why do you think there appears to be a mismatch between what young people want to do and the types of work placements they end up in?

2 What could be done to reduce gender segregation in training and work?

'Welcome to Spraggett Engineering. You're here to learn important technical skills and experience the latest in high-tech engineering.'

(Excellent! Someone to clean out the loos and make the tea – and we hardly have to pay him anything!)

Training schemes do not, therefore, appear to be breaking down traditional patterns of sex stereotyping found in employment and education; nor are they encouraging girls to move into non-traditional areas. In fact, they are structured so as to reproduce gender inequality. Buswell (1987) points out that the types of schemes into which girls are channelled, such as retail work, lead to occupations where they are low paid when young, and work part time when older, reflecting women's position in the labour market.

According to recent figures from the DfES, 6 per cent of Apprenticeships in hairdressing are taken up by males compared with 94 per cent by females. Retail fares slightly better with a 38/62 split, whereas in construction crafts, the male-to-female ratio is 99/1.

Many sociologists are sceptical about the claims for vocationalism. They argue that the central aim of giving students skills is fine in theory, but has been difficult to achieve in practice. **Competence-based learning** and assessment often become more about getting the right boxes ticked, rather than developing real skills. However, there have been some benefits arising from the new vocationalism – although it may be that these are simply the result of the extra resources being pumped into education to support all of the initiatives.

Bridging the vocational/academic divide?

Recent initiatives have aimed to start vocational education and training much earlier by bringing it into the compulsory phase of education in schools. All schools have now been encouraged to participate more fully in work-related learning, which, in 2004, became a part of the National Curriculum. Since September 1998, schools have had the flexibility to ignore aspects of the Key Stage 4 National Curriculum to arrange extended work-related learning for those students who want it or would benefit from it.

The changes brought about in post-16 education and training by Curriculum 2000 should, in theory, have enabled

synoptic link

social inequality and difference

Recent government research (Cabinet Office 2003) shows that disadvantaged ethnic minorities frequently face a range of barriers to success in the labour market. These include:

- disproportionate concentration in communities with weak employment bases
- relatively weak social networks that could open doors to employment
- employer discrimination.

Vocational education appears to be less accessible to Black and ethnic-minority groups. There are very few young Black women in Modern Apprenticeships and those that are in them are concentrated in low-paid sectors or gendered vocations such as nursing.

Of all those who started the higher level of Modern Apprenticeships in 2001/2, only 4 per cent came from ethnic-minority backgrounds. However, this figure varies across sectors, from 8 per cent for childcare to 1 per cent for construction.

Clearly, the barriers to success experienced by ethnic minorities in employment have some bearing upon the extent to which they are able to gain access to vocational training.

students to mix and match vocational and academic qualifications. Vocational A-levels can be studied alongside traditional subjects, and all students have been encouraged to achieve 'Key Skills' qualifications. However, there is, as yet, little evidence of this happening. Most middle-class White students are still opting for the traditional academic curriculum as before, while vocational courses continue to be dominated by working-class and ethnic-minority students. Partly as a result, the government set up the Tomlinson review of 14-to-19 education (Working Group on 14–19 Reform 2004) to try to end the vocational/academic divide for good. The division between compulsory and post-16 education, which has divided curriculum provision in the past, is to be overcome by the development of 'seamless' provision between the ages of 14 and 19 through an overarching diploma framework. A-levels and GCSEs were to be absorbed into the new diploma framework along with vocational qualifications.

Pre-16 learners would continue to follow the statutory curriculum, gaining recognition towards the award of a diploma where appropriate. They would be able to opt for a substantial element of vocational learning, but would not be able to specialize in specific occupational areas. Post-16 learners would have greater choice to select between:

- a range of specialized diploma lines, designed to provide a basis for progression within lines of learning covering the range of vocational and academic options
- open diplomas which enable the learner to select a mixed pattern of subjects or lines of learning.

All diplomas would have the same basic structure of a core – including numeracy, communication and computer literacy – combined with the opportunity for specialization in particular areas. However, in a white paper published early in 2005, the Labour education secretary rejected Tomlinson's proposals to do away with A-levels and GCSEs; as some observed, it may have been unpopular with voters.

The New Labour government is aiming to make the world of work more familiar to all pupils as they progress through school, to inform their future choices better and, it is hoped, to provide employers with sufficiently skilled workers in the future. Whether these aims cut across class, ethnic and gender lines, or whether educational segregation continues in the future as it has existed in the past, remains to be seen.

Check your understanding

1. **In your own words explain why Britain was seen to be at a disadvantage in terms of equipping people for industry.**

2. **What was the 'new vocationalism'? Give examples.**

3. **What is the difference between vocational education and vocational training?**

4. **What do you consider to be the three most serious criticisms of vocational training?**

5. **What is meant by the vocational/academic divide, and how has the government tried to remove this divide?**

6. **How has focus on work-related learning recently shifted from post-16, to 14 to 19?**

research ideas

1. Survey a group of post-16 students at your school or college. Choose a sample that includes students following both academic and vocational courses. Why did they stay on at the age of 16? What is motivating them, and what do they hope to achieve from their qualifications? Are there differences in the motivations of students following academic and vocational courses?

2. Conduct interviews with students who have undertaken work experience. Find out about their experiences and whether they feel that these have made them better equipped for a future job.

web.tasks

1. **Find out about government policies on training at the Department for Education and Skills website at www.dfes.gov.uk**

   Do you think that these will be successful? Do they represent real opportunities for young people, or might there be other motives behind the policies?

2. **Look into the proposed reforms of 14 to 19 education at www.dfes.gov.uk/14-19**

   Do you think these would have had more success in bridging the vocational academic divide than have past initiatives?

KEY TERMS

Competence-based learning – type of learning where the aim is to demonstrate that a particular skill has been acquired.

Vocational education – work-related courses offered in schools and colleges (usually with a small amount of work experience).

Vocational training – work-related courses offered through work experience (usually with a small amount of time in college).

Item A

Percentage of 16 year olds in full-time education by type of course, England, 2001 to 2003

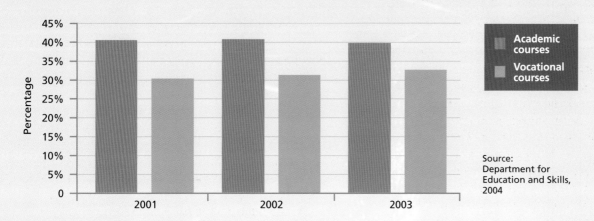

Source: Department for Education and Skills, 2004

Item B

There is often a gap between the image promoted of youth training and its reality. The literature of YT often suggested that it could open up exciting and creative opportunities for young people regardless of social background. However, youth trainees have long complained that they are being trained for 'Noddy jobs'. Certainly, there is evidence that the majority of YT places are provided by the big retailers – e.g. supermarkets and department stores, such as BHS and Marks and Spencer. Consequently, YT trainees have generally found themselves trained in a narrow range of skills, such as working on the till, shelf-filling and stocktaking, which are common to most retail jobs. One study found that 80 per cent of the jobs that YTS trainees went into required no entry qualification. There is also evidence that some employers are using YT as a screening device. If the trainee is uncomplaining, docile and flexible about the mundane tasks they are allocated, there is a good chance that they will be offered a post. Finally, while YT schemes emphasize equal opportunities for females and ethnic minorities, there is evidence that female training places reinforce traditional gender roles, while in some areas youth training places with major employers have been monopolized by White youth.

Adapted from Maguire, S. (September 1993) 'Training for a living? The 1990s youth labour market', *Sociology Review*, 3(1)

(a) Using **Item B**, explain what is meant by the term 'youth training'. (1 mark)

(b) Identify and briefly explain **two** trends in the bar chart in **Item A**. (8 mark)

(c) Suggest **three** reasons why the percentage of 16 year olds studying vocational courses increased between 2001 and 2003 **(Item A)**. (9 marks)

(d) Identify and explain **two** ways in which the 'new vocationalism' may reinforce social inequalities. (12 marks)

Exam practice

(e) Outline and assess the view that 'new vocationalism' both meets the needs of the economy and of young people today. (60 marks)

FOR MANY STUDENTS STUDYING SOCIOLOGY for the first time, it seems strange that we should investigate health and illness. Surely, they argue, this is something that is obviously biological rather than social. However, as we proceed through the various topics, it becomes clear that what appears at first sight to be completely natural and biological is heavily influenced by society. In Topic 1, for example, we see that some sociologists argue that the very concepts 'health', 'illness' and 'disease' are actually socially constructed, varying across societies, time and different social groups.

It is not just *definitions* of health and illness, however, that vary. Studies of health and illness of the British population suggest that these are not randomly distributed, but are closely linked to social class, geographical location and gender. In Topic 2, we examine the *distribution of health and illness* across the population and explore the contrasting explanations suggested by sociologists.

Inequalities are not found solely in the variations in health across the British population; they are also found in the *provision* of health services. Topic 3 explores this phenomenon of variation in the amount and quality of care within the NHS.

In the first three topics, we concentrate on the social dimensions of physical health, but in Topic 4, we look at the contribution of sociologists to the study of mental health. As many as one in five of the population suffer at some point in their lives from mental illness, so the distribution of mental illness – and the impact of being labelled as mentally ill – are important issues for sociologists.

In Topic 5, we examine the role of the medical professions. In particular, we explore how doctors have obtained the power they hold in society and who actually benefits from it. Some sociologists argue that the main beneficiary of how medicine is organized in Europe and the USA is likely to be the medical profession, rather than patients. Finally, a discussion of the role of the medical establishment in constructing the way we think about sexuality brings us back to the point where we began – the social construction of health.

OCRspecification	topics	pages
The social nature of health and illness		
The social construction of health and illness, mental health and disability. The importance of social reaction and labelling for identity.	Discussed in Topic 1. Mental health is the subject of Topic 4.	130–139 154–159
Deviance, social control and the sick role.	Covered in Topics 1 and 5.	130–9, 160–7
Trends and patterns in health and illness		
Problems of measuring health inequalities, including problems of measuring morbidity; health inequalities as a social artefact.	Covered in Topic 2.	140–147
Patterns, theories and explanations of health inequalities, according to social class, gender, ethnicity, region and over time: e.g. cultural, subcultural, social selection, social administration and structural explanations.	Covered in Topics 2 and 3.	140–153
Solutions to the problem of health inequality; the relationship between sociology and social policy. Recent changes in state and private healthcare provision. Gender and informal healthcare provision.	Solutions to health inequality are covered in Topic 2, as is the issue of gender and informal care. State and private healthcare are discussed in Topic 3.	140–153
Medicine, power and control		
The bio-mechanical model and the role of the medical professions: functionalist, Marxist, feminist, social action and postmodern critiques.	Models of health are explored in Topic 1. The medical professions are discussed in Topic 5.	130–139 160–167
Medicine and the redefinition, control and regulation of the body, mind and sexuality (e.g. in relation to reproduction, abortion, mental illness). The ideological role of such definitions, with particular reference to gender and ethnicity.	Mental illness is covered in Topic 4. The remaining issues issues are the focus of Topic 5 while parts of Topic 1 are also relevant.	154–167 130–139

UNIT 4
Health

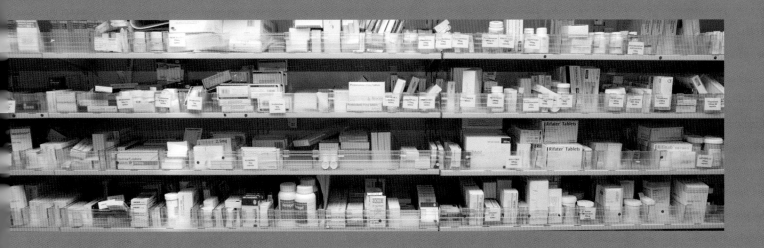

Defining health, illness and disability

gettingyouthinking

Look at the four photos on this page and then answer the following questions.

1 Which of these people are, in your opinion, 'abnormal' and which are 'normal'?

2 What suggestions can you make for helping 'abnormal' people make themselves 'normal'?

3 Next, indicate which of these people, if any, are 'ill'.

4 In small groups, compare your answers and explain how you made your decisions.

5 Do you think that health and illness and normal bodies have anything to do with society, or are they just natural, biological states?

This topic investigates the ways in which **health**, **illness** and **disability** are defined in our society and the implications for people who are defined as ill or disabled. The majority of the population pass most their lives taking for granted the normal, routine state of their bodies, until this 'normality' is disrupted in some way. At this point, people often say they are 'ill'. However, it is very unclear just what illness is. Surely, such an important concept does not vary simply according to how each individual feels? Anyway, how does anyone know what is 'normal'?

A second, linked area is the notion of 'abnormality'. If there is such a thing as 'normality', then there must be something which is 'abnormal'. This category might include those suffering from chronic (long-term) illness, such as multiple sclerosis, those with a 'mental illness' or those with a physical 'disability'.

Sociologists also want to understand how terms such as 'abnormality' and 'disability' are constructed and what implications there are for the people so labelled.

We begin by looking at how health and illness are defined and the implications of these definitions for society. We then extend our analysis to issues of disability and mental illness, and their implications for people labelled with these terms.

Definitions of health and illness

At some time, most of us will have woken up in the morning not really feeling very well. Despite telling our parents this, it may have been difficult to persuade them that we really were too ill to go to school or college (particularly if there was an exam that day or a particular lesson they knew we loathed). Only when we produced some real evidence, such as vomiting or a rash, were we believed. Our parents may also be rather less than supportive when it turns out that we have been drinking pretty heavily the night before. Ill or just hung over? And anyway, why is being hung over not being ill – after all, we feel

awful? The answer from disapproving parents might well be that being hung over is the price we pay for a night's drinking and that it therefore does not count as a 'real' illness.

This situation illustrates a number of issues. First, it is not clear exactly what we mean by being 'healthy' and being 'unwell'. It seems that these concepts may well have different meanings depending upon who is defining them. In this case, us and our parents. Furthermore, there is a 'moral' element involved. If feeling ill is a result of having drunk too much, then this may be classified as just a 'hangover' and hence our own fault.

Definitions of illness and their consequences (get the day off college or have to endure a miserable day attending) form the starting point for the sociology of medicine (see Figure 4.1).

To unravel this complex issue, we will look first at how ordinary, or **lay**, people construct their definitions of health and illness. We will then move on to look at the competing models amongst health practitioners themselves.

Lay definitions of health and illness

In the survey *Health and Lifestyles* (1990), Mildred Blaxter asked almost 10 000 people how they defined health. She discovered that three clear types of definition emerged:

1 *Positive definitions* – where health is defined as feeling fit and able to undertake any reasonable task.
2 *Negative definitions* – where health is defined in terms of being free from pain and discomfort.
3 *Functional definitions* – where people define health in terms of being able to perform a range of tasks.

Blaxter concludes that these different definitions mean that a particular level of discomfort for one person may indicate that

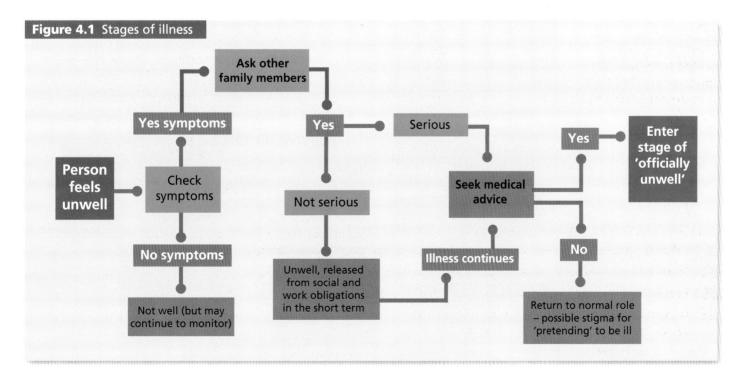

Figure 4.1 Stages of illness

they are ill, whilst, for another person, it may have no such meaning. Health and illness then seem less like objective, physical states than socially defined states, varying from person to person.

Factors influencing lay definitions of health and illness

If definitions of health and illness vary, then we need to know just what factors appear to influence the way in which individuals define their sense of being healthy or ill. Sociologists have suggested that culture, age, gender and social class are particularly important.

Cultural differences

Different social groups have differing ideas of what constitutes illness. For example, Krause (1989) studied Hindu and Sikh Punjabis living in Bedford, and in particular focused on their illness called 'sinking heart' (*dil ghirda hai*) which is characterized by physical chest pain. According to Krause, this illness is caused by a variety of emotional experiences – most importantly, public shame of some sort. No such illness exists in other mainstream cultures in Britain.

Age differences

Older people tend to accept as 'normal' a range of pains and physical limitations which younger people would define as symptoms of some illness or disability. As we age, we gradually redefine health and accept greater levels of physical discomfort. In Blaxter's national survey of health definitions, she found that young people tend to define health in terms of physical fitness, but gradually, as people age, health comes to be defined more in terms of being able to cope with everyday tasks. She found examples of older people with really serious arthritis, who nevertheless defined themselves as healthy, as they were still able to carry out a limited range of routine activities.

Gender differences

According to Hilary Graham (2002), men have fewer consultations with doctors than women and appear to have lower levels of illness. This is partly due to the greater number of complications associated with childbirth and menopause which women face, but it is also partly due to the fact that men are less likely to define themselves as ill, or as needing medical attention. The idea of 'masculinity' includes the belief that a man should be tough and put off going to the doctor.

Despite the greater propensity of men to define themselves as healthy and to visit **GPs** less often, men have considerably higher mortality (death) rates than women.

Social class differences

Blaxter's research also showed that working-class people were far more likely to accept higher levels of 'illness' than middle-class people. Blaxter describes working-class people as 'fatalistic' – that is, they accepted poor health as 'one of those things'. As a result, people from lower social classes are less likely to consult a GP than middle-class people. This may be because they will accept a higher level of pain and discomfort before considering themselves ill enough to visit a doctor.

Medical definitions of health and illness

There is a distinction in most people's minds between those who think they are ill and those who really are ill. In contemporary society, the role of deciding whether the person is truly ill lies with doctors. If they decide that a person is ill, then a series of benefits flow, both formal (in the provision of medical help, or time off work or college) and informal (such as sympathy, release from household tasks and so on).

However, if they decide that you are not really ill, then you receive no benefits and may, in fact, be open to accusations of **malingering**.

Doctors use a particular 'scientific' measure of health and illness in order to decide whether someone really is ill or not. This model is known as the **biomedical model**, and it is the basis of all Western medicine. The elements of this model include the following:

- Illness is always caused by an identifiable (physical or mental) reason and cannot be the result of magic, religion or witchcraft.
- Illnesses and their causes can be identified, classified and measured using scientific methods.
- If there is a cure, then it will almost always be through the use of drugs or surgery, rather than in changing social relationships or people's spiritual lives.
- This is because the cause almost always lies in the actual physical body of the individual patient.

At its simplest, this model presents the human body as a type of machine and, just as with a machine, parts can go wrong and need repairing. Over time, the body 'wears out' just as a machine does and will eventually stop working completely. This is why the contemporary medical model is sometimes referred to as the 'bio-*mechanical*' model.

Illness and disease

What emerges from the discussion of health and illness is that individuals, using lay concepts of health, may define themselves as 'ill' or not, depending upon a range of social factors. On the other hand, doctors claim that they can scientifically determine, via medical tests, whether or not a person is ill. Eisenberg (1977) has therefore suggested that we should make a distinction between illness and disease. Illness is an individual's subjective experience of symptoms of ill health, whilst diseases are clinical conditions defined by medical professionals.

It is therefore perfectly possible, as Blaxter has pointed out, to have an illness without a disease and a disease without an illness!

Lesley Cooper
ME: real or imagined illness?

Myalgic Encephalomyelitis (Chronic Fatigue Syndrome) has been the centre of a debate as to whether it is a real illness or not. Cooper wanted to explore the way that doctors responded to people who presented themselves at the surgery claiming to be suffering from ME. Cooper used the 'narrative method', where people were encouraged to tell their story (rather than being asked questions). Their stories were recorded and then analysed. The narratives were those of doctors, patients, researchers and psychiatrists.

What Cooper found was that individuals suffering from ME would experience a wide range of debilitating symptoms which they were unable to explain. When they were seen by doctors, their experiences were very different. Some people were diagnosed as having ME and received help and support. Others saw doctors who did not believe that ME exists as a specific illness and would either suggest that the symptoms were in the mind of the patient or that they had a virus and needed rest. Where doctors made a diagnosis of ME, sufferers were treated with some respect and concern by employers and family. However, where the diagnosis of ME was refused, this led to considerable trouble with employers and lack of support from family and friends.

Cooper's work illustrates the way that physical symptoms alone are not as important as definitions by doctors in being defined as ill.

Source: Cooper, L. (1997) 'Myalgic encephalomyelitis and the medical encounter', *Sociology of Health and Illness*, 19(2)

1 **What method did Cooper use to find out about people's experiences of ME?**

2 **How is this approach different to that normally used by doctors?**

3 **What was the effect of a doctor's decision whether or not to diagnose ME?**

Traditional and non-Western definitions of health and illness

The biomedical model contrasts markedly with concepts of illness in traditional and non-Western societies, where illness is seen as the result of a wider range of factors than just the body itself.

In traditional societies, for example, these factors could include witchcraft – where the blame for the illness lies in the bad wishes of others, or possibly the 'will of God'. A more complex model of health exists in non-Western societies, where the body and the mind are seen as completely linked. Any understanding of the body must be linked with the person's mental state, and the two need to be treated together.

However, over the last two hundred years, the biomedical model of health has come to dominate healthcare and has excluded other approaches. This supremacy is linked to the wider development of science and scientific methods as the predominant form of knowledge in modern societies.

Complementary medicine

In recent years, there has been a major growth in alternative or **complementary** forms of health provision. These include therapies such as homeopathy, herbal medicines and acupuncture. Following the ideas of Giddens (1991) about the development of new ways of thinking and acting in contemporary society, which he characterizes as **late modernity**, Hardey (1998) has argued that in late modernity, there has been a decline in the uncritical acceptance of the authority of professionals such as doctors. A second relevant feature of late modernity has been the growth in self-expression and individual choice. The idea that some people should give themselves completely into the power of doctors, and subject themselves to treatments which they may not even understand has therefore become increasingly questioned.

The result of this has been a partial rejection of the traditional biomedical model, in favour of seeking alternative therapies from the wide range available (see also pp. 165–6).

Criticisms of the biomedical and complementary models of health

According to Coward (1989), both the biomedical and the complementary models of health tend to stress that health problems are individual, both in terms of the causes and the cures. Coward argues that this ignores the wider social factors which cause ill health, such as poverty, poor housing, job-related stress and pollution, amongst others.

Defining disability

The dominance of medical definitions of health and ill health has had important implications for people with disabilities. According to Friedson (1965), the common perception of disability is that disabled people have some impediment that prevents them from operating 'normally'. This perception starts from the assumption that there is a clear definition of the 'normal' body, and a 'normal' range of activities associated with it.

However, it has been pointed out by critics such as Michael Oliver (1996) that the impediments imposed by society are at least as great as those imposed by the physical impairment. In other words, disability is a social construction, rather than just a physical one.

Not everyone is able to do everything as well as others – for example, run, catch or throw a ball – yet we do not describe those who are less able as being 'disabled'. We just accept these differences as part of the normal range of human abilities. This range of normality could be extended to include those defined as 'disabled'. This could occur, it is argued, if physical facilities and social attitudes were adjusted to include those with disabilities – for example, by altering the way we construct buildings, and by regarding sport played by disabled people as equal to 'traditional' types of sport.

It is with this in mind that the World Health Organization has distinguished between impairment, disability and handicap:

- *Impairment* refers to the abnormality of, or loss of function of, a part of the body.
- *Handicap* refers to the physical limits imposed by the loss of function.
- *Disability* refers to the socially imposed restriction on people's abilities to perform tasks as a result of the behaviour of people in society.

According to this approach, disability has to be understood as much in social terms as physical ones; so, a person can have an impairment without being disabled.

The origins of disability

If disability is a socially constructed concept, how did it come about? According to Finkelstein (1980), the modern idea of the dependent disabled person is largely the result of industrialization and the introduction of machinery. People with impairments were excluded from this type of work and came to be viewed as a burden. The rise of the medical profession in the early 19th century led them to become labelled as sick and in need of care.

Oliver (1990) takes Finkelstein's analysis further, by suggesting that the medical profession not only imposed the label of sickness and abnormality on people with impairments, but also helped to construct a way of looking at disability which saw it as a **personal tragedy**.

This concept of personal tragedy stresses that the individual disabled person has to be 'helped' to come to terms with the physical and psychological problems which they face. According to Oliver, this draws attention away from the fact that impairment is turned into disability by the wider economic, physical and social environment which discriminates against disabled people.

Stigma, illness and disability

Stigma is an important term in helping us to understand how people with disabilities are excluded from social activities. The idea of 'stigma' does not just apply to disabled people, but also to those with certain illnesses, such as Aids. The concept was first used in sociology by Erving Goffman (1963), who suggested that certain groups of people are defined as 'discredited' because of characteristics that are seen as 'negative'.

Types of stigma

Goffman suggested that there are two types of stigma.

1 *Discrediting* – These are obvious types of stigma, such as being in a wheelchair. People find it awkward to have

synopticlink

Perceptions about normality in body functions and shape have very powerful consequences for the people who are defined as abnormal or 'sick'. Disabled people, for example, suffer from various types of discrimination because they do not fit the pattern of what is considered 'normal'. In fact, it was not until 1995 that it became illegal not to provide facilities for disabled people that would allow them equal access to public buildings. When it comes to employment, however, people who have long-term illness or some form of physical disability are marginalized. Unemployment levels are higher for disabled people; they also have lower-status jobs and lower levels of earnings than able-bodied people. This does not reflect any lower levels of ability or intelligence, but discrimination on the part of the wider society.

social inequality and **difference**

Sociological explanations for stratification all offer different reasons for this discrimination:

- Weberian approaches suggest that disabled people are less powerful and so lose out when competing with other groups – thus having lower income and status levels.
- Marxist approaches point out that disabled people may be less able to produce the same levels of profits as able-bodied and are, therefore, marginalized.
- Finally, functionalist approaches suggest that society places greater value on able-bodied people than on disabled people. This latter approach implies that able-bodied people are in some way more useful to society, though most sociologists would distance themselves from such a suggestion.

normal social relations with those who are 'discredited'. They may be embarrassed, avoid eye contact or ignore the 'obvious' disability.

2 *Discreditable* – Here, the stigma is one of potential, dependent on whether other people find out about the discreditable illness or disability. Examples of this might include HIV status or epilepsy. In this situation, the person with the illness may find it difficult to act 'normally' in case they are 'found out'.

The concept of 'master status'

When the discrediting or discreditable status becomes the main way in which people are seen by others, then Goffman calls this a 'master status'. The stigma then completely dominates the way the person is treated, and any other attributes are seen as less important. The person who is unable to walk unaided is seen simply as 'wheelchair-bound' (not as an intelligent, articulate woman, for example), and the happy family man is seen as an 'Aids victim'. Finally, Goffman points out that the individuals themselves may accept this master status and come to see themselves solely in terms of their stigmatized status.

However, Goffman's argument that the individuals with stigma may well accept this as a master status has been criticized by other sociologists. According to Scambler and Hopkins (1986), for example, people with stigma may react in a number of different ways, using different tactics to manage their stigma:

- *Selective concealment* – If the stigmatizing condition is not obvious, the person may only tell a few trusted friends and family.
- *Covering up* – The person may tell no one.
- *Medicalizing the behaviour* – If the person cannot hide (or does not choose to hide) the condition, they could emphasize the medical aspect of it, as opposed to the social or moral aspect, and thus make a bid for sympathy (a link to the sick role here – see p. 136).
- *Condemning the condemners* – This is where people with a stigmatized condition take on those who impose the stigma and engage in forms of political action to have the stigma reviewed. Examples of this include the activities of HIV/Aids pressure groups and of pressure groups set up by disabled people.

The origins of stigma

Goffman never explained the origins of stigma, that is, why some people are stigmatized and others not. His main interest was in the effect of stigma on people and their interactions with others. However, other writers have suggested reasons why certain categories of people come to be stigmatized.

Clarke (1992) conducted a content analysis survey of magazines over a 20-year period and concluded that certain illnesses are linked to leading the 'wrong' sorts of lifestyles. HIV/Aids is viewed as discreditable, as are lung cancer and **obesity**. However, heart disease had no negative image.

focus on research

Gray (2002)
Stigma

Gray decided to research Goffman's concept of stigma with parents of autistic children. These children can behave in public in ways that are deeply embarrassing to parents. Gray wanted to find out if this stigmatized them in the eyes of other parents and also how they responded. Gray conducted semistructured, in-depth interviews with 33 families who were attending a clinic for autistic children. Originally, he had asked 40 families and seven refused to join the study.

Interviews lasted between two and three hours, and were recorded and later transcribed. The transcriptions were then analysed and certain themes were identified across the range of interviews. These themes of shame and methods of hiding the autism of their children were then explored in detail.

Gray concluded that autism is linked to 'discreditable' stigma and, as a result, parents try to conceal the autism of their children from other parents, as they fear that they will be branded 'bad' parents on account of their children's behaviour. Trying to conceal the autism of their children involves restricting their social life, keeping their children away from others and trying to pretend that everything is normal.

Gray, D. (2002) '"Everybody just freezes. Everybody is just embarrassed": felt and enacted stigma among parents of children with high functioning autism', *Sociology of Health and Illness*, 24(6), pp. 734–49

1 Suggest reasons why Gray used semistructured interviews in this research.

2 What themes were identified during the interviews?

3 How does the idea of stigma help understand the behaviour of the parents in this study?

Oliver (1990), as discussed earlier, sees the role of the medical profession as being crucial in defining how certain conditions are viewed.

The social construction of health

So far, we have seen that health is at least as much of a social concept as it is a physical one. Furthermore, this social notion of health is one that is *constructed* by people in their interaction. All the examples we have explored so far – the lay construction of health, the concept of disability and the notion of stigma – have been heavily influenced by interactionist forms of sociology. However, what is intriguing – and for sociology, very unusual – is that all the main perspectives agree that health has this socially constructed dimension. Naturally, what the social dimension actually is and what the implications are for society are bitterly contested. Both functionalist and critical writers have emphasized the social dimension in the construction of health and illness.

Functionalism

Functionalism starts by accepting that health and illness exist as 'real' states, but the meaning of health and illness is heavily influenced by the demands of the social structure. In *The Social System* (1951), Parsons introduced the idea of 'the sick role' (see Figure 4.2). Parsons argued that societies need people to continue to perform their allocated social roles in all circumstances if the social structure is not to collapse. The best way that society can deal with this problem is to treat illness as a form of deviance, from which people are coaxed or even coerced back into normal activity as soon as possible and this is the function of the sick role. The sick role brings with it two rights and two obligations. The two rights are benefits which sick people enjoy, but are conditional on fulfilling these two obligations.

The rights of the sick role are as follows:

1 The ill person does not have to fulfil their normal work and social tasks. The extent to which they avoid these tasks depends upon how serious the illness is deemed to be; here, the medical profession plays a key role in legitimating an illness as being serious or not.

2 The person is not blamed for being ill on the grounds that there is 'nothing they can do about it'. This also implies that the person has to be looked after by others. (There are some illnesses where the person is commonly deemed *not* to be an innocent victim – for example, the commonly held view of sexually transmitted diseases or problems associated with obesity.)

Balanced against these rights are two obligations, aimed at limiting social disruption caused by illness. These are:

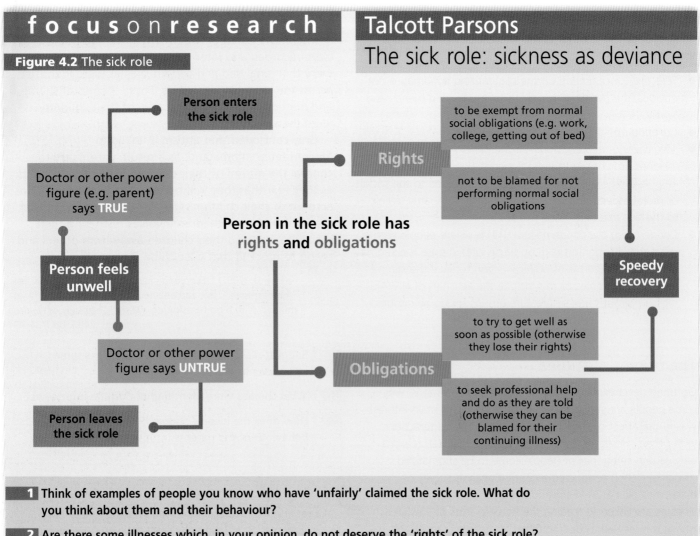

focuson**research**

Figure 4.2 The sick role

Talcott Parsons
The sick role: sickness as deviance

Person enters the sick role

Doctor or other power figure (e.g. parent) says **TRUE**

Person feels unwell

Doctor or other power figure says **UNTRUE**

Person leaves the sick role

Person in the sick role has rights and obligations

Rights

to be exempt from normal social obligations (e.g. work, college, getting out of bed)

not to be blamed for not performing normal social obligations

Speedy recovery

Obligations

to try to get well as soon as possible (otherwise they lose their rights)

to seek professional help and do as they are told (otherwise they can be blamed for their continuing illness)

1 Think of examples of people you know who have 'unfairly' claimed the sick role. What do you think about them and their behaviour?

2 Are there some illnesses which, in your opinion, do not deserve the 'rights' of the sick role?

1 The sick person must accept that being ill is undesirable and should try to get better as soon as possible.

2 The sick person must cooperate with those attempting to cure them.

Criticisms of the idea of the sick role

Parsons' concept of the sick role only applies to acute illness (such as flu), not chronic illness (such as diabetes). He also ignored the role of family and friends in defining whether someone was really ill or not, and placed too great an emphasis on doctors. Finally, Turner (1995) suggests that Parsons ignores the negative aspects on doctors' actions in defining certain people as ill or not (see Marxist approach).

Parsons' idea of the sick role is interesting for two reasons:

● It clearly demonstrates the intricate connection between illness and the smooth functioning of society.

● It links the idea of being sick to the concept of social deviance, and when an action is defined as deviant, this suggests that societies will have means of 'policing' the deviance.

Although Parsons did not really pursue this control or 'policing' idea in his writings, a number of other perspectives – particularly the Marxist or critical sociology approach – did so, and we shall examine these next.

The Marxist perspective on health

Marxist writers also stress the close connection between illness and the 'needs' of society. However, their interests lie in exploring the ways that the definitions of health and illness reflect the particular needs of *capitalist* society.

According to Navarro (1986), definitions of health and illness are crucially linked to the ability to work: if a person is capable of working, they are healthy; if they are incapable of work, they are ill. The task of the medical profession is to ensure that the workforce is actually fit enough to work and also to 'police' the boundaries between those who are genuinely ill and those who are not. Medicine also has an ideological function by explaining health and illness in individual terms. So a person is ill because of their individual life choices (they overeat/smoke/drink alcohol) or in terms of genetics or even chance. What medicine does not do is to link the different levels of illness to the varying income and living conditions of the social classes.

Critics have argued that this description of health provision in capitalism is inaccurate, as spending on (free) healthcare has continuously increased in capitalism. But Navarro argues that this growth in spending is largely a way of hiding the actual causes of ill health, which lie in the very nature of the inequalities inherent in capitalism. Medical techniques are largely ineffective in tackling the causes of ill health, but by spending so heavily on 'healthcare', people are persuaded that the capitalist state does care and is trying to eliminate ill health. Furthermore, according to Marxist writers, not only does the current way of understanding illness and how to 'cure' it have an ideological benefit for capitalism, it also has an economic benefit. The large pharmaceutical companies earn high profits from the design and production of drugs and other forms of medical technology. Capitalism therefore creates ill health and also profits from it.

The critical approach

The critical approach is closely linked with the Marxist critique of medicine, with overlapping arguments, but these writers do not necessarily subscribe to the wider Marxist analysis of society. McKeown (1976), in one of the best-known studies on the relationship between health and medicine, traced the history of various diseases such as whooping cough and measles. His research demonstrated that these diseases had their major decline *before* the availability of immunization (see Figure 4.3).

McKeown suggests that modern medicine, therefore, has constructed an image of health and medicine that ignores the wider factors of quality of life, which clearly have a much greater impact on illness than specific medical interventions.

Figure 4.3 The medical contribution to the decline in infectious diseases

Source: McKeown (1976)

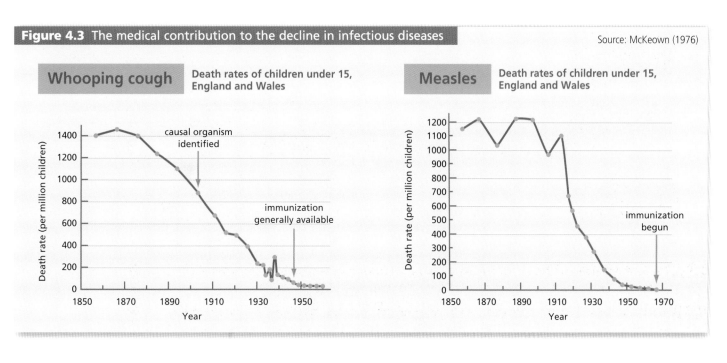

Illich (1990) takes this critique of capitalism further with his concept of **iatrogenesis**, by which he means the harm done to people by modern medicine. Illich argues that, far from helping people, modern medicine is actually dangerous. Indeed, it has been estimated that 10 per cent of all hospital patients contract some form of infection and that the process of surgery is partly responsible for 30 per cent of deaths after operations (and is the main reason in 7 per cent of cases). Illich suggested that iatrogenesis went wider than this direct medical harm. Other forms of iatrogenesis include:

- *social iatrogenesis* – whereby the notion of illness extends so that wide swathes of behaviour and feelings come to be defined as 'medical problems' that can only be dealt with through medical intervention
- *cultural iatrogenesis* – where people 'unlearn the acceptance of suffering' and believe that all forms of suffering and pain are not natural and can be eliminated by medicine.

Criticisms of the Marxist and critical approaches

Hart (1985) argues that capitalism has actually provided real healthcare gains for the majority of the population through increased standards of living. Furthermore, the critical and Marxist approaches are really only applicable to countries, like the USA, where healthcare has to be paid for.

Check your understanding

1 How does the public define health?

2 Identify and explain any three factors that affect the definition of health and illness.

3 Who 'sanctions' illness (officially approves it), and what are the benefits of being 'sanctioned' as ill?

4 Construct a table summarizing the three types of medical models: biomedical, traditional and complementary.

5 What is the difference between 'impairment' and 'disability'?

6 Explain the difference between stigma and disability.

7 Why might certain types of people become stigmatized?

8 How does the idea of the 'sick role' contribute to an understanding of how societies encourage people to perform their allocated roles?

9 How do Marxists argue that the provision of healthcare benefits capitalism?

10 How does McKeown argue that medicine is not very effective in improving health?

research ideas

1 Conduct interviews with a small sample of your peers at school or college. Who sanctions their 'illness' when they feel too ill to come in to school or college? How does the process of 'negotiating' absence work?

2 Select a small sample of people, ideally from different generations, and ask them to rate their degree of sympathy on a scale of 1 to 5 for people with the following 'illnesses': hangover, headache (not caused by a hangover!), impotence, cirrhosis of the liver (caused by drinking too much alcohol), anorexia, heart disease, breast cancer, lung cancer caused by smoking, sexually transmitted disease.

Do your results show any different attitudes to illness and disease amongst people? What explanations can you suggest for your findings?

KEY TERMS

Biomedical model of health – the conventional Western model. It sees the body as very much like a biological machine, with each part of the body performing a function. The doctor's job is to restore the functions by solving the problem of what is wrong. Ideas about the environment or the spiritual health of the person are not relevant.

Complementary medicine – alternative forms of health intervention, such as homeopathy.

Disability – the socially imposed restriction on people's abilities to perform tasks as a result of the behaviour of people in society.

General practitioner (GP) – a local doctor who deals with general health issues.

Health – a person's perception of the state of their body's wellbeing.

Iatrogenesis – the harm caused to people by modern medicine.

Illness – perception of feeling unacceptably worse than normal body state.

Late modernity – a term used to describe contemporary society where choice and individuality have become more important than conformity and group membership.

Lay definitions of health – 'lay' refers to the majority of the public who are not medical practitioners and who therefore use common-sense ideas about health and illness.

Malingering – pretending to be ill in order to avoid work or other responsibilities.

Obesity – a medical term for being overweight.

Personal tragedy – a term used by Oliver to describe the way disability is seen as a personal as opposed to a social problem.

web.tasks

1 **RADAR is an educational and campaigning organization for people with disabilities. Visit their website at** www.radar.org.uk

   The website has information sheets which are worth exploring for information on disability.

2 **Search online for information and advice on health – for example, *Men's Health Magazine* at** www.menshealth.co.uk

   Does the advice make an assumption about what is normal and abnormal in terms of body shape and styles of life?

3 **Search the world wide web for examples of traditional models of health and illness. Compare them with conventional Western models.**

exploring defining health, illness and disability

Item A

The Ndembu explain all persistent or severe health problems by reference to social causes, such as the secret malevolence of sorcerers or witches, or punishment by the spirits of ancestors. These spirits cause sickness in an individual if his or her family and kin are 'not living well together', and are involved in grudges or quarrelling.

The Ndembu traditional healer, the *chimbuki*, conducts a séance attended by the victim, their kin and neighbours. By questioning these people and by shrewd observation, he builds up a picture of the patient's social situation and its various tensions. The diviner calls all the relatives of the patient before a sacred shrine to the ancestors, and induces them 'to confess any grudges and hard feelings they may nourish against the patient'. By this process all the hidden social tensions of the group are publicly aired and gradually resolved. Treatment involves rituals of exorcism to withdraw evil influences from the patient's body. It also includes the use of certain herbal and other medicines, manipulation and cupping and certain substances applied to the skin.

Adapted from Helman, C. (2000) *Culture, Health and Illness*, Oxford: Butterworth/ Heinemann, pp. 197–8 (adapted)

Item B

In the biomedical model, information is gathered by means of indicators like X-rays, blood sugar levels, electroencephalograph readings or biopsies, which are thought to measure these biological processes directly. This framework is closely associated with developments in Western science. Physicians can readily reach agreement on the operation of the body by reference to well-defined criteria which are known to all members of the medical profession and which become progressively more precise with advances in scientific knowledge. The doctor will be able to use signs derived from these tests as objective indicators of biological malfunction or irregularity – regardless of whether the supposed patient actually feels ill.

Adapted from Dingwall, R. (1976) *Aspects of Illness*, Basingstoke: Palgrave

(a) Identify **one** form of treatment used by the traditional healer **(Item A).** (1 mark)

(b) Identify and briefly explain **two** characteristics of the biomedical model of health **(Item B).** (8 marks)

(c) Identify **three** factors that the Ndembu healer sees as being important in the diagnosis of illness **(Item A).** (9 marks)

(d) Identify and briefly explain **two** ways in which the Western model of health and illness **(Item B)** is different from the traditional model described in **Item A.** (12 marks)

Exam practice

(e) Outline and assess the view that definitions of health and illness are social constructions. (60 marks)

Health inequalities

gettingyouthinking

SMRs by social class for men aged 15/20 to 64 (England & Wales)

Year	I	II	III		IV	V	Ratio V:I
			IIIN	IIIM			
1921–3	82	94	95		101	125	1.52
1930–2	90	94	97		102	111	1.23
1949–53	86	92	101		104	118	1.37
1959–63	76	81	100		103	143	1.91
1970–2	77	81	99	106	114	137	1.78
1979–80/82–3	66	76	94	106	116	165	2.50
1991–3	66	72	100	117	116	189	2.86

Note: for 1921 to 1972, men aged 15 to 64 are included;
for 1979 to 1993, men aged 20 to 64 are included

Source: Shaw, M., Dorling, D., Gordon, D. and Davey Smith, G. (1999)
The Widening Gap, Bristol: Policy Press, p. 132

SMR stands for 'standardized mortality ratio'. This is a guide to the relative chances of dying for specific age ranges (in this case men aged 15/20 to 64). In this model, average chances of death are 100 and any figures above this indicate above-average chances of death. Any figures below indicate below-average chances. The letters 'I' to 'V' stand for social classes, 'I' being the highest and 'V' the lowest.

Remember when answering these questions that SMRs are *relative* figures – that is, they show differences between groups. It is not possible to make any statements about the *absolute* figures over time.

1 **In 1921–3, what were the SMRs for social class I and social class V?**

2 **What changes happened in the relative SMRs of the social classes:**
   (a) **between 1921 and 1953?**
   (b) **after 1972?**

3 **What long-term impact, if any, did the introduction of the National Health Service in the late 1940s have on inequalities in the SMR?**

4 **What reasons can you suggest for all the changes you have identified from the table?**

5 **Look at the photographs above and make a list of the reasons why, in your opinion, people in the 'lower' social classes are more likely to die young. Do you think the government could do anything about these issues?**

In 1979, the Labour government of the time commissioned a report on health and illness in Britain. Shortly afterwards, they lost the election and a new Conservative government came into power. The following year, the committee reported back on their findings. The new government was so embarrassed by these findings that they only printed 260 copies and gave the report no publicity, in the hope that no one would notice. Unfortunately for the government, they did, and what the press and the public read was quite shocking: after 35 years of a free health service, health and life expectation were still very closely linked to social class. Despite this revelation, a further report ('Independent Inquiry into Inequalities in Health'), commissioned by the next Labour government almost 20 years later, found that the 'health gap' between the poorest and the richest had actually widened.

Research has shown that health is closely linked to a number of social factors, including geography, social class, gender and ethnicity. We will look at each area in turn.

Measuring health and illness

Before we begin our examination of the statistics, we should just note the difficulties in measuring health and illness. In most official statistics on health, two measures are used: morbidity and mortality.

Morbidity

Morbidity refers to illness and is a measure of how healthy the population is. Morbidity statistics are collected in three main ways, i.e. from:

- the statistics collected from hospitals and GPs' reports of diagnosed diseases
- the numbers of people who are claiming various government benefits on the grounds of incapacity
- national surveys that collect self-reported accounts of health.

In some ways, the debates on health statistics mirror those of the crime statistics. Official figures depend upon the gatekeeping activities of GPs and hospitals. How they define and categorize illness is reflected in the official statistics published. Yet, as we have seen in the previous topic, doctors rely upon a medical model that is built on a range of beliefs about 'real' illness. The figures collected from incapacity benefits are also subject to considerable debate. During the early 1990s, when the government wished to demonstrate very low unemployment figures, it was relatively easy to obtain incapacity benefits, as people receiving these payments were 'sick' not unemployed. However, with the decline in unemployment figures to acceptable levels, the current government has taken a much stricter line as to who qualifies for incapacity benefits. The result is that the number of long-term sick has officially declined. Finally, self-report methods of measuring illness are entirely dependent upon the individual's perception of their own health and this leads to wide variations.

Mortality

Mortality refers to death rates. As everyone dies at some point, this does seem an objective measure. There are, however, some issues here. The actual measure used is the mortality rate, which refers to the number of people dying within any particular period, per 100 000 (or some other number) of the population. Mortality rates can be general, or they can refer to deaths among specific groups (such as the infant mortality rate) or to specific causes of death (the mortality rate for heart disease). An alternative measure, often used, is that of the standardized mortality ratio (or SMR) (see opposite page).

The basis for some of these figures is the cause of death as stated on the death certificate, but problems can arise here – as Hart (1985) has pointed out, what is written on the death certificate may not be a completely accurate description of death. Those dying of AIDS, for example, will be classified as dying from heart disease, skin cancer or respiratory disease. For older people, there may be numerous illnesses all contributing to the death, but only one is selected. A good example of this is the way that prostate cancer deaths have increased in recent years. A very significant proportion of men over 60 have prostate cancer, but until recently it was rarely referred to as the cause of death. In the last five years, there has been a growing interest (and diagnosis) of the disease and, as a result, death rates from this form of cancer have (officially) risen.

Geographical differences

In 1999, a team of researchers led by Mary Shaw looked at the **parliamentary constituencies** in Britain and gathered information on the health of the people living in each constituency. They compared the one million people living in the constituencies that had the very worst health records with the one million people living in the constituencies that had the very best health records. The gap between these groups surprised even the researchers themselves.

The comparison showed that, in the worst health areas:

- children under the age of 1 are twice as likely to die
- there are ten times more women under the age of 65 who are permanently sick (including those who are disabled)
- adults are almost three times as likely to state that they have a serious 'chronic' (long-term) illness or disability
- adults have a 70 per cent greater chance of dying before the age of 65.

These geographical differences generally reflect differences in income and levels of deprivation. However, they are not simply a reflection of these, because poorer people living in the richer areas tend to have higher standards of health. It seems that quality of life in poorer areas is generally lower and, as a result, health standards are worse.

Social class

Mortality

Over the last 20 years, **death rates** have fallen for both men and women, in all social classes. But they have fallen faster for those in the higher social classes, so that the difference in rates between those in the higher and lower social classes has actually grown. For example, in the early 1970s, the death rate among men of working age was almost twice as high for those in class V (unskilled) as for those in class I (professional). By the 1990s, it was almost three times as high. Men in social class I can expect to live for almost nine years longer than men from social class V, while women in social class I can expect to live six years longer than their social class V counterparts.

Despite its use as a general indicator of health, life expectancy takes no account of the *quality* of life. While males born in the United Kingdom in 2001 could expect to live 4.9 years longer and females 3.6 years longer than those born in 1981, those extra years may not necessarily be spent in good health. In 1981, the expected time lived in poor health for males was 6.4 years and for females 10.1 years. By 2001, this had risen to 8.7 years for males and 11.6 years for females (*Social Trends* 2005, p. 76).

Morbidity

Although death rates have fallen and life expectancy has increased, there is little evidence that the population is experiencing better health than 20 years ago. In fact, there has actually been a small increase in **self-reported** long-standing illness, and differences between the social classes are still quite clear. However, as we saw in Topic 1, what is defined as 'health' changes over time. So it may be that people are actually in better health but don't believe it.

Bearing this in mind, among the 45 to 64 age group, 17 per cent of professional men reported a limiting long-standing illness, compared to 48 per cent of unskilled men (1999). For women, the figures were 25 per cent for professional women and 45 per cent for unskilled women.

In adulthood, being overweight is a measure of possible ill health, with obesity a risk factor for many chronic diseases. There is a noticeable social-class gradient in obesity, which is greater for women than men. About 25 per cent of women in class V are classified as obese, compared to 14 per cent of women in class I.

Explanations for differences in health between social classes

Different ways of explaining class differences in mortality and morbidity have been suggested.

The artefact approach

An artefact is something observed in a scientific investigation that is not naturally present, but occurs as a result of the investigative procedure. Perhaps the link between class and health is not real but a statistical illusion. Illsley (1986) argues that the statistical connection between social class and illness exaggerates the situation. For example, he points out that the number of people in social class V has declined so much over the last 30 years that the membership is just too small to be used as the basis for comparisons with other social classes.

However, the recent 'Independent Inquiry into Inequalities in Health' showed that, even when the classes were regrouped to

Wilkinson (1996)
Health and social capital

In one of the most famous studies to uncover the relationship between social factors and health, Wilkinson compared the health and economic data for 23 different countries. He found very strong evidence to link the overall health of the population with the degree of economic inequality. Once a certain basic level of overall economic wealth had been attained by a country, then the greater the economic inequality which existed, the wider the health differentials. Interestingly, no matter how high the general standard of living became, as long as there were economic inequalities, there was no increase in the general standards of health. This meant that a country with a high standard of living, but considerable economic inequality, actually had lower standards of health for the majority of the population than a poorer country with greater social equality. Cuba, for example, despite being much poorer than the USA, has better standards of health and expectation of life overall than the USA.

Wilkinson's conclusions were that societies with low levels of inequality had high levels of 'social capital' – that is a sense of belonging and place in a society. This sense of belonging had the effect of increasing the sense of wellbeing, which in turn improved standards of health.

Wilkinson, R.G. (1996) *Unhealthy Societies: The Afflictions of Inequality*, London: Routledge

1 What is Wilkinson's explanation for the fact that Cuba has higher life expectancy than the USA?

2 What does Wilkinson mean by 'social capital'? How does it improve health?

include classes IV and V together, significant differences remained. For example, in the late 1990s, death rates were 53 per cent higher among men in classes IV and V, compared with those in classes I and II. Carr-Hill has pointed out (1987) that when he examined death certificates, he found that the 'profession' recorded on the death certificate was often incorrectly categorized and this meant that statistics based on death certificates may well be inaccurate.

individuals and to those around them. These forms of abnormal behaviour are classified as mental illness. Social realists such as Pilgrim and Rogers (1999) accept that, at different times and in different cultures, there are variations in what is considered as mental illness. Nevertheless, they argue that, although mental illness may have different names and may or may not be recognized in different cultures, it does actually exist as a real condition.

Social constructionism

Social constructionist perspectives have been very influential in sociological approaches to mental illness and start from the argument that what is considered normal varies over time and from society to society. For example, over the last two hundred years in Britain, alcohol consumption has been seen variously as normal, as morally wrong or even illegal, as a sign of being mentally ill and as a central part of a religious ritual. In fact, most of these different attitudes to alcohol can still be found in Britain today!

Even greater extremes of behaviour have been seen as normal in some societies and as evidence of madness in others. For example, saying that you are possessed by the spirit of your ancestor would suggest madness in contemporary Britain, but for native Americans, or in some West African religions, it would be a perfectly reasonable statement which most people would believe was true.

Mental illness: real or culturally created?

All sociologists agree that there are forms of behaviour that cause considerable stress to the individual involved, and which prevent them from engaging in any meaningful participation in society. They also recognize that how it comes to be defined depends upon cultural differences. Where the difference between realist and constructionist perspectives emerge is more in the stress they place on how far the cultural context determines the levels and types of mental illness.

The best way to understand the sociology of mental health is to see it as a continuum, with those who argue for the overwhelming importance of culture at one extreme and those who argue for the existence of common illnesses (which might go under different names, but are essentially the same) at the other extreme.

The labelling perspective

The degree of flexibility about what constitutes normal and abnormal behaviour has been taken furthest by so-called 'labelling theorists'. Labelling theory examines how labelling occurs in the first place and what effects it has on those who are labelled. Thomas Szasz (1973), for example, argues that the label 'mental illness' is simply a convenient way to deal with behaviour that people find disruptive. Labelling theory rests firmly upon a social constructionist definition of mental illness.

The effects of labelling

According to Scheff (1966), whether someone becomes labelled or not is determined by the benefits that others might gain by labelling the person 'mentally ill'. So, those people who become a nuisance, or who prevent others from doing something they want to do, are far more likely to be defined as being mentally ill than those who pose no threat or inconvenience, and may be ignored.

Once labelled, there are a number of negative consequences for the person, because it is then assumed that all their behaviour is evidence of their mental state. A famous study by Rosenhan (1973) illustrates this. In the early 1970s in the USA, Rosenhan asked eight perfectly 'normal' researchers to enter a number of psychiatric institutions after phoning up and complaining that they were 'hearing voices'. Once the researchers had been admitted into the institutions, doctors and staff regarded them as truly mentally ill and reinterpreted all their behaviour as proof of this. However, the researchers were under strict instructions to behave completely normally at all times.

In a later study, new staff in a psychiatric hospital were told that this experiment was to be repeated in their institution, and they were asked to uncover these researchers who were just pretending to be ill. In this study, staff routinely judged people who were 'genuinely ill' as merely pretending. It would seem, therefore, that there is some confusion as to how even experts can decide who is actually mentally ill.

Erving Goffman (1961) followed the **careers** of people who were genuinely defined as being mentally ill. He suggested that, once in an institution, people are stripped of their **presenting culture** – by which he means the image that we all choose to present to the world as 'us'. This may include a style of haircut, make-up, or the requirement that people address us as 'Mr' or 'Mrs' rather than 'Michael' or 'Sarah'. The 'patient' may also lose their right to make decisions about their life and may be required to take medication which can disorientate them.

Quickly, the self-image that a patient has – perhaps of being a respectable, witty, middle-aged person – is stripped away, leaving them bewildered, vulnerable and ready to accept a new role. In this powerless situation, any attempts to reject the label of mental illness can actually be interpreted as further signs of illness, and perhaps as indicating a need for increased medication or counselling. In fact, accepting the role of being mentally ill is seen as the first sign of recovery.

Criticisms of the labelling perspective

The labelling perspective on mental illness has not gone unchallenged. Gove (1982) suggests that the vast majority of people who receive treatment for mental illness actually have serious problems before they are treated and so the argument that the label causes the problem is wrong. Furthermore, he argues that labelling theory provides no adequate explanation for why some people start to show symptoms in the first place.

According to Gove, labelling may help explain some of the responses of others to the mentally ill, but it cannot explain the causes of the illness.

Mental illness: Foucault's perspective

A second, very distinctive version of social constructionist theory emerges in the work of the French sociologist, Foucault (1965). He explains the growth in the concept of mental illness by placing it in the context of the changing ways of thinking and acting which developed in the early 18th century. According to Foucault, during the **Enlightenment**, more traditional ways of thinking, based on religious beliefs and on emotions, were gradually replaced by more rational, intellectually disciplined ways of thinking and acting. These eventually led to the significant scientific and engineering developments which formed the basis of the 'industrial revolution'. Foucault argues that as rationality developed into the normal way of thinking, irrationality began to be perceived as deviant.

This shift away from the irrational and towards the rational was illustrated, according to Foucault, by the growth in asylums for those considered mad. Foucault suggests that having mad people in asylums, both symbolically and literally, isolated mad people away from the majority of the population. The asylums symbolized the fact that madness or irrationality was marked out as behaviour that was no longer acceptable.

Although Foucault's writing is very dense and complicated, the essential message is that madness, as we understand it, is a relatively modern invention which emerged from the development of modern 'rational' ways of thinking and acting.

Structuralist perspectives

Structuralist perspectives on mental health are closely tied to the social realist definition of mental illness. These approaches accept the reality of mental illness and set out to discover what factors in society might cause the illness. As a result of research by sociologists working within this tradition, evidence of clear mental health differences between social groups has emerged. Some of these are discussed next.

Mental illness and ethnicity

Members of ethnic minorities have significantly different chances of mental illness compared to the majority white population. According to Nazroo (2001) people of 'South Asian origin' have very low rates of mental illness, whilst those of African Caribbean origins have particularly high levels of **schizophrenia**, with levels between three and five times higher than the population as a whole. Writers within the structuralist perspective, such as Virdee (1997), explain this by arguing that the sorts of pressures and stresses that can cause people to develop mental illness are more likely to be experienced by members of ethnic minorities because they encounter racism and disadvantage throughout their lives.

However, labelling theorists have argued that some of the behaviour of Afro-Caribbean adults in particular, has been seen as inappropriate in British society, and has therefore been labelled as a symptom of mental illness. Nazroo points out that people of Bangladeshi origin, who are amongst the most deprived groups in the British population and are also recipients of racism, actually have lower levels of mental illness than the general population. They therefore argue that it cannot just be racism and deprivation.

Mental illness and gender

Women are more likely than men to exhibit behaviour defined as mental illness. Overall, women have rates about one third

synopticlink

Mental Illness is generally seen as a form of illness that can affect anybody at any time. This is true, but it is also true to say that certain groups are more likely to have higher levels of mental illness than others. In the government publication *Saving Lives; Our Healthier Nation*, the authors note that:

- suicide rates are higher for poorer groups in the population
- unemployed people are twice as likely to suffer from depression as people in work
- children in the poorest households are three times more likely to have mental ill health than children in the best-off households
- people sleeping rough or using night shelters are four times more likely to have a mental disorder than the general population
- people in prisons are at least 15 times more likely to have a psychotic disorder than the general population

social inequality and difference

- refugees have higher rates of mental disorder than the general population.

Mental illness is, therefore, linked to social disadvantage and forms just one element of a broader range of disadvantage shared by poorer and less powerful groups in society. However, not only does it reflect disadvantage, according to the government report, but it also contributes to it. The report notes:

<< *People with mental illness may have difficulties in sustaining supportive relationships with friends, family and colleagues; with parenting; with work and other daily activities. They may have higher rates of substance misuse. These social consequences of mental illness increase the stigma and social exclusion suffered by people with mental illness and that, in turn, makes the original condition worse.* >> (www.archive.official-documents.co.uk/document/cm43/4386/4386.htm)

higher than men, but in some specific forms of mental illness, the figures are much higher. For example, women are at least three times more likely to suffer from depression. Structuralists, such as Brown *et al.* (1995) argue that women are more likely to lead stressful lives – combining careers and the responsibility for childcare, for example, and being more likely to experience poverty and poor housing conditions.

However, labelling theorist and feminist sociologists such as Chesler (1972) go further and argue that the behaviour of women is more likely to be defined as evidence of mental illness because the defining is done by a male-dominated profession. Rather than looking for the real reasons – which are most likely to be stress and poverty – psychiatrists are more interested in defining the problem in terms of an individual's mental state.

Busfield (1988) has suggested that the structuralist position and the labelling approach are not irreconcilable and that women are both under pressure in their lives, which leads to higher levels of mental illness, but are also more likely to have their problems defined as mental illness by psychiatrists.

Inequality, social class and mental illness

Overall, when looking at which group is most likely to suffer from high rates of mental illness, the poorest and most excluded are massively overrepresented.

Link and Phelan (1995) reviewed all the evidence over a period of 40 years between social class and mental illness, concluding that all the research clearly pointed to the close relationship between deprivation and low levels of mental health. A government study (Green *et al.* 2005) found that children from the poorest backgrounds were three times more likely to have conduct disorders than those whose parents were in professional occupations. Structuralist writers, such as Myers (1975), have suggested a '**life-course**' model, which explains the higher levels of mental illness as a result of poorer people consistently encountering higher levels of social problems over their lifetimes, but having limited educational, social and economic resources to continue overcoming the problems. They argue that, eventually, the stress of coping emerges and is expressed through mental illness.

A second form of structuralist explanation is that of **social capital**. The concept of social capital derives from the writings of Putnam (2000) who argues that people who have social networks of friends and relatives are more likely to be happy, to have lower levels of stress and to feel they 'belong' to their local community. The result of this is that they are less likely to suffer from mental illness.

Pilgrim and Rogers (1999), however, point to the arguments of labelling and feminist theorists, who note that within the most deprived groups, there are also higher levels of women suffering from mental illness compared to men and they would suggest that women are more likely to have their problems defined in terms of mental illness.

Mental illness: conclusion

Mental illness is a highly contested issue in sociology. There are arguments over the very definition of the term and how to explain the differences in mental illness rates in the population.

focus on research

MIND (1998)
Mental health and poverty

For a number of years, sociologists had suggested that to see mental health solely as a health problem was to ignore the devastating affect it had on people's lives in general. In particular, it was argued, mental health led people to have high levels of unemployment, homelessness and poverty. In 1998, the mental health pressure group MIND conducted a national survey to find out the extent of poverty amongst people with mental illness. Of those mentally ill people who replied, 98 per cent received some form of state benefit, with 60 per cent entirely dependent on benefits.

They also found that 35 per cent of respondents were too ill to work. However, 38 per cent did some kind of unpaid voluntary work (often because they could not find paid work) and 16 per cent were actively looking for a paid job, but were unable to find one. MIND found that people who had suffered from mental illness and were looking for work, routinely encountered discrimination and stigma.

MIND's research, then, demonstrates that mental illness is more than a health issue, it is a social one too.

MIND (1998) *Mind Disability Benefits Survey*, London: Mind Publications

1 **Give examples of the 'devastating effect mental health problems may have on somebody's life'.**

2 **How representative of people with mental health problems do you think the MIND survey was? Explain your answer.**

3 **Explain in your own words the problems people suffering from mental illness experienced when looking for employment.**

However, the approaches are not entirely irreconcilable and Busfield's approach is one that has received much support. She argues that it is probably true that some groups are much more likely to find their behaviour defined as mental illness, compared to the behaviour of other groups. However, it is also true that these very same groups – ethnic minorities, women and the socially excluded – all suffer high levels of stress and so one would expect them to have higher levels of illness. Both processes reinforce each other.

web.task

Find the website of the mental health charity MIND at www.mind.org.uk. Use the 'links' section to explore the work of some of the organizations connected with mental health issues. Make a list of all the mental health issues covered. How important an issue is mental health in the UK today?

Check your understanding

1 **Identify the two sociological approaches to defining mental illness.**

2 **Explain the key differences between the two approaches you have identified.**

3 **How does the idea of 'labelling' help us to understand mental illness?**

4 **What is meant by a structural explanation for mental illness?**

5 **How does Busfield suggest that the structuralist and labelling approaches can be combined?**

6 **Why are people from certain ethnic minorities more likely to be defined as suffering from mental illness?**

7 **What argument do feminist writers use to explain why women are more likely to be defined as suffering from mental illness?**

Office for National Statistics

focus on research

Differences in levels of mental illness, 2004

1 The table below shows the differences for a range of social groups in their levels of mental illness. What differences in mental illness can you find for the following factors?

(a) social class   (b) ethnicity

(b) employment status   (c) marital status

Mean annual consultation rates per 1000 men at risk for specified psychiatric disorders

SPECIFIED PSYCHIATRIC DISORDER

		Bipolar affective disorders	Schizophrenia	Neurotic disorders	Personality disorders	Alcohol dependence	Drug dependence	Depression
SOCIAL CLASS	I	17.0	1.5	33.2	2.0	8.5	9.6	21.6
	II	13.4	1.4	40.4	1.8	4.9	6.6	32.8
	IIIN	13.1	7.1	55.9	7.4	7.8	15.9	35.0
	IIIM	13.3	4.6	48.2	3.2	8.8	23.6	41.7
	IV	16.3	12.1	58.4	8.1	13.0	25.4	50.9
	V	19.4	25.7	84.8	16.5	23.9	78.5	56.7
ETHNIC GROUP	White	14.5	7.7	49.4	4.6	8.9	20.7	38.5
	Afro-Caribbean	5.7	50.9	21.2	24.1	5.7	7.1	14.2
	Asian	9.1	2.8	39.1	9.8	4.2	0.7	5.6
	Other	7.6	0.0	50.8	5.1	1.3	10.2	25.4
EMPLOYMENT STATUS	Employed full-time	8.6	1.1	37.4	1.6	3.9	5.4	25.0
	Employed part-time	31.7	23.2	51.6	5.7	8.0	22.2	39.7
	Unemployed	24.4	16.0	84.8	15.3	24.3	102.4	66.3
	Student	7.7	4.8	22.2	2.3	0.5	13.4	16.6
	Permanently sick	79.8	102.5	195.7	41.0	66.0	113.4	201.4
	Other	24.8	7.1	58.3	5.8	10.7	17.0	59.3
MARITAL STATUS	Single	13.7	16.2	48.1	8.0	8.5	38.6	27.9
	Married	13.2	1.7	43.8	2.6	4.0	5.2	37.0
	Separated/divorced	26.4	21.1	101.2	11.0	57.7	60.6	101.4
	Widowed	25.9	17.6	97.3	4.1	9.3	70.4	73.5

Sociology A2 for OCR

Career – in this context, the gradual changes in people as a response to a label (for example, 'mental patient').

Enlightenment – a period of intellectual change in the 17th and 18th centuries.

Life course model – that the accumulation of social events experienced over a whole lifetime, not just individual important events, influence people and their mental state.

Presenting culture – a term used by Goffman to refer to how people like to portray themselves to others.

Schizophrenia – a form of mental illness where people are unable to distinguish their own feelings and perceptions from reality.

Social capital – a network of social contacts.

Social constructionism – the approach which suggests that mental illness (and all other social phenomena) exists because people believe it does.

Social realism – a sociological approach which suggests that mental illness does really exist.

research idea

Watch the film *One Flew Over the Cuckoo's Nest* (or read the original book by Ken Kesey). What perspective on mental illness does this film (or book) illustrate?

exploring mental health and mental illness

Item A

≪ It affects your mind. If you feel depressed that you are not treated as other people are, or they look down on you, you will feel mentally ill, won't you? It will depress you that you are not treated well racially, it will affect your health in some way. It will cause you depression, and that depression will cause the illness. ≫

Quoted in Annandale, E. (1998) *The Sociology of Health and Medicine*, Cambridge: Polity Press, p. 187

Item B

People of African-Caribbean origin are far more likely to reach the mental health system via the police, the courts and prisons, and to experience the more harsh and invasive forms of treatment (such as electro-convulsive therapy), than other groups.

With regard to mental illness, for all diagnoses combined, women's rate of admission to hospitals in England and Wales was 29 per cent above the rate for men.

Adapted from Annandale, E. (1998) *The Sociology of Health and Medicine*, Cambridge: Polity Press, pp. 143 & 186

Item C

Katz examined the process of psychiatric diagnosis among both British and American psychiatrists. Groups of British and American psychiatrists were shown films of interviews with patients and asked to note down all the pathological symptoms and make a diagnosis. Marked disagreements in diagnosis between the two groups were found. The British saw less evidence of mental illness generally. For example, one patient was diagnosed as 'schizophrenic' by one-third of the Americans, but by none of the British.

Adapted from Helman, C. (2000) *Culture, Health and Illness*, Oxford: Butterworth/Heinemann, p. 80

(a) Using **Item B**, identify **one** way in which not being 'treated well racially' (**Item A**) might influence your health. (1 mark)

(b) Identify and briefly explain **two** reasons why members of ethnic minorities might experience depression. (8 marks)

(c) Give **three** reasons why the British and American psychiatrists in **Item C** may have diagnosed the same individual differently. (9 marks)

(d) Identify and explain **two** reasons that might explain why women's rate of admission to mental hospitals is higher then men's. (12 marks)

Exam Practice

(e) Outline and assess the contribution of labelling theory to an understanding of mental illness. (60 marks)

The medical professions in society

getting you thinking

Untrained and out of control: health chiefs target rogue plastic surgeons

By F. Elliot and M. Fitzwilliams

MINISTERS are planning to overhaul Britain's booming cosmetic surgery industry after a review found shocking evidence that vulnerable patients are being exploited by untrained and unscrupulous medics.

Potentially dangerous procedures are being carried out by surgeons with no specific training on patients misled by exaggerated or false claims ... A string of high-profile blunders that have left women permanently disfigured has helped to alert the public to the dangers ... Botched tummy tucks, leaking breast implants and bodged botox injections are among a rising number of horror stories emerging.

The Independent on Sunday (12 September 2004)

1 Would you ever consider plastic surgery or other cosmetic treatment, such as botox injections? Why?

2 Do you think that people should have a right to plastic surgery?

3 Do you think that there are any grounds on which doctors should have the right to refuse to perform some plastic surgery if they think it inappropriate – even if you are willing to pay? If so, what are they?

4 Do you think that tattooists should have similar powers to refuse?

5 Which occupational groups (if any) do you trust more than doctors?

6 Why do you trust doctors?

Members of the medical profession are among the most prestigious and well-paid groups in society. But how did they get this superior status? Was it really through their greater abilities, as they would have us believe?

Sociologists are always suspicious of the claims groups make about themselves, and, as you might expect, their views are not always totally supportive of the caring, dedicated image the medical professions like to present. In this topic, we are going to explore the reasons sociologists suggest provide the basis for the power, prestige and affluence of the medical professions. This exploration of the medical professions is useful in its own right, helping us to understand the nature of medical provision in Britain, but it is also a helpful model for understanding how other occupational groups have arrived in their particular position. Some of these, such as the legal profession, have been successful in obtaining prestige and financial rewards, while others, such as the teaching profession, have been much less successful.

There are five main sociological approaches to understanding the position and role of the medical professions. These are:

- *the functionalist argument* – that the medical profession benefits society
- *the Weberian approach* – that the medical profession is just an occupational strategy to get higher income and status
- *the Marxist view* – that the medical profession acts to control the majority of the population and is rewarded for this by the ruling class
- *Foucault's suggestion* – that the power of the medical profession has emerged as a result of their ability to define what is prestigious knowledge
- *the feminist approach* – that the medical profession can best be understood by seeing how it has controlled and marginalized women.

The functionalist approach: professions as a benefit to society

The first approach to understanding the role of the professions developed from the functionalist school of sociology (see Unit 1

Topic 1), associated with the writing of Talcott Parsons, which seeks to show what functions the various parts of society play in helping society to exist.

Barber (1963) argued that professions, especially the medical professions, are very important for society because they deal with people when they are in particularly vulnerable positions. It is, therefore, in the interests of society to have the very best people, who maintain the highest standards, to provide medical care. These people must not only be competent but they must also be totally trustworthy. According to functionalists, true professions can be recognized by the fact that they share a number of 'traits'. These are as follows:

● They have a *theoretical basis* to their knowledge – Doctors have a full understanding of medical theories about the body. This allows them to make independent decisions about the cause of illness and the best cure.
● They are *fully trained* to the highest possible standards – Only the most intelligent can enter and succeed.
● Competence is *tested by examination* – There is no favouritism and doctors are in their position as a result of their ability alone.
● The profession has a *strict code of* '**ethics**' – Doctors deal with people at their most vulnerable and the code of ethics ensures that no patient is exploited.
● They are *regulated and controlled* through an organization (in the case of doctors it is the General Medical Council) which decides who can enter the profession and has the power to punish and exclude for any misconduct.

Critics of the functionalist approach,such as Waitzkin (1979), while agreeing that high standards and trust are all needed, argue that these 'traits' merely justify the high status of doctors. The medical profession simply uses them as barriers to prevent others from entering. This criticism was for a long time supported by the fact that entry to medicine remained largely the preserve of males from higher social-class backgrounds. Only in the last 20 years has there been a significant inflow of women and ethnic minorities into the medical profession. This inflow has largely coincided with an acceptance of the criticisms of the functionalist approach.

The Weberian approach: professionalization as a strategy

The second approach to understanding the power of the medical professions is that, rather than being constructed for the good of the community, they are, in fact, constructed for the good of the medical professions themselves. This argument has developed from the original writings of Max Weber, an early 20th-century sociologist who argued that all occupational groups are constantly vying with one another to improve their prestige and financial bargaining power. There are a number of different techniques used, but the two main ones are the creation of trades unions (which has traditionally been used by the working class) and the construction of professions (which has been used by the middle class).

Overall, **professionalization** of an occupational group has actually been a more effective method to gain status and financial rewards. It is for this reason that many other groups, such as teachers and social workers, have tried to gain professional status.

The process of professionalization has four important dimensions:

1 *The production of a body of* **esoteric** *knowledge* – This means creating an apparently complex body of knowledge which must be placed in the hands of experts.
2 *Educational barriers* – Professionals construct a series of specialist educational courses and qualifications in order to limit the numbers of entrants.
3 *Exclusion of competition* – The profession must wipe out any possible competitors, such as faith healers, homeopaths and herbalists. They do this by claiming that only scientific medicine and surgery are effective.
4 *Maintenance of privilege* – The professional group will fight all attempts to have others impose any control over them. So doctors will demand '**clinical freedom**' – the right to do what they think best – and they will fight any attempts to hand over part of their work to others, such as allowing nurses to prescribe medicines.

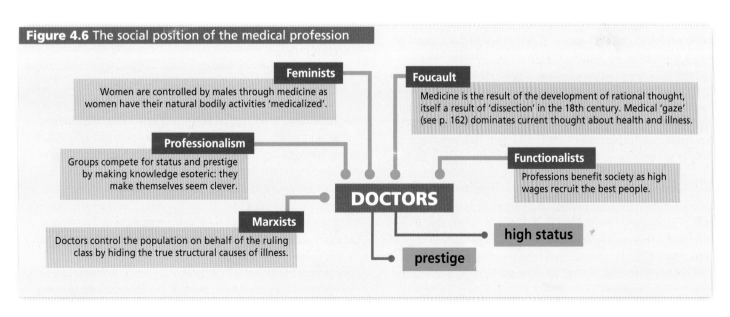

Figure 4.6 The social position of the medical profession

Feminists
Women are controlled by males through medicine as women have their natural bodily activities 'medicalized'.

Foucault
Medicine is the result of the development of rational thought, itself a result of 'dissection' in the 18th century. Medical 'gaze' (see p. 162) dominates current thought about health and illness.

Professionalism
Groups compete for status and prestige by making knowledge esoteric: they make themselves seem clever.

Functionalists
Professions benefit society as high wages recruit the best people.

Marxists
Doctors control the population on behalf of the ruling class by hiding the true structural causes of illness.

DOCTORS

high status

prestige

These four methods of professionalizing are very similar to the traits suggested by functionalist writers. From a Weberian perspective, therefore, the medical profession is looking after its own interests as well as those of the patients.

Marxist approaches

Marxists, such as Navarro (1977), argue that in capitalist societies such as Britain, a small ruling class exploits society for its own benefit. In order to hide this exploitation from people and to maintain its power, the ruling class employs a number of mechanisms, which involve distorting 'reality', so that people come to accept exploitation as 'natural'.

The medical profession plays an important role in this by misleading the population as to the real cause of their illnesses. The medical profession explains health and illness in terms of individuals' actions and genetics – they point the finger away from the poor working conditions, poverty, poor housing and inequalities in society, which are the true, underlying causes of ill health, according to Marxist writers. But what doctors do succeed in doing for the health of the population is to keep them fit enough to work.

Marxists also point out that health and illness in a capitalist society are carefully linked to being able to work or not. Doctors play a key role in deciding who is fit to work and who is sick enough to be eligible for state disability and sickness benefits.

Critics have pointed out that this perspective ignores the genuinely beneficial work that doctors do, and that to characterize their work as only misleading and controlling the population is inaccurate. Doctors do work very much within the framework of looking at individual problems, but stress in the workplace and the role of poverty are well known and recognized by doctors.

Foucault's approach

There is an old saying, 'knowledge is power', and in Foucault's analysis of society this is literally true. According to Foucault (1976), in every society, groups are 'battling' to look after their own interests. The best way of doing this is to get control of what is regarded as 'truth' or 'knowledge'. If other people believe that what you say is 'true' and what others say is 'false', then you have a high chance of getting them to do what you want. So you seek to create an overall framework of thought and ideas, within which all the more specific debates (what Foucault calls '**discourses**') are conducted. This argument is similar in some ways to the Marxist argument we saw earlier.

Foucault argues that, over time, doctors have led the way in helping to construct an idea of 'science', through their activities in dissecting bodies and demonstrating to people the ways in which bodies are constructed in the form of a 'biological machine'. This has resulted in a society where rational scientific thought is prized above all else, where other forms of thought are regarded as inferior, and where doctors have significant prestige and power.

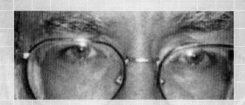

Harold Shipman

It is estimated that the doctor Harold Shipman killed over 250 of his patients. It is thought that he is the most prolific mass murderer in British legal history. He injected elderly patients with too high levels of morphine, thus killing them.

Although he had a much higher number of unexplained deaths than most GPs in Britain and he had one of the highest uses of morphine in Britain, he was able to get away with murdering his patients for almost 30 years.

1 If a relative of yours had died unexpectedly after a visit from a doctor, do you think that you would have questioned it? Please explain your answer.

2 Why do you think Harold Shipman managed to get away with murder for so long?

So medicine has played a major part in constructing the way we think and act in contemporary society. In the process, the medical professions have gained considerable benefits in terms of prestige and financial rewards.

The medical gaze

Foucault's writings move beyond simply exploring the role of the medical profession to the much wider areas of social control in society. He argues that at any particular period in society, one form of thinking about issues dominates – he uses the term 'discourse' to describe this. In some ways, the term is similar to the Marxist notion of 'ideology', as it provides a framework for perceiving the world.

Applied to medicine, the discourse provides ways of thinking and making sense of the human body, including disease, sexuality and reproduction. During the 19th and 20th centuries, medicine developed certain dominant discourses that framed the way in which the medical profession operated. This resulted in doctors viewing the human body as a biological organism that they could explore in order to find the illness, with the views or experiences of the patient becoming of little importance. The core task of medicine is, therefore, to examine the body in order to search for certain clues as to the illness, using visual inspection, touch and medical technology. As part of this examination, patients are compared with what is considered 'the norm' of the body. Variations from the expected normal body can, therefore, provide the clues as to the illness.

Foucault used the term 'the **medical gaze**' to describe these ways that doctors perceive the body and examine it for clues.

The medical gaze has two important implications for society as a whole:

- The first is actually in the development of social sciences, for Foucault sees this form of disinterested searching for deviations from the norm in order to understand and explain problems as just the task that sociology, psychology and the other social sciences engage in. As an example, he points to the study of explanations for inequalities in health (epidemiology), where sociologists have followed the methods of 'the medical gaze' in looking for clues as to the reasons in health differences by concentrating on how certain groups and individuals engage in health-related behaviour that deviates from the norm – for example the impact of smoking, of eating poor foods or excessive alcohol consumption.
- The second implication for the wider society of the medical gaze is the fact that certain body types and body mechanisms (pulse and heart rates, blood pressure) come to be seen as normal, and so those who have different body shapes and mechanisms come to be seen as deviant. Therefore, Foucault points out, society develops from this desirable and undesirable body types with the emergence of concept of obesity, for example. Furthermore, the need to categorize that emerges from the medical gaze has also helped to construct the clear distinction between heterosexual and homosexual, a categorization of sexual types that is relatively recent (see opposite page).

The significance of the discourse of modern medicine and the medical gaze do not stop at just the construction of body types, but, as just mentioned, implies that certain types of body, of sexuality and, indeed, ways of living are superior to others. In modern medicine and modern society, for example, it is regarded as deviant to be 'fat'. An entire industry has developed around this perceived need to slim. Foucault argues that medicine is heavily involved in a process that he calls 'disciplinarity', by which he means that medicine (along with a range of other professions, such as social work, teaching and psychiatry) are all engaged in controlling behaviour of people to coincide with what is believed to be medically and socially preferable. The methods of discipline used do not necessarily use coercion or punishment, but are much more likely to be based on appeals to common sense and to medical necessity, and to be based on caring.

Disciplinary practices have extended out of medicine to the situation whereby certain types of body shapes, child-rearing, sexual practices, food choices and leisure activities are regarded as desirable. A good example of this disciplinarity is the government's 10-year plan to increase standards of health by encouraging people to exercise, have regular health checks (including control of weight and blood pressure), engage in leisure activities, and limit drug and alcohol intake.

Foucault and body-centeredness

As the discourses centring on the best form of body and of lifestyle has developed, so too has a more wider concern with the body and 'looking after oneself'. The moral obligation to take care of the body goes beyond the medical; how the body looks to others takes on particular importance – body building, diet and cosmetics (as well as fashionable clothing) all become extremely important as people develop what has become known as '**body fetishism**', i.e. an extreme stress on how one appears in public. Fetishism leads beyond this, however, to the reconstruction of the body through surgical intervention to the face, bust and even the sexual organs.

However, this extension of the idea of the medical discourse has been criticised by Marxists, who argue that Foucault has missed the central point, which is that an entire industry has developed in late capitalism which profits through the obsession with body and which encourages the trend. Marxists argue that capitalism constantly seeks new markets to exploit and the concern with the body simply reflects this.

163

synoptic link

Doctors have high levels of social status in Western societies. How they have achieved this is a matter of some debate between Marxist, functionalist and Weberian writers, as we have seen in the text. According to Marxists, doctors perform the useful function in capitalism of maintaining health and ensuring that only the truly sick avoid working. Weberians concentrate instead on the way that doctors have used the strategy of professionalization to improve their status. Finally, functionalists have stressed the fact that doctors are highly educated and a scarce resource that must be well rewarded by society. In many ways, examining the class position of the medical professions provides a focused set of examples of the competing sociological explanations for the class position of the middle class in general.

social inequality and difference

Focusing on doctors also illustrates the changes which have taken place in the role of women in society. Fifty years ago, the overwhelming majority of doctors were male; women who aspired to be doctors had to fight against a significant number of barriers. Today, however, there are more female doctors being trained than male doctors (although the majority of doctors overall are male because of the historical legacy of so few women being trained in the past). It seems likely that in the next 50 years, the majority of doctors will be women. These changes simply reflect the changing position of women in employment in Britain and their movement into higher positions. However, despite the increased numbers of female doctors, just as in the wider employment market, the higher-status jobs in medicine are still dominated by men.

Feminist approaches

Feminist sociologists, such as Oakley (1986) and Witz (1992), suggest that the activities of doctors contribute to the social control of women, both as patients and as medical practitioners. They point out that medicine has traditionally been a male occupation, with women excluded or marginalized into junior roles. This simply reinforces the subordinate position of women in society. (However, in the last 15 years, roughly equal numbers of men and women have been training to be doctors.)

Historically, women had always held a key role in healing and traditional healthcare. For example, the women who we now refer to as 'witches' were very often herbal healers who were eagerly sought out in rural areas. There had always been a degree of competition between male and female healthcare practitioners and it was not until 1885 that a law was passed which legally recognized a closed medical profession. Although women were not legally prevented from entering the medical profession, because of the values of Victorian Britain, and because of the nature of the educational system which generally excluded women from higher education, the outcome of the act was that they were effectively prevented from becoming doctors.

Techniques to exclude women from the medical profession

According to Witz, the male-dominated medical profession was successful in excluding females for over half a century by using two techniques – exclusion and demarcation:

- *Exclusion* involves creating barriers so that it is virtually impossible for other groups (in this case females) to enter the profession.
- *Demarcation* involves creating a restricted area of competence and then allowing people to enter this area. At the same time, this area of competence is still controlled by the medical profession. Examples of this include nursing and radiography.

Witz further argues that to combat these techniques, women have used two strategies – inclusion and dual closure:

- *Inclusion* involves using any possible method of gaining entry through, for example, political and legal action.
- The aim of *dual closure* is to accept in part a restricted area of competence, but then to close this off to others and to seek to turn it into a profession. It is exactly this process that is happening to nursing.

The 'medicalization' process

Feminist sociologists, such as Lupton (1994), also claim that the male-dominated profession of medicine has successfully 'medicalized' a number of female problems. By this, they mean that normal or natural activities of women (such as childbirth and menopause), or problems faced more often by women (such as depression), have been taken over by the medical profession and turned into medical issues. So, for example, women are expected to give birth in the manner and in the place determined by 'the experts'. For Lupton, this means that male doctors can use this as a means of controlling how women ought to act. According to Lupton, through this process:

>> *Women are placed in a position of compliance with expert advice throughout their pregnancy and delivery, and their personal needs and wishes tend to be ignored.*>> (Lupton 1994, p. 148)

Depression

When it comes to an 'illness' such as depression – which feminists argue is partly a result of the restricted role of women in society – the medical profession turns it into a medical problem that can be solved by prescribing medicines. This shifts the issue away from the position of women in general, to the particular medical condition of a single woman. One example of the creation of female illness and resulting medical treatment, according to Wertz and Wertz (1981), was the treatment of upper-class women in Victorian Britain. Links were made between the female reproductive and sexual organs and a whole range of illnesses including headaches, sore throats, indigestion and 'inappropriate libido'. This resulted in 'routine' hysterectomies, removals of ovaries and clitorectomies.

Reproduction and childbirth

Lesley Doyal (1994) has suggested that medicalization has been particularly powerful when it comes to control of reproduction and childbirth. In terms of reproduction, Doyal argues that women do not have full control over the decision to become pregnant and to remain so. She argues that pregnancy and child-rearing is one of the major ways in which men control women, and that religious and social pressure in many societies limit women's access to contraception and abortion. In most Western societies, it is the medical profession that has become the main agency deciding on 'appropriate' use of contraception and abortion facilities. According to Doyal, it is the right of women to make choices in these areas rather than the medical profession.

Feminists, however, have focused most of their analysis on the way that doctors have taken control of the process of childbirth, as we mentioned above. Although childbirth is a natural process which historically women controlled themselves, during the 19th century a gradual process of medicalization occurred whereby women (including the original midwives) lost control of the process to the male-dominated medical profession. Childbirth shifted from a natural process to a medical process that required the expectant mothers to come under the control of doctors. Midwives, too, came to be responsible to doctors, losing their autonomy. As we saw earlier with Foucault, certain types of childbirth and behaviour during pregnancy came to be 'normal' and women were disciplined into following the 'correct procedures'. It is only relatively recently that feminist campaigning has given back elements of control to women.

The role of the medical professions in the construction of sexuality

It may seem strange to include a section on sexuality in a unit about health, yet the medical professions have played a key role in shaping our views on human sexuality.

Essentialism versus social constructionism

In Topic 1, we explored the way that a seemingly natural or biological event – illness – could also be understood as something that is socially constructed. Sexuality, too, can be viewed in much the same way. Some commentators, such as Wilson (1978), believe that sexual orientations are 'natural', and that people can be divided into categories such as heterosexual, homosexual and lesbian – or even paedophiles and 'perverts' – a position known as **essentialism**. Other sociologists, such as McIntosh (1968), put forward a social constructionist position that sees sexual 'identity' as being socially created. Indeed, McIntosh suggests that the very notion of homosexuals and heterosexuals never occurred before the 17th century and the term was not widely used until the 19th century.

Social constructions of homosexuality

One of the most influential writers who argued for the notion of the social construction was Foucault (1981), who suggested that the concept of a homosexual person first developed in the 19th century, when there was both an explosion of interest in the academic study of sexuality and, running parallel, a forceful repression of the expression of sexual activity. Before this period, sexual activity between men was relatively commonplace, but was not seen as indicating that the men involved were a different sort of person called a 'homosexual'; it was seen as just another form of sexual activity. However, as a result of the development of scientific methods based on the categorization of individual objects, people and animals into classes and categories in order to study and understand them, the medical profession began to categorize and distinguish between groups of people on the grounds of their sexual preference. One result, among many others, was the classification of people into groupings which were believed to have a real, objective existence. And so, the categories of homosexual and heterosexual came about. Interestingly, there was hardly any interest in the construction of the category of 'lesbian'. This possibly reflects the dominance of males in the medical, scientific and psychiatric professions.

Weeks (1992) has extended some of Foucault's ideas and suggests that since the 19th century, sex has gained an increasingly important role in the identities of individuals, to the point in contemporary society where it is seen as a central element in the identity of many men and women.

Reproductive model of female sexual identity

Foucault's argument that homosexual identity (as opposed to homosexual activity) was a construction of the 19th century challenged many established notions about sexuality, but the work of Laqueur is, if anything, more challenging. Laqueur (1990) argues that the modern notions of women as sexual beings completely distinct from males also came about in the 19th century. According to Laqueur, before that time, women and men were seen as being essentially the same, and women's need and desire for sexual pleasure was regarded as similar to that of men. The major difference was that the male body was seen as superior to the female body – based largely on its greater physique. The 19th century, however, saw the development of a distinctive 'reproductive model' of women, in which their role was to bear and look after babies. This period also saw the emergence of the idea that women lacked (or ought to lack) sexual feelings and desires.

Social construction of 'prostitute'

Medical activity also helped to stabilize the category of 'prostitute', according to Saraga (1998), through a similar process. Saraga points to the way that by defining women in a particular way, then different approaches to healthcare can be used. The modern concept of prostitute developed, along with other sexual types in the 19th century, as part of the general process of categorization described above. However, when sexually transmitted diseases were found to be a growing threat to the health of the population, medical advice to the government led to the passing of a series of Acts in the 1860s (the Contagious Diseases Acts) by which 'common prostitutes' could be forcibly examined every two weeks. Refusing or evading the examination could lead to a period in prison. However, the issue of examining men (the main group to spread the disease) never arose. Therefore, the newly constructed category of prostitute – itself partly an outcome of the growth of medicine – led to different health policies towards them.

The rise of complementary medicine

The traditional male-dominated medical profession's monopoly over healthcare has been strongly challenged over the last 20 years. Within the profession, there has been an influx of ethnic minorities and women, and from outside the profession the claim to sole expertise on health matters has been challenged by a wide range of groups. Perhaps the biggest external challenge

KEY TERMS	
Body fetishism – an extreme stress on how one appears in public.	**Essentialism** – belief that categories such as sexual orientation are 'natural' and that people can be categorized, for example, as heterosexual or homosexual.
Clinical freedom – the right of doctors to do what they think is best without other people having a say.	**Esoteric** – obscure and accessible only to a few.
Discourse – see Key terms on p. 147.	**Ethics** – a code of behaviour.
Disciplinarity – the way that medicine (and professions such as social work and teaching) seek to control people's behaviour so that it coincides with what is believed to be medically and socially preferable.	**Medical gaze** – the ways that doctors perceive the body and examine it for clues to illness, using visual inspection, touch and medical technology.
	Professionalization – a tactic used by occupational groups to gain prestige and financial rewards.

Cant and Sharma (2002)
Chiropractic

Cant and Sharma studied the rise in the status of complementary medicine, using chiropractic as an example. (Chiropractic is the manipulation of the spine, joints and muscles in order to realign them.) For over 60 years, chiropractors campaigned to gain legal recognition, which was finally granted in an act of parliament in 1994. Cant and Sharma point out that in order to get this recognition, chiropractors undertook a number of activities.

1 Divisions within the profession were resolved, with the more controversial wing of the profession – who claimed that chiropractic could heal a wide range of non-muscular/skeletal problems – accepting the need to drop their claims, as they were too controversial for the dominant medical profession.
2 They worked hard to gain the approval of the established medical profession, acknowledging its dominant position and dropping any claims to provide an alternative, competing model of healthcare.
3 The chiropractors had to accept that, within the NHS, they could only see patients if they were referred by doctors. This meant that they became dependent upon the goodwill of doctors.
4 They had to accept that they had no legal monopoly (as doctors do) to practise their techniques of bone and muscle manipulation. Anyone else can do this, but they cannot call themselves chiropractors.

Cant and Sharma's research is an excellent example of how the medical profession has continued to work to maintain its dominance of healthcare. Any group offering alternative models, such as chiropractors, has to accept an inferior role if they are to gain any form of legal recognition.

Source: Cant, S. and Sharma, U. (2002) 'The state and complementary medicine: a changing relationship?', in S. Nettleton and U. Gustafsson *The Sociology of Health and Illness Reader*, Cambridge: Polity

1 What compromises did chiropractors have to make in order to gain legal recognition?
2 How did the medical profession ensure that chiropractic had to 'accept an inferior role' in order to be recognized?

has come from complementary or alternative medicines, including homeopathy, herbal remedies, acupuncture and a range of other techniques (see Focus on research, left).

Giddens (1991) has argued that this is the result of the development of late modern society. Two particularly relevant characteristics of late modernity are:

1 decline in conformity, with a greater stress on individual desire and choice
2 disillusionment with the claims of professionals and experts in general to have a monopoly of knowledge, leading to a decline in the acceptance that 'doctor knows best' and an increased demand for choice in what 'cures' and interventions the ill person should undergo.

A third, less significant element of late modernity, which is particularly relevant to mental illness, is that a much wider range of behaviour is tolerated. This makes the distinction between deviant or marginally tolerated behaviour and mental illness far less clear.

Check your understanding

1 Give two examples of the 'traits' of a profession, according to functionalists.
2 According to the 'professionalization' approach, how do professions exclude other competing occupational groups?
3 How do the actions of doctors, in explaining why we are ill and then prescribing medicines, help capitalism?
4 Give one example of how doctors have 'medicalized' a normal activity of women?
5 According to Foucault, what is the relationship between knowledge and power over people?
6 What are the implications for society of Foucault's idea of the 'medical gaze'?
7 How does Foucault argue that the category of 'homosexual' is socially constructed?

web.tasks

1 **Visit the Royal College of Nursing website at www.rcn.org.uk**

What aspects of the discussion in this topic are illustrated here? (You could start with the image on the home page!) It is also useful to look at the section on the RCN's 'mission'.

2 **Visit the General Medical Council website at www.gmc-uk.org**

What points in this topic does this website illustrate (and also perhaps challenge!).

exploring the medical professions in society

Item A

« It is commonly held that nursing, since becoming a profession (the first register was set up in 1919), has progressed to become a higher-status, centrally recognized healthcare profession. Yet the crucial distinction between nursing and medicine remains: that of curing versus caring. Nursing's professional bodies are caught in a double-bind: in order to be of high status, the profession must lay claim to clinical and curative skills, but in order to remain as 'nursing', the practice must be centred on caring for, not curing, patients.

This dilemma has been addressed in part by the conscious formation of a body of theoretical knowledge, the nursing process, which is particular to nursing and distinct from medicine. To some extent, this has also been the rationale behind the most recent developments in nurse education, for example, the creation of the new Project 2000 and the possibility of a degree in nursing, which superseded the old apprentice-style ward-based training of 'pupil' nurses.»

Marsh, I. (2000) *Sociology: Making Sense of Society*, Harlow: Prentice Hall

Item B

« Professional bodies (such as the General Medical Council) are charged with supervising the profession. But, being members of that profession, they usually whitewash or ignore cases of incompetence, etc. Final sanctions, like striking a doctor off the medical register, are used only rarely and then more often for sexual misconduct than for gross incompetence.»

Trowler, P. (1996) *Investigating Health, Welfare and Poverty*, London: Collins Educational

Item C

« For functionalist sociologists the higher professions such as medicine are virtually beyond reproach. Professionals are seen as selfless individuals working for the good of the community, often making great personal sacrifices. They need to be of the highest intelligence and skill, have to undergo years of training and in their early careers earn very little. High levels of reward later, then, are necessary to attract, retain and motivate the best people into the professions.»

Trowler, P. (1996) *Investigating Health, Welfare and Poverty*, London: Collins Educational

(a) Using **Item B**, identify **one** example of a 'professional body'. (1 mark)

(b) Identify and briefly explain **two** ways in which nursing has attempted to improve its status in recent years **(Item A)**. (8 marks)

(c) Give **three** reasons why professional bodies might 'ignore cases of incompetence'. (9 marks)

(d) Identify and briefly explain **two** reasons why functionalists argue that professionals deserve high rewards. (12 marks)

Exam practice

(e) Outline and assess the view that professionalization in the medical professions is simply a strategy for ensuring high status and rewards. (60 marks)

---

research ideas

1 Ask a small sample of people to identify five characteristics they associate with doctors. Do your results support the points made in the topic?

2 Identify a small sample of people who have actually used some form of 'alternative' healing. Conduct unstructured interviews to uncover their motives in seeking the treatment and the meaning they gave to their experiences.

AT THE TIME OF WRITING, the main talking point in the academic journals is concerns the role of sociology in society. The head of the American Sociological Association has suggested that sociology ought to get its hands dirty and involve itself in policy issues rather than 'just' theorizing. The response on both sides of the Atlantic has been very strong – with some sociologists arguing that the role of sociology is to theorize and push the boundaries of knowledge, and others saying that sociology as a subject has lots of useful things to say and it should be influencing government policy. In this unit, we look at a number of very applied issues, exploring what sociology has to say about the welfare state. Perhaps it is this one area of sociology – generally known as 'social policy' – where the sociologists do get involved in examining issues that have very direct impact on the lives of everyone, but particularly the most disadvantaged in society.

We begin, in Topic 1, by examining the development of welfare in Britain. Many people believe that the welfare state simply developed over time – few realize the immense political battles that led to its creation shortly after the Second World War. Sociologists have taken very different approaches towards explaining why it emerged and we will explore these different ideas to see what insights they can give us.

The second topic is an extension of this theoretical debate. Social policy as an academic subject combines sociology with politics (and a bit of economics) and applies the resulting mix of ideas towards explaining welfare provision. This topic provides a detailed overview of the theoretical ideas and ideological perspectives that have been used to understand the welfare state.

The following three topics examine, in considerable detail, what might be considered the core elements of the welfare state (apart from health, which has already been explored as a topic in its own right) – these areas are housing, social care and social security.

For many people, housing is something they take for granted, yet for others the idea of adequate housing of decent quality remains simply a pipe dream. Housing differences are one of the clearest indicators of inequality in Britain, with some people sleeping on the streets and millions of others living in substandard or overcrowded homes.

Social security refers to the financial support system provided by the state. Although we still use the term social security, the old idea of unemployed people queuing outside an office to receive government benefits has now substantially been replaced by millions of people receiving tax 'credits' in their wage slips. How this came about and the significance for the society is discussed in some depth.

Finally, in Topic 5, on social care, we examine the work of all those people, voluntary and employed by local authorities or the NHS, who provide services for people who are in need of support. The topic examines the different sociological approaches to social care and the changing nature of provision – especially from residential to community care.

Social policy and welfare

The history of welfare

1 Using the photographs on the right, as well as your own ideas, identify which groups of people in British society you think are going to find it most difficult to provide for their own needs. Explain your answer.

2 Which of the two statements below do you feel most matches your own views? Explain your answer.

3 Do you think that government support for people creates any problems or dangers? Explain your answer.

- Statement A: **We need to support the most vulnerable people in society.**
- Statement B: **People should take responsibility for their own lives.**

The questions above raise some very basic issues about the relationship between the government – or state – and its citizens. Politicians and public alike have some strong views about the extent to which the government should intervene in people's lives by taking money in the form of taxation. There are also sharply divided opinions as to how the money should be spent. It might surprise you to know that these arguments are by no means new. To find their origin, we need to go way back to the reign of Elizabeth I.

Early welfare

Although most people think of the start of the welfare state as being 1945, in fact, the history of welfare provision by the state dates back at least 400 years before that. The first major attempt to help the old and the sick was the Elizabethan Poor Law (1601), which imposed upon parishes the requirement to provide almshouses (the equivalent of hospitals/old people's homes) for the local old and sick. Two solutions to the problem of poverty emerged. The first was to provide an institution where the poor were expected to work and earn their keep. An alternative was a system of **outdoor relief** where those who earned less than the local **minimum wage** received an additional sum from the parish. (This is very similar to current British policy of income support!)

Welfare in the 19th century

By the early 19th century, this system was near collapse as a result of changing values and the rapid demographic and economic changes brought about by industrialization. The outcome was the 1834 Poor Law Act. This was based upon the idea that there were two types of poor people:

- *the deserving poor* – those who were poor through no fault of their own (such as widows and disabled people)
- *the undeserving poor* – those whose poverty was a result of defects in the individuals, such as laziness or lack of planning.

The Act abolished 'outdoor relief' and introduced the **workhouse** where all the poor had to go. The conditions in the workhouse were to be so dire that only someone truly desperate would go there. This was the principle of **less eligibility**. The Poor Law Act was not finally abolished until the late 1920s, but by then it had changed dramatically and many of the elements of the welfare state as we know it today had come into being.

The 19th century also saw the first tentative beginnings of government intervention in education (1870) and, to a lesser extent, in providing housing (1875). Medical provision by the government was, however, limited to public hospitals for those with physical disability or suffering from mental illness. The general view was that the provision of health and welfare was not the duty of the government and was better left to charity. Nineteenth-century attitudes to poverty were based on the belief that poverty was the result of individual circumstance rather than the way society was organized. Debates on welfare focused primarily on how to distinguish between those who deserved welfare and those who did not. It was not until the turn of the 20th century that a group of writers and intellectuals known as **Fabians** began to question this view and to gain ground in their argument that the real causes of poverty were built into the system of uncontrolled capitalism.

1900 to 1945: the beginnings of the welfare state

The early part of the 20th century saw the beginnings of the modern system of welfare. Partly in response to the debates taking place as a result of a Royal Commission on the Poor Law and partly out of fear of the threat of the new Labour Party, the Liberal Governments in 1908 and 1911 introduced old age pensions (1908), compulsory health insurance for a section of the workforce (1911) and unemployment insurance (1911). Although these would now be regarded as of very low value and extremely limited in their scope, they were, in fact, major breakthroughs. The government, for the first time, was accepting responsibility for the welfare of its citizens in the areas of pensions, health and unemployment.

The system was not based upon **means-testing**, with its associated **stigma**, but on the principle that everyone paid **insurance** against the possibility of ill health and unemployment, and therefore had a right to claim – rather than it being charity. This was significant because before this, when poor or sick people asked for help from charities or local government, they had no rights. In fact, only if the organization providing the assistance felt that the individual deserved help would they give it. Means-testing, for example, involved finding out if there was anybody in the family who could provide help before there was the possibility of the charity or local government department taking any responsibility.

After the end of the 1914–18 War, the government also accepted that it had a duty to provide housing (or allow local authorities to do so) and so large-scale public housing estates were built. This was a direct result of declarations made by politicians during the 1914–18 War, when they promised 'homes fit for heroes' to the men in the trenches on their return home. Educational provision also expanded up to the 1939–45 War – largely in response to the need for a skilled and educated workforce.

1945 to 1970s: a welfare consensus?

In 1941, Sir William Beveridge was commissioned by the wartime Prime Minister, Churchill, to investigate improved welfare schemes. Beveridge's report in 1942 proposed a comprehensive welfare state, based upon tackling what he called the five 'giant evils' of:

1 'Want' = poverty
2 'Disease' = ill health
3 'Ignorance' = inadequate educational facilities
4 'Squalor' = poor housing
5 'Idleness' = unemployment.

Beveridge was viewed by the government as having gone beyond his brief in proposing the construction of a welfare state that would care for people from 'the cradle to the grave' and his work was initially ignored. However, the 1945 Labour Government took up his plan and it was introduced between 1946 and 1948.

The Beveridge welfare state

Poverty

Three steps were taken to tackle poverty:

● Family Allowances were introduced, a universal benefit that meant that every family received state payments for children under 16.
● National Insurance was provided to cover all workers, giving a wide range of **benefits**, including sickness benefit, unemployment benefit and maternity benefits, as well as a retirement pension. The government, employers and employees all contributed.
● National Assistance – this was a form of safety net where those who, for whatever reason, were unable to contribute to the National Insurance, could claim benefits. National Assistance was means-tested, so only those who were poor could claim it.

The outcome of these new benefits was that, for the first time, the entire population of Britain would be guaranteed not to fall into **absolute poverty**.

Health

Perhaps the most radical piece of legislation was the introduction of the National Health Service. Before the 1939–45 War, healthcare was based upon a mixture of private, charitable and local-authority provision. For a large proportion of the population, healthcare was unavailable as they could not afford to pay, and there was no guarantee that they would obtain care from the charity or local-authority hospitals. The new NHS was based on three principles, which were radical at the time:

● that all services would be free to patients
● that the service would cover everyone in Britain
● that the provision would be based upon medical need, not the ability to pay.

Unemployment

Prior to the Second World War, levels of unemployment were regarded as inevitable consequences of changes in the economy. Governments largely avoided intervening in the economy as this was not considered to be their role. However, Beveridge's report and the growing sophistication of economic analyses persuaded the postwar Labour government to attempt to manipulate the economy in order to maintain a high level of employment. Furthermore, government 'employment exchanges' (today's Job Centres) were set up to help unemployed people find work.

Education

Just as the health service was introduced on the principle of medical need rather than on ability to pay, so the reforms in the education system were based on providing children with the education that best fitted their abilities. The 'tripartite' system that was introduced in 1944 was based on the belief that there were three types of children – the academic, the skilled and the less able. Children were divided at 11 and sent to the type of school that was regarded as best fitting their abilities. Although this may seem crude now, it was regarded at the time as a great step forward. The age at which children could leave school was also extended from 14 to 15.

Housing

One area that had been addressed prior to the 1939–45 War was that of housing, with local authorities engaging in massive council-house building programmes. The period after the war saw a continuation of this, linked to strict controls on where buildings could be constructed.

The development of welfare in a period of consensus

The 1950s and 1960s were characterized by a general consensus or agreement between the major political parties. Both main parties (Labour and Conservative) accepted the general provision of state welfare through the welfare state and much of the appeal to the voters consisted of who could be more efficient in providing services. The consensus was based on two factors:

- There was general political agreement that the Labour Party had no intention of bringing in significant social change based on socialist ideas. On the other hand, the Conservative Party had no desire to turn the clock back to the period before the 1939–45 War.
- The period from the 1950s through to the 1970s was largely one of unprecedented economic prosperity and it was possible to fund the welfare state. Furthermore, with low unemployment and a relatively young population, the burdens of pensions, unemployment and healthcare were relatively inexpensive.

An end to consensus: the debate over welfare in late modernity

By the early 1970s, Britain had a fully developed welfare state that offered a range of health and income support services. The system was still largely that originally suggested by Beveridge. However, the economic, social and political circumstances in which it operated were significantly different from the late 1940s. Consequently, the system came under sustained attack from both right-wing and left-wing views. The right felt that it was inefficient and overbureaucratic (i.e. too much time and money was spent on administration), while the left believed that it had failed to address the problems of poverty, poor housing and so on, that it had been set up to overcome. By the late 1970s, it is accurate to describe the situation as a welfare state in crisis. How this crisis was understood varied. Four broad views can be identified:

- social democratic
- Marxist
- New Right
- feminist and antiracist.

Social democratic views

The social democratic approach argued that although the welfare state was a significant step forward, it had failed in its primary purposes of eliminating poverty, ill health and the class-based differences in educational attainment. Research by Abel-Smith and Townsend (1965) showed that poverty was still as evident as at the beginning of the welfare state. Later research

synoptic link

social inequality and difference

Changes in the patterns of stratification in Britain are closely mirrored by changes in the provision of welfare to different groups in society. The introduction of the welfare state during the 1940s very closely reflected the class and gender divisions of that time. The 1940s were a period in which the huge turmoil of the Second World War (1939-45) threatened the pre-war political and social status quo. Large numbers of working-class men were returning from the armed forces back into civilian life and they were reluctant to accept the huge inequalities of the pre-war era. The welfare state was aimed at providing a range of benefits for working-class men engaging in manual labour and working in factories. These benefits would then filter through to their families. This reflected the historical period of modernity. However, by the 1970s, Britain had entered a period of late modernity with as many women as men working; with industry beginning to

decline as the major employer and office work increasing. The increase in women working reflected and brought about changes in family life.

Furthermore, the ethnic composition of the British population had changed substantially. The 1980s onward saw a tremendous change in welfare provision, in terms of economic benefits being increasingly directed to women and to lone-parent families in particular. There was also a recognition that ethnic-minority populations had different needs that had to be catered for by health and welfare organizations.

Finally, the increase in overall prosperity meant that the population as a whole would no longer accept minimum or 'safety net' standards from the welfare state, but wanted high-quality services. All of this led to the huge changes in welfare provision from the late 1990s onward.

into ill health, education and housing revealed similar patterns of inequality.

The introduction of the welfare state by the Labour Party was based on the belief that not only could the 'great evils' be eradicated, but also that progressive taxation (where the rich are taxed more heavily than the poor) would smooth out the income and wealth inequalities. However, research by Titmuss (1964) showed that these inequalities had hardly changed since the introduction of the welfare state. Later research by Le Grand (1982) suggested that the welfare state might actually increase inequalities as the middle classes made greater use of health, welfare and educational services than the poor.

Marxist views

Marxist commentators on the welfare state have split into two groups. One group of writers see it as simply another means by which the ruling class continue their control of the mass of the population, whilst giving relatively little away. On the other hand, an opposing view is that the welfare state has been won from the ruling class as a result of class conflict. In the 1970s, a new approach was introduced by writers such as O'Connor (1973), whose analyses combined the previous views. According to O'Connor, the welfare state was set up to ensure the continuation of capitalism through the provision of a fit, educated and disciplined workforce. However, there is an inherent contradiction in the notion of a welfare state. The costs of welfare prevent the growth of 'capital accumulation' – that is, they prevent the rich getting richer. This leads to demands for cuts in welfare – an 'accumulation crisis'. However, doing this can lead to a backlash from the mass of the population, who have become accustomed to having a welfare system – a 'legitimation crisis'. For writers such as O'Connor, capitalism and the welfare state are, therefore, in contradiction with one another. Either the welfare state is maintained at the expense of increases in wealth for the few, or welfare is cut.

New Right views

The New Right attacked the welfare state from two angles. The first was economic. Bacon and Eltis (1976) argued that the welfare state had become an enormous economic burden to society and it was no longer possible for Britain to afford it. According to them, the high levels of taxation on companies and individuals starved industry of investment and so undermined the ability of Britain to produce wealth. It is this very wealth that allows Britain to have a welfare state in the first place. Bacon and Eltis' writings occurred at just the time that Britain was undergoing a series of major economic crises that were increasing unemployment and causing significant union unrest. They appeared to provide a compelling explanation of the collapse of the British economy. Writers from the right also began a sustained attack on the very idea of state welfare. According to Hayek (1960), the growth of the welfare state meant the extension of the power of the state into people's lives, and a decrease in personal freedom. Hayek suggested that the welfare state was leading people on the 'road to serfdom'. In a similar vein, Boyson (1971) claimed that the more the state interfered with personal decision-making and provided an alternative to family and other informal networks of support, the faster these traditional structures would collapse, leading to an increasing reliance upon the state. An extension of this argument was put forward by Murray (1990), who claimed that an 'underclass' was developing – a generation that relied upon state welfare, preferring this to working and taking on family responsibilities.

Feminist and antiracist views

Feminists and antiracists argued that by the 1970s, the values and social relationships underlying the creation of the welfare state were no longer valid. From the feminist perspective, the belief that the role of the woman was primarily to be a housewife and that the entire benefit system should be based on a two-parent family, with the male as primary earner, were no longer necessarily true. This belief meant that the system failed to provide for women adequately. Antiracist campaigners pointed out the way that the welfare system, particularly the NHS, was based on the low-paid employment of ethnic minorities, yet discriminated against them in the very operation of the system.

1970s to 1990s: crisis and transition

Whichever one or more of the above analyses of the welfare state was correct, the outcome of the crisis of welfare in the 1970s was to the benefit of the New Right. A right-wing Conservative government came into power in 1979 and remained there until 1997. The Conservative leader, Margaret Thatcher (prime minister from 1979 to 1990), largely accepted the New Right analysis of the cause of the welfare state's problems. As a consequence of this, the government committed itself to:

- cutting back spending on health and welfare
- introducing competition from private providers of health and welfare
- introducing more efficient working practices from the business sector into the welfare state
- reducing the power of administrators and professionals within the health and welfare services.

The government was only partially successful in its aims as there turned out to be a number of contradictory elements to the New Right philosophy when put into practice:

1 The costs of the welfare state actually rose during the 1980s as the economic policies followed by the government led to increased unemployment and consequent huge increases in the costs of unemployment benefits and income support.

2 Government was unable to privatize the NHS and introduce private healthcare insurance because of huge support for the NHS amongst voters. Instead, the government attempted to bring commercial practices and 'internal competition' into the NHS. This actually resulted in an increase in administrative and managerial posts rather than a decline.

However, one area in which the government achieved radical change was in council housing. The '**right-to-buy**' legislation in 1980 allowed people in local-authority housing to purchase their properties. This was extremely popular, but has led to a decline in the availability of decent, low-cost, rented properties.

The welfare state in late modernity

Disillusionment with Conservative governments influenced by New Right thinking led to a period of New Labour control from 1997. New Labour claimed to be influenced by an ideological approach called 'the Third Way'. Though the Third Way claimed to be a distinctive approach, it seemed largely to adopt and adapt many of the policies of the New Right, while at the same time claiming to follow the approach of social democracy. The current system is based upon several factors:

● *Full employment* – This limits the numbers of people claiming social-security benefits. Those on low incomes and/or in part-time employment can now receive 'tax credits' from the government, which effectively are a means by which the government tops-up low pay through the income tax system.
● *The use of private and charitable organizations* to help deliver health, welfare and educational services – The government claims that these organizations tend to be more responsive to changing demands than the huge state monopolies of old. According to New Labour, the use of private finance to fund hospitals and other welfare state buildings saves money.
● *Increases in spending on health and welfare services* – New Labour has significantly increased spending in health, social care and education, and is committed to high levels of expenditure. This is the main difference from previous Conservative governments.

Welfare pluralism or state provision?

One of the debates that rages unabated is the one between those who argue that the best organization to provide health and welfare is the government, and those who argue that it is better to let private companies and charities take over the provision of these services – an approach known as **welfare pluralism**. New Labour, influenced by the Third Way approach, has largely accepted the idea of welfare pluralism, despite its origins in New Right thinking.

Those who argue that the state should provide health and welfare, point to the situation before the introduction of the welfare state in the 1930s and the way that health and welfare were delivered in an uncoordinated way by a variety of local authorities, profit-making companies and charities. For example, those who were affluent could afford to buy healthcare, whilst the less well-off usually had to rely upon charity or local-authority help.

However, the defenders of private health and welfare provision argue that government departments tend to be inefficient and wasteful. They operate with the interest of the bureaucrats and professionals in mind, rather than the patients or clients. Furthermore, there are positive benefits from using a mix of private and voluntary provision. Voluntary work helps to draw people together, reinforcing a sense of mutual purpose and solidarity – very much in the way that Durkheim (1960, first published 1894) saw as being crucial to the functioning of society. This contrasts with the view of Marshall (1975), who argues that a sense of citizenship created by a welfare state promotes social solidarity.

Since the 1980s, and at an increasing pace under New Labour governments since 1997, there has been a move towards the privatization or quasi-privatization of services. Nursing homes for older people are largely private but state financed, and private medical organizations have been paid to provide additional services to those of the NHS. Rented housing is provided by charitable housing associations, but is largely funded through state grants. Linked to this is the growing use of private finance – the **Private Finance Initiative (PFI)**. PFI is a means whereby the government enters into agreements for hospitals and other health or welfare services to be built (and sometimes run) by private companies. Despite these developments, the state still remains the main provider of health and welfare.

The move towards welfare pluralism has been bitterly criticized by supporters of the traditional welfare state. Webb and Wistow (1982), for example, point out that when there is no welfare state, just a mix of provision, many groups – usually viewed as less deserving – may not receive help. So welfare pluralism is not comprehensive. What is more, if people are able to pay for better health and welfare services, then these will not be based upon need but upon the ability to pay. Therefore, the inequalities that exist in society will be strengthened rather than broken down.

Check your understanding

1. **What was the Elizabethan Poor Law?**
2. **What distinction did the 1834 Poor Law make between different sorts of poor people?**
3. **What happened to poor people as a result of this law?**
4. **What was the Beveridge Report?**
5. **Give two examples of welfare reforms introduced by the Beveridge Report.**

research idea

Ask permission to visit a day centre or club for older people and record some of their memories of childhood before the welfare state and during its introduction.

web.task

Explore the history of the welfare state at the BBC History website at www.bbc.co.uk/history Type 'The Welfare State' into the search engine on the opening page on the site.

KEY TERMS

Absolute poverty – total destitution.

Benefits – used to refer to all payments (and/or welfare services) provided by the state.

Fabians – theoretical tradition that argues for a gradual move to a socialist society; extremely influential in the initial moves towards a welfare state in Britain (named after a Roman general who argued for gradual change).

Insurance – in area of welfare, financial/health benefits given out by the state as a result of people paying a certain amount into an insurance fund, to which they can apply when in need.

Less eligibility – the concept underlying the 1834 Poor Law (which created workhouses); conditions in the workhouses had to be so much worse than anything outside that only the truly poor would go there.

Means-tested – before a benefit can be received, the personal/household income is checked to see that it is low enough to qualify.

Minimum wage – government-set minimum amount that a person can be paid per hour.

Outdoor relief – policy on poverty introduced by the Elizabethan Poor Law of 1601; those earning below a certain wage received an additional sum from their local parish.

Private Finance Initiative – scheme introduced by New Labour government whereby the government enters into agreements for hospitals and other health or welfare services to be built (and sometimes run) by private companies.

Right-to-buy – legislation introduced in 1980 that allowed people renting from local authorities to buy the properties at a low price.

Stigma – feeling of being negatively labelled.

Welfare pluralism – situation where some welfare services are provided by the government directly and others by private or voluntary organizations.

Workhouse – in the 19th and early 20th century, poor people were not given state benefits, but expected to go and live (and work, if able) in these institutions; conditions were generally very poor.

exploring the history of welfare

Item A

Churchill thought Beveridge was 'an awful windbag and a dreamer', promoting 'false hopes and visions of Eldorado' (paradise). A secret committee was set up to prepare a brief on the report for the leaders of the Conservative Party. It claimed that the payment of social security was too expensive and would 'encourage malingering and laziness'.

Adapted from: Lund, B (2002) *Understanding State Welfare*, London: Sage

Item B

Two accounts of the evolution of welfare states dominate the literature. Some argue that industrialization and the social needs it generates, particularly unemployment and poverty, make the provision of state welfare more or less inevitable. Others argue that state welfare is won through political competition and follows the coming to political power of representatives of the interests of industrial workers or, more recently, other key groups such as women, ethnic minorities and disabled people.

Baldock, J., Manning, N. and Vickerstaff, S. (2003) *Social Policy*, Oxford: Oxford University Press, pp.19–20

Item C

For three reasons, the continuing viability of the existing welfare state is being questioned across Europe. The first is simply that the status quo will be difficult to sustain given adverse demographic and financial conditions. The second is that the same status quo seems increasingly out of date and ill-suited to meet the great challenges ahead. Third, our existing systems of social protection may hinder rather than promote employment growth. They may also be inadequate in the face of evolving, and possibly far more intense, social risks and needs.

Adapted from Esping Anderson, G. (2002) *Why We Need a Welfare State*, Oxford: Oxford University Press

(a) Using **Item A**, identify **one** criticism of the Beveridge's proposal for social-security payments. (1 mark)

(b) Identify and briefly explain **two** differing explanations for development of the welfare state **(Item B)**. (8 marks)

(c) Give **three** reasons why Esping Anderson questions the continuing viability of the welfare state across Europe **(Item C)**. (9 marks)

(d) Identify and explain **two** welfare policies introduced by governments after 1997. (12 marks)

Exam practice

(e) Outline and assess the view that the history of the welfare state shows that governments have always taken total responsibility for the welfare of the population. (60 marks)

Theories and ideologies of social policy

The Biggest Social Responsibility of All

Steve Tibbett, Director of Campaigns and Policy, War on Want, 5 April 2004

ACCORDING TO YVES PICAUD, Managing Director of water company Vivendi, 'if you don't pay for something, you will not appreciate it'. In the context of water, this may seem ridiculous, but it is also unsurprising. In a world where water is becoming a scarce resource, business interest in privatized water and other public services has made them into commodities rather than necessities.

The people of Kwazulu Natal in South Africa might have something to say to Picaud. When they could no longer afford water – post-privatization – they drank from streams. The ensuing cholera outbreak killed more than 250 people – the worst outbreak ever recorded.

Picaud's company now controls large swathes of the world's drinking water, applying the profit motive, like some ideological fluoride, to failing water services throughout the world. In years to come, water will increasingly become a flashpoint, both ideological and strategic.

Vivendi themselves say they are the world's largest water company, and that's exactly the point – when a company controls an asset, then that asset, in the language of the boardroom, must be made to work for the shareholders. It's a simple concept, and a problematic one when applied to public services in poor countries.

Vivendi says they 'place a high priority on maintaining social dialogue and social cohesion throughout our company'. Indeed. It has done wonders for social cohesion in places like Tucuman, Argentina, where people solidly refused to pay for drinking water turned brown under the control of a subsidiary of Vivendi.

The problem water companies and other companies that want to run public services have in relation to corporate social responsibility (CSR) is that to a large extent they are trying to square a circle. Where water has been privatized, it has not been a popular move. The increasing tide of protest around the world proves that. But it is not just an issue of unpopularity. More often than not the responsible way to manage public services is in the public sector. Private companies bidding for contracts will inevitably find themselves in a 'profit-overprovision' bind.

The Observer, 21 March 2004

VOTERS OF ALL PARTIES are largely split on whether specific examples of private-sector involvement are effective: 49 per cent of voters want private companies to carry out NHS operations, including 45 per cent of Labour supporters. They are also uncertain about government plans to offer more choice in public services: 48 per cent think allowing people to choose which NHS hospital they are treated at is a good idea. Labour supporters, 57 per cent of whom agree with government policy, are more enthusiastic about choice.

Julian Glover, political correspondent, The Guardian, 27 September 2005

1 Do you agree with Yves Picaud, that people only appreciate what they pay for?

2 Are there any items or services that people should not have to pay for?

3 Why are these items or services different from other services?

4 How will these items or services be paid for if the users do not?

5 Do you think that if private companies provide healthcare, it would be any different from the NHS? Explain your answer.

Theories and ideologies

The exercise above should have shown you that the sorts of decisions that need to be made by politicians are likely to be heavily influenced by their views of what society and people are like. In other words, their **theories** of society will influence their actions. In other parts of this book, especially Unit 1, we have seen that there are a number of different, competing theories in sociology and these provide very different explanations for society. These theories form the basis of political **ideologies**: ideas about what actually ought to be done. According to George and Wilding (1994), ideologies are usually based upon a theoretical explanation of how society functions, but go one step further and suggest a political programme that should be followed as a logical outcome of the theory. For example, Marxist theory, which claims that those who own the economic base of a society will oppress the majority of those who are non-owners, leads to Marxism, which is the political creed that the non-owners ought to wrest control of the economic base from the ruling class that exploits them.

There is not necessarily a political link between sociological theories and social policy ideologies, as is the case with Marxism, but certainly functionalism does have links to the New Right, and there are definite echoes of Weber in the work of many social democratic approaches.

The academic subject of social policy

This debate leads us to the very heart of the distinction between sociology as traditionally studied in Britain and the academic subject known as social policy. If sociology uncovers and explains social phenomena, then social policy (that is the academic subject as opposed to government social policies) seeks to go one step further and to study what might happen when these theories become ideological perspectives and are put into effect by governments.

Ideologies in social policy

In the previous section, we looked at the way that theories provide explanations that shade into ideological perspectives when a political programme is developed on the basis of the theory. The main ideological perspectives on social policy are:

- social democracy – which derives from the writings of Max Weber
- Marxism
- the New Right – which has some elements of functionalism underpinning it
- feminism
- antiracism – which is based on sociological explanations of racism
- environmentalism – developed from the ideas of the green movement
- the Third Way – linked to the writings of the sociologist Anthony Giddens.

Social democracy

This remains the dominant ideological approach to welfare in Britain and stands in the very middle of all debates. Although the contemporary welfare state is moving away from some of the ideas of social democracy, its ideas still provide the basis for the welfare state.

The term 'social democracy' is itself rather wide and includes a range of different outlooks. What these all share is a belief that capitalism and the free market are inefficient, often unjust, and require state regulation to produce a better society. Social democratic approaches are based upon socialism, although they owe a debt to some religious traditions, such as the Quakers and Methodists. The socialist model they put forward is based upon gradual social reform and improvement, as opposed to revolution.

Explaining the welfare state

According to Crosland (1956), the development of a welfare state was the direct result of increases in the political power of the working class – through the trades unions and the Labour Party. Capitalism would not willingly give welfare benefits and it is primarily through political pressure that working-class people gained the welfare state. However, since it has been initiated in the 1940s, the welfare state has been accepted as an integral part of capitalism by both the labour movement and by capitalists. Changes in welfare are partly a response to the differences in power between the various groups in society.

Main characteristics of social democratic ideology

Paternalism

Paternalism is the belief that experts can determine the best way to solve social problems, and that research into social problems will provide the knowledge to solve those problems. This 'top-down' approach was very influential in British social policy and led to the centralized and often bureaucratic nature of public welfare provision, and a suspicion of private (for-profit) and voluntary alternatives to state services.

Reformism

Supporters of the social democratic approach believed that radical social upheaval could create as many problems as it solved and that a slow, piecemeal approach to reform was preferable to the Marxist idea of revolution.

Equality

According to the social democratic perspective, reducing inequality benefits society because it improves social harmony and integration and allows everyone to realize their full potential.

Citizenship

According to Marshall (1975), every person living in a society is entitled to have the rights of a citizen, including access to health and welfare services, the right to justice and the right to have their say in the political process. The welfare state takes care of the rights to health and welfare services.

Criticisms of the social democratic approach

- Critics of social democracy argue that the **reformist** strategy has not been successful, as poverty and health inequalities still remain. In fact, according to Le Grand (1982), the main groups to benefit from the welfare state have been the affluent middle classes rather than the poorest groups in society. It is the middle classes who make greater use of public services, especially education, health and welfare.
- New Right critics argue that the paternalism and **elitism** of the welfare state alienated the users of services and often made them feel like second-class citizens. Critics, such as Griffiths (1984), have also argued that many public welfare services operated as **monopolies** and functioned in the interests of service providers rather than service users. This meant that public services became very inefficient and unresponsive to claimants' needs.
- For Marxists, such as Harrington (1972), the social democratic argument is flawed as it sees the welfare state as a step forward when, in fact, it is merely a means of controlling workers. Furthermore, whereas social democrats such as Marshall can see the emergence of a fair society within capitalism, Marxists simply reject this view.

Marxism

Marx was engaged in a total analysis and criticism of capitalist society and was not very interested in issues of welfare. Marx thought that social policy was no more than a minor set of reforms to an economic and social system that was profoundly and inherently unjust. Consequently, Marx himself said very little about welfare and social policy; the Marxist analysis of welfare was developed by later Marxists who applied Marx's general outlook to this specific area.

The Marxist approach argues that those in control of the economic base of a society are able to control the entire society and exploit the majority of the population. A consequence of this exploitation is that society is characterized by conflict between the owners of wealth and the majority of the population. According to George and Wilding (1994), Marxists have a mixed view of the welfare state, with three broad positions being taken, i.e. seeing the welfare state as:

- the outcome of the class struggle
- a means of oppression
- a response to a legitimation crisis.

T.H. Marshall (1975)
The concept of citizenship

The social democratic approach places great emphasis on the notion of citizenship. In particular, they are concerned to tease out the meaning of the term and its implications for the right to social welfare. Marshall argues that citizenship has three elements – legal, political and social – that have developed separately over time. According to Marshall, legal citizenship came first, followed much later by political citizenship; the issue of social citizenship remains an issue of contention even today.

- *Legal citizenship* – This was the first form of citizenship that came about with the granting of equal legal rights to all. The 19th century was the period of greatest legal reform that aimed to apply the law equally to all citizens.
- *Political citizenship* – this emerged with the growth of free speech and democratic voting rights, largely during the early part of the 20th century.
- *Social element of citizenship* – This remains in doubt. To what extent do people have rights to health and welfare as they do to political and legal rights? According to social democratic writers, there is still no consensus on this issue. Whereas, social democratic writers argue that the right to free and high standards of welfare are simply another aspect of citizenship, for those on the political right, these are not rights but are privileges given by the state.

1 To what extent do you agree that legal and political citizenship exists for all in Britain today?

2 Why is there controversy about the idea of 'social citizenship'?

Outcome of the class struggle

Deacon (1977), in his analysis of the origin of unemployment benefits, sees the welfare state as a success for the class struggle, and a genuine concession that has been won from capitalists. According to Deacon, the main reason why these were introduced was because the ruling class was frightened of possible revolution.

A means of oppression

Alternatively, there are those, such as Ginsburg (1998), who see the welfare state bolstering and renewing capitalism. Its very existence makes capitalism seem more humane, as its apparent benefits hide the 'underlying brutality' of the system. The welfare state ensures that there is a healthy, educated and housed workforce available for employment. The welfare state also helps to make profits for the ruling class, as there is huge spending by the state on the construction and running of education, health and welfare services and buildings.

Legitimation crisis

O'Connor (1973) has argued that although there is truth in both of these positions, they ignore a core problem that capitalism faces when providing a welfare state. O'Connor argues that all capitalist states must fulfil two contradictory functions – accumulation and legitimation. Accumulation refers to the need for profits for capitalism, while legitimation refers to the need for the ruling class to persuade the working class that it (the ruling class) is acting according to the interests of the whole of society, not just itself. The welfare state plays a key role in legitimation, as it tells people that capitalism is not just interested in profits but the welfare of the whole nation.

However, O'Connor argues that once a welfare state is constructed, it is difficult for the ruling class to limit the demand for welfare. The result is that the costs of welfare threaten to diminish the accumulation of profits that capitalism seeks. Thus, we find the contradiction: the more that capitalism seeks to legitimate itself by providing welfare, the greater the threat to profitability. This leads to a crisis and the cutting back of state expenditure on welfare.

Policy and Marxism

Unlike most of the other perspectives we consider in social policy, Marxism is not really interested in making policy recommendations for the effective running of the welfare state. As far as Marxists are concerned, social welfare is limited by capitalism and cannot challenge the fundamental nature of this exploitative system. The only long-term welfare solution is to replace capitalism in a socialist revolution in which there is a redistribution of wealth so that a welfare state as such is no longer necessary.

The New Right

One of the most influential ideological perspectives in recent social policy – and in politics generally – has been the New Right. It owes its origins to Hayek (2001, originally 1944), and was later developed by writers such as Friedman (1962) and Murray (1984). The policies of the New Right were enthusiastically adopted by Conservative governments from 1979, and they have had considerable influence on New Labour (and its ideology of the Third Way) since 1997.

Four related ideas are central to New Right social theory.

Primacy of freedom/liberty

Freedom, from a New Right point of view, means that people are left alone to behave as they wish, free from state intervention.

Minimal state intervention

The idea of liberty is closely related to the New Right principle of reducing the role of the state to a minimum. The New Right support the ideal of **laissez-faire**, or minimal state activity. The function of the state is to maintain law and order, to protect the individual by providing an army, and to provide the bare essential of public services (e.g. sanitation, street lighting). Engaging in activities to provide healthcare or to try to reduce inequalities is seen as interfering with personal freedom.

What point is the cartoon making about the welfare state?

That's incredible! This is the exact place that **my** great-grandfather offered sympathy to **your** great-grandfather!

Centrality of the free market

According to the New Right viewpoint, **the market** (or 'free market') is efficient, sensitive and speedy in its response to demand. Because they are directed by what people actually want and will pay for, rather than by government officials, free markets are the most effective way of distributing goods and services. Where there are no markets (as in public welfare services) there is inefficiency, as 'producers' (in the case of the welfare state: doctors, administrators and social workers) are more concerned about satisfying their own needs rather than those of clients. Such a system is also ineffective as it delivers what bureaucrats think people *should have*, rather than what they actually want and would choose in a free market.

The New Right and the welfare state

The New Right are therefore suspicious of the welfare state, as it involves the imposition of a system by the state and takes away freedom of choice. According to Willetts (1992), state welfare 'crowds out' other forms of welfare provision, such as that offered through the voluntary sector (e.g. charity) or within the family. This can weaken moral bonds and communal feeling in society. This in turn leads to irresponsibility and reduces self-reliance, creating a 'dependency culture' where people come to expect that the government will do everything for them instead of looking after themselves. New Right theorists, such as Green (1988), favour **privatizing** welfare services as far as possible, either by selling them off to private companies or by encouraging individuals to 'opt out' of public provision and subscribe to private services such as private occupational pensions and healthcare.

Feminism

While there are many different strands of feminism, they all share the view that the disadvantages faced by women in comparison with men are social and systematic rather than individual and random. Therefore, feminism aims to understand the structure and organization of society that keeps women at a disadvantage in comparison to men. For feminists, mainstream social theory has been inadequate because it has been 'gender-blind' – in other words, traditional social theory and social policy were based on male assumptions and did not account for the very important differences between men and women. In short, social theory pursued a 'malestream' agenda in which women's interests and rights were either neglected or completely ignored.

Feminism and the welfare state

According to Williams (1989), feminists have mixed feelings about state welfare provision. On the one hand, they recognize that the welfare state has done some good in advancing the cause of female independence, e.g. through child benefit and a range of lone-parent benefits that are more likely to help women. On the other hand, feminists such as Siim (1990),

complain that the welfare state may also reinforce traditional gender roles. Although the majority of employees of the NHS are female, they are significantly more likely to be in less senior posts, and also to be employed in what are seen as traditional 'caring' female roles, such as nursing. Sapiro (2002) argues that the majority of people who use the welfare state – both as claimants and service users – are women. This means that it is of particular importance for feminists. Also, while the staff of the welfare state are largely women, the majority of people providing informal, family or voluntary care are also women. Despite this, the key decisions regarding welfare are taken by men. Finally, Sapiro points out that welfare-state professionals may act in ways that regulate and control women's freedom in terms of decisions on reproduction, childcare, healthcare and state benefits.

Criticisms

Feminism has been criticized for sometimes assuming a unity of female experience and interests. This has been challenged by Black feminists and postmodernists, for example, who emphasize difference and diversity among women. According to George and Wilding, feminism may also be accused of committing a mistake attributed to Marxists: confusing the outcomes of a system (such as the welfare state) with its intentions. For example, simply because something has a particular effect (e.g. gender discrimination) does not mean it was designed with the purpose to achieve this; it may have come about for other reasons.

Antiracism

Issues of race and the welfare state have been raised ever since its foundation. As Ahmad and Craig (1998) point out, one of the reasons discussed by Beveridge for the introduction of the welfare state was to ensure that there would be a healthy White workforce in Britain, capable of running an empire. Antiracists define racism as 'the process whereby discrimination … is structured and perpetuated' (Penketh and Ali 1997). Such racism need not be intentional: the routine procedures of an organization may be racist without any of the individuals who operate them being deliberately prejudiced. This is known as 'institutional racism'.

According to those within the antiracist perspective, institutional racism can be found in much of British government policy and this includes welfare. Ethnic minorities are more likely than most other groups in Britain:

- to encounter the welfare state as clients or recipients as they are more likely to be unemployed
- to be low paid
- to be amongst the poorest groups in society (Modood *et al.* 1997).

Furthermore, they are less likely to be well housed and young women of African Caribbean origin have higher levels of lone motherhood than other groups.

Theories and ideologies of social policy in many ways mirror explanations for inequality in society. New Right thinkers reflect functionalist thinking, particularly the ideas of Davis and Moore (1955). Davis and Moore claim that inequality of rewards ensure that the best people are motivated to enter the functionally most important roles for society. By offering welfare provision, governments break up this functionally important link between rewards and social position. The result is, according to functionalists, that the society stagnates economically and everyone becomes poorer. Welfare systems are, therefore, a very important area of debate for functionalist sociologists.

At the other extreme of political/sociological thinking, Marxists also have their doubts about the welfare state and its link with inequality. For some Marxists, the welfare state serves to even out extremes of inequality and the

marginalized groups who would be most likely to lead any revolution are effectively 'bought off' by the provision of minimum welfare standards. Patterns of inequality then are also powerfully influenced by welfare provision.

Sociologists influenced by a Weberian perspective also see the welfare state as having a significant impact on inequality. The best way to understand their approach is to perceive the welfare state as an 'arena of struggle'. So, levels of welfare and decisions about which groups receive benefits depend upon the power that they can muster to make stronger claims than other groups. Welfare benefits, therefore, do redistribute some wealth across groups, but this is the result of the ability for some groups to muster enough power to persuade others to channel benefits to them.

British policy initiatives towards 'race'

British policy towards 'race' has stressed one of two approaches, both of which are believed by antiracists to have helped to maintain racism.

Assimilationism

Assimilationism is the policy of integrating ethnic minorities into the 'mainstream' culture. According to the antiracist viewpoint, this strategy is based on the idea of the cultural and racial superiority of the dominant (White) group and the belief that minority groups should be absorbed into this culture. Little or no provision is made within the mainstream culture for diversity and the result is that too many people from ethnic minorities are excluded from full citizenship.

Multiculturalism

The **multiculturalist** approach, which has been adopted more recently, accepts diversity, in the belief that contact and familiarity with different groups will reduce ignorance and prejudice among the White population. However, the antiracist perspective argues that multicultural policies in Britain have, in fact, used multiculturalism as a reason for only making minor adjustments to institutions (such as welfare organizations) while leaving the basic 'racist fabric' of society untouched.

Antiracism and the welfare state

The welfare state is regarded as a good example of institutional racism. For example, social workers and healthcare workers often work with an implicit set of cultural values and expectations regarding appropriate behaviour. It has been suggested for example, that this is part of the reason for the high rate of people from African Caribbean origins who are diagnosed as suffering from mental illness. Furthermore, many ethnic minority members face demands

that they produce evidence to prove that they are British citizens. Members of the ethnic minorities have high levels of employment in the NHS, but are concentrated in the lowest grades within it.

Environmentalism/greenism

All political ideologies advocate changing society in some way, but arguably none support such significant changes as those proposed by environmentalists, such as Carson (1962) and Schumacher (1974). The environmentalist movement is much more than a single-issue pressure group and its programme for change is far-reaching (Meadows and Meadows 1977). Environmentalists such as Lovelock (1979) challenge the assumptions and starting points of alternative perspectives. These, they say, are 'anthropocentric' (human-centred) when they should be 'ecocentric' (centred on the needs of the earth and its ecosystem).

Unlike most other perspectives, environmentalism does not regard nature simply as a resource that is available to be exploited for human wellbeing. In fact, environmentalism questions the view that economic development actually represents an advance for humans or for the planet as a whole. Environmentalism broadens the idea of what counts as 'human wellbeing' by arguing that we must see this in the context of global ecological needs. Only by existing in harmony with nature can we achieve high standards of life quality.

Environmentalism and the welfare state

According to Cahill (1998), the Greens approach the issue of the welfare state in a very different way from most other perspectives. They support the objectives of welfare provision but are critical of some of the means used to achieve them. Environmentalists argue for a more **holistic** idea of welfare and wellbeing, one that takes into account the place of people within the wider ecological system. So, healthcare should shift away from traditional, scientific, medical models of curing people and instead look to the harm done by pollution and stress.

They also reject the current form of centralized, bureaucratic welfare state, and would replace it with decentralization and greater emphasis on community and voluntary support in the family and within local areas, which, they claim, would lead to higher levels of participation by citizens.

Criticisms

Antienvironmentalists accuse Greens of being irrational in their approach to technical problems and prioritizing plants and animals over human needs. It is viewed as the luxury of the wealthier nations who, having achieved a high standard of living through exploiting the planet, now wish to deny that to poorer nations.

The Third Way

The term 'Third Way' is used to distinguish this new approach from two older political traditions. The 'first way' is the New Right; the 'second way' is traditional social democracy. Proponents of the Third Way, such as Giddens (1999), claim that it is an attempt to combine the best elements from each. Giddens sees the Third Way as a contemporary version of social democracy, which is more in tune with the political, economic and social changes that have taken place in late modernity. Traditional notions of left and right have been abandoned and policies are drawn from both the New Right and from social

democratic approaches, as well as from environmental, antiracist and feminist perspectives.

The underlying argument is that Britain is in the period of postmodernity, in which the traditional class and occupational structures have broken down, and that a fluid society needs a more flexible welfare system. Separately, the influence of globalization and, in particular, international competition has led to the need to restrict welfare spending in order to remain competitive in this world market.

Check your understanding

1. **What is meant by an ideology?**

2. **Which perspective is most associated with the welfare state? Explain why.**

3. **What views do feminists hold on the welfare state?**

4. **How would the New Right provide welfare?**

5. **Marxists give two quite different reasons for the existence of the welfare state. What are they?**

6. **Identify the two approaches that are in favour of all or some privatization of welfare? Explain your answer.**

7. **Explain the meaning and the significance of the term 'ecocentric' for understanding welfare.**

8. **What is the Third Way and what are the other two 'ways'?**

9. **Which sociologist is associated with the idea of the Third Way?**

KEY TERMS

Assimilationism – the policy of integrating ethnic minorities into the 'mainstream' culture.

Elitism – a small, powerful group control the society.

Holistic – when every factor is taken into account; the greens use it to refer to the need to take environmental factors into account in all activities.

Ideology – a set of beliefs about how best to act, based upon a particular theoretical perspective.

Laissez-faire – a belief that governments should not intervene in the economy by restricting the activities of companies.

The market (or free market) – the situation where people can buy and sell services.

Multiculturalism – the policy of allowing people to have their own cultures within one society.

Monopoly – when there is only one provider of services and people have no choice.

Paternalism – when powerful people believe they know what is good for others.

Privatization – when an activity previously performed by the state is handed over to a private, profit-making company.

Reformism – incrementalism or gradualism: a slow pace of change rather than dramatic changes.

Theories – explanations that give an account of the nature, workings and origins of different aspects of society.

web.task

Visit the Social Policy site at Robert Gordon University, which is edited by Paul Spicker – this contains a wide variety of updated information on Social Policy. Go to: www.rgu.ac.uk/public policy/introduction/socpolf.htm

research idea

Design a questionnaire to discover the views of a sample of people towards the welfare state. Ask a range of questions covering the sorts of issues raised in the 'Getting you thinking' exercise at the beginning of this topic. Analyse the results by trying to identify which of the perspectives described here are closest to each respondent's views.

exploring theories and ideologies of social policy

Item A

The scope of government must be limited. Its major function must be to protect our freedom both from the enemies outside our gates and from our fellow-citizens, to preserve law and order, to enforce private contracts, to foster competitive markets. Most of the present welfare programmes should never have been enacted. If they had not been, many of the people now dependent on them would have become self-reliant individuals instead of wards of the state. The heart of the new right philosophy is a belief in the dignity of the individual in his freedom to make the most of his capacities and opportunities. Government action can never duplicate the variety and diversity of individual action. At any moment in time, by imposing uniform standards in education, housing and so on, governments could undoubtedly improve the level of living of many individuals, but in the process would substitute uniform mediocrity for variety and replace economic success with stagnation.

Adapted from Friedman, M. (1962) *Capitalism and Freedom*, Chicago: University of Chicago Press; and Friedman, M. and Friedman, R. (1980) *Free to Choose*, London: Secker & Warburg

Item B

We have discerned two factors of importance in explaining the growth of the welfare state: the degree of class conflict … and the ability of the capitalist state to formulate and implement policies to secure the long-term reproduction of capitalist social relations.

Gough, I. (1979) *The Political Economy of the Welfare State*, Basingstoke: Macmillan

Item C

The politics of the Third Way recognizes that the range of questions that escape the old left/right divide in politics is greater than ever before. It operates in a world where the views of the old left have become obsolete, and those of the new right are inadequate and contradictory. It also stems from a radicalization of the political centre. It is a new and pragmatic response to the political issues facing society today. (It is) simply modernized social democracy – sustaining socialist values and applying them to a globalized world.

The aim is to help people negotiate the revolutions of our time – globalization, transformations in personal life and institutions, and our relationship to nature. It tries to respond to changing patterns of inequality. The poor today are not the same as the poor of the past: they include proportionately more children and single parents, for example, and proportionately fewer older people. Likewise, the rich are not the same as they used to be.

Adapted from Giddens, A. (2001) London School of Economics website (www.lse.ac.uk)

(a) Using **Item A**, identify **one** role of the state. (1 mark)

(b) Identify and briefly explain **two** ways in which Marxists might explain the development of the welfare state **(Item B)**. (8 marks)

(c) Using **Item A** and any other material, give **three** reasons why the New Right criticize the provision of welfare by the government. (9 marks)

(d) Identify and explain how the 'Third Way' differs from traditional right/left approaches to welfare **(Item C)**. (12 marks)

Exam practice

(e) Outline and assess the social democratic view of the welfare state. (60 marks)

Housing

gettingyouthinking

1. Are there clearly defined areas in your town that contain different sorts of houses? Are there clear social differences between the people who live in these areas? Why do you think these divisions occur?

2. People often talk about the 'right to healthcare', or the 'right to a decent education' – in the same way, do you think that people have a 'right' to housing?

3. In health services, we give people treatment on the basis of their need – should housing be allocated solely on need too? How might this work?

4. Why do you think people are homeless?

Housing as a social issue

Housing is not simply a matter of bricks and mortar. People invest much of their income in buying or renting their properties. They also express their identities in the way they decorate and treat their properties. Houses also have meaning for the people who live in them, as they have come to represent a private sphere where the individual and their family can relax and express themselves.

Poor housing, or lack of housing altogether, can significantly affect people's health and wellbeing, and can also have a destructive effect on family relationships. Housing patterns also paint an interesting picture of the divisions within society. As Rex and Moore (1967) point out, housing is a **scarce resource**, and different groups in the population will use what financial, political and social resources they have to obtain the better housing. The outcome is that different areas of towns and cities are clearly distinguishable from each other, not just by quality of housing, but also by their occupancy by different social classes and ethnic groups.

Historical background

In the 19th century, inadequate housing and town planning had been clearly linked on the one hand to poverty and, on the other, to such things as poor health and other social problems. As a result, from the mid-19th century, charitable organizations began to set up housing schemes to try to provide better housing conditions for the working class. However, it was not until the early part of the 20th century that **local government**

became involved in a serious way in providing houses for the less well off. By the 1930s, an average of 50 000 homes were built each year for **local authorities** to rent out. After the 1942 Beveridge Report, both Labour and Conservative governments provided financial support for local authorities to engage in a massive project of house-building for rent. The governments also encouraged homeownership through the use of tax relief on **mortgages**.

By the end of the 1970s, with the **crisis of welfare** (see Topic 1), the Conservative government, influenced by New Right thinking, became ideologically committed to cutting back the role of the state – and local authorities in particular. According to Doling (1993), they therefore introduced the right of local-authority **council-house** tenants to buy their own homes, while at the same time preventing local authorities from building new homes. The lower paid who could not afford to buy property were encouraged to turn to **housing associations**. This policy has remained unchanged, despite the return of Labour governments since 1997. These changes have been accompanied by a significant change in British culture, in that most people now seek to buy their own homes. Today, about 75 per cent of households are either purchasing or already own their own homes.

The significance of tenure

Tenure is the term used to describe the ownership patterns of housing. There are three main types of tenure:

1. **Owner occupancy** – The person living in the property is buying or actually owns the property.
2. **Privately rented** – The person living in the property pays rent to the owner, who is renting the property simply to

make money. The property can be rented with furniture or without.

3 **Social housing** – The person living in the property pays rent to the owner. The owner, however, is providing the property as a social service, rather than for profit. There are two main providers of social housing. Local authorities provide what people traditionally call council housing, while registered social landlords and housing associations are private, not-for-profit organizations.

Tenure is significant in that it is one of the key components of social class in contemporary Britain. Social housing increasingly takes the majority of lower-income and socially excluded groups and provides the location for a high proportion of social problems such as drug use, crime, poverty and unemployment.

Local-authority housing

At the beginning of the 20th century, most people could not afford to buy their own homes and would rent from private landlords. However, conditions were often so appalling that, from 1919, local authorities intervened and began building homes for rent. In 1939, at the outbreak of the Second World War, half a million high-quality houses had been built. Although social housing today caters mainly for the poor, and there is some stigma attached to living in social-housing estates, in the 1930s the local-authority homes were relatively expensive to rent and were regarded as very prestigious. The criteria to become a tenant meant that the majority of those renting were from the skilled working class, with the unskilled and lower paid having to rent privately.

By the 1960s, living in local-authority housing started to become associated with poverty and increasingly became the housing safety net for those who could not afford to buy. In 1980, the then Conservative government's right-to-buy scheme was introduced, allowing tenants the right to buy that property at discounts on the market value of up to 50 per cent. Since 1980, 2.27 million flats and houses have been bought under this scheme. Most of the properties bought have been the better-quality ones, meaning that, increasingly, council stocks are of poorer quality. It also means that the supply of council housing available for rent has effectively disappeared.

Reasons for the right-to-buy legislation

The Conservative government objected to local-authority provision of housing for three main reasons:

● *Ideological belief in the market* – The government believed that it was not the role of governments to provide housing. They argued that housing is not a social service but a private choice.
● *Self-help* – The Conservatives believed that people should look after themselves and 'stand on their own feet', not rely on the state to provide things.
● *Unresponsive bureaucracies* – Local-authority housing departments were good examples of unnecessary bureaucracies that looked after their own interests rather than those of the tenants.

The government did recognize, however, that there were people on low incomes who could not afford to purchase housing and were not catered for by private landlords. It therefore enhanced the role of housing associations. All these arguments were drawn directly from New Right political ideology.

The consequences of right-to-buy legislation

The social consequences of the right-to-buy legislation were quite profound in that the better-quality houses and flats were bought, in more attractive locations, by the better-off tenants. Linked to the increasing tendency of more affluent working-class families to purchase their own homes without applying for social housing in the first place, the change in social composition of the local-authority housing sector has been quite marked. Local-authority tenants are more likely to be the poorest groups in society, and strikingly often have no earners in the household and/or are lone-parent families. For example, the numbers of non-earning households in local-authority housing rose from below 10 per cent in the 1970s to over 60 per cent by the late 1990s. The corresponding figures for owner-occupiers were approximately 20 and 28 per cent.

Local-authority tenants are also more likely to be at the extremes of ages, typically being younger people and older people, with the middle-aged now moving into owner occupation. Finally, local-authority housing had traditionally encompassed a mixture of the skilled and unskilled working class. By the 1990s, the more skilled had increasingly moved into owner occupation. The process by which local-authority housing has become largely the preserve of the non-employed and the unskilled is known as **residualization**.

Housing associations/registered social landlords

In order to limit the role of local authorities in providing and running housing, the 1980s Conservative government increasingly switched its funding to housing associations (registered social landlords or RSLs), i.e. non-profit making organizations providing affordable housing. Some 5 per cent of all housing stock is owned by RSLs and they have raised £10 billion in private finance. Labour governments since 1997 have continued to support RSLs and to transfer housing from local-authority stocks to housing associations (over 474 000 between 1980 and 2000). As for new buildings completed, in 1999/2000 for example, local authorities built 100 houses in total while RSLs completed 17 000. Despite all these problems and the shift to housing associations, local authorities are still responsible for accommodation. However, the right-to-buy legislation has led to the sale of over one and a half million local-authority houses. This has taken away the opportunity for the poorest in society to obtain housing, and as people from ethnic minorities are overrepresented among the poorest, they have been particularly hard hit. Most noticeable has been the overrepresentation of African Caribbeans among those in, or seeking, local-authority accommodation. Howes and Mullins (1999) have suggested that White tenants have been given a disproportionate number of the better-quality properties, while Bangladeshis, in particular, were allocated the worst accommodation, on the worst estates.

Tenure and poverty

The assumption that most people would make that there are more poor people in the rented sector of housing has been challenged recently by Burrows (2003), who conducted a national survey of poverty and tenure. He concludes that although a higher proportion of people living in rented accommodation are poor, the rise in the number of people in owner-occupied housing, means that more than half of all people living in poverty either own their own homes or are buying them. Burrows suggests that there are interesting differences between the sorts of people who are in poverty who are owner occupiers and those who rent.

- Poor homeowners are more likely to live in households where people are in employment.
- 48 per cent of poor homeowners are couples with dependent children, compared with 26 per cent of renters.
- Poor people in the rented sector tend to be younger than poor homeowners.
- There are clear socioeconomic differences, with a higher proportion of poor homeowners coming from non-manual (37 per cent) or skilled manual backgrounds (37 per cent), whereas 71 per cent of poor renters are from manual backgrounds.
- There are also regional differences: in the North, the South, London and Scotland, similar or higher proportions of poor people live in the rented sector than in homeownership, whereas in the Midlands and Wales higher proportions of poor people live in their own homes than rent them.
- Poor homeowners are more likely to be members of a Black or ethnic-minority group (14 per cent) than are poor renters (8 per cent).

Homelessness

Defining homelessness

Although the term 'homeless' seems obvious, in fact the definition has been the source of considerable discussion. In 2001, 104 000 'households' in England and Wales were homeless (according to the official definition). This covers over a quarter of a million people, about half of whom are children.

Until 1977, the official definition of homelessness included only families that had been placed in temporary accommodation by the 'welfare authorities'. The local authorities were not obliged to place people in temporary accommodation and more people were turned away than accepted. This meant that 'homelessness' depended on the actions of local authorities. Between 1996 and 1997, this was amended to give priority to certain categories of homeless people. But it was not until The Homes Act 2001 that local authorities were legally obliged to house certain groups, such as pregnant women and families with dependent children, in 'suitable accommodation', if they are unintentionally homeless.

However, the official definition of homelessness is disputed by many, who point out that about 1000 households each day approach local authorities claiming that they are homeless but over half are turned away as they do not fit the official definition of homelessness. Shelter (a housing pressure group) estimates that the real extent of homelessness in Britain may well be over one and a half million.

The idea of intentional and unintentional homelessness is a very good example of a theme that has run through British social policy: the belief that one can distinguish between those who deserve help and those who do not. The 19th-century Poor Law (see Topic 1) was based upon the distinction between the deserving and the undeserving, and much New Right philosophy is based on distinguishing between those who

synoptic link

Housing and social differentiation are very closely linked. Indeed, sociologists point out that if there is one very clear indicator of the continuing existence of social and economic inequality in Britain, it is housing. First, homeownership is the most common form of wealth across Britain. Those people who own their own houses are able to pass these on to their children and this is one major way in which inequalities of wealth continues. Second, housing is rarely 'mixed' in the sense that, until relatively recently, it has not been a planning requirement for different forms of housing (social, 'affordable', owner-occupied, etc.) to be built near each other. This has resulted in distinctively different areas, with the middle class living within one area and working-class groups in another. This division between social classes in terms of neighbourhoods has had significant knock-on effects for education and medical services. Comprehensive schools that draw from a largely middle-class area are

social inequality and difference

profoundly different in composition from those drawing from working-class areas and this is reflected in examination results, with their consequent importance for future life-chances. Medical services in middle-class areas are more likely to provide a range of services than in working-class areas, and indeed there is considerable difficulty found in recruiting doctors to work in surgeries on large social-housing developments. But housing divisions are not only based on social-class differences but reflect and sharpen ethnic divisions too. People from African, Caribbean and Bangladeshi backgrounds are more likely to be in social housing than the majority population and, within the range of social housing, to have the worst properties. People from Asian backgrounds (excluding Bangladesh) have high levels of owner occupancy, but with some of the poorest housing conditions.

ought to get help from the state and those who are in the predicament because of their own fault. This can be contrasted with a more radical approach, influenced by Marxism, which suggests that it is more important to look at structural influences rather than individual characteristics.

Groups more at risk of homelessness

Homelessness is more likely to occur to some groups of people than others:

- *Low income groups* – Those with the lowest incomes are least likely to be able to afford accommodation. Over 80 per cent of those applying for housing are on state benefits.
- *Lone parents* – Lone parents are ten times more likely to be homeless and comprise over 60 per cent of households with children applying for housing.
- *Young people* – Younger people are more likely to be homeless than the rest of the population because they tend to be poorer and to have a higher proportion of lone parents. About 40 per cent of those applying for housing are under 25, and 75 per cent are under 35 years of age.
- *Larger families* – Larger number of children means the need for a larger home that costs more. Larger families are also overrepresented amongst the poorer families.
- *The unemployed* – This group makes up 60 per cent of those applying for accommodation.

Causes of homelessness

There are two approaches to explaining homelessness, focusing respectively on immediate and structural causes.

Immediate causes

The immediate causes of homelessness are the final, specific reasons that force a person or family to seek help from the local authority or housing association. These include parents, families or friends being no longer willing or able to provide accommodation, partners separating, the loss of rented property through disputes with landlords, inability to keep up mortgage repayments or rent arrears. Immediate causes focus on the specific problems of the individuals and seem to suggest that homelessness is the fault of the individual or their family or landlord.

Structural causes

An alternative explanation is that, as governments have failed to provide an adequate supply of affordable houses to rent or buy, families have been forced to take on very high mortgages in order to obtain accommodation. The blame should therefore be placed on wider economic inequalities rather than the individuals involved. According to the homelessness charity, Shelter, up to three million people in Britain simply cannot afford to pay the rents or to purchase a home. The issue could therefore be regarded as one of poverty rather than homelessness.

This can be closely linked to employment patterns. Because of high unemployment levels in areas outside the South East, people are forced to move to the areas where rents and house prices are at their highest. Furthermore, demographic changes, such as the increase in single parents and the decline in the stability of relationships, mean that there are far more people seeking accommodation.

Responses to homelessness

The government response to homelessness is a mixture of short-term measures. A variety of temporary accommodation may be provided. This includes bed-and-breakfasts, hostels, shelters, refuges and short-life tenancies in poor-quality accommodation that no one else wants. Today, this form of accommodation provides for about half of those accepted as homeless:

- *Shelters* provide a place to sleep overnight, somewhere to wash, and sometimes food. These are usually provided by charitable organizations.
- *Hostels* are run either by local authorities or by voluntary organizations and offer longer-term accommodation.

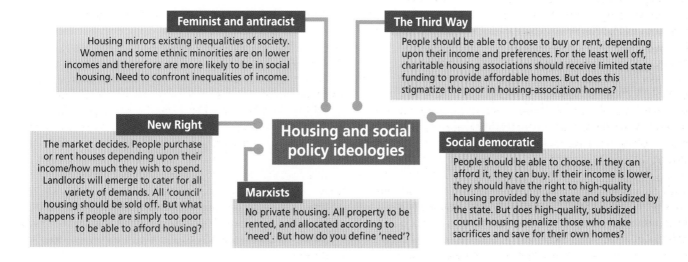

Figure 5.1 Housing and social policy ideologies

Feminist and antiracist
Housing mirrors existing inequalities of society. Women and some ethnic minorities are on lower incomes and therefore are more likely to be in social housing. Need to confront inequalities of income.

The Third Way
People should be able to choose to buy or rent, depending upon their income and preferences. For the least well off, charitable housing associations should receive limited state funding to provide affordable homes. But does this stigmatize the poor in housing-association homes?

New Right
The market decides. People purchase or rent houses depending upon their income/how much they wish to spend. Landlords will emerge to cater for all variety of demands. All 'council' housing should be sold off. But what happens if people are simply too poor to be able to afford housing?

Housing and social policy ideologies

Marxists
No private housing. All property to be rented, and allocated according to 'need'. But how do you define 'need'?

Social democratic
People should be able to choose. If they can afford it, they can buy. If their income is lower, they should have the right to high-quality housing provided by the state and subsidized by the state. But does high-quality, subsidized council housing penalize those who make sacrifices and save for their own homes?

They are meant to be places for moving homeless people into before they begin work or training, or find permanent accommodation.

- *Short-life tenancies* – Where properties are about to be demolished or their condition is so poor that most people will not accept living there, local authorities may use them on a temporary basis for those accepted as homeless. They are the second most common form of accommodation offered to those accepted as homeless by local authorities.

Regeneration: social problems, structural causes and housing

Successive governments have tried to regenerate the most deprived urban areas by involving tenants in setting up their own organizations to improve their areas. Separately, the European Community introduced the Single Regeneration Budget in 1993 to tackle unemployment, social disorder and educational improvements, as well as housing. Since 1998, the New Deal for Communities has provided funding for the most deprived neighbourhoods. The government argues that housing should not be seen in isolation from wider social problems and that it is therefore necessary to tackle the problems that caused the need for regeneration in the first place. The New Deal aims to combat 'welfare dependency' by improving the skills needed for employment and reducing health problems, crime and disorder, and poverty.

However, critics have pointed out that the small-scale nature of the projects can have very little impact on the widescale deprivation and poverty that lead to poor housing. They argue instead that a much broader and ambitious antipoverty programme is needed that will eliminate poverty and so enable people to afford better housing.

focus on research

Palmer *et al.* (2005)
Monitoring poverty & social exclusion

Over 100 000 homeless households are now living in temporary accommodation, more than double the numbers in 1997.

Around 200 000 households were accepted as homeless by their local authority in 2003, a quarter higher than in 2000. All of this rise has been households without dependent children, who accounted for two-thirds of all the households accepted as homeless in 2003. Statistics from Scotland suggest that the vast majority (95 per cent) of homeless households are single adult households (equivalent data is not available for England).

By far the biggest reason for becoming homeless is loss of accommodation provided by relatives or friends. An estimated two and a half million people live in overcrowded conditions (such that at least one of the adults does not have a bedroom of their own).

Source: Palmer, G., Carr, J. and Kenway, P. (2005) *Monitoring Poverty and Social Exclusion 2004*, York: Joseph Rowntree Foundation and New Policy Institute

1 What problems are researchers likely to face when trying to discover the number of homeless people?

2 What does the extract imply is the link between homelessness and overcrowding?

Check your understanding

1 In what way can housing be seen as a social issue?

2 What was the predominant form of tenure at the beginning of the 20th century?

3 What significant legislation was passed in 1980 that radically altered the tenure patterns in local-authority social housing?

4 In what way did New Right ideas influence the right-to-buy legislation?

5 Give two examples of the relationship between housing patterns and gender.

6 Give two examples of the relationship between housing patterns and ethnicity.

7 What are the differences between structural and immediate causes of homelessness?

8 What is the New Deal for Communities and how has it been criticized?

web.task

Prepare a report and/or give a presentation on one of the following issues:

- **antisocial behaviour**
- **community and neighbourhood**
- **homelessness**
- **street homelessness.**

The information can be downloaded from the 'The Policy Library' section of the Shelter website (select 'Policy and Practice' from the home page) at www.shelter.org.uk

KEY TERMS

Council housing – a term traditionally used for local-authority social housing.

Crisis of welfare – the period in the 1970s when, for the first time, politicians began to argue that the welfare state was too expensive and cumbersome, and that it was time to think of alternatives.

Housing associations/ registered social landlords – non-profit-making organizations that provide housing for rent; they have taken over the role from local authorities.

Local government/local authorities – the local borough or county council.

Mortgages – large loans taken out to pay for property.

Owner occupancy – a type of tenure, where the person living in the property is buying (or owns) the property.

Privately rented – a type of tenure where a tenant rents a property from a private individual or company.

Residualization – the process by which those left in local-authority housing are more likely to be the poorest.

Scarce resource – anything that is socially desired, but there is not enough of for everyone who wants it.

Social housing – type of tenure where tenant rents property from an organization that is operating as a social service rather than for profit.

Tenure – whether a person owns or rents a property.

exploring housing

Item A

It has been shown that housing policy is not simply or even primarily aimed at those in greatest housing need. Housing policy was very slow to develop in the 19th century and the driving forces then and since have been political. Since the 1960s, it has been increasingly used to pursue party political objectives, even when this meant helping the better off more than those in greatest housing need. The promotion of owner-occupation, the decline in the provision of council housing, and the attempt to introduce market rents for social tenants are clear illustrations of this. This could happen because the voices of those in housing need and those representing them are often very weak compared with the voices of financial institutions and builders and the voting strength of the majority. Governments calculate the votes to be won and lost before introducing new policies. Since governments have numerous policy goals, it should not be expected that policy in an area such as housing is driven by a single goal such as meeting housing need.

Pickvance, P. (2003) 'Housing and housing policy', in J. Baldock, N. Manning and S. Vickerstaff (2003) *Social Policy*, Oxford: Oxford University Press

Item B

Sixty-six people were interviewed: 24 men and nine women. The research revealed a high degree of overlap between experiences of begging and rough sleeping. Almost all of those interviewed had slept rough; four-fifths had begged.

Most interviewees had a family background characterized by disruption and trauma. Almost half had been in residential care/school or foster care and over a quarter reported drug- or alcohol-misusing parents. A number of interviewees, particularly women, reported being abused as children; their experiences included rape, sexual assault, incest, beatings and mental cruelty. Other traumas endured were bereavement, domestic violence, and family or relationship breakdown.

Many interviewees also had experience of institutional living. Two-thirds had received custodial sentences, often for relatively minor offences such as non-payment of fines. Many of these had no criminal record or experience of prison prior to becoming homeless. One-fifth of the sample had received psychiatric care, but seldom for a sustained period.

One-third of the sample reported alcohol dependencies and over one-fifth were current heroin users. Many had developed these substance dependencies early in life as a means of coping with traumatic experiences, and several interviewees reported that their habits had worsened as a result of life on the streets or in hostels.

People's involvement in begging almost always followed their experience of rough sleeping. Indeed, only seven interviewees who had begged were not sleeping rough when they started.

Fitzpatrick, S. and Kennedy, C. (2000) *Getting By: Begging, Rough Sleeping and* The Big Issue *in Glasgow and Edinburgh*, York: Joseph Rowntree Foundation

(a) Using **Item B** identify what percentage of those interviewed had begged. (1 mark)

(b) Identify and briefly explain **two** government policies towards housing since the 1960s **(Item A)**. (8 marks)

(c) Suggest **three** reasons why family background might be related to begging **(Item B)**. (9 marks)

(d) Identify and explain **two** reasons for homelessness. (12 marks)

Exam practice

(e) Outline and assess the view that housing in Britain reflects wider social inequalities. (60 marks)

Social security

gettingyouthinking

1 Do you think the reasons for unemployment have changed since the 1930s? Explain your answer.

2 Do you think that all unemployed people should receive state benefits (such as Jobseeker's Allowance)? If not, then who shouldn't?

3 Family Allowance, a payment to parents for all children still attending school, is paid to every family with children in Britain, no matter what their income. Do you think this is sensible? Can you think of any reasons why it might be a good idea?

4 In England and Wales (but not Scotland), when older people are unable to look after themselves and have to move to a care home, they must pay for themselves until their savings have fallen to a limit set by the government. This almost always means that they have to sell their homes, as these count as savings. People with no savings or who rent their property have their care paid for. Do you think this is fair? Does it penalize those who have led careful lives or is it only right that richer people should have to pay?

By **social security**, we mean the system of payments made by the state to help people in need. These range from pensions to Jobseeker's Allowance for the unemployed. Social security payments are the main method used by the government to confront poverty. About 70 per cent of all British households – 30 million people – receive some income from state benefits. Each year, the government spends over £100 billion on social security benefits – in fact it is the single biggest area of spending, about the same as health and education put together!

The origins of social security

Social security as we know it is less than 100 years old, and was first introduced between 1906 and 1911, with the provision of old age pensions and unemployment benefit for men. However, the main elements of the social security system that we recognize today were introduced between 1946 and 1948 as part of the reforms recommended by the 1942 Beveridge Report.

Contributory and non-contributory benefits

Beveridge made an important distinction between **contributory** (or insurance-based) benefits (known as National Insurance) and **non-contributory** (or assistance) benefits (known as National Assistance).

Contributory benefits were intended to offer protection against unemployment and illness in return for compulsory 'contributions' or deductions from their wages. Employers and the government also pay into the fund. Beveridge did not invent social insurance; there had been a form of National Insurance protection for unemployment, sickness and pensions in the UK as early as 1908, copied from an even earlier system in Germany.

In the event of unemployment or illness, and during retirement, every person who has made enough payments has a right to claim the relevant benefits through the National Insurance system. The National Insurance system introduced by Beveridge was based on a number of principles. These included:

- *Comprehensiveness* – The system was to cover the bulk of the (male) working population.
- *Flat-rate benefits and contributions* – The contributions were to be paid at the same rate, regardless of earnings. Similarly, the benefits were to be paid at a flat rate.
- *Adequate benefits* – State benefits should offer a decent minimum standard which would allow a reasonable standard of living.

Non-contributory benefits were to be a 'safety net' for all those who could not be included in the National Insurance scheme. These benefits were given to people to prevent them from falling into destitution.

The crucial distinction between the two forms of payments was that contributory benefits were regarded as a form of insurance which had been paid for, whilst non-contributory benefits were regarded as a guarantee that no citizen would be allowed to fall below a decent standard of living.

Changes in social security

1948 to 1979

A gradual change took place in the nature of British social security benefits from their introduction in the late 1940s until the 'crisis of welfare' in the 1970s. Most significantly, the levels of payment from the contributory-based insurance benefits were never high enough to provide people with an adequate standard of living, and so more and more people had to turn to additional non-contributory benefits (such as today's **Income Support**). What Beveridge saw as a contributions-based system, in which everyone was entitled to benefits because they paid for them, increasingly became a means-tested system.

Non-contributory, means-tested benefits increased social security spending each year from the very beginnings of the welfare state, so that by the mid-1970s, many felt that the social security system which Beveridge had designed for the post-war years was out of date. Critics from the right felt it was also too expensive. Around the same time, a global **economic recession** meant that cutbacks in **public expenditure** were imposed and ideas for a more drastic overhaul of the social-protection system began to emerge.

1980s to 1997

In 1979, a Conservative government was elected with very clear views about the future of social security. In their view, the system had drifted away from its original aim of providing help for those who were unable to find work or who were unable to perform work because of ill health or disability. They believed that social protection had instead become a wasteful bureaucratic structure that actually discouraged people from working. They therefore embarked on a series of measures, as follows.

Cut back on social security spending

The government was influenced by the argument that the costs of welfare were so great that they were causing the British economy serious problems. In order to cut costs, the government broke the link between increases in benefits and increases in earnings, and instead linked benefit rises to increases in prices. As price increases are usually lower than wage rises, the longer-term outcome was that social security and benefits, including pensions, fell behind average wages.

Target the 'most needy'

The government believed that welfare payments were being given to those who had no real need of them, and that greater means-testing was needed.

Attack the culture of dependency

It was felt that a generation of people had grown up in a 'welfare society' where they expected the state to look after them and were not prepared to take responsibility for themselves or their families. The increase in the numbers of lone parents was particularly emphasized.

1997 onwards

Since 1997, Labour governments have accepted the aims of attacking the '**dependency culture**' and of lowering social security expenditure, but they have followed a different approach.

Stress on employment

Despite all attempts by governments to lower the cost of social security payments, the costs have continued to rise. The Labour government therefore decided that above all else, they should attempt to encourage as many people as possible into employment – even if it is part-time.

The poverty trap

The **poverty trap** refers to the situation that many poorer people found themselves in when they moved from living on social security benefits to employment. This occurred for two reasons:

- Prior to 1997, wages could actually be lower than benefit levels.
- A considerable number of benefits were linked to being on social security – once people were employed, they lost these benefits because they crossed the threshold line for eligibility.

As a result, going into employment meant that people's total income could actually decline.

The minimum wage

In order to counter this situation, the government introduced a **minimum wage** – that is, a minimum amount that could be paid to a worker per hour. This immediately raised the income of millions of poorly paid cleaning, care and unskilled workers.

Tax credits

However, it was still possible to have a lower income on a minimum wage than on social security payments – for example, in the case of part-time workers. In order to encourage people into lower-paid work or part-time work, the government has now introduced **tax credits**. The government decides what the minimum decent income is for any particular size of family, and then tops up the main earner's income through the tax system. This is sometimes known as 'negative income tax', where the government pays you rather than deducts money from your paypacket. Tax credits have the advantage of encouraging people back into work, particularly lone-parent families, thus partially cutting the social security bill and also attacking welfare dependency.

Debates on social security

New Right approaches

The New Right attacks the idea that governments should provide insurance against unemployment or ill-health, believing that these are best left to free enterprise. Friedman (1962) argues that compulsory state-based insurance systems are less efficient than private insurance. According to Friedman, if there were a number of private companies offering insurance in competition with each other, instead of a state monopoly, then the cost of insurance would fall. He also suggests that compulsory insurance by the state is an attack on individual liberty: it is up to an individual to decide whether or not they want to insure against unemployment or sickness – it is not the role of the state.

However, the New Right is not opposed to helping the poor. Hayek (1976) for example, has argued that the state should provide a basic income which would prevent absolute poverty, but this should be strictly means-tested.

Marxist approaches

Ginsburg (1979) argues that social security should be seen less as a way of preventing poverty and more of a system for social control. Social security systems actually camouflage the exploitative nature of capitalism. Ginsburg argues that it does this in the following ways:

- People are forced into accepting low-paid work because benefits are so low.
- Social security maintains a cheap labour supply by providing a minimum income for the unemployed to live off until other poorly paid work becomes available – a '**pool of labour**' is maintained.
- The system humiliates claimants and individualizes their situation – hiding the fact that it is the system, not their own inadequacies, that makes them unemployed.
- It also ensures that workers want to remain employed as they fear the **stigma** of being a claimant.

Feminist approaches

Feminist critiques of social security point to the way the system sets out to discipline them into traditional 'female' roles:

- Glendinning and Millar (1992) argue, for example, that contributory benefits are generally based upon long-term, regular contributions, which is exactly the opposite of many women's employment history. Typically, women break off their work for child-bearing and child-rearing and then restart work. This can mean that they are excluded from the higher-paying benefits.
- Williams (1992) points out that social security benefits have, until recently, been based on the assumption of a male worker and a dependent wife (and children). This reflects and reinforces the dependency of women.
- Oppenheim and Harker (1996) argue that one of the poorest groups in society are lone parents and that 90 per cent of these are female. They argue that social security benefits have largely ignored the plight of lone parents and thereby the poverty of women. What is more, the system has consistently stigmatized lone parents as 'spongers'.

Antiracist approaches

Mann (1992) suggests that not only does the social security system exacerbate class differences by failing to redistribute resources, but it also fails to confront the specific racial dimensions of poverty. Mann points out that people from ethnic minorities are much more likely to suffer from poverty, but the social security system fails to address this. Indeed, according to Mann, ethnic minorities are likely to be discriminated against in the social security system. For example, those of African-Caribbean origins are twice as likely to be dependent upon means-tested benefits and less likely to claim benefits to which they are entitled.

Universalism versus means-testing

Universalism refers to the policy by which every person (within a particular category) receives social benefits or free healthcare, irrespective of their income or wealth. An example of a universal benefit is child allowance. Every family in Britain receives an allowance for children under 16 living at home. Other universal benefits are the health service (free to all who are sick) and state pensions.

The alternative to universalism is means-testing, the policy whereby people only receive social benefits or free healthcare if the government considers them poor enough to be eligible. An example of a means-tested benefit is family credit, an allowance given to those on lower incomes, depending upon their savings.

The debate

The universalist position is traditionally associated with social democratic approaches. Supporters of this position argue that means-testing humiliates people because they have to prove to others how little they have. Demonstrating one's poverty, it is claimed, is embarrassing and demeaning. Universalism also creates a feeling of social bonding by giving people the right to claim the assistance of all through the state. According to Titmuss (1964), this is a key element of citizenship (see Topic 2, p. 178). More practically, universal payments are actually cheaper and easier to provide as there is very little bureaucratic cost involved in paying them. Means-tested benefits require someone to work out a person's income and then calculate how much they ought to receive. Some means-tested benefits for people with disabilities actually cost almost as much to administer as they give out.

focus on research

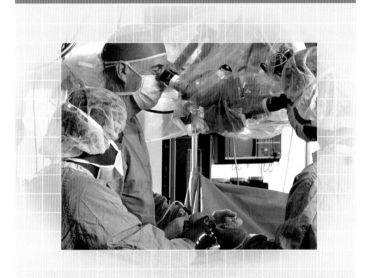

The idea of need

Much of the division between the New Right and other groups regarding the appropriateness of giving financial and social benefits to people 'in need', stems from what precisely is meant by the word 'need'. Those from the right argue that the term 'need' is consistently misused by supporters of welfare. In fact, this argument over need is the difference between absolute and relative measures of poverty. For the right, people in need are those who would be absolutely destitute without help, while for the majority of supporters of the welfare state, people need to have a standard of living more or less equal to the mass of the population. In order to clarify the concept of need for debates on social policy,

Bradshaw (1972) has suggested that there are, in fact, four types of need:

- *Normative need* – What an expert thinks someone should have. This is the sort of need that is assessed by professionals such as doctors or by employees of the state in calculating whether individuals or groups can be defined as 'in need'.
- *Felt need* – What a person or group believes they should have. This links closely to expressed needs (below) and refers to individuals feeling that they are being unfairly refused something they want.
- *Expressed need* – This is the felt need which has come to be a political demand by certain groups. Expressed needs can also be seen as 'wants', particularly where a group of people feel that they are unjustifiably being prevented from fulfilling their aspirations. Expressed needs have been suggested as the reason for inner-city riots, for example. Merton's concept of anomie (see Unit 2, p. 33) is based on similar ideas.
- *Comparative need* – This is a need which is defined in terms of an individual or group comparing their situation with others. A good example of this is the notion of 'relative poverty', which is defined in terms of what is socially expected, rather than what is needed to exist.

Forder (1974) has added another type of need:

- *Technical need* – This is a newly invented need which may reflect new technology or changes in values. A good example is the increasing need for healthcare, as technical breakthroughs in health provision raise the standard of what can be expected.

1 **In what ways does Bradshaw's categorizing of needs illustrate that the idea of the state fulfilling the needs of the population is more complex than first appears?**

There has always been a bitter political debate about who has the right to receive state benefits. On the one side are those who argue that a minimal level of payments ought to be made to those in desperate need, but who are also judged to be in need through no fault of their own. Arguing against them are writers who suggest that it is the right of any citizen of Britain to receive a decent standard of living and it is not up to the state to add in the element of a moral judgement about who is genuinely deserving of help or not. The key distinction between the two positions is partly about the level of state benefits payable, but more significantly over whether people should be judged as 'deserving' or not.

The issue of the underclass focuses this argument quite sharply. The modern debate was first started by Charles Murray in 1984, when he argued that in the USA there was emerging a significant proportion of younger people in the population who had never worked and were not interested in regular employment. They preferred to live off state benefits, inhabit state-subsidised housing and top up their incomes by engaging in minor criminal acts. Furthermore, Murray suggested that the women were highly liable to be lone parents and that both males and females were likely to have numerous sexual partners. In the USA, Murray linked this underclass to ethnic-minority groups, though in his analysis of Britain he saw no particular 'racial' element. Murray's work has been influential in creating the image of a subgroup within the working class that has its own particular subculture, described as the 'dependency culture' because of its reliance on state benefits. Murray's arguments have been subjected to particular criticism by Hartley Dean (2002), who argues that there is no such thing as an underclass and that this notion is simply a way of blaming the unemployed for the wider structural problems of society which cause them to be in this position.

Those who support means-testing are often associated with the New Right. They argue that giving assistance to everyone will inevitably mean that those who are not in need or who could pay for the services, will benefit. This is both unfair (why should affluent people be supported by the less well off?) and wasteful. They argue that only those truly in need should receive help, and the resulting savings could be used to lower taxation or to provide higher-quality services for the genuinely 'needy'.

Supporters of universal benefits point out that, although the argument for means-testing seems sensible, in practice it often draws people into 'the poverty trap' (see p. 192). In effect, means-testing rewards many people for not trying to improve their income and for not saving.

Social security, taxation and the redistribution of income and wealth

Another key debate concerns the extent to which the welfare state actually redistributes wealth so that the poorest groups become better off. There are two ways of looking at redistribution: vertical and life-cycle:

- *Vertical redistribution* – the redistribution from wealthier groups to poorer ones, e.g. housing benefit paid to the poorest groups only.
- *Life-cycle redistribution* – the redistribution of resources from one part of a person's life-cycle to another, e.g.

pensions, received when older but paid for during our working lives.

In 1997, Hills studied redistribution patterns and his findings are summarized below.

Vertical redistribution

Hills found that the poorer 50 per cent of households received 2.4 times as much from cash benefits as those in the wealthier 50 per cent, and the poorest 10 per cent received four times more than the richest 10 per cent. The significance of state benefits for the poor is indicated by the fact that the poorest 10 per cent receive about 70 per cent of their total household incomes from state benefits.

Interestingly, the poorest 10 per cent actually receive less in benefits than the next 20 per cent of low-income groups in the population because they fail to claim and/or they are simply not entitled to some other benefits.

When it comes to income tax, it is clear that this is a **progressive tax** – with people paying more the greater their income. However, if we include **indirect taxes** such as VAT, where everyone pays the same regardless of their income, then the poorest 10 per cent actually pay more out in tax than any other group in the population.

However, in any one year the bottom 50 per cent of the population gain from income transfers created by tax and government benefits, and the more affluent 50 per cent lose out. Hills goes on to argue, however, that this vertical redistribution may not be the case when totalled over a person's entire life.

Life-cycle redistribution

Hills' research suggests that life-cycle redistribution of benefits does take place to shift our income from our highest-earning period (20 to 50) to when we are older.

The next step in Hills' analysis was to combine vertical and life-cycle calculations together. There is also clear evidence that the poorest benefit over their lifetime from the rich who make a 'loss' over their lifetime in terms of benefit costs.

However, the situation is more complex in that 75 per cent of the lifetime gain for the poor is actually life-cycle redistribution – in other words the benefits they gain overall over their lifetime are actually self-financed, with only 25 per cent of the gain coming from the rich. To put it another way, 'nearly three-quarters of what the state does ... is a "savings bank", only a quarter is "Robin Hood" redistribution between different people' (Hills 1997).

The welfare state, then, does redistribute, but not to any very great extent.

Social security and stigma

As mentioned in the last section, one of the reasons for the poorest groups failing to receive state benefits is the fact that they simply do not apply for benefits to which they are entitled. One significant reason for this revolves around the idea of stigma. The concept of stigma was used by Goffman (1968) to suggest that a person has low status in the eyes of others, and is aware of this.

Spicker (1984) has suggested that five forms of stigma can be identified in relation to social policy:

- stigma linked to poverty and social exclusion
- stigma related to having a physical disability or long-term illness
- stigma associated with mental illness and drug abuse
- moral stigma linked to certain forms of behaviour such as begging or antisocial behaviour
- the stigma attached to the use of welfare services.

People always seek to avoid stigma if possible as they experience it as humiliating, and this has led to them avoiding seeking social services and state benefits. Indeed, there is considerable underclaiming of state benefits, especially by older people, and this is closely linked to the notion of means-testing. If people have to undergo some test in order to obtain state benefits, they may well regard this as demeaning and discreditable and therefore not apply. The welfare state is built upon the idea that people should be encouraged to save for themselves – and only if they have not done so (or were not able to do so) should the state look after them. According to Carol Walker (1993), a degree of stigma is therefore implicit in the welfare system, as governments seek to limit the numbers of people who apply for state benefits.

Benefit take-up figures suggest that there is a degree of stigma attached to applying for state benefits. About 25 per cent of people do not take up their full Jobseeker's Allowance entitlement, with about the same percentage not taking up Council Tax Benefit and about 8 per cent of people not taking up Housing Benefit. It is estimated that, on average over the last five years, a minimum of £2 billion a year of income-related benefits have not been claimed.

The architects of the welfare state were aware of the stigma that many people felt when asked to reveal all their personal and financial details in order to obtain benefits. It was with this in mind that Beveridge wanted most benefits to be universal and it also underpinned the stress on contributory pensions in welfare: if a person had paid insurance, then they were entitled to benefits. However, if the benefits were non-contributory, many people felt that they were getting charity and so were being 'looked down on'.

Walker (1993) argues that stigma is not an accidental element of claiming benefits, nor is it some historical leftover,

Figure 5.2 Theoretical approaches to social security

Marxist
The social security system supports capitalist exploitation by keeping benefits so low that people have to accept low-paid work. It also creates the impression that poverty is the individual's fault, thus hiding the exploitative nature of capitalism.

Feminist
The system of social security disciplines women into traditional roles by making assumptions about their domestic role and forcing them into dependence on men.

Theoretical approaches to social security

New Right
Individuals should be free to choose whether or not to buy insurance against unemployment or sickness. Little support for the compulsory state system.

Antiracist
The welfare state fails to deal with the racial aspects of poverty and sometimes actually discriminates against individuals and groups from ethnic-minority backgrounds.

but is the result of the demonization by the media of those who claim benefits. The outcome of this is that it has been estimated by the Social Security Select Committee (an official committee of the House of Commons) that as much as £3.5 billion of income-related benefits is not claimed each year; some benefits, such as Housing Benefit, reach 95 per cent take-up, while for others, such as the Social Fund (an emergency loan to people on Income Support), take-up is as low as 70 per cent. However, at the other end of the scale, the welfare state faces a huge number of fraudulent claims. No one is sure of the amount of fraud, but the Social Security Select Committee estimated that the figure was around £1 billion.

KEY TERMS

Contributory benefits – state benefits based on payment of National Insurance contributions; people receiving these are not usually means-tested.

Dependency culture – a situation where it is believed that people prefer to live off state benefits rather than work.

Economic recession – when there is a high rate of unemployment and decline in people's incomes.

Income Support – form of state benefit which acts as a safety net paid to all those whose income falls below the minimum set by government.

Indirect taxes – taxes such as VAT, which everyone pays equally, regardless of their income.

Means-testing – the policy whereby people only receive social benefits or free healthcare if the government considers them to be poor enough.

Minimum wage – in 1999 the government introduced a minimum wage per hour that employers had to pay.

Non-contributory benefits – safety net benefits not based on National Insurance contributions; people receiving these are usually means-tested.

Pool of labour – a Marxist term referring to unemployed people; Marxists believe that capitalism wants a high number of unemployed in order to frighten those in employment with the idea that there is always someone who wants their job.

Poverty trap – a situation which occurs when a person's income actually declines when they move from living on state benefits into employment, as their wages do not bring in the same income as state benefits.

Progressive tax – tax such as Income Tax where the rich pay proportionately more than the poor.

Public expenditure – the total spending made by a government.

Social security – the system of payments made by the state to help people in need.

Stigma – suggests that a person has low status in the eyes of others, and is aware of this.

Tax credit – low earners can receive additional payments from the Inland Revenue.

Universalism – the policy by which every person (within a particular category) receives social benefits or free healthcare, irrespective of their income or wealth.

Check your understanding

1. How much is spent each year in social security payments by the government?

2. Explain in your own words the difference between contributory and non-contributory benefits.

3. What were the aims of the 1979 Conservative government towards social security?

4. How, if at all, have the aims of the Labour Party governments since 1997 differed from those of the previous Conservative government?

5. Give any two feminist criticisms of the social security system.

6. Compare the advantages of universal and means-tested benefits.

7. What is the difference between vertical and life-cycle redistribution?

8. How does the idea of stigma help us understand the low take-up of some social security benefits?

research idea

Child Benefit is a universal benefit paid to all families with children, regardless of their income. Conduct a small-scale survey aimed at finding out the extent to which this benefit is supported. Include a sample of adults living in families with children and a sample without children. Try to include both middle-class and working-class adults. Are there any differences in attitudes? Do differences relate to their family situation or income?

web.task

Go to the website of the Department for Work and Pensions at www.dwp.gov.uk. Select 'Resources' and then 'Research and Statistics'. Select some up-to-date statistics that relate to any one of the themes raised in this topic. Identify the trends or patterns they reveal and attempt to explain them.

exploring social security

Item A

Universal welfare provision works its damaging effects on everyone, not just the poorest. The expectations that society, the state, the government, 'they', will look after our problems tricks us into abdicating from self-reliance and social responsibility. This is a major cause of escalating crime, the collapse of the family, inadequate schools, and healthcare, and economic decline. Despite what universal welfare provision pretends, it is down to each of us, individually and in voluntary cooperation.

We should encourage those at the bottom of the pile to aspire and struggle to improve their lives. Universal welfare provision instead locks them tight into undercaste dependency. For example, it offers incentives for staying unemployed, or underemployed, though work is the major source of independent dignity

By ridiculing competition and excellence, it deprives the children of the welfare-dependent underclass of self-improvement through education – in the past the salvation of even the most disadvantaged...

Adapted from D. Marsland (1989) 'Face to face', *Social Studies Review*, November, Oxford: Philip Allan

Item B

Frank Field does a brilliantly devastating critique of the evils of means-testing, how it warps people's morals, encouraging them to show how incapable they are instead of what they can do. It rewards helplessness and fecklessness instead of endeavour. Everyone who hears him in full flow is always knocked out by it, especially the right. But his critique was never matched by a workable solution. Means-testing is easy to criticize but there just isn't a better alternative.

His theme was high universal benefits for everyone backed by insurance, so that anything extra the poor earned was theirs to keep. It would do away with means-testing and the need for people to prove to the state their various incapacities.

The trouble was his sums, which made no sense.

Universal benefits big enough to do away with means-testing require a vast unacceptable rise in taxes, at the same time as paying out colossal sums to the great majority of the population who don't need any help. Furthermore, there are great difficulties in deciding what conditions qualify people for benefits, in the case of disabled or chronically sick people, we might remove the stigma of the test of income, but there will still be a test to see if the person is adequately sick or disabled to be eligible for the benefit.

Beveridge intended to develop a system of universal benefits but he never made it work either. His state pension always fell below the National Assistance level, so the poorest pensioners always had to be means-tested. The poor have never been lifted out of means-testing, so universal benefits have never helped them.

The truth is we don't spend too much on social security. Set to rise at around 2 per cent more than inflation, it level pegs with our rising GDP*. If it was taking a growing slice of GDP, there might be a reason to worry.

* GDP refers to the overall economic activity of a country and is generally seen as a measure of how wealthy a country is.

Polly Toynbee, *The Guardian*, 21 May 1999

(a) Identify the ideological perspective associated with Marsland's views in **Item A**. (1 mark)

(b) Identify and briefly explain **two** reasons why the provision of social security is harmful, according to Marsland in **Item A**. (8 marks)

(c) Suggest **three** reasons why universal benefits are criticized **(Item B)**. (9 marks)

(d) Identify and explain **two** ways in which the concept of stigma can be applied to debates about social security **(Item B)**. (12 marks)

Exam practice

(e) Outline and assess the view that the social security system should be based on means-tested benefits. (60 marks)

Social services

gettingyouthinking

In February 2000, the little girl pictured here, Victoria Climbié, was murdered by her great aunt, Marie Therese Kouao, and Kouao's boyfriend, Karl Manning. Over a number of years she was brutally beaten, starved and tortured. According to the Laming inquiry (2003) into the circumstances of her death, the local personal social services department, social workers and staff at the local hospital all shared some of the blame. In their defence, the social workers said that they were overworked and the department was underfunded.

1 Do you think it is fair to blame social workers for the death of Victoria? Surely they are just caring people who are doing their job?

2 What is your image of social workers: do-gooders, interfering busybodies or people trying to do something to combat social problems?

3 Is it possible for social workers to solve society's social problems, or are these simply a product of poverty and social exclusion?

Personal social services departments are run by local authorities who receive the bulk of their total funding (about £10 billion) from central government. The main tasks undertaken by personal social services departments include:

- the protection and care of children who are regarded as being at risk of harm or neglect
- organizing care and providing support for older people
- providing support for people with disabilities that prevent them living entirely independent lives
- supporting those people who are **socially excluded**, such as the homeless, refugees and migrants.

Although personal social services are usually associated with the idea of social work and social workers, only about 15 per cent of employees of personal social services departments are actually social workers. The majority of staff are care workers looking after people in residential institutions, day centres or in their own homes.

In many ways, social services departments represent the safety net of the state; they deal with those who have no one else to turn to. However, they represent a tiny proportion of the total care given in Britain, the vast bulk being provided by families. For example, only 30 per cent of people aged 85 or over ever turn to personal social services departments; the figure is less than 4 per cent for children living in families on

state benefits and less than 2 per cent for children with disabilities.

It is important to note that not all personal social services are provided by local authorities – there are numerous charities and other organizations that also provide services.

The origins of personal social services

The origins of social services lies in the work of the **Charity Organisation Society (COS)**, founded in 1869 to regulate the dispersal of funds to help the poor. COS workers would assess the claimants, using 'scientific' criteria to assess whether they were truly in need of help and what form the help should take. COS workers divided the poor into the deserving and undeserving based on the detailed study of individual circumstances – providing the deserving with support and recommending the undeserving to apply to the workhouse. This approach to helping the poor was based on the simple idea that the situation people found themselves in was the result of their individual choices and actions. We shall see how significant this is in the discussion of ideological approaches to social work below.

The COS was a powerful institution and its belief in individual blame for poverty was extremely influential in government circles. However, it gradually declined during the first half of the 20th century and the modern social-work profession, which developed from it, was created at the same time as the introduction of the welfare state.

Initially, there were no local-authority social-work departments as such, but instead there were children's departments and health and welfare departments. However, it was felt that the division was too confusing and as a result of the Seebohm Report in 1971, these were merged into the modern-day personal social services departments run by local authorities. After this, social services departments grew rapidly and took on a range of problems. Alongside this growth, a heated debate about the aims and methods of social work developed.

Ideological approaches to social work

Marxist approaches

According to writers such as Stedman Jones (1971) and Saville (1957), the role of personal social services is to promote social stability and the conformity of working-class people to the capitalist system. Social work does this in a number of ways:

- It persuades people that the reasons they are poor or facing social problems are located in their own, individual failings. This diverts attention away from wider, structural factors in society.
- It works with the poorest and most socially excluded groups in order to reintegrate them into society. However, it is just these people who might provide the real opponents to capitalism as they are the people with the least to lose and, according to Marx, the revolution would come precisely when significant numbers of the working class had nothing to lose.
- It promotes a sense of wellbeing in society. The very existence of social workers appears to demonstrate that the state actually does have the best interests of the workers at heart and does not wish to allow members of society to live in misery.
- Social work enforces certain patterns of behaviour as being correct and others as being incorrect. Social workers help to reinforce the message that it is important to conform to the values of capitalist society.

Other Marxist writers are less critical of social work and see it as offering the potential for some degree of liberation, while accepting that it is primarily there for control reasons.

Methods of social work

Marxist thinking spawned an attempt at a radical form of social work that sees its role as:

- the empowerment of clients so that they recognize and resist oppression
- supporting and encouraging collective action that challenges the actual cause of social problems, which, they suggest, is capitalism itself.

Social democratic approaches

For social democrats, social work has been successful in helping many of the poorest in society. There are real gains for the least powerful and to dismiss the work of social workers as simply 'control' is to miss the fact that social workers really can make a difference to the lives of their clients – whether or not capitalism is the wider social structure that generates the conditions that have led to their problems.

Methods of social work

Traditionally, social democratic approaches to social work have been based on resolving problems on an individual basis. This has involved a number of different techniques, depending upon what is considered to be the most appropriate model of social-work practice to use. Approaches therefore varied between psychologically based approaches to alter behaviour, to supporting local community activity.

Increasingly, however, in response to the government shift to **community care**, much of their work is seen as sorting out appropriate packages of care.

Feminist approaches

Perhaps the most interesting and effective attack on social work has been mounted by the feminist movement. The first point noted by Brooke and Davis (1985) is that social work has largely been an activity undertaken by women – usually upper-class and middle-class – for other women – usually working-class. It developed out of the concerns of women for the social conditions of the poor, and they organized and provided much of the assistance. However, typical of a patriarchal society, the management and control of the social-work organizations have been in the hands of men.

The actual practice of social work is of great significance to feminist analysts. Gieve (1974) has highlighted the way in which social work reinforces the position of women in the family, as it takes for granted the caring role of the woman and rarely challenges the status quo. The outcome of social work, then, is to shore up the family, which in itself is one of the organizations in society that does so much to exploit women. According to Ehrenreich and English (1979), a basic idea of social-work practice is that the quality of maternal care is crucial for the development of normal children. Being a competent mother often involves staying at home to care for children, thus becoming financially dependent upon a male partner. This leads to the subjection and potential exploitation of women.

Social work also operates with the idea of what is normal female behaviour. This will usually involve taking on the caring role for whichever members of the family are in need. Earlier, we saw that only a small proportion of caring is provided by the state, with the vast bulk being provided by families. In actual fact, as Finch and Groves (1983) point out, that burden tends to fall on the female family members.

Methods of social work

Feminist approaches to social work have focused on **antidiscriminatory** and **antioppressive** work. As traditional social work has accepted the status quo and sought to reintegrate those with social problems back into society, feminists have refused to do this. Instead, they seek to alter the practices of discrimination and oppression that cause women to have social problems. Williams (1989) has argued that the feminist approach to social work should also apply to those from ethnic-minority backgrounds, whose problems are largely caused by an oppressive and racist society.

New Right approaches

For the New Right, the distinction made between the deserving and undeserving remains true. Simply by giving welfare to the poorest and least successful in society solves nothing, as the cause of the social problem lies either with the individual or their culture. According to Bremner (1968), for example, all that social work does is to help continue the problems that it is supposed to deal with.

For Bremner, it is the role of the family to care for its members. By taking away responsibility, the state is actually weakening the family unit, thereby creating yet more dependency upon the state. The increasing burden on the state of providing personal social services, according to Bacon and Eltis (1976), simply increases taxes, places greater burdens on employers and leads to unemployment, which generates more poverty.

The growth of the social services departments and of social work as a profession has been fuelled, according to Gray (1992), by the way that social workers have colonized the right to speak about the poor and the socially disadvantaged. They have created an industry of social work where none is actually needed.

Methods of social work

For the New Right, social-work departments need to be replaced by charitable organizations that can distinguish between the deserving and undeserving.

Contemporary personal social services

In 1990, the Health and Community Care Act brought in radical changes to social services departments:

- Wherever possible, people were to be looked after in the community rather than in institutions (see below).
- The traditional model of personal social services, whereby the state provided all services, was dismantled. Since 1990, a mixed economy of welfare has been introduced, with

local authorities purchasing care from any appropriate organization. This could be private, charitable or from local government itself. Although the act was introduced by a Conservative government that relied heavily upon advice from the New Right, the ideas have been continued by New Labour.

The role of social workers was increasingly to involve 'care planning'. This involves the social worker assessing a particular person who has asked for help and then organizing a set of services for them from the range of provider organizations. These services will be paid for by the local authority and by the people themselves, as many of them are provided only after the person is means-tested.

Health and social care

As a result of the government's 'modernization agenda', in which all government services were encouraged to reorganize themselves and to adopt modern management methods, social care is increasingly becoming integrated into the health services. In the 1999 Health Act, all health and social care services had to form 'local strategic care partnerships' that involved them working much more closely together.

Community versus residential care

It has been estimated that there are well over ten million people in the UK who need someone to help them look after themselves. As we saw before, the overwhelming majority of these people receive adequate levels of help from members of their own friends or family – usually female. However, there are many whose needs are so great that they cannot be satisfactorily looked after by friends, neighbours and family members, or else it could be that they have no family to look after them and are socially isolated.

There are two possible ways of organizing care for these people:

- **Residential care** – Care in institutions such as hospitals, children's homes or elderly persons' homes. The sociologist Erving Goffman (1968) termed these '**total institutions**', as the individuals being cared for live there permanently – eating, sleeping and having their leisure there.
- *Community care* – The approach that provides care in the person's home, if possible. There are considerable variations within this definition, however, as individuals may be living in a group home, where three or four people share accommodation (often used when moving mentally-ill people out of long-stay hospitals), or it may be that the person lives in accommodation that is watched over by a warden (such as sheltered housing).

Community care

Today, the model of community care is the dominant one in Britain, although until the 1960s, residential care had been

'Caring' as a concept was taken up by feminist writers in the 1980s. Initially, they were interested in it as an example of how women were expected to shoulder an unfair proportion of this work for family members – particularly older relatives and any disabled family members. This initial interest then began to broaden out. The next stage in feminist writings on the subject of caring focused on the assumption made by the welfare system that it was the responsibilities of women to undertake family care. This was based, in turn, on traditional ideas concerning the role of women in society and within the family. Welfare benefits assumed that women would care for family members and only if they were unable to do so would the state step in.

social inequality and difference

On the other hand, whereas women were socially expected to care, men could discharge their family obligations by passing on the responsibility to their wives.

Feminist writers, therefore, set about highlighting these issues. They went further, pointing out that caring is a form of hard physical labour, undertaken in unrewarding circumstances with little public recognition of its importance. In doing this, they began to challenge the way that the expectations of women to undertake a wide range of household and caring tasks play a crucial role in limiting women's lives and restricting access to decent jobs and positions outside the family.

---

favoured. The move towards community care came about for four main reasons:

- cost
- demographic change
- ideology
- concerns about residential care.

Cost

By 1986, the government was spending approximately £6 million in the area of residential care, but by the 1990s, it was paying out over £1.6 billion. Such sustained rises led the government to feel that it was becoming too expensive to maintain.

Demographic changes

The reason for the growth in costs is the result of increased numbers of older and disabled people. There are over four million people over the age of 75 (16 per cent of the population) today and at least 1.25 million people over the age of 85, compared to 700 000 in 1986. This second figure is important because it is at around 85 that older people need substantial assistance from the state. There has also been a similar growth in the numbers of severely disabled people (though there is considerable overlap between the groups), with over 6.2 million people in the UK with a physical disability of some kind.

Ideology

We have seen that social-policy decisions are crucially influenced by ideologies, and the development of community care was no exception. At the time of the policy change to community-based care, the government was influenced by the ideas of the New Right, which, as we have seen before, stress self-reliance, independence and the family. In particular, the government asked why it was that the state was having to provide institutional care for people who could have been looked after by family members.

Linked to this was the acknowledgement that there were already over 1.5 million people acting as unpaid carers for family members (the majority of whom were women) and it was felt that funding should shift away from the state-provided residential allowance towards giving those carers financial support.

Concerns about residential institutions

When people are looked after in residential accommodation, they depend almost totally upon the staff who work there. There have been numerous examples of poor treatment from care staff who work in highly stressed conditions for low pay.

Even where staff work to the best of their abilities, the nature of residential life, where residents live their entire lives in an isolated environment, tends to generate a culture of its own. The best known research into this is by Erving Goffman (1968).

Goffman studied a large mental hospital in Washington in the USA. What he wanted to explore was the impact of living in a total institution upon the person's identity. Although the study was of a mental institution, Goffman claims it can apply to any institution in which people live for 24 hours each day – this could therefore be as true for a prison, army or a monastery. According to Goffman, on entering a total institution, people are stripped of their old identity. They may have their hair cut in an institutional way and/or have their own clothes taken away, to be replaced by the institution's own. Often the person is then forced into a process he calls 'the mortification of self', whereby they undertake a series of degrading or humiliating actions, as required by the institution's staff. This could be abuse by officers (army) or being bathed without privacy (homes for older people). The next stage in the process, according to Goffman, is that the person is gradually taught another personality (or self) that is supposed to fit into the requirements of the institution. People are rewarded for behaving according to the formal or informal rules of the staff.

However, Goffman argues that people respond in very different ways to this process and he suggests that there are five 'modes of adaptation':

- *Situational withdrawal* – The individual withdraws into themselves.
- *Intransigence* – The individual refuses to cooperate.
- *Colonization* – The individual becomes fully at home and does not wish to leave.
- *Conversion* – The individual identifies with the staff and takes on some of their behaviour patterns.
- *Playing it cool* – A very 1960s term for simply trying to get through the experience of the institution without too much self-damage.

It is important to remember that Goffman's research took place in the 1950s and we need to be careful about applying it to contemporary institutional care.

Criticisms of community care

Community care has not been the great success that its supporters had hoped. The ideal of care at home has not been matched by the reality of provision. The following are some of the reasons suggested:

- *Funding* – It was thought that community care would be cheaper than residential care. However, this has not turned out to be true. Furthermore, many community care services are means-tested so that the costs have been borne by those living at home.
- *Inequality of provision* – The quality of community care varies across the country depending upon the organization delivering it. There is no one standard.
- *Carers* – Community care has continued to rely upon family and friends to provide support and care.
- *Resistance* – One form of community care has been to set up small hostels for groups of mentally-ill people and those with learning difficulties. However, local residents often oppose these.
- *Potential danger* – Some groups of people who live in the community pose a potential danger. There is a small number of mentally ill people, for example, who are dangerous if they do not take their medication.

Residential care

Although the vast majority of care is now taking place in the community, there has been a swing back towards residential care for some groups of people, such as those with the most severe disabilities and those who are unable to look after themselves for whatever reason. Residential care is provided by a range of organizations that include local authorities and the NHS, voluntary organizations and private profit-making organizations.

Despite the criticisms of residential care, there are of arguments in favour of it:

- There is no alternative – For some groups of people, there is simply no realistic alternative, as they need levels of care or support that can only be achieved by being cared for in an institution.
- Residential care has been reformed – The criticisms of residential care are outdated. Government reports have led to the introduction of a number of reforms. These included staff monitoring, improved links with the local community and the application of national standards.

Direct payments

The most recent innovation in care services has been the widespread introduction of direct payments. Traditionally, most people defined by social services as 'in need' have been provided with the services that are regarded as necessary. However, in the new model of direct payments, individuals – in particular people who are disabled and older people – are given money directly, instead of receiving services; they can then choose themselves what services they wish to buy with the money.

KEY TERMS

Antidiscriminatory – activities that challenge behaviour or policies that benefit one group over others.

Antioppressive – activities that challenge behaviour or policies that oppress particular groups in society.

Charity Organisation Society (COS) – organization set up in the later part of the 19th century to help the poor; very influential in creating the idea of social work.

Community care – help given in the home of the person or in small-scale institutions located in residential areas.

Residential care – help and care given in large-scale institutions, such as care homes for older people.

Socially excluded – people without access to the normal quality of life, such as the homeless and the poor.

Total institutions – a term used by Goffman to refer to the fact that people living in institutions are totally cut off from the wider society and develop certain, particular forms of behaviour.

Check your understanding

1. What are the main tasks of personal social services departments?

2. What was the COS? What was its view on the causes of poverty?

3. What do Marxists believe is the true role of social services?

4. What do feminists believe is the role of social services?

5. What changes were introduced by the 1990 Health and Community Care Act?

6. What reasons lay behind the introduction of community care?

7. What is meant by a total institution?

8. What responses to life in a total institution did Goffman identify?

research idea

Look up cases of child abuse using the website of a newspaper. For example, *The Guardian* runs regular discussions on social care issues. Conduct a content analysis of the way in which social work and social workers are represented.

web.task

Look at the job adverts at
www.community-care.co.uk
What sorts of agencies employ social workers? How does this illustrate the debates over the mixed economy of welfare?

exploring social services

Item A

One of the most significant changes in the 1990s for voluntary organizations involved in the delivery of welfare services in the UK, was the implementation in 1993 of the 1990 NHS and Community Care Act. This legislation encouraged:

- a shift from institutional to community care
- an emphasis on needs-led rather than supplier-led services

- a decentralization of policy and management
- the development of a mixed economy of care involving for-profit and non-profit providers as well as the state.

The consequences were mixed. The advantages were that the increased funding led to better organized and efficient voluntary services and an increase in the training and skills of volunteers. But there were also negatives – especially the increase in dependence on government funding and the squeezing out of smaller, voluntary organizations that were unable to compete for funds in the new 'marketplace'.

Scott, D. (2003) 'The role of the voluntary and non-governmental sector', in J. Baldock, N. Manning and S. Vickerstaff, *Social Policy*, Oxford: Oxford University Press

Item B

The key concept informing social-care development has been that of 'normalization'. Originally developed in Scandinavia through the work of Wolfensberger (Race 2003), normalization aims to ensure that people with disabilities share the same lifestyles and choices as non-disabled people. These ideas have emerged from sociological concepts of labelling and deviance, whereby people with disabilities have been stigmatized and isolated from the wider social community and as a result have been socially devalued

and excluded. According to the principles of normalization, people with disabilities should be integrated with the rest of society – using the same facilities, living in ordinary households and taking part in social and community life. Their surroundings and clothes should not be marked out as different – second-best, shabby or demeaningly childish. They should be allowed to progress through the life-cycle with all the normal expectations, including sexual relationships, marriage, parenthood and full employment. In

Wolfensberger's work, particular emphasis is placed upon social-role valorization, whereby the demeaning and negative stereotypes projected onto disabled people by society are reversed through their positive involvement in socially valued activities. These ideas have been particularly influential in Britain in the deinstitutionalization movement and the integration of disabled people into mainstream life.

Twigg, J. (2003) 'Social care', in J. Baldock, N. Manning and S. Vickerstaff, *Social Policy*, Oxford: Oxford University Press

(a) Explain what is meant by a 'for-profit provider' **(Item A)**. (1 mark)

(b) Identify and briefly explain **two** changes brought about by the 1990 NHS and Community Care Act **(Item A)**. (8 marks)

(c) Identify **three** responses to institutionalization identified by Goffman. (9 marks)

(d) Identify and explain **two** advantages of 'normalization' for people with disabilities **(Item B)**. (12 marks)

Exam practice

(e) Outline and assess the view that the disadvantages of residential care outweigh the advantages. (60 marks)

WE ALL HAVE SOME EXPERIENCE OF POWER. Some of us wield it. Most of us are on the receiving end of it. However, it is not an easy concept to define because it takes so many different forms. Sociologists, therefore, take a keen interest in both the nature of power and its sources. This is the main focus of Topic 1.

You will have noticed that power is openly used by a variety of people, including your parents, your teachers, the police, your employers and the prime minister. You, too, probably have some power – you may be a prefect at school or a supervisor at work, but you also exercise more subtle and hidden forms of power as consumers and voters. Topic 2 looks at the distribution of power in society and asks whether it is evenly shared out or whether it is concentrated in the hands of a select few.

Whether you like it or not, the government plays a major role in your lives – the state defines and supervises all aspects of your existence from cradle to grave.

Topic 3, therefore, investigates the function of the state and the central role that it plays in society.

Many young people seem to be turned off by mainstream politicians and political parties. However, this does not mean that they are turned off by politics. Young people often get angry about a range of issues, such as debt in the developing world, animal experimentation, environmental degradation and human rights abuses. Topic 4 explores some of the reasons why these issues attract attention and what organizations exist to help people tackle them.

Disorder and riots have been a fairly regular occurrence in many cities both in the UK and across the world over the last few years. Topic 5 turns its attention to these issues and explores the various explanations for urban disorder – is it just a matter of lawlessness or are people making a political statement?

OCRspecification	topics	pages
The context of political action		
Defining political action: types of governments, political parties, pressure groups and new social movements.	Definitions of key terms are contained in Topic 1 although types of political movement are the subject of Topic 4.	206–213 228–237
Globalization, global social movements and nationalism.	Discussion of globalization occurs at various points in the unit, but the main discussion of these issues is in Topic 4.	228–237
The changing patterns of political action		
Types of direct action, for example riots, terrorism, demonstrations and strikes.	Primarily covered in Topic 5 although some relevant material in Topic 4 in the context of the tactics of new social movements.	228–243
The relationship between direct action and social class, age, gender, ethnicity, sexuality, disability and nationalism.	These issues are discussed in Topics 4 and 5.	228–243
Explanations of the forms and patterns of political action and how these relate to social structure, economic deprivation, rational responses to problems such as powerlessness and racism, and collective/subcultural identities.	Covered in Topics 4 and 5	228–243
Power, culture and identity		
Power, authority, legitimacy, ideology and hegemony, and their impacts on the development of new social movements.	These key areas of political sociology are covered in Topics 1, 2 and 3. New social movements are covered in Topic 4.	206–237
Differences and the formation of identities through protest, for example social class, age, gender and ethnic identities.	Protest movements are the focus of Topic 4 although some relevant material can also be found in Topic 5.	228–243

UNIT 6

Protest and social movements

Defining power

All of the people shown above exercise some sort of power.

1 What type of power do you think they exercise?

2 How do these types of power differ from each other?

3 Rank these individuals in hierarchical order on the basis of how much power they exert over your life.

4 How might Madonna's success have equipped young females today with more power than their mothers?

The above exercise should have shown you that power can take several different forms and can be exercised in a number of direct and indirect ways. For example, you are unlikely to meet George Bush or Osama Bin Laden, but they still exercise considerable power over your life. For example, terrorism on the streets of Britain in 2005 is seen by some as a result of the policies of these two individuals. In 2005, the power of the police to stop and search you, and even use violence on you, considerably increased as a result of these terrorist attacks. Similarly, it can be argued that if you are a female, Madonna's success impacts directly on your capacity to exercise power. You exercise more power than your mother because Madonna's career over the years has contributed to an acceptance of a wide range of activities for women that were once considered deviant.

Max Weber and power

In the most general sense, power refers to any kind of influence exercised by individuals or groups on others. For example, Max Weber defined power as the chance or probability of an individual or group of people imposing their will on others despite resistance, i.e. where A has power over B to the extent that A can get B to do something that B would not otherwise do. This conception of power – the **zero-sum view of power** – implies that the exercise of power involves negative consequences for some individuals and groups because it involves repression, force and constraint. Weber believed that such power could be exercised in a range of social situations.

<< *Positions of power can emerge from social relations in a drawing room as well as in the market; from the rostrum of a lecture hall as well as the command post of a regiment, from an erotic or charitable relationship as well as from scholarly discussion or athletics.* >> (Lukes 1986)

Weber distinguished between two main types of power implied here – coercion and authority:

- Coercion is force, usually in the form of violence or military resources.
- Authority depends upon consent – that is, people believe that the power is **legitimate**.

f o c u s on . . .

Max Weber's types of authority

Weber argues that legitimacy can be derived from three sources.

- *Charisma* – Some individuals are able to direct the behaviour of others because they have exceptionally powerful personalities that inspire strong feelings of devotion and loyalty. These may be political leaders such as Adolf Hitler, religious leaders such as Gandhi or the Reverend Jim Jones and sporting personalities such as José Mourinho or Sir Alex Ferguson. Note how some of your teachers may use their charisma to motivate you.
- *Tradition* – Power can be derived from historical precedent, such as that embodied in the succession of the Royal Family in the UK. Many people in the UK believe that the Queen has inherited the 'right' to rule and so consider themselves as loyal subjects.
- *Rational–legal* – Most authority in Britain, whether that of the prime minister, a police officer or a teacher, derives from formal rules which often take the form of laws. Such authority is thought to be impartially applied to everyone and enforced without bias. Consequently, people consent to obey this type of power, which is usually administered by a hierarchical **bureaucracy**. Morgan (1999) refers to this as 'the routinization of obedience'. The option of force still exists but it is used only as a final resort.

Some sociologists have highlighted other forms of power halfway between coercion and authority, e.g. influence (where people are persuaded to change their minds) and manipulation (where individuals are cynically deceived perhaps through control over education, knowledge, information and news).

Functionalism and power

Functionalists view power as a positive resource, characterized by consensus and legitimacy. Talcott Parsons (1963) argued that power results from the sharing of resources in order to achieve collective social and cultural goals. If A and B work together, they will both increase their power as well as benefit society. Power is therefore a functional resource working for the benefit of everybody and helping to maintain social order and strengthen social solidarity.

Parsons argued that if power is to be used to pursue collective goals effectively, it needs direction and organization. For this reason, members of society authorize some individuals via democratic elections (namely, politicians) to exercise power on their behalf. Parsons argues that if society is unhappy with the use of that power, members of society simply will not vote for them. In this way, power can never be monopolized and is always used to benefit the greater good. However, this view of power has been criticized as naive, as it fails to acknowledge that power can be accumulated in the hands of individuals with more interest in pursuing their own sectional interests than collective goals or common good.

Marxism and power

Marxists argue that power arises out of the social **relations of production** that characterize the economic system of production found in **capitalist societies** (see Unit 1 *Sociological theories*, p. 5). These social relations exist between two groups characterized by their access (or lack of access) to economic resources:

- the **bourgeoisie** or ruling class – a minority group who own and control the **means of production**, such as capital, land, factories, technology and raw materials
- the **proletariat** or working class – the majority group who have only their labour power, which they hire out to the bourgeoisie in return for a wage.

This class inequality is further deepened by the bourgeoisie's exploitation of the proletariat's labour power, in that the wealth of the dominant class is increased by the fact that the value of the goods produced by the worker always far exceeds the wage paid. This surplus value is pocketed by the bourgeoisie in the form of profit. Marxists argue, therefore, that inequalities in ownership and control – along with exploitation – lead to economic inequality, and this is the source of political and social power in society. In other words, power derives from class relationships.

Hegemony

Class domination and economic power are maintained through coercion (although this tends to be used as a last resort) and ideological **hegemony** (the control of ideas). Marxists argue that this latter concept is much more effective than force in controlling a proletariat which has the potential to be very disruptive if it decides that the organization of the capitalist infrastructure is unfair and unjust in how income and wealth are distributed. Hegemony or cultural dominance by the ruling class is needed in order to make sure that the working class regard bourgeois power as legitimate, and so reduce the potential for revolutionary protest.

According to Bocock (1986), hegemony occurs when the intellectual and moral ideas of the ruling class provide the dominant cultural outlook for the whole of society. Marxists such as Althusser (1971) argue that the bourgeoisie achieve this cultural dominance by using its economic power to define what counts as knowledge, ideas, art, education, news and so on. Social institutions such as the education system, the legal system, the political system, the mass media and religion, which Marxists see as making up the '**superstructure**' of capitalist society, play an important role in transmitting ruling-class ideology so that it is accepted by the mass of the population as 'normal' or 'natural'.

Westergaard (1996) argues that the result of hegemonic power is that workers fail to understand their own structural position correctly – that is, they fail to realize their true interests as exploited workers. This false class-consciousness means that they rarely realize their potential power for bringing about revolutionary change. The Frankfurt School of Marxism (see Unit 1, pp. 5–6) in a similar analysis argue that the working class has become 'ideologically incorporated' into capitalist society. Marcuse (1964) argued that this incorporation takes the form of encouraging 'one-dimensional thought': the general population is encouraged to indulge in uncritical and sterile forms of entertainment or mass culture that reduce their appetite for critical and creative thought and action that might challenge hegemonic power. Following on from Marcuse, White (2004) argues that Western culture today is dominated by a 'Middle Mind' – a mainstream consensus that is shaped by consumer culture that pleases everyone but moves, challenges or shocks no one. He notes:

>> When we accept the Middle Mind as our culture (or, worse yet, when we demand it as consumers), we are not merely being stupid or unsophisticated or "low brow". We are vigorously conspiring against ourselves. We murder our own capacity for critique and invention as if we were children saying, 'Can you do this for me?'.>>

According to Gramsci (1971), hegemony, and the resulting consent of the people, has enabled the ruling class to deal with any threats to its authority without having to use force. However, Gramsci argues that hegemony does not mean that subordinate classes will always lack power or that the power of the dominant class is absolute. He argues that power is potentially available to the subordinate classes if they become sufficiently class-conscious and politically organized to seize or

focus on . . .

Giddens and power

Leading sociologist Anthony Giddens (1968) is critical of functionalist analyses of power. He suggests that power is part of all social relations and interactions.

>> What slips away from sight almost completely in the Parsonian analysis is the very fact that power is always exercised over someone! Parsons virtually ignores, quite consciously and deliberately, the hierarchical character of power, and the divisions of interest which are frequently consequent upon it. However much it is true that power can rest upon 'agreement', it is also true that interests of power-holders and those subject to that power often clash. >>

>> All interaction involves the use of power because all interaction is concerned with the production and reproduction of structure, drawing upon rules and resources. Power relates to those resources which actors draw upon in interaction, in order to 'make a difference'. >>

Giddens, A. (1968) '"Power" in the recent writings of Talcott Parsons', *Sociology*, 2(3)

1 Explain Giddens' criticism of Parsons in your own words.

2 Giddens argues that all interaction involves power. Explain how power might be involved in:

a a group of friends talking
b a family deciding which TV programmes to watch in the evening
c a doctor–patient interaction
d a parents' evening at school.

to challenge the control of the means of production. Importantly, Gramsci argues that people in capitalist societies experience 'dual consciousness', i.e. their beliefs are only partly shaped by capitalist ideology because their beliefs are also influenced by their personal day-to-day experiences of society –

these sometimes contradict or challenge dominant ideology and so encourage some resistance and opposition to it. This 'resistance' might take an overtly political form (for instance, active campaigning or taking to the streets to oppose G8 talks) or a 'symbolic' form (such as setting out to challenge dominant institutions and beliefs through the use of 'shock', e.g. through fashion statements or simply substituting a hedonistic lifestyle for the 9 to 5 lifestyle demanded by capitalism).

Neo-Marxists such as Stuart Hall (Hall and Jefferson 1976) have developed **relational conceptions of power** – that is, they recognize that power is a process which involves **ideological struggle** between the capitalist class and groups such as working-class youth. The capitalist class is normally able to impose cultural hegemony and so obtain the consent of most of the people to rule. However, pockets of **symbolic resistance** among sections of the working class indicate that power is not a one-way process. Gilroy (1982a) suggests that working-class crime may well be political, a means by which subordinate groups can enjoy some power through hitting back at the symbols of capitalist power such as wealth and property. The work of the Birmingham Centre for Contemporary Cultural Studies similarly suggests that working-class deviant youth subcultures may be symbolically resisting hegemonic definitions of respectability by adopting forms of style and behaviour that set out to shock. For example, the Punk subculture of the late 1970s incorporated conformist symbols, such as the Queen and Union Jack, as well as deviant symbols, such as Nazi insignia, into its dress codes in a deliberately provocative way.

Criticisms of the Marxist theory of power

Michael Mann (1986) takes issue with the Marxist view that all power is rooted in class relationships. He argues that there are two broad types of power:

- distributional power – exercised by individuals
- collective power – exercised by social groups ranging in size from nation states to families.

Mann notes that power has a number of unique characteristics:

- It can be *extensive* – It can involve the ability to co-opt large numbers of people across huge distances to work together in common interest. For example, some Muslim people, regardless of their nationality or ethnic group, express loyalty first and foremost to their religion.
- It can be *intensive* – It can command extreme loyalty and dedication from followers. For example, the power wielded by some leaders of religious groups, most notably Jim Jones of The People's Temple, has resulted in mass suicide.
- It can be *authoritative* – It is organized around rules and commands which are largely regarded as legitimate. For example, your head teacher or principal has the power to exclude you from school or college.
- It can be *diffused* – It results from natural or spontaneous processes rather than an individual or group issuing commands or physically imposing themselves on a subordinate group. For example, a fall in consumer demand for a particular product might force a manufacturer out of business.

Mann agrees with Marxists that economics (or class) is an important source of power but, as the examples above illustrate, he acknowledges other sources of power:

- World religions often wield ideological power independently of the economic system.
- Military power, particularly in the developing world, may be separate from economic power, as seen in the number of economic elites who have been deposed by military coups.
- The state has political power, which may result from democratic elections in the case of politicians and **meritocracy** in the case of civil servants. Mann notes that political power is not always used in ways which benefit the economically dominant classes – for example, the minimum wage legislation brought in by the Labour Government in 1999 was opposed by big business interests.

synoptic link

social inequality and difference

Functionalists, such as Davis and Moore (1955), see stratification and social inequality as a functional necessity in modern societies, because certain social positions, e.g. occupational roles, are more important than others. In order to attract those with the most talent, high rewards are attached to these positions. Those in the top positions often wield economic power in that they enjoy a superior standard of living. They often make decisions that affect the economic wellbeing of other members of society, e.g. where to locate a new business. They also exercise authority legitimated by both law and state bureaucracy, e.g. head teachers can suspend pupils. Functionalists argue that this power is generally used for the benefit of society and our consent for its use is an important contributor to social order.

Marxists, on the other hand, see social class inequalities as the natural outcome of the social organization of capitalism. The bourgeoisie control the means of production and exploit the labour power of the working class. The vast profits made by the bourgeoisie give them political power. Consequently, they can use coercion and repression, if they so wish, in order to protect their interests through control of agencies such as the police, the security services and the armed forces. However, Marxists note that in modern capitalist societies, the bourgeoisie are more likely to use cultural and ideological forms of power, through agencies such as education and the mass media, to persuade the subordinate class that society is organized in a just fashion.

Hegemony and resistance

1 **Explain how the people in the two photos above could be seen to be symbolically resisting hegemony.**

Mann argues that it is rare that any one social group in a single society is able to dominate more than two sources of power, especially as power is increasingly globalized – power networks now extend across the world and consequently no single interest group is able to monopolize power.

Abercrombie *et al.* (1980) are dismissive of claims that a dominant ideology characterizes contemporary society. They put forward three key reasons:

- Capitalism today is characterized by conflicts between capitalist interests such as small businesses, finance capital, industrialists, multinational companies and state corporations. This conflict undermines the idea that the capitalist class is transmitting strong and unified ideological messages.
- The subordinate class often rejects the so-called dominant ideology – as can be seen in surveys of working-class people

who recognize that we live in a class society characterized by inequality. Such workers may express resistance through strikes and membership of trade unions.

- The simple fact that workers have to work in order to preserve their standard of living leads to their cooperation and participation. People conform, not because of ideological hegemony but quite simply because they fear unemployment and poverty.

Poststructuralism and power

Michel Foucault

Foucault (1980) rejects the link between social structure and power. He suggests that power is an inescapable part of everyday life. In particular, power plays a major role in the construction of identity.

According to Foucault, there is a significant relationship between power, knowledge and language. He argued that there exist bodies of knowledge and language which he terms **'discourses'**. These dominate how society sees, describes and thinks about how we should live our lives, in terms of family, sexuality, discipline and punishment, health and illness, and so on. Our power to behave in certain ways – and the power of others to prevent us behaving in those ways – is dependent upon dominant discourses.

In illustration, Foucault showed how, during the 18th century, there was a shift away from coercive forms of power associated with physical punishment (e.g. execution) to what he calls **'disciplinary power'**. This type of power saw a move to identify and categorize 'normality' and 'deviance' in the form of discourses in the fields of criminality, sexual behaviour and illness. Bauman (1983) notes how this type of power is based on the construction and imposition of surveillance (watching for deviation from normality), routine and regulation. 'It wanted to impose one ubiquitous [i.e. universal] pattern of normality and eliminate everything and everybody which the pattern could not fit.'

Disciplinary power

Foucault's conception of disciplinary power, i.e. discourses that control everyday behaviour via surveillance and discipline, first developed in state institutions such as prisons and asylums. For example, Foucault notes that people were no longer simply punished for crimes – rather there was an attempt to judge why people had committed particular crimes, i.e. to categorize them into specific types. A range of expert professions emerged with the power to observe, judge and categorize people's behaviour in terms of 'normality' and 'deviance'. These included psychologists, psychiatrists and social workers. Foucault notes how, over the course of the 20th century, such surveillance and judgement has expanded into institutions such as schools and workplaces. For example, educational psychologists now attempt to explain a range of behaviours exhibited by children in the educational system, ranging from high achievement through to truancy. At the same time, people who choose not to work are dismissed by experts as 'inadequate' or as 'social problems'. Foucault is therefore suggesting that our identity as well as our behaviour patterns are the result of these powerful judgements or discourses about what should count as 'normal' or 'conformist' behaviour.

Bio-power

Foucault identified a second conception of power which he termed '**bio-power**'. Bio-power is concerned with controlling the body and how it is perceived by the general population. Foucault sees bio-power as especially influential in structuring discourses on sexuality and in shaping attitudes and behaviour among the mass of the population towards different types of sexuality. He claims that, from the 19th century onwards, discourse on sexual behaviour rapidly became dominated by professionals working in the fields of psychiatry, medicine and social work. He argues that this discourse on sexual behaviour has power over all of us because it defines what is and what is not 'normal' and 'what is and what is not available for individuals to do, think, say and be' (Clegg 1989).

Foucault suggests that the dominant discourse favours heterosexuality at the expense of homosexuality and other alternative sexualities. This power to impose definitions of 'normality' has become part of institutionalized life and results in individuals being criticized, treated prejudicially and punished for being different – that is, for indulging in non-heterosexual behaviour or for holding attitudes that challenge the dominant heterosexual discourse. Moreover, Foucault argues that bio-power is extremely influential because it shapes our own sense of identity. We unconsciously internalize aspects of the discourse and engage in self-discipline. We avoid behaviour and attitudes that are likely to provoke even more surveillance and discipline from official agencies. For example, if we are attracted to people of the same sex, we may avoid forms of behaviour which other people interpret as 'homosexual' in order to avoid judgement and perhaps prejudice and discrimination. Foucault claimed that such self-discipline leads to 'docile bodies' – that is, people who conform and consequently do not threaten social order.

Power and resistance

Foucault does not see power as an entirely negative concept. He sees that it has a positive dimension too, as people generally enjoy the freedom to choose to resist such power. He argues that the knowledge on which power is based can be challenged. For example, there are signs that in the West, homosexuality is becoming more socially acceptable (and therefore, less deviant), as the medical and psychological knowledge used to justify the repressive treatment of homosexuals in the past is challenged. It can be argued that the weakening of the dominant medical and psychological discourse about homosexuality has resulted in less surveillance, discipline and punishment, as illustrated by the virtual decriminalization of such behaviour in the Western world (although negative social attitudes towards homosexuality in some sections of the population still illustrate the power of the previously dominant discourse).

Evaluating Foucault's work

Foucault's work has been criticized for not being empirical in a conventional research sense. He tended to support his arguments with selective historical examples rather than systematically gathered contemporary data. Moreover, his work tended to be overly descriptive at the expense of explanation – for example, it is not entirely clear why disciplinary power and bio-power evolved, nor who exercises these types of power. Foucault did argue that no one group dominates disciplinary power but it may be unrealistic to suggest that no one group benefits more than others from exercising this type of power. However, his work has value in that it convincingly explores the relationship between knowledge and power. His observation that the wielding of power produces resistance which may lead to positive change is an interesting contrast with those theories which define power in more absolute and repressive terms.

Gender and power

Westwood and postfeminism

Westwood (2002) notes that feminist thinkers who focused on the concept of patriarchy insisted that the key issue in gender relations was power. Feminism saw itself 'as fighting for a reversal of the status quo in which men were seen to be dominant'. However, Westwood argues that this type of approach was crude and alienated women, because it cast women as powerless subordinates, oppressed and exploited by patriarchal power.

Westwood argues for the development of 'postfeminism', in which sociologists use Foucault's work on discourse to show how women can take control of their lives and identities. She cites Rubin (1998), who argues that females can exercise power through a series of strategies focusing on the microprocesses of power. Women can use their bodies, intuition and control of gestures to gain power and to construct their identities. Westwood uses the example of Diana, Princess of Wales, to demonstrate how the microprocesses of power can be amplified through the media. Westwood concludes that Diana was able to exercise power subtly by presenting herself as a victim of both adultery and institutional power. She made herself highly visible through the media and used her role as the mother of the future king to ensure her voice was heard.

Westwood argues that the Diana story raises many of the issues seen in a Foucauldian reading of power relations. For example, Diana's struggle for power stemmed from her attempts to construct an identity or individuality that was at odds with a discourse that stated that she should be an obedient subject of the monarchy. Such a discourse led to attempts to discipline her and control her behaviour. In her case, this disciplinary power eventually failed because she was able to develop visibility and utilize aspects of the microprocesses of power (especially in the field of sexual politics) that monarchy and society could not ignore.

Bio-power – term used by Foucault to describe concern with controlling the body and its perception.

Bourgeoisie – Marxist term describing the ruling (or capitalist) class in capitalist society.

Bureaucracy – form of organization associated with modern societies, consisting of a hierarchy of formal positions, each with clear responsibilities.

Capitalist societies – where one social class owns the means of production, while another class does the work.

Disciplinary power – the power to identify and categorize what is 'normal' and what is 'deviant'.

Discourse – ways of talking and thinking that dominate how society sees, describes and thinks about how we should live our lives.

Hegemony – situation where the ideology of the dominant class becomes accepted as the shared culture of the whole of society.

Ideological struggle – cultural conflict between the capitalist and subordinate classes.

Legitimate – justified and accepted.

Means of production – Marxist term referring to the material forces that enable things be produced, e.g. capital, land, factories.

Meritocracy – a society in which people are rewarded on the basis of merit, i.e. intelligence and ability, usually via examinations and qualifications.

Proletariat – in Marxist terms, the working class, who hire out to the bourgeoisie in return for a wage

Relational conception of power – power seen as a process that involves ideological struggle between the capitalist class and subordinate groups.

Relations of production – Marxist term referring to the allocation of rules and responsibilities among those involved in production.

Superstructure – Marxist term used to describe the parts of society not concerned with economic production, such as the media, religion and education.

Symbolic resistance – rebellion which takes an indirect form.

Zero-sum view of power – idea that power involves one person or group gaining and another person or group losing.

Criticisms of Westwood

Westwood may be guilty of exaggerating the degree of power that women have in patriarchal societies. It can be argued that women still do not enjoy equal power and status with men in fields such as work, wealth, income and politics. Moreover, Princess Diana's power to resist the will of the monarchy may have been the result of her social-class position as much as her gender. Her wealth and social position afforded her the celebrity status that allowed her access to the media in order to promote her version of reality. Diana may also be a unique example in that the mass of ordinary women are unable to use their 'bodies, intuition and gestures' to gain power or get themselves heard.

In fact, the work of Foucault can be used to criticize Westwood's postfeminist position that women can control their own identities. Feminist sociologists have pointed to the way in which dominant discourses about female bodies shape female identity and self-esteem in ways that reinforce female powerlessness. For example, as Bartkey (1992) notes, dominant discourses about femininity celebrate thinness and this results in a strong disciplinary power over women's bodies focusing on weight, shape and appearance. Women, in response, may practise self-discipline by engaging in dieting, slimming, exercise, surgery, and even anorexia and bulimia.

web.task

Search the worldwide web for lists of powerful men and/or women in Britain. What is the basis of the power of those who make up these lists?

Check your understanding

1. How does the 'zero-sum of power' model define power?

2. What is the difference between coercion and authority?

3. What type of power is exercised by the prime minister?

4. What is the function of power according to Parsons?

5. Where does political power originate according to Marxists?

6. What is the function of the superstructure in regard to power?

7. According to Gramsci, how is the consent of the people gained by the ruling class?

8. Suggest two ways in which subordinate groups can acquire power according to Marxists.

9. How does Foucault suggest the exercise of power has changed over time?

10. How does Westwood use the example of Princess Diana?

1   Construct a spider chart with a box in the centre symbolizing yourself. Draw lines to other boxes containing the names of significant people in your life, e.g. friends, brothers and sisters, parents, other relatives, teachers, employers, workmates. Use a different colour pen to symbolize the type of power relationship you have with these people – for example, if the relationship is based on authority draw a red line, as you would from you to your teacher. Some of your relationships may be based on coercion, persuasion, influence, manipulation, even ideology – use different colour lines to symbolize these. You may have to add categories or adapt existing ones.

2   Ask a small sample of other people (try to include people of different ages, gender, ethnic and class backgrounds) to construct similar diagrams. Compare the diagrams. What similarities and differences do you find?

exploring definitions of power

Item A

Power as a continuum

| Force and violence | Influence and manipulation | Legitimacy and consent |

Source: Morgan, I. (1999) *Power and Politics*, London: Hodder & Stoughton, p. 8

Item B

We are all affected by institutional power, i.e. the relatively routine arrangements of power involved in, say, the bringing-up of children within a family, the management of an office within a large company, or indeed the exercise of judgement by government officials over who is deserving of welfare and who is not. Institutional power is usually experienced as something quite ordinary: it is often, for example, the kind of thing that you only really know about when you are on the receiving end of it – when as a child you may have complied with or rebelled against the discipline laid down by your parents or a teacher, or later in life found yourself following, perhaps against your will, the instructions given by a bureaucratic manager, a doctor or a police officer. In particular, you may have found yourself doing something you did not want to do.

Adapted from Allen, J. (2000) 'Power: its institutional guises (and disguises)', in G. Hughes and R. Fergusson (eds), *Ordering Lives: Family, Work and Welfare*, London: The Open University/Routledge, pp. 8–9

(a) Examine **Item A** and identify which of the three sets of characteristics on the continuum is associated with 'authority'. (1 mark)

(b) Identify and briefly explain **two** ways in which power is legitimated in the UK. (8 marks)

(c) Using material from **Item B** and elsewhere, identify **three** ways in which institutional power is exercised. (9 marks)

(d) Identify and explain **two** problems that sociologists face in exploring who has power in modern societies. (12 marks)

Exam practice

(e) Outline and assess the view that power originates in consensus and order rather than exploitation and conflict. (60 marks)

The distribution of power

gettingyouthinking

Read through the following fictional scenario and then answer the questions that follow.

Imagine you are attending a Public Inquiry into whether a new road should be built between the port of Grimsby and the A1. There are two proposed routes. Route A will cost £210 million and will run straight through the only known habitat in the north of England of the rare wide-mouthed frog. It will also involve the blasting of a tunnel through the Lincolnshire Wolds, an area of outstanding natural beauty. Route B will cost £160 million but will run through the greenbelt around the historic city of Lincoln, as well as involve great disruption to traffic in the area while a bypass is especially built to take traffic away from the city centre. Five groups will give evidence to the Inquiry.

A Lincoln Chamber of Commerce

We favour Route B. The motorway will bring extra business and trade to the city which is good for our members. Hauliers and builders will especially benefit. In particular, it will increase the tourist trade to the city. The motorway will affect the surrounding countryside but there is plenty of it to enjoy that will not be affected. (Report prepared by John Smith of Smith Road Haulage Ltd and Stephen Brook of Brook Building Quarries Ltd.)

B Department of the Environment, Food & Rural Affairs

We approve of Route B for cost reasons. It will also attract foreign investors to the area because of the fast road-links to London. It will increase the status of the area and attract commuters in from London who can take advantage of rail links from Lincoln. Employment opportunities will increase, leading to full employment and higher wages. However, the department is also content with Route A because the Ministry of Defence requires a fast road from the Grimsby area to facilitate the efficient movement of nuclear waste in and out of RAF Binbrook. (This information is highly confidential and should not be disclosed to the Inquiry.)

C Friends of the Earth

We oppose both routes on the grounds that wildlife and the countryside will suffer. We are particularly concerned about the survival of the wide-mouthed frog, which is in danger of extinction across the country. Both roads will be a blot on the landscape. Existing rail services can easily deal with the container traffic from the port of Grimsby.

D North Lincolnshire Ramblers' Association

We oppose both routes. We are concerned that the natural beauty of the area will be ruined. We are concerned about the danger to children from more traffic, especially in terms of accidents and pollution. There may be an influx of new people into the area. Some of these may be undesirables and bring crime to the area. The value of our properties may fall considerably.

E National Farmers' Union

We favour Route A. This route involves less damage to the environment compared with Route B. The danger to the wide-mouthed frog is overestimated. It can be moved to another habitat. The land around Route B currently attracts about £200 million in EU subsidies – the NFU estimates that we would only receive about £70 million from the Ministry of Transport if the land is compulsorily purchased whereas our members would receive approximately £90 million for the less fertile land around Route A.

1 Look carefully at the five briefs. If you were representing these organizations, what information would you disclose to the Inquiry? What would you hold back and why?

2 What does this exercise tell you about the decision-making process?

The point of this exercise is to demonstrate that decision-making is not a straightforward process. You will have noticed that four of the groups have a vested interest in either one or both routes. Moreover, they probably made decisions not to divulge all of the information they had because it might have prejudiced the Inquiry against them. The Inquiry, then, is basing its conclusions on incomplete information. There are three groups who would benefit enormously whichever road is built. Only one group has nothing to hide. Ironically, this group, Friends of the Earth, is most likely to lose.

What this exercise tells us is that decision-making is not an open process. Rather there are hidden dimensions to it that we rarely see. It is important to examine the distribution of power if we want to gain insight into the decision-making process in modern societies.

Pluralism

Robert Dahl (1961) carried out an **empirical** study of decision-making in New Haven, USA surrounding three contentious issues. He employed a range of methods which he believed would precisely measure the exercise of power. These included:

- looking at changes in the socioeconomic background of those who occupied influential political positions in the community
- measuring the nature and extent of the participation of particular socioeconomic groups
- determining the influence of particular individuals
- randomly sampling community-based activists and voters
- analysing changing voting behaviour.

Dahl's research concluded that:

1 Power in modern societies is **diffused** and distributed among a variety of community elites who represent specific interests in fairly unique areas. No one group exerts influence in general.
2 Moreover, each group exercises **countervailing** power – that is, each serves as a check on the others thus preventing a monopoly of power.
3 Power is also **situational**, tied to specific issues. If one group does succeed in dominating one area of policy, it will fail to dominate others.
4 All elites are **accountable** because they rely on popular support and must constantly prove they are working in the public interest rather than in their own.

Dahl concludes, therefore, that societies are characterized by democratic **pluralism**. Power is open to all through political parties and pressure groups. No interest group or individual can have too much of it.

Elite pluralism

Grant (1999) is an elite pluralist, meaning that he accepts that power in the UK is in the hands of **elites** or leaders of pressure groups, political parties and government departments, rather than all members of society having equal access to power. He argues the following:

- Power is widely dispersed between a greater range of pressure groups than ever before.
- Most interest groups in the UK are now represented.
- There now exist multiple arenas in which these pressure groups can influence policy on behalf of their clients, such as Parliament, regional assemblies in Scotland and Wales, the European Union, the mass media and the courts.

As well as lobbying politicians, many of these pressure groups use direct action, such as demonstrations, blockades, advertising, boycotts of consumer goods, internet canvassing and sometimes even violence. Grant acknowledges that some groups have more influence than others, but argues that pressure-group politics is generally a just way of managing the democratic process.

Pluralism: the critique

Dahl was criticized by Newton (1969), who notes that about 50 to 60 per cent of the electorate fail to vote in US presidential elections. It is therefore not enough to assume that inclusion within a community is evidence of sharing in the power process. Newton suggests that Dahl overstates the 'indirect influence' that voters have over leaders for five reasons:

- Votes are often cast for packages of policies and personnel rather than leaders, and it is extremely difficult for a sociologist to work out what a vote actually stands for. Consider, for example, votes for the Labour Party in the 2005 election. Could the Labour leader, Tony Blair, regard these as support for the Iraq War? Some people voting Labour may have been against the war, but voted the way they did because Labour's other policies – on the economy, poverty, and so on – remained attractive or because they were not attracted to the policies of the other political parties.
- Indirect influence via the medium of voting assumes voters' interests are similar and that these are clearly communicated to politicians. Clearly, however, the motives of a stockbroker working in the City of London in voting for Labour are going to be different to those of a traditional trade unionist.
- It is also assumed that voters are represented by selfless politicians. There is a failure to recognize that power may be wielded in self-interest or on behalf of powerful groups that have little in common with the electorate.
- The needs of groups such as the poor, the unemployed, the young, single mothers and asylum seekers can be ignored because they lack the economic and cultural power to be heard.
- The power of elected officials may be severely constrained by permanent officials such as civil servants. Ambitious plans to bring about great social change may be slowed down or watered down because of advice and pressure from those responsible for the day-to-day implementation of such policy. The television comedy series *Yes, Minister* is both a realistic and humorous illustration of this process.

However, in his defence, Dahl did acknowledge that political apathy, alienation, indifference and lack of confidence among the poor and ethnic-minority sections of US society did create obstacles to effective participation in political life.

Second and third dimensions of power

Bachrach and Baratz (1970) note that Dahl only looked at what Lukes (1974) calls the 'first dimension of power' – decisions that can be seen and observed. Dahl neglected the second dimension of power – the ability to prevent issues from coming up for discussion at all. Power, then, is not just about winning situations but confining decision-making to 'safe' issues that do not threaten powerful interests. In short, power may be expressed through '**non-decision-making**'. Non-decision-making can work in three ways:

1 The powerful can ignore the demands of the less powerful. If these demands are put on the political agenda, they can effectively be undermined via fruitless discussion in endless committees and public inquiries.
2 Some issues may not be raised simply because opposition is anticipated. See Lukes' second dimension of power.
3 Dominant interests can **mobilize bias** in that they can shape the values, beliefs and opinions of the less powerful so that they support the interests of the powerful or, at the very least, do not challenge the decision-making process. See Lukes' third dimension of power.

Lukes takes this critique further by identifying a third dimension of power. He suggests some groups exercise power by deliberately manipulating or shaping the desires of less powerful social groups. However, he also acknowledges that powerful groups may pursue policies that they genuinely believe will benefit the whole community, but which in the long term actually benefit the interests of the powerful more than others. He argues, therefore, that we need to identify who benefits in the long term from particular decisions. For example, a couple may make a joint decision that the female will stay at home to raise the children, but the male may benefit in the long term from this decision in terms of career development, income, influence over decision-making, etc. Lukes argues that this third dimension of power is the most potent type of power because it is rarely questioned or challenged.

A study by Saunders (1979) of two policies in a rural community illustrates this point. The two policies were the preservation of the environment and the maintenance of low rates (a form of property tax). These would appear to be in everybody's interests, but the reality was different:

● Preserving the environment ensured that private housing was scarce and expensive, and council house-building was restricted. Farm labourers were forced into tied housing and therefore dependence upon their employers. No new industry was allowed to develop and this resulted in farmers being able to maintain the low wage levels paid to their employees.
● Low rates meant that little was spent on services that would benefit the poor, such as public transport, welfare and education provision.

Elite theory

Classical elite theory stresses that power is concentrated in the hands of an elite – a closed minority group. Pareto (1935) argued that concentration of power is an inevitable fact of life. In any society, power is exercised by the active few, who are supposedly better suited to such a role than the passive masses because they possess more cunning or intelligence, or because they have more organizational ability. Some elite theorists simply suggest that some elites are 'born to rule'.

Pareto saw power as a game of manipulation between two dominant elites who compete with each other for power:

● the foxes (who used cunning and guile) – e.g. politicians and diplomats
● the lions (who exercise power through force) – e.g. military dictators.

Pareto argued that all states are run by these elites and all forms of government are forms of elite rule. Political change is merely the replacement of one elite by another, as the elite in power becomes either decadent, i.e. soft and ineffective, or complacent, i.e. set in their ways. In fact, Pareto argues that history is simply a 'circulation of elites'.

Similarly, Mosca (1939) argued that the masses will always be powerless because they don't have the intellectual or moral qualities to organize and run their societies. He suggested that a minority were more cultured, rational, intellectual and morally superior compared with the masses and were more suited to rule over them. He argued that elections are merely mechanisms by which members of this elite have themselves elected by the masses. Mosca believed in government *for* the people, and dismissed the idea that government could ever be government *by* the people. Mannheim (1960) agreed, but went further, arguing that democracy could not work because the masses were 'irrational', i.e. incapable of rational decision-making.

focusonpluralism

Abercrombie and Warde (2000) argue that the pluralist view of power in Britain is undermined by four processes:

1 Many interests are not represented by pressure groups and political parties. For example, fewer than half the workforce is represented by trade unions. Sections of society such as the poor, single mothers, women in general, ethnic minorities and young people lack specific groups that represent their interests in the political arena.
2 Some interests (in particular finance capitalism and employers) are overrepresented in terms of powerful interest groups working on their behalf.
3 Many campaigning groups are undemocratically organized and dominated by self-perpetuating **oligarchies**.
4 There is evidence that key institutions in the UK are run by elites who share similar economic, social and educational backgrounds.

1 What is meant by the pluralist view of power?

'Cultured' and 'rational' elites, he claimed, were essential to maintain civilization.

Some critics have suggested that this is a very simplistic view of power and politics because real differences between governments are dismissed. Both socialism and democracy are seen to conceal elites. However, no criteria are provided by which we can measure the so-called superior qualities of elites. It is merely assumed that the masses are inferior and that the elite is superior.

C. Wright Mills: the power elite

The American sociologist C. Wright Mills (1956) regarded the USA as a society characterized by elite rule. He argued that three key elites monopolize power in modern societies like the USA:

- the economic or business elite, symbolized by the growth of giant corporations controlling the economy
- the political elite, which controls both political parties and federal and state governments
- the military elite.

Mills argued that the activities of each elite were interconnected to form a single ruling minority or 'power elite' dominating decision-making in the USA. The cohesiveness of this group is strengthened by their similarity of social background, i.e. White, male, Protestant, urban and sharing the same educational and social-class background. Moreover, there is interchange and overlap between these elites in that company directors sit on government advisory committees, retired generals chair business corporations, and so on. Such unity, argues Mills, means that power elites run Western societies in their own interests; the bulk of the population is manipulated by the elite through their control of education and, particularly, the newspaper and television news media.

Moore (2001, 2003) and Phillips (2004) have both documented the 'special relationship' between what Phillips calls the 'American dynasty' of the Bush family, the American political **establishment**, economic corporations such as Haliburton and Enron, military incursions in both Afghanistan and Iraq, and an uncritical mass media, especially symbolized by Fox-News. Both authors generally agree that the power elite dominates American politics today and the brand of 'crony capitalism' that it attempts to impose on the rest of the world is alienating vast sections of the world's population, particularly in the Islamic world. Moore's film *Fahrenheit 9/11* is a particularly interesting critique of this power elite.

Marxism and the distribution of power

Marxists believe that elites constitute a ruling class whose major aim is the preservation of capitalist interests. Marxists argue that exploitation of the working class has led to the concentration of wealth in the hands of the few. For example, in the UK the wealthiest one per cent of the population own

about 23 per cent of total wealth, and the wealthiest 10 per cent own 56 per cent of all wealth – mainly in the form of company shares (Inland Revenue 2004). This economic elite is united by common characteristics, such as inherited wealth and public school and Oxbridge connections. Marxists argue that the class structure is of central significance because those who own what Abercrombie and Warde (2000) call 'property for power' – the means of production such as **finance capital**, land, technology and factories – are able to exert power over everyone else.

Direct and indirect rule

Miliband (1970) argued that the capitalist class rules both directly and indirectly in the UK.

- *Direct rule* – The capitalist class rules directly by forming Conservative governments. Miliband argued that direct and open rule by the ruling class is common in history, as is their willingness to confront working-class dissent and protest.
- *Indirect rule* – The ruling class also rule indirectly by occupying powerful positions in the **civil service** and **judiciary**. The upper levels of the civil service (responsible for advice and policy) are mainly drawn from the same background as the economic elite. Like other members of this elite, their outlook tends to be conservative and suspicious of change.

Miliband argued that the groups that constitute the political elite (that is, members of the government, politicians in general, top civil servants and so on) and the economic elite share similar educational backgrounds in terms of public school and Oxbridge experience. They often have family connections and are members of the same London clubs. They are therefore similar enough to constitute a ruling class. Moreover, elite members often 'swap' roles. For example, top civil servants on retiring often take up directorships in business whilst prominent businessmen often appear on government committees.

Economic power and ideological power

Marxists also suggest that economic power results in ideological power. The ruling class exerts influence over the ideas transmitted through a range of social institutions. Miliband, for example, focused on the role of the media in promoting the view that the national interest is best served by capitalist interests. This can be seen in advertising campaigns that promote companies such as BP as symbolizing 'security, reliability and integrity'. Television programmes and tabloid newspapers reinforce capitalist values by encouraging people to see the way to fulfilment as being through the acquisition of material goods. Such ideological power leads to hegemony or cultural domination. People accept that the culture of capitalism (based on consumerism, materialism and individualism) is good for them and so consent to power being held by the capitalist class or its representatives, who are seen to manage the economy effectively and thus maintain their standard of living.

Divisions within the capitalist class

Miliband therefore argued that the ruling class rules but does not necessarily govern – instead it rules the government by the fact of common background and therefore class interest.

If we examine the statistical evidence in regard to social and educational backgrounds, it does seem to support Miliband's argument that those in elite occupations do share characteristics and there is considerable overlap between these groups. Scott (1991) refers to this overlap as 'the establishment' and claims it monopolizes the major positions of power and influence.

However, in criticism of this Marxist argument, other sociologists have pointed out that government economic policy has generally failed to benefit those groups who dominate capitalism. Some actually suggest that the economic elite is characterized by conflict and division. Scott points out that the interests of industrialists may be different from those of finance capital. He notes the existence of 'power blocs' within the capitalist class which form alliances to promote their interests. He notes how different power blocs dominate the political and economic decision-making process at different points in history in Britain. For example, **manufacturing capital** was dominant in the 1950s, while in the 1980s and 1990s, finance capital (i.e. the City) was dominant. It could be argued that power today is dominated by transnational companies and currency speculators, as economies become increasingly globalized. However, Marxists argue that it does not matter which power bloc dominates, the overlap between them guarantees that capitalist interests are generally promoted before the interests of the rest of society.

Poulantzas: power and the capitalist system

Poulantzas (1973) suggested that the common social background of the ruling class is less important than the nature of capitalism itself. It does not matter whether elite groups rule directly or indirectly because the ruling class will always benefit as long as capitalism exists. Most governments across the world, whether they are on the right or left of the political spectrum, accept that economic management of their economies involves the management of capitalism in such a way that they do not lose the confidence of international investors or The Stock Exchange. Moreover, legislation in favour of subordinate groups, such as pro-trade union or health and safety laws,

benefit the capitalist class in the long term because it results in a healthy, fit and possibly more productive workforce.

Poulantzas argued that the capitalist class will always ultimately benefit unless the whole system is dismantled. The capitalist class does not have to interfere directly in decision-making – the fact that the decision-making process is happening within a capitalist framework will always benefit it.

Conclusion: pluralism or elitism?

The overall evidence seems to support the view that elites dominate decision-making in both Britain and the USA. There is no doubt that these elites share some elements of a common social background and culture. However, this is not the same as suggesting that these elites constitute a unified ruling class working to promote its own economic and political interests. At best, the evidence for this is speculative.

Check your understanding

1. **What does Dahl mean when he says that power is diffused?**
2. **What does Lukes identify as the three dimensions of power?**
3. **What is the most potent type of power, according to Lukes?**
4. **Outline the contribution of 'foxes' and 'lions' to our understanding of power.**
5. **What is the power elite?**
6. **In what ways does a ruling class rule both directly and indirectly according to Miliband?**
7. **How does the term 'the establishment' assist an understanding of the distribution of power?**
8. **Why are the common social backgrounds of elites not that important, according to Poulantzas?**

KEY TERMS

Accountable – those in power can be held responsible for their decisions and actions.

Civil service – paid officials who work in government.

Countervailing power – an alternative source of power that acts as a balance to the prevailing power source.

Diffused – spread widely.

Elite – small, closed, dominant group.

Empirical – based on first-hand research.

Establishment – informal network of the powerful, linked by shared social, economic and educational backgrounds.

Finance capital – financial investment institutions.

Judiciary – judges.

Manufacturing capital – businesses that make products.

Mobilization of bias – a situation where dominant interests control the way in which a political system operates in such a way that some issues are never actually discussed.

Non-decision-making – the power to prevent some issues from being discussed.

Oligarchy – control by a small elite.

Pluralism – the theory that power is shared amongst a range of different groups in society.

Situational – holders of power vary from issue to issue, no one individual or group is dominant.

research idea

- Interview a small sample of teachers about the distribution of power at your school or college. You could ask them to explain one or two recent decisions and how they were taken. To what extent does the evidence you have collected support pluralist or elite theories?

web.task

Find out the names of the politicians who make up the Cabinet and Shadow Cabinet. Examine the biographical data available on some of these people by looking at their websites. Access can be gained from www.parliament.uk/directories/hciolists/alms.cfm. Investigate the educational and occupational backgrounds of the elite to see whether they share any common ground.

exploring the distribution of power

Item A

Pluralists believe that elections, or the certainty that an election must come, mean that a governing party must always conduct itself in a way that will ultimately appeal to the majority of the electorate. There is evidence that widespread retrospective voting does occur: many voters do remember major features in the overall performance of an administration, and this acts as a check upon it. When the election comes, the government knows that, to win, it must have the backing of a 'majority of minorities'.

Adapted from O'Donnell, M. (1992) *A New Introduction to Sociology* (3rd edn), London: Nelson

Item B

There are three pieces of evidence that support the view that a ruling class exists in the UK:

1 No elected government in Britain has sought to abolish the capitalist economy based on private ownership. No government has seriously tried to reorganize industry so that firms are managed by their workers, or extended welfare services so that they provide adequate provision for all the population from the cradle to the grave.

2 Business interests are not merely one group amongst a number, but are the best organized and wealthiest of all groups and were able, as in the early 1970s, to mount extensive newspaper campaigns against nationalization.

3 The best organized social grouping within Britain is finance capital, popularly known as the City of London. British economic policy has been mainly devoted to protecting finance capital through keeping a strong value of the pound sterling, enabling these institutions to invest abroad on a massive scale.

Adapted from Abercrombie, N. and Warde, A. (2000) *Contemporary British Society* (3rd edn), Cambridge: Polity Press

(a) Using **Item A** only, identify the ultimate check on the power of governing parties. (1 mark)

(b) Using material from **Item B** and elsewhere, identify and briefly explain **two** ways in which the ruling class have protected their interests. (8 marks)

(c) Identify **three** features of British politics that suggest that it is characterized by pluralism. (9 marks)

(d) Identify and explain **one** way in which a capitalist class may rule directly and **one** way in which a capitalist class may rule indirectly in British society. (12 marks)

Exam practice

(e) Outline and assess the view that power in modern capitalist societies is concentrated in the hands of a few. (60 marks)

The state

1 What do you think the people in these images have in common?

2 What role do the people in these occupations play in your life?

3 Do you think the role they play is an important one?

4 Who pays for these people and institutions? How?

All the uniformed people pictured in these images are servants or employees of the state. The state serves the society of which you are a member, so all these state institutions play a crucial role in your life whether you realize it or not. The police protect you from crime, and help maintain law and order. The army exists to ensure you are defended if the country is invaded by a foreign army. Doctors and nurses are dedicated to keeping you alive and healthy. All of these things come courtesy of the state!

What is the state?

Abercrombie and Warde (2000) note that the state is made up of a combination of major social institutions that organize and regulate British society.

>> *The state consists of that set of centralized and interdependent social institutions concerned with passing laws, implementing and administering those laws, and providing the legal machinery to enforce* **compliance** *with them. These institutions rest upon the state's monopoly of legitimate force within a given territory, which means that most of the time the laws of Britain are upheld. The powers of the state ultimately rest upon this threat of legitimate force.* >>

A state, then, is a central authority that exercises legitimate control over a given territory. It can use political violence against either its own citizens or other states to enforce that control.

Abercrombie and Warde argue that the British state is characterized by six significant and far-reaching powers:

- It has an almost unlimited ability to make and enforce law, although final appeals can now be made to the European Courts.
- It is able to raise large sums of money via taxation.
- It employs about one-fifth of the UK's total labour force.
- It is a major landowner.
- It controls instruments of economic policy, especially control over currency exchange and interest rates.
- It regulates the quality of provision of both services and commodities on behalf of the general public. Ofsted, for example, inspects the quality of schools on behalf of the state.

We can add another power which has increased in recent years: surveillance and recording. Supporters of human rights have become very concerned at the state's ability to observe our behaviour via CCTV and at its accumulation of information about its citizens through birth, marriage and death registration data, taxation and social security details, criminal records, and so on. Human-rights campaigners are concerned about the proposal, announced by the Labour government in 2003, that all citizens will be required to carry ID cards, linked to a National Identity Database. In 2002, the police announced that all genetic samples taken from citizens, whether guilty of a crime or not, would be kept on police file.

A brief history of the British state

The state as it is today is the result of a long historical process in which power has been effectively transferred from the monarchy to the people. The 19th century, in particular, saw the power of the House of Commons increase as the vote was

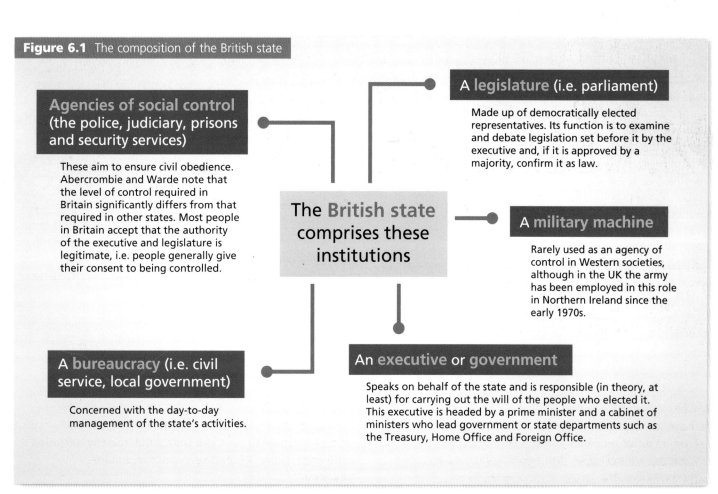

Figure 6.1 The composition of the British state

The British state comprises these institutions

Agencies of social control (the police, judiciary, prisons and security services)

These aim to ensure civil obedience. Abercrombie and Warde note that the level of control required in Britain significantly differs from that required in other states. Most people in Britain accept that the authority of the executive and legislature is legitimate, i.e. people generally give their consent to being controlled.

A legislature (i.e. parliament)

Made up of democratically elected representatives. Its function is to examine and debate legislation set before it by the executive and, if it is approved by a majority, confirm it as law.

A military machine

Rarely used as an agency of control in Western societies, although in the UK the army has been employed in this role in Northern Ireland since the early 1970s.

A bureaucracy (i.e. civil service, local government)

Concerned with the day-to-day management of the state's activities.

An executive or government

Speaks on behalf of the state and is responsible (in theory, at least) for carrying out the will of the people who elected it. This executive is headed by a prime minister and a cabinet of ministers who lead government or state departments such as the Treasury, Home Office and Foreign Office.

Figure 6.2 Organizations controlled, regulated and administered by the state

Economic bodies

The Bank of England is part of the state despite its relative autonomy from the Treasury. The state provides a range of economic services to the general public such as the Post Office, and regulates the economic activities of those industries that were once under state control, such as the railways, gas, electricity and water.

Education

The state finances institutions such as schools, colleges and universities and has played a vital role in defining the content and assessment of the curriculum.

The state controls, regulates and administers the activities of a range of organizations:

Communications

The BBC is essentially also part of the state. It was set up by Royal Charter. Its political independence is supposedly guaranteed by not being dependent upon the state for its finance, the main bulk of which comes from the licence fee. However, the cost of the licence fee is decided by the state. Parliament must vote on this. Moreover, the executive is responsible for appointing the BBC's Chairman and Governors.

Health

The National Health Service (NHS) is the product of the state's decision to take responsibility for the health and welfare of its citizens.

extended to the middle classes. This led to the emergence of distinct political parties with distinct ideologies and high-profile leaders. Elections resulted in the party with the largest share of the vote forming the government and its leader becoming the prime minister. Nineteenth-century governments generally adhered to **laissez-faire** policies (meaning that they were generally reluctant to interfere in the daily social and economic lives of their citizens). Consequently, state policy involved minimal legislation.

During the 20th century, elections became even more important, as the vote was extended to all citizens aged 21 and over in 1928. Political parties produced manifestos of their policies in order to attract voters and, once in power, governments saw it as the state's responsibility to manage the economy and look after the welfare of its citizens.

The post-1945 period saw a massive transformation in the size, range and power of the state. As Abercrombie and Warde (2000) observe:

>> *It has at its disposal enhanced powers of observing, recording and repressing the population (particularly through computer databases). It provides a wide range of services administered by large bureaucracies (both the civil service and local authorities). And it plans and acts on behalf of society as a whole, since, if matters were left to each individual, many would suffer unnecessary deprivation.* >>

For example, the Labour government of 1945–51 extended the role of the state in a number of extraordinary ways.

- It **nationalized** key industries such as the railways, mines, iron and steel.
- It set up the National Health Service (NHS).
- It extended state services in regard to social welfare and the alleviation of poverty.
- The 1944 Education Act extended state control over all aspects of education with the exception of the private sector.

Up to 1979, a consensus existed between the main political parties on welfare and economic policy. State management by both these parties when in government was remarkably similar. However, after Conservative leader Margaret Thatcher's election victory in 1979, there was a fracturing of this consensus, as the Conservative government committed itself to 'roll back' the frontiers of the state. Nationalized industries were **privatized**, public utilities and council housing were sold, taxation was lowered and there were attempts, albeit unsuccessful, to reduce the size of the welfare state.

The Labour government that came to power in 1997, after 18 years of Conservative government, has committed itself to a so-called '**third way**'. This is usually taken to mean the state taking **paternalistic** responsibility for the '**socially excluded**' while encouraging the general population to take responsibility for their own actions. The 'third way' also extends to the state taking responsibility for maintaining stable economic conditions, although, as we shall see later in this topic, global influences can undermine state actions in this area.

Theories of the modern state

Pluralist theories of the state

As we saw in Topic 2, pluralists like Robert Dahl (1961) argue that modern democratic societies are characterized by power being dispersed between a plurality of elite groups, as represented by political parties and pressure groups. Although these elites share a basic consensus on social values and goals (e.g. they agree that violence is not a legitimate strategy), they are often in conflict with each other. The function of the state, according to pluralist theory, is to act as a neutral, independent referee or 'honest broker', whose role is to reconcile and accommodate competing interests. Aron (1967) saw the state as in the business of compromise. Resources such as power and capital are primarily in the hands of the state and its role is to distribute such resources to deserving causes on the basis of public or national interest. The state therefore regulates competing interest groups and operates to ensure that no one group gets its own way all of the time. Aron argued that the state and its servants, such as the civil service, are neutrally serving the needs of all by ensuring that all competing interest groups have some influence on government policy.

Marxist theories of the state

Marx and Engels (1848) described the state as a 'committee for managing the affairs of the whole bourgeoisie'. Marxists argue that while the state gives the illusion of serving the general will of the people, in reality it serves class interests. Althusser (1971) noted that agencies of the state are essentially ideological apparatuses that function to cultivate a picture of the state as being above any specific interest. However, the reality is that the state serves to reproduce, maintain and legitimate capitalism, ruling-class interests and therefore class inequality.

There are, however, variations in the Marxist approach, outlined below.

Instrumental Marxism

Miliband (1970) and other 'instrumental Marxists' see the state as an instrument controlled directly and indirectly by the ruling class. This view argues that the state is operated and controlled by those representing the interests of capitalism. Miliband argued that the view that the civil service and judiciary are neutral institutions is an ideological one aimed at disguising their true function – to protect the economic interests of the ruling class. Instrumental Marxists argue that political and economic elites are unified by social and educational background and therefore constitute a ruling class.

Structuralist Marxism

Structural Marxists such as Poulantzas (1973) argue that the social backgrounds of those who occupy key positions doesn't really matter. The state is shaped by the economic structure of capitalist society and therefore its actions will always reflect the class relations built into the structure of capitalism. The social relations of capitalism are characterized by class inequality, so the state will always reproduce such inequality unless capitalism is dismantled. However, Poulantzas argued that in order to fulfil its role unchallenged, the state needs to be **relatively autonomous** or free from the direct control of the ruling class. There are a number of reasons for this:

- The bourgeoisie have their own internal conflicts. The state must be free of interference from these in order to represent their interests as a whole.
- The state may need to make concessions to subordinate classes every now and then in order to prevent social disorder. These concessions may not benefit the ruling class in the short term, although they are likely to benefit their objective interests in the long term.
- The state can promote the ideology that it represents the national interest or consensus.

The work of Westergaard (1995) suggests that the state, even when managed by Labour governments, has done very little to challenge the inequality inherent in modern capitalist Britain. Economic inequalities in terms of the distribution of income and wealth continue to persist whilst health inequalities have actually widened in recent years. For example, the incomes of the richest 1 per cent have risen sharply since 1997, the wealthiest 10 per cent of the population now own 56 per cent of the UK's wealth, and the gap in life expectancy between the bottom fifth and the general population has widened by 7 to 8 years. From a Marxist perspective, these are indications that state social policy is generally benefiting the bourgeoisie. As Hastings (2005) notes:

<< Until the 20th century, disease was no respecter of purses. The wife of a Victorian financial colossus was almost as vulnerable to the perils of childbirth as a maid in his household. The tombstones of the great reveal how many died before their natural spans were exhausted. Today, medical science can do many extraordinary things for people able to pay. There has never been a wider gulf between the remedies available to the rich and those on offer to most of the poor, even in societies with advanced public healthcare systems.>>

Hegemonic Marxism

Hegemonic Marxists point out that the mass of the population consent to the state managing capitalism, despite the fact that it mainly benefits the ruling class rather than society in general. Gramsci (1971) argues that the ruling class are able to manage the state in such a way that hegemony – cultural and ideological domination – is achieved. People accept the moral and political leadership of high-status groups without question because the ruling class control the ideas and beliefs held by members of society, using state agencies and the mass media.

However, Gramsci noted that the bourgeoisie was unable to exercise total control over the flow of ideas in any society. Sections of the working class, especially intellectuals amongst them, can gain access to ideas and beliefs that challenge hegemony, giving the proletariat some influence over the policies of the state, e.g. through trade-union and welfare-state legislation. However, Westergaard and others have suggested, using Lukes' concept of a third dimension of power (see Topic 2, p. 216), that in the long run such policies have generally benefited the bourgeoisie more than the proletariat.

Hall (Hall and Jefferson 1976) used the concept of hegemony in explaining Margaret Thatcher's victories in three general elections in 1979, 1983 and 1987. He argues that her management of the state was characterized by '**authoritarian populism**'. She was able to use the ideological apparatus of the media to portray herself as a strong, resolute and moral leader – the Iron Lady – and to convince the general public that a good dose of strong economic medicine, whilst painful, was good for them. She convinced a substantial section of the nation that those who dissented from her vision were the 'enemy within' and threatened the security of the nation, the state and the family. Some Marxists have suggested that this analysis might be useful in explaining the election victory of Tony Blair in 2005, despite the extensive opposition to his decision to join in the invasion of Iraq in March 2003.

Evaluation of the Marxist view

Despite differences of interpretation, all three Marxist positions agree that the state serves the interests of the dominant class. However, as we saw in Topic 2, this is a difficult assertion to prove. We can see economic and social connections between the political elite and members of the economic elite, but this does not necessarily mean that they are using the mechanisms of the state to advance ruling-class interests.

Concepts such as 'ideology' and 'hegemony' are difficult to operationalize and to use as a means of measuring degrees of power. It is also unlikely that hegemony is experienced universally. Over the past 30 years, the state has consistently faced opposition in the form of urban riots by the powerless, strikes, new social movements and terrorism, and it has been forced to use coercion and force on a number of occasions.

synopticlink

social inequality and difference

The Marxist theory of social stratification sees capitalist society as characterized by an economic system in which a capitalist minority owns and controls the means of production, while appropriating the surplus value produced by the labour power of the proletariat. The economic system or infrastructure, therefore, produces a class system in which the ruling class exploits the working class. However, this class inequality is always under threat from the possibility that the subject class may object to this state of affairs and turn to revolutionary action in order to reverse it. Marxists argue that the capitalist class has developed a superstructure of social institutions whose function is to reproduce and legitimate the class inequality found in the infrastructure. The superstructure is made up of the state, i.e. its executive (the government), the civil service, the legislature (parliament), the judiciary and laws, agents of social control (such as the police, security services, the armed forces and the BBC) and institutions such as the educational system, the welfare-state and healthcare system, as well as social institutions not directly controlled by the state, such as religion and the mass media. The function of this superstructure is to transmit ruling-class ideology, i.e. capitalist values and beliefs, in order to convince all members of society, but especially the working class, that the way capitalist society is economically and socially organised is natural and just. Marxists argue that the superstructure is so effective that it produces false class consciousness –

The BBC: part of the state's superstructure?

members of the working-class are not aware that they are being exploited and oppressed and never become conscious of the conflict of interest between themselves and the bourgeoisie.

The view that the British state is an instrument of the capitalist class can also be criticized because a great deal of economic policy has been unsuccessful. The state has been unable to prevent events such as stock market crashes, devaluation of sterling and the decline of heavy industry and manufacturing. If the state is an agent of the ruling class, its success is far from complete.

Jessop and the workfare state

Jessop (2002) rejects the theories of both Miliband and Poulantzas, although he accepts that capitalism has a powerful effect upon state activities and policies. He argues that the state is not an agent of capitalism. Rather, he argues that the state enjoys 'operational autonomy', meaning that it can operate in ways that can cause damage to capitalist interests, although it generally operates to make sure that capitalism behaves responsibly and for the general good of society. However, he does acknowledge that as a global system, capitalism exerts more influence than the state – it enjoys what he calls 'ecological dominance', in that capitalist investment secures mass employment which is good for society. Moreover, the profit-driven market approach now dominates most areas of social life, including even education and health.

Jessop notes that there has been a sea-change in state regulation of capitalism that itself has been shaped by the global expansion of capitalism. Up to the mid-1970s, state regulation was characterized by intervention in the economy aimed at securing full employment and low inflation, as well as by social democratic schemes of welfare-state provision. Jessop argues that this welfare-state regulation has been replaced by what he calls the 'workfare state', where the state and private corporations work in partnership to ensure that British companies can compete healthily in the global marketplace. This cooperation between public and private has also expanded into the public sector, especially in health and education. Moreover, the workfare state encourages members of society to take more individual responsibility for their welfare and future. Jessop notes that, as a result, the state has lost some of its functions, but he argues that it still exerts great influence as a result of its willingness to be flexible in its response to globalization.

Criticisms of the modern state

- Abercrombie and Warde are critical of what they call the 'secret state'. They note that civil servants rarely appear in public to explain or justify their actions. Judges and senior police officers are generally not accountable for their decisions or actions. The security or intelligence services also largely operate outside the law.
- Some commentators have become concerned with the concentration of political power in the hands of the prime minister and a core of close advisers. Many of the latter are not elected officials or civil servants. Tony Blair was criticized for his presidential approach between 1997 and

2005 because the huge majority Labour enjoyed in parliament allegedly led to Labour MPs merely rubber-stamping executive decisions.
- New Right sociologists are still critical of what they term the '**nanny state**'. They see state policy as undermining personal responsibility and creating what they label as a '**dependency culture**'.
- State bureaucracy is seen by some as unnecessarily bulky and insensitive to the needs of ordinary people.
- The state is also accused of **institutional racism**. The immigration laws are the most obvious example, but sociological evidence indicates that institutional racism may be embedded in the everyday practices of the police, the judiciary, the prison service, the NHS – especially the mental-health sector – and in education.
- Feminist sociologists argue that the state is patriarchal. State agencies have until fairly recently been dominated by male personnel. State policy is also accused of being patriarchal, especially in the fields of family welfare and in its failure to get to serious grips with gender inequalities.

The future of the state

Recent research, for example by Abercrombie and Warde, suggests that the state and its power to act is under threat from a number of trends:

- *Regionalization* – as a result of increasing regional pressure, the Labour government has devolved some state powers to a Scottish Parliament, Welsh Assembly and Northern Ireland power-sharing assembly.
- *Europe* – the European Union (EU) has some legal authority over the British state especially in the fields of economic policy and trade. There are some concerns that this is eroding the power of ordinary people to take part in the democratic process because the agencies of the EU are not elected.
- *Internationalization* – British foreign policy is increasingly tied in with that of Europe or the USA. In the aftermath of the events of 11 September 2001, concerns were expressed that Britain had become a 'poodle' of the US administration.
- *Globalization* – It is argued by sociologists such as Held (2000) and Sklair (2004) that globalization threatens the very existence of the nation state for four reasons:

1 States find it almost impossible to control the international flow of money which can severely affect exchange rates and undermine economies. Some global currency speculators, such as George Soros, have the power to undermine state economic policy.
2 Transnational economic behaviour can severely disrupt economic policy by shifting investment and therefore employment between countries. It is argued that modern states, especially those in the developing world, are the puppets of global corporations. Such nation-states have to compete with each other for

international investment and may even have to compromise some of their policies on taxation and welfare in order to attract it. For example, international organizations such as the International Monetary Fund (IMF) have insisted they will only give aid if countries agree to change their economic or welfare policies.

3 The global economy means that recession in one part of the world can undermine the economy in another part.

4 Global communications and the internet have made it difficult for states to regulate the flow of information across borders. There are concerns about transnational media influence, **cultural imperialism** and the use of the internet to encourage global dissidence and, especially, terrorism.

It is therefore argued that globalization challenges the traditional contexts in which states have operated, because they are less able to resist external events and forces. According to Held and McGrew (2002), there are very few states in the world today (UK included) that can make decisions without reference to other states or transnational interests in the form of economic corporations or international organizations such as the United Nations, European Union, NATO, World Bank, World Trade Organization or IMF. They argue that the modern state is undergoing transformation as its sovereignty is challenged and compromised by these global pressures.

Held and McGrew argue for new forms of cross-national institutions to assist the state in dealing with global challenges and conflicts in the fields of trade and currency, the environment, security and new forms of communication. They see a bright future in a more democratic EU and the transformation of the United Nations into a world parliament that would deal with global issues such as debt, AIDS, refugees, environmental pollution and famine.

Check your understanding

1 What is the role of (a) the state executive and (b) the state legislature?

2 In what sense is the BBC a state institution?

3 Identify four ways in which the state was expanded between 1945 and 51?

4 What is the role of the state according to pluralist theory?

5 What are the key differences between Miliband and Poulantzas in regard to the role of the state?

6 Why is the neo-Marxist notion of 'rule by consent' problematical?

7 Why are Abercrombie and Warde critical of the state?

8 What problems has the state caused according to New Right sociologists?

9 Why is globalization a threat to the British state?

10 What effect has regionalization had on the British state?

research idea

Take a sample of broadsheet newspapers such as *The Times, Guardian, Independent* and *Daily Telegraph*. Conduct a content analysis to ascertain the influence of the state on our daily lives.

- What proportion of articles are concerned with the state or some agency of the state?

- Is foreign news dominated by accounts of government action?

- Do the articles indicate consent in regard to the role of the state or are they critical of it?

web.task

Charter 88 is a pressure group that aims to reform the British state, especially in terms of its lack of openness and accountability. Visit their website at www.charter88.org.uk

- What issues are they raising about the British state?

- What concerns do they have about the power and openness of government?

- What are they doing about it?

Authoritarian populism – the view that strong leaders attract popular support.

Compliance – conformity.

Cultural imperialism – situation where one culture dominates and overrides other cultures. American culture is often accused of cultural imperialism.

Dependency culture – a way of life where people become incapable of independence

and rely on the state to meet their needs.

Institutional racism – racism that is built into the routines and practices of an organisation.

Laissez-faire – to leave alone.

Nanny state – term used by the New Right to imply that the state acts as a 'nanny' to people by providing for their every need and not leaving them alone.

Nationalization – policy that involved governments taking important industries (e.g. coal) into state (public) ownership.

Paternalistic – fatherly, tending to be patronising.

Privatization – selling off previously nationalized industries to the private sector.

Relatively autonomous – term used by Marxists to show that the state can still represent capitalist interests

even if it is not made up of capitalists.

Socially excluded – those members of the population who are not a part of mainstream society because of poverty and lack of opportunity.

Third way – political philosophy favoured by New Labour, a middle way between socialism and capitalism.

exploring the state

Item A

Just about everywhere we turn in modern life we encounter the State. The State in some form is present when we post letters, use money to buy stamps, watch BBC television, travel abroad bearing passports, go to school or attend further or higher education. The State obliges birth,

marriage and death to be registered. It takes a cut from every pound you earn. The roads you walk and drive on belong to the State. The State can declare you insane and institutionalize you. It can kick your door down at five in the morning and arrest you under the Prevention

of Terrorism Act. It can conscript you and send you to fight in a foreign land. The State can remove all your belongings if you don't pay your taxes. Clearly, the State is a powerful and diverse organisation.

Barnard, A. and Burgess, T. (1996) *Sociology Explained*, Cambridge: Cambridge University Press

Item B

The agencies of the State are both highly secretive and powerful. Leading judges, who in theory are bound by the laws made by parliament, are actively engaged in making the law because they are continuously involved in interpreting existing laws. Likewise, the police are powerful because they have the scope to exercise discretion. Among

the millions of law-breakers, the police decide who to stop on suspicion, and they do so in terms of a number of crude stereotypes of possible criminals. The security services also enjoy a very high degree of autonomy in their operations and operate largely outside the law. The elected parts of the State have little idea of the activities of the security

services, or of the scale of their operations. On occasions, even the prime minister has not been made aware of the scale of operation of the secret security forces.

Adapted from Abercrombie, N. and Warde, A. (2000) *Contemporary British Society* (3rd edn), Cambridge: Polity Press

(a) Using **Item A** only, identify how the State regulates birth and death. (1 mark)

(b) Using information from **Item B** and elsewhere, identify and briefly explain **two** aspects of the 'secret state'. (8 marks)

(c) Identify and briefly explain **three** features of the British state. (9 marks)

(d) Identify and explain **two** reasons why globalization may be undermining the effective functioning of the British state. (12 marks)

Exam practice

(e) Outline and assess the view that the State works in the interests of the powerful rather than the electorate. (60 marks)

Pressure groups and new social movements

gettingyouthinking

A strong rural force

The National Farmers' Union is the democratic organization representing farmers and growers in England and Wales. Its central objective is to promote the interests of those farming businesses producing high-quality food and drink products for customers and markets both at home and abroad.

The NFU takes a close interest in the whole range of rural affairs and works with politicians and officials – both in the UK and internationally – and other groups and organizations to advance rural interests.

Another key aspect of the NFU's work is encouraging a greater understanding of farming and rural life among school children and the wider public.

As well as representing its members' interests, the NFU provides a wide range of services to them including help with legal, planning and taxation matters, marketing and food promotion.

Mission statement

Greenpeace is an independent, campaigning organization that uses non-violent, creative confrontation to expose global environmental problems, and force solutions for a green and peaceful future. Greenpeace's goal is to ensure the ability of the Earth to nurture life in all its diversity.

Greenpeace does not solicit or accept funding from governments, corporations or political parties. Greenpeace neither seeks nor accepts donations that could compromise its independence, aims, objectives or integrity. Greenpeace relies on the voluntary donations of individual supporters, and on grant support from foundations. Greenpeace is committed to the principles of non-violence, political independence and internationalism. In exposing threats to the environment and in working to find solutions, Greenpeace has no permanent allies or enemies.

Animal liberation

The ultimate struggle. All too often animal liberation is seen, by those who do not understand, as a radical form of animal welfare. It's not about welfare, it's about freedom from oppression, it's about fighting abuses of power and it's about achieving a world in which individuals – irrespective of gender, race or species – are at liberty to be themselves. The state, the establishment and the multinationals seek to control our lives and imprison or kill us when we resist.

Compassion in World Farming

campaigns to end the factory farming of animals and long-distance transport, through hard-hitting political lobbying, investigations and high profile campaigns.

CIWF was started in 1967 by dairy farmer Peter Roberts. Peter and his wife Anna were becoming increasingly concerned with the animal welfare issues connected to the new systems of intensive factory farming that were becoming popular during the 1960s.

CIWF campaign through peaceful protest and lobbying and by raising awareness of the issue of farm animal welfare. We also produce fully referenced scientific reports. Our undercover teams provide vital evidence of the suffering of farm animals.

North West Hunt Saboteurs Association

18th February 2005 saw a day that many decent people had thought to believe may never come – the day that hunting with hounds was relegated to the history books.

The North West Hunt Saboteurs Association (NWHSA), is an organisation that is dedicated to the saving of the lives of hunted animals. Whilst the 18th February marked a very special day, it did not signal the end of that fight. There is still much work to do to ensure that the hunters do indeed desist with their sick pastime, make the switch to drag hunting, or face the consequences of breaking the law.

The ban is workable, can be enforced and bring an end to hunting as we know it. And this is where the continued role of hunt saboteurs comes in ... We do know that some blatant infringements of the law are taking place. And it's in cases such as these that hunt sabs are possibly best placed to gather evidence, as after all we are the people who have always been in the field with the hunts, know what constitutes illegal hunting and aren't afraid to get in amongst the action to get what is required. This of course doesn't mean that we won't intervene to save the life of the hunted animal – after all, that remains our sole aim as hunt saboteurs.

They seek to profit from the imprisonment or murder of those from the other species. They seek to own and control the land, the oceans and the skies which should be free to all. Animal Liberation is the struggle – indeed the war – against such tyranny in all its forms. We must fight this tyranny in all its forms. We must fight for the defenceless and the innocent. We must fight for a more compassionate world. We can, we must and we will win the ultimate struggle. When Animal Liberation is achieved, we shall all be free... free to enjoy the true liberty that has been denied us for far too long!

Examine the manifestos (statement of beliefs) of the five organizations on the previous page.

1 Allocate these organizations to the following categories:

  A   Those that conform to mainstream political rules and work within the law to achieve their aims
  B   Those that use both politically acceptable and unlawful means of drawing attention to their cause(s)
  C   organizations that are generally in confrontation with the authorities.

  Under each category, clearly state why the organization's beliefs and tactics may be acceptable or unacceptable forms of political action.

2 Are any of these organizations influential enough to shape their members' sense of personal identity?

You will have noticed that the organizations above occupy very different positions on a continuum of political protest. At one extreme are organizations such as the National Farmers' Union (NFU), which work within the existing political system to represent the interests of their members. The NFU is typical of what we call a '**pressure group**'. Two other organizations also operate within the conventional political world – Greenpeace and Compassion in World Farming (CIWF) – but reserve the right to work outside the democratic process in order to draw attention to particular causes. For example, CIWF uses undercover agents in factory-farming enterprises to gather evidence for animal cruelty. Both these organizations qualify as pressure groups, but they can also be classed as part of '**new social movements**', because membership usually involves a type of dedication to a cause which shapes the identity of the member. We can particularly see this in the case of social movement organizations and groups that lie *outside* the political mainstream. Membership of groups like the Hunt Saboteurs Society and especially the Animal Liberation Front (ALF) involve their members in actively opposing the democratic mainstream. Moreover, the fact of their membership tends to lie at the very heart of the identity of their members – in other words, an Animal Liberationist is likely to see membership of the ALF as a central defining component of their existence.

Pressure groups

Pressure groups are organized bodies that aim to put pressure on decision-makers such as government ministers, Members of Parliament, representatives in the European Union and local government. This pressure may take the form of mobilizing public opinion and/or lobbying behind the scenes in order to encourage policymakers either to make *no* change to existing policies and practices, or, more likely, to insist on reform and even radical innovation. Pressure groups seek to influence rather than to get elected.

Types of pressure group

It is generally accepted by sociologists that two broad types of pressure group exist.

- *Interest* or *sectional pressure groups* aim to protect the interests of their members or a section of society. This category would include the following:
  - trade unions representing workers
  - employer and trade associations, such as the Confederation of British Industry (CBI) and Institute of Directors
  - professional associations, such as the British Medical Association and the Law Society
  - even organizations such as the National Trust and Automobile Association.

  All of these protect the interests of particular social groups.

- *Promotional pressure groups* focus on specific issues or causes that members feel strongly about. Examples would include:
  - Greenpeace and Friends of the Earth, which aim to protect the environment
  - Oxfam, which aims to promote greater understanding and sensitivity towards issues such as poverty and debt in developing countries
  - Gingerbread which seeks to alleviate the problems and poverty of single-parent families.

However, this distinction is not watertight. For example, some interest pressure groups, such as trade unions, may also pursue causes that are in the wider public interest, such as the need for greater corporate responsibility in terms of health and safety. Professional associations such as the British Medical Association have drawn attention to the need to increase public spending to reduce health risks, such as specific types of cancer.

In addition, Morgan (1999) identifies the following types of pressure groups:

- Ad hoc or 'fire brigade' groups – formed to deal with specific new proposals, such as the building of a motorway. These are often disbanded once their aims and objectives are achieved.
- 'Idea' or think-tank groups – aiming to provide an ideological rationale or to carry out research for the aims and objectives of specific causes or issues. For example, the Fabian Society has provided the intellectual rigour that has underpinned socialism and the actions of trade unions, whilst the Adam Smith Institute has provided much of the New Right philosophy underpinning those organizations in

favour of free-market government policies. Groups such as the Joseph Rowntree Foundation often provide the research and evidence in antipoverty campaigns.

- 'Political cause' groups – seeking to change the organization of the political system. For example, Charter 88 aimed to change the nature of democracy in the UK. It can be argued that the Human Rights Act in 2001 was a direct consequence of their campaign.
- 'Latent' groups – those which have not yet fully evolved in terms of organization, representation and influence. There are some social groups, such as the poor and minority ethnic groups, who experience a 'poverty of politics or protest' in that they have no formal organizations to speak out on their behalf. However, their 'representatives' may be consulted by the government or media, especially when moral panics develop around 'problems' perceived to be associated with such groups.

However, Morgan's typology is also by no means comprehensive or watertight. In recent years, we have seen the evolution of the 'celebrity' pressure group, with rock stars such as Sir Bob Geldof, Sting and Bono using their celebrity status to raise the public profile of issues such as famine, the degradation of the Amazonian jungle and debt in the developing world, in order to influence governments to change or modify their policies.

Insider and outsider status

Another useful way to look at pressure groups is to work out whether they have 'insider' or 'outsider' status when it comes to exercising power over the decision-making process.

Insider pressure groups

Pressure groups with insider status are often invited to send representatives to sit on official committees and to collaborate on government policy papers. Civil servants and ministers regularly consult with them. Such groups tend to use 'political brokers' or professional lobbyists who have inside knowledge of how the political process works and/or have official and non-official access to influential politicians and public servants. Such groups prefer to keep a low profile. This is not surprising because, as Duverger (1972) notes, some of these pressure groups, especially those representing the interests of capital, have 'unofficial power' – 'they actually have their own representatives in governments and **legislative bodies**, but the relationship between these individuals and the groups they represent remains secret and circumspect'.

Outsider pressure groups

Outsider groups, on the other hand, do not enjoy direct access to the corridors of power. Such groups attempt to put government under pressure by presenting their case to the mass media and generating public opinion in their favour. Their campaigns are likely to involve demonstrations, boycotts and media campaigns, writing to those with influence and occasionally giving evidence to government committees. Some pressure groups have gone further than this and either disobeyed the law or challenged the law through the courts.

Pressure groups and the distribution of power

Sociological theories of power have generally allocated pressure groups a central role in debates relating to the social distribution of power.

Pluralists see competition between pressure groups for the attention of policymakers as evidence of '**polyarchal democracy**'. In other words, modern democracies like the USA and Britain are seen as being characterized by many sources of power and influence. Pressure groups are seen as part of a diffused power network and are regarded as a force for democracy because they give ordinary people and minority groups an effective voice in the political process. It is suggested that pressure groups increase awareness of issues among the general public and that this prevents complacency among politicians. Moreover, pressure groups monitor government power in order to make sure that the state does not act in unjust or illegal ways. Such pressure may even result in changes in government policy. In this sense, pressure groups are a vehicle for social change which governments dare not ignore if they are to retain public support.

However, this view has been criticized for a number of reasons:

- **Neo-pluralists** suggest that pluralism exaggerates the openness of democratic societies. They argue instead that Britain is a '**deformed polyarchy**', meaning that some pressure groups, especially insider groups, have more influence than others because they are strategically better positioned to bargain with policymakers. Their control over scarce resources such as labour, skills, capital and expertise may mean that they always have insider status – they can use threats to withdraw these resources as a way of ensuring substantial influence over decision-making. It was believed that trade unions had such power until the late 1970s, whilst pressure groups representing capital may use their powerful influence over levels of financial investment to shape government economic policy.
- Marxists point out that the influence of some pressure groups may be disproportionate because of the nature of their membership. For example, some groups recruit exclusively from the more powerful and vocal sections of the community, such as the White middle class, and so exercise more power and influence than groups such as the elderly or ethnic minorities. Marxists also argue that powerful capitalist interests, such as finance capital and global corporations, dominate political decision-making and, therefore, competition between pressure groups. However, as we have already seen in Topic 2, it is relatively easy to identify these groups but generally impossible to prove the extent of their influence on the decision-making process. Moreover, analysis of economic government policy over the last 50 years indicates that these economic power blocs have not always benefited from such policy.
- Pressure groups are rarely democratic institutions themselves – members often have little say in the day-to-day running of such organizations.

- New Right analysts claim that the existence of pressure groups threatens to destabilize democracy. They argue that there are too many of them vying for political influence. Such **hyperpluralism** makes it increasingly difficult for governments to govern. For example, it is argued that in the 1970s, governments were weakened by competing demands (especially from trade unions), and this led to political stagnation and national decline.
- Recently, there has been concern about the disproportionate influence that global transnational corporations might be exercising over the domestic decision-making of national governments.

New social movements

Recent political sociology has moved away from the study of pressure groups to examine the emergence of new social movements (NSMs).

Hallsworth (1994) defines the term new social movement as:

<< *the wide and diverse spectrum of new, non-institutional political movements which emerged or (as in the case of feminism) which re-emerged in Western liberal democratic societies during the 1960s and 1970s. More specifically, the term is used to refer to those movements which may be held to pose new challenges to the established cultural, economic and political orders of advanced (late-20th-century) capitalist society.* >>

Storr (2002) notes that NSMs are a form of extra-parliamentary politics, i.e. they tend to operate outside of the formal institutions of parliament or government.

At this stage, it is useful to distinguish between new social movements and old social movements (OSMs). The term OSM is used to refer to older, more established political organizations, such as the socialist movement, or organizations representing working-class alliances, such as trade unions or employers' associations. OSMs mainly focus on bringing about economic change and tend to be class-based with formal and centralised organization.

In contrast, Diani (1992) argues that the key characteristics of a new social movement are:

- an informal network of interactions between activist groups, individuals or organizations
- a sense of collective identity
- a sense of opposition to or conflict with mainstream politics with regard to the need for social change.

Using Diani's definition, we can see that NSMs focus on broad issues such as environmentalism, animal rights, antiglobalization, anticapitalism, anarchism, human rights, gay rights, travellers' rights, etc. If we examine the NSM of environmentalism, we can see that it includes a wide diversity of groups and organizations, including pressure groups such as Greenpeace and Friends of the Earth, eco-warriors and anarchist groups such as Reclaim the Streets. The Reclaim the Streets group is also an excellent example of how interconnected NSMs are. The group was originally formed by a group of squatters in protest at the extension of the M11 in East London in the early 1990s, so it was originally an antiroad group. However, its activities have expanded to take in action in support of sacked Liverpool dock workers, organizing global carnivals 'against capital', as well as being heavily involved in antiglobalization protests in cities where the World Trade Organization hold

synoptic link

It is useful when looking at the evidence for inequality in all its shapes and forms to consider the role of both old and new social movements.

OSMs such as socialism and trade unionism were very focused on social-class inequalities. They played a major role in the introduction of social policies that tackled poverty and class-based inequality in the UK, such as pensions, welfare benefits, the comprehensive education system and the National Health Service.

NSMs, on the other hand, are more likely to focus on single issues, such as human rights, animal rights, the environment and antiglobalization, as well as identity politics focused on women's rights, disability or sexuality – for example, gay rights have been promoted by groups such as Outrage and Stonewall. Interestingly, NSMs have tended to attract a very middle-class membership. Some sociologists suggest that NSMs are now more influential than OSMs because social class has declined as a source of identity in people's lives. However, survey evidence suggests that social class is still perceived by manual

social inequality and difference

Trade unionism: an example of an OSM

workers as the major cause of their low socioeconomic position. Groups representing the poorest groups continue to play a key role in encouraging the government to see the eradication of poverty as a priority.

meetings. Reclaim the Streets also protest using environmental actions such as 'guerilla gardening', whereby activists plant trees in unexpected places.

Some sociologists have suggested that some NSMs can be composed of ideas and informal networks, rather than specific organizations pursuing particular goals. A good example of this is feminism – it is difficult to identify a particular campaign group or set of influential women that works either defensively or offensively in the pursuit of a feminist or antipatriarchal agenda. Rather there exists a network of female academics who identify themselves as liberal, Marxist or radical feminists, pressure groups such as Gingerbread and the English Collective of Prostitutes, and voluntary groups such as Rape Crisis, that recognize a common theme – that most women in the UK share similar experiences in terms of how a patriarchal society views and treats them.

Types of NSM

Hallsworth argues that if we examine the ideological values underpinning the activities and philosophy of NSMs, we can see two broad types:

● defensive NSMs
● offensive NSMs.

Defensive NSMs

These are generally concerned with defending a natural or social environment seen as under threat from unregulated industrialization and/or capitalism, impersonal and insensitive forms of state bureaucracy and the development of **risk technology** such as nuclear power or genetically modified (GM) crops. Examples of such organizations include animal-rights groups such as the Animal Liberation Front, environmental groups such as Friends of the Earth and the antinuclear movement. Such groups call for an alternative world order built on forms of **sustainable development** in tune with the natural world, as well as social justice for all.

A variation on defensive NSMs is a form of association that Hetherington (1998) calls the '**bunde**', made up of vegetarian groups, free-festival goers, dance culture, squatters, travellers, and so on. This social network of groups has characteristics similar to defensive NSMs. They generally resist the global marketplace, are anticapitalist, and oppose the rituals and conventions that modern societies expect their members to subscribe to, such as settling down in one permanent place or abiding by social standards of hygiene. The bunde therefore create their own spaces, such as 'Teepee valley' in Wales, and gather in 'tribes' at key events and places, such as Stonehenge and Glastonbury, to celebrate symbolically their alternative lifestyles. The bunde can experience intense hostility from society. For example, the police have been accused of singling out traveller convoys for regular surveillance and harassment.

Offensive NSMs

These aim to defend or extend social rights to particular groups who are denied status, autonomy or identity, or are marginalized and repressed by the state. The concept of difference, therefore, is central to these movements. Hallsworth argues that such NSMs are concerned with exposing institutional discrimination and advancing the social position of marginalized and excluded groups such as women, gay men and lesbians, minority ethnic groups, refugees and those denied human rights.

Whether defensive or offensive, NSMs are generally concerned with promoting and changing cultural values and with the construction of identity politics. People involved in NSMs see their involvement as a defining factor in their personal identity. NSMs provide their members with a value system which stresses 'the very qualities the dominant cultural order is held to deny' (Hallsworth 1994). This value system embodies:

● *active participation* – people genuinely feeling that they can help bring about change as opposed to feeling apathy and indifference towards formal politics
● *personal development* – wanting personal as opposed to material satisfaction
● *emotional openness* – wanting others to see and recognize their stance
● *collective responsibility* – feeling social solidarity with others.

The organization of NSMs

Often the organizational structure of NSM organizations is very different to that of other political organizations. OSMs are often characterized by high levels of bureaucracy, oligarchic control by elite groups, limited participation opportunities for ordinary members and employment of full-time officials. Hallsworth notes that the internal organization of NSM groups is often the diametric opposite of this. They are often characterized by low levels of bureaucracy, the encouragement of democratic participation at all levels of decision-making for all members and few, if any, full-time officials. Often such organizations are underpinned by local networks and economic self-help, both of which deliberately aim to distance their activities from traditional political institutions and decision-making. Mainstream politicians are mainly concerned with raising economic standards and improving standards of living. Those actively engaged with NSMs are more likely to be motivated by postmaterialist values – for example, they may wish to improve quality of life for animals and people, or encourage lifestyles that are more in harmony with the environment.

The social characteristics of the members of NSMs

Research into the social basis of support for NSMs suggests that members and activists are typically drawn from a restricted section of the wider community, specifically from the youth sector. Typical members of NSMs are aged 16 to 30 and tend to be middle class in origin; they are likely to be employed in the public and service sector of the economy (teaching, social work, and so on), or born to parents who work in this occupational sector. Other typical members are likely to be peripheral to (i.e. on the margins of) the labour market, such as students and the unemployed. However, Scott (1990) points out that it is difficult to make accurate generalizations about the membership of NSM groups. For example, many of the anti-veal export campaigners at Brightlingsea in Sussex in the late 1990s were middle aged or retired.

Cohen and Rai (2000) are critical of those sociologists who distinguish between OSMs and NSMs. They point out that organizations such as Amnesty International, Greenpeace and Oxfam are not that new, and have often used very traditional methods such as lobbying ministers, MPs and civil servants to pursue their interests. Moreover, it is too narrow to say that political parties and trade unions are mainly concerned with class politics or sectional economic interests. Political parties, particularly those of a socialist and liberal tendency, have been involved in identity politics, promoting and protecting the legal and social rights of women, minority ethnic groups, refugees, asylum seekers, and gay men and lesbians, as well as campaigning for human rights and democracy abroad. Both the Green and Liberal Democratic parties have long been involved in environmental campaigns.

Cohen and Rai do acknowledge that the nature of social movements has changed in two crucial respects:

● New media technology, particularly the internet and e-mail, have improved the ability of social movements to get their message across to much larger audiences than in the past. This has put greater pressure on politicians to bring about social change.

● Some social movements have taken advantage of this new media technology to globalize their message. For example, Greenpeace has members in over 150 countries.

NSMs and political action

The type of political action adopted by some NSMs deliberately differs from the activities of OSMs and pressure groups. The latter generally work within the existing framework of politics and their last resort is the threat of withdrawal of whatever resource they control – for example, labour or capital investment. Many NSMs tend to operate outside regular channels of political action and tend to focus on 'direct action'. This form of political action includes demonstrations, sit-ins, publicity stunts and other obstructive action. Much of this action is illegal, but it often involves fairly mild forms of mass civil disobedience, such as antiroads protesters committing mass trespass in order to prevent bulldozers destroying natural habitats, the Reclaim the Streets movement disrupting traffic in the centre of London, and Greenpeace supporters destroying fields of GM crops. However, there have been instances of action involving more serious forms of illegal and criminal action – for example, damaging nuclear-weapons installations or military hardware, fire-bombing department stores that sell fur goods, breaking into animal-testing laboratories and attacking scientists with letter and car bombs.

Kate Burningham & Diana Thrush

The environmental concerns of disadvantaged groups

NSMs mainly attract a middle-class clientele, so how do disadvantaged people perceive environmentalism and organizations such as Greenpeace? This research carried out focus-group interviews with 89 members of disadvantaged groups in Glasgow, London, North Wales and the Peak District. It found that the poor are more interested in local issues, such as the rundown state of the areas they lived in, rather than national or global environmental concerns. This stemmed from real anxieties about meeting basic economic needs, which left little time for them to think or worry about wider or more abstract concerns. They gave priority to their most immediate problems, and so environmental concerns were viewed as too distant. They knew little about environmental organisations or eco-warriors beyond the media stereotypes, and generally perceived activists as too extreme. No one in the sample belonged to an environmental NSM, although this was put down to the lack of a local presence from such organizations rather than lack of interest. Finally, the sample expressed confusion about green consumerism, particularly about the merits of organic food and non-genetically modified foods. Most felt that buying environmentally friendly food was too expensive anyway.

Burningham, K. and Thrush, D. (2001) *Rainforests Are a Long Way from Here: The Environmental Concerns of Disadvantaged Groups*, York: Joseph Rowntree Foundation

1 What problems of reliability and validity might arise in the use of focus-group interviewing?

2 Using evidence from the above study, explain why working-class people appear to be less interested than middle-class people in the goals of NSMs.

The nature of politics

Many sociologists (e.g. Scott) argue that the emergence of NSMs in the 1960s indicates that the nature of political debate and action has undergone fundamental change. It is suggested that up to the 1960s, both political debate and action were dominated by political parties and pressure groups that sought either to protect or challenge the economic or material order. In other words, politics was dominated by class-based issues. However, the emergence of the women's movement and the civil-rights movement led to a recognition that wider social inequalities were of equal importance and resulted in a concern to protect, and even celebrate, the concept of 'social difference'. It was argued that affluence in Western societies meant than economic issues became subordinated to wider concerns about long-term survival, reflected in increased interest in social movements related to antinuclear technology, peace, the environment and global issues such as debt.

Theories of NSMs

The Marxist Habermas (1979) saw membership of NSMs as arising out of the nature of postcapitalism, in which the majority of people enjoy a good standard of living and are supposedly, therefore, less interested in material things. In such societies, priorities change – economic matters are of less importance than issues such as protecting human rights and democracy from an ever-encroaching state bureaucracy. NSMs, therefore, are a means by which democratic rights are protected and extended.

Touraine (1982), another Marxist, agrees, arguing that NSMs are a product of a postindustrial society that stresses the production and consumption of knowledge rather than materialism, consumerism and economic goals. The focus on knowledge has led to a critical evaluation of cultural values, especially among the young middle class, who have experienced greater periods of education. NSMs are therefore concerned with the promotion of alternative cultural values encouraging quality of life, concern for the environment and individual freedom of expression and identity. Touraine sees NSMs as at the heart of a realignment of political and cultural life. He suggests that they are in the process of replacing political parties as the major source of political identity.

Marcuse (1964) argued that NSMs are the direct result of the **alienation** caused by the capitalist mode of production and consumption. He suggested that capitalism produces a superficial **mass culture** in order to maximize its audience and profits. However, the emptiness of this culture has led some middle-class students whose education has given them critical insight, to reject materialism. NSMs, therefore, are a form of **counterculture** that encourages people to focus on unselfish needs, such as concern for other people or the environment.

Other writers believe that NSMs are the product of a search for identity rather than the product of common political ideology or shared economic interests. Alberto Melucci (1989) argues that the collective actions and political campaigns associated with NSMs are not organized in a formal sense. It is this informality or looseness that appeals to its membership. This belonging to a vast unorganized network is less about providing its members with a coherent and articulate political

focus on...

Animal liberation

A good example of a new social movement is the Animal Liberation Front (ALF). Some observers have noted that membership of the ALF is like membership of an extraordinary fundamentalist religion. Since its foundation in 1976, animal rights terrorists have targeted butchers' shops, science laboratories, fur farms, live exports, dog-breeding farms and high-street chemists. Most animal rights activists begin their career around the family kitchen table as young teenagers by refusing to eat meat, and then going on to become vegans – who reject the use of all animal products, such as milk, cheese or leather. This rejection is based not on taste but the moral conviction that killing animals for human consumption is wrong. In their own minds, ALF members are possessed of a blinding religious truth: our society is built on the unnecessary killing of animals and they are morally bound to use all means, including violence, to stop the daily holocaust of animal lives.

Adapted from Kevin Toolis, *The Guardian*, Wednesday 7 November 2001

manifesto or ideology than about providing a sense of identity and lifestyle. In this sense, Melucci argues that NSMs are a cultural rather than political phenomenon. They appeal to the young in particular because they offer the opportunity to challenge the dominant rules, whilst offering an alternative set of identities that focus on fundamentally changing the nature of the society in both a spiritual and cultural way.

Melucci suggests that NSMs have made a significant cultural contribution to society because direct action, even if unsuccessful in conventional terms, reveals the existence of unequal power structures and makes people aware that these require challenging. In fact, Melucci argues 'that to resist is to win' – in other words, the mere fact of a protest action is a kind of success, because it is a challenge to existing power structures. Road protesters might fail to prevent a road being built, but, as Field (quoted in Storr 2002) notes:

<< resistance to road building is not just about stopping one particular project. Every delay, every disruption, every extra one thousand pounds spent on police or security is a victory: money that is not available to spend elsewhere. 'Double the cost of one road and you have prevented another one being built' is an opinion often expressed by activists. In such an unequal struggle, to resist is to win.>>

Postmodern accounts of NSMs

Postmodernists argue that the meta-narratives that were used to explain the world are in decline, as the modern world evolves into a postmodern world. Meta-narratives are the 'big theories' – science, religions and political philosophies (e.g. socialism, conservatism, nationalism, liberalism and social democracy). The search for truth, self-fulfilment and social progress through these meta-narratives has largely been abandoned as people have become disillusioned by the failure of these belief systems (as seen in the fall of communism) and/or the damage caused by them in terms of war, genocide, environmental destruction and pollution. The postmodern world is characterized by global media technology, which has led to knowledge becoming relative, i.e. it is accepted that all knowledge has some value. Moreover, in the postmodern world, knowledge is also an important source of power and personal identity. Access to the knowledge marketplace allows people a greater degree of choice about how they should consume knowledge in order to shape their personal identity. Postmodernists see NSMs as offering nuggets of relative knowledge that contribute important dimensions to personal identity. For example, people may partly define themselves by making statements that involve membership of causes such as vegetarianism, the antiglobalization movement or the Make Poverty History campaign.

Crook et al. (1992) argue that in postmodern society, sociocultural divisions (e.g. differences in consumption and lifestyle) are more important than socioeconomic divisions (e.g. differences between social classes). Consequently, the traditional 'them-versus-us' conflict between employers and the working class has gone into decline and politics is now concerned with more universal moral issues. This has led to the emergence of new political organizations – NSMs that generally appeal to people's moral principles as well as their lifestyles. For example, we may be convinced by the moral arguments advanced by environmental organizations to consume in an ecologically responsible fashion and to dispose of our waste by recycling. Getting involved in NSM activities, therefore, is both a political statement and a lifestyle choice.

Commentators such as Ulrich Beck (1992) and Anthony Giddens (1991) note that in a postmodern world dominated by global media and communications, there is a growing sense of risk – people are increasingly aware of the dangers of the world we live in. In particular, there is a growing distrust of experts such as scientists, who are seen as being responsible for many of the world's problems. Giddens uses the concept of 'increasing **reflexivity**' to suggest that more and more people are reflecting on their place in the world and realizing that their existence and future survival increasingly depend on making sure that key political players, such as governments and global corporations, behave in a responsible fashion.

However, not all sociologists agree that we have entered a postmodern age. Meta-narratives still seem important. Religious meta-narratives, in particular, have re-emerged as important explanations of terrorism and suicide bombings in the UK. Crook and colleagues have been criticized for overstating the decline of social class, and for suggesting that sociocultural differences in consumption and lifestyle are not connected to socioeconomic differences. As Marxist critics have noted, the poor do not enjoy the same access to cultural consumption or NSMs as other sections of society.

Global social movements

There is evidence that NSMs are becoming increasingly globalized. Klein, in her book *No Logo* (2001), suggests that global capitalism, with its strategy of **global branding** and marketing, is responsible for the alienation fuelling an emerg   global anticorporate movement. She identifies five aggressive branding and marketing strategies adopted by global corporations that have resulted in the superficial mass culture that has led to this alienation:

● *Logo inflation* – The wearing of logos such as the Nike swoosh or FCUK on clothing has become a universal phenomenon.
● *Sponsorship of cultural events* – Rock festivals are increasingly sponsored by global corporations. Even the visit of Pope John Paul II to the USA in the late 1990s was sponsored by Pepsi.
● *Sport branding and sponsorship* – Corporations such as Nike and Adidas have attempted to turn sport into a philosophy of perfection by recruiting sports icons such as Michael Jordan and David Beckham to promote their products.
● *The branding of youth culture* – Youth trends such as snow-boarding, hip-hop and skate-boarding have been hijacked by corporations in order to make brands 'cool' and 'alternative'.

- *The branding of identity politics* – Some corporations, most notably Nike and Benetton, have identified their products with liberal issues that young people are likely to identify and sympathize with, e.g. antiracism.

Klein argues that young people are disillusioned with capitalism. This, she claims, is the result of their increasing realization that what counts as youth identity in modern society is often a product of corporate branding rather than individual choice. Moreover, people are beginning to understand that excessive branding has led to corporate censorship – the elimination and suppression of knowledge that does not support corporate interests – as well as the restriction of real choice, as two or three corporations dominate particular markets. The antiglobalization social movement has also drawn people's attention to how the activities of global corporations in the developing world sustain debt, subsistence wages and child labour. Consequently, people see governments of all political persuasions as colluding with global corporations or as ineffective in the face of corporate global power. Klein argues that what unites all these people as they join a loose network of antiglobalization groups and organizations is their desire for a citizen-centred alternative to the international rule of these global brands and to the power that global corporations have over their lives. Examples of this alternative in action include consumer boycotts of environmentally unfriendly goods and goods produced by child labour or regimes that regularly engage in human-rights abuse. The global anticorporate movement has also provided networks in which high-profile organizations such as Greenpeace and Oxfam have been able to collaborate and exert pressure on governments and transnational companies.

NSMs – the end of class politics?

There has undoubtedly been a huge surge of interest in NSMs in the past 30 years, but it is a mistake to conclude that this indicates the end of class politics. An examination of the distribution of power, studies of voting behaviour and the activities of pressure groups indicates that class and economic interests still underpin much of the political debate in Britain. It is also important not to exaggerate the degree of support that NSMs enjoy. Most people are aware of such movements but are not actively involved in them. However, conventional political parties and pressure groups can still learn a great deal from such movements, especially their ability to attract the educated, articulate and motivated young.

Check your understanding

1 **What are the main differences between sectional and promotional pressure groups?**

2 **What is the difference between an 'insider' and an 'outsider' pressure group?**

3 **How do pluralists and neo-pluralists differ in their attitudes towards pressure groups?**

4 **Why are Marxists critical of pressure groups?**

5 **Identify three differences between old social movements and new social movements.**

6 **What are the main differences between defensive NSMs and offensive NSMs?**

7 **In what ways might membership of NSMs be related to anxieties about postindustrial society?**

8 **How do Marxists like Marcuse explain the emergence of NSMs?**

9 **How is the notion of 'increasing reflexivity' related to membership of new social movements?**

10 **What evidence is there that NSMs have become globalized?**

research idea

Choose an issue, such as vivisection, testing drugs on animals or using animals in testing perfumes, and research one or more of the following:

1 The depth of feeling about the issue in your school or college. Find this out either by conducting a brief questionnaire or by asking people in your school or college to sign a petition asking for it to be banned.

2 The plans of conventional political parties with regard to the issue.

3 What pressure groups and/or social movements exist in regard to your issue and what tactics are they adopting to bring the issue to public attention?

web.task

www.resist.org.uk/ is the coordinating site for most of the organizations that make up the antiglobalization social movement. Click on their website and go to the 'Links' page. This lists all the organizations/issues that are affiliated. Choose a sample of organizations and find out their aims and tactics.

KEY TERMS

Alienation – an inability to identify with an institution or group to which you might belong.

Bunde – term used by Hetherington to describe a new form of association made up of vegetarian groups, free-festival goers, dance culture, travellers, and so on.

Counterculture – a culture that is in opposition to authority.

Deformed polyarchy – situation where some pressure groups have more influence than others because they are strategically better positioned to bargain with policymakers.

Global branding – attempts by global corporations to make their image and products recognizable worldwide.

Hyperpluralism – a situation where there are too many pressure groups competing for influence.

Legislative bodies – the state, parliament, the judiciary, i.e. agencies that have the power to make laws.

Lobbying – a means by which pressure groups and NSMs inform politicians and civil servants of their concerns and/or pass on information that will assist their cause; pressure groups often employ lobbyists to promote their cause in parliament.

Mass culture – a superficial entertainment culture propagated by the mass media that undermines people's capacity for critical thinking.

New social movements – loosely organized political movements that have emerged since the 1960s, based around particular issues.

Neo-pluralists – writers who have updated the idea of pluralism.

Polyarchal democracy – society in which many sources of power and influence exist.

Pressure group – organized body that aims to put pressure on decision-makers.

Reflexivity – the ability to reflect on your experiences.

Risk technology – technology that poses dangers to society, such as nuclear power.

Sustainable development – strategies for modernizing the developing world that result in a fairer distribution of wealth and resources.

exploring pressure groups and NSMs

Item A

Social movements are not organizations, not even of a peculiar kind. They are networks of interaction between different actors that may either include formal organizations or not, depending on shifting circumstances. As a consequence, a single organization, whatever its dominant traits, is not a social movement. Of course, it may be part of one, but the two are not identical.

Adapted from Diani, M. (2002) 'The concept of social movement', in P. Hamilton and K. Thompson (eds) *The Uses of Sociology*, London: The Open University/Blackwell

Item B

'New social movement' is a collective term which refers to a political movement that is broad, middle-class based, and organized around identity politics (e.g. the promotion of gay rights, human rights, animal rights or feminism) or the quality of life in the community (e.g. the protection of the environment). These movements are composed of a range of organizations, action groups, websites and individuals, and are less hierarchical and more loose-knit in structure than traditional pressure groups and political parties. Some sociologists see them as a form of counterculture that aims to resist the materialism, bureaucracy, globalization and alienation associated with the capitalist world.

Adapted from Chapman, S. (2002) *Sociology: Essential Word Dictionary*, Oxford: Philip Allan

(a) Using **Item A** only, identify what is meant by a social movement. (1 mark)

(b) Using **Item B**, identify and briefly explain two differences between new social movements and pressure groups. (8 marks)

(c) Identify **three** reasons why young people are particularly attracted to new social movements. (9 marks)

(d) Identify and explain **two** forms of direct action unique to the belief-systems and organisation of new social movements. (12 marks)

Exam practice

(e) Outline and assess sociological explanations for the emergence of new social movements. (60 marks)

237

Unit 6 Protest and social movements

Urban disorder

1 Look at each photograph carefully. What types of people do you think riot?

2 What do you think motivated each of the groups above to take to the streets?

3 What types of crimes constitute rioting?

4 Is rioting ever a legitimate form of protest?

5 Do riots ever achieve anything positive?

Above left: Riot police use baton charges to ring fence protesters in Edinburgh, just before the G8 summit at Gleneagles, July 2005

Above right: rioting in Bradford, July 2001

Riots are a form of **direct action**. They can generally be defined as a type of collective urban disorder. They usually involve some degree of violence, especially against property, and most commonly take the form of confrontation with the police. Such street disorders tend to be focused in inner cities characterized by high levels of social and economic deprivation. Rioting may be perceived as being the only option available to some social groups who lack access to legitimate means of political protest. Mainstream political parties, pressure groups and trade unions fail to represent their interests. Street riots may be the only means by which grievances can be voiced so that they are noticed.

Riots are not a modern phenomenon. John Beynon (1986) points out that the history of Britain has been characterized by frequent outbursts of urban disorder. In June 1780 a total of 285 people died in the Gordon Riots (anti-Catholic riots), and serious riots occurred throughout the 19th century in cities such as Bristol, Manchester, Birmingham, Nottingham, Derby and London. In 1887, three people were killed and 200 injured in Trafalgar Square after the police clashed with unemployed people. In 1910, troops were called in to deal with violent disorder in South Wales at Tonypandy, whilst four people were shot by troops in Liverpool and Llanelli. In 1919, people were shot dead in race riots in Cardiff. The 1930s were also years of considerable disorder.

Much of the sociological explanation that has evolved to explain rioting came about as a result of urban disorder that occurred in the 1980s. In 1980 and 1981, riots broke out in the St Paul's area of Bristol and in Brixton and Southall in London. In 1985, serious rioting broke out in Handsworth, Brixton and Broadwater Farm in Tottenham. The latter resulted in the death of a police officer.

Beynon's four types of explanations for urban disorder

- The conservative view generally regards collective violence as a criminal enterprise motivated by greed, excitement and imitation. Some commentators see urban disorder as the result of declining morality and a culture of poverty that encourages its young people to challenge the law.
- The liberal perspective sees rioting as the inevitable consequence of conditions such as high unemployment and widespread social disadvantages, such as **racial discrimination**, insensitive policing and lack of political representation. Riots are generally seen as a radical means of drawing attention to such problems. However, liberals view riots as problematical, not least because they contribute to the negative stereotyping of groups involved.

- The radical view sees urban disorder as a conscious and deliberate form of direct action by groups who have no other opportunities to bring their grievances to public attention. In this sense, radicals, who tend to be Marxist, see urban disorder as a political act and consequently a legitimate form of resistance. It may even be interpreted as the first signs of revolutionary protest.
- A fourth, recent perspective has been offered by the radical feminist, Bea Campbell (1993). She has linked urban disorders in the late 1990s to the so-called '**crisis in masculinity**' which sociologists such as Mac An Ghaill (1994) see arising out of the decline in traditional manual work in this period. Campbell believes that young working-class men may be attempting to reassert their masculinity in a social world in which femininity is increasingly valued and the traditional male role is in decline.

The conservative perspective

This perspective is made up of a number of interlinked explanations that tend to focus on law and order issues, in that they very clearly see no excuse for what is interpreted as criminal and immoral behaviour. Such theories take a number of forms:

- Some conservative writers and commentators see urban disorder as an expression or symptom of social change. It is argued that rapidly changing values have brought about a moral decline in behaviour. This view sees the inhabitants of inner-city areas as morally corrupt, and consequently it is suggested that those who take part in urban riots see themselves as being outside the moral and legal restraints of wider society.
- Poor or inferior socialization is often linked to this moral decline. Conservative commentators suggest that the main responsibility for the criminal behaviour of youth lies with parents who either do not care about what their children do or who cannot control them. It has even been suggested by some that the Black community suffers from a 'weak' family structure compared with the White community. The African-Caribbean community has a higher proportion of female-headed, single-parent families and it is has been suggested that these mothers lack control over their sons. It is argued that this lack of disciplinary control experienced by African-Caribbean boys is responsible for poor educational performance, street crime and urban disorder.
- Some conservative sociologists suggest that urban disorder is the product of 'alien' values imported into Britain through immigration. It has been suggested that ethnic minorities have a more confrontational attitude towards law and order than Whites. Solomos (1993) notes that young Blacks were seen by some right-wing politicians as carriers of negative cultural values that resulted in them adopting a '**ghetto mentality**' that was aggressive in its attitude towards agents of social control such as the police. The Rastafarian religious sect was often cited by the mass media as the main disseminator of these alien 'anti-White' and 'anti-authority' values among young African-Caribbeans.

- The New Right position associated with Charles Murray suggests that inner-city areas in the UK are inhabited by an 'underclass', that is, a distinct lower-class grouping which subscribes to 'deviant', rather than mainstream, values which it transmits to its children. Murray suggests that this class is characterized by commitment to a life of unemployment, dependency on benefits, **fatalism**, criminality, hostility towards the police and authority, poor parenting, ill-disciplined children and immoral behaviour. This theory is often invoked to explain urban disorder, especially that which characterized White council estates in cities and towns like Newcastle, Sunderland, Oxford and Lincoln during the mid-1990s.

Solomos points out that the conservative approach has been extremely influential in shaping the general public's perceptions of inner-city riots. One reason for this is that the mass media, especially the tabloid press, have tended to take a conservative view of urban disorder. This has had two consequences:

- *The **criminalization** of the problem* – The social and sociological reasons for such behaviour have been neglected and society at large has been persuaded that such problems are the product of an 'alien' minority, and consequently not typical.
- *The **racialization** of the problem* – It is suggested that this type of urban disorder is a racial problem, i.e. it arises out of the unique culture of Black people, rather than being a legitimate or understandable reaction to poor social conditions.

The liberal perspective

Lord Scarman's (1981) report into the Brixton riots of that year is typical of the liberal response to the social problem of urban disorder. Scarman highlighted three crucial causes of these riots:

- *Insensitive policing of young people in Brixton* – The use of 'stop and search' tactics and racist language had led to great hostility among young Blacks towards what they perceived as a racist police force.
- *Social and economic disadvantage* – Scarman concluded that young Blacks in Brixton experienced higher than average levels of unemployment, poor housing and amenities, and widespread racial discrimination. Although Black people experienced the same type of deprivations as Whites, they experienced them more acutely.
- *Feelings of rejection* – Young Blacks felt rejected by British society. Such feelings of frustration, deprivation and **marginalization** were reinforced by what they perceived as police harassment and the non-existent level of Black political representation.

Scarman concluded that these factors created a set of social conditions which 'create a **predisposition** towards violent protest'. He noted that many young Blacks believed with justification that violence was an effective means of protest because it attracted the attention of the media, thus allowing them to get their message across.

Scarman's conclusions are not dissimilar from the theory of left realism associated with John Lea and Jock Young (1993) (see Unit 2, p. 76). This theory argues that some working-class and Black youth turn to street crime and urban disorder because of **relative deprivation**. In comparison with their peers (middle-class and White youth), they feel deprived in terms of education, jobs, income and standard of living. They feel they have little power to change their situation, that they are picked on by the authorities and that nobody listens to them. As a result, some young people may resort to **collective responses** (such as criminal subcultures) or collective social disorder (such as urban rioting). Lea and Young note that the former response is more likely but particular circumstances may come together to precipitate urban disorder. For example, Lea and Young are very critical of the 'military-style' policing tactics that were adopted by the London Metropolitan Police in the 1980s. Such policing involved saturating the local community with officers on the beat, stopping and searching young Blacks and engaging in dawn drug-raids in which excessive violence was used. These tactics allegedly raised tension in Brixton, Toxteth and Broadwater Farm immediately prior to the outbreak of urban disorder.

Other liberal explanations have focused on political exclusion. Bachrach and Baratz (1970) conclude that riots are the 'ballot boxes of the poor' and are attempts to force onto a political agenda demands that otherwise would be neglected or ignored. The poor, therefore, have no other way of being heard. Wedderburn (1974) notes that mainstream political parties have little time for the poor because they are perceived as exerting little power compared with the articulate and wealthy middle classes.

Mason (2000) notes that the inner-city race riots of the 1980s share certain features:

- They challenged the idea of assimilation, i.e. the idea that Black people would quietly and unproblematically blend into British society and culture.
- They were almost always triggered to some degree by community responses to heavy-handed and insensitive policing.
- The riots were an attempt by those who took part to assert a degree of control over their urban space. This was in response to what were perceived as intrusions by the police or right-wing groups such as the British National Party, as well as a protest against urban deprivation and unemployment. In this sense, riots can be seen as a symbolic demonstration of control and resistance.

Cashmore (1989) argues that rioting has four constructive consequences:

- 'Riots provide a spontaneous outlet for built-up emotional energies. Riots for young Blacks are occasions for symbolic revenge against a system they despise. Youth, in burning the property of their own neighbourhoods, were attacking symbols of their entrapment in the ghettos'.
- Riots draw public attention to the social and economic deprivation that triggered off the protest. Cashmore notes that young Blacks are often denied access to conventional means of protest because politicians show little interest in them. A riot, however, gets their attention.

- Riots often lead to educational reform because it is recognized that urban violence is partially the result of prolonged unemployment, which in turn is linked to poor school performance.
- Riots result in the economic revitalization of the inner cities as governments pour funds into them in order to attract business and hence jobs.

Sociological research indicates that liberal explanations are supported by strong evidence of institutional forms of racism across many areas of British society. For example, the Macpherson Report (1999) into the death of the Black teenager Stephen Lawrence suggested that there are still serious concerns about police officers' treatment of ethnic-minority citizens (see Unit 2, p. 76). Macpherson concluded that the Metropolitan Police Service was institutionally racist, which he defined as follows:

<< *The collective failure of an organization to provide appropriate and professional service to people because of their colour, culture or ethnic origin. It can be seen or detected in processes, attitudes and behaviours which amount to discrimination through unwitting prejudice, ignorance, thoughtlessness and racist stereotyping which disadvantage minority ethnic people.* >>

MacPherson noted that institutional racism could be seen in stop and search tactics which were disproportionately used against Black youth. Moreover, it was reflected in the lack of confidence Black people had in the police in relation to reporting racist attacks against them. Moreover, Mason (2000) points out that there have been widespread and persistent reports of police officers acting unjustly and with unnecessary violence towards ethnic-minority citizens, as well as claims of racial abuse and harassment. There is also evidence that policing practices, especially definitions of what constitutes 'suspicious' or 'criminal', may be shaped by stereotypes about Black people.

Beynon documents a range of other evidence that supports the view that extreme forms of economic and social deprivation may be underlying causes of urban disorder:

- Ethnic unemployment is high and especially affects the young. Moreover, there is evidence that Black rates of unemployment are significantly higher than the national average. For example, on the Broadwater Farm estate, youth unemployment was 60 per cent.
- Housing occupied by the poor, especially Black families in inner cities is often substandard. There has been a lack of adequate investment in council housing in many inner-city areas. Moreover, many of these areas lack adequate and appropriate youth amenities.
- Schools in inner-city areas are often short of funds, experience a high turnover of staff and consequently compare badly in terms of examination results when compared with suburban schools. Moreover, there is some evidence of institutional racism in the form of teacher attitudes towards African-Caribbean boys, which may be reflected in the disproportionate number of school exclusions experienced by this group.
- Racial discrimination by employers is still fairly common.

- Racist abuse, harassment and attacks are a fact of life in many parts of Britain.
- The poor and especially ethnic minorities are very rarely in a position to influence decisions made about them. They are very rarely consulted. Surveys indicate that they feel they are not listened to.

The radical approach

The Marxist approach to urban disorder generally sees riots or urban disorder in terms of resistance and rebellion, even uprisings. Urban disorder is presented as a legitimate reaction against an oppressive and racist state. This approach is very similar to that of the 'new criminology' which saw crime as a conscious political act (see Unit 2 Topic 4). Taylor, Walton and Young (1973) suggested that working-class people choose to commit crime or riot because of their experience of the injustices of capitalism. It is a deliberate and conscious reaction to being placed at the bottom of the socioeconomic hierarchy. Paul Gilroy (1982b) argued that Black participation in urban disorder is political, in that it is a conscious and deliberate reaction to young Black people's anger at the way White society has historically treated Black people via slavery, colonialism and everyday prejudice and discrimination.

The Marxist view has been criticized as naive and overromantic. It would make sense if affluent areas were being attacked and capitalist property was being destroyed. However, the victims of urban disorder tend to be other poor people as it is property and amenities in the inner cities that are destroyed.

The 'flashpoints' model

This analysis essentially combines liberal and radical approaches. It emphasizes the relationship between a precipitating incident (such as overpolicing) and existing and longstanding grievances. This model sees a range of factors as influencing the potential for riot:

1 *Structural factors* – Rioters experience inequalities in power, resources and life-chances. Inner-city residents may feel relatively deprived and frustrated because the state seems uninterested or unwilling to relieve their problems.
2 *Political/ideological factors* – Rioters lack political representation. They feel that no one cares and that they have little to lose.
3 *Cultural factors* – The police and other agencies of social control may not be able to relate to young people's culture, such as hanging around in the street. If the groups have different or incompatible definitions of a situation, then the potential for conflict is increased.
4 *Contextual factors* – Those who riot may be responding to a past history of conflict between themselves and the authorities. Media rumour and prediction may lead to siege mentality and self-fulfilling prophecies about disorder.
5 *Situational factors* – Riots may evolve spontaneously in response to a particular situation, such as what is seen as a wrongful arrest.
6 *Interactional factors* – The quality of interaction between police and members of a community may be poor. 'Flashpoints' occur as some actions, especially by the police, may be seen by participants as breaking unwritten rules governing behaviour – for example, unfair arrests and excessive police violence.

Recent riots

In 2001, the towns of Oldham, Burnley and Bradford saw violent confrontations between young Asians and the police. Kundnani (2002) has identified a number of possible explanations for these riots:

- High Asian unemployment has stemmed from the closure of textile mills. Young Asians in towns across Lancashire and Yorkshire experience unemployment rates of about 50 per cent.
- Local-council housing policies mean that Whites dominate council estates in these areas. For example, only 2 per cent of Bradford's stock of council housing has been allocated to Asians. Asians have had to buy or rent cheap housing in particular areas which have then become dominated by Asian families. Whites and Asians therefore live in mutually exclusive or segregated areas.

synoptic link

social inequality and difference

Urban disorder may be a direct response to aspects of social inequality that exist in the UK today. The riots of the 1980s were certainly linked to the multiple deprivations experienced by ethnic minorities, particularly African-Caribbeans, which took the form of poverty, unemployment, poor educational achievement, poor housing and a perception that policing was characterized by institutional racism. Most importantly, there existed the perception that White politicians were not that interested in Black people in general because ethnic minorities generally lack the power or political organizations to participate in a noticeable way in the political process. Direct action in the form of rioting drew public attention to the range of deprivations experienced by ethnic minorities and led to government attempts to address these inequalities.

The riots that featured in Northern British towns in the summer of 2001 were also connected to social inequality and difference, especially to the perception among sections of the White community living on disadvantaged council estates that they were not getting a fair share of scarce resources, such as housing.

- Segregation in housing has led to segregation in education. In some districts, school catchment areas contained nearly 100 per cent populations of just one ethnic group. This has produced Asian ghetto schools in which institutional racism in the form of expectations of failure and negative assumptions about Asian culture by White teachers is common. The growing popularity of **faith schools** has encouraged mutual distrust between the White and Asian communities.
- Young Asians born and bred in Britain are less willing to be the victims of racial attacks and are fully prepared to take the law into their own hands in order to protect their areas. Violent confrontations between racist Whites and Asians attracted police attention, but young Asians feel that the police generally tend to criminalize them for defending themselves. Moreover, Asian areas have become increasingly targeted by the police, who believe Asian gangs are getting out of control.
- The leaders of Asian communities have sold their communities short. They are more concerned with being seen as members of the respectable middle class than with serving the real needs of their communities.

Check your understanding

1 Explain what is meant by a riot.

2 What is the alleged relationship between family, culture and urban disorder according to Conservative thinkers such as Charles Murray?

3 In what way can Conservative theories of inner-city rioting be seen as racist?

4 What effect has Conservative thinking on inner-city riots and mass-media representations of them had on the general public's perception of this problem?

5 What were the three causes of the inner-city rioting of 1981 according to Lord Scarman?

6 In what ways is the left-realist theory of urban disorder similar to the conclusions of the Scarman Report?

7 What is meant by Bachrach and Baratz when they describe riots as the 'ballot boxes' of the poor?

8 Identify five types of economic and social deprivation that may trigger urban unrest.

9 Explain how police institutional racism may provoke inner-city unrest.

10 Why do Marxists use the term 'uprising' to describe inner-city rioting?

11 What six elements go to make up the 'flashpoints' theory of urban disorder?

12 What were the main causes of the 2001 rioting according to Kundnani?

Kundnani argues that the Labour government has reacted in a conservative way to these riots:

>> *Blair spoke of thuggery, refusing to look beyond a narrow law-and-orderism, refusing to see in the riots the reflection of his own failed ambitions to tackle 'social exclusion'.*>>

Even the community leaders blamed the riots on a lack of discipline, a decline in Muslim values and the undue influence of Western values. He concludes that the mistakes of the past are being repeated because nobody is consulting the young Asians who took to the streets.

Back (2002) agrees and notes that:

>> *Journalists, politicians and the pundits have viewed the events of 2001 through a distorted lens. The voices that are conspicuously absent from the public attention are those of the 'rioters' themselves ... They are much talked about, but they do not speak, although we may see the shape and colour of their faces in images of 'the mob'.*>>

Back also argues that sociological analyses of urban disorder and riots as racial events may distract from the fact that these events generally tend to revolve around young males. He suggests that rioting may be an aspect of the masculine culture that young Asians and African-Caribbeans share with their White peers. He notes that 'violent confrontations are racialized, to distinguish between groups of young men who in many other respects mirror each other. Black, White and Asian men behave and carry themselves in similar ways as they move through the city' (p. 4). In other words, Back is suggesting that urban disorder may be a product of how young British men, regardless of ethnicity, interpret and use their masculinity to solve problems, rather than it being a specific product of 'poor race relations'.

research idea

Using either your local library or the internet, access newspapers such as *The Guardian*, *Daily Telegraph*, *The Times*, *Independent* and *Yorkshire Post* for July/August 2001. Conduct content analysis of the language and images used by journalists to describe the riots that occurred in Bradford, Burnley and Oldham. In particular, look closely at headlines, photographs and editorials. Who or what do these newspapers blame? Are there differences in their interpretation of events? Are they taking a conservative, liberal or radical line?

web.task

Access the Socialist Worker newspaper's reports on the 2001 riots on www.socialistworker.co.uk/archive/1780/sw178009.htm

How does its coverage of the riots differ from mainstream newspapers?

Collective response – a group or gang response.

Criminalization – shaping the perception of the general public so that they always see the activities of a particular group as criminal or potentially criminal.

Crisis in masculinity – the idea that young working-class men are experiencing anxiety as traditional jobs disappear and women take over the breadwinning role.

Direct action – Attempt to remedy a perceived wrong or to improve conditions through readily available means such as strikes, demonstrations and riots.

Faith schools – religious schools.

Fatalism – the feeling that nothing can be done about the future.

Ghetto mentality – feeling under siege.

Marginalization – lacking power, being forced to live at the edge of society.

Predisposition – natural inclination towards doing something.

Racial discrimination – the practice of refusing to give people jobs, promotion or housing on the basis of skin colour or other 'racial' characteristics and/or the physical and verbal abuse of people from ethnic minorities through racially motivated attacks and name-calling.

Racialization – shaping the perception of the general public so that they always associate a particular social problem with Black people.

Relative deprivation – feeling of being poor arising from a comparison with a peer group.

exploring urban disorder

Item A

Conservative reactions to the inner city riots of 1985, as in 1980 and 1981, ascribed the riots to criminality and greed, hooliganism and 'mindless violence', extremists and subversives, imitation, base impulses in human nature and general evil, or to a failure in education and a breakdown in family life and proper values. Douglas Hurd (the then Home Secretary) said after the Handsworth disorder that it was 'not a social phenomenon but crimes': it was 'not a cry for help but a cry for loot'. Mr. Norman Tebbit, Conservative Party Chairman, said after the Tottenham riots that they were the result of 'wickedness', and he later suggested that the moral degeneration was a legacy of the permissive society of the 1960s. Police officers, on the other hand, favoured explanations drawn from the basic social and political flaws category. The Chief Superintendent of Police in Tottenham said that social disadvantage and unemployment were important factors. Black community leaders blamed police harassment and abuse, as well as racial discrimination and disadvantage.

Adapted from J. Beynon (1986) 'Turmoil in the cities', *Social Studies Review*, January

Item B

The 2001 summer of race riots on British streets in Oldham, Burnley, Bradford and Leeds was fuelled partly by resentment among local groups, who believed other races were being favoured for Government grants, a groundbreaking official report says. The report paints a picture of dangerously fragmented communities, with ethnic groups segregated into virtual 'ghettos' at home and at school for fear of racist attack if they tried to move away from what was regarded as their territory. Political and community leadership was alarmingly weak, making little effort to bridge the divide or to listen to young people who have become increasingly disenfranchised, according to the review. White and Asian inner-city areas ended up 'pitted against each other, competing for resources', with jealousy and suspicion on both sides. Areas with high ethnic-minority populations often scored highest for deprivation and received more funding. When a mainly White estate saw an Asian estate receiving funding, or vice versa, suspicions were swiftly aroused. A Home Office source said 'with regeneration money, because the communities have become so distant and because they are not talking to each other, you end up with rumours about "that side of the fence getting lots more money" and so on.'

Gaby Hinsliff, Sunday 9 December 2001, *Society Guardian* © Guardian Newspapers Limited 2001

(a) Using **Item A** only, identify the reasons given for inner-city riots by the police. (1 mark)

(b) Using **Item B** and other material, identify and briefly explain **two** reasons why resentment between ethnic groups led to riots in 2001 in places such as Burnley and Oldham. (8 marks)

(c) Identify **three** positive consequences of urban disorder. (9 marks)

(d) Identify and explain **two** aspects of racism that might trigger inner-city rioting. (12 marks)

Exam practice

(e) Outline and assess the view that urban riots are the result of the frustration caused by extreme economic and social deprivation rather than criminality. (60 marks)

SOCIOLOGISTS SHARE A PASSION for understanding the world around them with many other people: writers, journalists, politicians and others have their opinions about the causes of, and remedies for, social problems, for example. However, what distinguishes sociologists from these other groups of people is, first, that they generate and use theory to explain society and, second, that they carry out research activities that provide the evidence for these theories. In the first unit of the book, we drew an outline of the various sociological theories, which you have been filling in during your study of the other units in this book. Here, we focus on applying research methodology.

You will already have studied research methods at AS-level. This unit covers significant areas of new ground, but also reviews much of the AS material, taking a deeper and more academic look at the issues which have been raised earlier. For this reason, it is recommended that you study this unit in conjunction with Unit 6 of *Sociology AS for OCR* (*Sociological research skills*).

Here we begin by examining the use of quantitative methods in sociology – in particular, the advantages and disadvantages of using surveys and statistical methods in research. The following topic explores more interpretive models of society, which attempt to understand how people think and act by observing them in their daily lives, and, wherever possible, joining in with them. These approaches are generally known as qualitative methods.

Topic 3 then sees how both quantitative and qualitative researchers go about asking people questions – in particular, it explores the different uses of questionnaires and interviews. Finally, Topic 4 looks at the use of secondary sources in sociology. This involves a detailed exploration of the advantages and pitfalls in using official publications, the work of other sociologists and the use of fictional and biographical sources.

AQA specification	AS topics	A2 topics
Research design and sociological theory		
Generating research questions or hypotheses: reviewing the field and the theoretical background.	Covered in Topics 1 and 2.	These issues are explored in the context of quantitative (Topic 1), qualitative (Topic 2) and secondary (Topic 4) data.
Operationalizing concepts and categories (e.g. 'race', 'ethnicity' 'class' 'gender' 'attitudes').	Covered in Topic 5.	Covered in Topic 3.
Research design. Generalization, reliability and representativeness. The role of piloting. Sample design.	Key concepts are explained in Topic 1; research design is covered in Topics 1 and 2. Sampling is discussed in Topic 3.	Piloting is covered in Topic 1 and sample design in Topics 1 and 2. The other issues are discussed in Topics 1, 2, 3 and 4.
Ethical issues in research design.	Discussion of ethical issues in Topic 2.	Discussed in Topics 2 and 3.
Techniques of data collection		
Ethical and safety issues in negotiating access and conducting research.	Discussion of ethical issues in Topic 2.	Discussed in Topics 2 and 3.
Quantitative and qualitative techniques of collecting and recording data. Questionnaires, interviews, participant and non-participant observation, use of secondary sources.	The main methods of primary and secondary data collection are the subjects of Topics 3 to 6.	Covered in Topics 2, 3 and 4.
The context of data collection. Validity, researcher effect, observer bias, intercultural issues (e.g. gender, race, class, etc.).	These issues are explored in Topics 1, 2, 4 and 5.	Discussed in Topics 2 and 3.
Interpreting, evaluating and reporting data		
Quantitative analysis. The meaning of tables and graphs. Trends, similarities and differences.	Interpreting data is discussed in the context of theory in Topic 2. Opportunities to interpret and evaluate quantitative data are provided in Topics 3 and 5.	Quantitative data is the subject of Topic 1. The analysis and presentation of quantitative data is also covered in Topic 3.
Qualitative analysis. Interpreting and coding qualitative data. Interpretive bias and 'standpoint' research (e.g. feminist perspectives).	Interpreting data is discussed in the context of theory in Topic 2. Opportunities to interpret and evaluate qualitative data are provided in Topic 4.	Qualitative data is the subject of Topic 2. Feminist approaches are also covered here. The analysis and presentation of qualitative data is also covered in Topic 3.
Reporting research. Conventions, referencing and transparency in reporting the research process. The reflexive researcher. Accountability to research participants.	The effects of reporting research results are discussed in Topic 2.	Covered in the context of qualitative research in Topic 2 and in terms of asking questions in Topic 3.

Applied sociological research skills

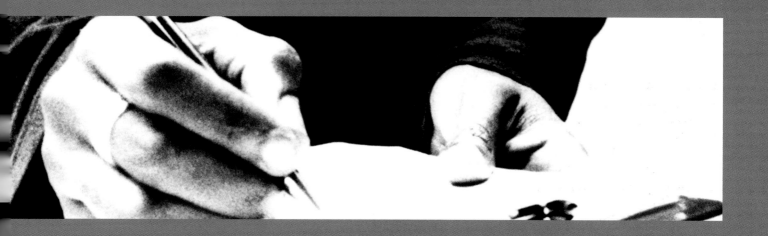

Doing quantitative research

Petty squabbles cause empty pews

Research suggests that people leave the Church because of trivial issues rather than religious doubts

IT ISN'T the big questions that stop people going to church – it is the little irritations, research has suggested.

Most churchgoers who abandon their weekly worship do so because they have had a dispute with a fellow member of the congregation. A disagreement on a range of issues, from the way the organ is played to the content of the sermon, was the reason that nearly three quarters of respondents to a survey gave for why they felt people had left the Church.

The study, which surveyed more than 500 people about why they felt worshippers left, was conducted by Spring Harvest and Care for the Family, two Christian organisations, as research for a conference next February to help leaders to retain their congregations.

Attendance in the Church of England and the Roman Catholic Church has stabilised at about one million in each, but there has been a trend of decline in attendance since the 1960s, something that many churches are trying to reverse. This weekend the Manchester diocese is holding its second 'Back to Church Sunday' in an attempt to win back churchgoers. All have been encouraged to bring their friends to church. Last year more than 880 people returned as a result.

Rob Parsons, the author of Bringing Home the Prodigals, said that people who stopped going to church did so for the most trivial of reasons. He said: "It is not big doctrinal issues. Typical arguments take place over types of buildings, styles of worship, youth work. If not that, then they argue over the flower rota.

"People often tell me they don't feel the need to attend church any more, and I can understand why they may feel that way."

Of those surveyed, more than half said that the style of church meetings had caused them to leave. The survey found that people felt the Church was no longer a place where worshippers needed to dress smartly. Only 5 per cent said that it was important to dress smartly for church.

About 74 per cent of respondents thought that people had left the church because of disagreements with other church members while 40 per cent said that the church did not need to be more welcoming to non-Christians.

Nearly all the respondents to the research were regular churchgoers, and more than half of them had attended the same church for ten years or longer.

Ruth Gledhill, *The Times*, 25 August 2005, p. 22

1 According to the research – why did people stop going to church?

2 How do you know the contents of this article are true?

3 The churches want to use the results to help people to come back to church – do you think they have chosen the best sample to achieve this?

4 How would you redesign this piece of research if you had the opportunity?

Throughout your AS and A2 courses, statistical evidence will have been used to support or criticize arguments. Despite our caution about accepting anything as 'the truth', for most sociologists, a well carried-out piece of survey research that produces a set of statistics is as near as we can get to producing facts. Research projects that produce statistics are referred to as '**quantitative research**', while those that set out to uncover the meaning of social action rather than measure it through statistics are known as 'qualitative research'. In the AS course, you explored the nature and use of both approaches and we would strongly recommend that you go back and review that material before, or at the same time as, working through this unit.

In this first topic, we are going to look at the research process used in quantitative research while Topic 2 will examine qualitative methods. However, it will first be helpful to focus on the differences between qualitative and quantitative approaches in a little more detail.

Theory and research

The aim of sociology is to help us understand the social world. This is an easy statement to make, but the real problem is what methodology should be used to go about this task. Two overlapping, but distinctive traditions have developed. The first is **positivism**, which holds that sociology should use the same sort of approaches as those used in the natural sciences such as physics and chemistry. This involves testing hypotheses using rigorous techniques of data collection. Positivists seek out valid indicators to represent the variables under investigation in order to study them in a reliable way. This approach strongly favours the use of quantitative methods such as surveys using questionnaires.

The alternative approach is often referred to as **interpretive sociology**. This is much more concerned with digging deep into how people feel and behave. Interpretive researchers largely reject the use of quantitative methods and prefer qualitative research, the subject of Topic 2.

However, rather than splitting them into two completely irreconcilable camps, it is better to think of sociologists as either more sympathetic to the use of traditional scientific methods (positivists) or more sceptical that this is the most useful way to proceed (interpretive sociologists).

Bryman (2004) has argued that, if there is one distinction to be made regarding the different aims of positivist and interpretive research, it is this: positivist research sets out to explain human behaviour through *analysing* the forces that act upon it, while interpretive sociology sets out to understand varieties of human behaviour by being able to *empathize* with it. He goes on to identify the key differences between qualitative and quantitative methods.

Differences between qualitative and quantitative methods

Bryman (2004) suggests that the differences between qualitative and quantitative methods include:

- *Numbers versus words* – Qualitative methods tend to describe social life in words, while quantitative research uses far more numbers to paint the sociological picture.
- *Point of view of researcher versus point of view of participants* – In quantitative research, the researcher is the one who decides what questions to ask and how to classify the responses. However, in qualitative research, the researcher starts from the point of view of the participants, writing up what they say, no matter how confusing or contradictory.
- *Researcher is distant versus researcher is close* – In quantitative research, the sociologist usually stays 'outside' and is uninvolved with the participants. All the sociologist wants is to distribute and collect the questionnaires or interview results, which are then analysed. In qualitative research, the sociologist is heavily involved with the people being researched, as they attempt to understand what is going on.
- *Theories tested versus theories emerge* – In quantitative research, the sociologist usually has a hypothesis that they wish to test and this forms the basis for the research. In qualitative research, however, the theory may well emerge from the actual process of research. This is known as 'grounded theory'.
- *Structured versus unstructured* – Quantitative research is usually very well structured as the information needs to be gained in a way that is **reliable**. Qualitative research, on the other hand, is usually far less structured, and is more flexible and open. Incidentally, this does not mean that it is less well organized.
- *Hard, reliable data versus rich, deep data* – Quantitative research almost always aims to be generalizable. So a survey should provide information about the population as a whole. Qualitative research places much greater emphasis on a detailed understanding of the particular group being studied. Qualitative research rarely claims to be generalizable.

focus on... A qualitative study

Ethnographers usually live in the communities they study and establish long-term, close relationships with the people they write about. In other words, in order to collect 'accurate data', ethnographers become **intimately involved** with the people they study.

I spent hundreds of nights on the street and in crackhouses **observing** dealers and addicts. I regularly **tape-recorded their conversations and life histories**. Perhaps more important, I also visited their families, attended parties and intimate reunions. I interviewed **and in many cases befriended**, the spouses, lovers, siblings, mothers, grandmothers of the crack dealers featured in these pages.

Adapted from Bourgois, P. (2003) *In Search of Respect* (2nd edn), Cambridge: Cambridge University Press

1 This term is sometimes used to describe someone who engages in long-term participant observation.

2 This links to the point about hard data versus rich, deep data. Great for depth, but think about the problems of bias. How can the researcher be objective?

3 Therefore finding out how they actually behave, not just how they *say* they behave.

4 Words not statistics here. Also, these conversations could not have been structured.

5 This suggests that he sees things from their viewpoint and any theories are generated from the interaction. It is unlikely that he could be testing any hypothesis here. Finally, it tells you how close he has got to his subjects.

The British Crime Survey is a regular **survey**, funded by the Home Office, that takes place every year. The main object of the survey is to obtain information on **the extent of crime**.

The sampling frame is the Postcode Address File, which provides a comprehensive coverage of the population apart from homeless people. A multistage cluster sample is used to obtain **an accurate representation** of the population. In all approximately 13 000 addresses are chosen for the survey. There is a **23 per cent non-response rate**. Respondents are asked to choose all the crimes that have been perpetrated against them from a list provided. **Interviews last on average 50 minutes**. A smaller sample are also asked to complete a self-report questionnaire on their attitudes towards crime.

1 The most common form of quantitative method is the survey.

2 Hard data (statistics) required.

3 This tells us the importance of generalizing for quantitative research.

4 This is a major issue with quantitative surveys because of the fact that no relationship is built up and so the subject may feel no obligation to do the questionnaire.

5 This is likely to be a highly structured questionnaire. The situation will be controlled by the interviewer.

Triangulation and multistrategy research

In order to understand the different research strategies used by sociologists, we have distinguished between quantitative and qualitative research. However, in real-life research, things are rather more complicated. Although one group of sociologists is largely in favour of using quantitative methods wherever possible and other sociologists are largely in favour of using qualitative methods, both groups will dip into the 'other side's' methods if they think it will be useful.

So, quantitative researchers may well back up their work by including some observation or some in-depth, unstructured interviewing, while qualitative researchers may well engage in some structured interviewing or draw upon secondary sources in order to strengthen their research. This use of multiple methods is generally known as **triangulation** (though, strictly speaking it is really 'multistrategy' research).

The term 'triangulation' originally referred to the use of different indicators in quantitative research as ways of measuring social phenomena. The aim was to overcome the problem of loss of **validity** where a faulty indicator was used. However, over time the term has come to mean the use of multiple methods in research, with the aim of improving the validity, reliability and generalizability of a particular piece of research. An example is provided in the 'Focus on research' below.

focus on research — Grimshaw *et al.* (2004)

Triangulation

Roger Grimshaw and colleagues (2004) carried out a research project that aimed to find out the impact of news reporting on levels of racist attitudes and activity against refugees and asylum seekers in London. They used the following methods:

- analysing press coverage over a two-month period in a representative sample of the national and London press

- conducting focus groups with participants from London boroughs with high levels of refugees and asylum seekers to explore the impact of the media
- interviewing local refugee groups and local authority officials
- interviewing the editors of national and local newspapers
- engaging in a literature search of material on relationship between the press and racism.

They concluded that there was unbalanced and inaccurate reporting of refugee and asylum seeker issues and that this did have an impact on feelings towards these groups.

Grimshaw, R., Smart, K., Tait, K. and Crosland, B. (2004) *Media Image, Community Impact*, London: ICAR Kings College

1 In what ways is this research an example of triangulation?

Surveys

The most common types of quantitative research are surveys and experiments. We will start by looking at surveys.

A social **survey** involves obtaining information in a standardized manner from a large number of people. This is done in order to maximize reliability and **generalizability**. There are two main types of survey – longitudinal and cross-sectional. If you are undertaking either form of survey, then you would obtain your information by using standardized questionnaires or standardized interviews. (See Topic 3 for more information on questionnaire and interview designs.) It is important to remember that if the questionnaires and interviews are not asked in a standard way from person to person, then the reliability would be destroyed and the survey would be of little use.

When to use a survey

You would certainly want to use a survey in the following situations:

- If you want to uncover straightforward factual information about a particular group of people, e.g. their voting intentions or their views on punishment of convicted offenders – This is because a survey allows you to gather information from a large range and number of people.
- Where you wish to uncover differences in beliefs, values and behaviour between people, but only when these are easily and clearly measured – If it is hard to find unambiguous indicators for the beliefs and attitudes, or they are complex or difficult, then qualitative research may be more appropriate.
- It is a useful method for testing a hypothesis, where you need to gain more information to confirm or deny it.

The major weakness of all surveys – indeed of all quantitative research – is that the information to be obtained must be very clear and unambiguous. As a method, it cannot easily uncover complex views. This means that there is always an issue regarding the validity of quantitative research. It is essential to **operationalize** and find indicators for concepts effectively (see Topic 3).

Types of surveys

Cross-sectional surveys

Cross-sectional surveys are often called 'snapshot' studies as they gather information at one particular time. These are the most common surveys that we are used to reading about in newspapers and textbooks, and are often referred to as 'opinion polls'.

Cross-sectional surveys are extremely widely used in both social science and market research, and provide the backbone of statistical information that sociologists use. The method is very useful for finding out information on a particular topic at one specific moment. If organized properly, it is quick to do, the results can be collated and analyzed very quickly and findings

are likely to be highly generalizable. However, the real difficulty with cross-sectional surveys lies in ensuring that the indicators or questions chosen to measure, for instance, opinions about a particular subject are accurate. If they are not, then the research is not valid.

When to use a cross-sectional survey

You would use this method of research if you wanted to find out about attitudes that people claim they hold and/or behaviour that people claim they engage in. You want to find this information out quickly and you wish to ensure that the information you have obtained from the people studied is most likely to be true of the population in general. However, it is important to remember that the information can only be claimed to be true for the moment in which the questioning takes place. A cross-sectional survey cannot plot changes over time.

Longitudinal surveys

Longitudinal studies are surveys that take place over a period of time – sometimes years. This type of survey addresses the particular weakness of cross-sectional surveys: that, despite their high reliability and the generalizability of their findings, they provide information for one particular moment only. Neither can they measure changes in attitudes or behaviour over time, nor longer-term factors that might influence behaviour. So when quantitative sociologists are particularly interested in change, they often switch to using a longitudinal survey. By following groups of people over a period of time, sociologists are able to plot the changes that they are looking for.

Such surveys provide us with a clear, moving image of changes in attitudes and actions over time. The British Household Panel Survey is a longitudinal study that has studied over 10 000 British people of all ages, living in 5500 households. The interviewing started in 1991 and has continued every year since then. The information obtained covers a vast area, including family change, household finances and patterns of health and caring. It is used by the government to help inform social policies.

When to use a longitudinal survey

Longitudinal studies are almost always concerned with changes over time and so are suitable for researchers seeking patterns of change or investigating how different factors influence people at different times.

However, longitudinal surveys suffer from some quite serious drawbacks. The biggest of these is the drop-out rate. Answering questions over time and being the object of study can lead to people getting bored or resentful. In addition, people move addresses, colleges and friendship groups, so tracking them becomes a complex and expensive task. For both these reasons, longitudinal surveys suffer from low retention – a major problem because then the survey will start to lack reliability and generalizability. If the retention rate becomes too low, then the views and behaviour of those who remain may well differ from the views of those who have left the survey.

synoptic link   social inequality and difference

Debates over the extent of poverty have raged as long as sociology has existed, but these arguments between sociologists tell us as much about sociological methods and sociologists' political biases as they do about the extent of poverty itself.

Attempts to measure the extent of poverty using strictly quantitative methods always take as their starting point what we mean by the term 'poverty'. How poverty is defined will largely determine how much poverty exists. This is a basic stumbling block for all social-science quantitative research, as what is being measured must first be defined by the researcher; if there is no general agreement on this, then the figures obtained will be disputed by other sociologists. The earliest studies on the extent of poverty, conducted by Rowntree around the turn of the 20th century, were based on an absolute definition that Rowntree constructed by saying that anyone with less than a specified level of income would be unable to feed, clothe or house themselves adequately to survive. Everyone in his surveys with lower incomes was, therefore, poor. This approach had the great strength that it was difficult, if not impossible to dispute and it was relatively easy to measure.

However, in the 1970s, other researchers, such as Townsend, began to argue that simply drawing a poverty line at absolute destitution did not reflect the reality of society. Townsend's crucial breakthrough was to suggest that what is regarded as poverty is relative and that 'poverty as destitution' needed to be replaced by a more subtle poverty line based on what people regard as acceptable in society. The measure of poverty for quantitative researchers therefore shifted to a more complex relative definition.

Over time, the relative definition of poverty has become ever more sophisticated. However, despite the starting definition including an interpretive or socially constructed definition, the research methods were still quantitative, in that the researchers used traditional questionnaire methods and analysed the officially produced statistics on incomes and costs of living. The output too has been to produce yearly figures on numbers below the poverty line – essentially a quantitative output.

However, a second tradition that can be traced back as far as the mid-19th century, to researchers such as Booth and Mayhew, has been to seek to understand the viewpoint and experiences of those who are regarded as 'the poor'. Rather than collecting statistics, these researchers have collected the experiences of poor people. It was partly through this tradition of research that the modern notion of 'social exclusion' emerged in the 1990s. This argues that financial poverty is only one of a range of disadvantages that the poor (or the socially excluded) face. They also suffer from poor experiences of health, education, bullying and social stigma. This 'package of exclusion' was missed by quantitative researchers, who, in their search for statistically valid measurements of the extent of poverty, missed the broader experience of social exclusion.

This is not to say that the qualitative approach, which draws out the *experiences* of social exclusion, is any better than quantitative methods, which provide the *extent* of poverty. Both methods reveal compatible, but different, stories about poverty.

Pilot surveys

Pilot surveys are not an alternative form of survey to cross-sectional or longitudinal, but are small-scale trial studies that most quantitative researchers carry out before the main survey. The point of these is to identify any possible problems that could emerge in the full-scale survey.

Pilot surveys can be very small. In Graham and Bowling's (1995) national study on crimes committed by young people, in which the full survey involved 2529 people, this is how they describe the pilot survey:

>> *Thirty-seven interviews were achieved, after which debriefing sessions were held with the interviewers and the questionnaire was redrafted before the main stage of the fieldwork.* >>

Surveys and response rates

The validity and generalizability of all surveys are dependent on having high response rates. Response rates refer to the proportion of people approached in the survey who actually respond to the questionnaire or interview. The greater the proportion of people who return the questionnaires or agree to be interviewed, the greater the chance the survey has of being valid. This is because we know nothing about the views of people who refuse to respond to questions. For example, if 100 students are sent a questionnaire asking if they enjoy sociology and 10 people return it, all of whom say 'yes', then you can say 100 per cent of all those who replied agreed that they enjoyed sociology. However, we know nothing about the views of the other 90 per cent. They too may enjoy sociology, or some might enjoy it and others not, but it could also be true that all 90 hate sociology so much they simply couldn't bring themselves to hand the questionnaire back. Clearly, then, researchers must strive for the highest response rate possible.

Experiments

An **experiment** is a form of research in which all the **variables** are closely controlled, so that the effect of changing one or more of the variables can be understood.

Experiments are very commonly used in the natural sciences, but are rarely used in sociology. In the physical sciences, experiments are regarded as the best form of scientific research method, as the researcher can be sure that no other factors are influencing what is going on. This is simply not the case in sociology, where it is almost impossible to isolate a social event from the real world around it – in other words, researchers cannot control all the variables.

Furthermore, experiments often involve manipulating people in ways that many people might regard as immoral.

Finally, even if these two problems can be overcome, then another problem that has been found to occur is 'experimenter effect', where the awareness of being in an experiment affects the normal behaviour of the participants. Think of your own behaviour when you know you are being photographed, even if you are asked to 'look natural'.

Howell and Frost (1989) conducted a sociological experiment to see which of the three forms of authority identified by Weber (see Unit 6, p. 207) were most effective in getting tasks done. They found 144 student volunteers and divided them into groups. Each group was given tasks to perform, led by actresses who used different authority methods to undertake the tasks. They concluded that charismatic leadership was the most effective form of authority.

One form of experimental method that has been used more often by sociologists is the **field experiment**, where a version of an experiment is undertaken in the community. Garfinkel (1967) used this method to research ethnomethodology. He asked his students to behave 'inappropriately' at home, by refusing to take anything for granted that people said and questioning them on what they really meant.

Sampling in quantitative research

One of the main strengths of survey research is that it uses processes that ensure the people in the survey are **representative** of the whole population. When the people selected are representative, then the results of the survey are likely to be true for the population as a whole and therefore generalizable.

It is very difficult for sociologists to study large numbers of people as the costs of devising and carrying out the research is just too high. Instead, as we have seen throughout this book, sociologists tend to study a small but representative cross-section of the community. If this small sample truly mirrors the bigger population, then the results from studying this chosen group can be said to be true of the larger population too.

Quantitative surveys have two different methods of ensuring that their sample is representative: **probability** (or **random**) **sampling** and **quota sampling**. There are also other forms of sampling – snowball and theoretical – which are more commonly used in qualitative research. (These are discussed in Topic 2.)

Probability or (random) sampling

Probability or random sampling is based on the same idea as any lottery or ticket draw. If names are chosen randomly, then each person has an equal chance of being selected. This means that those chosen are likely to be a cross-section of the population and so provide a representative sample.

The sampling frame

In order to make a random sample, sociologists usually prefer to have a **sampling frame**, i.e. some form of list from which the sample can be drawn. British sociologists typically use Electoral Registers (lists of people entitled to vote) or the Postcode Address File (the way that The Post Office links names and addresses to postcodes). However, for smaller studies, sociologists could ask for permission to use the lists of students attending a school, or members of a club that keeps lists of names.

As Bryman (2004) points out, any piece of random sampling can only be as good as the sampling frame, so if this is inaccurate or incomplete, then the sampling itself will not be accurate.

The different forms of random sampling

If the names are picked out entirely randomly, then this is known as 'simple random sampling'. However, when given a list of names, it is apparently quite difficult to pick in a truly random way, so very often a method is used whereby every 'nth' name (for example, every fifth or tenth name) on a list is chosen. This is known as **systematic (random) sampling.**

Stratified sampling is a further refinement of random sampling, and requires the use of a sampling frame. Here, the population under study is divided according to known criteria (for example, it could be divided into 52 per cent women and 48 per cent men, to reflect the sex composition of the UK). Within these broad strata, people are then chosen at random from the sampling frame. In reality, these strata can become quite detailed, with further divisions into age, social class, geographical location, ethnic group, religious affiliation, etc.

The final form of random sampling is known as **cluster sampling** and is used when the people the researcher wishes to interview (rather than use postal or e-mail questionnaires) are in a number of different locations. In order to cut costs and save time travelling to many different places, the sociologist simply chooses a number of locations at random and then individuals within these locations. This means that it is possible to generalize for the whole population of Britain by interviewing in a relatively few places. This approach has also been developed into the multistage cluster sampling, in which smaller clusters are randomly chosen within the larger cluster.

Random sampling is generally very easy to use, and even if there is no sampling frame, it is possible to stop every 'nth' person in the street or college and ask them. It also has the enormous advantage that if certain statistical tests are used, then it is possible to say with a degree of statistical certainty how accurate the results are.

Problems with random sampling

Although random sampling is very commonly used, there are a number of problems that can occur. First, it is often difficult to obtain a sampling frame, particularly in the last few years since laws restricting access to information held on computers have been introduced.

Where systematic sampling is undertaken, often by asking every 'nth' person in the street or another appropriate location, it can be extremely difficult for the researcher to maintain the necessary discipline to ask the correct person. If the person looks unpleasant or threatening, then researchers often skip that person and choose the next one! Also, factors such as the time of day or the weather can have an important influence on how representative the people in the street (or college) are. For example, stopping every tenth person in the high street of a town between 9 am and midday, usually results in a high proportion of retired and unemployed people. The sample is not representative and the results are therefore not generalizable.

Nazroo (2005)
Sampling ethnic minorities

Sometimes sociologists do *not* want a representative cross section of the population and therefore must 'slant' their sampling deliberately to access the particular group they are interested in. A good example of this is Nazroo's research on British ethnic minorities (Nazroo 2005).

Nazroo wanted to look at the views and attitudes of ethnic minorities in Britain, but finding a large enough sample was very difficult, as there is no easily available sampling frame available for ethnic-minority people in Britain. He therefore started by using the Postcode Address File and randomly selected geographical addresses. However, he selected more addresses in areas where ethnic minorities are more likely to live and fewer addresses in areas where ethnic minorities are less likely to live.

Nazroo, J. (2005) *A Longitudinal Survey of Ethnic Minority People: Focus and Design*, www.ccsr.ac.uk/methods/events/lsem/summary.pdf

1 To what extent was Nazroo's sample likely to be representative of the British population as a whole?

2 To what extent was Nazroo's sample likely to be representative of the ethnic-minority population of Britain?

Non-random (or non-probability) sampling

The main alternative to random sampling in quantitative sociological research is quota sampling.

Quota sampling

For research based on interviews, the main alternative to random sampling, which is commonly used by market research companies, is quota sampling. This can be used in any situation where the key social characteristics of the population under study are already known. For example, census information can give us a detailed picture of the UK population in terms of the proportion of people in each age group, income band, occupational group, geographical location, religious affiliation and ethnicity. There is therefore no reason to try to seek a representative sample by random methods. All that has to be done is to select what the key characteristics are and then ask the interviewer(s) to use their judgement to select the same

MORI (2003)

Quota sampling

This report presents the findings of a survey conducted by MORI Social Research Institute for the Refugee Council among 15 to 24 year olds. The objectives of the research were to explore young people's attitudes towards refugees and asylum seekers.

Methodology: a nationally representative quota sample of 289 adults (aged 15 to 24) was interviewed throughout Great Britain by MORI in 195 different sampling points. These points are specially selected to be representative of the whole country by region, social grade, working status, tenure, ethnicity and car ownership.

Interviews were conducted face to face, in respondents' homes, using CAPI (Computer Assisted Personal Interviewing), between 8 and 12 May 2003.

These quotas are devised from an analysis of the 1991 Census combined with more recent ONS (Office of National Statistics) data. Overall, quotas are a cost-effective means of ensuring that the demographic profile of the sample matches the actual profile of GB as a whole, and is representative of all adults in Great Britain aged 15 and over.

Source: http://www.unhcr.org.uk/pdfs/mori_2003.doc
MORI Refugee Week 2003: A survey of 15–24 year olds (May 2003)

1 **How many respondents are used in this 'nationally representative' research?**

2 **What steps were taken to make the sample representative of the whole country?**

3 **Computer-assisted personal interviewing (CAPI) can enable respondents to type their own answers in to a laptop. What are the advantages of this method of recording data?**

proportion in the sample as in the main population. Each interviewer is then allocated a quota of people exhibiting the key characteristics. This guarantees that there is a representative coverage of the population.

The main reason for the popularity of quota sampling over random sampling is the very small number of people needed to build up an accurate picture of the whole population (as long as you know what key characteristics to look for). For example, the typical surveys of voting preferences in journals and newspapers use a quota sample of approximately 1200 to represent the entire British electorate.

Problems with quota sampling

Quota sampling has a number of significant drawbacks:

- Unless the researcher has the correct information on the proportion of people in each key category, then the method is useless. In this situation, it is always better to use random sampling.
- The statistical tests that can be used with random sampling to ensure that the results of the survey are accurate, cannot be used with quota sampling.
- The most important drawback, though, is that quota sampling usually relies upon a researcher choosing people who fall into the quotas they have been given. Relying upon the interviewer's perception of who to interview can lead to all sorts of problems including the researcher making mistakes in deciding if people fit into the appropriate categories (for example, thinking people are younger than they are).

Convenience sampling

This refers to a sample made simply on the basis that it is easily available. Think of a television discussion show where the host asks the audience to vote on the views presented to them, or the teacher in class asking for a show of hands after a discussion. **Convenience sampling** is commonly used in quick surveys simply because it is convenient. By its very nature, it is unlikely to be a true reflection of the population as a whole, and so any research based on this type of sample is unlikely to be generalizable.

A subtype of convenience sampling is volunteer sampling, which involves asking people to volunteer to answer questions. The drawback of this is that the people who do choose to volunteer usually have strong opinions on a topic and so, once again, the sample is not representative of the general population.

Case studies

A **case study** is a detailed study of one particular group or organization. Instead of searching out a wide range of people via sampling, the researcher focuses on one group. The resulting studies are usually extremely detailed and provide a depth of information not normally available. However, there is always the problem that this intense scrutiny may miss wider issues by its very concentration. Case studies are used widely by both quantitative and qualitative researchers. McKee and Bell (1985) studied a small community to explore the impact of high rates of unemployment on family relationships.

The main problem with case studies is that there is never any proof that the particular group chosen to be studied is typical of the population as a whole, and so it may not be possible to generalize from the findings to other groups.

focus on research

Goodman *et al.* (2003)
Convenience sampling

Goodman and her colleagues wanted to find out about the use of information technology by older people and used a convenience sample. This is how they describe it:

≪ The sample comprised 353 older adults from Scotland, 25 per cent aged 50 to 64, 43 per cent 65 to 74, 27 per cent 75 to 84 and 5 per cent 85 or older. The gender distribution was female (68 per cent) and male (32 per cent). We used various methods of convenience sampling, distributing 42 per cent of the received questionnaires through organizations, 38 per cent directly through a researcher, using a variety of contact means, 17 per cent through a relative or friend, and 3 per cent through other means. These methods have more sampling bias than, for example, probability sampling using mail shots. However they allow more personal contact, and so richer, more in-depth information can be elicited, helping us to get to know the group better. They also let us develop contacts, both with organizations and individuals, for future work. For our survey these factors were important goals. ≫

Goodman, J., Syme, A. and Eisma, R. (2003) 'Age-old question(naire)s', in the proceedings of *Include 2003*, Helen Hamlyn Institute, London, March 2003

1 Why does convenience sampling create more 'sampling bias' than other methods of sampling?

2 What are the advantages and disadvantages of having 'more personal contact' between researchers and respondents?

Check your understanding

1 Explain the difference between positivism and interpretive sociology in your own words.

2 What are the advantages of triangulation for sociological researchers?

3 What forms of quantitative research are there?

4 Identify one advantage and one disadvantage of a longitudinal survey.

5 Why do sociologists use pilot surveys?

6 Give one reason why sociologists tend not to use experiments.

7 Why is it important for researchers to get the sampling correct?

8 Identify two types of random sampling, and give one example of when each would be useful.

9 What is 'quota' sampling? What is the main advantage of quota sampling?

10 Why is it unwise to generalize from the results of a case study?

web.tasks

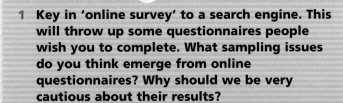

1 Key in 'online survey' to a search engine. This will throw up some questionnaires people wish you to complete. What sampling issues do you think emerge from online questionnaires? Why should we be very cautious about their results?

2 Go to the Office for National Statistics www.statistics.gov.uk/. This is the government's website where most of its quantitative statistics are collated. Then click on the link at the bottom centre that will take you to their methodology section at www.statistics.gov.uk/about/default.asp Under 'Serving the public' there is information about the ONS longitudinal study – find out all you can about this.

research idea

Suggest how you could attempt to achieve a representative sample of students at your school or college using each of these three methods of sampling: quota sampling, stratified sampling and systematic sampling.

Case study – a highly detailed study of one or two social situations or groups.

Cluster sampling – the researcher selects a series of different places and then chooses a sample at random within the cluster of people in each area.

Convenience sampling – a sample that is easily available to the researcher.

Cross-sectional survey – survey conducted at one time with no attempt to follow up the people surveyed over a longer time.

Experiment – a highly controlled situation where the researchers try to isolate the influence of each variable.

Field experiment – an experiment undertaken in the community rather than in a controlled environment.

Generalizability – the ability to make general statements about the whole of a sample population, on the basis that the sample selected is representative of the sample population.

Interpretive sociology – an approach to sociological research that stresses the need to use qualitative methods to investigate in depth how people feel and behave.

Longitudinal survey – a survey that is carried out over a considerable number of years on the same group of people.

Operationalize – to define a concept in such a way that it can be measured accurately.

Pilot survey – small-scale survey carried out before the main one, to iron out any problems.

Positivism – an approach to sociological research that advocates using the same sort of approaches as those used in the natural sciences; it involves testing hypotheses using rigorous quantitative methods.

Quantitative research – research based on the collection of statistical data.

Quota sampling – the interviewer is given the task of selecting participants in various categories that reflect the characteristics of the sample population. For example, they might be asked to interview 10 males below the age of 25 and ten males over the age of 25. This method is commonly used in street interviewing.

Probability (random) sampling – where a representative sample of the population is chosen by entirely random methods.

Reliability – quality of repeatability: if the same piece of research were to be done by another sociologist, then it should produce the same results.

Representative – a sample is representative if it is an accurate cross section of the whole

population being studied; this allows the researcher to generalize the results for the whole population.

Sampling frame – a list used as the source for a random sample.

Stratified sampling – where the population under study is divided according to known criteria, such as sex and age, in order to make the sample more representative.

Survey – a large-scale piece of quantitative research aiming to make general statements about a particular population.

Systematic sampling – where every nth name (e.g. every tenth name) on a list is chosen.

Triangulation – mixing methods to provide a broader picture or to check the data collected.

Validity – the extent to which data give a true picture of the subject being studied.

Variable – a measurable characteristic that can be tested in an experiment.

exploring quantitative research

Item A

National asthma survey reveals continuing morbidity

<< A preliminary analysis of a survey of 44 177 people with asthma has revealed that for many the condition causes frequent symptoms and substantially interferes with daily life. There is also a trend for older people with asthma to experience more problems. More information about treatment was seen by many as the best way to improve care. The Impact of Asthma Survey was conducted by Gallup on behalf of the National Asthma Campaign with funding from Allen & Hanburys. Questionnaires were given to people with asthma via surgeries, pharmacies, retail outlets, over a period of one week; the respondents were therefore self-selected and may not be representative of the population with asthma. Asthma symptoms were experienced on most days or daily by 41 per cent of survey respondents, ranging from 18 per cent of the under-11s to 55 per cent of pensioners. Waking every night with wheeze, cough or breathlessness was reported by 13 per cent and 43 per cent say they are woken by symptoms at least once a week. About 20 per cent consider that asthma dominates their life, ranging from 17 per cent in children to 37 per cent in the over-60s; over 40 per cent of each age group say the condition has a moderate impact on their quality of life. >>

Prescriber, 19 March 1996, p. 15

(a) Using only **Item A**, identify **two** reasons why the findings from the survey may not be representative of all people who have asthma. (6 marks)

(b) Identify **one** strength and **one** weakness of using cross-sectional surveys to research the views of people with asthma. (6 marks)

(c) In your own words, summarize the findings of the research in **Item A**. (12 marks)

(d) Outline and explain the research process that you would adopt in collecting quantitative data to find out the impact on people's lives in England and Wales, of having a serious disability. (22 marks)

(e) Assess the potential weaknesses of your research proposal, briefly explaining how you would overcome them. (44 marks)

Doing qualitative research

Madonna uses secret nightclub 'focus groups' to pick songs for new album
By Chris Hastings, Arts Correspondent

They have been used to sell everything from washing powder to New Labour. But now it seems that even Madonna has woken up to the power of focus groups. The most successful female artist in chart history has chosen songs for her next album after secretly trying them out on nightclubbers.

The tunes, with her distinctive vocals removed, were played in clubs from Liverpool to Ibiza throughout June. The reaction of the crowds were filmed and used by the 47-year-old mother of two to determine the final track listing for Confessions On A Dancefloor, her 10th studio album.

Stuart Price, 28, the DJ and producer revealed rock music's first flirtation with market research in an interview for the singer's official website. "Whenever I was DJ-ing I'd take dub or instrumental versions out with me and test them at the club that night," he said. "I had my camera with me and the next day I'd tell Madonna, 'This is what a thousand people in Liverpool look like dancing to our song'."

He added: "You can work on a song for 12 hours but I guarantee you'll know within just 10 seconds of putting it on at a club whether it works or not. So these songs were tested on unwitting subjects throughout Europe."

Daily Telegraph, 13 September 2005

1. **Do you think that music artists ought to do the music they believe in or what they think the audience wants?**

2. **Do you think this sort of market research is going to help Madonna? Explain your reasons.**

3. **Advertisers use focus groups to decide how to promote goods and services. Why do you think this is the case?**

4. **If you were promoting Madonna's music, what would you think is the best way to understand people's needs and motivations?**

The aim of sociology is to help us understand the social world. This is an easy statement to make, but the real problem is what methodology should be used to go about this task. Two overlapping, but distinctive, traditions have developed. The first is quantitative research, which we explored in the previous topic. This method is concerned much more with providing statistical information on attitudes and behaviour. The alternative method, and the subject of this topic, is qualitative research. This is much more concerned about digging deep into how people feel and behave. If quantitative research reports are largely filled with numbers, qualititative ones consist much more of words.

Interpretive approaches and method

Interpretive researchers largely reject the use of quantitative methods (that is, statistical surveys and other positivist approaches) and prefer instead **qualitative research**. Qualitative research methods refer to any approach in sociology that sets out to uncover the meaning of social action rather than measure it through statistics.

Interpretive researchers prefer qualitative methods for the following reasons.

Meaning

As we have just noted, qualitative research allows sociologists to search for the meaning for participants of events, situations and actions in which they are involved. This reflects the belief of interpretive approaches that only by understanding how individuals build up their patterns of interaction can a full understanding of society be presented.

Context

Interpretive research usually studies small-scale groups and specific situations. This allows the researcher to preserve the

Bonnell (1999)

Theoretical approaches and qualitative methods

Qualitative methods are linked with interpretive theories. Bonnell studied why some HIV+ gay men continued to have unprotected sex.

The social world is one which has been given meaning by the people in it. Therefore, to explore this world, it is necessary to draw upon the concepts that people themselves use. Consider the difference between the work of a virologist (a scientist who studies viruses) and a sociologist. Viruses do not speak and do not decide their own behaviour. However, a sociologist who wishes to explore why gay men have unsafe sex must explore what gay men themselves understand by terms such as 'unsafe', 'protection' and 'sex'.

Bonnell, C. (1999) 'Gay men: drowning (and swimming) by numbers', in S. Hood, B. Mayall and S. Oliver (eds), *Critical Issues in Social Research*, Buckingham: Open University Press

1 **How does the extract link qualitative research to interpretive theories?**

individuality of each of these in their analyses (in contrast with positivistic research which is based on large samples). Interpretive-based research provides the researcher with an understanding of the events, actions and meanings as they are influenced by specific circumstances. It is only within the contexts that action makes sense.

Unanticipated phenomena and influences

Positivistic research tends to fall into a format whereby researchers look for evidence to back up a hypothesis and then amend or reject it. In other words, positivistic researchers tend to anticipate certain outcomes – research does not start in a vacuum, but is based on a fairly clear idea of what should happen if variables react as expected.

In qualitative research, the researcher does not necessarily have to have a clear idea of what they are looking for (see 'grounded theory', in the panel on the left) – researchers often start with an interest in a particular area and absolutely no idea of where it might lead. Without the 'blinkers' of the hypothetico-deductive model, researchers are much more open to the unexpected, and to fresh ideas.

Process

Positivistic forms of research are generally interested in outcomes (what happens if), however qualitative research is more interested in the process (what is happening). This reflects a belief by positivists that they are looking for patterns that can be generalized across society – they are not interested necessarily in the details of the actual processes that lead to the outcome. Interpretive sociologists, on the other hand, will be interested in the actual dynamics of the situation – the process.

Types of qualitative research methods

Qualitative research covers a wide range of methods, but the most common are: observational research (**ethnography**), focus groups and qualitative interviewing (qualitative researchers sometimes use secondary sources too). In this topic we will concentrate on just observational research and focus groups, leaving the interviewing and secondary sources to be discussed in the next two topics.

A note on ethnography: We will be using the term *ethnography* quite often in this topic and it can be quite confusing. Ethnography is a general term commonly used by sociologists for participant observation or observation plus in-depth interviewing. So it is best to think of ethnography as a useful term for sociologists immersing themselves in the lives of the people under study, generally joining in as much social activity as possible, so that they can gain an in-depth understanding of the lives of a particular group.

Ethnographic research

Any sociologist undertaking this form of research has quite a number of decisions to make about what is the best form of observational research for their purposes.

The key decisions facing the researcher are:

● the extent of involvement with the group under study
● the amount of information that the sociologist gives the group about their research.

The following two examples illustrate the differences between the methods.

Extent of involvement with the group under study

Sociologists can choose the extent of their participation in a group from one extreme of simply being an external observer with no contact with the group whatsoever – this is known as **non-participant observation**, through to the other extreme of complete immersion in the group – in fact, actually becoming a full group member – known as **participant observation**. Of course, in reality, observational research usually falls somewhere in between.

In deciding the extent of their involvement in the group, the researcher has to decide what they wish to obtain from their research and weigh up the advantages and disadvantages of the role they adopt. Usually, qualitative researchers ask themselves three questions:

1 *What is possible?* – Is it actually possible to become a member of the group and be accepted? Differences in age, social class background, gender, lifestyle and education can all have an impact on this.
2 *What is ethically correct?* – Is it acceptable to join a group that is possibly engaging in harmful activities. What harm will come to them by the sociologist's actions? There is also an ethical dimension to the decision. It is one thing to observe a group engaging in immoral or illegitimate activity; it is quite another actually to be involved.
3 *What method will produce the most valid results? Will becoming a full member of the group actually improve the quality of the research?* – The more the researcher becomes involved with the group, the greater their chances of really getting in-depth information. The sociologist is able to see the situation through the eyes of the group being studied and so will be able to emphasize with the group.

On the other hand, by not getting too involved with the group being studied, the sociologist can avoid getting their personal feelings mixed up with their research perceptions and are much less likely to influence the group in any way (which would ruin the research).

Amount of information the sociologist gives

The sociologist has the choice to be completely honest about the role they are playing – this is known as **overt** observation, or the sociologist can tell the participants nothing and pretend to be a full member of the group – this is known as **covert observation**.

Once again, the sociologist will make the choice by balancing the three elements:

1 *What is possible?* – Is it actually possible to get away with being a member of the group? Will they find out and the cover be blown. For example, even if the sociologist is young looking and can get accepted by a youth group, how is it possible to hide their job and background?
2 *What is ethically correct?* – Is it acceptable to pretend to be a member of a group without letting them know what is really happening ? The ethical guidelines that most sociologists follow insist that informed consent is always obtained. What harm will come to them by the sociologists actions?
3 *What method will produce the most valid results?* – If by pretending to be a member of a group, the researcher is able to enter groups normally closed to researchers and is able to obtain information that results in greater sociological knowledge, then there is a strong argument for using this form of observation.

By balancing these three issues, in terms of the overt/covert and participant/non-participant decisions, the researcher can then decide exactly what form of observational research role they will use.

Gold (1958) has suggested that the result of making these decisions can lead to the researcher taking one of four roles:

- complete participant
- participant as observer
- observer as participant
- complete observer.

These roles lie along a continuum, as shown in Figure 7.1 below.

The process of participant observation

Making contact and gaining entry to the group

Participant observational research by its very nature is interested in groups about whom it is difficult to gain

---

Figure 7.1 Gold's four roles in ethnographic research

According to Gold (1958), making decisions about the extent of their involvement with the group can lead researchers to take one of four roles, along a continuum:

Participant/Covert			Non Participant/Overt
Complete participant	**Participant as observer**	**Observer as participant**	**Complete observer**
A fully functioning member of the group, acting in a covert role	The researcher joins in as a participant, but is overt about their role	The researcher is mainly there to interview and observe	The researcher simply observes what is going on around them, making no attempt to interview or discuss.

information by survey methods. In the majority of cases, it involves studying groups who are marginal to society in some way, very often engaging in deviant behaviour. Most sociologists are not already members of such groups!

The first problem is to make contact and then find some way to gain entry to the group. Most researchers use a contact or gatekeeper who opens the door for them. In Bourgois' study of East Harlem in the 1990s, it was a local part-time crack dealer, Primo, who befriended him. However, not all groups studied are deviant; many researchers simply ask their colleagues if they can study them (see 'Convenience sampling' on pp. 262–3), or get a job, or perhaps join a society where they can observe people.

Lee Monaghan, for example, undertook a number of studies involving participant observation. The first one was about the culture of body builders and their use of drugs. Monaghan (1999) joined a gym and used his hobby as a body builder to study those who attended the gym. In a later study (2005) he used these contacts to get a job as a doorman in a club, where he undertook a further participant observational study on this form of employment.

Acceptance by the group

Gaining access and being introduced to a group does not necessarily mean that the group will accept the researcher as a member or observer. The next stage is to work out how one is going to be accepted. This has two elements: role and relationships

Role refers to the decision of whether to be covert or overt. Most sociologists take a fairly pragmatic view of what role to take, in the sense that they will adopt the role that gives them the greatest chance of getting the research material they want. The factors limiting that will be relationship issues, which we explore next and ethical issues (see p. 261) about how much harm the researcher may cause by acting covertly.

Relationships refer to the similarities and differences between the researcher and the group being studied. Age, ethnicity, gender, religion and social class are amongst the wide range of factors that influence the possibility of the researcher getting close to the people being studied and being able to empathize with them.

Participant observation Advantages and disadvantages

Advantages		Disadvantages	
Experience	Participant observation allows the researcher to fully join the group and see things through the eyes (and actions) of the people in the group.	*Bias*	The main problem lies with bias, as the (participant) observer can be drawn into the group and start to see things through their eyes. Loses objectivity and therefore validity.
Generating new ideas	Often this can lead to completely new insights and generate new theoretical ideas. Also good for validity.	*Influence of the researcher*	The presence of the researcher may make the group act less naturally as they are aware of being studied, unless the researcher is operating covertly.
Getting the truth	One of the problems with questionnaires, and to a lesser extent with interviews, is that the respondent can lie. Participant observation prevents this because the researcher can see the person's actual behaviour. This leads to high levels of validity.	*Ethics*	How far should the researcher allow themselves to be drawn into the activities of the group – particularly if these activities are immoral or illegal?
Digging deep	Participant observation can create a close bond between the researcher and the group under study, and individuals in the group may be prepared to confide in the researcher. Excellent for validity.	*Proof*	There is no way of knowing whether the findings of participant observation are actually true or not, since there is no possibility of replicating the research. In other words, the results may lack reliability.
Dynamic	Participant observation takes place over a period of time and allows an understanding of how changes in attitudes and behaviour take place. Again can raise level of validity.	*Too specific*	Participant observation is usually used to study small groups of people who are not typical of the wider population. It is therefore difficult to claim that the findings can be generalized across the population as a whole.
Reaching into difficult areas	Participant observation is normally used to obtain research information on hard-to-reach groups, such as drug users and young offenders.	*Studying the powerless*	Most (participant) observational studies are concerned with the least powerful groups in society. What about the powerful and their activities?
• Scores very high for validity.		• Scores very low for reliability and generalizability.	

Recording the activities of the group

Once settled into a group, one of the biggest problems faced by the researcher in participant observation is how to record information. This is particularly problematic for researchers engaged in covert observation. There are a number of answers to the problem of how to keep a **field diary**.

The first is simply to remember as much as possible and then to write this up as soon after the events as possible. This has the enormous advantage of allowing the researcher to pay full attention to what is going on at the time, rather than being distracted by writing notes. Indeed, in covert observation, this is probably the only possible method. But the big problem is that the researcher is bound to forget things, and of course, it may be the things they forget that are the more important.

The second method is to make notes wherever possible as the action is unfolding. This leads to great accuracy, but is almost guaranteed to disrupt normal social interaction, as one person in a group making copious notes of what is going on

rather stands out! In Ditton's (1977) study of workplace 'fiddles', he used to go to the toilets to write up his research, using the toilet paper for his notes!

Getting at the truth: influencing the group/getting influenced by the group

In observational research, it is hard to remain objective. Close contact with the group under study means that the sociologist's feelings almost always slip into their field diaries and research notes at some time. The closer to the group the researcher gets, the more likely it is that bias of some sort will creep in. So Bourgois (2003) became close friends with some of the crack dealers in his study, for example: 'I interviewed and in many cases befriended, the spouses, lovers, siblings, mothers, grandmothers … of the crack dealers featured in these pages.'

Not only can the activities of the group influence the researcher positively or negatively, but the researcher can also influence the group. If the group is small and perhaps less

focus on research

Tom Hall was a young researcher who undertook a piece of ethnographic research in 'Southerton' in the South of England.

<< I determined simply enough to spend as much time as I could in the company of, and in conversation with, those young people I first met at the Lime Street hostel, keeping a daily written record of things said and done. I rented a small bedsit room five minutes from Lime Street and spent the best part of most days and every evening there. Over time I was introduced to a wider group of young people. Eventually, my room became a venue for residents and ex-residents. My movements on any given day were by and large determined by those I happened to be with or bump into.

In the first few months of my fieldwork, I made use of a tape-recorder toting it around with me and recording casual discussion. But conversations recorded this way tended to be stilted, so I pretty much stopped using my tape-recorder after the first few months. Instead I used fieldnotes. I spent several hours almost every day writing up my field diary. I seldom took detailed notes in company because it proved impractical to do so, as I couldn't keep up with conversations. But I did keep a

Tom Hall (2003)
Better times than this

small notebook with me at all times in which I made (surreptitious) scribbled notes and jottings whenever the opportunity presented itself. These were useful when last thing at night and first thing in the morning I sat down in my room to write.

From the outset I was open and honest with any young people I met on Lime Street as I felt was right and reasonable, and as least as honest with them as they were with me. Everyone I met were aware that I was 'doing a project thing or something' in which they might feature. And just about everyone I met was happy enough, so far as I could tell to leave it like that.>>

Some months later...

<< Away from the field, back at my desk and working through my fieldnotes and because these were friends of mine, I have found myself fretting and anxious. It has been hard to write disinterestedly about life on Lime Street, having known it and lived it intimately.>>

Hall, T. (2003) *Better Times Than This*, London: Pluto

1. How did Hall gain access to the young people at the hostel?

2. What approach to sampling is used? What problems does this approach bring?

3. What problems did Hall face in making a record of his data?

4. To what extent do you think Hall gained informed consent from the young people in his study?

5. How does Hall's experience illustrate the problems of values entering into participant observation research?

educated than the sociologist, then the researcher's ideas might influence the group – thereby ruining the research. In his classic study of youths in Liverpool, Howard Parker actually gave them legal advice when they were caught by the police for stealing from cars (Parker *et al.* 1998).

Leaving the group

Everyone engaging in participant observation or ethnographic research must, at some time, leave the group. There are two issues here. The first is when to leave? Glaser and Strauss (see 'Theoretical sampling', on p. 263) argue that the correct time to get out of an ethnographic study is when new information does no more than confirm what the sociologist has already found out. They use the term 'theoretical saturation' to describe this situation.

The second issue is actually how to leave. This can be a very difficult thing. If the researcher likes the group and gets on well with the group being studied, then it might be very emotional to leave and may upset both group members and the researcher. On the other hand, if the researcher is engaged in deviant behaviour, it may actually be very dangerous to leave and so a strategy must be developed. In one classic study which studied a violent Glasgow youth gang, 'James Patrick' the researcher used a false name to infiltrate the gang, knowing that if they found him after he left, they would get their revenge. Indeed, to this day his real name is not widely known.

Of course, some people never quite leave. Philippe Bourgois (2003) admits to regularly going back to East Harlem in New York and has kept in touch with his principle gatekeeper (the person who gets the sociologist into the group in the first place and keeps the researcher linked in) – Primo. Interestingly, Primo was heavily influenced by Bourgois and turned from a crack user and part-time dealer into a small time businessman who gave up alcohol and drugs.

Causing harm: The ethical dimension of ethnographic studies

Possibly of all forms of research, apart from experiments, participant observation carries the most difficult ethical dilemmas. At virtually any stage in the proceedings, participant observation (particularly covert) can lead to harm to the researcher, to the participants or to the public.

But even if no harm comes to others, there is still the controversial issue that anyone undertaking covert participant observation does not get the consent of the people who they are studying. This contradicts one of the bases of all modern research, that those being studied give their informed consent. Holdaway (1982) for example was a police officer studying his colleagues without their knowledge. He knew that he was leaving the police force to work at a university once his research was completed. When the research, which was critical of his colleagues was published, some were angry as they felt that he had taken advantage of them

Sociologists therefore have to be very careful about what they do, and this can lead to many moral dilemmas. This is the last part of the introduction to Bourgois' (2003) study of East Harlem (New York) where he studied crack dealers and users.

<< *Finally, I want to thank my family. I will always be grateful to Charo Chacon-Mendez for coming with me to El Barrio, where we married at the very beginning of the research project. Her help was invaluable. I apologize for imposing so much anxiety on her when I regularly stayed out all night on the street and in crackhouses for so many years. I hope that it is not one of the reasons why we are no longer together. If it is, I regret it profoundly.* >>

Focus groups

A second very common form of qualitative research method is the focus group. A focus group consists of a relatively small number of people, usually less than 12, who are requested to discuss a specific topic. Focus groups ideally are representative of a particular population and are obtained through the most appropriate sampling techniques. (These can include both traditional qualitative or quantitative sampling methods.)

Focus groups give researchers an opportunity to hear an issue being discussed, with people able to discuss and challenge each other's views. Compared with the rather static interview method, focus groups are much more dynamic, with people demonstrating the thought process involved in how they came to their views. In the actual discussions, issues emerge that researchers may never have thought of and so those groups are often innovative. Finally, the focus group members have the power to concentrate more on issues they consider important than on the researcher's priorities. See the panel below for a summary of advantages and limitations of focus groups.

Focus groups Advantages and limitations

Advantages

- Allows researcher to understand *why* people hold certain opinions
- People can modify and change views, so demonstrating how strongly held their views are.
- Because it is a discussion the focus group will prioritize issues it thinks are more important. This may be different from the researcher's ideas.
- Focus groups are dynamic, with people probing each other's views and defending their own views.
- Focus groups study group views and interactions.

Limitations

- Researchers have limited control over what happens. The group discussion can veer off into irrelevant (for the researcher) areas.
- Membership of focus groups needs to be carefully run to ensure real discussion, and 'louder' people who dominate discussion need to be controlled.
- Focus groups generate a huge amount of material which is not clearly structured, this means that analysing the material is very difficult.

Feminist research and qualitative methods

Feminist sociologists tend to favour qualitative research, though recently there has been a strong attack on this position from those, such as Oakley (1998), who claim that feminist work needs to be more quantitative and positivistic in style.

According to Mies (1993), quantitative research suppresses the voices of women, either by ignoring them or by submerging them in a torrent of facts and statistics. She also argues that the typical research process disempowers women, as they simply become objects of research and have no ownership of it. This reflects their position in society. Finally, the typical tradition of value-freedom in research actually means that women are unable to get their views across. In Mies' view, feminist research should be for the benefit of women – and should specifically set out to be so.

According to Mies, qualitative research is much more sympathetic to feminist concerns. It allows women's voices to be heard, and their views expressed. Mies also states that the research should be conducted in such a way that researcher and participant are equal and engage in defining and conducting the research together. Feminist research should never impose categories or meanings upon women.

However, in a series of articles, the well-known feminist sociologist Oakley (1999) rejects this. She argues that the use of qualitative research methods in feminist studies reflected a desire to distance feminist perspectives from the traditional scientific/positivist approaches which were much favoured by the male sociology 'establishment'. According to Oakley, that time has now passed and it is important for feminist researchers to use quantitative methods in their research. This will allow them access to the prestige, funding and influence on government policy currently enjoyed by those following more positivistic methods.

Sampling in qualitative research

There are three main types of sampling associated with qualitative research.

Convenience sampling

This refers to any group used for research that is easily available to the researcher. Convenience sampling is very commonly used in ethnography because problems of entry and acceptance by the group being studied are kept to a minimum. Typically

focus on research

Reger (2001)
A 'failed' participant observation

As a feminist-oriented researcher, Reger wished to study a local feminist/activist bookshop. Eventually Reger decided to give up the research.

≪ When I began doing the participant observation, the intention was to be fully and adequately 'sociological'. As a scholar of social movements, feminist and activist, I thought I had found the perfect place to research. I decided on participant observation because I had always been interested in the method but had not yet tried it. The process of participant observation sounded simple. Sit, listen, observe, record – all things I could do.

From the moment I started, the project did not feel right, but being a 'good' researcher, I ignored it. I was clear on the fact that researcher's emotions are not acceptable in the realm of research. I attributed my discomfort to the newness of the method. Surely, I thought, as I grew more comfortable the emotional uneasiness would pass. My first step was to approach

the women I worked with at the bookstore and get permission for the study. They quickly agreed, just like I knew they would. But I felt I had not told the truth, and revealed my intent. I was going to study them, and I was going to do it covertly. They trusted me so completely. I felt like warning them that I could do all sorts of things.

I continued to work at the bookstore, but on the sly I would secretly jot down observations I would later record in greater detail. I kept those notes on scraps of paper hidden in my clothing.

I felt like a spy. I felt dishonest. I felt like I had betrayed the customers, the women of the collective and myself. I was too close to the people already. I felt like I knew too much about the customers. It hurt to observe them. I was not a 'participant' observer, I felt I was a 'parasitic' observer using their lives for my own academic gain. To watch customers' movements felt like a violation of their privacy. The bookstore was a place of personal exploration and safety, and I was violating that with my notes. ≫

Reger, J. (2001) 'Emotions, objectivity and voice: An analysis of a "failed" participant observation', *Women's Studies International Forum*, 24(5), pp. 605–16

How does Reger's experience illustrate:

1 the problems associated with covert observation?

2 some feminist criticisms of conventional research?

Despite the passing of equal-pay legislation as far back as 1970, statistics from a wide variety of sources have shown that, on average, women still earn less than men, are less likely to be in senior management positions and are likely to be found working in a fairly narrow range of employment positions, often linked to traditional caring roles. The statistics providing evidence for this inequality in the workplace have largely come from official statistics and from quantitative surveys conducted by researchers. Similar research methods have been used to explain women's position in the workplace. However, there is a limit to what these statistical studies can tell us about the daily experience of women in the workplace. In order to understand this, qualitative methods are more likely to provide insights. A good example of this is the experience of sexual

harassment in the workplace. Here, a questionnaire is unlikely to be able to provide the sense of harassment that a study using an ethnographic or in-depth interviewing approach might provide. In particular, an ethnographic approach can allow the researcher to build up a relationship with the women subjects of research. By doing this, it is more likely that the women will be prepared to confide in the researcher. For example, Simpson and Cohen (2004) explored the way that women were bullied and sexually harassed in higher-education institutions. Their qualitative research indicated that women varied greatly in how they defined what was harassment or bullying, with some women accepting as normal behaviour, actions which others would immediately define as harassment.

convenience sampling is used for research into occupational groups such as nurses, teachers and students.

Though this is widely used, it can have serious drawbacks. Engaging in covert research can make a person feel like a spy. As seen earlier, where colleagues know and accept the researcher, any results that are critical of them may lead to problems between the researcher and colleagues after the research is over.

Snowball sampling

This is used in all forms of qualitative research – but is most common in studying deviant groups. This method involves finding one person initially who agrees to act as gatekeeper and then through them building up an ever bigger network of contacts. The main problem with this form of sampling is that the sample tends to be restricted to one group who have contacts. This may result in a very partial picture of social interaction.

<< A snowball sample of men and women was built up by making contacts through various institutions such as luncheon clubs, local history groups and other social networks. Many were recommended to us by someone who had already participated, and we were able to interview some members of the same family.>> (Hood and Joyce 1999)

Theoretical sampling

Theoretical sampling is different from the other types of sampling in that it is closely associated with a particular methodology known as grounded theory. In this approach, instead of starting off with a hypothesis and setting out to prove/disprove it, the researcher chooses an area of interest, begins the research and hopes that ideas will emerge from the process. Glaser and Strauss (1967) developed this approach based on the idea that the source of data collection would

have to change as new ideas emerged in the research. At each stage of the research, Glaser and Strauss decided what next group or secondary source was needed to further their research and concentrated their efforts on finding this. When they had reached theoretical saturation (no new ideas are emerging) then it was time to finish.

<< ... but after ten interviews I gradually realized that I needed more interviewees of certain types. For example, initially I found I had only interviewed families with harmonious relationships and so I asked if they could find me families with problems.>> (Darlington and Scott 2002)

Criticisms of research methods used in interpretive sociology

Positivist sociologists have not been shy in criticizing the methods used by qualitative researchers in the following ways.

Values

Positivists argue that although a value-free sociology may not be possible, there are reasonable limits to observe. Qualitative research is shot through with issues related to value bias, and it is almost impossible to untangle the personal biases of the researcher with the research 'insights' generated. The approach taken by feminists such as Mies, which commits itself to a particular value approach, is seen as going beyond the acceptable limit. However the very opposite can occur too. In Lee-Treweek's (2000) study of carers in homes for the elderly, she found that she increasingly disliked the 'carers' she was studying. Their attitudes to the old people so angered her that it was difficult to continue her study in value-neutral position as she wished.

Transferability

Qualitative research is often small scale and specific to a particular group. Positivists claim that it is difficult to transfer the results of research in one specific situation to others – that is, there are problems with **transferability**.

Lack of transparency

According to Bryman and Burgess (1994), the qualitative methods associated with interpretive sociology are often unclear in how they reach their conclusions, resting heavily upon the intuition and understanding of the researcher. The reader of the research has to take it on trust that the perception of the situation as described by the interpretive researcher is accurate.

Comparing research methods

Qualitative research can justifiably claim to provide extremely useful insights into the nature of social action. It seeks, above all, to find out how people perceive the world about them and how this influences their actions – and the consequences of these actions for both themselves and others. Whether qualitative approaches are 'better' or 'worse' than quantitative approaches is like asking whether in theory, structural approaches are 'better' or 'worse' than interpretive approaches. There is no simple answer, except to say that each approach asks different questions that need to be studied in different ways.

Conclusion: the reflexive researcher

All researchers, whether quantitative or qualitative, need to bear in mind that the choices they make in research – choice of method, wording of questions, interpretation of data and final conclusions – are inevitably influenced by their own values, either consciously or unconsciously. For this reason, researchers need constantly to question their own choices and so become **'reflexive researchers'**. According to Hardy et al. (2001), reflexivity 'involves reflecting on the way in which research is

carried out and understanding how the process of doing research shapes its outcomes'. The reflexive researcher will:

- question their own background and values
- strive to identify any questions and issues they may have ignored in the research
- discuss their approaches, interpretations and conclusions with their colleagues and with those participating in the research.

Reflexivity allows both quantitative and qualitative researchers to get closer to the reality of the social phenomenon they are attempting to explain.

Check your understanding

1 **Identify and explain three reasons why interpretive sociologists prefer the use of qualitative methods in research.**

2 **What advantages does observational research have over quantitative methods?**

3 **What strategies do participant observers use to gain entry to the group they are studying?**

4 **What problems do participant observers face in recording information?**

5 **Explain the difference between covert and overt research.**

6 **What ethical problems do sociologists face using participant observation?**

7 **Give an example of a piece of research where the use of focus groups might be appropriate.**

8 **Why do some feminist sociologists favour qualitative methods?**

9 **Why do qualitative methods have a problem with generalizability?**

10 **Why is it important for researchers to be 'reflexive'?**

research ideas

1 Design a research strategy using positivist ideas to discover why some young people are attracted to 'clubbing'. Now, design an alternative piece of research using interpretive ideas. How is the research different? How could each piece of research be criticized?

2 If there is a school or college canteen, spend half an hour observing the way that different people interact. You could choose to compare males and females, or couples versus groups of friends. How do people behave if they are sitting alone?

Next (and with the permission of the tutor) undertake a participant observational study of another class you attend (or perhaps your workplace).

Back in class, compare notes on your observations. What did you observe, if anything? What issues arise when doing this sort of research?

Incidentally, if you have studied people in some detail or engaged in participant observation (for example with your group of friends), then you should ask them for their permission to discuss their behaviour in class and you should certainly promise not to use their names in discussion.

Covert observation – where the sociologist does not admit to being a researcher.

Ethnography – term used to describe the work of anthropologists who study simple, small-scale societies by living with the people and observing their daily lives. The term has been used by sociologists to describe modern-day observational studies.

Field diary – a detailed record of events, conversations and thoughts kept by participant observers, written up as often as possible.

Non-participant observation – where the sociologist simply observes the group but does not seek to join in their activities.

Overt observation – where the sociologist is open about the research role.

Participant observation – where the sociologist joins a group of people and studies their behaviour.

Qualitative research – a general term for approaches to research that are less interested in collecting statistical data, and more interested in observing and interpreting the ways in which people behave.

Reflexive researcher – one who constantly questions every aspect of their research.

Transferability – the ability to transfer the results of research in one specific situation to others.

web.tasks

1 **Go to the Joseph Rowntree website at www.jrf.org.uk**

 Select a summary of one piece of research. Why do you think the researchers used the particular methods they did?

2 **Increasingly, sociologists are conducting ethnographic research on the internet. Go to the chat room, The Student Room at www.thestudentroom.co.uk/ and explore the informal rules of conduct that govern the interaction.**

exploring qualitative research

Item A

Webb and Palmer studied 'fiddles' at Telco, a British-based subsidiary of a Japanese manufacturing company over a two-month period. Fiddles were shop-floor activities which got around official work rules and gave workers greater control over their lives.

<< The material for this paper was gathered during an eight-week period working as a shop-floor operator at Telco – a British-based subsidiary of a Japanese manufacturing company.

The choice of participant observation as a method was guided by a number of factors. Most significant, the nature of the research issue under investigation – fiddles – requires a research methodology that looks below the surface of the formal organizations and views workers in their 'natural environment'. Participant observation allows the researcher to experience work routines at first hand, to see people at work and to discuss their actions and motives with them. This juxtaposition of personal experience, observation and interaction allows the researcher to provide a detailed and reflexive account of the social world of the shop-floor. However, it is not possible to generalize from such a restricted study to all employment situations.

We found that the opportunity for fiddling stems from the company's inability to strictly control the quality of the work and the activities of its workers. Moreover, the results suggest that the fiddles operate mainly with the consent of the supervisors (in the factory) and are ultimately not in conflict with the interests of management as they ensure that the production targets are met. If quality control measures were strictly adopted and there were no fiddles, it is unlikely that the output targets could be attained. >>

Webb, M. and Palmer, G. (1998) 'Evading surveillance and making time: an ethnographic view of the Japanese factory floor in Britain', *British Journal of Industrial Relations*, 36(4), pp. 611–27

(a) Using only **Item A**, identify **two** reasons why the research required the use of participant observation. (6 marks)

(b) Identify **one** strength and **one** weakness of using participant observation to study the issue of 'fiddles' in the workplace. (6 marks)

(c) In your own words, summarize the findings of the research in **Item A**. (12 marks)

(d) Outline and explain the research process that you would adopt in collecting qualitative data to find out the extent of fiddling in a large office environment. (22 marks)

(e) Assess the potential weaknesses of your research proposal, briefly explaining how you would overcome them. (44 marks)

Questionnaires and interviews in research

Which Austen heroine are you?

1 You identify most with:

a   Sleeping Beauty
b   Cinderella
b   Beauty and the Beast
d   The wicked queen (in Snow White)
e   Tinkerbell
f   The Little Mermaid

2 Your favourite movie star is:

a   Dark, French and sexily brooding
b   George Clooney
b   Colin Farrell
d   Matthew McConaughey
e   Viggo Mortensen
f   Harrison ford

...

10 What do you drink?

a   What have you got?
b   Champagne
b   White wine/spritzers
d   The latest trendy cocktail
e   Red wine, vodka, and/or brandy
f   You don't really drink much.

11 You flirt:

a   With anyone who'll flirt back – gender immaterial
b   With any good-looking man who crosses your path
c   With men you like, but it's more mutual teasing and quick-witted banter than sexual innuendo
d   Discreetly. It may feel to you like flirting, but your friends would never call you a flirt
e   Yes, but you're uncomfortable if the conversation gets too sexually provocative
f   Not really. It's rare that you meet someone you really connect with.

12 You dress:

a   Down – jeans, sweaters, trainers
b   Classy but sexy – you like to be noticed
c   Attractive, but not flashy
d   In the latest trends, and you like to show skin – low-rise jeans and a belly-button piercing
e   Feminine – skirts, pretty tops, kitten heels
f   To express your personality.

Scoring

Q1   a 2 b 1 c 3 d 4 e 5 f 6
Q2   a 4 b 3 c 5 d 2 e 6 f 1
Q10 a 5 b 4 c 2 d 3 e 6 f 1
Q11 a 4 b 5 c 3 d 1 e 2 f 6
Q12 a 1 b 4 c 3 d 5 e 2 f 6

41–51 You are Elizabeth
(Pride and Prejudice) – outgoing, funny and direct. You want a serious relationship, but it's essential for you to find someone you can have fun with or teach to have fun. Your best matches are: Mr Darcy, Henry Tilney, Captain Wentworth ...

64–71 You are Lydia
(Pride and Prejudice) – flirty, wild and thoughtless. You're not ready for a serious relationship – what you need is a series of fun flings, and any of these wild boys will do nicely – Henry Crawford, Willoughby, Mr Wickham ...

Source: The Times, 29 August 2005

1 This is part of a 15-question quiz about personality types published in *The Times*. The questionnaire and answers are good fun – but if we were serious in asking questions about personality types, what sorts of questions might you ask?

Asking questions

The most common form of research in social science is based on simply asking questions and noting down the answers. Questions, either as questionnaires or interviews, are used in both qualitative and quantitative research equally. In this topic, we will explore the best way to construct questionnaires and interviews. We will also examine their strengths and weaknesses, and discuss what form of questioning is most appropriate for different research requirements.

Key issues in asking questions

- *Validity* – Do the questions actually get to the truth of the matter?

- *Reliability* – Is every interview or questionnaire conducted in the same way?
- *Ethics* – Do the questions have the potential to embarrass or humiliate the person responding?

What types of questions are there?

In sociological research, as in normal life, questions fall along a range from those which simply require a response to a very specific question – e.g. Do you like pasta? How many students are entering the exam? – to questions that require an explanation or complex information – e.g. Why do you like playing guitar? How do I pass the exam?

When a question requires a very specific answer and the respondent chooses from alternatives, it is known as a

- **Validity** – Do the questions actually get to the truth of the matter? Crucially, this depends upon whether the sociologist has operationalized (put them in a form that can be measured) concepts through the use of indicators (things that are real, measurable).

- **Reliability** – The sociologist has ensured that, as far as possible, every interview or questionnaire is the same as the other. This means that they can be counted as the same.

- **Replicability** – That the research is organized in such a clear way that if the study was conducted by someone else, they would get exactly the same results.

- **Generalizability** – The result of reaching high levels of reliability and validity is the confidence that the research outcomes are true for a much wider population than those studied.

- **Ethics** – The questions must never embarrass or humiliate the person responding and they must be certain that their answers will not be used in a way that could lead to this.

'**closed question**'. When a question requires a more complex answer and the respondent is free to say what they want, it is known as an '**open question**'.

This distinction is crucial in determining the differences and uses of questionnaires and interviews and their relationship to quantitative and qualitative research designs.

Questionnaires and interviews

Questionnaires generally consist of written questions which respondents are requested to complete by themselves. To emphasize this and distinguish them from structured interviews, questionnaires are often referred to as '**self-completion questionnaires**'. These are likely to contain a majority of closed questions.

Interviews consist of a series of questions asked directly by the researcher to the respondent and the responses are recorded by the researcher. Interviews may contain some open questions.

Quantitative approaches usually use self-completion questionnaires, as these allow the researcher to create statistics out of the data obtained; qualitative approaches usually use interviews, as they allow exploration of ideas and feelings.

Self-completion questionnaires

Questionnaires are used by sociologists when they are looking for specific information on a topic (often to support a hypothesis). They are extremely useful in surveys, as they can

Karl Marx (1880)
Designing a questionnaire

The questions below come from a questionnaire written by Karl Marx in 1880. Twenty-five thousand copies of the questionnaire, which contained 101 questions were distributed, but hardly any were returned.

1   What is your occupation?
3   State the number of persons employed in your workshop.
12 Is the work done by hand or with the aid of machinery?
13 Give details of the division of labour in your industry.
56 If you are paid piece rates, how are the rates fixed?
73 If you are employed in an industry in which the work performed is measured by quality or weight, as is the case in mines, does your employer or his representative resort to trickery in order to defraud you of a part of your earnings?

Fulcher, J. and Scott, J. (2003) *Sociology* (2nd edn), Oxford: Oxford University Press, p. 87

1 **Critically analyse each question.**

reach a large number of people, since the printed questions can be handed out, mailed out, or put on the internet. Even though they are distributed to a large number, or a widely dispersed group of people, they are still very easy to administer and can be very quick to get organized and distributed. They provide clear information, which can be converted into statistical data through the use of coding.

In terms of the sorts of questions asked, most questionnaires generally use closed, rather than open, questions, as without a researcher present, people may become confused if the questions are complex. Questionnaires are also particularly useful when it comes to asking embarrassing questions where having an interviewer present may make the respondent feel uncomfortable.

Reliability

Questionnaires are highly standardized, so clearly everyone receives the same questions in the same format. This should make them highly reliable. However, it is never possible to know if everyone interprets the questions in the same way, so the questionnaires are not strictly the same.

Generalizability and representativeness

Questionnaires are widely used in survey work and, if the sampling has been correct, then the questionnaire should produce questions that are generalizable to the whole population. However, postal or internet questionnaires need not necessarily be answered by the person they were sent to. Anyone in the household or with access to a computer could complete the questionnaire. This throws some doubt on representativeness and generalizability.

The second main problem with all self-completion questionnaires is the low **response rate**. Unfortunately, many people cannot be bothered to reply to questionnaires – unless there is some benefit to them, such as the chance to win a prize. This is a serious drawback of questionnaires in research. A low response rate (that is when only a small proportion of people asked actually reply) makes a survey useless, as you do not know if the small number of replies is representative of all who were sent the questionnaire. Those who reply might have strong opinions on an issue, whereas the majority of people may have much less firm convictions – without an adequate number of replies, you will never know. This often occurs when questions are asked about moral issues, such as experiments on animals, or abortion/termination. The issue of response rates is crucial, as it impacts on the generalizability of any research using self-completion questionnaires.

Validity

Questionnaires can have high validity if they are well designed and seek out answers to relatively simple issues. However, there are a number of problems that they have to overcome to ensure these high levels of validity. People who reply to the questionnaire may interpret the questions in different way from that which the researcher originally intended. So their replies might actually mean something different from what the researcher believes they mean. Even more problematic than this is the danger of people deliberately lying or evading the truth. There is little that the researcher can do, apart from putting in 'check questions' – questions that ask for the same information, but are phrased differently. However, without an interviewer present, the researcher can never really know if the answers are true. Parker *et al.* (1998) used questionnaires

focus on... Questions used in questionnaires

1 **Category**
I don't think voting is very important: ☐ Agree ☐ Disagree

2 **Quantity or information**
What is your weekly income? _____

3 **Scale**
If there was a general election tomorrow, how likely would you be to vote, on a scale of 1 to 10?

   1   2   3   4   5   6   7   8   9   10

Absolutely certain not to vote   *Absolutely certain to vote*

4 **List or multiple choice**
In what way, if any, would you like to vote if there was a general election tomorrow?
☐ Text ☐ Internet ☐ By post
☐ Don't mind ☐ Would not like to vote

5 **Ranking**
What do you see as the most important issue facing Britain today? Please rank all those relevant in order from 1 downwards.
☐ Crime ☐ Drugs ☐ War
☐ Terrorism ☐ Racism ☐ Animal welfare
☐ other (please specify) _____

6 **Open ended**
What is your view of New Labour?
_____
_____

1 These are usually 'either/or' questions.

2 The respondent should write in one specific piece of information. Increasingly, these are being replaced by multiple-choice questions in self-completion questionnaires.

3 Used to measure emotions or beliefs. A major problem of validity emerges here in terms of the indicators 1 to 10. How do we know what anyone means when they put down a particular choice? Your '3' might mean a completely different thing from my '3'.

4 Very common in self-completion questionnaires. People drawing up the questionnaire have to be sure that the categories they specify are correct and cover all possibilities. This raises the issue of operationalizing concepts into indicators.

5 If people are being asked to rank things, then the choice of things to rank must cover all possibilities and also must be 'rankable'. For example, you could not ask people to rank such things as illnesses or natural disasters.

6 Not too common in self-completion questionnaires, as very hard to code and quantify.

Questions taken from 'Young People's Attitudes towards Politics', *Nestlé Family Monitor*, 16, 2003

to find out what sorts of drugs young people were using over a period of time. Later in follow-up interviews, one respondent said:

> << The first time we had this questionnaire, I thought it was a bit of a laugh. That's my memory of it. I can't remember if I answered it truthfully or not. It had a list of drugs and some of them I'd never heard of, and just the names just cracked me up.>>

Designing a good questionnaire

When constructing a questionnaire, the sociologist has to ensure:

- *that the indicators are correct* – so that it asks the right questions, which unearth exactly the information wanted – in sociological terms, 'the concepts have been well operationalized'
- *that there is clarity* – the questions are asked in a short, clear and simple manner that can be understood by the people completing the questionnaire
- *that it is concise* – that it is as short as possible, since people usually cannot be bothered to spend a long time completing questionnaires
- *that it is unbiased* – the respondent is not led to a particular viewpoint or answer.

Collating and analysing self-completion questionnaires

As these are usually closed questionnaires, sociologists use a system known as 'coding'. This consists of allocating each answer a particular number and then putting all the answers into a type of spreadsheet. This spreadsheet can then be interrogated for information. All the different answers to the questions can be summarized and compared one against the other. Sociologists have numerous statistical software packages for this.

Interviews

Sociologists generally use interviews if the subject of enquiry is complex, and a self-completion questionnaire would not allow the researcher to explore the issues adequately.

Types of interviews

Interviews fall between two extremes: **structured** and **unstructured**.

- At their most *structured*, they can be very tightly organized, with the interviewer simply reading out questions from a prepared questionnaire. Effectively, they are oral questionnaires in which the researcher writes down the answers (hence the use of the term 'self-completion questionnaire' to distinguish from the highly structured interview).

- Highly *unstructured* interviews are more like a conversation, where the interviewer simply has a basic area for discussion and asks any questions that seem relevant.
- In between is *the* **semistructured interview**, where the interviewer has a series of set questions, but may also explore various avenues that emerge by probing the respondent for more information.

There are three further types of specialist unstructured interviews sometimes used by sociologists:

- *Oral-history interviews* – Respondents are asked about specific events that have happened in their lifetimes, but not necessarily to them. These interviews are almost always used to link up with other secondary sources.
- *Life-history interviews* – These are a second form of unstructured interview in which people are asked to recount their lives. Like oral-history interviews, this method is almost always linked to secondary sources.
- *Group interviews* – Interviews are usually conducted on a one-to-one basis, but there are occasions when group interviews are useful and these have similar issues in terms of reliability and validity to focus groups (see Topic 2, p. 261). Group interviews are commonly used where the researcher wants to explore the dynamics of the group, believing that a 'truer' picture emerges when the group is all together, creating a 'group dynamic'. An example of this is Mairtin Mac an Ghaill's *The Making of Men: Masculinities, Sexualities and Schooling* (1994), in which a group of gay students discuss their experiences of school.

Reliability

Interviews always involve some degree of interaction between researcher and respondent. As in every interaction there is a range of interpersonal dynamics at work. Differences in age, ethnicity, social class, education and gender, amongst many other things, will impact on the interview. The less structured the interview the greater the impact of these factors. Reliability levels are, therefore, much lower than with questionnaires and are directly related to the degree of structure of the interview. According to May (2001), the greater the structure, the higher the reliability – as the greater the chance of these variables being excluded and of the different interviews being comparable. However, Brenner *et al.* (1985) argue that 'any misunderstandings on the part of the interviewer and interviewee can be checked immediately in a way that is just not possible when questionnaires are being completed'. So, they believe that reliability is actually greater.

Representativeness and generalizability

Interviews are much more likely to be used in qualitative research, as they allow for greater depth and exploration of ideas and emotions. Qualitative research tends to be more interested in achieving validity than representativeness. There is no reason why interviews should be any less generalizable than questionnaires, but as they are more likely to be used in non-representative studies, interviews have a reputation for being less generalizable. However, there is a much higher response rate with interviews than with questionnaires, as the process is more personal and it is often more difficult to refuse a researcher who approaches politely.

Validity

Interviews, particularly unstructured ones, have high levels of validity. The point of an unstructured interview is to uncover meaning and untangle complex views. Interviewing also has a significant advantage over self-completion questionnaires in that the interviewer is present and can often see if the respondent is lying or not. However, there are some problems ensuring that validity is high in interviewing.

We saw earlier that every interview is a social interaction with issues of class, gender, ethnicity and so on impacting on the relationship between the two people. Not only does this make each interview slightly different, it also means that validity can be affected. In particular, this can lead to the specific issue of **interviewer bias** – the extent to which the relationship between interviewer and respondent can change the

respondents' answers to questions. There is a whole range of possibilities from respondents wishing to please the interviewer at one extreme to seeking to mislead them at other.

In fact, there is no reason why people should tell the truth to researchers, and this is particularly true when a sensitive issue is being researched. When questioned about sexual activities or numbers of friends, for example, people may well exaggerate in order to impress the interviewer. This can influence the **validity** of the research project. So it is rare now for interviews to be used for personal or embarrassing issues, with sociologists preferring self-report questionnaires.

It is easy for researchers, unknowingly, to slip their values into the research. Usually this happens in questionnaires as a result of the language used. In interviews there is a much wider possible range of influences to bias the research – as well as the language, there is the body language or facial expression of the researcher, or even their class, gender or ethnic background. In particular, interviewers should avoid leading questions.

Loaded words and phrases can also generate bias, i.e. the researchers use particular forms of language that either indicate

focus on research

Wellings and colleagues wished to study sexual behaviour in Britain, but were well aware that there might be some degree of embarrassment and that people might not be too keen to disclose very personal information to researchers they did not know. They were also concerned over the sort of language to use – clinical language or slang? Would it be better to let people complete questionnaires by themselves or should they be interviewed? Would respondents be convinced that their answers really were going to be confidential?

After a small pilot survey, they decided to conduct the research face to face. This would allow the researchers to put people at their ease.

A combination of self-completed questionnaire and interview was chosen. The interview dealt with less personal issues such as family background, early sexual experiences and sex education.

The self-completed questionnaire asked about more private issues, including visits to prostitutes and details of sexual activity. There was an interviewer present, however, who used prompt cards for some questions. These cards listed the possible answers and the

Wellings *et al.* (1994)
Sexual behaviour in Britain

respondent could indicate the number or letter rather than saying the words – the idea here was to avoid embarrassment.

The form of language used was a matter of considerable debate, but in the end, the researchers used more formal language – 'sexual intercourse' rather than 'making love' (or more potentially offensive terms). However, they still had problems over this, as sexual intercourse was interpreted in a variety of ways by respondents.

Although the researchers used the neutral term 'sexual partner' to refer to the person(s) that the respondents were engaging in sexual acts with – there was considerable criticism that the study underestimated the extent of same-sex sexual activity as a result of inadequate methods and inaccurate reading of the findings. The survey suggested that about 1 per cent of men and about 0.3 per cent of women engaged in 'sexual experiences' which were 'mostly or only homosexual', and that 5.2 per cent of men and 2.6 per cent of women had at least one experience of homosexual activity, whereas a commonly accepted figure is in the region of 10 per cent.

Wellings, K., Field, J. and Wadsworth, J. (1994) *Sexual Behaviour in Britain: The National Survey of Sexual Attitudes and Lifestyles*, Harmondsworth: Penguin

1 **What efforts did the researchers make to ensure their data was valid and reliable?**

2 **How successful do you think they would have been?**

Racism and interviewing

One of the areas that has most interested sociologists is that of racism, both its causes and the experiences of those subjected to it. In trying to obtain information on the experience of racism, sociologists encounter some major methodological issues. One of the most common forms of research has been to interview people from ethnic-minority backgrounds in order to find out what their experiences are – however, there are some real problems in doing so. The interviewer may wish to keep the atmosphere as neutral as possible and so may use closed questions and a highly structured form of interview. However, in dealing with sensitive subjects such as racism, most sociologists would opt for a less structured form of interview or, at the very least, open-ended questions. In opting for a more flexible approach involving interaction between both interviewer and interviewee, some problems emerge. Central to the success of an unstructured interview about a sensitive subject is the importance of creating an atmosphere of

social inequality and difference

trust – or rapport – between interviewer and interviewee. Yet, if the interviewer is from a different ethnic background than the person being interviewed, this may present difficulties – particularly if the interviewer is from the same ethnic background as those engaging in racist practices. On the other hand, if both interviewer and interviewee are from the same ethnic background, then there is the possibility that the person being interviewed may wish to please the interviewer by providing evidence of what they imagine the interviewer is seeking (e.g. by exaggerating experiences of racism). Interviewer and interviewee may also have very different understandings of what is meant by racism and this can lead to the researcher failing to grasp the perception of the interviewee towards racism.

Interviewing is a highly complex research tool and when dealing with sensitive issues, there is a high possibility that some form of bias may intrude.

---

a viewpoint or may generate a particular positive or negative response. For example, 'termination of pregnancy' (a positive view) or 'abortion' (a negative view); 'gay' or 'homosexual'.

Prompts and probes

In interviews, **prompts** and **probes** are almost always used:

● *Prompts* – These consist of possible answers to the question.
● *Probes* – These are tactics by which the interviewer can encourage the interviewee to expand on an answer or to explain it more closely. This can range from asking them directly to expand, to simply remaining silent as if expecting more detail from the respondent.

Choosing structured or unstructured interviews

The more structured the interview, the more it takes on the strengths of questionnaires in terms of reliability and the capacity to produce statistics. On the other hand, the more structured it is, the more it can lose in validity. Quantitative researchers almost always used structured interviews, though they may also include some less structured ones in order to deepen their understanding. On the other hand, the more unstructured an interview, the higher the chances of it achieving good levels of validity, but losing out on reliability. Most qualitative researchers use some form of less structured interview as they seek to uncover values and meaning. However, not only do they lose out on reliability, but they also have less chance of claiming high levels of generalizability.

Designing a good unstructured interview

When constructing a good unstructured interview, a sociologist has to take the following steps:

● *Ensure that the questions are fairly short* – It is the respondent who is meant to talk, not the interviewer.
● *Keep the questions clear and avoid jargon* – People can become confused by long or complex questions.
● *Avoid leading and biased questions* – These will produce the replies that the sociologist wants, but will not necessarily reflect the real feelings of the respondent.
● *Ensure there is trust* – The person being interviewed must feel comfortable to talk and must have trust in the researcher.

The advantages of interviewing

● Interviewers can pick up non-verbal cues from interviewees.
● The interviewer can see whether the respondent might be lying, by seeing the situation through their own eyes.
● There is a higher response rate than with questionnaires.
● Interviews take place where interviewees feel comfortable.
● The more structured the interview, the higher the chance of replicating it and therefore of high reliability.
● The less structured the interview, the higher the validity as meaning can be explored.

Ethical issues in interviews

There can be significant ethical issues when using interviews in research, as the interviewer can gain considerable information about the interviewee – some of which is potentially embarrassing for the interviewee. Trust needs to be established very early on and the person being interviewed has to have a reassurance that the information will be confidential. Any information that is published will be done in such a way that the interviewee remains anonymous.

Dorothy Scott studied child abuse in a children's home (Darlington and Scott 2002).

>> *Confidentiality also proved to be difficult as I became increasingly aware of the the difficulty of presenting findings of research based on an intensive analysis of cases without using illustrations which might be recognizable to the staff or the clients.* >> (p. 38)

Collating and analysing interview data

Interviews are usually recorded and then this recording is **transcribed** (written up) into notes. This is an extremely time-consuming activity. For example, Tizard and Hughes (1991) recorded interviews with students to find out how they went about learning – and every one hour of interview took 17 hours to transcribe and check. However, researchers still prefer to do this, as taking notes at the time of the interview usually disrupts the flow, disrupting the atmosphere. The transcription is then studied for key themes. Increasingly, sociologists use special software that can be set up to look for key words or phrases and will then collate these into categories. By recording and transcribing interviews, sociologists have got independent evidence to support their claims, and which they can also provide to other researchers should they wish to replicate the research. This is very important for qualitative sociologists, who are often criticized by quantitative researchers for their failure to provide independent evidence.

Conclusion

However skillfully questions are asked, one key problem remains: people will only reveal what they want to reveal and what they aware of. Darlington and Scott put it this way:

>> *Interviews and questionnaires allow access to what people say, but not to what they do. The only way to find out what 'actually happens' in a given situation is through observation.* >>

An alternative approach is to getting round this problem is to use 'unobtrusive measures' – that is, to exploit the vast amount of information that already exists, from official statistics to the contents of your dustbin – in other words, to use secondary data. These are the subject of the next topic.

Check your understanding

1 Why is the operationalizing of concepts so important in achieving validity in questionnaires?

2 Explain the difference between open and closed questions.

3 What is meant by loaded questions and leading questions? Illustrate your answer with an example of each and show how the problem could be overcome by writing a 'correct' example of the same questions.

4 Why are 'response rates' so important?

5 Distinguish between oral-history and life-history interviews.

6 In what situations is it better to use questionnaires rather than interviews?

7 When would it be more appropriate to use unstructured interviews?

8 Give any two advantages of structured interviews compared to unstructured ones.

9 What do we mean by 'transcribing'?

10 What problem do all methods of questioning face in collecting valid data?

research ideas

Your aim is to find out about a sample of young people's experience of schooling. Draft a closed questionnaire to collect this data. Collect and analyse the data quantitatively. Then draft guide questions for an unstructured interview to find out about the same issue. Conduct two or three of these interviews, either taping or making notes of the responses.

Compare the two sorts of data. What differences are there? Why do those differences occur? Which method do you think was most effective for that particular purpose? Why?

web.tasks

1 Go to the MORI website at www.mori.com Find the social and political section of the website and look at the 'latest research' (or you can search the archive). You will find a wide range of examples of questionnaires. How do MORI go about asking the questions?

2 Now search the worldwide web for other examples of questionnaires. Assess the strengths and weaknesses of the question design.

Closed questions – questions that require a very specific reply, such as 'yes' or 'no'.

Interviewer bias – distortion of a respondent's answers resulting from any aspect of their relationship with the interviewer.

Open questions – questions that allow respondents to express themselves fully.

Probes – tactics by which the interviewer can encourage the interviewee to expand on an answer, e.g. by asking them directly to expand or simply remaining silent as if expecting more detail from the respondent.

Prompts – possible answers to a question.

Response rate – the proportion of the questionnaires that are returned (could also refer to the number of people who agree to be interviewed).

Self-completion questionnaire – questionnaire filled in by respondents themselves.

Semistructured interview – where the interviewer has a series of set questions, but may also explore avenues that emerge by probing the respondent for more information.

Structured interview – where the questions are delivered in a particular order and no explanation or elaboration of the questions is allowed by the interviewer.

Transcribing – the process of writing up interviews that have been recorded.

Unstructured interview – where the interviewer is allowed to explain and elaborate on questions.

Validity – refers to the problem of ensuring that the questions actually measure what the researcher intends them to.

exploring questionnaires and interviews

Item A

<< We set out to compare how crime has been perceived by ordinary working-class people at different periods over the last 60 years. We therefore decided to gather testimony from three generations of people. Fifty-four full-length tape-recorded interviews were completed (with 34 men and 20 women). Informants were drawn from various parts of the London Borough of Tower Hamlets. We aimed to find people who could provide testimony which would allow experiences, memories and interpretations of the past. There were obvious problems in interpreting and comparing testimonies about life in the East End over the last 50 years. We recognized that the recalling of images of the past would be affected by a number of factors: selective amnesia, telescoping of events, reinterpretation in the light of previous experiences, suppression of unpleasant memories or exaggeration of one's own involvement. We certainly came across informants who talked of the 'good old days' recounting stories of bed-bug infestation and chronic overcrowding while still insisting that 'life was better then'.

Of the three generations, those brought up before the 1940s emphasized the shame of and social stigma of being seen as a thief. Furthermore, they argued that crime was low as there was little to steal. The fifties generation changed attitudes to some extent but there was a clear continuity with the values of the older generation. The current generation, however, views things very differently, with an ambiguity towards crime. People condemned theft but were prepared to buy stolen goods. Trust and community solidarity were noticeably less.

Our testimonies obviously refer only to particular experiences and perceptions of some of the people who lived in the area at particular points in time. Care should therefore be taken in comparing these testimonies for purposes of validating their reliability, authenticity and representativeness, with others gathered in different places and at different times. In oral histories of this kind, it is not a question of deciding which is valid evidence, but the findings should be seen as an illustration of the life experiences within a working-class community. >>

Hood, R. and Joyce, K. (1999) 'Three generations: oral testimonies on crime and social change in London's East End', *British Journal of Criminology*, 39(1)

(a) Using only **Item A**, identify **two** reasons why the researchers used interviews to understand how the perceptions of crime has changed over the past 60 years. (6 marks)

(b) Identify **two** problems of using interviews to study the issue of how people have perceived crime over a period of 60 years. (6 marks)

(c) In your own words, summarize the findings of the research in **Item A**. (12 marks)

(d) Outline and explain the research process that you would adopt in collecting interview data about the changes in perceptions of crime over a period of 60 years. (22 marks)

(e) Assess the potential weaknesses of your research proposal, briefly explaining how you would overcome them. (44 marks)

Secondary data

gettingyouthinking

The photo on the right was taken in the early part of the 20th century and used to illustrate an article in the magazine *History Today*. The article explores the way in which European colonialists exploited Africans around this period and, in particular, the way that Belgian colonialists would chop limbs off children if they failed to collect enough rubber. Below is the list of sources quoted by the writer that he used for his article.

Joseph Conrad (1995) *Heart of Darkness* (edited by D.D.R.A. Goonetilleke), Broadway Literary Texts 1

Frederick Karl and Laurence Davies, *The Collected Letters of Joseph Conrad*, Cambridge University Press

Marvin Swartz (1971) *The Union of Democratic Control in British Politics During the First World War*, Oxford: Clarendon Press

Wm. Roger Louis *The Triumph of the Congo Reform Movement 1905–1908*, Boston University Papers on Africa

Roger Anstey (1971) 'The Congo Rubber Atrocities – A case study', *African Historical Studies*, Vol. IV, 1

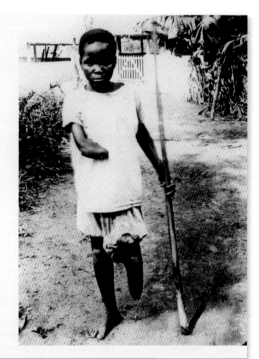

Source: Angus Mitchell (1998) 'New Light on the *Heart of Darkness*', *History Today*, December 1999, pp. 20–1

1 List the variety of sources used by the author (for example, are there any academic articles or novels?).

2 Why do you think that he used this range of material?

3 If you wanted to study a topic which happened in 1904, what would you do?

4 Can you think of any problems that might result from using the range of sources mentioned above?

In our explorations of research so far, we have examined the variety of research methods that sociologists use to generate their own **primary data**, such as surveys, observation and experiments. In this topic, we explore the way that sociologists can make use of material collected by other people for whatever reason. Because these resources have been collected by other people and are 'second-hand' when the sociologist comes to examine it, these data are known as '**secondary data**'. However, it is important to remember that secondary data have equal status amongst sociologists with primary data, and can be just as difficult to collect and interpret. Both qualitative and quantitative researchers make use of secondary sources for a variety of reasons, which we will explore in this topic.

Types of secondary data

A huge range of material can be considered as secondary data. Bryman (2004) suggests the following categories.

- *Life (personal) documents* – These include diaries, letters, e-mails, photographs and video recordings. They may be written down, or in visual or aural (i.e. can be heard) form.

- *Official documents* – These derive from the state and include official statistics, government and local authority reports, minutes of government meetings and of Parliament, and the whole range of officially sanctioned publications available.

- *Other documents that derive from organizational sources* – By this, Bryman means the publications of profit-making companies, charities and any other form of organization that produces some form of formal output.

- *The contents of the mass media* – This is a whole area of study by itself. The mass media refers to all organizations producing information and entertainment for a public audience. This includes radio, television, the internet, newspapers and magazines and novels.

- *Previous sociological research* – This covers all previously published sociological research and datasets.

Webb *et al.* (1981) also argue for the use of **trace measures** – the physical changes produced by human action, such as the number of lager cans left around a building after a group of young people go home after hanging around for the evening.

The advantages to sociologists of using secondary sources

Rather than starting afresh, all sociological research begins with a **literature search**, or **review**, which consists of finding and reading all relevant previous sociological research on the particular topic under investigation.

If the information required already exists, though perhaps in a different form, the researcher does not have to repeat the original research. Alternatively, the researcher may use the original data to reexamine previously published data or studies in order to interpret them in a new theoretical light.

Often, sociologists want to look back in history for information but there is no one able to provide a life or oral history. In these cases, the sociologist must use secondary sources, such as **official documents** and letters.

Sometimes, it is impossible for the researcher actually to visit or talk to the group directly. This could be for financial reasons, or because the group may be geographically too distant or scattered. More commonly, the sociologist thinks that studying the group directly would be too obtrusive. This is where trace measures are often used.

Sociologists studying crime and deviance are often faced with situations where direct studies of the group might be considered unethical – a good example is research on children where it may not be possible to get informed consent. Although some sociologists are prepared to engage in participant observational methods, for example, that can involve them in illegal or immoral activities, other sociologists prefer to study these activities by the use of secondary data.

Finally, and overlapping with the previous point, there are groups engaged in activities that they do not want sociologists to study, because they may be illegal, deviant or immoral. For sociologists studying these groups, one of the few ways to gain information is to access any secondary data available.

Disadvantages of using secondary sources

All secondary sources (except trace sources) are created for a reason; this could well create **bias** and distortion. Government statistics are often neutral, but they are also often constructed in such a way as to throw a positive light on events or statistics. At worst, they can be simple propaganda. Private organizations such as companies, are concerned to produce a positive image of themselves. They will, therefore, only produce information that promotes this image. This applies equally to charities and any other form of organization. **Life documents**, such as a diary, give a very one-sided view of what happened and are almost always bound to be sympathetic to the writer.

Historical sources contain the possibility of bias, which we have already noted for other secondary sources, but there is the even greater problem, according to May (2001), of their being influenced by particular historical events or cultural ways of thinking that the sociologist may not be aware of.

Finally, as we have seen throughout the book, the work of sociologists may contain errors and biases.

Assessing the quality of secondary data

Scott (1990) suggests that there are four criteria to use when judging the usefulness of secondary data to the researcher. These are:

- *Authenticity* – Is the origin of the data known and does the evidence contained there seem genuine?
- *Credibility* – Are the data free from error and distortion?
- *Representativeness* – Is the evidence shown by the data typical of its kind?
- *Meaning* – Is the evidence clear and comprehensive?

We will use these to guide us through the usefulness of each type of secondary sources.

Approaches to secondary data

Sociologists take different approaches towards analysing and using secondary data. There are three main approaches.

Extraction

Extraction simply involves taking statistics or research examples from the original texts. It is commonly used when sociologists examine previous sociological sources and data bases.

Content analysis

In **content analysis**, documents and other sources are examined in great detail to see what themes run through them. There are two ways of doing this:

- Qualitative content analysis stresses exploring the meaning and looking for examples to illustrate the themes. This method is particularly commonly used in studies of the mass media.
- On the other hand, quantitative analysis will almost certainly use computer programs, which will count the number of times certain words (which are regarded as indicators of themes) or themes are used.

Semiotics

Semiotics is the study of signs. A sign is something that stands for something other than itself. For example, a Mohican haircut may indicate a rebellious attitude or a St George's Cross painted on a face signifies support for an England sports team Semiotics is often used in the study of youth culture, and is apparent in

FOREST

Research into smoking

Forest is a pressure group that supports the right of people to smoke cigarettes. It is largely funded by the tobacco industry. In May 2004, it produced the results of a report, a random sample of 10 000 adults aged 18+ in eight cities. Below are the answers to one question asked and the summary by the report: 'Which one of the following statements is closest to your view about the way smoking should be dealt with in pubs, clubs and bars?'

- Smoking should be allowed throughout
  all pubs, clubs and bars   6%
- All pubs, bars and clubs should be mainly
  smoking with separate non-smoking areas   19%
- All pubs, bars and clubs should be mainly non-
  smoking with separate areas for smoking   49%
- Smoking should be banned completely
  in all pubs, bars and clubs   24%
- Don't know   1%
                                          ALL (10 000)

Source: Forest (2004) Smoking in Public Places

The replies were summarized in the report as follows:

<<*Presented with four options of how smoking should be handled in pubs, clubs and bars – 74 per cent prefer to retain some smoking facility rather than banning it altogether, with 24 per cent agreeing with a complete ban on smoking. Just over two-thirds of non-smokers (67 per cent) agreed with one of the options that would retain some smoking facility, compared with 90 per cent of smokers. The proportion of non-smokers opting for a complete ban was 32 per cent compared with only 24 per cent of smokers. Of those visiting pubs frequently or often, only 19 per cent would prefer to see a ban.*>>

1 **Assess the validity of the summary of the findings of this research.**

2 **How could you explain any possible distortion you find?**

the work of both Marxist cultural studies writers and of postmodernist writers. Both these groups seek to analyse the meaning of the particular clothes, music and 'argot' used by young people. Similarly, sociologists interested in semiotics try to uncover the hidden meaning within the secondary data. It is particularly used in the study of life documents, especially photos and in music.

Life documents

Life documents include virtually all written, aural and visual material that derives from people's personal lives, including diaries, letters, e-mails, photographs and video recordings.

Traditionally, the material used by sociologists was written, but increasingly, there has been a growth in visual material such as photographs and home videos.

Life documents can give sociologists a detailed and very personal look into people's lives; as a way of seeing events through their eyes, it is an unrivalled method. They are also particularly useful when there is no other way to get hold of information, for example if the events have happened a long time ago and there is no one to interview. However, the writers may have distorted views of what happened, or they may well be justifying or glorifying themselves in their accounts.

Plummer (2000) suggested that the main forms of life documents include diaries, letters, photographs, film and what he calls '**miscellanea**', which consist of anything else reflecting one's life. We will examine each of these in turn.

Diaries

The key thing about diaries is that they chronicle events as they happen, rather than being filtered by memory or later events, as is the case with autobiographies. Diaries are also very detailed as they cover events day by day. This daily writing is also useful as if gives the sociologist a real idea of the exact timing of when things happen.

However, diaries cannot be relied upon for 'the truth', as people are not objective about their own lives. Instead they filter what happens around them according to their own biases and perceptions. It is also important to remember why the diaries were being written, as many politicians and journalists have published diaries that were specifically written for later publication (for example, the diaries of the politician Tony Benn). This would suggest that the contents will be biased to ensure that they come to be perceived by the reader in a positive fashion.

Letters

The most famous example of the use of letters in sociology is Thomas and Znaniecki's *Polish Peasant* (1918). This is a study of the correspondence of recent immigrants to the United States with their families back in Poland. Thomas and Znaniecki placed an advert in the Chicago newspaper offering to pay for each letter handed to them, and received hundreds of letters. The letters gave them insights into the ordinary lives of immigrants and the issues that concerned them in their new lives in the USA. It also told them about the changes that occurred in family life and relationships as a result of the movement. The letters were divided into various categories by Thomas and Znaniecki, including ceremonial letters (marking formal occasions such as marriages, deaths and birthdays), informal letters about everyday life, sentimental letters (e.g. about love) and letters asking for and sending money and financial advice.

However, letters are always written with some purpose in mind and to convey a particular image of a person. For example, in Thomas and Znaniecki's work, the immigrant letter writers wanted to demonstrate to the people left in Poland what a success they had made with their lives, and so this 'filter' had to be taken into account when reading the letters.

Visual images

Millions of photographs and images are produced every year by families as the most common form of documenting their lives. Photographs have a very long history in sociology and in the early days of sociology in America, almost all research was illustrated with photographs. More recently, some sociologists have used photographs to 'capture' images of people's lives as a form of ethnographic study. Jackson (1978) used mainly photographs to explore the lives of prisoners and Harper (1978) photographed the lives of homeless people. These two sociologists argued that using image rather than text provides a powerful insight into people's lives.

Sutton (1992), however, is very critical of the use of photographs in sociological research. He points out that photographs are almost always taken when groups or families are engaged in holiday or festive occasions and that the photographs are also constructed to reflect a happy image ('Say cheese!'). He conducted a study of visits to Disneyland and concluded that these happy images reinforced the pleasant memories that families had of their visits, helping to forget the more negative experiences. Sutton therefore suggests that to use photographs (and videos) in research has serious drawbacks. However, as Plummer (2000) points out, photographs of events are not restricted to family holidays and occasions, and there is a wide variety of photographic images available which are not necessarily biased.

Miscellanea

Plummer uses this category to include the huge variety of other personal 'documents' that sociologists have used. For example, Schwartz and Jacobs (1979) studied people's suicide notes to try to understand the thoughts and emotion of people in their last hours before death.

However, the same point has to be made regarding miscellanea as for all other life documents. The documents were produced for an effect; they do not necessarily represent the truth or even what people really thought. Taking the example of suicide notes, Schwartz and Jacobs point out that they were often intended to make other people feel guilty and to punish them. They were, therefore, written for an audience and may not necessarily tell their true feelings.

Official publications

Statistics compiled by governments and reputable research organizations are routinely used by sociologists. Governments have entire departments devoted to the production of statistics. In the UK, the Office for National Statistics produces these and collates them from other departments. These statistics provide far greater scale and detail than sociologists can generally achieve and offer a source of information that is readily available, comprehensive and cheap to access.

Usually, the government will produce these statistics over a number of years – for example, the government statistical publication *Social Trends* has been published for over 35 years. This makes it is possible to make comparisons at various points in time.

Although these official statistics have many advantages, there are also some problems facing researchers using them. The statistics are collected for administrative reasons and the classifications used may omit crucial information or classify groupings or activities in a way that is inappropriate for the researcher. So a researcher might be interested in the link between religion and income, but the official statistics may be collated on the grounds of ethnic origin or gender and average income.

Official statistics may also be affected by political considerations, as government will always seek to present the statistics in a positive light as possible. They may also reflect a complex process of interaction and negotiation – as is the case with crime statistics – and may well need to be the focus of investigation themselves!

Reports and government inquiries

The Civil Service and other linked organizations will often produce official reports that investigate important problems or social issues. However, although they draw together much information on these issues, they are constrained by their 'remit', which states the limits of their investigations. The government and other powerful bodies are therefore able to exclude discussion of issues that they do not want to become the centre of public attention. For example, McKie *et al.* (2004) examined official government policy documents on health improvements for families in Britain. They used a particular perspective in their analysis, in that they explored exactly what benefits there would be for women as opposed to other family members. They conclude that there were significant gender inequalities in the official documents, with assumptions about the role of women being to care for other family members.

Documents from other sources

An enormous range of documents is produced by non-governmental organizations (NGOs) – that is, private companies, charities and other social groups. These include annual reports, press releases, advertisements and a range of statistical information about the company's aims and achievements. Increasingly, these are brought into the public domain via the internet.

Official statistics are one of the sources most commonly used by sociologists to obtain information. They are usually authoritative, well-researched and statistically sophisticated. But there are three particular strengths that they have which make them attractive to sociologists:

- They very often provide a national picture, rather than the smaller-scale one that individual sociologists may have to use because of lack of funding.
- They are often able to provide a set of figures over time, thus allowing sociologists to explore trends.
- The government often has the legal power to require individuals to provide information, e.g. census data.

Of particular interest to sociologists exploring inequality are the figures on the unequal distribution of wealth. Each year for tax purposes, the Inland Revenue and Customs (HMRC) collect statistics on the distribution of wealth. These are obtained from the tax forms that people are legally obliged to complete. They ought to be highly accurate, as those who lie are liable for prosecution. What the figures show is that there is very great inequality of wealth in Britain and, perhaps more surprising, that wealth inequality has actually been growing since the mid 1990s. Today, according to the

Inland Revenue, the top 1 per cent of the population own 23 per cent of all the wealth, and these are the figures routinely provided by the government. However, these figures heavily underestimate the degree of inequality, as they include the values of people's homes. To what extent a person's home is a source of wealth is a debatable question – clearly, if someone has a huge mansion or a number of 'homes', this could be considered as wealth, but is the same true for the majority of people who have the one home in which they live? If we exclude the value of a person's house, then the top1 per cent of the population own 35 per cent of all wealth. Similar sorts of questions can also be asked about pensions – to what extent is a private pension 'wealth'?

What emerges from looking more closely at official statistics is that they are statistical 'artefacts', that is they reflect the definition of the researchers, rather than 'reality'. Official statistics are created for reasons that are different from the interests of sociologists. In the case of wealth statistics, the Inland Revenue and Customs are interested in obtaining taxation, and are not concerned with gathering other information on wealth distribution that does not help them in that task. The sociologist must, therefore, treat these statistics with caution.

However, sociologists are even more wary of taking NGOs' materials than they are of taking government ones. Most companies – and even non-profit-making organizations – have a vested interest in ensuring that their public image is positive. It is, therefore, extremely unlikely that negative information will be published by a company about itself. The complexity of using formal information produced by NGOs is illustrated by Forster's (1994) study of career-development opportunities in a large, multinational corporation. The more detail that Forster went into, the more contradictory the information he received:

<< One of the clearest themes to emerge was the apparently incompatible interpretations of the same events and processes amongst the three subgroups within the company – senior executives, HQ personnel and regional personnel managers. These documents were not produced deliberately to distort or obscure events or processes being described, but their effect was precisely to do this. >> (p. 160)

The mass media

The mass media produce an overwhelming amount of information each day, which not only reflects the concerns and values of society but also helps to shape these values. The mass media thus provide fertile ground for sociological researchers.

Content analysis is used by sociologists order to discover how particular issues are presented. They can do this in two ways:

- Using quantitative techniques, researchers simply count the number of times a particular activity or term appears in the media being analysed. This helps to prove a particular hypothesis, e.g. regarding the numbers of people from minority-ethnic backgrounds appearing on television. A slightly more sophisticated version of this might be to construct a content analysis grid, where two or more themes can be linked, e.g. the number of times that newspapers run stories that link people from minority-ethnic backgrounds with negative events.
- In a similar way to the second form of quantitative analysis, researchers may use a qualitative form of content analysis to draw out general themes from the newspapers, film or television. They will, for example, seek to establish not just whether there is a negative association between ethnicity and social problems, but what forms any such association might take.

Quantitative approaches are useful because they provide clear, unambiguous statistics on the number of times topics appear in the press or are broadcast. They can also clearly state the criteria they use for the selection of themes. They are also replicable, because other sociologists can return to the original sources and check their accuracy. However, qualitative approaches have the strength of being able to explore the meaning of the theme or item being researched. Just having the number of times that an item is mentioned in the media does not give a true image of what is being discussed or the importance of the discussion. So, qualitative analyses tend to be more valid but less reliable.

Content analysis is very widely used in sociology, because it is simple and relatively cheap to access mass-media material and analyse it. Furthermore, there are no problems in finding a representative sample, as it is possible to obtain a wide variety of newspapers or television programmes. Importantly, it is an unobtrusive method of research – recording a television programme and then analysing it for its content themes does not impact in any way on the making of the programme.

However, Macdonald and Tipton (1993) suggest there is considerable risk of bias and distortion, for two main reasons:

● There are errors of various kinds, most importantly errors of fact, as the standards of journalists are not as high as academics.
● There is distortion of the facts – Newspapers and television programmes have various preferences as to what can be considered news and what 'angle' to approach the news from. The influences include journalistic values, proprietor's values and, perhaps most important in a competitive market, the audience at which the journalists perceive themselves to be aiming the news.

Furthermore, as Cohen (2002) points out, there is no single correct way to 'read' a newspaper's or television programme's hidden meanings. Each sociologist will approach the interpretation of the contents from their own perspective. Therefore, both reliability and validity are low in content-analysis studies.

One final further difficulty sociologists have in content analysis is actually knowing how the viewers or readers interpret the media output. We know from Morley's research (1980) that people approach and understand television programmes from very different perspectives. Sociologists cannot assume that the interpretation they have – even as a group of researchers agreeing on the content's meaning – will be the same as that of the viewer.

The internet

Possibly the single biggest source of material is available on the Internet. A search engine will quickly throw up hundreds of sources on any topic of interest to a sociologist. However, there is no guarantee of the quality or accuracy of any of this material. The following questions need to be asked:

● Who produced the web pages?
● Why were they produced?
● Was the person or group that produced the information in a position to write authoritatively about the subject?
● Is the material genuine?
● Did the person or group have a particular viewpoint? Can you identify this?

● Is the information typical of its kind? If not, is it possible to establish how untypical it is?
● Is there supporting or competing information elsewhere on the internet?

Sociological research and data archives

There are a number of **data archives** in Britain where the results of large research studies are stored. These can be accessed and the information reused by other researchers. Many of these can be found at The Data Archive (www.data-archive.ac.uk), based at the University of Essex. This holds over 4000 datasets from government, academic researchers and opinion poll organizations.

The huge advantage of these datasets is that they provide ready-made material, but the information that the researchers were originally seeking may not be the same as what is needed by the researcher using them as secondary data. If the researcher is not careful, it is possible to be led astray by the focus of the original research.

Although we have categorized data sets as purely sociological research, it is worth knowing that some are wholly or part-funded by the government. However, as they tend to collect information that is sociological in character rather than politically sensitive, most sociologists classify government-sponsored datasets as sociological research.

Perhaps the best-known data set is the Census, a survey of all people and households in the country, which takes place every ten years (the last Census was 2001, the next is 2011). All households in Britain are required to complete this by law. It is intended to be the most complete picture of Britain available. In recent years, there has been some concern that not everyone completes the Census – in particular, certain minority-ethnic groups, refugees and asylum seekers, and transient populations such as the homeless and travellers. It may, therefore, underrepresent certain categories of the population.

Other well-known data sets include the longitudinal British Household Panel Survey and the General Household Survey which collects information on:

● household and family information
● housing patterns
● ownership of consumer items
● employment
● education
● health services usage
● income
● demographic changes
● smoking and drinking.

Previous sociological research studies

Previous studies as a starting point

Whenever sociologists undertake a study, the first thing they do is to carry out a literature search – that is, go to the library or the internet and look up every available piece of sociological research on the topic of interest. They can then see the ways in which the topic has been researched before, the conclusions reached and the theoretical issues thrown up. Armed with this information, the researcher can then construct the new research study to explore a different 'angle' on the problem or simply avoid the mistakes made earlier.

Reinterpreting previous studies

Often, sociologists do not want to carry out a new research project, but prefer instead to examine previous research in great detail in order to find a new interpretation of the original research results. So the secondary data (that is, the original piece of sociological research) provide all the information that is needed. Sometimes, sociologists might conduct a **meta-analysis**. This is a formal term for the process of looking at the whole range of research on a topic and seeking to identify and draw together common findings.

A good example of how previous sociological work was used as secondary data is provided by Goodwin and O'Connor's (2005) reexamination of a little-known sociological study undertaken in the early 1960s on the lives of young people as they left school and entered work. They compared this with the transition from school to work today. The early work provided them with a detailed and rich database from which they could form hypotheses and make comparisons with contemporary research.

Sometimes, however, there are methodological errors in published research, as well as possible bias in the research findings. There have been many examples of research that has formed the basis for succeeding work and that only many years later has been found to be faulty. A famous piece of anthropological research which was used for 40 years before it was found to be centrally flawed was Mead's *Coming of Age in Samoa* (1945). Mead made a number of mistakes in her interpretation of the behaviour of the people she was studying, but as no one knew this, many later studies used her (incorrect) findings in their work.

Trace measures

One of the problems faced by all sociological researchers is the degree to which their presence and activities actually changes the natural behaviour of the participants. This problem is well recognized in participant observation and experimentation, but also exists to a lesser degree in survey work.

Webb has argued that sociology should use 'unobtrusive measures' in research wherever this is possible, so that this problem is eliminated (Webb *et al.* 1966). He points out that when people interact, they will often leave behind them some physical sign of their activities, the trace measures referred to earlier. According to Webb, there are two types of trace measures:

● *Erosion measures, referring to things missing* – The most famous example of erosion measures (and the origin of the term) was the fact that the tiles around a particular exhibit in the Chicago Museum of Science and Industry which showed real chicks hatching out from their eggs, had to be replaced every six weeks because they became worn out by the sheer numbers of people visiting this exhibit. However, the rest of the museum only needed its tiles replacing after some years.
● *Accretion measures, referring to things being added* – They were used by Rathje and Murphy (2002) in their study of rubbish thrown out by households, but they have also been used in studying graffiti in Belfast (to indicate 'ownership' of particular areas) and litter patterns (to demonstrate public use of space).

Check your understanding

1. **What are secondary data?**
2. **What do we mean by the term 'hermeneutics? Give one other example of ways of approaching the study of documents.**
3. **Why do sociologists use secondary sources?**
4. **What are the disadvantages of using secondary sources?**
5. **What are the advantages and disadvantages of using official statistics and other government documents?**
6. **What are the advantages and disadvantages of using qualitative secondary data, such as diaries?**
7. **Give two examples of data archives. How can these be used by sociologists?**
8. **How can sociologists use trace measures in research?**

researchidea

You can conduct a simple trace measure experiment. Go around your house/garden and look at the objects lying around (anything from a photograph or a scratch in some wood to a CD) and think about the memories that these bring up. Think about the changes in you and your family since these first appeared, and what your feelings are.

web.task

Read more details about the research mentioned in the Focus on research on p. 248 (Topic 1). Go to www.icar.org.uk and then to the publications link and choose 'Media Image, Community Impact'.

KEY TERMS

Bias – where the material reflects a particular viewpoint to the exclusion of others; this may give a false impression of what happened and is a particular problem for secondary sources.

Content analysis – exploring the contents of the various media in order to find out how a particular issue is presented.

Data archives – where statistical information is stored.

Extraction – taking statistics or research examples from the original texts.

Life (personal) documents – personal data in written, visual or aural form, including diaries, letters, e-mails, photographs and video recordings.

Literature search/review – the process whereby a researcher finds as much published material as possible on the subject of interest, usually done through library catalogues or the internet.

Meta-analysis – studying a range of research on a particular topic in order to identify common findings.

Miscellanea – a term used by Plummer (2000) to refer to a range of life documents other than letters and diaries.

Official documents – publications produced by the government.

Primary data – Data collected by the sociologists themselves.

Secondary data – data already collected by someone else for their own purposes.

Semiotics – the study of the meaning of signs; data are examined for symbolic meaning and reinterpreted in this light.

Trace measures – physical changes as a result of human actions.

exploring secondary data

Item A

The following pages show the results of a quantitative content analysis carried out on a sample of the UK press during the period November 2002 to March 2003. The purpose of the analysis was to assess to what extent the UK press was either supportive or critical of the US position on Iraq during the non-military phase of the crisis. The time-scale was dictated by the negotiations at the United Nations, starting in the weeks immediately preceding discussions on the legality of the invasion of Iraq, and finishing at the point when it became clear that the differences between UK/US and French/German/Russian policy would prevent a second resolution being passed to confirm the legality of invasion (early March 2003). The titles used as the basis of the sample were: *Daily Telegraph, Guardian,*

Daily Mail and *Daily Mirror*. This sample is representative of the national daily press in terms of spread of political alignment and distribution by media sector. All articles mentioning the word 'Iraq' during the stated time frame were downloaded from a web version of the titles. Many of these articles only mentioned Iraq in a marginal fashion, in the context of some theme other than the crisis; these articles were not analysed.

The analysis records the numbers of positive/negative mentions of US policy and related matters during

this period, in a stratified sample of articles in the sample titles which had as their main theme the Iraq crisis; the sample is approximately 10 per cent of 'Iraq main theme' articles in each title. It also analyses the distribution of these positive and negative mentions across four identified themes.

The table below shows the percentage distribution of articles for two newspapers having the Iraq crisis as their major theme across the sample of titles.

http://jcamd.londonmet.ac.uk/department/mediat.html
(accessed 23/09/05) amended

Title	No. of articles mentioning Iraq	No. of articles with Iraq crisis as main theme	% of all articles with Iraq crisis as main theme
Daily Telegraph	1032	610	59
Daily Mail	790	316	40

(a) Using only **Item A**, identify **two** reasons why the research could claim to be representative of newspaper articles published about Iraq. (6 marks)

(b) Identify and explain **two** strengths of quantitative content analysis when researching attitudes and beliefs. (6 marks)

(c) In your own words, summarize the findings of the research in **Item A**. (12 marks)

(d) Outline and explain the research process that you would adopt in collecting qualitative data on the impact of newspapers on attitudes towards asylum seekers and refugees. (22 marks)

(e) Assess the potential weaknesses of your research proposal, briefly explaining how you would overcome them. (44 marks)

SOCIOLOGISTS POINT OUT that inequality and difference lie at the heart of all our social experiences. This is the reason why this unit is a synoptic unit because our experience of social life, whether it be in the family, the educational system or at work, is largely shaped by factors such as our socioeconomic status, our gender and our ethnicity. Our chances of going to university, getting a good job, owning our own home and enjoying a long life are all linked to our place in society. In other words, social inequality is a fact of life in modern capitalist societies.

Topic 1 explores the different ways in which different societies grade and rank their citizens, whether that is through religion and patriarchy (as in many developing countries) or according to occupation (as in the UK). This topic examines how occupation is used to produce social categories that we call 'social classes'.

Topic 2 examines sociological explanations for why most societies have stratification systems. In particular, it examines explanations for social-class systems.

Topic 3 explores the effect of social class upon our life-chances. For example, examination of health statistics allows us to say fairly confidently that if you come from an unskilled manual background in terms of your father's occupation, that you are less likely to live beyond 65 years compared with the child of a professional person. Topic 3, therefore, examines a range of outcomes that differ according to social class.

Social commentators are very fond of announcing the death or decline of social class. They suggest that it no longer plays a significant role in our lives and that people today rarely see social class as an important facet of their identity. Topic 4 looks closely at the organization and social character of those broad groupings that we call social classes in order to ascertain the validity of these arguments.

A particularly controversial area of the class structure lies at its base: the issue of poverty. Topic 5 discusses whether a satisfactory definition of poverty can be found before going on to look at recent trends in poverty and identifying the groups most at risk. Finally, the possible causes of poverty are discussed and evaluated.

It has long been argued by feminist sociologists that gender is just as important as social class in shaping division, inequality and identity. Topic 6 examines the extent of gender influence in areas such as education, work and health, and assesses how influential patriarchy actually is.

There has been some concern in recent years that, despite years of antidiscrimination legislation, racism is still very present in modern UK society. In a number of social fields, particularly education and employment, we can see that some ethnic-minority groups are experiencing inequality compared with the White population. Topic 7 investigates both the extent of, and explanations for, these differences in ethnic opportunity and outcome.

Social inequality and difference

Social inequality, difference and stratification

gettingyouthinking

Examine the photo on the right.

1 All these children enjoy equal access to education, but does this mean that they will enjoy similar lifestyles when adults?

2 What social factors may create barriers for them?

3 Look at the photographs below. What ways of measuring class do they indicate?

4 How do the photographs below relate to the criteria listed in the table?

5 Which of the criteria suggested in the table would you use to judge a person's social class and why?

When a random group of respondents were asked to identify the criteria they would use to assess a person's class, the results were as shown in the table on the right.

Adapted from Hadford, G. and Skipworth, M. (1994)
Class, London: Bloomsbury, p. 19

	%		%
Neighbourhood	36	How they talk	17
Job	31	What they wear	15
Pay	29	Parental background	13
Educational background	27	Use of leisure time	11
Wealth (assets such as property and material goods)	22	Political party support	11

It is generally believed that modern societies provide their citizens with the opportunities to better themselves. We all enjoy access to education and the chance to obtain formal qualifications; we all have access to a job market that offers decent incomes and promotion opportunities; we all enjoy the possibility of acquiring wealth. Or do we? The exercise above suggests that these opportunities may not exist for all social groups, or if they do, that some social groups have greater or easier access to these opportunities. In other words, inequalities between social groups are a fact of life in modern societies. The job of sociologists working in the field of stratification is to identify which social groups enjoy unfettered access to economic and social opportunities, and which are denied them, and why.

Differentiation and stratification

All societies **differentiate** between social groups – men and women, the young and the old, the working class and the middle class, and ethnic groups such as Whites, Asians and African-Caribbeans are often perceived to be socially different in some way. When these differences lead to greater status, power or privilege for some over others, the result is **social stratification**. This term – borrowed from geology – means the layering of society into strata, from which a hierarchy emerges reflecting different ranks in terms of social influence and advantage. The degree to which a society has a fixed hierarchy is determined by the degree of opportunity its members have to change their social position.

The sociological term for a person's social importance is **social status**. Status can be gained in two ways:

- **Ascribed status** is given at birth either through family (e.g. the Queen was 'born to rule') or through physical, religious or cultural factors (e.g. in some societies, women and girls are regarded as second-class citizens simply because they are female).
- **Achieved status** is the result of factors such as hard work, educational success, marriage, special talent or sheer good fortune (e.g. winning the lottery).

Societies that allow for and reward achievement are called **open societies**, whereas those that ascribe social position are known as **closed societies**. Politicians tend to see the degree of openness in society as a measure of the freedoms they have helped to create, but they often overemphasize the extent to which society is open. Modern Britain, for example, may have free education for all up to the age of 18 or 19, but, as we shall see in Topic 3, those who are rich enough to attend a top public school have significant advantages in life.

In reality, few societies are totally open or closed and each could be placed somewhere along a continuum (see Fig. 8.1). Traditional societies tend to be more closed because of the greater influence of religion and tradition, which means that people can play a limited range of roles and these tend to be fixed at birth. Modern societies, which seem more fluid and open, may actually experience significant levels of closure, in that some groups face social barriers and obstacles when attempting to improve themselves.

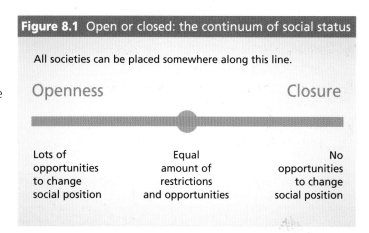

Figure 8.1 Open or closed: the continuum of social status

All societies can be placed somewhere along this line.

Openness — Closure

| Lots of opportunities to change social position | Equal amount of restrictions and opportunities | No opportunities to change social position |

285

Table 8.1 Examples of traditional societies based on ascribed status

	The caste system	The feudal estate system
Place and time	Although officially banned in India today, the Hindu **caste system** of stratification is still enormously influential.	The **feudal estate system** was found in medieval Europe.
Structure	There are four basic castes or layers, ranging from the Brahmins (religious leaders and nobles) at the top, to the Sudras (servants and unskilled manual workers) at the bottom. 'Untouchables' exist below the caste system and are responsible for the least desirable jobs, such as sewage collection.	The king owned all the land and, in return for an oath of loyalty and military support, he would allocate the land to barons who, in turn, would apportion parts of it to knights. The majority (95%) were peasants or serfs who had to work the knight's land and, in return, were offered protection and allowed to rent land.
Restrictions	People are born into castes and cannot move out of them during the course of their lives. There are strong religious controls over the behaviour of caste members – for example, you cannot marry a member of another caste, nor can you do certain jobs because these are assigned exclusively to certain castes.	Feudal societies, too, were mainly closed societies – people's positions were largely ascribed and it was rare for people to move up. Marriage between groups was rarely allowed and feudal barons even restricted the geographical movement of the peasants.
Possibility of social mobility	The system is based upon religious purity – the only way people can be promoted to a higher caste is by living a pure life and hoping that they will be reincarnated (reborn) as a member of a higher caste.	On rare occasions, exceptional acts of bravery could result in a gift of land.

Unit 8 Social inequality and difference

Social class

Social class is the stratification system found in modern industrial societies such as Britain. **Social classes** are groups of people who share a similar economic position in terms of occupation, income and ownership of wealth. They are also likely to have similar levels of education, status and power. Class systems are different from previous systems in the following ways:

- They are not based on religion, law or race, but on economic factors such as occupation and wealth.
- There is no clear distinction between classes – it is difficult to say where the working class finishes and the middle class begins, for example.
- All members of society have equal rights irrespective of their social position.
- There are no legal restrictions on marriage between the classes.
- Social-class societies are open societies – you can move up or down the class structure through jobs, the acquisition of wealth or marriage.
- Such systems are usually **meritocratic** – that is, people are not born into ascribed roles. Individuals are encouraged to better themselves through achievement at school and in their jobs, by working hard and gaining promotion.

Just how meritocratic social-class societies really are, and the extent to which factors such as race, gender and age can affect access to opportunity, will be a key focus of this unit.

Measuring social class

Question 3 in the 'Getting you thinking' on p. 284 should have shown that measuring social class is not an easy exercise. People define social class in different ways and some even deny its existence altogether.

Why is there a need to measure class?

Various groups such as sociologists, advertisers and government agencies have vested interests in **operationalizing** the concept of social class in a consistent way for a number of reasons:

- Sociologists want to address class differences in all areas of social life in order to identify reasons why inequalities come about.
- Advertisers want to target particular social groups in order to maximize sales.
- Governments need to formulate social policies in order to address inequalities.

Each interest group has tended to operationalize the concept of social class in a different way. For example, governments and sociologists tend to approach social class as an objective reality that results in patterns of behaviour and inequality in areas such as health, life expectancy and education. Advertisers are more interested in how people subjectively interpret their class position, because this may affect their consumption patterns and their leisure pursuits.

Occupation as an indicator of social class

The single most objective measurable factor that corresponds best with the characteristics most often associated with class is occupation. It is something that the majority of the population has in common. It also governs other aspects of their life, such as income, housing and level of education. Occupation, therefore:

- governs a significant proportion of a person's life
- is a good indicator of income and wealth, and consequently lifestyle
- is a good indicator of similar skill and knowledge levels
- is an important influence on a person's sense of identity.

However, this still leaves out those who do not work, such as the extremely rich and the long-term unemployed. Objective measures using occupation have, however, enabled social class to be measured statistically. However, getting such measures right has proved to be more of a problem and the various occupational scales that have been constructed have all been criticized for failing to present a true picture of the class structure.

Scales of social class

The Registrar General's scale

This occupational scale was used by the government from 1911 until 2000 and involved the ranking of thousands of jobs into six classes based on the occupational skill of the head of household:

- Class I: Professional, e.g. accountants, doctors
- Class II: Lower managerial, professional and technical, e.g. teachers
- Class IIINM: Skilled non-manual, e.g. office workers
- Class IIIM: Skilled manual, e.g. electricians, plumbers
- Class IV: Semi-skilled manual, e.g. agricultural workers
- Class V: Unskilled manual, e.g. labourers, refuse collectors.

This scheme differentiated between middle-class occupations (non-manual jobs were allocated to classes I to IIINM) and working-class occupations (manual jobs were allocated to classes IIIM to V). The Registrar General's scheme has underpinned many important social surveys, particularly those focusing on class differences in educational achievement and life expectancy.

Criticisms of the Registrar General's scale

The Registrar General's scale was the main way in which class was measured in official statistics. Most sociological research conducted between 1960 and 2000 uses this classification system when differentiating between different classes. However, it does have disadvantages:

- Assessments of jobs were made by the Registrar General's own staff – Hence, there was a bias towards seeing non-manual occupations as having a higher status than manual occupations. However, as we shall see in later in this unit, Marxists argue that the working conditions of some white-collar workers, particular those found in workplaces such as call centres, is remarkably similar to that of manual workers employed in factories.

- It failed to recognize those people who do not work – The unemployed were classified according to their last job. However, the increasing number of never-employed unemployed undermined this system.
- Feminists criticized the scale as sexist – The class of everyone in a household was defined by the job of the male head of household. Women were assigned to the class of their husbands (or their fathers, if unmarried).
- It glossed over the fact that workers allocated to the same class often had widely varying access to resources such as pay and promotion.
- It failed to distinguish between the employed and self-employed – This distinction is important because evidence shows that these groups do not share similar experiences. For example the **black economy** is much more accessible to the self-employed – they can avoid paying tax and VAT by working at a cheaper rate 'for cash', which cannot be traced through their accounts, or by not fully declaring all the work they do.

The Hope-Goldthorpe scale

Sociologists were often reluctant to use government-inspired scales as they lacked sufficient sociological emphasis. In order to study **social mobility**, John Goldthorpe created a more sociologically relevant scale that has proved very popular with social researchers. Goldthorpe recognized the growth of middle-class occupations – and especially the self-employed – and based his classification on the concept of **market position**, i.e. income and economic **life-chances**, such as promotion prospects, sick pay and control of hours worked. He also took account of **work** or **employment relations**, i.e. whether people are employed or self-employed, and whether they are able to exercise authority over others. The Hope-Goldthorpe scale also acknowledged that both manual and non-manual groups may share similar experiences of work and, for this reason, Goldthorpe grouped some of these together in an **intermediate class**. Instead of the basic non-manual/manual divide used by the Registrar General's scale, Goldthorpe introduced the idea of three main social divisions into which groups sharing similar market position and work relations could be placed: he referred to these as the **service class**, the intermediate class and the working class.

Goldthorpe's scale was first used in studies conducted in 1972, published in 1980. The scale more accurately reflected the nature of the British class system, but it was still based on the male head of household. He defended this position by claiming that, in most cases, the male worker still determines the market situation and lifestyle of a couple, i.e. the male is still the main breadwinner. However, many feminists remained unconvinced by this argument. They argued that scales based on the idea of a male 'head of household':

- overlook the significance of dual-career families, where the joint income of both partners can give the family an income and lifestyle of a higher class
- ignore situations where women are in a higher-grade occupation than their husbands
- overlook the significance of the increasing number of single working women and single working parents, who are classified according to the occupation of their ex-partners or fathers.

A feminist alternative: the Surrey Occupational Class Schema

This scale was developed by the feminist sociologists Arber, Dale and Gilbert (1986) in an attempt to overcome what they saw as the patriarchal bias inherent in the Hope-Goldthorpe scale. In this scheme, women are classified on the basis of their own occupations, whether they are married or not. The gendered nature of work in contemporary society, especially the growing service sector of the economy, is also taken into account. This is most evident in class 6 which is divided into 6a (sales and personal services – female dominated) and 6b (skilled manual – overwhelmingly male).

However, the inclusion of women in such occupational classifications does present some difficulties because women's relationship to employment is generally more varied than that of men. More women work part time or occupy jobs for short periods because of pregnancy and childcare. It is, therefore, difficult to know whether the class assigned provides a meaningful insight into their life experience as a whole or whether it merely reflects a short-term or temporary experience that has little impact on lifestyle and life-chances.

Table 8.2 The Hope-Goldthorpe Scale		
Service class	**Intermediate class**	**Working class**
1 Higher professionals High-grade administrators; managers of large companies and large proprietors	3 Routine non-manual (clerical and sales)	6 Skilled manual workers
2 Lower professionals Higher-grade technicians; supervisors of non-manual workers; administrators; small-business managers	4 Small proprietors and self-employed artisans (craftspersons) 5 Lower-grade technicians and supervisors of manual workers	7 Semi-skilled and unskilled manual workers Source: Goldthorpe, J.H. (1980) *Social Mobility and Class Structure*, Oxford: Clarendon Press

We can see from this topic that defining and measuring social class is a major problem for sociologists. This is because social class is an abstract social concept that needs to be operationalized. In other words, indicators of what identifies the social class of individuals must be identified. Most sociologists and civil servants faced with this problem have tended to use occupation and level of educational achievement as the indicator, although in their study of educational inequality, Boyland (cited in Gold 2003) also chose to use as his indicators receipt of free school meals alongside occupation. However, not all sociologists agree with these indicators. Goldthorpe actually acknowledges that a person's job is made up of a complex interplay of factors, while the NS-SEC (see below) focuses on a range of indicators related to work, such as authority over others, pay, autonomy over working practices and promotion potential. Finally, the debate about how to measure social class is complicated by the fact that people's subjective awareness of their class position and identity can differ from objective definitions. However, Pawson (1989) notes that, while people may be able to place themselves within class categories, these may not mean a great deal to them. Evans (1992) has demonstrated that people's attitudes towards inequality, for example, often have very little to do with their awareness of their class position.

Table 8.3 The Surrey Occupational Class Schema

1	Higher professional
2	Employers and managers
3	Lower professional
4	Secretarial and clerical
5	Supervisors, self-employed manual
6a	Sales and personal services
6b	Skilled manual
7	Semi-skilled
8	Unskilled

Source: Arber et al. (1986)

A new scale for the 21st century: the National Statistics Socio-Economic Classification (NS-SEC)

The NS-SEC scale, which essentially is a variation on the Hope-Goldthorpe scale, fully replaced the Registrar General's scale for government research and statistics and was used for the first time to classify data from the 2001 census (see Table 8.4).

Like the Hope-Goldthorpe scale, the NS-SEC is based on:

- **employment relations** – whether people are employers, self-employed, or employed and whether they exercise authority over others
- **market conditions** – salary scales, promotion prospects, sick pay, how much control people have over the hours they work, and so on.

Table 8.4 The National Statistics Socio-Economic Classification (NS-SEC)

Occupational classification		% of working population	Examples
1	Higher managerial and professional	11.0	Company directors, senior civil servants, doctors, barristers, clergy, architects
2	Lower managerial and professional	23.5	Nurses, journalists, teachers, police officers, musicians
3	Intermediate	14.0	Secretaries, clerks, computer operators, driving instructors
4	Small employers and self-accountable workers	9.9	Taxi drivers, window cleaners, publicans, decorators
5	Lower supervisory, craft and related	9.8	Train drivers, plumbers, printers, TV engineers
6	Semi-routine	18.6	Traffic wardens, shop assistants, hairdressers, call-centre workers
7	Routine	12.7	Cleaners, couriers, road sweepers, labourers
8	Long-term unemployed or the never-worked		

Source: Rose, D. and Pevalin, D. (with K. O'Reilly) (2001) *The National Statistics Socio-economic Classification: Genesis and Overview*, London: ONS

Strengths of the NS-SEC

- It no longer divides workers exclusively along manual and non-manual lines. Some categories contain both manual and non-manual workers.
- The most significant difference between the Hope-Goldthorpe scale and the NS-SEC is the creation of Class 8, i.e. the long-term unemployed and never-employed unemployed. Some sociologists, most notably from New Right positions, have described this group of unemployed as an 'underclass'.
- Goldthorpe has finally acknowledged the feminist arguments and women are now recognized as a distinct group of wage-earners. They are no longer categorized according to the occupation of their husbands or fathers.

Potential weaknesses of the NS-SEC

- The scale is still based primarily on the objective criteria of occupation. This may differ from what people understand by the term 'social class' and their subjective interpretation of their own class position.
- Those who do not have to work because of access to great wealth are still not included.
- Some argue that the scale still obscures important differences in status and earning power, e.g. headteachers are in the same category as classroom teachers.
- Some critics have suggested that ethnicity and gender may be more important in bringing about social divisions and shaping identity.

Subjective measurements of social class

Social surveys suggest there is often a discrepancy between how objective measurements of social class classify jobs and how people who actually occupy those jobs interpret their social status or class position. For example, many teachers like to describe themselves as working-class despite their objective middle-class status. This is because many teachers have experienced upward mobility through educational qualifications from working-class origins and feel that their perspective on the world is still shaped by working-class values and experience. This subjective awareness of class position often conflicts with official objective interpretations.

More important, it is the subjective interpretation of class position that is responsible for the sharp boundary lines that exist between the social classes in the UK. In other words, there is some evidence (which will be explored in more detail in later sections) that those people who interpret themselves as 'working-class', 'middle-class' and 'upper-class' have very clear ideas about what characteristics people who 'belong' to their class should have. Moreover, they tend to have very strong views about the characteristics of other social classes. These subjective interpretations may have little or nothing in common with official and objective attempts to construct broad socioeconomic classifications based on employment. As Reay (1998, quoted in Bottero 2005) has noted:

Savage, Bagnall & Longhurst (2001)
Class identities

Mike Savage and his colleagues carried out in-depth interviews with 178 people living in four sites in and around Manchester. They identified three groups of people in terms of subjective class identity:

- First, there was a small minority of their sample who strongly identified themselves as belonging to a specific class. These were often graduates who had the cultural confidence to express their class position in an articulate fashion.
- The second group was also well educated, but did not like to identify with a particular class position. Rather, this group tended either to reject the notion of social class, because they saw themselves as individuals rather than a product of their social-class background, or they preferred to debate the nature of social class rather than acknowledge their belonging to any particular group. Some felt happier differentiating themselves from other social classes rather than focusing on their own membership of a particular social class.
- The third group, which made up the majority of the respondents, actually identified with a social class, but did so in an ambivalent, defensive and uncommitted way. Some of this group prefaced their 'belonging' with remarks such as 'I suppose I'm …' or 'probably, I'm …'.

Savage and colleagues concluded that identification with the concepts of 'working-class' and 'middle-class' for this part of their sample was based on a simple desire to be seen as normal and ordinary, rather than any burning desire to be flagwavers for their class. They conclude that, in general, the notion of class identity was 'relatively muted'.

Savage, M., Bagnall, G. and Longhurst, B. (2001) 'Ordinary, ambivalent and defensive class identities in the North West of England', *Sociology*, 35(4),

1. **Suggest reasons why Savage's research team used in-depth interviews in this study.**

2. **Explain how the findings of Savage and colleagues led them to conclude that class identity is 'relatively muted' (i.e. unclear, muffled).**

<<*Class is a complicated mixture of the* **material**, *the* **discursive**, *psychological predispositions and sociological dispositions that quantitative work on class location and class identity cannot hope to capture ... Now what is required are British-based ethnographic examinations of how class is 'lived' in gendered and raced ways to complement the macro versions that have monopolized our ways of envisaging social class for far too long.* >> (p. 83)

Studies of subjective class identities confirm this observation. Marshall *et al.* (1988) found that 53 per cent of their sample saw themselves as 'working-class' despite the fact that the majority of their sample were in white-collar, non-manual jobs. However, Savage *et al.* (2001) are not convinced that identification with such class categories has any real meaning beyond the need to feel normal and ordinary. They argue that people identify with the term 'middle-class' because they see it as the least loaded of the terms offered to them by sociologists. In fact, Savage and colleagues argue that, by saying they are middle-class, people are actually saying they are typical, ordinary people, who are neither particularly well off nor particularly badly off. Bradley (1999) notes, too, that when people identify themselves as working-class, this does not

involve a strong sense of group or collective loyalty or attachment to traditional working-class institutions such as trade unions. Again, it is more likely to indicate a claim to be an ordinary and typical working person. In other words, subjective interpretations of social class may have very little to do with the characteristics allocated to social class by objective official classifications.

Check your understanding

1. What is the difference between social differentiation and social stratification?
2. Why might those at the bottom of the caste system accept their lot?
3. What determined one's position in the hierarchy in the feudal estate system?
4. Why are most modern societies more open than most traditional societies?
5. Why is occupation considered to be the most defining characteristic for the measurement of social class?
6. What problems are created by using occupation as the key indicator of social class?
7. What were the strengths and weaknesses of each of the scales used before 2000?
8. How does the NS-SEC scale address the weaknesses of the other scales?
9. How might the NS-SEC scale still be said to be lacking?

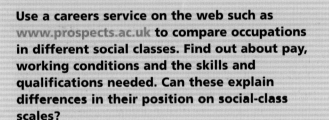

web.task

Use a careers service on the web such as www.prospects.ac.uk to compare occupations in different social classes. Find out about pay, working conditions and the skills and qualifications needed. Can these explain differences in their position on social-class scales?

KEY TERMS

Achieved status – the degree of social honour and prestige accorded to a person or group because of their achievements or other merits.

Ascribed status – the degree of social honour and prestige accorded a person or group because of their origin or inherited characteristics.

Black economy – illegal ways of increasing income.

Caste system – Hindu system of stratification, now officially banned in India but still influential.

Closed societies – societies with no social mobility or movement within or across each stratum.

Differentiation – perceived social differences between

people, e.g. on lines of gender, age or race.

Discursive – up for discussion or debate.

Employment relations – see 'Work relations' below.

Feudal estate system – stratification system of medieval Europe.

Intermediate class – according to Goldthorpe, a lower grouping of the middle class containing those with the poorer work and market situations than the service class, e.g. clerical workers, small proprietors and lower-grade technicians.

Life-chances – opportunities for achieving things that provide a high quality of life, such as good housing, health and education.

Market position or conditions – income and

economic life-chances, such as promotion prospects, sick pay, and control over hours worked and how work is done.

Material – physical, often economic, things such as money and consumer goods.

Meritocratic – rewarding hard work or talent, rather than inherited wealth or position.

Open societies – societies with a high degree of social mobility, where status is usually allocated on the basis of achievement and merit.

Operationalize – define something in such a way that it can be measured.

Service class – according to Goldthorpe, those with the highest work and market situations: the upper middle class, e.g. large proprietors as

well as administrators, managers and professionals who service the economy.

Social class – hierarchically arranged groups in modern industrial societies based on similarities in status, wealth, income and occupation.

Social mobility – the movement of individuals up or down the social scale.

Social status – degree of social honour, prestige and importance accorded to a person or group.

Social stratification – the hierarchical layering of a society into distinct groups with different levels of wealth, status and power.

Work relations – whether people are employed or self-employed, and are able to exercise authority over others.

1 Imagine you are conducting sociological research on social class at a horse-racing track or a cricket match, using observation only – you are not allowed to distribute questionnaires or conduct interviews. What sorts of things might you listen or look out for that might give you clues as to a person's social class?

2 Undertake a piece of research using a structured interview to measure the class distribution of students on various school or college post-16 courses. Pilot it with a random sample of ten students across the institution. After each interview write down any

issues that may affect the validity, representativeness or reliability of the evidence gathered. For example:

- Did respondents understand the questions, answer truthfully or exaggerate aspects of lifestyle/income?
- Did they find the questions too intrusive or personal? Were they confused by the terminology you used?
- Identify the main problems you encountered in trying to operationalize social class.
- Did you note any differences between people's subjective interpretations of their social class position and how the NS-SEC ranks them?
- What, if any, conclusions can you draw from your findings?

exploring social inequality, difference & stratification

Item A

Subjective class identities

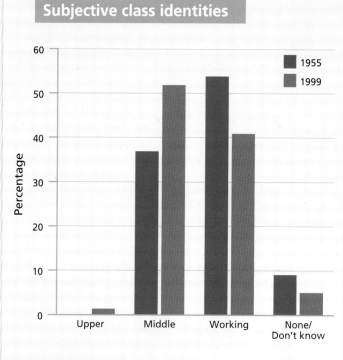

Legend: 1955, 1999

Categories (x-axis): Upper, Middle, Working, None/Don't know

y-axis: Percentage (0 to 60)

Source: Travis (1999)

Item B

Both the Registrar-General's and Goldthorpe's class schemes have been useful in highlighting class-based inequalities, such as those related to health and education, as well as reflecting class-based dimensions in voting patterns, political outlooks and general social attitudes. However, such schemes suffer from several significant limitations.

Occupational class schemes are difficult to apply to the economically inactive, such as the unemployed, students, pensioners and children. Such schemes are also unable to reflect the importance of property ownership and wealth to social class. Occupational titles alone are not sufficient indicators of a person's wealth and overall assets. The rapid economic transformations occurring in industrial societies have made the measurement of class even more problematic. New categories of occupations are emerging; there has been a general shift away from factory production towards service and knowledge work, and an enormous number of women have entered the workforce in recent decades. Occupational class schemes are not necessarily well suited to capturing the dynamic processes of class formation, mobility and change that are provoked by such social transformations.

Adapted from Giddens, A. (2001) *Sociology*, Cambridge: Polity Press, pp. 288–90

(a) Using **Item A**, identify **two** trends in how people's perceptions of their social class have changed between 1955 and 1999. (6 marks)

(b) Identify **two** 'economic transformations occurring in industrial societies [that] have made the measurement of [social] class even more problematic', according to **Item B**. (6 marks)

(c) Identify and explain **two** problems of using occupation as the main criteria for measuring social class. (12 marks)

(d) Using your wider sociological knowledge, outline the evidence for the view that social-class inequality is a common experience in UK society. (22 marks)

(e) Outline and assess the strengths and weaknesses of the different models of social class employed by sociologists in the last 30 years. (44 marks)

Theories of inequality

gettingyouthinking

Look at the photograph of a richer and a poorer person.

1 Using your knowledge of sociological theory, suggest how the following perspectives might explain the relative class position of the people in the picture:

(a)   Marxism
(b)   functionalism.

2 What do you think are the advantages and disadvantages for societies of having:

(a)   a high level of social inequality?
(b)   a low level of inequality?

In the broadest terms, you may have been able to work out that Marxists explain class differences in terms of exploitation – the rich owners of large businesses pay as little as possible to their workers, while benefiting from the existence of a group of poor and unemployed people, who help keep the general level of wages low and who can do some low-paid work when necessary. For functionalists, however, inequality can actually benefit society by motivating people to work hard and fulfil their potential. It is this latter view that we consider first.

Functionalism

The founding father of functionalism, Emile Durkheim (1858–1917), argued that class stratification existed because it was functional or beneficial to social order. He saw modern societies as characterized by a specialized occupational **division of labour**, in which people have very different functions, skills and abilities. In other words, it is characterized by social divisions. However, he argued that members of society are happy to take their place within this division of labour because they believe in its moral worth, i.e. there is common agreement or consensus about how society and its institutions, such as work, should be organized. This **value consensus** also means that members of society accept the legitimacy of stratification, i.e. they accept that occupations should be graded in terms of their value to society and that those occupying the more functional or valued positions should receive greater rewards for their efforts. Durkheim, therefore, saw the stratification system

as a moral classification system embodying and reflecting common values and beliefs.

He argued that stratification is beneficial because it sets limits on competition and people's **aspirations**, in that it clearly links criteria such as skills and qualifications to particular roles so that people do not become overly ambitious and therefore disappointed and resentful. Because the system is regarded as fair and just, members of society are relatively contented with their lot, and so social order is the norm.

Durkheim did acknowledge some potential problems with this system that might cause conflict and, therefore, possible breakdown in social order. He noted that if people are unable to compete freely for jobs or roles – if they are forced into certain types of work – then moral consensus and solidarity could break down. Durkheim believed that ascription (the arrangement whereby roles are allocated on the basis of fixed inherited criteria such as gender and ethnicity) would lead to conflict because those allocated to roles had no choice in the matter. On the other hand, Durkheim believed that the possibility of acquiring skills and qualifications gave people an element of choice and so reaffirmed their moral commitment to society. He also believed that this moral order could be disturbed by sudden shifts in a society, such as economic recession or the accumulation of too much power in the hands of one individual or group, because these shifts could destabilize what people expected from the stratification system. For example:

● Recession could lead to a rapid and sudden rise in unemployment and deflation in wages.

- A dictatorship could lead to people being put into functionally important and highly rewarded roles on the basis of patronage rather than ability, thus fuelling resentment and conflict.

Talcott Parsons (1902–79) saw stratification as a ranking system based on moral evaluation – that is, based on respect, prestige, social honour, social approval and disapproval. He argued that modern class stratification reflects a **normative** consensus about what society values, especially with regard to kinship (family status), personal qualities (gender, age, beauty, intelligence, etc.), achievement (qualifications and skills), possessions, authority (the ability to influence others because of a particular status, e.g. doctor) and power (the ability to get our own way regardless of resistance).

Parsons noted that those qualities associated with the labour market, e.g. achievement and skills, are the most highly valued in contemporary Western societies according to the consensus into which we are all socialized. Parsons therefore argues that stratification is the outcome of general agreement in society about how roles should be ranked in terms of their functional importance or value to society. Those most highly valued are consequently more highly rewarded. As Bottero notes (2005):

<< People have little choice but to accept the general value placed on the different positions in a hierarchy. They may not like it, but – if they want to get on – they have to live with it and play by the rules. >> (p. 49)

These classical functionalist ideas of Durkheim and Parsons were built upon by Davis and Moore in the 1950s. Table 8.5 below outlines both their views and those of their critics.

Is stratification really good for society?

A similar view to that of Davis and Moore has been proposed by the New Right thinker, Peter Saunders (1996). He points out that economic growth has raised the standard of living for all members of society, and social inequality is thus a small price to pay for society as a whole becoming more prosperous. Saunders is influenced by Hayek (1944), who argued that capitalism is a dynamic system that continually raises everybody's standards of living, so the poor in contemporary society are much better off than they were 30 years ago. Moreover, **capitalist societies** offer incentives to those with talent and enterprise in the form of material wealth. If these incentives did not exist, Hayek argues, then many of the consumer goods that we take for granted today, such as cars, ballpoint pens, computers and Ipods, would not exist, because talented people would not have been motivated to produce them. However, this perspective, like functionalism, downplays the argument that the disparity of rewards may create resentment and dissatisfaction that could lead to deviance and social disorder.

Marxism

According to Marx (1818–83), the driving force of virtually all societies is the conflict between the rich and powerful minority who control the society, and the powerless and poor majority who survive only by working for the rich and powerful. These two classes are always in conflict as it is in the interests of the rich to spend as little as possible in paying their workers.

Table 8.5 The functionalist theory of stratification	
Davis and Moore (1955)	**Criticisms**
All societies have to ensure that their most important positions are filled with the most talented people. They therefore need to offer such people high rewards.	Does this really happen? Lots of occupations can be seen to be essential to the smooth running of society but are not highly rewarded, such as nurses. There are also plenty of idiots in high places!
Class societies are meritocracies – high rewards in the form of income and status are guaranteed in order to motivate gifted people to make the necessary sacrifices in terms of education and training. Educational qualifications (and hence the stratification system) function to allocate all individuals to an occupational role that suits their abilities. People's class position is a fair reflection of their talents.	Some groups may be able to use economic and political power to increase their rewards against the will of the majority. High rewards sometimes go to people who play no functionally important roles but who simply live off the interest generated by their wealth. Do the three to five years of training at college and/or university merit a lifetime of enhanced income and status? Isn't higher education a privilege in itself?
Most people agree that stratification is necessary because they accept the meritocratic principles on which society is based.	There is a substantial level of resentment about the unequal distribution of income and wealth as illustrated by the controversy over 'fat-cat' levels of pay. Unequal rewards may be the product of inequalities in power.
Stratification encourages all members of society to work to the best of their ability. For example, those at the top will wish to retain their advantages while those placed elsewhere will wish to improve on their position.	The **dysfunctions** of stratification are neglected by Davis and Moore. For example, poverty is a major problem for people and negatively impacts on mortality, health, education and family life.

Causes of conflict

The heart of this class conflict is the system of producing goods and services – what Marx called the **mode of production**. This is made up of two things:

- the **means of production** – the resources needed to produce goods, such as capital (money for investment), land, factories, machinery and raw materials
- the social **relations of production** – the ways in which people are organized to make things, i.e. the way in which roles and responsibilities are allocated among those involved in production.

Marx described modern Western societies as capitalist societies and suggested that such societies consist of two main classes:

- the **bourgeoisie** – the capitalist or ruling class, who own the means of production; they are the owners or, today, the large shareholders in businesses, and control decisions about employment, new investment, new products, and so on.
- the **proletariat** – the working or subordinate class, who sell their ability to work (labour power) to the bourgeoisie; most people make a living by working for a profit-making business, but they have no say in business decisions or how they are put to work, and rely on the success of the company they work for.

The social relations of production between the bourgeoisie and proletariat are unequal, exploitative and create class conflict. Capitalism's relentless pursuit of profit means that wages are kept as low as possible and the bourgeoisie pockets the difference between what they pay their workers and the value of the goods produced by workers. This '**surplus value**' forms the basis of their great wealth. Moreover, workers lose control over their jobs as new technology is introduced in order to increase output and therefore profits. Workers become **alienated** by this process and are united by a shared exploitative class experience. This common class experience means that the working class is a **class-in-itself**.

So, according to Marx, capitalism is a pretty dreadful kind of society. However, if this is the case, why do most people happily accept it – even believing it to be superior to other kinds of societies? Marx had an answer for this, too. Workers very rarely see themselves as exploited because they have been 'duped' by **ideological apparatuses**, such as education and the media, into believing that capitalism is fair and natural. The working class are 'suffering' from **false class consciousness**.

Marx believed that the conflict inherent in the capitalist system would come to a head, because the increasing concentration of wealth would cause the gap between rich and poor to grow and grow, i.e. to become **polarized**, so that even the most short-sighted members of the proletariat would see that the time for change had come. Marx predicted that, eventually, the proletariat would unite, overthrow the bourgeoisie, seize the means of production for themselves and establish a fairer, more equal society – known as **communism**. For Marx, then, radical social change was inevitable as the working class was transformed from a class-in-itself into a revolutionary **class-for-itself**.

Evaluation of Marx

Marx's ideas had a huge influence in the 20th century. Communist revolutions occurred in many countries, such as China and Russia, and it could be argued that his ideas have had more impact on more people than have the teachings of Jesus Christ and Mohammed put together. However, his ideas have come in for a great deal of criticism, especially since the communist regimes of Eastern Europe crumbled in the 1990s.

- Marx is accused of being an economic **determinist** or **reductionist**, in that all his major ideas are based on the economic relationship between the bourgeoisie and proletariat. However, many contemporary conflicts, such as those rooted in nationalism, ethnicity and gender, cannot be explained adequately in economic terms.
- Marx is criticized for underestimating the importance of the middle classes. He did recognize a third (in his view, relatively minor, class) made up of professional workers, shopkeepers and clerks, which he called the **petit-bourgeoisie**. However, being outside the system of production, they were deemed unimportant to the class struggle. In his view, as the two major camps polarized, members of this class would realign their interests accordingly with either one. Some **neo-Marxists** have argued that the upper middle class have aligned themselves with the bourgeoisie in that they act as agents for that class in their role of managers and professionals – in other words, the service class 'service' their employers. Others, most notably Braverman (1974), argue that white-collar workers have more in common in terms of their working conditions with the proletariat. These issues are explored further in Topic 4.
- In particular, Marx's prediction that the working class would become 'class conscious' because they would experience extreme misery and poverty, and therefore seek to transform the capitalist system has not occurred. As we saw in Topic 1, working-class people do have a sense of class identity but this is limited. Most people who see themselves as working class do so not because they recognize their exploited status but because they wish to claim their typicality in terms of being working people. Furthermore, although Western capitalist societies may have problems such as poverty and homelessness, they do have a reasonably good record in terms of democracy and workers' rights. Moreover, the living standards of the working class have risen. It may be then that working-class people are sensibly reconciled to capitalism rather than being 'falsely conscious'. In other words, they appreciate the benefits of capitalism despite being aware of the inequalities generated by it.

Neo-Marxism

Neo-Marxists have tended to focus on the relationship between the **infrastructure** (i.e. the capitalist economy and particularly the social relationships of production characterized by class inequality, exploitation and subordination) and the **superstructure** (i.e. all the major social institutions of society, such as education, the mass media, religion, the law and the political system). Neo-Marxists argue that the function of the superstructure is the reproduction and legitimation of the class inequality found in the infrastructure. In other words, the superstructure exists to transmit ruling-class **ideology** and, in particular, to make sure that the mass of society subscribes to ruling-class ideas about how society should be organized and does not complain too much about the inequality that exists, e.g. in income and wealth. The function of the superstructure, therefore, is to encourage acceptance of class stratification and to ensure that false class consciousness continues among the working class.

Education is seen by neo-Marxists as a particularly important ideological apparatus working on behalf of the capitalist class. Marxists, such as Althusser (1971), suggest that education transmits the idea that it is a meritocracy – i.e. that ability is the major mechanism of success. However, this disguises the reality of the stratification system: that those born into ruling- or middle-class backgrounds are much more likely to achieve, because what goes on in the educational system, in terms of both the academic and hidden curriculum, is the product of bourgeoise values. The **cultural capital** of the children of the upper and middle class (along with the material advantages they enjoy, such as private education) ensure that class inequality is reproduced in the next generation. The children of the working class, on the other hand, lack this cultural capital and so are condemned to a life of manual work, as they are ejected from the educational system at the age of 16. However, these working-class children rarely blame the capitalist system for their 'failure'. Rather, the ideology of meritocracy ensures that they blame themselves, with the consequence that the working class rarely challenge the organization of capitalism or see stratification as a problem.

Other neo-Marxists have focused on the ideological power of the mass media and how the bourgeoisie might be using this to their advantage. The Frankfurt School of Marxists, for example, writing since the 1930s, have focused on the role of the media in creating a popular culture for the masses that has diverted working-class attention away from the unequal nature of capitalism to consumerism, celebrity culture and trivia. Marcuse (1964), for example, noted that capitalism has been very successful in bedazzling the working class with what he saw as 'false needs' to buy the latest consumer goods. Neo-Marxists argue that the latest soap storylines, and the lifestyles of the rich and famous, are now given more priority by the media, especially the tabloid newspapers and commercial television, than political and economic life. Consequently, the mass of society is now less knowledgeable and more ignorant about how society is politically and economically organized. The result of this ideological barrage is that the working class is less united than ever, as people compete with each other for the latest material goods. As a result, stratification and class inequality are rarely challenged.

In criticism of neo-Marxism, Saunders (1990) argues that such writers suffer from the same two problems:

- How is it that they know the truth when it is hidden from everybody else? The answer, says Saunders, smacks of arrogance: 'Marxists know the true situation because Marxist theory is true' (p. 19).
- Marxist theory does have the unfortunate habit of dismissing what working-class people say and think about their situation as the product of ideology and false class consciousness. As Parkin (1972) notes, there is a haughty assumption in Marxist ideology theory that the working class are experiencing a kind of collective brain damage.

synoptic link   education and mass media

It is worth thinking through the roles of agencies such as the mass media and education with regard to stratification. Functionalist theories stress the central role of value consensus and agencies of socialization in preparing people to take their role voluntarily in the specialized division of labour and to accept that the organization of this system benefits all sections of society. Education obviously plays a major positive role in this process by socializing us into key values, such as achievement, competition and individualism. The mass media reaffirm our commitment to a meritocratic society by positively reporting on individual success and by celebrating values such as wealth, hard work and equal opportunity.

Marxists, on the other hand, argue that conflict and inequality lie at the heart of a deeply divisive capitalist society. They see agencies such as education and the mass media functioning in an ideological way to convince those groups at the bottom of the socio- economic order that inequality is fair, just and deserved. Both education through the hidden curriculum and the mass media (by stressing entertainment at the expense of serious news) work to hide the real facts of inequality in capitalist societies from the working class.

Sociologists who have been influenced by Weber generally agree with this Marxist analysis.

Feminists who argue that women generally occupy a lower status position than men, even when occupying the same class position, often complain that both education and media generally operate in favour of males.

Finally, postmodernists see both education and especially the globalization of mass media as partly responsible for the death of social class as a primary source of identity. Postmodernists argue that education and mass media have made many more choices available to us and consequently our identities are a mixture of different influences.

Max Weber

Another classical theorist, Max Weber (1864–1920), disagreed with Marx's view on the inevitability of class conflict. Weber also rejected the Marxist emphasis on the economic dimension as the sole determinant of inequality. Weber (1947) saw 'class' (economic relationships) and 'status' (perceived social standing) as two separate but related sources of power that have overlapping effects on people's life-chances. He also recognized what he called '**party**' as a further dimension. By this, he meant the political influence or power an individual might exercise through membership of pressure groups, trade unions or other organized interest groups. However, he did see class as the most important of these three interlinking factors.

Like Marx, Weber saw classes as economic categories organized around property ownership, but argued that the concept should be extended to include 'occupational skill' because this created differences in life-chances (income, opportunities, lifestyles and general prospects) among those groups that did not own the means of production, namely the middle class and the working class. In other words, if we examine these two social classes, we will find status differences within them. For example, professionals are regarded more highly than white-collar workers, while skilled manual workers are regarded more highly than unskilled workers or the long-term unemployed. These differences in status lead directly to differences in life-chances for these groups.

The significance of status in inequality

People who occupy high occupational roles generally have high social status, but status can also derive from other sources of power such as gender, race and religion. Weber noted that status was also linked to consumption styles (how people spend their money). For example, some people derive status from conspicuous consumption – e.g. from being seen to buy expensive designer products. This idea has been taken further by postmodernists, who suggest that in the 21st century, consumption and style rather than social class will inform people's identity.

Weber defined social classes as clusters of occupations with similar life-chances and patterns of mobility (people's opportunities to move up or down the occupational ladder). On this basis, he identified four distinct social classes:

1 those privileged through property or education
2 the petty-bourgeoisie (the self-employed, managers)
3 white-collar workers and technicians (the lower middle class)
4 manual workers (the working class).

Weber's ideas have influenced the way in which social class is operationalized by sociologists such as Goldthorpe (1980a) and by the government through the recent NS-SEC scale – see Topic 1. The notion of market situation and work relations is based on the notion that status differences (and therefore, life-chances) exist between particular occupational groups.

Weber was sceptical about the possibility of the working class banding together for revolutionary purposes – i.e. becoming class conscious – because differences in statuses would always undermine the notion of common cause. Social classes were too internally differentiated, and this destabilized the idea of group identity and common action.

The concept of 'status groups' rather than social classes is central to Weber's theory of stratification. Weber noted that people make positive and negative judgements about other people's standing and esteem, and these can affect a person's life-chances. These judgements tend to focus on qualities which are shared by groups. Therefore, we might make judgements about people's education ('they are brilliant' or 'thick'; 'they went to university'), their religion ('they are extremists' or 'they treat women negatively'), their age ('they cannot cope with the responsibility'), their ethnicity ('they are all criminals'), their gender ('they are too emotional') and even their bodies ('they are too thin, too fat, ugly, beautiful'). Status groups, then, are those who share the same status position, as well as a common awareness of how they differ from other status groups. In other words, their identity is bound up with their exclusiveness as a group, and this will shape their lifestyle in terms of how they interact with others – for instance, they may only socialize with people like themselves.

Evaluation of Weber

Class, status and wealth

Marxists argue that Weber neglected the basic split between capitalists and workers, and argue that class and status are strongly linked – after all, the capitalist class has wealth, high status and political power. Weber recognized that these overlap, but suggested that a person can have wealth but little status – like a lottery winner, perhaps – or, conversely, high status but little wealth – such as a church minister. He suggested that it is very rare that high-status groups allow wealth alone to be sufficient grounds for entry into their status group. He noted that such groups may exclude wealthy individuals because they lack the 'right' breeding, schooling, manners, culture, etc. This practice of 'social closure' will be explored in more depth in later topics. Conversely, someone may be accepted as having high status by the wealthy, despite being relatively poor in comparison, such as the aristocrat who has fallen on hard times. Weber rightly points out that high status and political power can sometimes be achieved without great economic resources.

Party

Party or power plays a role in this too. Weber saw this third type of inequality as deriving from membership of any formal or informal association that sets out to achieve particular goals. Such associations might include political parties, trade unions, the freemasons, old boy networks and even sports clubs. Membership of these can influence the social status a person has in the community. For example, membership of the freemasons might increase a person's potential to make social and business contacts, and, therefore, their wealth, while many middle-class men may be keen to join the local golf club because of the prestige that such membership may confer on them.

Gender and ethnicity

Weber's analysis helps explain why some groups may share economic circumstances but have more or less status than others, for example, due to gender or ethnic differences. Weber saw gender and ethnicity as status differences which have separate and distinct effects on life-chances compared with social class. In other words, the working class might have less status than the middle class, but working-class Black people and working-class women may have less status than working-class White men.

Status and identity

Savage et al. (2001) take issue with the importance of 'status' in terms of shaping people's identity or giving us insight into the nature of inequality. Savage notes that people rarely make status claims, and suggests that they are wary of 'appearing to demonstrate openly their cultural superiority'. In fact, Savage's research suggests that people are more concerned with stressing how ordinary or how mainstream they are. Very few social groups assert that they are a special case. However, Savage does acknowledge that Weber did note that as a general rule, class, status and party do go together. As Bottero (2005) notes:

>> The rich tend to be powerful, the powerful to be wealthy, and access to high-status social circles tends to accompany both. >> (p. 41)

Conflict and stability

Bottero concludes that, unlike the Marxian theory of stratification, Weber provides an adaptable 'history-proof' model of stratification which may be more valid in analyzing the variety of stratification arrangements that exist. However, she notes that both Marx and Weber fail to explain why societies organized around conflict or difference are so stable, orderly and reasonably free of major conflict between the social groups who occupy them.

Interpretive sociology

Most of the accounts that we have examined – especially functionalism and Marxism – are structural theories. This type of stratification theory is often accused of over-determinism: reducing all human behaviour to a reaction to either social or economic structure, and presenting people as puppets of society, unable to exercise any choice over their destiny. Interpretivist sociologists suggest that the social actions of individuals are more important than the organization of society, – that is, its social structure. These sociologists argue that subjective meanings are important because they allow us to choose how to behave – for instance, we might decide that our ethnicity is more important to us than our social class and act accordingly.

Bottero, however, notes that this focus on **agency** or action assumes that social life is patternless. She argues that this ignores the constraints within which people must continue to live, in that structured social inequalities continue to set 'substantial limits on choice and agency for all and create situations in which some are more free to act than others' (p. 56). She notes that Marx recognized the role of agency when he stated that 'men make their own history', but he also recognized that social structure shaped action when he said that 'they do not make it under circumstances chosen by themselves'.

Giddens and structuration

Giddens (1973) developed these ideas in his theory of structuration, in which he argued that individuals create structural forces, such as social class, by engaging in particular actions. For example, he noted that class advantages can be passed on to the younger generations through family interaction. He also noted that consensus about the status or standing of occupations, as well as our acceptance that some people have the authority to tell us what to do at work, creates a hierarchy of occupations and, therefore, a stratification system based on social class. In other words, we judge people by the type of house or area they live in, by the car they drive, by the clothes or logos they wear, by the consumer goods they buy. He argues that this consensus about consumption also contributes to stratification.

However, in 1990, Giddens decided social class was no longer as significant as it had been in the past. Rather, the major social division in society was between the employed and the unemployed or socially excluded. Social class no longer constrained the activities and lifestyle of a whole mass of people – it was now individuals who experienced constraints and opportunities. Moreover Giddens set himself on the postmodernist road when he argued that lifestyle and taste were now more significant than social class in the construction of identity.

Gate Gourmet supplies in-flight meals for airlines. Its workers went on strike in August 2005, disrupting British Airways flights. Many of its workers at Heathrow Airport are from ethnic minorities – in particular, the West London sikh community. Discuss the Gate Gourmet workers in terms of Weber's categories of class, status and party.

Postmodernism

Postmodernists reject what they see as the **grand narratives** of the stratification theories discussed so far. They instead focus on the concepts of 'identity' and 'difference'. They argue that the increasing diversity and plurality found in postmodern social life has led to the break-up of collective social identity, and especially class identity. It is argued that the group categories of 'social class', 'ethnicity', and 'gender' no longer exist in an homogeneous form. Subjective individual identity is now more important than objective collective identity. Best (2005) argues that, for postmodernists, ' the problem of identity is one of avoiding a fixed identity and keeping one's options open, avoiding long-term commitments, consistency and devotion'.

Postmodernists, such as Waters (1995), argue that social class is in terminal decline as a source of identity and that consumption – how we spend our money – is now central in terms of how we organize our daily lives. As Best notes, 'we are all cast into the roles of consumers'. Increasing affluence and standards of living have led to individuals being faced with a variety of consumer choices about their lifestyle rather than being forced into particular forms of cultural behaviour by forces beyond their social control, such as social class. In particular, postmodernists argue that people now use a variety of influences, particularly those stemming from globalization, to construct personal identity. Waters, for example, suggests that as a result, postmodern stratification is about lifestyle choices, fragmented association (we never belong to or identify with one group for very long), being seduced into conspicuous consumption by advertising and constant change in terms of what we are supposed to be interested in, the choices available to us and how we are supposed to feel.

Topics 3 and 4 examine social class and its relationship to future life-chances and identity and, consequently, it is recommended that you use the evidence from those topics to judge the validity of this postmodernist view of the influence of social class.

Check your understanding

1. **Why is social stratification acceptable, according to Durkheim?**
2. **In what circumstances might stratification be dysfunctional to society, according to Durkheim?**
3. **Why, according to Davis and Moore, do some people deserve more rewards than others?**
4. **Why do functionalists like Davis and Moore see social stratification as good for society?**
5. **What, according to Marx, determines a person's social class?**
6. **What is false class consciousness and how does it aid stratification?**
7. **Marx is accused of being an economic reductionist – what does this mean?**
8. **What is the role of the superstructure with regard to stratification?**
9. **What three sources of inequality does Weber identify as important in modern societies?**
10. **How does the concept of status help explain gender and ethnic differences?**
11. **How do postmodernists view class identity?**

KEY TERMS

Agency – social action.

Aspirations – ambitions.

Alienation – lack of fulfilment from work.

Bourgeoisie – the ruling class in capitalist society.

Capitalist societies – societies based on private ownership of the means of production, such as Britain and the USA.

Communism – system based on communal ownership of the means of production.

Class-for-itself – a social class that is conscious of its exploited position and wishes to change its situation.

Class-in-itself – a social group that shares similar experiences.

Cultural capital – attitudes, ways of thinking, knowledge, skills, etc., learnt in middle-class homes that give middle-class children advantages in education.

Determinist or reductionist – the view that phenomena can be explained with reference to one key factor.

Division of labour – the way the job system is organized.

Dysfunctions – the negative effects of social actions, institutions and structures.

False class consciousness – where the proletariat see the society in a way that suits the ruling class and so pose no threat to them.

Grand narratives – postmodernist term for big structural theories, such as functionalism and Marxism.

Ideological apparatuses – social institutions that benefit the ruling class by spreading the ideas that help maintain the system in their interests, e.g. the mass media, education system.

Ideology – set of beliefs underpinning any way of life or political structure. Used by Marxists and neo-Marxists to refer specifically to the way powerful groups justify their position.

Infrastructure – in a Marxist sense, the capitalist economic system that is characterized by class inequality.

Means of production – the material forces that enable things to be produced, e.g. factories, machinery and land.

Mode of production – economic base of society that constitutes the entire system involved in the production of goods.

Neo-Marxists – those who have adapted Marx's views.

Normative – accepted by all, taken for granted.

Party – term used by Weber to describe political influence.

Petit-bourgeoisie – term used by Marx to describe the small middle class sandwiched between the proletariat and bourgeoisie.

Polarization – at opposite ends of the spectrum.

Proletariat – the working class in capitalist societies.

Relations of production – the allocation of roles and responsibilities among those involved in production.

Superstructure – social institutions such as education, mass media, religion, which function to transmit ruling-class ideology.

Surplus value – term used by Marx to describe the profit created by the work of the proletariat but taken by capitalists.

Value consensus – moral agreement.

research idea

Conduct a piece of research to discover young people's explanations of inequality. Design an interview schedule to assess the ways in which your sample explains inequality. Do they take a functionalist position and see inequality as beneficial, motivating and meritocratic? Alternatively, do they agree with Marxists that inequality is damaging, unfair and demotivating?

web.task

Use the search facility at the Social Science Information Gateway – www.sosig.ac.uk – to find out about key sociologists and their views on inequality, stratification and social class.

A useful website covering the work of Marx is www.anu.edu.au/polsci/marx/marx.htm

exploring theories of inequality

Item A

The Marxist model of class formation

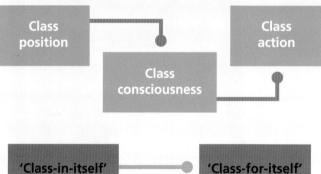

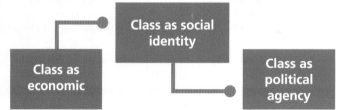

Item B

The Marxian analysis revolves around the concept of class, and Marx's great insight was to see the exploitation of the working class by the factory owners as the determining factor in social division. People's behaviour is determined by the class grouping in which they find themselves. Furthermore our ability to make perceptions of the world and act on the basis of those perceptions is class determined.

According to Marxian analysis, the state is viewed as an institution that helps to organize capitalist society in the best interests of the bourgeoisie. The legitimacy of the capitalist system is maintained by ideology; working-class people are victims of a false consciousness. In other words, working-class people are said to hold values, ideas and beliefs about the nature of inequality that are not in their own economic interests to hold. Working-class people have their ideas manipulated by the media, schools and religion, for example, and regard economic inequality as fair and just.

Adapted from Best, S. (2005) *Understanding Social Divisions*, London: Sage, p. 14

(a) Using only the information in **Item A**, identify **two** consequences of social-class position. (6 marks)

(b) Identify **two** ways in which the legitimacy of the capitalist system is maintained by ideology according to **Item B**. (6 marks)

(c) Identify and explain **two** methodological problems facing sociologists who wish to research ideology and false class consciousness. (12 marks)

(d) Using your wider sociological knowledge, outline the evidence for the view that status differences characterize many areas of social life in Britain today. (22 marks)

(e) Outline and assess the usefulness of sociological explanations that stress conflict in explaining fundamental social divisions in Britain today. (44 marks)

Life-chances and social class

gettingyouthinking

GIVENCHY

1 Look at the photographs. How do they show that consumption and lifestyle may be becoming increasingly important as sources of identity?

2 How available are the lifestyle choices illustrated above to all social groups? Who may be denied access and why?

You may have concluded from the exercise above that the ground rules regarding the expected behaviour of different social classes are changing. You may also have concluded, however, that material factors still govern lifestyle choices and that these are class related. Some sociologists argue that class identity has come to depend not only on market situation but on differences and similarities in power and status, as well as **consumption** and lifestyle.

Does class still matter?

Savage (2000) argues that since 1979, when it suffered the first of four successive election defeats, the Labour party has deliberately avoided talking about class and has focused instead on the concept of '**social exclusion**'. Consequently, political debate has focused on the idea that groups such as the long-term unemployed, single mothers and the residents of socially deprived areas are somehow excluded from the benefits most of us take for granted. In response, social policy has been devised in the fields of education, training and welfare with the concept of '**social inclusion**' in mind – that is, it has aimed to target these groups so that they can become part of mainstream society again. However, Savage argues that the concepts of 'social exclusion' and 'social inclusion' are deliberately 'bland and inoffensive' – they reflect the New Labour or **Blairite** view that social-class divisions are no longer important because we allegedly now live in a society 'where most social groups have been incorporated into a common social body, with shared values and interests'. Britain in the 21st century is perceived as a classless society, or if social class is to be acknowledged at all, a society in which the vast majority of us share in middle-class lifestyles and aspirations – as Tony Blair once said, 'we are all middle-class now'. Sociologists have also taken up this baton of classlessness. New Right sociologists such as Peter Saunders, as well as postmodernists such as Pakulski and Walters, have argued that social class is no longer important as a source of personal identity for people in the 21st century. These sociologists, despite their theoretical differences, have suggested that consumption patterns and '**cleavages**' are far more important than social class in shaping lifestyle and life-chances today.

Equality of outcome or equality of opportunity?

Another way to look at the relevance of social class today is to see a debate between those who argue for **equality of outcome** and those who argue for **equality of opportunity**.

The traditionalist view

Those sociologists and politicians who believe that equality of outcome should be the priority see class divisions and conflict as the key characteristics of British society; they believe that New Labour politicians have abandoned their commitment to equality and social justice for those exploited by the organization of capitalism, i.e. the working class. These 'traditionalists' believe that New Labour has betrayed its working-class roots because it has done nothing to redistribute wealth and income from rich to poor, nor to address the fundamental flaws that they see as inherent in the capitalist system. Rather, traditionalists accuse the government of tinkering with policies under the banner of social exclusion that raise the opportunities of groups such as the poor and single-parents without addressing what traditionalists see as the main cause of their inequality: the concentration of vast amounts of wealth in the hands of an obscenely rich few.

The new egalitarian view

Giddens and Diamond (2005), however, claim that the arguments of the traditionalists are both simplistic and misguided, especially in their insistence that equality of outcome and equality of opportunity are somehow vastly different objectives. As Giddens and Diamond argue: 'the promotion of equal opportunity in fact requires greater material equality: it is impossible for individuals to achieve their full potential if social and economic starting-points are grossly unequal' (p. 101).

Giddens and Diamond argue that since 1997, New Labour's policies on social exclusion have significantly lowered levels of poverty, especially among children and the elderly, and have put a break on any further rises in income inequality, especially inequalities in disposable material resources. However, they accept that there is still a long way to go in reducing inequalities of opportunity. They note that 'the life-chances of individuals today are still significantly influenced by the economic and social position of their parents' (p. 104). However, Giddens and Diamond are reluctant to acknowledge the argument that 'economic and social position' has anything to do with social class.

Giddens and Diamond refer to themselves and others who subscribe to the equality of opportunity argument as the '**new egalitarians**'. They note that the 'new egalitarianism' stresses the following:

- Economic efficiency created by a dynamic, competitive and flexible capitalist economy is a necessary precondition for the future redistribution of wealth and income.

- Levelling-up through the provision of educational and training opportunities, tax breaks for the poor and minimum wage legislation rather than levelling-down by taxing the rich is more likely to equalize life-chances.
- There is some 'social exclusion at the top', however, which could be addressed in order to bring about a fairer society. This includes practices such as tax avoidance, tax evasion and irresponsible corporate behaviour.
- The large-scale entry of women into the labour force and the rise of mass consumerism have disrupted traditional patterns of class affiliation.
- Social and economic divisions today are more likely to be between groups such as dual-earner families and lone-parent households rather than between social classes.
- Tensions within society are likely to result from getting the balance right between ethnic and cultural diversity, and the need to incorporate and integrate newcomers into a unified national identity.

Giddens and Diamond, therefore, argue that the claim that social class lies at the heart of inequalities in capitalist societies is dated. Moreover, they strongly defend the use of the concept of social exclusion. They note that the term was invented by academic sociologists rather than New Labour in order to 'capture the range of deprivations' that make up the experience of poverty and prevent people from taking a full part in society. They note that government-sponsored studies have tended to use four indicators or measures of social exclusion:

- the number of people not in employment, education or training
- the number of those earning below 60 per cent of the average wage
- the number of those experiencing low levels of social interaction
- the number of those who believe that they live in an area characterized by high crime, vandalism or material dilapidation.

Such studies have concluded that less than 1 per cent of the UK's population is excluded on all four counts. Giddens and Diamond, therefore, conclude that **multiple deprivation** of this kind affects specific neighbourhoods rather than the working-class as a whole.

Segmented society

Will Hutton (1996) takes a similar new egalitarian line in his 30–30–40 thesis of economic inequality. He argues that society is now divided into segments (he avoids the use of the term 'social class'!) based on inequalities in income and wealth. He argues that the top 40 per cent comprises all those with secure jobs, the bottom 30 per cent comprises the disadvantaged – the unemployed and the poor – while the middle 30 per cent comprises the marginalized – those workers who are both insecure and low paid.

So, who is correct? The traditionalists or the new egalitarians? We need to examine the evidence in more detail before we can come to any firm conclusions.

Trends in income and wealth

A number of observations can be made about the distribution of income and wealth between 1945 and now.

Income

Between 1979 and 1997 (during an unbroken period of Conservative government), income inequality between the rich and poor in Britain widened until it was at its most unequal since records began at the end of the 19th century. No other Western industrialised country, apart from the USA, had experienced this level of inequality.

Average income rose by 36 per cent during this period, but the top 10 per cent of earners experienced a 62 per cent rise, while the poorest 10 per cent of earners experienced a 17 per cent decline. In 2000, those in the service class (professional, managerial and administrative employees) earned well above the average national wage, whereas every group of manual workers (skilled, semi-skilled and unskilled) earned well below the national average. In 2002/03, the richest 10 per cent of the population received 29 per cent of total disposable income (compared with 21 per cent in 1979), while the poorest 10 per cent received only 3 per cent (compared with 4 per cent in 1979).

Income inequality and market forces

Roberts (2001) notes that the most popular explanation for income inequality is market forces. It is argued that income inequalities have widened because skill requirements have been rising and workers with the right skills, most notably finance professionals working in the City of London, have benefited. New egalitarians, such as Giddens and Diamond, suggest that the economically successful often bring benefits to the wider society in terms of drive, initiative and creativity, and should not be penalized in the form of excessive taxes. However, Roberts notes that the facts do not support the market-forces view. He points out that pay rarely corresponds with labour shortages or surpluses. For example, he shows that universities today produce more graduates compared with 30 years ago and, logically, average graduate pay should have fallen. However, in practice, graduate pay has actually risen – pay differentials between graduates and non-graduate employees have widened. Roberts argues that only class theory can explain this, in that upper-middle-class occupations, such as company executives and senior managers, generally fix their own salaries. They also often supplement their salaries with other financial incentives, such as being given stock options, bonuses and profit-sharing deals, as they have overall day-to-day operational control over corporations and in some cases, actually own the majority of shares in the company. The reduction in tax rates for top earners from 83 per cent to 40 per cent in 1979 enormously benefited this group. Roberts notes that while some middle-class professionals can negotiate their salaries, the vast majority of lower-middle-class and working-class occupations either have to negotiate collectively as part of trade unions or they are told how much they will earn.

Corporate moral responsibility

In recent years there been some concern about the salaries of these so-called 'fat-cats'. It has been suggested that corporations should be more morally responsible in the context of a society in which poverty, deprivation and debt is a norm for many people. For example, in October 2005, Philip Green, the chief executive of Arcadia was criticized for being greedy in paying himself £1.4 billion in salary. Moreover, there are signs that society is increasingly unhappy because top executives are not only rewarded for success, but seemingly also for failure, in that many executives are paid off with 'golden goodbyes' often totalling hundreds of thousands of pounds.

Wealth

The 20th century did see a gradual redistribution of wealth in the UK. In 1911, the most wealthy 1 per cent of the population held 69 per cent of all wealth, yet by 1993, this had dropped to 17 per cent. However, this redistribution did not extend down into the mass of society. Rather it was very narrow – the very wealthy top 1 per cent distributed some of its wealth to the wealthy top 10 per cent via trust funds in order to avoid paying taxes in the form of death duties. The result of this redistribution within the economic elite is that in 2000, the top 10 per cent owned 50 per cent of the nation's wealth and the wealth of the most affluent 200 individuals and families doubled. This polarization of wealth in the UK has also been encouraged by a soaring stock market (investments in stocks and shares) and property values, which as Savage notes 'have allowed those who were already wealthy to accumulate their wealth massively'.

The privatization of public utilities such as British Telecom and British Gas in the 1980s widened share ownership, so that by 1988, 21 per cent of people owned shares. However, the evidence suggests this was a short-term phenomenon as people who had never owned shares before sold their shares quickly as their value rose. Today, although about 17 per cent of all people own shares, the richest 1 per cent of the population still own 75 per cent of all privately owned shares. As Roberts notes:

>> *We are certainly not all capitalists now. In 1993, the least wealthy half of the population owned just 7 per cent of all personally-held wealth; around 30 per cent of adults do not own the dwellings in which they live; a half of all employees do not have significant occupational pensions. In fact, a half of the population has near-zero assets, and many are in debt when account is taken of outstanding mortgages, bank overdrafts, hire-purchase commitments, loans on credit cards, store cards and all the rest. It is only roughly a half of the population that has any significant share in the country's wealth.* >> (pp. 178–9)

The fact that nearly half the population have a share in the country's wealth may sound impressive, but Roberts points out that most of these people will liquidate assets such as savings and pension funds in old age in order to safeguard the standard of living they have enjoyed in the latter half of their life. As Roberts notes, it is only the extremely wealthy

Problems of defining and measuring wealth

Wealth is defined as the ownership of property, shares, savings and other assets. However, within that overall definition, there is some debate about exactly what we should include as property and 'assets'. For example, does a person's house constitute wealth? Yes, of course, if they sold it, they would receive a large amount of money – but where would they live? But even that is too simple. Some people live in houses which are enormous and far exceed what they need – so does the excess beyond their needs count as wealth?

A similar debate surrounds pensions – some argue that pensions must be defined as wealth, because they are savings, while others argue that pensions are essential and so they do not actually constitute wealth.

So how we define wealth is not as easy as first appears. The answer to this problem of definition faced by sociologists is that we normally talk about 'marketable wealth'. By this we mean the range of assets that a person is reasonably able to dispose of, if they should so wish. This is generally taken to mean that marketable wealth excludes house and pension.

A further problem with wealth is actually measuring it. Unlike income, the Inland Revenue does not conduct a yearly assessment of wealth. So researchers obtain their information in one of the following two ways:

- looking at the assessment of wealth made for tax purposes when someone dies
- asking a sample of rich people the extent of their wealth.

Some problems arise with both methods:

1 *Inland Revenue statistics based on inheritance tax –* Using information obtained from wills usually only provides us with out-of-date figures. What is more, wealthy people will attempt to limit the amount of wealth that they declare for tax purposes. Charitable trusts, early distribution of wealth to younger family members before death, and financial holdings abroad are all common ways to avoid tax. All of this means that the wealth of the rich may be underestimated. On the other hand, poorer people who do not pay inheritance tax are excluded from Inland Revenue statistics, so their wealth may be underestimated too.

2 *Surveys –* Because of these problems, sociologists turn to surveys, but rich people are extremely reluctant to divulge their true wealth. Either way, the figures will probably be inaccurate.

Problems of defining and measuring income

Like wealth, income is difficult to measure. Once again, those with large amounts of income will seek to minimize their income levels on their income tax returns, and will employ accountants and tax experts to do just that.

But there are also methodological problems that sociologists face in trying to measure income levels. They have to decide whether to calculate income by household or by individual (poverty statistics, for example, are increasingly based on households). They must decide which is more important: income before tax, or income after tax? And what about people who work for 'cash in hand'? Finally, many people receive state benefits, but also receive some services free (bus passes, for example) which others have to pay for – is this income?

---

who can expect to die with most of their wealth intact. A lot of wealth that people have is also tied up with property in which people live. Homeowners can make money out of their property but this is not the main reason most people buy their houses. Most people own one house, while the extremely wealthy may own several houses as well as land bought for its future investment value. Finally, Roberts notes that the proportion of the population with enough wealth that they do not have to work for others is still less than 1 per cent. This elite group employ others to work for them. On the other hand, the life-chances of the vast majority of the population depend on the kinds of jobs they can obtain. Roberts concludes:

> << Despite the spread of wealth, this remains a clear class relationship and division. It is, in fact, the clearest of all class divisions, and it still splits the population into a tiny minority on the one side, and the great mass of the people on the other. >> (p. 180)

Health

Bottero (2005) claims that 'social inequalities are written on the body' and 'hierarchy makes you sick'. She notes that if illness was a chance occurrence, we could expect to see rates of **morbidity** (i.e. illness and disease) and **mortality** (i.e. death) randomly distributed across the population. However, it is clear from Department of Health statistics that the working class experience an overproportionate amount of illness. In general, health across the population has improved over the last 30 years but the rate of improvement has been much slower for the working class. Generally, the working class experience poorer mortality rates and morbidity rates than the middle classes. For example, 3500 more working-class babies would survive per year if the working-class infant mortality rate was reduced to middle-class levels. In other words, babies born to professional fathers have levels of infant mortality half that of babies born to unskilled manual fathers.

Class and death rates

If we examine death rates we can see that, between 1972 and 1997, death rates for professionals fell by 44 per cent, but fell by only 10 per cent for the unskilled. Bartley *et al.* (1996) note that men in Social Class I (using the old RG scale) had only two-thirds the chance of dying between 1986 and 1989 compared with the male population as a whole. However, unskilled manual workers (Social Class V using the old RG scale) were one-third more likely to die compared with the male population as a whole. In other words, despite the NHS providing free universal health care to all, men in Social Class V were twice as likely to die before men in Social Class I.

Bottero notes that:

<< *There is a strong socio-economic gradient to almost all patterns of disease and ill-health. The lower your socio-economic position, the greater your risk of low birthweight, infections, cancer, coronary heart disease, respiratory disease, stroke, accidents, nervous and mental illnesses.* >> (p. 188)

Moreover, she points out that there are specific occupational hazards linked to particular manual jobs which increase the risk of accidental injury, exposure to toxic materials, pollution, etc. Poor people are more likely to live in areas in which there are more hazards, such as traffic and pollution, and fewer safe areas to play. Consequently, poor children are more likely to be run over and to suffer asthma.

The health gradient

Some studies have suggested that there exists a **health gradient**, in that at every level of the social hierarchy, there are health differences. Some writers, most notably Marmot *et al.* (1991), have suggested that social position may be to blame for these differences. They conducted a study on civil servants working in Whitehall, i.e. white-collar staff, and concluded that the cause of ill health was being lower in the hierarchy. Those low in the hierarchy had less social control over their working conditions, greater stress and greater feelings of low self-esteem. These psychosocial factors triggered off behaviour such as smoking and drinking, poor eating habits and inactivity. The net result of this combination of psychosocial and lifestyle factors was greater levels of depression, high blood pressure, increased susceptibility to infection and build-up of cholesterol. If we apply Marmot's findings to society in general, it may be the fact that working-class occupations are the lowest in the hierarchy that may be causing their disproportionate levels of morbidity and mortality.

Other sociologists, most notably Wilkinson (1996), argue that the health gradient is caused by income inequality. He argues that relative inequality affects health because it undermines **social cohesion** – the sense that we are all valued equally by society which affirms our sense of belonging to society. Wilkinson argues that inequality disrupts social cohesion because it undermines self-esteem, dignity, trust and cooperation and increases feelings of insecurity, envy, hostility and inferiority, which lead to stress. As Wilkinson notes:

<< *To feel depressed, cheated, bitter, desperate, vulnerable, frightened, angry, worried about debts or job and housing*

insecurity; to feel devalued, useless, helpless, uncared for, hopeless, isolated, anxious and a failure; these feelings can dominate people's whole experience of life, colouring their experience of everything else. It is the chronic stress arising from feelings like these which does the damage. It is the social feelings which matter, not exposure to a supposedly toxic environment. >> (p. 215)

Wilkinson notes that egalitarian societies have a strong community life, in that strong social ties and networks exist in the wider society to support their members. In other words, members of these societies have access to '**social capital**' – social and psychological support from others in their community which helps them stay healthy. It is argued that in societies characterized by extreme income inequality, social capital in the form of these networks is less likely to exist and health inequalities continue to grow. We can see this particularly in residential areas in the UK characterized by high levels of council housing.

Housing

Government spending on health and education has increased by over 30 per cent since 1981, but the reverse is true of expenditure on public housing (the 5 million council houses managed by local authorities and the 800 000 managed by housing associations). Since the 1980s, the availability of such housing has actually fallen, for two reason:

- Many council houses were sold off to their tenants as a result of the Conservative government's '**Right to buy**' scheme, or were transferred to housing association control.
- Capital investment in new council housing has been so low that very few new homes have been built.

For example, in 1981, 32 per cent of the housing stock was made up of council housing, but this had fallen to 22 per cent by 2000. There has been a corresponding decline in the percentage of people renting private houses, flats, bedsits, etc. For example, in 1945, 62 per cent of the housing stock was privately rented, but this had fallen to 5 per cent by 2000. This public-housing shortage has led to both local authorities and housing associations allocating housing to those in greatest need. This has had the effect of concentrating socially deprived groups in particular areas, thus creating new class divisions locally and nationally. This tendency for lower-income households to be more concentrated in council housing is not new; the trend was clearly well-established before 1980. However, there was a degree of choice involved in where people wanted to live, giving residential areas a more comprehensive and socially cohesive feel. This choice no longer exists today.

Council estates and social capital

The trend towards home ownership in the UK has also contributed to the polarization of social classes in terms of areas in which people live. For example, in 1945 only 26 per cent of homes were privately owned, yet this figure was 76 per cent in 2000. This has led to an overconcentration of the poor

Peter Saunders (1990)
A nation of homeowners

Saunders carried out a local household survey aimed at a sample of 500 respondents in three predominantly working-class towns; Burnley, Derby and Slough. People were interviewed using a questionnaire composed of both open and closed questions about the experience and meaning of home ownership in their daily lives. He found that 91 per cent of his sample expressed a preference for home ownership over council tenancy. He argued that home ownership was starting to change the character of wealth ownership in the UK – investment in housing was bringing capital gains to the 'middle mass' and benefiting future generations who were inheriting wealth because of their parents' ownership of property. Saunders, therefore, rejects the class traditionalist view that increased owner-occupancy has contributed to a polarization in inequality between social classes. However, his study does acknowledge a new division between the middle mass, who own their property, and a marginalized minority located on undesirable council estates, who experience multiple deprivations. Interestingly, he also discovered that 43 per cent of council tenants associated the home with family, love and children compared to only 33 per cent of home owners, and were twice as likely to view community as an important aspect of their daily lives.

Saunders, P. (1990) *A Nation of Homeowners*, London: Unwin Hyman.

1 **In what sense, might Saunders qualify as a new egalitarian?**

2 **Saunders argues that council tenants should be able to buy their own homes at subsidised prices. Why?**

3 **In what way might Saunders' findings about community contradict the findings of Wilkinson?**

on council estates. For example, in 1963, only 1 in 4 council tenants were made up of those on the lowest incomes, but this had increased to 1 in 2 by 2000, with less council housing stock to be distributed amongst them. For example, in 1979, there were 8 million council houses with 4 million tenants with low incomes. By 2000, there were only 5 million council houses with the same number of low-income tenants. Council estates, therefore, have large concentrations of people on income support, such as the unemployed, single mothers, the elderly, the low paid and asylum-seekers. According to the General Household Survey (2001), 51 per cent of single-parent families are council tenants compared to 15 per cent of the general population. In 2001, it was estimated that 45 per cent of tenants in publicly owned housing were on state benefits of one type or another. This trend has created less desirable residential areas and pockets of deprivation, with dysfunctional communities, failing schools and a disproportionate level of social problems such as crime. For example, it is estimated that 42 per cent of all burglaries happen to the homes of those belonging to the poor and single parents, the vast majority of whom are living on council estates.

Council estates are generally poorly resourced in terms of shops, recreational facilities, public transport and healthcare services such as GPs and hospitals. Very importantly, there is evidence of low social cohesion on these estates, and as a result, there may be high rates of depression, isolation, hostility and anxiety. Social capital in the form of supportive formal and informal social networks is also likely to be absent because of family breakdown, economic cutbacks in council services and a lack of community spirit fostered by people constantly moving in and out of the area, a high crime rate, fear of crime, antisocial behaviour and intensive policing.

Education

We can see distinct class differences in achievement in that working-class children perform much worse in education than all other social groups at all levels of the education system. For example, more working-class children leave school at the age of 16 with no qualifications than middle-class 16-year-olds, and while the number of working-class 18-year-olds entering university has increased, the number of middle-class undergraduates still far exceeds them. Connor and Dewson (2001) found that only one in five young people from working-class backgrounds participated in higher education. Moreover, as Savage and Egerton (1997) found, ability does not wipe out class advantage. For example, their study found that less than half of the 'high-ability' working-class boys in their study made it into the service class (compared with three-quarters of the 'high-ability' boys with service-class fathers). Furthermore, 65 per cent of their 'low-ability' service-class boys were able to avoid dropping down into manual work.

Cultural capital

The evidence suggests that middle-class children benefit from living in better areas (with better schools). This, of course, is assisted by the better incomes earned by their parents, which means they can afford to buy into areas which have schools with good league-table standings. Income increases educational choices, so, for instance, parents can choose to send their children to private schools or to hire personal tutors. The evidence overwhelmingly shows that children who attend the elite private schools in the UK (the public schools) have easier access to Oxbridge and the redbrick universities. Moreover the 'old school tie' network ensures important and valuable social contacts for years to come, particularly in the finance sector of the economy. Middle-class parents are also able to use their knowledge, expertise, contacts and greater confidence in expressing themselves and in dealing with fellow professionals, – their cultural capital – to ensure that their children are well served by the educational system.

Conclusions

The new egalitarians are undoubtedly correct in drawing our attention to the fact that a diversity of social groups, such as the long-term unemployed, single mothers and asylum-seekers, are socially excluded from mainstream society and so experience a range of social and economic deprivations. However, their reluctance to acknowledge the role of social class and its indicators (such as inequalities in income, wealth, housing, health and education) is incomprehensible given the weight of the evidence available. As Savage concludes:

<< In recent years, whatever people's perceptions of their class might be, there is no doubting that class inequality has hardened. People's destinies are as strongly affected and perhaps more strongly affected, by their class background than they were in the mid-20th century. >>

The evidence in this section also challenges the postmodernist view that social class has ceased to be the primary shaper of identity and that people exercise more choice about the type of people they want to be, especially in terms of lifestyle and consumption. Postmodernists and New Right thinkers, such as Saunders, neglect the fact that lifestyle choices and consumption depend on educational qualifications, the jobs we have and the income we earn. Unfortunately, members of the working class are less likely to qualify on all three counts for the postmodern lifestyle. Moreover, they are well aware that it is their social class more than any other social factor that is holding them back from making the sorts of choices that are taken for granted by social classes above them.

Check your understanding

1. **What groups are typically socially excluded according to the new egalitarians?**

2. **What is the main difference between traditionalists and new egalitarians?**

3. **What is the new egalitarian attitude towards the rich?**

4. **Why have income inequalities widened in the UK over the last thirty years?**

5. **What have been the main trends with regard to wealth redistribution in the UK over the past 30 years?**

6. **Give three statistical examples of health differences between classes.**

7. **What effect has the health gradient had on the social make up of some residential areas?**

8. **What evidence is there that council housing is becoming increasingly the domain of the socially deprived?**

9. **What problems do those living on council estates face?**

10. **How do educational inequalities support the view that social class may still be important?**

KEY TERMS

Blairite – ideas uniquely associated with Tony Blair or New Labour.

Cleavage – a term used by Saunders to describe differences in the spending patterns of social groups.

Consumption – spending on goods and services.

Equality of opportunity – the idea that individuals should begin from the same starting point in terms of opportunities.

Equality of outcome – the idea that social groups should be able to achieve results on the basis of ability rather than wealth. Believers in equality of outcome suggest equality can never be achieved so long as inequalities in wealth and income continue to persist and be reproduced generation by generation.

Health gradient – the fact that the chances of dying or becoming ill progressively increase or decline the lower or higher you are on the occupational hierarchy.

Material deprivation – the lack of physical resources needed in order to lead a full and normal life.

Morbidity rate – reported ill health per 100 000 of population.

Mortality rate – number of deaths per 100 000 of population.

Multiple deprivation – the experience of a range of factors which inhibit life-chances, e.g. unemployment, single motherhood, residing in a high-crime area.

New egalitarians – a group of sociologists and politicians who believe that social-class divisions are in decline and that policies to socially include deprived groups are working.

Right to buy initiative – a Conservative government scheme whereby councils were instructed to allow long-term council tenants to buy their rented homes at a fraction of their market value (typically half).

Social capital – social relationships that benefit people, e.g. in finding a job.

Social cohesion – the idea that people feel a sense of belonging to society because they feel valued and wanted.

Social exclusion – the fact that some people are excluded from what everyone else takes for granted usually because of poor educational, family or economic circumstances.

Social inclusion – being part of the mainstream because of the opportunities offered by government policies, e.g. training, education.

research idea

Get an A to Z of your local area. Enlarge a residential area that you know to be a high-demand area. Similarly, enlarge an area in low demand. Annotate each as far as possible to highlight differences in facilities/resources. Conduct a survey of residents in each area to discover the level of services and facilities on offer there.

Compare and contrast the two areas to test the extent to which people in low-demand areas suffer a variety of social exclusions.

web.task

Go to the government statistics site at www.statistics.gov.uk.

Select Neighbourhood statistics. Choose your own postcode or the district or postcode where your school or college is situated. You will be able to investigate a variety of indicators of wealth and deprivation. How does your area compare with other parts of the region or with Britain as a whole?

exploring life-chances and social class

Item A

Standardized mortality rates (per 100 000) by social class, men aged 20 to 64, England and Wales

	YEAR		
Social class	1970–2	1979–83	1991–3
Professional	500	373	280
Managerial and technical	526	425	300
Skilled (non-manual)	637	522	426
Skilled (manual)	683	580	493
Partly skilled	721	639	492
Unskilled	897	910	806
England and Wales	**624**	**549**	**419**

Abercrombie, N. and Warde, A. (2000) *Contemporary British Society* (3rd edn), Cambridge: Polity Press

Item B

In Wilkinson's view, the widening gap in income distribution creates resentment, social exclusion in terms of the poor and social isolation, where the more wealthy cut themselves off to protect their assets. Social cohesion is affected. People become isolated from their community. People are unable to cope with stress, which is reflected in poor health. Wilkinson argues that social factors such as the strength of social contacts, ties within communities, availability of social support and a sense of security are the main determinants of the relative health of a society. However, areas vary greatly in terms of safety, environmental conditions and the availability of services and public facilities. For example, deprived areas tend to have fewer basic services such as banks, food shops and post offices than do more desirable areas. Community spaces such as parks, sports grounds and libraries may also be limited. Yet people living in disadvantaged spaces are often dependent on local facilities as they lack the funds and transport that would allow them to use facilities and services provided sometimes more cheaply elsewhere.

Adapted from Giddens, A. (2001) *Sociology* (4th edn), Cambridge: Polity Press, pp. 150

(a) Using only the information in **Item A**, identify **two** trends in mortality that reflect social class differences between 1970 and 1993. (6 marks)

(b) Identify and briefly explain **two** social factors that are determinants of the relative health of a society, according to **Item B**. (6 marks)

(c) Identify and explain **two** reasons why official statistics might be regarded as a reliable way of collecting information about people's relative life-chances. (12 marks)

(d) Using your wider sociological knowledge, outline the evidence for the view that many people in the UK experience social exclusion. (22 marks)

(e) Outline and assess sociological explanations of the view that social and economic divisions today are more likely to be between groups such as dual-career families and lone-parent households rather than between social classes. (44 marks)

Changes in the class structure

gettingyouthinking

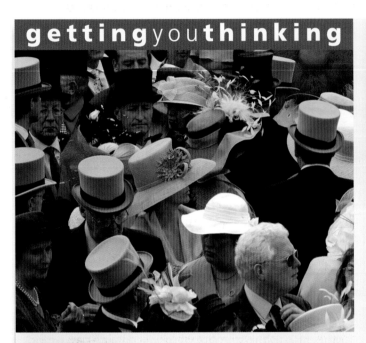

1. What do you think are the main differences between the people in the photographs above?

2. Which would you call 'posh' and why?

3. Why do you think Victoria Beckham was often referred to as 'Posh' when she performed with the Spice Girls?

4. With which social class do you most associate the Beckhams? Explain your answer.

5. What do the terms 'working class', 'middle class' and 'upper class' mean to you?

6. What factors other than class affect the way people are perceived today?

Your answers to the above questions may demonstrate that class is a difficult thing to define nowadays and that status is no longer a matter of being on the right side of the class divide. The old idea of the class structure was that it comprised a triangular shape, with numbers increasing towards the base, which was composed of a vast number of unskilled manual workers providing a strong industrial-based manufacturing sector. This model implied a strict hierarchy, with higher levels of income, status and power towards the top. Although this was never actually the true shape (because manufacturing jobs have never accounted for the majority of the workforce), there has been a dramatic shift in Britain's industrial structure with only about 18 per cent of the population working in manufacturing today. At the same time, numbers of those working in **tertiary** or **service-sector jobs** (those providing services such as transport, retailing, hotel work, cleaning, banking and insurance) have increased dramatically from 25 per cent to 75 per cent.

The upper class

It has been argued that the upper class (the extremely wealthy, property-owning elite who do not need to work in order to maintain their lifestyle), especially the aristocratic and traditional rich, have declined in wealth, power and influence over the course of the 20th century. In particular, it has been argued (Roberts 2001) that high death duties (now called 'inheritance tax') have resulted in a substantial number of upper-class families losing their family seats (the country houses where their family lived for generations) and experiencing downward social mobility. Some have even been forced to take up salaried employment in the service sector. In other words, it is argued that the upper class is in danger of being assimilated into the upper middle-class. So, how true are these assertions? A number of observations can be made on the basis of the evidence available.

Inherited wealth

The upper class is still very wealthy. We saw earlier how the top 1 per cent have got 'poorer', but only because they have made real efforts to avoid inheritance tax by transferring their wealth via trust funds to the top 5 per cent. Moreover, the top 1 per cent still own about one-third of the country's wealth.

The evidence suggests that we should talk about wealthy families rather than individuals. In this context, inheritance is very important. In general, individuals or families are wealthy because their fathers were also rich. Inheritance is responsible for most of the inequality in the distribution of wealth.

Positions of economic leadership

Scott (1982) argues that there now exists a unified propertied class which has actively used its wealth to maintain its privileged position at the top of the socio-economic structure. He argues that the core of the upper class – the richest 0.1 per cent

(between 25 000 and 50 000 people) – occupy positions of leadership in manufacturing, banking and finance. He suggests that this core is made up of three groups:

- entrepreneurial capitalists, who own (or mainly own) businesses founded by their family
- internal capitalists, the senior executives who head the bureaucracies that run the big companies
- finance capitalists, who usually own or run financial institutions such as merchant banks and firms of stockbrokers.

It can be argued that the traditional landed gentry, mainly aristocratic in character, has managed since the turn of the 20th century, through investment and marriage to the 'nouveau riche', to become an integral part of the three groups that make up the core of the modern upper class.

Networks and social closure

The upper class is also supported by networks that permeate throughout that class. These may be based on marriage or kinship. For example, there is a tendency for members of the upper class to marry other upper-class individuals. This obviously gives the class a unity based on marriage and kinship, and is instrumental in strengthening business and financial ties between families.

Membership of the upper class is strengthened by **social closure** – the ability to control mobility into upper-class circles. This is partly achieved by networking and being part of an 'in crowd'. Another major means of ensuring social closure is the emphasis on public-school education in generation after generation, especially at those schools seen as the 'great and good', such as Eton, Harrow, Winchester, Westminster, Charterhouse and Rugby. The large movement of such pupils into the elite universities of Oxford and Cambridge reinforces such students' belief in their 'difference' from the rest of society. The 'old-boy network', based very much on common schooling, results in self-recruitment to the upper class. This means that current members of the upper class are likely to be the offspring of wealthy individuals who attended the same schools and universities, as will their sons and daughters.

Scott notes evidence relating to interlocking directorships. He found that in 1976 eleven people had a total of 57 directorships in the top 250 companies and had many others in smaller companies. Such interlocking directorships provide a powerful network that cements connections between members of the upper class.

The 'Establishment'

Scott argues that the upper class's influence is not confined to business. There is overwhelming evidence that those in top positions in politics, the civil service, the church, the armed services and the professions come disproportionately from upper-class families. Scott refers to this group as the 'establishment' – a coherent and self-recruiting body of men with a similarity of outlook who are able to wield immense power. However, exactly how this group interacts and whether they do so for their own benefit is extremely difficult to prove.

Although the basis of the wealth of the upper class is no longer primarily land, this class still retains many of the characteristics it possessed 50 years ago, especially an emphasis on public-school education, thus helping to ensure that social closure continues unchallenged.

The idea of a post-industrial economy

Many writers, notably Daniel Bell (1973), have suggested that society is moving from an industrial to a post-industrial stage in which jobs will no longer be characterized by dirty, physical work but will be based more on intellectual creativity. Bell also believed that companies will become less concerned with profit and more concerned with satisfying their workforces through better working conditions and job security, having invested heavily in their training and personal development.

Kumar (1978), however, argues that, even in the 19th century, those in the service industries were often substantially worse off in terms of income than those in manufacturing. The ideal of the knowledge-based society seems some way off today (as we will see when we examine further the true plight of the lower middle-classes). Service-sector companies have been struggling to maintain their workforces in the wake of increased competition and the transfer of routine non-manual tasks to computer technology – for example, consider the impact of online banking, insurance and travel on the personnel working in these sectors. However, as Roberts (2001) points out, there are many non-manual operations now performed because of new technology that simply would not have been previously possible (e.g. telephone banking, flight/holiday booking, car insurance quotations). This may have led to some increases in the service sector, albeit at the lower end (in most cases in call-centre work).

Another striking development has been the feminization of the workforce. This has not only affected status differences in the workplace, but has also, for most households, had a massive effect on household income. This has, in turn, made a major difference to the lifestyle and consumption patterns of all classes.

The middle classes in modern Britain

The expansion of the middle classes

In 1911, some 80 per cent of workers were in manual occupations. This number fell to 32.7 per cent in 1991 and is approximately 25 per cent today. Non-manual workers (traditionally seen as middle-class) have therefore fairly recently become the majority occupational group in the workforce. As Savage (1995) points out, there are now more university lecturers than coal miners in the UK.

Reasons for the expansion

The number of manual jobs in both primary and **secondary industries** has gone into decline since the 1970s. The decline has been caused by a range of factors, including new technology, the oil crisis and globalization (i.e. the same raw materials and goods can be produced more cheaply in developing countries). The tertiary or service sector of the economy that is focused around education, welfare, retail and finance has expanded hugely in the past 20 years. Mass secondary education and the expansion of both further and higher education have ensured the existence of a well-educated and qualified workforce. The service sector is made up of a mainly male professional workforce at its top end but, as a result of changes in women's social position, the bulk of workers in this sector are female.

The boundary problem

Studying the middle classes can be problematic because not all sociologists agree who should be included in this category. This is the so-called '**boundary problem**'. Traditionally, differentiating between the middle class and working class was thought to be a simple task involving distinguishing between white-collar, or non-manual, workers on the one hand and blue-collar, or manual, workers on the other. Generally, the former enjoyed better working conditions in terms of pay, holidays and promotion possibilities. Today, however, this distinction is not so clear cut. It is generally agreed that many **routine white-collar workers**, who are mainly women, especially those who work in call centres, now have similar conditions of work and pay to manual workers and, therefore, cannot be seen as a higher class.

A fragmented middle class

The term 'middle class' covers a wide range of occupations, incomes, lifestyles and attitudes. Roberts et al. (1977) argued that the middle class was becoming fragmented into a number of different groups, each with a distinctive view of its place in the stratification system. They suggest that we should no longer talk of the middle class, but of the 'middle classes'. Savage et al. (1992) agrees that it is important to see that the middle class is now divided into strata, or '**class fractions**', such as higher and lower professionals, higher and middle managers, the petit bourgeoisie and routine white-collar workers.

Professionals

Savage et al. (1992) argue that higher and lower professionals mainly recruit internally – in other words, the sons and daughters of professionals are likely to end up as professionals themselves. The position of professional workers is based on the possession of educational qualifications. Professionals usually have to go through a long period of training – university plus professional examinations before they qualify. Savage argues that professionals possess both **economic capital** (a very good standard of living, savings, financial security) and **cultural capital** (seeing the worth of education and other cultural assets such as taste in high culture), which they pass on to their children. Moreover, they increasingly have social capital (belonging to networks that can influence decision-making by other professionals such as head teachers). Professionals also have strong occupational associations, such as the Law Society and the British Medical Association, that protect and actively pursue their interests (although the lower down the professional ladder, the weaker these associations/unions become). The result of such groups actively pursuing the interests of professionals is high rewards, status and job security.

Savage concludes that professionals are aware of their common interests and quite willing to take industrial action to protect those interests. In this sense, then, professionals have a greater sense of class identity than other middle-class groups. However, as the public sector has become increasingly privatized, many professionals are facing an increased threat of **redundancy** and reduced promotional opportunities as a result of de-layering (a reduction in the number of 'tiers' of management in an organization).

Managers

Savage and colleagues suggest that managers have assets based upon a particular skill within specific organizations. Such skills (unlike those of professionals) are not easily transferable to other companies or industries. Many managers have been upwardly mobile from the routine white-collar sector or the skilled working class. Often they lack qualifications such as degrees. They may even have worked their way up through an organization. Their social position, therefore, is likely to be the result of experience and reputation rather than qualifications. Savage notes that most managers do not belong to professional associations or trade unions. Consequently, they tend to be more individualistic in character and are less likely to identify a common collectivistic interest with their fellow managers – who are much more likely to be seen as competitors. Savage argues that managers actively encourage their children to pursue higher education because they can see the benefits of a professional career. However, managers, despite being well paid, are less likely to have the cultural capital possessed by professionals.

Savage argues that job security differentiates professionals from managers – managers are constantly under threat from recession, mergers and **downsizing**. Savage points out that it is middle managers such as bank managers whose jobs are under threat and who are more likely to be downwardly mobile.

However, higher managers, e.g. executives, are likely to be on spectacular salaries and to have share options worth millions. The Income Data Services showed that nearly half of all senior executives of Britain's 350 largest public companies made more than £1 million a year, with eight directors on packages of £5+ million (Cohen 2005). Adonis and Pollard (1998) claim that this 'superclass' of higher-salaried people (i.e. salariat) now

makes up approximately 15 per cent of middle-class occupations. They note that it is mainly located in the South East of England, and employed mainly by banks that deal in currency speculation, stockbroker companies and the privatized utilities, many of which are based in the City of London. According to Adonis and Pollard, the lifestyle of this superclass revolves around nannies and servants, second homes, private education for their children, private health schemes, exotic foreign holidays and investment in modern art. The superclass tends to live on private urban estates patrolled by private security companies.

The self-employed

Between 1981 and 1991, the number of people **self-employed**, or '**petit-bourgeois**', has risen from 6.7 per cent of the workforce to over 10 per cent. Research by Fielding (1995) examined what the self-employed in 1981 were doing in 1991. He showed that two-thirds of his sample were a relatively stable and secure part of the workforce in that they remained self-employed over this ten-year period. However, the character of the self-employed has changed in some respects too. The number of managers who prefer to work for themselves (for example, as consultants) rose considerably in the 1980s, especially in the finance and computer industries. Some writers argue that many firms now prefer to contract services to outside consultants rather than employ people themselves. A large number of people, again mainly managers, have businesses 'on the side' while continuing to be employees.

Routine white-collar workers

Marxists such as Harry Braverman (1974) argue that routine white-collar workers are no longer middle class. Braverman argues that they have been subjected to a process of **proletarianization**. This means that they have lost the social and economic advantages that they enjoyed over manual workers, such as superior pay and working conditions. Braverman argues that in the past 20 years, employers have used technology, especially computers, to break down complex white-collar skills, such as book-keeping, into simplistic routine tasks. This process is known as '**de-skilling**' and is an attempt to increase output, maximize efficiency and reduce costs. Control over the work process has, therefore, been removed from many non-manual workers.

These developments have been accompanied by the parallel development of the feminization of the routine white-collar workforce (especially in the financial sector), because female workers are generally cheap to employ and are seen by employers as more adaptable and amenable to this type of work. Braverman concludes that de-skilling means that occupations that once were middle class are today in all respects indistinguishable from those of manual workers.

Marshall et al. (1988) challenged the idea of proletarianization. In a national random sample of female workers, they found that it was mainly manual workers who claimed that their work had been de-skilled. Over 90 per cent of non-manual workers felt that little had changed, and that they were as likely to identify themselves with the middle class as they were with the working class. Finally, they were more likely to vote Conservative than Labour. Marshall and colleagues therefore concluded that proletarianization among routine white-collar workers was not taking place.

New-technology workers

In further contrast to Braverman however, Clark and Hoffman-Martinot (1998) highlight the growth of a technological elite of 'wired workers' – new professionals who are as productive through the use of technology as entire offices of routine non-manual workers, spending most of their days behind computers working in non-hierarchical settings. They enjoy considerable **autonomy**, are paid extremely well, often working flexibly, engaged in dynamic problem-solving activities. Such workers can be found in a wide range of new occupations regarded as part of the 'infotech sector' – jobs such as web designers, systems analysts, in e-commerce, software development, graphic design and financial consultancy.

However, at the lower end of this sector, Denscombe (1999) notes that information and communication technologies have developed rapidly since the 1980s and have had a profound effect on the nature of work in the finance and service sectors of the economy. In particular, these technical advances have led to the setting up of a new type of office or white-collar employment – the call centre. This form of white-collar work is economically attractive to employers because 'call centres provide customer services and sales more economically than face-to-face facilities which require more staff, and premises with the attendant costs. Huge databases of information can be accessed electronically at a stroke and people can pay for services using credit and debit cards over their own telephones'. He notes that in 1999 that between 300 000 and 400 000 workers were employed in call centres. Many of these workers, although technically middle-class according to official classifications, are low-paid, usually female, casual workers (many of them students). They spend all day, usually in self-contained booths, on the telephone in front of a VDU, often working in conditions in which they are closely controlled and monitored by management – for example, supervisors often listen in to calls and the workers are only allowed to go to the toilet at certain times. This work involves little creativity as workers often have to read off a preprepared script. Denscombe notes that such work is not unlike factory assembly-line production and, unsurprisingly, there is a high turnover of staff. The increase in this type of work may, therefore, support the proletarianization thesis, especially as it seems to be fairly insecure work. Increasingly, British employers such as banks and insurance companies are making the decision to globalize their operations by closing British-based call centres and opening up new ones abroad, particularly in India.

We can see from this section that the middle classes are, therefore, an important and vibrant part of the class structure. What was once the minority, perceived as a class apart from the working class in terms of income, lifestyle, status, and culture, has become a much larger, more heterogeneous (diverse) body.

The working class

When sociologists talk about the working class, they are often referring to people employed in manual jobs and their dependants. This might seem straightforward in terms of social-class categorization. However, many households in the UK are composed of couples occupied in both manual and non-manual work, therefore making it difficult for objective classifications to categorize households and families into particular social-class groupings. Moreover, as we have already seen, categorization is also made more difficult because of changes in the nature of both manual work and non-manual work. In other words, social processes such as embourgeoisement and proletarianization may be occurring, which makes it difficult to determine where particular occupational groups lie within the middle-class/working-class continuum. However, some sociologists argue that differences between manual and non-manual groups can be detected in terms of the former's strong subjective sense of belonging to the working class.

Changes in class solidarity

Fulcher and Scott (1999) point out that until the late 20th century, the working class had a strong sense of their social-class position. Virtually all aspects of their lives, including gender roles, family life, political affiliation and leisure, were a product of their keen sense of working-class identity. Lockwood's (1966) research found that many workers, especially in industrial areas, subscribed to a value system he called '**proletarian traditionalist**'. Such workers felt a strong sense of loyalty to each other because of shared community and work experience, and so were mutually supportive of each other. They had a keen sense of class solidarity and consciousness. They tended to see society, therefore, in terms of conflict, in terms of 'them versus us'.

However, later research has claimed that this type of class identity is in decline because the service sector of the economy has grown more important as the traditional industrial and manufacturing sectors have gone into decline and transnational companies have taken advantage of economic globalization by relocating production to the cheaper developing world. Roberts (2001) notes that the decline of employment in manufacturing and extractive industries (e.g. coal mining) has been steep, from around 70 per cent of all jobs in 1841 to 30 per cent of all jobs in 2000. In 2004, well over 70 per cent of all jobs were in services. Today, the main source of employment growth is consumer services – retailing, hotels and catering, and other leisure industries. Consequently, the working class has shrunk in size as the number of manual workers has declined.

It is argued that recession and unemployment have undermined traditional working-class communities and organizations such as trade unions. However, Cannadine (1998) argues that this idea – that once upon a time the working class subscribed to a collective class consciousness and an adversarial view of society – is exaggerated and the evidence lacking. He argues that the history of the working class suggests no clear consistent pattern of class consciousness – collectivism only emerges at particular times and in particular contexts, and even then, is rarely universally shared.

Middle-class lifestyles?

In the 1960s, Zweig (1961) argued that a section of the working class – skilled manual workers – had adopted the economic and cultural lifestyle of the middle class. This argument became known as the '**embourgeoisement** thesis' because it insisted that skilled workers had become more like the middle class by supporting bourgeois values and the Conservative party as well as enjoying similar income levels.

This view was investigated in Goldthorpe and Lockwood's famous study of a car factory in Luton (1969). They found little evidence to support Zweig's assertion. Economically, while wages were comparable to those of members of the middle classes, they did not enjoy the same working conditions or fringe benefits, such as expense accounts, company car, sick pay or company pensions. They had to work longer hours and had less chance of promotion. They did not readily mix with members of other classes, either inside or outside work, and 77 per cent of their sample voted Labour. Goldthorpe and Lockwood did, however, argue that there were signs of **convergence** between working-class and middle-class lifestyles, but concluded that, rather than an increase in the middle class, what had emerged was a new working class.

Privatization

Goldthorpe and Lockwood identified a new trend, the emergence of the 'privatized instrumentalist' worker who saw work as a means to an end rather than as a source of identity. These affluent workers were more home-centred than traditional working-class groups; they were also less likely to subscribe to the notion of working-class community and 'them-versus-us' attitudes. Fiona Devine (1992) undertook a second study of the Vauxhall plant at Luton, in which she argued that Goldthorpe and Lockwood's study may have exaggerated the degree of working-class privatization. She found that workers retained strong kinship and friendship links, and were critically aware of class inequalities such as the unequal distribution of wealth and income.

Although the concept of embourgeoisement is now rarely used, it is frequently argued that the working class have fragmented into at least two different layers:

focus on research

Simon Charlesworth
A phenomenology of working-class experience

Simon Charlesworth's study focuses on working-class people in Rotherham in Yorkshire, the town where he grew up. Charlesworth based his study on 43 unstructured, conversational interviews, though he clearly spoke to large numbers of people whom he knew socially. Many of the people to whom he spoke were male, but at least a third were female. Charlesworth finds class seeping into all aspects of life in Rotherham and the lives of the people are ones of suffering. The loss of a man's job, for instance, has a physical consequence because it can lead to fear and panic consequent on loss of earnings. Older people are faced with the difficulties of learning to cope with a changing world, and even his younger respondents are often surprised by the behaviour of those even younger than themselves. One of the main points is that miserable economic conditions seem to cause people to feel both physically and psychologically unhealthy.

Many of the workers experience a lack of identity and a sense of being devalued because of the loss of status accompanying the lack of paid work. Others see no point in education or qualifications because even if they acquire them, they are not able to obtain decent work. There are further problems for those who do go to university or college in that they feel out of place and excluded from the culture because they are not fully part of it. The culture of the working-class lad demands that he be respected.

Changes in the social climate have left people without a sense of belonging to each other or of understanding how the world is developing. They have little sense of hope in the future and worry for their children. This has been one of the direst results of the years of Thatcherism and recent government policies that have not fully challenged the views of the New Right. He claims people feel rage and suffering; unemployment is destructive to people because it forces them into poverty. The culture that develops is one of having to make do, or to buy only what is necessary. It is marked by social and spiritual decay. Language is marked by heavy use of swearing and often friendship is displayed through a form of public insult.

Adapted from Blundell, J. and Griffiths, J. (2002) *Sociology since 1995*, Vol 2, Lewes: Connect Publications

1 Identify two criticisms that might be made of Charlesworth's methods as described in the passage above.

2 What factors have caused working-class culture in Rotherham to be marked by a 'social and spiritual decay'?

- The traditional working class in the north of England as shown, for example, in films like *The Full Monty* – This group still subscribes to the proletarian traditionalist ideas identified by Lockwood.
- A new working class found in the newer manufacturing industries, mainly situated in the south who enjoy a relatively affluent lifestyle but still see themselves as working-class – This group is more likely to own their own home, to holiday abroad and to engage in consumer spending not dissimilar from that of the middle class. Although this group sees itself as working-class, this no longer involves automatic loyalty to either trade unions or the Labour Party. The decision to vote Labour or to join a trade union is taken on instrumental rather than ideological grounds, i.e. whether it economically benefits the individual and their family.

Roberts (2001) notes the emergence of a new working class in the 1990s employed typically in shopping centres, hypermarkets, restaurants and hotels and in other businesses connected with leisure, sport and tourism. Such work is usually mundane, low paid, low level, part time and casual. However, because it is highly visible, involving constant contact with the general public, the group most often employed are young attractive people, who are aesthetically pleasing to the public's eye, so boosting 'the company's image, appearing human and interested in their commitment to customer satisfaction'. However, Roberts notes that such work can be stressful and demeaning. There is also a less public, new working class working behind the scenes in work that is also insecure, poorly paid, at odd and variable hours and offering little future career development, with security firms, in fast-food outlets such as McDonalds and with contract cleaners. Roberts, therefore, argues that the working class, like the middle class, is fragmented.

False consciousness?

Marxists reject the view that there is a fragmented working class. They argue that there is still a unified working class made up of manual workers – both Black and White, male and female, and routine white-collar workers. They would argue that the sorts of divisions discussed above are the product of ruling-class ideology, which attempts to divide and rule the working class. The fact that some groups do not see themselves as working class is dismissed by Marxists as false class-consciousness. They would argue that in relation to the means and social relations of production, all so-called 'class fractions' are objectively working class because they are alienated and exploited by the ruling class, whether they realize it or not.

Does class identity still exist?

Postmodernists argue that class identity has fragmented into numerous separate and individualized identities. Social identity is now more pluralistic and diverse. Pakulski and Waters (1996) argue that people now exercise more choice about what type of people they want to be. Gender, ethnicity, age, region and family role interact and impact with consumption and media images to construct postmodern culture and identity.

However, postmodern ideas may be exaggerated as recent surveys indicate that social class is still a significant source of identity for many (e.g. Marshall *et al.* 1988). Members of a range of classes are still aware of class differences and are happy to identify themselves using class categories. Savage, too, agrees that class identities continue to exist, but he argues that people only use them to indicate themselves as 'ordinary' or 'middling'. Class is rarely viewed as an issue by most people. According to Savage, class identities have declined in importance because of changes in the organization of the economy (for example, the decline of **primary industries** and factory work, the expansion of white-collar work as well as the rise of more insecure forms of manual and non-manual work), which Savage argues have dissolved class boundaries.

Check your understanding

1 How has the structure of the upper class changed in the last 50 years?

2 What is the 'establishment'?

3 Why do some writers suggest that we should no longer talk of the middle class but of the 'middle classes'?

4 How do managers differ from professionals?

5 Why do Marxists see white-collar workers as experiencing proletarianization?

6 How does the nature of call-centre work support the theory of proletarianization?

7 What was the 'embourgeoisement thesis' and how was it challenged?

8 How do Marxists challenge the view that the working class has fragmented?

9 Identify two recent trends with regard to the nature of working-class work.

10 What do postmodernists like Pakulski and Waters argue has happened to identity?

research ideas

1 Ask a sample of adults across a range of occupations how 'flexible' their work is. Ask them about their job security, the sort of tasks they do, their working hours, how much freedom they have, and so on.

2 Conduct a survey of your peers in casual part-time employment to find out the conditions of work they experience.

KEY TERMS

Autonomy – freedom to organize one's own workload.

Boundary problem – the constantly shifting nature of work makes it more difficult to draw boundaries between classes of workers.

Class fractions – subdivisions within particular mass groupings.

Convergence – coming together, e.g. of working-class and middle-class lifestyles.

Cultural capital – social advantages associated with the middle classes.

De-skilling – reducing the skill needed to do a job.

Downsizing – reducing the size of the permanent workforce.

Economic capital – money in shares (and so on) which generates more money.

Embourgeoisement – the idea that the working class is adopting the attitudes, lifestyle and economic situation of the middle classes.

Primary industries – those involved in extraction of raw materials, e.g. mining, agriculture, fishing.

Proletarianization – a tendency for lower-middle-class workers to become de-skilled and hence to share the market position of members of the working class.

Proletarian traditionalist – members of the working class with a strong sense of loyalty to each other because of shared community and work experience.

Redundancy – losing your job because a company is down-sizing.

Routine white-collar workers – clerical staff involved in low-status, repetitive office work.

Secondary industries – those involved in producing products from raw materials.

Self-employed/petit-bourgeois – owners of small businesses.

Social closure – the process by which high-status groups exclude lower-status groups from joining their ranks.

Tertiary or service sector – jobs providing services such as transport, retailing, hotel work, cleaning, banking and insurance.

exploring changes in the class structure

Item A

Employment by gender and industry (UK)

Social class	MALES (%)		FEMALES (%)	
	1981	2001	1981	2001
Manufacturing	32	22	17	8
Distribution, hotels, catering and repairs	17	22	26	27
Financial and business services	11	19	12	18
Transport and communication	9	9	3	4
Construction	9	5	2	1
Agriculture	2	2	1	1
Energy and water supply	4	1	1	–
Other services	17	18	38	41
All employee jobs (millions)	13.2m	12.8m	10.0m	12.7m

Source: Short-term Turnover and Employment Survey, Office for National Statistics

Item B

<< Middle-class occupations are no longer as secure as they used to be. The drive to cut costs, boost labour productivity and reduce staffing levels which began in factories has spread through offices and has infected the management and professional grades. Mergers and takeovers have also sometimes led to site closures, rationalizations and redundancies, and sometimes to new businesses taking on new functions. For example, most banks and building societies have become multipurpose financial service providers. An outcome has been the creation of new management and professional specialisms, which have required staff to adapt. Many of these changes have been enforced rather than voluntary. Also, more of the moves have been sideways or downwards rather than upwards. As a result, we see less satisfaction and fulfilment in these jobs because the the 'onward and upward' view of management careers is now outdated.>>

Source: Roberts, K. (2001) *Class in Modern Britain*, Basingstoke: Palgrave

(a) Using only the information in **Item A**, identify **two** trends in employment in the UK between 1981 and 2001. (6 marks)

(b) Identify **two** factors that may have led to managers and professionals being less secure and satisfied in their work (**Item B**). (6 marks)

(c) Identify and explain **two** reasons why researching the upper class might be more difficult than researching the middle and working classes. (12 marks)

(d) Using your wider sociological knowledge, outline the evidence for the view that all social classes enjoy a similar standard of living. (22 marks)

(e) Outline and assess the usefulness of sociological explanations for the view that changes in the workplace mean that there are no longer distinct differences between non-manual and manual workers in the UK today. (44 marks)

Poverty

gettingyouthinking

1 Write down the first four words that come into your head when you look at the photo above.

2 If a homeless person were to ask you for money, what would you reply?

3 Compare your responses to questions 1 and 2 with those of with people sitting around you. Discuss with them the reasons for your replies.

4 Why do you think people like the man shown in the photo live the way they do? Is it their own fault? Bad luck? The fault of an unjust society?

5 How would you resolve their problems?

Arguments about the causes of poverty can be traced back as far as we have written records. Intriguingly, it seems that, although the terminology has changed, the actual explanations for the existence of poverty have remained the same through the centuries. On the one side, there are those who claim that affluence is a combination of natural ability and hard work; on the other side, there are those who argue that the poor are unfortunate, or that the 'system' is against them. So, one argument lays the blame at the feet of the poor themselves, while the other blames the society that condemns some people to poverty.

How do we identify the poor?

As Denscombe (2004) points out, poverty is a very complex issue, especially when it comes to defining and measuring it.

This is because, as we shall see, there are a number of competing definitions of poverty and, therefore, ways of measuring it.

The official approach to poverty

The official definition of poverty used by government agencies in Britain is '60 per cent of **median household income** after deducting household costs'. Essentially, this means that households were regarded as poor by the government in 2002 if they had less than £146 per week coming in. As Denscombe (2004) notes, this is a measure of relative inequality in society. He notes that:

≪In a developed economy, the concern is not so much about people lacking the resources to survive, but about whether people have the necessary income to participate

in normal social activities. It is about the equitable distribution of income and wealth and the extent to which those at the end of the spectrum are able to avoid the social exclusion that results from not having enough money to buy the kinds of things, and do the kind of things, that might be regarded as 'normal'.>>
(pp. 46–7)

Absolutist approaches to poverty

An alternative way of defining and measuring poverty is to adopt an absolutist approach. This is based on the idea that minimum resources such as nutritious diet, clothing, shelter and heating can be identified in terms of the income needed to maintain human needs. All who fall below this income are defined as being in absolute poverty. This scheme was adopted by Rowntree in his poverty surveys of York in 1899. However, this approach is largely rejected today for several reasons:

- Basic needs are not universal – they differ even in the same society between social groups, by region, etc.
- Basic needs change as living standards change, i.e. often, things that were seen as 'comforts' and 'luxuries' in the past come to be seen as 'necessities', e.g. indoor flush toilets, hot water.
- What is perceived as a basic need is really a value judgement.
- People's quality of life is not always determined by money – it could be enhanced, for example, by social and emotional supports from extended kin and community.

The government rejects the absolutist approach for the following reason:

<< *Only in countries at a very low level of economic development is it sensible to take an absolutist, 'basic needs' approach, which costs the bare essentials to maintain human life and uses this as the yardstick against which incomes are measured.* >> (*Social Trends 32*, 2002, quoted in Denscombe 2003)

Relative approaches to measuring poverty

Using the official definition of relative poverty, we can see that poverty in Britain increased substantially throughout the 1980s (ironically, during a period of economic growth) with over 14 million people on incomes below 50 per cent of the national average (a threshold of 60 per cent was adopted in 2002).

There are, however, signs that the numbers living in poverty have now stabilized to 12.5 million people living in relative poverty in 2002. This figure comprises 6.6 million adults of working age, 2.2 million pensioners and 3.8 million children. Another way of looking at this is that 22 per cent of the population is in poverty – 22 per cent of all pensioners, 35 per cent of all lone parents and 30 per cent of all children.

Children and poverty

The dramatic increase in single parents has also affected the proportion of children in poverty. Between 1979 and 1997, the number of children living in poverty in the UK increased by 40 per cent. A report by the Labour think tank the Institute for Public Policy Studies (Robinson 2001) suggested that the UK is the worst place in Europe to grow up. The report showed that over a third of children live in poverty in the UK, significantly more than in any other EU country. By way of comparison, in 2003, Denmark had the lowest rate of child poverty at 5 per cent. Research published by the charity Save the Children claimed that one in ten children experience severe poverty lasting five years or more. Such children lack warm and waterproof clothing, properly fitting shoes and often go without proper meals.

In 2003, the government announced that Britain would aim to become 'among the best in Europe' on child poverty. A report published in December 2003, *Measuring Child Poverty* (Department for Work and Pensions 2003), announced new indicators of child poverty to replace the household income measure. The main focus will be a survey in which 24 000 families whose household income is less than 70 per cent of the national median income will be asked 20 questions relating to deprivation and the possessions and activities of children, including heating, the adequacy and availability of shoes and clothing, holidays, hobbies, insurance and leisure equipment.

The survey is very similar to the Breadline Britain surveys carried out by Mack and Lansley in 1983 and 1990, which operationalized poverty in three stages:

1 They asked 1800 people what they considered to be necessities that average families should not be without.
2 They asked their sample population what they lacked from this consensual index or list. People were considered poor if they lacked three or more items.
3 They asked their sample population whether this was a matter of choice or not.

On this basis, they calculated that 11 million people were living in poverty in 1990.

However, this consensual model of relative poverty did run into criticisms because Mack and Lansley were using subjective judgements to compile their original lists of potential necessities while necessities on their list often lacked specifics – for example, they included 'three meals a day' for children, but this could include a nutritionally balanced meal or a takeaway from McDonalds.

There are signs that the *Measuring Child Poverty* survey could run into similar difficulties because, as Denscombe notes, the questions are based on ethnocentric assumptions about what constitutes 'normal' social life in the UK that might apply to some groups more than others. Moreover, the questions focus on goods and services that not everybody would regard as necessities, such as holidays, having friends or family around for a drink or a meal at least once a month, having children's friends around for tea once a fortnight or going on a school trip once a term.

The unemployed and low paid

About 1.8 million children come from households with no parent in employment. But it is not just children who are hit by unemployment. About 75 per cent of unemployed people now live in poverty.

Those who are unemployed for a long time face much greater problems than those who are out of work for a short period. These problems include a lower level of income, the gradual exhaustion of savings, and deterioration in the condition of clothing, furniture and general possessions. After three months of unemployment, the average disposable income of a family drops by as much as 59 per cent. It is not just financial losses that occur as a result of long-term unemployment – there are psychological effects too, such as lack of confidence, stress and depression. These further undermine people's ability to obtain work.

The Low Pay Unit (2000) estimated that 45 per cent of British workers were earning less than two-thirds of the average wage. Low-paid workers are often caught in a **poverty trap.** This means they earn above the minimum level required to claim benefits, but the deduction of tax, etc. takes them below it. Similarly, many on benefits could end up even worse off in low-paid work as they would then be no longer eligible for state support. New Labour introduced a minimum wage policy in 1999, but this is yet to have a significant impact.

The feminization of poverty

Some sociologists have noted an increase in the number of women in poverty. This feminization of poverty has come about for a number of reasons:

● The majority of elderly are female because women live longer than men. They are less likely to have occupational pensions to supplement their state pensions because they have spent long periods in the home as mothers and housewives.
● Over 50 per cent of lone parents in Britain live in poverty. Lone-parent families are more likely to be poor for two, possibly overlapping, reasons. First, there is a higher risk of women from poorer backgrounds becoming lone parents in the first place. So they are already more likely to be at risk of poverty before they have children. Second, any lone parent is likely to be poorer because they have to combine childcare with employment. This means that they are more likely to work part time, so their incomes on average will be lower. But it is important to remember that not all lone mothers are poor – it is just that they are more at risk of poverty.
● Women do not earn as much as men – they are more likely to be in low-skilled and part-time work and may be more likely to experience the poverty trap.

Ethnic minorities and poverty

There is some evidence that people from ethnic-minority groups may be more likely than White people to experience poverty. Some 69 per cent of Pakistani and Bangladeshi people, 46 per cent of African-origin people and 32 per cent of African-Caribbean origin people are poor.

Ethnic-minority groups have substantially higher rates of unemployment than the majority of the population. This holds true even if the person has the same educational qualifications as the majority population. Those of African-Caribbean origin and a majority of those of Asian origin have a greater chance of earning lower wages than the majority population. They are also more likely to work in the types of employment where wages are generally low. Racial discrimination and institutional racism across a range of organizations is increasingly being recognized as a major contributor to poverty among these groups.

Region and poverty

The chances of living in poverty vary considerably across the country and within cities. Indeed, in relative terms, Britain lies only second to Mexico in the industrialized world for the extent of regional inequalities in living standards.

People living in Wales, the North East, Inner London and Yorkshire are most likely to be poor, and those living in outer London and the South East are least likely to be poor. These largely reflect differences in rates of pay and of levels of unemployment.

Sick and disabled people

According to government statistics, there are approximately 6.2 million adults (14 per cent of all adults) and 36 000 children (3 per cent of all children) who suffer from one or more disabilities. Of these, 34 per cent are living in poverty. The average income for a disabled adult, under pensionable age, is 72 per cent of that for non-disabled people. The impact of disability also goes beyond the individual person concerned, with 52 per cent of working-age adults with a disabled child themselves living in poverty.

There are several reasons for the poverty of disabled people and carers. They may be unable to work, or the work they can do may be limited to particular kinds of low-paid employment. At the same time, people with disabilities often have higher outgoings, such as having to pay for a special diet, or having to pay for heating to be on all day.

The link between poverty and social exclusion

The problem for the government with using a relative approach to poverty is that the goal posts keep moving, in that average incomes tend to rise every year and so the poverty line gets higher. This makes getting rid of poverty almost impossible because there will always be disparities between the rich and the poor. Consequently, the Labour government of Tony Blair prefers to use the term 'social exclusion' because it captures the range of deprivations that make up the experience of poverty and prevent people from taking a full part in society. Targets to allow participation in normal life can more easily be set, measured and attained than those linked to relative poverty levels. Government-sponsored studies now use four indicators or measures of social exclusion:

- the number of people not in employment, education or training
- the number of those earning below 60 per cent of the average wage
- the number of those experiencing low levels of social interaction
- the number of those who believe that they live in an area characterized by high crime, vandalism or material dilapidation.

Poverty: a risk not a state

When we talk about poor people, it is rather misleading, because it gives the impression that there is a group of people who live in poverty all their lives. This is true for some people, but the majority of the poor are people who live on the margins of poverty, moving into poverty and out again, depending upon a range of economic factors, government decisions, family responsibilities and their earning possibilities.

Explaining the existence and persistence of poverty

Dependency-based explanations

Dependency-based explanations argue that the poor are, in some way, the cause of their own poverty. At their most extreme, they suggest that the welfare system in Britain actually makes people dependent on it by providing an attractive alternative to work.

Three different approaches exist, based on the following notions:

- **individual deficiency**
- the **culture of poverty**
- the **underclass**.

Individual deficiency

Explanations that centre on the concept of dependency stress that people who are poor are in that state because of some personal or cultural deficiency. Essentially, it is their fault if they are poor.

Two lines of thought, in particular, have emerged:

- *The individual as scapegoat* – This is the approach that many 19th-century writers took, and it remains, to some extent, in the idea of the '**scrounger**'. There is little evidence that this could explain any more than a tiny proportion of poverty. However, the myth of the scrounger was used powerfully in the 1980s as a justification for cutbacks in welfare.
- *The dependent individual* – This idea was developed by Marsland (1996) who argued that the individual's will to work was undermined by excessively generous state welfare

Beresford *et al.* (1999)
Poverty first hand

Beresford and his colleagues pointed out that most research undertaken on poverty had been by 'experts' and pressure groups. Typically, they collected statistics on poverty and then worked out the numbers of people in that situation. Even the definition of poverty was provided by these experts. Beresford and colleagues wanted to find out the views and attitudes of poor people themselves. In order to do so, they approached a wide variety of local groups across the country, mainly composed of people on low income, and then interviewed representatives from each. In all, 137 people were interviewed.

The results showed that living in poverty was a difficult and demoralizing situation, in which they felt stigmatized by the attitudes of others. The majority of the people believed that the causes of poverty were in the way society was organized, rather than in individual failings. They vehemently rejected the notion of the underclass. They would like to find work if they could or, if they were already in employment, in better-paid work.

Beresford, P. , Green, D., Lister, R. and Woodard, K. (1999) *Poverty First Hand*, London: CPAG

1 Typically, who does most research on poverty?

2 How representative of the poor do you think the sample was likely to be?

3 What were the views of the sample on the causes of poverty?

benefits, and that the need to look after other family members was weakened by the extensive provision of state services. The result was a high level of dependence on the state.

The culture of poverty

This idea was originally suggested by Oscar Lewis (1966) in his study of poor people in Mexico. Lewis argued that poor people in a 'class-stratified and highly individualistic society' were likely to develop a set of cultural values that trapped them in their poverty. It is important to stress the ideas of class and **individualism**, for Lewis is not arguing that these people are necessarily deficient. He believes that they are caught in a society that really does put barriers in their path – but that the poor themselves help ensure that they are trapped by developing a set of values that prevent them from breaking out of poverty. These cultural values include:

- a sense of **fatalism** and acceptance of their poverty
- an inability to think long term
- a desire for immediate enjoyment.

Critics of this approach argue that there is no such thing as a culture of poverty – rather, such cultural values are a perfectly rational reaction to conditions of hopelessness. In the USA, the poorest groups really are excluded, and they are unlikely to be allowed to break out of their poverty. In such a situation, the poor may feel that there is no point in planning long term.

The question of the underclass

The concept of the underclass has entered everyday speech to describe those living at the margins of society, largely reliant on state benefits to make ends meet. However, the concept is rejected by many sociologists due to its negative and sometimes politically charged connotations. Members of the political right, such as Charles Murray (1994) in the USA, have focused on the cultural 'deficiencies' of the so-called underclass, blaming them

for their situation, and accusing them of relying on benefits and even manipulating their own circumstances to increase the amount that they can claim from the state. Sometimes, it is also argued, they supplement their income through petty crime, or compensate for deprivation through excessive drug and alcohol abuse. Murray has focused on a Black underclass which, he alleges, is to be found in most American cities. Similar points have been made about members of non-working groups in deprived areas of Britain (Dennis and Erdos 1993).

A matter of choice?

Many New Right commentators (such as Saunders 1995) suggest that a large number of the poor see 'poverty' as a choice, a way of life preferable to work. Young mothers are often cited as examples of this – for example, by having a second child in order to secure a flat that will be paid for by the state.

Roberts (2001) notes that it is difficult to see one culture underpinning an underclass with a common commitment to values that stress dependency, criminality and immorality. He notes that:

<< *The long-term out-of-work, and the recurrently unemployed, are a variety of distinct groups with very different reasons for their prolonged or repeated unemployment. There are displaced workers who are nearing the normal retirement age. Then there are lone parents. Then there are convicted repeat offenders. Then there are people with chronic disabilities. Does it help in diagnosing any of these groups' situations to lump them all together?* >> (p. 114)

Various studies, such as those by Morris (1993) and Gallie (1994), have examined the extent to which the poor possess cultural differences that may account for their situation. They find that there is little evidence of an underclass culture and, if

synopticlink

families and households – education – wealth, poverty and welfare – crime and deviance

The underclass

The concept of 'underclass' is a useful tool to use to construct synoptic links. The New Right see the growth of a criminal and antisocial underclass as fuelled by the rise in numbers of single teenage mothers, who are failing to control their delinquent children. Combined with the decline of marriage, and the growth of divorce and cohabitation, this group is seen as a threat to the stability of the nuclear family and social order.

In terms of education, the underclass is also seen by the New Right as mainly responsible for problems such as poor classroom discipline, exclusion, truancy and poor levels of achievement in state schools in inner-city areas. It is argued that the poor attitude held by parents in the

underclass towards education is more important than poverty or other forms of material deprivation in explaining educational underachievement.

In the field of welfare and poverty, the New Right suggest that members of the underclass 'choose' to be poor and are happy to be dependent on welfare benefits.

Finally, the underclass are seen by the New Right as constituting a criminal class, in that, for them, the benefits of crime far outweigh the costs because they lack the normal range of controls that law-abiding people have in their lives.

anything, find the most disadvantaged groups have greater commitment to the concept of work than many other groups. Research also shows that the majority of lone parents would like a stable relationship; and there is no evidence of an automatic overlap between lone-parent families and crime.

Rather than blaming the cultural deficiencies of the poor, critics of the underclass thesis prefer to use the concept of social exclusion to explain poverty. Social exclusion can take many forms, the accumulated effects of which can lead to extreme poverty. Consider the current refugee 'crisis' concerning Eastern European immigrants to Britain: these people are excluded from gaining anything but casual low-paid work; they may be ineligible for state benefits; they have language barriers to contend with and may also be socially excluded due to xenophobic attitudes and racism.

It is perhaps understandable that social exclusion may build resentment that can lead to other social ills such as crime or increased suicide rates. Young (1999) suggests that crime rates may be reflecting the fact that a growing number of people do not feel valued or feel that they have little investment in the societies in which they live.

Exclusion-based explanations

Exclusion-based explanations argue that the poor are poor because they are prevented from achieving a reasonable standard of living by the actions of the more powerful in society.

This approach stresses differences in power between the various groups in society. Those who have least power – the

disabled, older people, women, ethnic minorities and, of course, children – have significantly higher chances of living in poverty. Within this approach we can distinguish three strands:

1 poverty, powerlessness and the **labour market**
2 **citizenship** and exclusion
3 poverty and capitalism: the economic-system approach.

Poverty, powerlessness and the labour market

In all societies, the least powerful groups are the most likely to lose out economically and socially, and they will form the bulk of the poor. Indeed, poverty and powerlessness go hand in hand. The powerless include women, lone parents (usually women), the very young and the very old, as well as those with disabilities. When these powerless groups do get employment, it is likely to be in short-term, low-paid, temporary and possibly 'unofficial' work. For many supporters of the welfare state, it is these groups who deserve help, because they are blameless 'victims' of the economic system.

Citizenship and exclusion

Field (1989) has developed this argument, and linked it to the idea of 'citizenship'. Field argues that three groups in society have, over the last 20 years, been excluded from the rights that citizens should enjoy, including the right to a decent standard of living. These are:

● the long-term unemployed
● lone-parent families
● those on state retirement pensions.

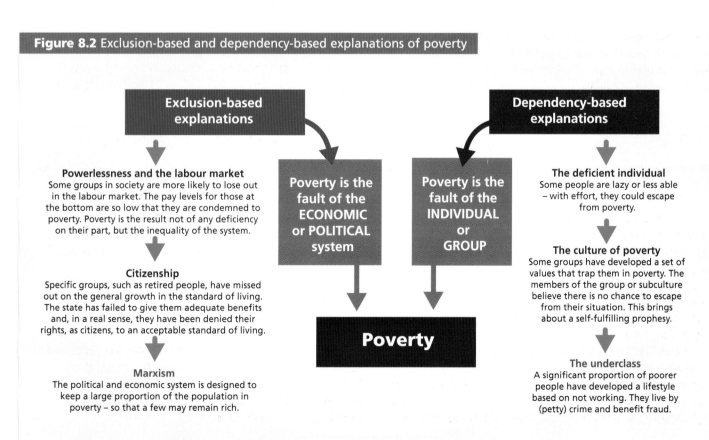

Figure 8.2 Exclusion-based and dependency-based explanations of poverty

Together these groups comprise what he calls (rather confusingly) the 'underclass'. Field argues that these groups have been particularly hit by several factors:

- government policies, which have increased the gap between rich and poor
- increases in the core number of long-term unemployed
- an increasing tendency to **stigmatize** and blame the poor for their poverty, rather than look at wider economic and social factors.

Once again, the answer to the problem of poverty lies in a better-organized and comprehensive welfare state.

Poverty and capitalism: the economic-system approach

The final, and most radical, explanation for poverty is provided by those in the Marxist tradition (see Unit 1, p. 5). They see poverty as an inevitable outcome of the capitalist system. According to Marxist theory, the economy is owned and run by a small ruling class, who exploit the majority of the population who work for them. Poverty emerges from three main causes:

1. The wealth of the ruling class is created from paying the lowest possible wages to people – because it is the profits that produce the wealth.
2. The poor act as a warning – having a group in poverty provides a direct warning to the rest of the workforce of what could happen to them if they didn't work hard.
3. Poor people provide a 'starting point' against which other workers can measure their own income (rather than against the income of members of the ruling class).

For Marxists, the welfare state is a means of hiding exploitation, and it is used by the rich and powerful to provide just enough in the way of health care and income-support benefits to prevent a serious challenge to their authority.

research ideas

1. Get a copy of the *Measuring Child Poverty* survey from the Department for Work and Pensions website or from p. 49 of *Sociology Update* 2004. Distribute the questions among 20 randomly selected people from all age groups and ask them whether they agree that these questions measure poverty? What questions would people subtract or add?

2. Ask a sample of people to estimate the numbers of the various groups 'at risk of poverty' who are actually living in poverty. Then show them the actual figures (Item A opposite). How closely do their estimates match the figures? Are they surprised at the figures?

Check your understanding

1. Identify five groups likely to experience the risk of poverty.

2. What is meant by the feminization of poverty?

3. How do absolutist measurements of poverty differ from relative approaches?

4. What is meant by the phrase 'poverty trap'?

5. What is meant by the term 'underclass'? Why is it a controversial concept?

6. What is meant by the concept social exclusion? How does this concept provide a more sociological explanation of poverty?

7. Identify three explanations of poverty which suggest that individuals are to blame for their own poverty.

8. How does Frank Field's theory of the underclass differ from that of Charles Murray?

9. How do Marxists explain poverty?

10. How are the concepts of citizenship and social exclusion related?

web.tasks

1. **Find out the latest figures on 'households below average income', and the latest figures for the 'poverty line'. Search the website of the Child Poverty Action Group at www.cpag.org.uk to find this and much more information.**

2. **What particular problems are faced by groups who run a high risk of poverty? Why do they often find it hard to break out of poverty? Search the World Wide Web to find out more about the disabled, single-parent families, child poverty, ethnic minorities, the unemployed, older people and the low paid.**

3. **The BBC News website gives a simple summary of some of the facts on the extent of poverty:**

   http://news.bbc.co.uk/1/shared/spl/hi/
   pop_ups/03/uk_poverty_and_social_
   exclusion/html/1.stm

KEY TERMS

Citizenship – refers (in this particular case) to the belief that people living in British society have certain 'rights', including the right to have a decent standard of living.

Culture of poverty – a set of values that some poorer people in society share, which they pass on to their children. The result is that they get trapped in poverty.

Dependency – the state of being dependent. It is used to refer to the idea that some people live off the hard work of others.

Fatalism – acceptance that what happens is the result of luck or 'fate'.

Individual deficiency – refers to a person's specific faults or weaknesses which make them unable to get on in society and be successful.

Individualism – the belief that individuals are far more important than social groups.

Labour market – refers to the sorts of jobs and employment conditions that people have.

Median household income – the middle range of incomes.

Poverty trap – earning so little that you are eligible for benefits but unable to escape poverty because receiving more income would reduce eligibility for benefits.

'Scrounger' – someone who claims welfare benefits they are not entitled to, and/or who manipulates the benefits system to their own advantage.

Stigmatize – to mark something out as bad.

Underclass – a derogatory term applied to the very poor who are seen to be to blame for their own circumstances and many social ills, e.g. crime.

exploring poverty

Item A Types of people in income poverty

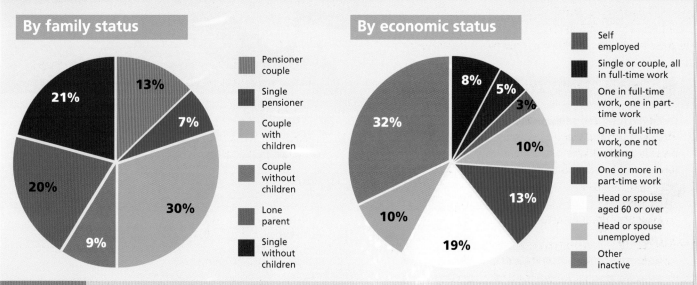

By family status

13%, 7%, 30%, 9%, 20%, 21%

- Pensioner couple
- Single pensioner
- Couple with children
- Couple without children
- Lone parent
- Single without children

By economic status

8%, 5%, 3%, 10%, 13%, 19%, 10%, 32%

- Self employed
- Single or couple, all in full-time work
- One in full-time work, one in part-time work
- One in full-time work, one not working
- One or more in part-time work
- Head or spouse aged 60 or over
- Head or spouse unemployed
- Other inactive

Item B

One explanation of poverty is that it is generated by the cultural attitudes and lifestyle of the poor. The culture of poverty argues that poverty cannot be eradicated by giving more money to the poor because they have developed a way of life which does not allow them to improve their position simply by having more money. Their culture is said to be characterized by short-term horizons, indifference to work, apathy and feelings of resignation. Furthermore, this culture is said to be transmitted from one generation to another, setting up a cycle of deprivation and a culture of dependency.

The culture of poverty thesis is largely discredited because it seemed to ignore structural causes of deprivation.

Goldthorpe, J. (1980, 1999) *Social Mobility and the Class Structure in Modern Britain*, Oxford: Clarendon

(a) Using only the information in **Item A**, identify the **two** family types most at risk of income poverty. (6 marks)

(b) Using the information in **Item B**, identify **two** possible links between culture and poverty. (6 marks)

(c) Identify and explain **two** problems facing sociologists using social surveys to measure poverty in terms of people's inability to pay for particular activities and items. (12 marks)

(d) Using your wider sociological knowledge, outline the evidence for the persistence of child poverty in the contemporary UK. (22 marks)

(e) Outline and assess the view that poverty is caused by social exclusion rather than cultural attitudes and lifestyle. (44 marks)

Gender and inequality

gettingyouthinking

Table 8.6 Qualifications gained 2005

GCSEs and equivalent	Girls (%)	Boys (%)
5+ grades A* to C	61.6	51.5
5+ A* to G grades	92.5	87.7
No graded results	1.8	3.3

DfES (2005) *GCSE and equivalent results for young people in England 2004/5 (provisional)*

Table 8.7 Occupations 2004

Employees and self-employed aged 16 and over (Great Britain)

Selected occupations	Women (%)	Men (%)
Receptionists	95	5
Educational assistants	93	7
Nurses	88	12
Care assistants & home carers	88	12
Primary & nursery teachers	87	13
Cleaners and domestics	80	20
Secondary teachers	54	46
Chefs and cooks	46	54
Retail & wholesale managers	35	65
Marketing & sales managers	26	74
IT managers	18	82
Software professionals	17	83
Production, works & maintenance managers	9	91

Adapted from ONS (2004) *Labour Force Survey Spring 2004*

Table 8.8 Full-time and part-time earnings 2004

Mean earnings of employees on adult rates

Hourly earnings	Women (£ per hour)	Men (£ per hour)	Gender pay gap*
Full-time	11.21	13.73	18%
Part-time	8.19	9.36	40%
Weekly earnings	(£ per week)	(£ per week)	
Full-time	420	557	25%
Annual earnings	(£k per year)	(£k per year)	
Full-time	21.7	30.1	28%

* The gender pay gap is 100 – (women's earnings as a percentage of men's full-time earnings). Women's full-time and part-time earnings are each compared to men's full-time earnings.

Adapted from ONS (2004) *Annual Survey of Hours and Earnings, 2004*

Table 8.9 Full-time and part-time employment 2004

Employees and self-employed aged 16 and over

Great Britain	Women (%)	Men (%)
Full-time	56	89
Part-time	44	11

Adapted from ONS (2004) *Labour Force Survey Spring 2004*

1 Identify the main patterns in each of the tables on this page.

2 Using ideas you have developed from studying your Sociology course, suggest explanations for each of these patterns.

You will probably have noted patterns in each of the tables above and realized that, despite all the improvements in the social position of women, gender differences in paid work are still very noticeable. You should also have been able to offer some explanations drawn from your past study of the subject. These may well match up with some of those introduced later in this topic, which examines gender inequality in the UK, focusing particularly on paid work. There are many other aspects of gender inequality in British society and you will have covered these as a part of your study of other modules at both AS- and A2-level.

Gender inequality in employment

In the past 30 years, the number of female workers in the UK rose by 2.45 million whereas the number of male workers rose by only 0.5 million. Although the numbers of males and females in employment have been evening out, there are still significant differences in the distribution of male and female workers throughout the occupational structure. In 1979, Catherine Hakim noted that occupational segregation by gender existed in Britain (Hakim 1979). She defined occupational segregation as existing when 'men and women do different kinds of work, so that one can speak of two separate labour forces, one male and one female, which are not in competition with each other for the same jobs'. So men and women may both be in paid employment, but they are usually doing different kinds of jobs. Hakim goes on to identify two types of occupational segregation:

- **Horizontal segregation** – Men and women 'crowd' into different types of jobs in different sectors of the economy.
- **Vertical segregation** – Women occupy the lower levels of pay and status in particular jobs.

Horizontal segregation

Table 8.7 opposite gives a clear picture of the high concentrations of men or women in many occupations. In the public sector, women are mainly employed in health and education, where they make up 80 per cent and 72 per cent of the workforce respectively. In the private sector, women are overconcentrated in clerical, administrative, retail and personal services, such as catering, whereas men are mainly found in the skilled manual and upper professional sectors (ONS 2004).

There is some evidence that horizontal segregation may be in decline because of the general decline in traditionally male sectors. Recent trends in female educational success may further assist the breakdown of this type of segregation.

There is also some evidence that men may be moving into traditionally female areas such as nursing and primary-school teaching. This may have negative implications for women in terms of vertical segregation – for example, while 50 per cent of male primary teachers were head teachers, the equivalent figure for females was 15 per cent.

Vertical segregation

Skill and status

Within each occupational layer, women tend to be concentrated at the lower levels. Even when women have gained access to the upper professional or management sector, they may encounter a '**glass ceiling**' – they can climb the ladder so far but then reach a barrier whereby they can see where they want to go, but cannot climb any further. In 2004, 58 per cent of professionals and 67 per cent of managers and senior officials were male. The higher up the occupational ladder you look, the fewer women there are. In 2004, women made up only 8.3 per cent of senior judges and police officers, 9.7 per cent of top business leaders and 9.1 per cent of national newspaper editors (EOC 2005a).

Pay

The gender gap between women's and men's average incomes was 46 per cent in 2002/3. There has been virtually no change in this since the mid-1990s. In 2004, the average hourly earnings for women working full time were 18 per cent lower than for men working full time. The weekly pay of all women is only 75 per cent of men's weekly earnings (EOC 2005b). In 1999, the EOC concluded that:

<< Throughout their working lives women earn significantly less than men, whether they are lawyers or sales assistants. At the present rate of change, women will have to wait until the year 2040 to achieve equality in pay. >>

Work situation

Women are more likely than men to be employed in part-time work. In 2004, 44 per cent of female employees worked part time, compared with only 11 per cent of male employees. McDowell (1992) argues that the changes brought about by **post-Fordism** require a core of multi-skilled workers on the one hand and part-time ancillary workers on short-term or part-time contracts on the other. Women mostly make up the latter, with few making it into the core. Part-time work tends to have worse working conditions, less job security and fewer promotion prospects than full-time work. The high demand for work has enabled employers to reduce part-time pay rates which, calculated as a percentage of full-time pay, fell from 81 per cent in 1980 to 75 per cent by the end of the decade. In 1999, women in part-time work earned, on average, 60 per cent of the average hourly pay of male full-time employees (Grimshaw and Rubery 2001).

What about men?

While men generally enjoy a greater range of work opportunities, more status and more pay, there is evidence of change in the experience of work for some men, particularly working-class men. This change is caused by economic recession and unemployment in traditional industries and manufacturing. Some writers suggest that this has led some men to feel frustrated at their inability to fulfil their traditional role as breadwinner and protector.

Scott MacEwen (1994) notes that there are two ways of measuring segregation. The first is an objective measure using survey or census data to calculate the numbers of women and men in an occupation. This is precise but measures broad occupations rather than specific jobs. It is at the level of specific jobs that segregation is most extreme. For example, the occupation 'cleaner' obscures the fact that it is mainly men who are 'street cleaners' and women who are 'office cleaners'. Similarly, the occupation 'teacher' glosses over the fact that the vast majority of primary teachers are female.

The second method is to measure occupational segregation subjectively. Here, interviews or questionnaires are used to ask people whether their type of job is done exclusively or mainly by men or women or shared equally. This method does have its problems – it relies on the judgement of the respondent for example – but it does focus on the more direct level of a person's job.

Adapted from Pilcher, J. and Whelehan, I. (2004)
50 Key Concepts in Gender Studies, London: Sage

This is made worse by the fact that women are more successful at getting the jobs that have replaced manufacturing, such as those in the new service sector. In so doing, they are felt to be taking over from men as breadwinners. This, in turn, may threaten marital stability and play some part in causing higher divorce rates in such areas. As Mac An Ghaill (1996) has argued, there is a general crisis in masculinity.

Willott and Griffin (1996) have explored this so-called 'crisis'. They researched a group of long-term unemployed men in the West Midlands. Their respondents typified the kinds of men most likely to be marginalized, having little hope of finding steady employment. While their role as provider was undermined, their other masculine characteristics (in particular their sense of authority over their families) remained. Willot and Griffin concluded that rather than there being a crisis of masculinity, as a whole, there was merely a weakening of certain elements of traditional masculinity.

Further discussion of masculinity can be found in Unit 1, Topic 2, p. 12.

Sociological explanations of gender stratification in employment

Functionalism and human capital theory

You should be familiar with the functionalist position associated particularly with the work of Talcott Parsons in the mid-20th century. Parsons felt that separate gender roles for men and women were helpful to societies. Women were more suited to what he called 'expressive roles' – those emphasizing

caring and emotions – while men were the ideal candidates for 'instrumental roles', those that required qualities of competition, aggression and achievement. This view implies that men are more suited to paid employment, women to domesticity. The implications of Parsons' view are that women will be less motivated and less suited to the labour market than men. Therefore, it is not surprising that they will, on average, be paid less.

Some economists have gone on to suggest that the pay gap between men and women is justified because it reflects the fact that men have more '**human capital**' than women because of their greater orientation to paid work. Women are more likely to take career breaks and opt for part-time work in order to continue to care for their families. Men, however, will be able to build up their skills, qualifications and experience through unbroken employment, education and training, and thus be able to command higher pay.

Human capital theory has been criticized by Olsen and Walby (2004). They used data from the longitudinal British Household Panel Survey to investigate the causes of pay differences between men and women. Although they accept that pay differentials in part reflect the fact that women tend to have less full-time employment experience than men and take more career breaks, they argue that women face 'systematic disadvantage in acquiring human capital'. For example, pay is lower in occupations where there are high concentrations of women. This could well be because these jobs provide less training and promotion prospects than jobs where men predominate. Furthermore, human capital theory assumes that experience of employment increases wages, yet experience of part-time work (undertaken by many women – see Table 8.9 on p. 324) is actually associated with a slight reduction in wages.

Dual labour-market theory

Many sociologists have looked for explanations within the structure of the labour market as a whole. Barron and Norris (1976) argue that a **dual labour-market** exists, i.e. the labour market is divided into two sectors:

- a primary sector consisting of secure, well-paid jobs with good prospects
- a secondary sector characterized by poor pay, insecurity and no ladder of promotion.

It is very difficult to move from the secondary to the primary sector. Women are more likely to be found in the disadvantaged secondary sector for a number of reasons, outlined below.

Women's 'unsuitability'

Employers may hold stereotypical beliefs about the 'unsuitability' of women for primary-sector roles. West and Zimmerman (1991) and Hartnett (1990) note that there are still powerful cultural myths subscribed to by some employers in the 1990s, as follows:

- Workers do not like working for a female manager (making women less eligible for promotion to management positions).
- Women are less dependable (and so cannot be trusted to fulfil delegated tasks).
- Women are financially dependent on men (and so have less need of pay rises/promotion).
- Women will stop work when they marry and have children (and so there is little point investing in their long-term training).
- Working mothers cause their children damage (so for the children's sake, women should stay at home and should not be given management jobs since these can require long or unsociable hours).

Disrupted career development

Jobs with good promotion prospects often recruit people young and require from them several years of continuous service. Few mechanisms exist to enable staff to take time out and return to a similar position. Social pressure to have a family leads to some women finding that child-rearing, even for a couple of years, can mean going back to square one of their career. Caplow (1954) argues that the husband's career may even dictate the geographical movement of the family, and wives are sometimes forced to leave their jobs as a consequence, affecting their chances of a continuous career.

Weak legal and political framework supporting women

Both the Equal Pay and Sex Discrimination Acts are ineffective in failing to protect women's employment rights. Coussins (1976) described the Sex Discrimination Act as 'feeble', as there are many areas of employment to which it does not apply. Further, she doubted the commitment of governments to eliminate gender inequality. There was limited access to nursery care at the time she wrote and little support for employers to provide crèche facilities. Recent changes in the legal position of part-time workers have, however, benefited women considerably and some attempt has been made to recognize that men, too, have some responsibility for child-rearing, with the introduction of recent legislation to allow unpaid leave for either partner.

Evaluation of dual labour-market theory

Dual labour-market theory has two strengths as an explanation of vertical segregation:

- It stresses that the social organization of work in Western societies is essentially **patriarchal**, with men in the positions of power making discrimination against women and their lower status appear 'natural'.
- It undermines the popular assumption that better qualifications and increased ambition for women would automatically dismantle gender divisions in employment. Women with the same qualifications as men will continue to be disadvantaged as long as these two sectors are allowed to exist and are underpinned with patriarchal assumptions about the role of women.

However, Bradley (1996) points out that the theory fails to explain inequalities in the same sector. For example, teaching is not a secondary labour-market occupation, yet women are less likely than men to gain high-status jobs in this profession. While 70 per cent of teachers are female, only 35 per cent of senior jobs in teaching are held by women.

Feminism

Perhaps the most significant contributions to understanding gender stratification have come from the range of perspectives classified as feminist. These are described in some detail in Unit 1, Topic 2 (see pp. 11–12). Here, we focus on the ways feminists have explained the position of women in employment.

Liberal feminism

Liberal feminists argue that gender-role socialization is responsible for reproducing a sexual division of labour in which masculinity is largely seen as dominant and femininity as subordinate.

Ann Oakley (1974) argues that the main reason for the subordination of women in the labour market has been the dominance of the mother–housewife role for women. She argues that ideas such as the maternal instinct have justified male dominance. The fact that female professional workers are three times more likely not to be married than their male counterparts also supports the view that the wife's role is primarily domestic.

In the 1990s, liberal feminists suggested that these processes were coming to an end. Sue Sharpe's work on the attitudes of teenage girls (1994) suggests that education and careers are now a priority for young women, while females have also enjoyed great educational success in recent years. Liberal feminists have an optimistic view of the future for women. Both partners will, they suggest, accept equal

Gender, life-chances and stereotyping

Although girls now outperform boys in terms of numbers of GCSEs and A-level qualifications, there are clear differences in subjects studied. English Literature and Sociology each had 70 per cent of entries from girls, while 76 per cent of Physics entries were by boys. In vocational training, gender differences are even more marked, with females heavily dominating early-years care and hairdressing, while males dominate plumbing, electrical work and construction.

Although women make up 46 per cent of the workforce, they are underrepresented in many jobs with power and influence. For example, only 18 per cent of MPs are women and only 8.3 per cent of senior police officers and top judges.

Women constitute only 9.1 per cent of editors of national newspapers and 4.3 per cent of the chief executives of large media companies. The media are a continuing source of conventional gender stereotyping.

Toy manufacturers also develop and market toys specifically for girls or boys. Not only are they stereotyped, but many boys' games and toys are noticeably violent and aggressive.

Even before birth, expectations based on gender may affect how a child is perceived by its parents. Some parents, especially fathers, hope their firstborn will be a son in order to continue the family name and to be a protector to any younger (girl) children that follow. Once a child is born, it is treated in gendered ways, and studies have shown that a mother will react differently to a baby depending on whether they are told that it is a girl or a boy.

More examples of gender stereotyping from the topics you have studied can be found throughout this book and its AS-level companion.

Adapted from various pamphlets and the website of the Equal Opportunities Commission (www.eoc.org.uk)

responsibility for domestic work and child-rearing, and dual-career families where both partners enjoy equal economic status will become the norm. Legislators are also beginning to recognize male responsibility for childcare with the recent increases in paternity rights.

Liberal feminism has been subject to some criticisms:

- Although there is evidence that masculinity and femininity are socially constructed, it does not explain why this leads to men dominating and women being oppressed.
- It also implies that people passively accept their gender identities, underestimating the degree to which women may resist.
- It fails to acknowledge that women's experiences differ according to social class and race.
- In seeing gender equality as simply a matter of time, real obstacles to progress are being overlooked. During World War II, when women were required to work in munitions factories, for example, free crèche places were made available. Over half a century later, only a small percentage of workplaces provide this facility.

Marxist feminism

Women's subordination within the labour market is seen by Marxist feminists as suiting the needs of capitalism. Women form a classic example of a '**reserve army of labour**', drawn upon by prosperous firms in times of rapid expansion and disposed of when recession sets in. Women constitute a more disposable part of the workforce for a number of reasons:

- They change jobs more frequently than men, so they are more vulnerable at times of redundancy.

- They are generally less skilled, relatively underunionized and often part time. As a result, it is easier for employers to sack them.
- Capitalist ideologies locate women in the home. The idea that married women have less right to a job than men is common among management, unions and women themselves. Therefore, when women are made unemployed, such ideology suggests 'women have gone back to their proper jobs'.

The reserve army of labour theory has been criticized because it does not explain why male and female labour is put to different uses. In other words, it fails to explain why there are men's jobs and women's jobs. It fails to explain why women occupy the mother–housewife role.

Margaret Benston (1972) focused on domestic labour and its role in maintaining capitalist society. The male wage, in fact, pays for two people as the woman works for free to create a new labour force. The housewife also provides emotional support for her husband, rejuvenating him sufficiently to enable him to return for the next day's alienated labour. According to Ansley (quoted in Bernard 1976), she may even soak up his frustration and alienation in the form of domestic violence.

Marxist feminism can be criticized for overlooking the fact that patriarchy can be as influential in its own right – the implication being that once capitalism is abolished, gender inequality will disappear.

Radical feminism

According to radical feminists, oppressive and unequal relationships between men and women originate not in the wider society, but in the intimacy of personal relationships, in sexual partnerships, and in families and households of various kinds. Personal relationships are also 'political', in that they are based upon different and unequal amounts of power, which are determined by sex and which are reinforced by every aspect of the wider society. Culture, government, tradition, religion, law, education and the media all reflect patriarchal leadership and power.

Radical feminists focus on the power relationships that are experienced in private – in particular, the significance of sexuality and the use of violence. Patriarchal definitions of women's sexuality are used to control women for the benefit of men. Women are told how to look, dress and behave. When patriarchal ideology fails, then women are constantly under the threat of male violence and sexual aggression, which limits their capacity to live as free and independent beings.

Radical feminism has been criticized for failing to acknowledge historical change or to take account of divisions between women based on class or ethnicity.

Black feminists have been critical of the **ethnocentricity** of most feminist approaches, which have assumed that all women experience patriarchy in the same way. Black feminists have been among the first to point out how different forms of inequality brought about by different oppressions actually intersect. Bhavani (2000) puts the following question: 'When comparing racism to sexism, which is more fundamental?' In her view, the question is unanswerable. It is like asking which number in a multiplication is more important in terms of the answer. Racism and sexism inform each other and both are, in turn, affected by class.

Walby on patriarchy

A key concept for many feminists is patriarchy – the system of male domination of women. Sylvia Walby (1990) has examined the idea of patriarchy in some detail. She argues that patriarchy has moved from private patriarchy, where women were limited to the domestic sphere, to public patriarchy where women have entered the public arenas of employment, politics and so on, but are still disadvantaged. As she puts it, 'women are no longer restricted to the domestic hearth, but have the whole society in which to roam and be exploited'.

Walby argues that patriarchy intersects with capitalism and racism to produce gender stratification. She identifies six key patriarchal social structures:

- *the area of paid work* – where women are restricted because of the ideology that 'a woman's place is in the home'; this leads to low pay and discrimination
- *the household* – where female labour is exploited in the family
- *the state* – which acts in the interests of men rather than women in terms of taxation and welfare rules, the weakness of laws protecting women at work, and so on
- *cultural institutions such as the mass media* – which represent women in narrow social roles such as sex objects and mother–housewives
- *sexuality* – where a double standard persists that values multiple sexual partners for men but condemns the same behaviour in women.

- *violence against women* – in the form of sexual assault and domestic violence.

Walby does acknowledge that inequalities between men and women vary over time and in intensity. For example, young women are now achieving better educational qualifications than men. The intensity of patriarchy has to some extent lessened. Nevertheless, women remain disadvantaged. In her book *Gender Transformations* (1997), Walby reviewed progress made since the 1980s. She notes continuing disparities, particularly for groups of women such as single parents. She also notes that the most powerful positions in all aspects of society continue to be held by men. She concludes that patriarchy continues to exist but that different **gender regimes** affect groups of women differently.

Preference theory

Catherine Hakim (2000) has examined data about gender and work from across the world. She argues that reliable contraception, equal-opportunities legislation, the expansion of white-collar and part-time jobs and the increase in lifestyle choices give women in modern societies more choices than ever before. But women do not respond to these choices in a uniform way. She identifies three main types of work–lifestyle preferences.

- *Home-centred* – For about 20 per cent of women, family life and children are their main priorities so they prefer not to be in employment.
- *Adaptive* – The majority of women (about 60 per cent) are those who want to combine family and paid work in some way.
- *Work-centred* – The 20 per cent of women whose priority is paid work or other involvement in public life. Childless women are concentrated in this category.

Hakim goes on to argue that, given the variety of women's preferences, conflicts are created between different groups of women – the policies and practices that suit one group do not necessarily work in the interests of the others. Men, however, are much more alike in their preferences – most fit into the 'work-centred' category. This is one cause of the continuation of male dominance or patriarchy.

Hakim's work has provoked much debate, particularly within feminism. For example, Ginn *et al.* (1996) point out that all too often it is employer attitudes rather than women's work orientation that confine women to the secondary labour market or the home.

Postfeminism

Postfeminism has two strands. The first asserts that feminism is no longer necessary, as women have largely won equality and, in any case, went too far in criticizing men, the family and femininity. Faludi (1992) sees this as a male-inspired backlash against feminism. She notes how politicians, business leaders and advertisers among others have, on the one hand, recognized women's equality, while on the other highlighting its cost to women. Magazines in the USA, for example, claim that professional women are prone to alcoholism, hair loss and infertility, while women without children suffer more hysteria and depression.

The second strand abandons the feminist grand theories to adopt a more postmodern position. Brooks (1997) argues that there needs to be a shift from the old debates about equality to debates about difference. Postmodern feminists consider that terms like 'patriarchy' and 'women' overgeneralize and ignore the different influences of male ideology in different contexts and among different groups and that all women do not experience oppression in the same way. They consider there to be a range of masculinities and femininities and attack the idea that some characteristics should be preferred over others. They concentrate on the differences between women and some writers have actually become known as 'difference feminists'.

Conclusion: which is more important, gender or class?

Feminists, particularly radical feminists, have pointed to the importance of gender inequalities in society. For many of these writers, despite cosmetic improvements to the position of women, gender is the most significant social division in modern societies.

However, for many years when sociologists talked about social inequality, they meant social class. This concern with social class is a longstanding tradition, especially in British sociology. However, Pilcher and Whelehan (2004) identify three key developments since the 1970s that have threatened the predominance of class analysis:

- Social and economic changes – These include the rise of flexible working, unemployment and the growth of political movements based on factors such as gender and ethnicity.
- The criticisms of traditional analysis of class made by feminists – Writers such as Walby (1990) have pointed out that much conventional sociology has either ignored gender or failed to recognize the importance of gender in structuring other forms of inequality.
- The emergence of postmodern perspectives which have directed attention towards diversity, difference and the analysis of specific situations – These have undermined the traditional focus on large social and economic groupings such as classes.

Today, rather than claim that class, gender or any other form of social inequality is more important, sociologists focus on the way different sources of social inequality and identity are interwoven. For example, Skeggs' (1997) research on a group of white, working-class women leads her to conclude that class cannot be understood without gender and vice versa. Similarly, Anthias (2001) argues that class, gender and ethnicity each involve distinctive features, but together create the conditions we live in and the opportunities we have.

The next topic considers the third in her list: ethnicity.

Sociology A2 for OCR

Check your understanding

1 Using your own words, explain the difference between horizontal and vertical segregation.

2 What is the relationship between vertical segregation and the glass ceiling?

3 How can dual labour-market theory be used to explain vertical segregation?

4 Why have some sociologists argued that a 'crisis of masculinity' exists?

5 How does human capital theory justify the gender pay gap? How can it be criticized?

6 How does Walby use the concept of patriarchy to explain gender stratification?

7 According to Hakim, why are women now able to have different 'preferences' for their work/lifestyle balance?

8 What does Faludi mean by the 'backlash'?

9 How does postmodern feminism differ from other forms?

10 Why is class analysis less popular with sociologists than 50 years ago?

research ideas

1 Try to get hold of a staff list from your school or college. Find out which of the staff are in which positions. To what extent does the institution you are studying in reflect vertical segregation?

2 Interview a sample of younger and older women about feminism. What meaning do they give to feminism? To what extent do their views reflect different types of feminism?

web.task

1 Find out the range of feminist views on a series of different issues by exploring the site: http://feminism.eserver.org/

2 Find the latest statistics on the position of men and women in British society at the website of the Equal Opportunities Commission at www.eoc.org.uk

KEY TERMS

Dual labour-market theory – see Key Terms p. 339.

Ethnocentricity – the view that your own culture is 'normal' and all others 'abnormal'.

Gender regimes – term used by Walby to illustrate how patriarchy continues to exist but affects different groups of women in different ways.

Glass ceiling – invisible barrier preventing women from gaining high-status positions in employment.

Horizontal segregation – gender division in the workplace whereby men and women work in different jobs in different occupational sectors.

Human capital – education, training and employment experience believed to give some employees pay advantages.

Patriarchy – system of male domination.

Postfeminism – recent views on gender influenced by postmodernism.

Post-Fordism – flexible methods of producing goods focused on variety of consumer choice. ('Fordism' refers to car-maker, Henry Ford, who invented the production line where every item produced was identical.)

Reserve army of labour – Marxist concept used to describe an easily exploitable pool of workers who can be moved in and out of the labour market as it suits capitalists.

Vertical segregation – gender division in the workplace whereby women occupy the lower levels of pay and status in particular jobs.

exploring gender and inequality

Item A

Changes in the pay gap over time

Ratio of women's to men's pay, based on average hourly pay of full-time employees, excluding overtime

Source: *New Earnings Survey*

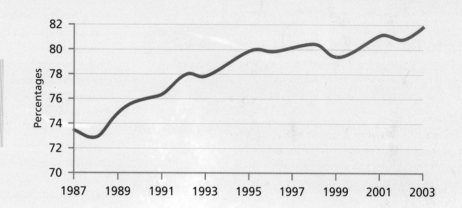

Item B

During her lifetime, a woman will earn over a quarter of million pounds less than the average man – and this is without taking motherhood into account, which adds another £140 000! The pay gap is not only disastrous for women, but for everyone because it reduces family incomes. But why are women earning less than men?

First, women work in low-paid sectors of the economy, such as retail and caring. Second, the existence of the 'glass ceiling' – men predominate in management, with women clustered in the lower-paid roles of organizations. Pay discrimination – inequality and lack of transparency in pay systems – discriminates against women.

Finally, women still take the major responsibility for caring and domestic duties, leaving them unable to have real choices about their working lives.

Adapted from Equal Opportunities Commission (2005) *Equal Pay Year* brochure, EOC

(a) Using **Item A**, identify **two** trends in pay differences between men and women that occur during the course of women's working lives. (6 marks)

(b) Identify **two** reasons why women are earning less than men according to **Item B**. (6 marks)

(c) Identify and explain **two** ways that sociologists might research women's attitudes towards inequality at work. (12 marks)

(d) Using your wider sociological knowledge, outline the evidence for the view that gender is still a major source of inequality in UK society. (22 marks)

(e) Outline and assess sociological explanations of the view that gender rather than class is the most important social division in modern industrial societies. (44 marks)

Ethnicity and inequality

gettingyouthinking

Blue Mink (shown left), a group with both White and Black members, from both Britain and the US, released the song 'Melting Pot' in 1969. The boy band, Boyzone released a cover version in 1996 with slight changes to the lyrics (see below – original lyrics in brackets).

Melting Pot (Blue Mink 1969/Boyzone 1996)

Take a pinch of white man
Wrap it up in black skin
Add a touch of blue blood
And a little bitty-bit of red
  indian boy
Curly, black and kinkies
Oriental sexy (mixed with
  yellow Chinkees)
If you lump it all together
Well, you've got a recipe for
  a get-along scene
Oh what a beautiful dream
If it could only come true
You know, you know

Chorus:
*What we need is a great big
  melting pot,*
*Big enough to take the world
  and all it's got*
*Keep it stirring for a hundred
  years or more*
*And turn out coffee-coloured
  people by the score*

Rappers in the fires (Rabbis
  and the friars)
Bishops and the gurus
  (Vishnus and the gurus)
We had (You got) the Beatles
  or the Sun-Gods (a long
  time ago – it's true)
Well it really didn't matter
  (Well it really doesn't
  matter)
What religion you choose
No no no

Mick and Lady Faithful and
  everyone who's graceful
  (and Mrs Graceful)
You know that living could be
  tasteful
We should all get together in
  a lovin' machine
I'd better call up the Queen
It's only fair that she knows
You know, you know

1 The song originally came out at a time when racial tension was high in the USA. What way forward does the song propose to promote racial harmony?

2 Many people would argue that the route proposed to racial harmony, although well intentioned, is racist. Why?

3 Why do you think the later version amended the lyrics of the original? Did this make it any more acceptable?

There is some evidence of a shift in thinking over the past 30 years, from treating everyone the same to positively recognizing and accommodating difference. This can be seen in the many multicultural celebrations throughout British cities every summer. A government report (Foster *et al.* 2005) assessing the impact of the Stephen Lawrence enquiry (into the murder of an 18-year-old Black youth who died from stab wounds following a racist attack in 1993) further highlights this shift:

>> *Every individual must be treated with respect. 'Colour-blind' policing must be outlawed. The police must deliver a service which recognizes the different experiences, perceptions and needs of a diverse society.* >>

Miles (1989) has argued that a key factor in the positioning of most ethnic-minority groups at the bottom of the stratification system is **racism**. This can be seen as a system of beliefs and practices that exclude on the basis of racial or ethnic background. The term '**race**' was once used to suggest biological differences between groups, but has since been discredited in that sense and abandoned in favour of the term '**ethnicity**' or 'ethnic minority'. However, it has reemerged recently as a useful term for focusing attention on power differences between groups. Ethnicity, meaning cultural grouping, lacks this power dimension. As Kenyatta and Tai (1999) note:

<< In abandoning the concept of race, there is a serious tendency to abandon discussions of power, domination, and group conflict ... I cannot help but notice in works on ethnicity how quickly the discussion there turns to matters of culture and identity, not at all to questions of economic exploitation, political power, and powerlessness. >>

Racism

Racism has three key elements: **cultural attitudes/prejudice**, racial discrimination and institutional discrimination.

Cultural attitudes/prejudice

Racism represents a way of thinking that relies heavily on stereotypes that are usually factually incorrect, exaggerated and distorted. These are used to legitimate hostility towards ethnic groups perceived to have negative characteristics.

Prejudice is part of a society's culture and passed from generation to generation through the agencies of socialization. It is only fairly recently, for example, that children's reading books have begun to reflect ethnic diversity, and many offensive racist images are still to be seen. Despite the increase in Black footballers over the last 30 years, racist chanting from the terraces has still not entirely disappeared, while the terrorist attacks on New York in 2001 and the UK in 2005 have increased Islamophobia, with the result that many Asians of all religions have experienced prejudice.

When ethnic difference is actually recognized, many feel that there is insufficient attention paid to the specific origins and experience of the group concerned. As Bhopal et al. (1991) pointed out:

<< The term 'Asian' is applied to people who have come to Britain from many different parts of the world, most notably India, Pakistan, Bangladesh, Uganda, Kenya and Tanzania, and from peasant or urban middle class backgrounds; they are also differentiated in their religion, language, caste, kinship obligations, diet, clothing, health beliefs, and birth and burial practices, and yet there is an inbuilt assumption through the use of the term that they all share a common background and experience. >>

Barker (1982) notes that the New Right, in an attempt to exploit fears about unemployment in the 1980s and 1990s, have focused on the concept of 'cultural differences'. They have suggested that traditional British/English culture is under threat from ethnic-minority culture or that ethnic minorities are not committed to integration. The mass media too, especially tabloid newspapers, such as the *Sun* and *Daily Mail*, have tended to portray Black people, Muslims and migrants from Eastern Europe as a 'problem' and a threat to the British way of life. There are many problems with these views:

- They offer an oversimplified view of what traditional English culture is like – e.g. warm beer and cricket on village greens.
- They exaggerate the 'strangeness' of other cultures, further fuelling prejudice.

- They play down the problem of racism and imply that if the problem does exist, the fault lies with the 'reluctance' of ethnic minorities to adopt a British way of life.

In part hastened by the bombings in London by British-born Muslims on 7 July 2005, the government announced plans in 2005 to introduce a new test of 'Britishness' for all those hoping to become British citizens. Applicants may have to answer questions on everything from Geordie accents and single-parent families, to workers' rights and elections, the Church of England, how to visit Parliament, and minimum ages for buying alcohol. British history and culture, however, are not included. The 45-minute multiple-choice test must be passed before someone can become a British citizen.

Racial discrimination

This is evident in the discrimination by landlords, building societies and council housing departments that has been well documented. It may take the form of racial attacks – this includes racist name-calling and street violence. The murder of Stephen Lawrence brought the enormity of this problem to the British public's attention. This case also highlighted the prejudice of the police officers involved in the enquiry who initially did not take Stephen's injuries seriously enough, did not accept that he was the victim of a racial attack and then mishandled the apprehension of known assailants.

Furthermore, many Black youths experience police harassment. They are more likely to be stopped and arrested on suspicion than White youths (see Synoptic link on p. 335). There is also a body of evidence showing police violence against ethnic minorities and some have suffered injury and even death in police custody (see Unit 2, pp. 75–6).

Institutional racism

Some sociologists argue that racism is a basic feature of the rules and routines of Britain's social institutions, such as the police and courts, the immigration service, central and local government, the mass media, the education system, and the employment and housing markets. Racism is taken for granted and is so common that it is not even recognized as racism. For example, chief constables have been accused of being complacent about the amount of racial prejudice among police officers.

Britain's immigration laws are often cited as an example of institutional racism. The laws restrict the entry of Black people while allowing White migrants easier entry. There is also evidence that the laws have been implemented in a racist manner. For example, Black visitors are more likely than White visitors to be stopped for questioning by immigration control. Both the Home Office and the London Metropolitan Police have admitted that their organizations are institutionally racist (Select Committee on Home Affairs 1999).

Institutional racism is not conscious nor intentional. That said, it would not be true to say that all members of key institutions are nonracist – they may or may not be. But it is the manner in which some institutions operate that has racist outcomes. Teachers, for example, may be committed to antiracist education but schools still expel four times as many Black pupils as White.

One way of tackling institutional racism is to increase the numbers of ethnic-minority employees working within key institutions, especially in the higher positions. Also, close monitoring of inclusion and exclusion of ethnic-minority groups can highlight imbalances that can then be addressed through equal-opportunities strategies.

Ethnic minorities and life-chances: empirical evidence

Ethnic minorities are disadvantaged in many areas of social life. However, it is very important to be aware of the significant differences between the various minorities, and of the way inequalities also link with gender and class differences. For example, the majority of Muslim immigrants entered Britain at the bottom of the socio-economic ladder. Many (mostly Pakistanis and Bangladeshis) are still concentrated in semi-skilled and unskilled sectors of industry. These communities suffer from unemployment, poor working conditions, poverty, overcrowded housing, poor health, and low educational qualifications. The 2001 disturbances in Oldham, Burnley and Bradford highlighted how multiple social deprivation leads to deep disaffection, alienation and frustration. The areas most affected suffered from relatively high levels of youth unemployment, inadequate youth facilities, and a lack of strong civic identity or shared social values to unite the diverse local communities. Those communities remain strongly polarized along ethnic, cultural, religious and economic lines. A feeling of 'us' and 'them' developed between communities, enabling divisive racist organizations such as the British National Party (BNP) to exploit anti-Muslim feelings among many White people. However, a degree of social mobility exists within British Muslim communities. In the early 1990s, the proportion of Pakistanis in professional occupations already exceeded that for White people; successful business ventures in property, food, services and fashion have continued to expand. Many Pakistanis have moved to affluent suburbia. There is a high proportion of skilled Arab settlers employed in professional positions as engineers, professors, doctors and businesspeople. Currently, there are over 5000 Muslim millionaires in Britain.

synoptic link

health – education – wealth, poverty and welfare

Health

- Infant mortality is 100% higher among the children of African-Caribbean or Pakistani mothers than among children of White mothers.
- Pakistani and Bangladeshi people are five times more likely to be diagnosed with diabetes and 50% more likely to have coronary heart disease than White people.
- African-Caribbean women have 80% higher rates for diagnosed hypertension than Whites.
- 2000 fully qualified asylum-seeking and refugee doctors are either prohibited from working or are forced into unskilled work.

Education

- In 2002, 2000 asylum-seeking children did not receive formal education.
- Bangladeshi, Pakistani and Black pupils achieve less than other pupils at all stages of compulsory education. African-Caribbean children have equal, if not higher, ability than White children on entrance to school, but African-Caribbean boys do least well at school. In 2003, only 41% of Pakistani pupils, 37% of Black pupils, and 45% of Bangladeshi pupils achieved 5 or more GCSEs at grades A* to C, compared with 51% of White pupils and 65% of Indian pupils.
- African-Caribbean pupils are over four to six times more likely to be excluded than White pupils, and three times more likely to be excluded permanently. Many of those excluded are of higher or average ability, although the schools see them as underachieving.

- Over half of children from Traveller and Gypsy/Roma heritage and Asian Bangladeshi groups were eligible for free school meals (an indicator of low income). Children who were eligible for free school meals were far less likely to achieve the expected outcomes for Key Stages 1 to 4.

Public services

- 35% of Black people believe they will receive worse treatment than others from the police.
- About a third of Black people believe immigration services will treat them worse than they treat others.
- 28% identified prisons and courts as places where they could expect poorer treatment than other people.

Housing

- 70% of all people from ethnic minorities live in the 88 most deprived local authority districts, compared with 40% of the general population.
- Almost half of all people from ethnic-minority groups live in London, where they make up 28% of all residents.
- A fifth of the housing occupied by asylum seekers is unfit for human habitation.
- Some ethnic-minority groups are more likely to live in poor housing (English House Condition Survey 1996). 30% of Bangladeshi and 22% of Pakistani households live in overcrowded housing (all types of tenancy), reflecting a lack of larger housing and lower incomes (from the Survey of English Housing 1999 to 2002).

Work

- One in eight people from ethnic-minority groups reported discrimination at a job interview.
- The number of employment tribunal claims under race discrimination was 3183 in 2001/02, almost double the number of cases in 1995. Statistics demonstrate that race discrimination cases remain the least likely to succeed of all tribunal cases and thus the percentage chance of success is very low indeed. Thus recent research indicates that only 16% of race discrimination cases win at tribunals. This figure is startlingly low, when one considers the level of apparent discrimination suffered by certain minorities at work.
- Those interviewed report being passed over for promotion, putting up with racist language, management only paying lip service to equal opportunities, and more subtle discrimination (TUC).
- Unemployment is considerably higher among ethnic-minority communities. In 2002, on average, 4.7% of White people of working age were unemployed, but among people from ethnic minorities it was nearly treble that at 14%. It was 16% for Pakistani people and 21% for Bangladeshi people.
- The disparity is even greater among the young, with 37% of Bangladeshis aged 16 to 24 and 35% of Pakistanis unemployed compared with 11% of White.
- An African-Caribbean graduate is more than twice as likely to be unemployed as a White graduate, while an African is seven times as likely.
- Ethnic-minority men are overrepresented in the service sector. The distribution industry (including restaurants and retail businesses) is the largest single source of service-sector jobs for men from ethnic-minority groups, employing 70 per cent of Bangladeshi and 58 per cent of Chinese men. In contrast, only 17 per cent of White and 19 per cent of Black men work in this industry (Labour Market trends 2000).

The legal system

- Racial harassment incidents are widespread and underreported — it is estimated that only 5% of incidents are reported to the police.
- Ethnic minorities are overrepresented throughout the criminal justice system from 'stop and search' to prison.
- Black people were eight times more likely to be stopped and searched than White people, and Asian people were almost three times more likely to be stopped and searched than White people.
- In a recent publication, *Race Equality in Prison*, the Commission for Racial Equality (CRE) found that for every 100 000 White people in Britain, 188 were in jail. For Black people, this figure was 1704. Black people are, therefore, over nine times more likely to be in prison than their White counterparts.
- People from ethnic minorities made up 18% of the male prison population and 24% of the female prison population, with Black people alone accounting for 12% of the male and 18% of the female prison population.
- 89% of young Black prisoners were sentenced for over 12 months compared to 75% of young White and 77% of Asian prisoners.

Sources: Commission for Racial Equality 2002; Home Office (2001) *Home Office Citizenship Survey: People, Families and Communities*, HORS 270; Trade Union Congress: *Black and Excluded* 2002, *Black and Underpaid* 2002, *Labour Research*, April 2002; Employment Tribunal Service 2001/02; DFES 2003.

Explanations of racism and racial inequality

Cultural explanations

Stereotypes associated with cultural racism probably originate in Britain's colonial past. People pick up these stereotypes today in the course of normal socialization. A great deal of prejudice is, therefore, the result of faulty stereotypes and a lack of accurate knowledge about the true nature of Black people. This is particularly so for those who live outside the inner city where most ethnic-minority people reside. However, The Chair of the Commission for Racial Equality Trevor Phillips, commented at the CRE Race in Media Awards 2005 that reality TV has done more for racial understanding than any other media creation in recent years. He said shows like Big Brother gave people a more varied view of what Asian and Black people could be like. So-called 'reality TV', he said, has given many British people a chance to encounter people from other ethnic groups they would never meet in their own everyday lives.

The host–immigrant model

A good example of an early sociological approach that stressed the importance of culture is the host–immigrant model (Patterson 1965), which shares many of the assumptions of functionalist sociology.

This theory depicted Britain as a basically stable, homogeneous and orderly society with a high degree of consensus over values and norms. This equilibrium was disturbed by the arrival of immigrant 'strangers' who subscribed to different sets of values. Patterson described the culture clash between West Indians (boisterous and noisy, and not in the habit of queuing at bus stops!) and the English hosts (who valued privacy, quiet and 'keeping oneself to oneself'). The host–immigrant model interpreted these clashes in terms of understandable fears and anxieties on the part of the host community. The hosts were not actually racist, just very unsure about how to act towards the newcomers. Their confusion sometimes spilled over into suspicion and resentment because the migrants competed with hosts for jobs and houses. For Patterson, the main problem was not so much racism or Black–White hostility, as cultural 'strangeness'. She was reasonably optimistic about the long-term prospects for racial harmony. She thought Britain's Black migrants would eventually move toward full cultural assimilation by shedding their 'old' ethnic values and taking on the values of the host society.

Criticisms

- The host–immigrant model focuses so much on culture that it tends to end up 'blaming the victim' or scapegoating them, by attributing the difficulties of ethnic groups to their 'strange' cultures.
- Racial hostility has not declined as predicted by Patterson. The basic structure of British society remains unchanged and the struggle over jobs, housing and money continues. This may create racial tension.
- Patterson underestimated the persistence and vitality of ethnic-minority cultures.

Today the goal of 'assimilation' has largely been abandoned by policymakers. Instead 'cultural pluralism' (where ethnic minorities retain their own cultures while adjusting to a society which accepts cultural diversity) is the norm.

Weberian explanations

Explanations based on the thinking of Max Weber (1864–1920) fall into three categories.

Status inequality

There is not only a class struggle for status, income and wealth, but there is also an ethnic struggle. However, status and power are in the hands of the majority-ethnic group, thereby making it difficult for ethnic-minority groups to compete equally for jobs, housing, etc. Ethnic minorities who do manual jobs are technically part of the working class, but are likely to face prejudice and discrimination from the White working class because they suffer from status inequality as well as class inequality. Even middle-class Asians doing professional jobs may experience status inequality in the form of prejudicial attitudes held by members of both the White middle and working classes.

Organization of the job market

Such prejudice and discrimination can be seen in the distribution of ethnic minorities in the labour force. The '**dual labour-market**' theory focuses on ethnic inequalities as well as gender inequalities in employment. There are two markets for labour:

- the primary sector, characterized by secure, well-paid jobs, with long-term promotion prospects dominated by White men

- the secondary sector consisting of low-paid, unskilled and insecure jobs.

Barron and Norris (1976) point out that women and Black people are more likely to be found in the secondary sector. They are less likely to gain primary-sector employment because employers may subscribe to racist beliefs about the unsuitability of Black people – and even practise discrimination against them, either by not employing them or by denying them responsibility and promotion.

Furthermore, the legal and political framework supporting Black people is weak. Trade unions are generally White-dominated and have been accused of favouring White workers and being less interested in protecting the rights of Black workers. The Race Relations Act 1976 (which was supposed to protect Black people from discriminatory practices) was generally thought to be feeble. However, the recent amendment to the Race Relations Act which came into force in 2001, increases the need for greater clarity concerning the meaning and status of race. Building on the Macpherson report into the murder of Stephen Lawrence, it extends coverage of the Race Relations Act 1976 to the functions of public authorities in general – not just the police. It also 'places a general duty on public authorities to work towards the elimination of unlawful discrimination and promote equality of opportunity and good relations between persons of different racial groups'. With this amendment, the Race Relations Act has a much wider impact – seeking to ensure that racial discrimination is outlawed throughout the public sector and placing a duty on all public bodies and authorities to promote good race relations. It is too early, though, to say whether this amendment has had any real impact.

Underclass

Rex and Tomlinson (1979) argue that ethnic-minority experience of both class and status inequality can lead to poverty, which is made more severe by racism. Consequently, a Black underclass may be created of people who are marginalized and feel alienated and frustrated. Sometimes, if young Blacks feel they are being harassed by the police and socially excluded, these feelings may erupt in the form of inner-city riots.

In criticism, there is considerable overlap between the White and Black population in terms of poverty and unemployment, but the constant threat of racism does suggest some sort of break with the interests of the White working class. In addition, the concept of status inequality does help to explain the apparent divisions between the White and Black working class.

Marxist explanations

Marxists argue that Black people are part of the exploited working class and it is this, rather than any lack of status due to ethnicity, that determines their fate in capitalist society. Racial conflicts are usually the symptoms of some deeper underlying class problem.

Marxists suggest that racism and racial inequality are deliberately encouraged by the capitalist class for three ideological reasons:

Tariq Modood *et al.* (1997)
Ethnic minorities in Britain

The fourth major survey of ethnic minorities in Britain, carried out in 1997 by the independent Policy Studies Institute, together with survey specialists SCPR, showed that ethnic-minority groups should no longer all be seen to be in the same position. The differences between minority groups are as important as the Black–White divide. The study also suggested that some groups can no longer be considered economically disadvantaged.

Ethnic Minorities in Britain: Diversity and Disadvantage is still the largest study of ethnic minorities ever carried out in Britain. It was based on detailed interviews with 5196 people of Caribbean, South Asian and Chinese origin, while 2867 White people were also surveyed to provide a comparison.

The study extended the scope of race-relations research by investigating several issues in new ways. Among its key findings:

- Ethnic variations in health can be explained by socio-economic circumstances rather than biological or cultural factors.
- Racial prejudice, discrimination and harassment were still problems which concern all minority groups, and a quarter of a million people suffer harassment every year.
- Distinct cultural practices are giving way among the British-born to more culturally mixed lifestyles; younger generations have a more assertive attitude to their ethnic identity, certainly compared with their grandparents, who typically arrived with a desire to fit in, even if that meant suppressing their own traditions.
- Of those born in Britain, half of Caribbean men and a third of Caribbean women have a White partner. Getting on for half of 'Caribbean' children have one White parent.

Modood, T., Berthoud, R., Lakey, J., Nazroo, J., Smith, P. , Virdee, S. and Beishon, S. (1997) *Ethnic Minorities in Britain: Diversity and Disadvantage*, London: Policy Studies Institute

1 How do the findings support the view that ethnic-minority groups are not to blame for the inequalities that they experience?

2 What evidence is there both from the report and elsewhere that the 'melting pot' idea of racial harmony (see 'Getting you thinking', p. 332) has some validity?

- *Legitimization* – Racism helps justify low pay and poor working conditions because Black workers are seen as second-class citizens. Capitalist employers benefit from the cheap labour of ethnic minorities.
- *Divide and rule* – If Black and White workers unite, then they are in a stronger position to campaign for better wages and conditions. Marxists such as Castles and Kosack (1973) argue that employers prefer them to be divided by racism so they can be played off against one another. Employers may use the Black workforce as a '**reserve army of labour**' to prevent White workers from demanding higher wages.
- *Scapegoating* – When a society is troubled by severe social and economic problems, then widespread frustration and aggression can arise. Instead of directing this anger at the capitalist class, Whites are sometimes tempted to pick on relatively vulnerable groups. They use Black people as scapegoats and it may be Blacks who are blamed for unemployment and housing shortages. Scapegoating is in the interests of the richer and more powerful groups

because it protects them from direct criticism and reduces pressures for radical change.

Miles (1989) argues that the class position of Black people is complicated by the fact that they are treated as socially and culturally different. They become the victims of racist ideologies which prevent their full social inclusion. Miles argues that ethnic minorities are members of '**racialized class fractions**'. While most Black people are members of the working class, they also recognize the importance of their ethnicity. While members of the White working class may stress the importance of ethnicity through prejudice and discrimination, Black people may react by stressing their ethnicity in actions such as campaigning for recognition of their need to observe particular religious or cultural traditions.

Miles acknowledges that some ethnic minorities may become part of the middle classes and see their interests lying with capitalism. Furthermore, their ethnicity may be a crucial influence in their business practices and financial success. However, the fact of their ethnicity probably makes it impossible for them to be fully accepted by the White middle class.

Recent approaches

It would be a mistake to think that all Black people 'lose out'. Owen and Green (1992) cite Indians and Chinese as two ethnic groups that have made significant economic progress in the British labour market since the 1980s. Recent figures indicate that their average earnings are indeed similar to those of White workers. More generally, evidence suggests that increasing numbers from the ethnic minorities are entering the ranks of the professional middle class. Sociologists are also starting to notice the growth of 'Black businesses' and the spread of self-employment among ethnic minority groups. Even though groups such as Indians are moving into white-collar work, it is quite possible that Whites fill the higher status positions within this sector.

However, some sociologists have questioned whether self-employment is really a privileged sector of the economy. Minorities may be forced into setting up their own businesses because racial discrimination prevents them from getting employment. Sometimes, these businesses are precarious ventures in extremely competitive markets, offering small returns for long hours and with the owners only managing to survive because they are able to draw upon cheap family labour.

Postmodernist approaches

Postmodernists, such as Modood (1992), reject the notions of Weberian and Marxist sociology that seek to generalize and offer blanket explanations for ethnic groups as a whole. They stress difference and diversity among ethnic groups and focus on identity. They argue that the globalization of culture has led to national cultural identities being eroded. British culture is not immune, and all ethnicities, including White, have begun to 'pick and mix', producing an array of new **hybrid identities**. Racial difference becomes a matter of choice and racial disadvantage is impossible to discuss as ethnic identity is not fixed.

The extent and impact of racism will differ from person to person as identities are chosen and interact. Postmodernists argue that once identity is better understood, targeted ethnic disadvantage can be addressed. Once we know that Jamaican boys not born in Britain in a particular area are more likely to drop out of school, for example, then something meaningful could be done to address this problem.

While postmodern ideas are illuminating, they can be accused of neglecting social and economic factors that impact on life-chances.

Check your understanding

1. **How can it be argued that the term 'race' has more explanatory value than the term 'ethnicity'?**

2. **Where does racial prejudice come from? Give examples to back up your arguments.**

3. **Explain why members of organizations deemed 'institutionally racist' may not necessarily be racist individuals.**

4. **How can institutional racism be tackled?**

5. **What is wrong with early functionalist explanations of ethnic inequality?**

6. **Why has assimilation been abandoned by policymakers?**

7. **Briefly summarize three Weberian accounts of ethnic inequality in the workplace.**

8. **How do Marxists argue that racism benefits capitalism?**

9. **Why do postmodernists reject Weberian and Marxist explanations of ethnic inequality?**

research ideas

1. Carry out a piece of research to explore local people's knowledge of ethnic differences. Do they understand the distinctions between the various Asian groups? Do they understand the significance of particular festivals? Do they know of prophets or holy books? Can they point on a world map outline to the countries of origin of the various groups?

2. Assess the extent to which an organization such as your school or college might be deemed to be institutionally racist. Look at the distribution of ethnic groups on the various courses. Try to acquire statistics on exclusions, achievement rates and progression. What problems might you encounter in your research and how might you overcome them?

web.tasks

1. **Go to the guardianunlimited website at** www.guardianunlimited.co.uk. **Search the archive by typing in 'race equality'. Read the articles highlighting a range of issues from institutional racism, social policy reform to rural racism and racial harassment.**

2. **The website of the Commission for Racial Equality, at** www.cre.gov.uk/, **contains a range of research findings and factsheets. Select one or two and write summaries.**

Cultural attitudes/prejudice –
a style of thinking that relies
heavily on stereotypes that are
usually factually incorrect,
exaggerated and distorted.

Dual labour-market theory –
the view that two labour
markets exist: the first has
secure, well-paid jobs with good
promotion prospects, while the
second has jobs with little
security and low pay; vulnerable
groups such as women, the
young, elderly and ethnic
minorities are concentrated in
this second sector.

Ethnicity – cultural heritage
shared by members of a
particular group.

Hybrid identities – new
identities created by ethnic
mixing.

Institutional racism – where the
sum total of an organization's
way of operating has racist
outcomes.

Race – variation of physical
appearance, skin colour and so
on between populations that
confers differences in power
and status.

Racialized class fractions –
term used by Miles to describe
splits in the working class along
racial lines.

Racism – systematic exclusion of
races or ethnic groups from full
participation in society.

Reserve army of labour –
Marxist concept used to
describe an easily exploitable
pool of workers drawn from
vulnerable groups such as
women, ethnic minorities and
the old and young.

exploring ethnicity and inequality

Item A

Economic activity rates: by ethnic group and sex,
2001–02

United Kingdom	Male %	Female %
White	85	74
Mixed	79	62
Indian	79	62
Pakistani	73	28
Bangladeshi	69	22
Other Asian	76	57
Black Caribbean	77	72
Black African	72	56
Other Black	76	62
Chinese	69	57
Other	69	53
All ethnic groups	**84**	**72**

Adapted from ONS (2002) *Annual Local Area Labour Force Survey,
2001/02*

Item B

Why is ethnic monitoring necessary? Without the
information provided by ethnic records, it is virtually
impossible for employers to assess realistically whether
or not people are being racially discriminated against in
their institution. Given the Policy Studies Institute's (PSI)
finding that as many as a third of private employers
discriminate directly against Asian and Afro-Caribbean
job applicants, no major employer can reasonably be
satisfied that direct or indirect discrimination is not
occurring. Industrial tribunals have shown that even
where a senior manager, personally, is not
discriminating, some of his or her employees may be
operating their own informal racial barriers against
ethnic-minority job applicants or employees seeking
promotion, etc. It is the employer, however, who is
liable for the unlawful acts of his or her employees – if
it cannot be shown that all reasonably practicable steps
were taken to prevent them. In any case, personnel
practices which appear to be 'colour blind' may,
however, unintentionally include requirements or
conditions that indirectly discriminate against people
from ethnic-minority groups; they would therefore be
unlawful under the Race Relations Act 1976.

Source: Commission for Racial Equality 2005

(a) Using **Item B**, identify **two** ways in which ethnic minorities may be discriminated against in the
workplace. (6 marks)

(b) Using **Item A**, identify **two** ways in which the employment rates of Bangladeshi men and
women differ from other ethnic groups. (6 marks)

(c) Identify and explain **two** advantages of conducting interviews to collect data on inequalities
experienced by ethnic minorities. (12 marks)

(d) Using your wider sociological knowledge, outline the evidence for the view that some ethnic
minorities are disadvantaged more than others. (22 marks)

(e) Outline and assess sociological explanations of why some Black and Asian minorities are
disadvantaged in the contemporary UK. (44 marks)

THE A2 SOCIOLOGY COURSE IS WORTH exactly the same proportion of A-level marks as the AS course: that is, 50 per cent. The mark out of 300 that you gained at AS level is simply added to your total A2 mark (also out of 300) to get a final A-level score. You need 480 out of 600 to achieve a grade A, 420 for a B, 360 for a C, 300 for a D and 240 for an E. You should know your AS-level score, so it is a simple matter to work out the score you require at A2 to achieve a particular grade. But don't think you can pick up easy marks at A2. Bear in mind that the A2 course is designed to be more demanding than AS. You have to:

- use more sociological theory
- apply your knowledge and understanding of research methods in more depth
- link the key themes of the course together in the synoptic module (*Social inequality and difference*).

Your performance in the OCR A-level course will be judged either totally by exams or through a combination of exams and coursework. Either way, you need to be completely confident about the organization of the exams: how long they last, how the questions are phrased, and what knowledge and skills are being tested. You also need to be aware of the nature of the coursework task, how it is broken down and how marks are allocated.

This unit guides you through the OCR exams and coursework. It provides essential information about the content and assessment of the course, including some really useful tips for both exams and coursework. After working through this unit, you should feel a lot more confident about the way your performance will be judged and be in a good position to get full value for all the work you've put in to your A-level Sociology course. Remember that the examiner and moderators are there to ensure that you get the grade your work deserves. They mark what is written on the paper, but they can cope with the odd spelling mistake, or slip of the pen. As long as they are confident about what you meant, they can and will award you the marks. The questions have been carefully designed to be as clear as possible, and to allow students to display their knowledge to the best of their ability. If you deserve full marks, then you will be given full marks. After you have read this unit, you should feel you know what you need to do to get the mark you deserve.

Preparing for the A2 exam

What will I study?

Aim/ rationale of course

The OCR A-level specification aims to offer you a sound introduction to sociology. In particular, it aims to develop in you a sociological knowledge and understanding of social processes, structures and theories that is both contemporary and relevant to your life in the 21st century. You are positively encouraged by this specification not only to reflect on your own social identity and experience of the social world in which you live, but also to apply your knowledge and understanding of sociology to everyday life. Your experience of this specification should equip you with the necessary skills:

- to engage in sociological debate
- to be able to interpret, apply and evaluate relevant evidence
- to construct convincing sociological arguments.

Finally, this specification is designed to offer you choice and flexibility in terms of its content, its varied assessment system and its coursework options.

Themes

The A2 specification has five interlinked themes:

1. It aims to build upon knowledge and understanding acquired at AS-level relating to how and to what extent individuals shape and are shaped by social structures.
2. The specification aims to explore those agencies that exercise power and control over our daily lives and to examine how such agencies contribute to the construction of our personal identities.
3. The specification aims to build on your understanding of the concepts and skills associated with sociological research. In particular, the focus will be on practical application and evaluation of research techniques and concepts in a range of sociological contexts.
4. It aims to identify and explain the level and pattern of inequality in contemporary Britain, and how inequality and difference underpin much of our everyday experience.
5. Most importantly, the specification aims to develop in you a deeper understanding of the connections between the nature of sociological thought, research methods and all the topics that you have covered both at AS- and A2-levels. This is known as 'synoptic understanding'.

Modules

There are three modules at A2-level:

- Module 2536: Power and Control
- Module 2537: Applied Sociological Research Skills **OR** Module 2538: Personal Study
- Module 2539: Social Inequality and Difference (the synoptic unit).

Topics

- The *Power and Control* module builds upon your understanding of the social construction of norms and values, and considers issues of power, control and ideology. It includes the options of:
  - crime and deviance
  - education
  - health
  - popular culture
  - social policy and welfare
  - protest and social movements.
- The *Applied Sociological Research Skills* module enables you to build on your methodological understanding acquired as part of AS Sociological Research Skills or the Research Report.

- The *Social Inequality and Difference* module is the synoptic unit and will aim to assess your understanding of social inequalities and differences relating to class, gender and ethnic inequalities, and how these relate to research methods, sociological theory and other topics studied throughout AS and A2. This module places particular emphasis on workplace inequalities and change.

How will I be assessed?

Skills

For A2 sociology, you will be tested by the following assessment objectives:

Assessment Objective 1 (AO1): Knowledge and understanding

After studying A2, you should be able to demonstrate knowledge and understanding of abstract concepts and, particularly, theory in some depth. It is necessary to have a detailed and wide-ranging knowledge and understanding of empirical evidence and how this links to theory within the context of sociological debate. You will also need a good holistic knowledge and understanding of the connections between the core theme of social inequality and difference and one or more other topic areas, plus links between substantive topics and how these connect to theory/method.

Assessment Objective 2 (AO2a): Interpretation and Analysis

This skill essentially involves showing the ability to select and analyse a broad and diverse range of data and evidence. In particular, it involves the ability to apply and link sociological evidence to specific sociological arguments in a focused fashion in support of particular debates. It also involves the ability to interpret quantitative and qualitative data, i.e. to work out what it is saying and/or put it into your own words.

Assessment Objective 2 (AO2b): Evaluation

It is important to be able to demonstrate a highly developed critical appraisal of theory, empirical evidence and debate.

The reliability and validity of sociological evidence and its links to theory and/or debate may form the basis of this skill.

Exams

See Table 9.1 below for details of the exam papers you will need to sit.

Coursework

Unit 2538 Personal Study is offered as an alternative to the written examination in unit 2537 and represents 30% of the A2-level and 15% of the full A-level.

How can I do well in the exams?

Guidance follows on how to do well in exams unit by unit. For each unit, we consider timing and the style of questioning, offering guidance on how best to tackle that unit.

2536 Power and Control

Timing

The Power and Control examination lasts 1 hour and is worth 60 marks. You have to do one essay in that period from a choice of 12, two for each topic area. You should aim to spend 5 to 10 minutes planning this essay and 50 minutes writing it. Aim for at least three sides of the examination booklet.

Style of Questioning

This is an essay question that will ask you to 'Outline and assess' a particular 'view', i.e. a sociological debate about a particular social or sociological problem. It is highly recommended that you plan your response to this question and that your response should adopt the following format:

- *Construct a brief introduction* identifying the theoretical or empirical source of the 'view' contained in the essay title. This introduction should 'set the scene' or context of the debate, i.e. clearly state who the debate is between in terms of theories or sociologists, and/or define any technical or conceptual terms used in the title, e.g. 'hidden curriculum'.

Table 9.1 Units of assessment

Unit code	Title	Exam	% of A2-level	% of full A-level
Unit 2536	**Power and Control**	You answer one essay question in 1 hour.	30	15
Unit 2537	**Applied Sociological Research Skills**	You answer one compulsory data-response question in 1 hour 30 minutes.	30	15
Unit 2539	**Social Inequality and Difference**	You answer one data-response question in 1 hour 30 minutes	40	20

Your introduction should be approximately half a page in length.

- *Outline the point of view* in the essay title in some depth and detail.
- *Elaborate and/or illustrate that point of view* with reference to theories, empirical studies and data that support it. This is crucial, and it means learning theories, studies and statistical data, and using contemporary evidence when appropriate. Always link the evidence that you use to the view in the question. The prompt words 'This means ...' or 'This shows ...' should ensure that you are interpreting the data used.
- *Assess the point of view* contained in the essay title with specific criticisms backed up by empirical studies and/or by outlining alternative views or theories. With regard to the latter course of action, do not be content just to outline another theory. Be quite clear in what way alternative theories differ from the original view.
- *Construct a brief conclusion* based on the content of your essay. Look at the title again. Have you addressed the essential elements of the question? Clearly state which point of view your evidence supports.

2537 Applied Sociological Research Skills

Timing

The Applied Sociological Research Skills examination lasts 1 hour 30 minutes and is worth 60 marks. It comprises one compulsory five-part question. The first three parts (worth 24 marks) pose questions relating to a piece of data (Item A) on a particular sociological problem. From January 2006, the data in Item A will contain some quantitative and some qualitative evidence and will be placed in a box.

The final two parts (worth 36 marks) will require students to outline and evaluate a research design on a given topic. It is recommended that you spend 30 minutes on parts (a) to (c) and 1 hour on parts (d) to (e).

Style of Questions

This is a five-part data response question. Parts (a) to (c) are focused on **Item A**, i.e. a description of how some sociological research has been carried out and its findings. This will be presented in both a textual and statistical form, i.e. in the form of a table, chart or graph.

- Question (a) will use the phrase *'Using only Item A, identify two reasons why....'* and will always relate to the research mentioned in Item A. Do not do more than the question asks. For example, you only have to identify what is in the Item and then use that data to answer the question directly. Look for words in the question like 'how' or 'why' and make sure that you respond to these in your answer. This question is worth 6 marks.
- Question (b) will be worded *'Identify and explain two strengths (or weaknesses)'* of a particular method. The method may not necessarily be mentioned in the Item, but

is likely to be strongly related to it. Note that this question requires an explanation of what you have identified. This question is worth 8 marks.

- Question (c) will be worded *'Summarize what the research findings in Item A tell us about...'*. Make sure that you summarize both the statistical and textual data from Item A. Try to use phrases such as: 'more than', 'greater than', 'less than', 'the same as'. This question is worth 10 marks.

Item B will outline a research problem. It is likely to state that an organization/institution requires either quantitative or qualitative data in order to investigate a specific social or sociological problem. The proposal will state that you have been invited as a sociological researcher to design a proposal that targets a representative sample of whatever research population the problem is focused on. For example:

> << *A local town council requires qualitative data to discover the reasons for an increase in graffiti in the town centre.*
>
> *You have been asked as a sociological researcher to design a research proposal that will collect qualitative data from an appropriate sample.*>>

- Question (d) will be worded *'Outline and explain the research process you would adopt in collecting quantitative (or qualitative data) on'* whatever the problem is. You need to outline a strategy, naming relevant method(s). Consider issues such as sampling, access and ethics. It is crucial that you then justify your strategy. This means stating how your chosen research process meets the specific requirements of the research problem. The question is worth 14 marks.
- Question (e) will always be worded *'Assess the potential weaknesses of your research proposal, briefly explaining how you intend to overcome them'*. You are aiming here to respond to particular weaknesses of your strategy in (d). This means offering criticisms of what you have designed, and offering solutions to these problems as well. The best (e) answers respond directly to each point they have stated in (d), integrating solutions as they write. You should aim to have at least four weaknesses and solutions, more if you can. The question is worth 22 marks.

2539 Social Inequality and Difference

Timing

The synoptic Social Inequality and Difference examination lasts 1 hour 30 minutes and is worth 90 marks. You have to do one five-part data response question from a choice of two, on the themes of workplace inequality, poverty and inequalities, and/or differences based on either social class or gender or ethnicity. Questions (a) and (b) are worth 6 marks each, question (c) is worth 12 marks, question (d) 22 marks and question (e) 44 marks. Consequently, you should allocate your time so that one minute is equal to one mark.

Style of Questions

This five-part data response will be accompanied by two Items. One of these will be text-based, whilst the other is likely to take the form of a graph, chart, etc.

- Question (a) will ask you to *'Identify **two***' of something from the data, usually in Item A. The following words are likely to be used: 'ways', 'trends', 'changes', 'reasons', 'examples', 'features', 'characteristics'. It is essential that you use some of the data in your answer, whether it is numerical or text-based. The question is worth 6 marks.
- Question (b) will also ask you to *'Identify **two'*** ways, patterns, changes, trends, etc., related to Item B. Follow the same guidance as in (a). It is also worth 6 marks.

Note that both questions (a) and (b) are merely asking you to use the data. Neither is asking you to explain what you have identified, although you should make clear your identification by illustrating it with an example from the Item.

- Question (c) will ask you to *'Identify and explain **two***' problems, difficulties, advantages, disadvantages, strengths, weaknesses, etc., of a particular method of collecting information about inequality and difference. This is a *synoptic* question because it focuses on the relationship between inequality and the research methods used to research it empirically. It is worth 12 marks. Note the added action word 'explain' – you now have to justify your choice of whatever it is you have identified in relation to the context of the question.
- Question (d) will ask you, *'Using your wider sociological knowledge'* to *'outline the evidence for'* class, gender, ethnic and workplace inequalities or poverty. This too is *synoptic* because you are expected to go beyond the unit of Inequality and Difference to gather evidence to answer this question. You should use evidence gleaned from at least **two** other areas of the specifications. It is perfectly legitimate for you to use evidence gained from both AS and A2 components. You are asked to produce evidence, so your answer should contain whatever you know in relation to the question – studies, theories, concepts and contemporary examples are all likely to be relevant. This question is worth 22 marks.
- Question (e) is an essay question and will always ask you to *'outline and assess'* sociological theories/explanations. It is worth 44 marks. It is important that you plan your response to this question and adopt the essay-format style recommended above in the Power and Control section. Your answer should be theoretical in the main.

How do I do well in coursework?

Requirements

The Personal Study requires you to produce an extended piece of work on a sociological topic of a maximum of 2750 words. You are required to design a sociological investigation using

primary data and to try out this design by assembling a limited but illustrative amount of data. It is possible to use only secondary data in your study but as the emphasis is on the technical process of carrying out research, students are well advised to carry out primary research wherever possible. Very few candidates produce Personal Studies based on only secondary data. The emphasis of the Personal Study is on the design of the research, on piloting the design and evaluating the research process.

The first stage of this process involves you completing a Proposal Form that is sent to a coursework adviser at OCR. The Proposal Forms are available from your school/college and require you state a title, some aims and an outline of the methods you intend to use in your investigation. This form needs to be with the adviser by 28 February of the year in which you submit the coursework for assessment, although most forms reach the adviser before this date. The adviser will comment on your proposal, often suggesting some modifications to it, and will return it to your centre. The adviser's comments are intended to help you and you should consider them carefully. In consultation with your teacher, you should act on their recommendations; if you choose not to, it is a good idea to explain the reasons for this in your evaluation section. Occasionally, advisers will reject a proposal on ethical grounds or because the methods identified are unworkable. If this happens, you need to resubmit another proposal form.

When you have received the proposal forms back, you can begin the investigation in full. Credit is given for the width and breadth of the design of the investigation and its evaluation, rather than for the quantity and type of any data collected.

You should aim to complete:

1. A *rationale* focusing on the central research issue, question or hypothesis to be addressed, with a clear statement of the sociological reasons for carrying out the study, together with a description, explanation and justification of the research design and procedures. This section should include a set of carefully formulated aims that are achievable. A background study or sociological context should inform the study.

   Your explanation of the research design needs to include a method, theoretical perspective, operationalization of concepts, sampling procedures, access and ethics. It is recommended that this section should be in the range of 1000 words. Emphasis is on the methodology, so this should be around 750 words. Some candidates choose to write a rationale and then a separate methodology section, which is permitted.

2. The *research section* should focus on the report of the testing of the actual research design and procedures, followed by analysis and presentation of the research findings, along with conclusions reached. You should present your findings and provide an analysis or commentary of how they relate to your aims and how they compare and contrast to the study in the Rationale. Place one clean copy and one used copy of your research tool (e.g. questionnaire) in an appendix for the examiner to refer to. It is recommended that this section should be in the range of 750 words.

3. The *evaluation section* should include an evaluation of the overall research design and strategy. Aims and methodology used should also be evaluated, as well as the sampling techniques employed and some assessment of how your research findings relate to your hypothesis/aims and any ideas for the further development of the research. Researcher bias/objectivity should also be explored. It is recommended that this section should be in the range of 1000 words.

Coursework tips

- Choose an accessible topic that allows you to use straightforward research methods – one on which there is plenty of information available in textbooks.

- Spend time on your aims, making them achievable and clear. You should not need more than three aims, and two may be sufficient in many cases.

- You must keep to the word limit, otherwise your research will not be able to achieve full marks, no matter how good it is.

- It is essential to use the key concepts of reliability, validity and representativeness/generalizability throughout the sections.

- The focus is on 'doing sociology', so make sure you dedicate discussion to the operationalization of concepts in your Rationale, explaining how you intend to access the population under study via particular sampling techniques and/or gatekeepers.

- Don't overdo the presentation of your findings in regard to graphs, charts, etc. Choose two or three key findings and present them in this way. The rest can be presented textually. Make sure that you interpret your findings – don't let charts or quotations speak for themselves. Relate them back to your aims.

- Make sure your teacher has seen anything you design before you go out and do the research.

- Remember that ethics are important, so make sure that your proposed respondents have given their consent and that you have referred to the British Sociological Association's Ethical Guidelines.

- Your safety is crucial – make sure all plans are discussed with, and agreed by, your teacher.

Abel-Smith, B. and Townsend, P. (1965) *The Poor and the Poorest*, Occasional Paper on Social Administration, No. 17, London: Bell

Arber, A., Dale, S. and Gilbert, N. (1986) 'The limitations of existing social class classification of women' in A. Jacoby (ed.) *The Measurement of Social Class*, Guildford: Social Research Association

Abercrombie, N. and Warde, A. (2000) *Contemporary British Society* (3rd edn), Cambridge: Polity Press

Abercrombie, N., Hill, S. and Turner, B.S. (1980) *The Dominant Ideology Thesis*, London: Allen and Unwin

Abraham, J. (1996) *Are Girls Necessary? Lesbian Writing and Modern Histories*, London: Routledge

Acheson, Lord (1998) *The Independent Inquiry into Inequalities in Health* (The Acheson Report), London: The Stationery Office

Adler, I. (1975) *Sisters in Crime*, New York: McGraw-Hill

Adonis, A. and Pollard, S. (1998) *A Class Act: the Myth of Britain's Classless Society,* Harmondsworth: Penguin

Adorno, T.W. (1991) The Culture Industry: Selected Essays on Mass Culture, London: Routledge

Ahmad, W. and Craig, G. (1998) 'Race and Social Welfare', in P. Alcock, A. Erskine and M. May (eds*) The Student's Companion to Social Policy*, Oxford: Blackwell

Akers, R.L. (1967) 'Problems in the sociology of deviance: social definitions and behaviour', *Social Forces* 46(4)

Alexander, J. (1985) *Neo-Functionalism*, London: Sage

Alford, R.R. (1975) *Health Care Politics: Ideological and interest group barriers to reform,* Chicago: The University of Chicago Press

Althusser, L. (1969) *For Marx*, Harmondsworth: Penguin

Althusser, L. (1971) *Lenin and Philosophy and Other Essays*, London: New Left Books

Anderson, E. (1999) *Code of the Streets: Decency, Violence and the Moral Code of the Inner City*, New York: W.W. Norton

Anderson, S., Kinsey, R., Loader, I. and Smith, C. (1994) *Young People, Crime and Policing in Edinburgh,* Aldershot: Avebury

Annandale, E. (1998) *The Sociology of Health and Illness*, Cambridge: Polity Press

Annandale, E. (2004) 'Gender differences in health', in S. Taylor and D. Field (eds) *Sociology of Health and Illness*, Oxford: Blackwell

Anthias, F. (2001) 'The concept of social division and theorising social stratification: looking at ethnicity and class', *Sociology*, 35(4), pp.835–54

Arber, A., Dale, S. and Gilbert, N. (1986) 'The limitations of existing social class classification of women' in A. Jacoby (ed.) *The Measurement of Social Class*, Guildford: Social Research Association

Arnot, M., David, D. and Weiner, G. (1999) *Closing the Gender Gap,* Cambridge: Polity Press

Aron, R. (1967) 'Social class, political class, ruling class' in R. Bendix and S.M. Lipset *Main Currents in Sociological Thought,* Vols 1 and 2, Harmondsworth: Penguin

Aubert, V. (1952) 'White collar crime and social structure', *American Journal of Sociology*, 58

Bachrach, P. and Baratz, M.S. (1970) *Power and Poverty: Theory and Practice*, Oxford: Oxford University Press

Back, L. (2002) 'Youth, "race" and violent disorder', *Sociology Review*, 11(4), April

Bacon, R. and Eltis, W. (1976) *Britain's Economic Problem: Too Few Producers*, Basingstoke: Macmillan

Ball, S. (1981) *Beachside Comprehensive*, Cambridge: Cambridge University Press

Ball, S. (1995) 'Education, Majorism and the curriculum of the dead', in P. Murphy, M. Selinger and J. Bourne (eds) *Subject Learning in the Primary Curriculum*, London: Routledge

Ball, S. (2002) *Class Strategies and the Education Market: The Middle Classes and Social Advantage*, London: RoutledgeFalmer

Ball, S., Bowe, R. and Gerwitz, S. (1994) 'Market forces and parental choice', in S. Tomlinson (ed.) *Educational Reform and its Consequences*, London: Rivers Oram Press

Barber, B. (1963) 'Some problems in the sociology of professions', *Daedalus*, 92(4)

Barker, P. (1982) *The Other Britain: a New Society Collection*, London: Routledge & Kegan Paul

Barron, R.G. and Norris, G.M. (1976) 'Sexual divisions and the dual labour market', in D.J. Barker and S. Allen (eds) *Dependence and Exploration in Work and Marriage*, London: Longman

Bartkey, S.C. (1992) 'Reevaluating French feminism', in N. Fraser and S.C. Bartkey (eds) *Critical Essays in Difference, Agency and Culture*, Bloomington: Indiana University Press

Bartley, M., Carpenter, L., Dunnell, K. and Fitzpatrick, R. (1996) 'Measuring inequalities in health: an analysis of mortality patterns using two social classifications', *Sociology of Health and Illness*, 18(4) p.455–74

Baudrillard, J. (1980) *For a Critique of the Political Economy of the Sign*, New York: Telos Press

Baudrillard, J. (1994) *The Illusion of the End*, Cambridge: Polity Press

Bauman, Z. (1983) 'Industrialism, consumerism and power', *Theory, Culture and Society*, 1(3)

Beck, U. (1992) *Risk Society: Towards a New Modernity*, London: Sage

Beck, U. (1999) *World Risk Society*, Cambridge: Polity Press

Becker, H. (1963) *The Outsiders*, London: Macmillan

Becker, H. (1970) 'Whose side are we on?', in H. Becker, *Sociological Work*, New Brunswick: Transaction Books

Becker, H. (1971) 'Social class variations in the teacher–pupil relationship', in B. Cosin (ed.) *School and Society*, London: Routledge & Kegan Paul

Bell, D. (1973) *The Coming of Post-industrial Society*, New York: Basic Books

Benn, C. and Chitty, C. (1996) *Thirty Years On: Is Comprehensive Education Alive and Well or Struggling to Survive?*, London: David Fulton

Benston, M. (1972) 'The political economy of women's liberation' in N. Glazer-Mahlbin and H.Y. Wahrer (eds) (1972) *Women in a Man-made World*, Chicago: Rand MacNally

Bernard, J. (1976) *The Future of Marriage*, Harmondsworth: Penguin

Bernstein, B. (1971) *Class, Codes and Control* (Volume 1), London: Routledge & Kegan Paul

Best, L. (1993) '"Dragons, dinner ladies and ferrets": sex roles in children's books', *Sociology Review*, 2(3), February, Oxford: Philip Allan

Best, S. (2005) *Understanding Social Divisions*, London: Sage

Beynon, J. (1986) 'Turmoil in the cities', *Social Studies Review*, January

Bhavani, K. (2000) *Feminism and Race*, Oxford: Oxford University Press

Bhopal, R., Phillimore, P. and Kohli, H.S. (1991) 'Inappropriate use of the term "Asian": an obstacle to ethnicity and health research', *Journal of Public Health Medicine*, 13, pp.244–6

Blackman, S. (1995) *Youth: Positions and Oppositions, Style, Sexuality and Schooling*, Aldershot: Avebury

Blair, M., Bhattacharyya, G. and Ison, L. (2003) *Minority Ethnic Attainment and Participation in Education and Training: The Evidence,* London: DfES

Blaxter, M. (1990) *Health and Lifestyles*, London: Tavistock

Blaxter, M. (2004) *Health*, Cambridge, Polity

Blumer, H. (1962) 'Society as symbolic interaction', in N. Rose (ed.) *Symbolic Interactionism*, Englewood Hills, NJ: Prentice-Hall

Bocock, B.J. (1986) *Hegemony*, London: Tavistock

Bonger, W. (1916) *Criminality and Economic Conditions,* Chicago: Little Brown

Bordieu, P. and Passeron, J. (1977) *Reproduction in Education, Society and Culture*, London: Sage

Bottero, W. (2005) *Stratification: Social Division and Inequality*, London: Routledge

Bourgois, P. (1995, 2nd edn 2002) *In Search of Respect*, Cambridge: Cambridge University Press

Bowles, S. and Gintis, H. (1976) *Schooling in Capitalist America: Educational Reform and the Contradictions of Economic Life*, New York: Basic Books

Bowling, B. (1999) *Violent Racism: Victimisation, Policing and Social Context* (revised edn), Oxford: Oxford University Press

Bowling, B. and Phillips, C. (2002) *Racism, Crime and Justice*, Harlow: Pearson

Box, S. (1981) *Deviance, Reality and Society* (2nd edn), Eastbourne: Holt Rheinhart Wilson

Box, S. (1983/1993) *Crime, Power and Mystification*, London: Tavistock

Boyson, R. (ed.) (1971) *Down with the Poor*, London: Churchill Press

Bradley, H. (1996) *Fractured Identities: Changing Patterns of Inequality*, Cambridge: Polity Press

Bradley, H. (1999) *Gender and Power in the Workplace*, Basingstoke, Macmillan

Bradshaw, J.R. (1972) 'The taxonomy of social need', in G. McLachlan (ed), *Problems and Progress in Medical Care*, Oxford: Oxford University Press

Braithwaite, J. (1984) *Corporate Crime in the Pharmaceutical Industry*, London: Routledge

Brake, M. (1980) *The Sociology of Youth and Youth Subcultures*, London: Routledge

Braverman, H. (1974) *Labour and Monopoly Capitalism*, New York: Monthly Press

Bremner, M. (1968) *Dependency and the Family*, London: IEA

Brenner, M., Brown, J. and Canter, M. (1985) *The Research Interview: Uses and Approaches*, London: Academic Press

British Youth Lifestyles Survey (2000) Home Office Research Study 209

Brooke, E. and Davis, A. (1985) *Women, the Family and Social Work*, London: Tavistock

Brooks, A. (1997) *Postfeminisms: Feminisms, Cultural Theory and Cultural Forms*, London: Routledge

Brown, G.W., Harris, T.O. and Hepworth, C. (1995) 'Loss, humiliation and entrapment among women developing depression', *Psychological Medicine*, 25, pp.7–21

Bryman, A. (2004) *Social Research Methods* (2nd edn), Oxford: Oxford University Press

Bryman, A. and Burgess, A. (1994) *Analysing Qualitative Data*, London: Routledge

Burns, J. and Bracey, P. (2001) 'Boys' underachievement: Issues, challenges and possible ways forward', *Westminster Studies in Education*, 24, pp.155–66

Burrows, R. (2003) *Poverty and Home Ownership in Contemporary Britain*, Bristol: The Policy Press

Busfield, J. (1988) 'Mental illness as a social product or social construct: a contradiction in feminists' arguments?', *Sociology of Health and Illness*, 10, pp.521–42

Buswell, C. (1987) *Training for Low Pay*, Basingstoke: Macmillan

Cabinet Office (2003) *Ethnic Minorities and the Labour Market: Final Report*, London: HMSO

Cahill, M. (1998) 'The green perspective', in P. Alcock, A. Erskine and M. May (eds) *The Student's Companion to Social Policy*, Oxford: Blackwell

Cain, M. (1986) 'Realism, feminism, methodology and law', *International Journal of the Sociology of Law*, 14

Campbell, B. (1993) *Goliath: Britain's Dangerous Places*, London: Methuen

Campbell, C. (2001) *Developing Inclusive Schooling: Perspectives, Policies and Practices*, London: University of London, Institute of Education

Cannadine, D. (1998) *Class in Britain*, London: Yale University Press

Caplow, T. (1954) *The Sociology of Work*, New York: McGraw-Hill

Carlen, P. (1988) *Women, Crime and Poverty*, Milton Keynes: Open University Press

Carlen, P. (1992) 'Criminal women and criminal justice: the limits to and potential of feminist and left realist perspectives', in R. Matthews and J. Young (eds) *Issues in Realist Criminology*, London: Sage

Carlisle, S. (2001) 'Inequalities in health: contested explanations, shifting discourses and ambiguous policies', *Critical Public Health*, 11(3), p.267–81

Carrabine, E., Iganski, P., Lee, M., Plummer, K. and South, N. (2004) *Criminology: A Sociological Introduction*, London: Routledge

Carr-Hill, R. (1987) 'The inequality and health debate: a critical review of the issues', *Journal of Social Policy*, 16, pp.509–42

Carson, R. (2000, originally 1962) *The Silent Spring*, Harmondsworth, Penguin

Carson, W.G. (1970) 'White collar crime and the enforcement of factory legislation', *British Journal of Criminology*, 10

Cashmore, E. (1989) *United Kingdom? Class, Race and Gender since the War*, London: Unwin Hyman

Castles, S. and Kosack, G.C. (1973) *Immigrant Workers and Class Structure in Western Europe*, Oxford: OUP

Chambliss, W.J. (1975) 'Towards a political economy of crime', *Theory and Society*, Vol. 2 pp.149–170

Charlesworth, S. (2000) *A Phenomenology of Working-Class Experience*, Cambridge: Cambridge University Press

Chesler, P. (1972) *Women and Madness*, New York: Doubleday

Clark, T.N. and Hoffman-Martinot, V. (eds) (1998) *The New Political Culture*, Boulder CO: Westview

Clarke, J.N. (1992) 'Cancer, heart disease and AIDS: What do the media tell us about these diseases?', *Health Communication*, 4(2)

Clarke, M. (1990) *Business Crime: Its Nature and Control*, Bristol: Policy Press

Clegg, S.R. (1989) *Frameworks of Power*, London: Sage

Clinard, M.B. and Meier, R.F. (2001) *Sociology of Deviant Behaviour* (11th edn), Fort Worth: Harcourt College Publishers

Cloward, R. and Ohlin, L. (1960) *Delinquency and Opportunity*, London: Collier Macmillan

Coard, B. (1971) *How the West-Indian Child is Made Educationally Sub-normal in the British School System*, London: New Beacon Books

Cohen, A. (1955) *Delinquent Boys*, New York: The Free Press

Cohen, N. (2005) 'Capital punishment', *The Observer*, 6 November

Cohen, P. (1984) 'Against the new vocationalism', in L. Bates, J. Clarke, P. Cohen, R. Moore and P. Willis, *Schooling for the Dole*, Basingstoke: Macmillan

Cohen, R. and Rai, S. (eds) (2000) *Global Social Movements*, Athlone: Continuum International Publishing Group

Cohen, S. (1972) *Folk Devils and Moral Panics*, London: Paladin

Cohen, S. (1980) *Folk Devils and Moral Panics* (2nd edn), Oxford: Martin Robinson

Cohen, S. (1985) *Visions of Social Control*, Cambridge: Polity Press

Cohen, S. (2002) 'Moral panics as cultural politics (New introduction)', in *Folk Devils and Moral Panics: The Creation of the Mods and Rockers* (3rd edn), London: Routledge

Collinson, M. (1995) *Police, Drugs and Community*, London: Free Association Books

Collison, M. (1996) 'In search of the high life', *British Journal of Criminology*, 36(3), pp.428–44

Colman, A. and Gorman, L. (1982) 'Conservatism, dogmatism and authoritarianism amongst British police officers', *Sociology* 16(1)

Conklin, J.E. (1977) *Illegal but not Criminal: Business Crime in America*, Englewood Cliffs, NJ: Prentice Hall

Connell, R.W. (1995) *Masculinities*, Cambridge: Polity Press

Connolly, P. (1998) *Racism, Gender Identities and Young Children*, London: Routledge

Connor H. and Dewson S., with Tyers C., Eccles J., Regan J. and Aston J. (2001) *Social Class and Higher Education: Issues Affecting Decisions on Participation by Lower Social Class Groups*, DfEE Research Report RR267

Coussins, J. (1976) *The Equality Report*, NCCL Rights for Women Unit: London

Coward, R. (1989) *The Whole Truth; The Myth of Alternative Health*, London: Faber

Coxall, B. (1981) *Parties and Pressure Groups*, Harlow: Longman

Craib, I. (1992) *Anthony Giddens*, London: Routledge

Croall, H. (2001) *Understanding White-collar Crime*, Milton Keynes: Open University Press

Crook, S., Pakulski, J. and Waters, M. (1992) *Postmodernisation: Change in Advanced Society*, London: Sage

Crosland, C.A.R. (1956) *The Future of Socialism*, London: Cape

Cuff, E.C., Sharrock W.W. and Francis, D.W. (1990) *Perspectives in Sociology*, London: Routledge

Dahl, R. (1961) *Who Governs: Democracy and Power in an American City*, New Haven: Yale University Press

Dalton, K. (1964) *The Pre-menstrual Syndrome and Progesterone Therapy*, London: Heinemann Medical

Darlington, Y. and Scott, D. (2002) *Qualitative Research in Practice*, Buckingham: Open University Press

Davey Smith, G., Shipley, M. J. and Rose, G. (1990) 'The magnitude and causes of socio-economic differentials in mortality: further evidence from the Whitehall study', *Journal of Epidemiology and Community Health*, 44, pp.265–70

Davis, K. and Moore, W.E. (1955) 'Some principles of stratification', in R. Bendix and S.M. Lipset (eds) *Class, Status and Power* (2nd edn 1967), London: Routledge & Kegan Paul

Davis, M. (1990) *City of Quartz*, London: Verso

Deacon, A. (1977) 'Coercion and concession: the politics of unemployment insurance in the twenties', in A. Briggs and J. Saville (eds), *Essays in Labour History 1918–1939*, London: Croom Helm

Dean, H. (2002) *Welfare Rights and Social Policy*, Cambridge: Pearson Education/Prentice Hall

Delamont, S. (2001) *Changing Women: Unchanged Men: Sociological Perspectives on Gender in a Post-Industrial Society*, Buckingham: Open University Press

Delphy, C. (1977) *The Main Enemy*, London: Women's Research & Resources Centre

Dennis, N. and Erdos, G. (1993, 3rd edn 2000) *Families without Fatherhood*, London: IEA

Denscombe, M. (1999, 2003, 2004) *Sociology Update 1999/2003/2004*, Leicester: Olympus Books

Denscombe, M. (2001) 'Uncertain identities and health-risking behaviour: the case of young people and smoking in late modernity', *British Journal of Sociology*, 52, March

Department for Work and Pensions (2003) *Measuring Child Poverty*, www.dwp.gov.uk/consultations/consult/2003/childpov/final.asp

Department of Health (1999) *Our Healthier Nation*, London: The Stationery Office

Devine, F. (1992) *Affluent Workers Revisited*, Edinburgh University Press: Edinburgh

DfEE (2000) *Statistics of Education, Permanent Exclusions from Maintained Schools in England* (10/00), London: Department for Education and Employment

DfES (2002a) *Government Supported Work-Based Learning in England 2001/2: Volumes and Outcomes*, SFR 27/2002, London: Department for Education & Skills

DfES (2002b) *Youth Cohort Study: Activities and Experiences of 18 Year Olds: England and Wales 2002*, London: Department for Education & Skills www.dfes.gov.uk/rsgateway/DB/SFR/s000382/V4sfr04-2003.pdf

DfES (2003) *Statistical Bulletin: Permanent Exclusions from Maintained Schools in England 2001/02* (ref 08/2003), London: Department for Education & Skills

DfES (2004) *Statistics of Education: Variation in Pupil Progress 2003* (Issue No 0204), London: The Stationery Office

DfES (2005) *Ethnicity and Education: The Evidence on Minority Ethnic Pupils*, London: Department for Education & Skills

Diani, M. (1992) 'The concept of social movement', *Sociological Review*, 40, pp.1-25

Discovery Home and Health (2000) 'Underachievement in boys', see www.discoveryhealth.co.uk/men/m_story.asp?storyid=103660&oldstoryid=91852&feature=tv

Ditton, J. (1977) *Part-time Crime: An Ethnography of Fiddling and Pilferage*, London: Macmillan

Dodd, T., Nicholas, S., Povey, D. and Walker, A (2004) *Crime in England and Wales 2003/4*, London: Home Office

Doling, J. (1993) 'British housing policy: 1984–1993', *Regional Studies*, 27(6), pp.583–8

Douglas, J.W.B. (1964) *The Home and the School*, London: MacGibbon and Kee

Downes, D. (1966) *The Delinquent Solution*, London: Routledge

Doyal, L. (1979) *The Political Economy of Health*, London: Pluto

Doyal, L. (1994) *What Makes Women Sick*, London: Pluto

Drew, D. (1995) *Race, Education and Work: The Statistics of Inequality*, Aldershot: Avebury

Durkheim, E. (1960) *The Division of Labour in Society*, Glencoe: Free Press

Durkheim, E. (1982, originally 1895) *The Rules of Sociological Method* (ed. S. Lukes), London: Macmillan

Duverger, M. (1972) *Party Politics and Pressure Groups*, London: Nelson

Education Network (2002) *England's Divided Schools and Policy Briefing on New Admissions Code of Practice*, London: The Education Network

Ehrenreich, B. and English, D. (1979) *For Her Own Good*, London: Pluto

Eisenberg, L. (1977) 'Disease and illness: distinction between professional and popular ideas of sickness', *Culture, Medicine and Psychiatry*, 1, pp.9–23

Elliot, A. (2002) 'Beck's sociology of risk: a critical assessment', *Sociology*, 36(2), pp.293–315

EOC (2005) *Free to Choose: Tackling Gender Barriers to Better Jobs*, London: Equal Opportunities Commission

EOC (2005a) *Sex and Power: Who Runs Britain?*, Manchester: Equal Opportunities Commission

EOC (2005b) *Facts about Women and Men in Great Britain*, Manchester: Equal Opportunities Commission

Etzioni, A. (1993) *The Spirit of Community*, New York: Crown Publishers

Evans, G. (1992) 'Is Britain a class-divided society? A re-analysis and extension of Marshall *et al.*'s study of class consciousness', *Sociology*, 26(2), pp.233–58

Faludi, S. (1992) *The Undeclared War against Women*, London: Chatto & Windus

Farrington, D.P. (2002) 'Key findings from the first 40 years of the Cambridge study in Delinquent Development', in T.P. Thornberry and M.D. Krohn (eds) *Taking Stock of Delinquency: an Overview of Findings from Contemporary Longitudinal Studies*, New York: Kluwer/Plenum

Farrington, D.P. and Morris, A.M. (1983) 'Sex, sentencing and reconviction', British Journal of Criminology, 23, pp.229–48

Farrington, D.P. and Painter, K.A. (2004) *Gender Differences in Offending: Implications for risk focussed prevention*, Home Office Online Report 09/04 www.homeoffice.gov.uk/rds/onlinepubs1.html

Feeley, M. and Simon, J. (1992) 'The new penology', *Criminology*, 30(4)

Fenwick, M. and Hayward, K.J. (2000) 'Youth Crime, Excitement and Consumer Culture' in J. Pickford (ed.) *Youth Justice: Theory and Practice*, London: Cavendish

Field, F. (1989) *Losing Out: The Emergence of Britain's Underclass*, Oxford: Blackwell

Fielding, A. (1995) 'Migration and middle-class formation in England and Wales' in T. Butler and M. Savage (eds) (1995) *Social Change and the Middle Class*, London: UCL

Finch, J. and Groves, D. (1983) *A Labour of Love: Women, Work and Caring*, London: Routledge

Finkelstein, V. (1980) *Attitudes and Disabled People: Issues for Discussion*, New York: World Rehabilitation Fund

Finn, D. (1987) *Training without Jobs*, Basingstoke: Macmillan

Firestone, S. (1971) *The Dialectic of Sex*, London: Cape

Fitzgerald, M., Stockdale, J. and Hale, C. (2003) *Young People's Involvement in Street Crime*, London: Youth Justice Board

Forder, A. (1974) *Concepts in Social Administration: A framework for analysis*, London: Routledge Kegan Paul

Forster, N. (1994) 'The analysis of company documentation' in C. Cassell and G. Symon (eds) *Qualitative Methods in Organizational Research*, London: Sage

Forsyth, A. and Furlong, A. (2003) *Socioeconomic Disadvantage and Experience in Further and Higher Education*, Bristol: Policy Press

Foster, J., Newburn, T. and Souhami, A. (2005) *Assessing the Impact of the Stephen Lawrence Inquiry*, Home Office Research Study 294, London: Home Office Research, Development and Statistics Directorate

Foucault, M. (1965) *Madness and Civilization*, New York: Random House

Foucault, M. (1976) *The Birth of the Clinic*, London: Tavistock

Foucault, M. (1977) *Discipline and Punish*, London: Allen Lane

Foucault, M. (1980) *Power/Knowledge: Selected Interviews and Other Writings 1972–77* (ed. C. Gordon), Brighton: Harvester Press

Foucault, M. (1981) *The History of Sexuality*, Vol. 1, Harmondsworth: Penguin

Francis, B. (1998) *Power Plays: Primary School Children's Constructions of Gender, Power and Adult Work*, Stoke-on-Trent: Trentham Books

Francis, B. (2000a) *Boys, Girls and Achievement: Addressing the Classroom Issues*, London: Routledge Falmer

Francis, B. (2000b) 'The gendered subject: students' subject preferences and discussions of gender and subject ability', *Oxford Review of Education*, 26(1), pp.35–48

Friedman, M. (1962) *Capitalism and Freedom*, Chicago: University of Chicago Press

Friedson, E. (1965) 'Disability as social deviance' in M.B. Sussman (ed.) *Sociology of Disability and Rehabilitation*, Washington, DC: American Sociological Association

Fulcher, J. and Scott, J. (1999) *Sociology*, Oxford: Oxford University Press

Fuller, M. (1984) 'Black girls in a London comprehensive', in R. Deem (ed.) *Schooling for Women's Work*, London: Routledge

Furlong, J. (1984) 'Interaction sets in the classroom', in M. Hammersley, *et al.* (eds) *Life in Schools*, Milton Keynes: Open University

Gallie, D. (1994) 'Are the unemployed an underclass: some evidence from the Social Change and Economic Life Initiative', *Sociology*, 28

Garfinkel, H. (1967) *Studies in Ethnomethodology*, Englewood Hills, NJ: Prentice-Hall

Garland, D. (1996) 'The limits of the sovereign state: strategies of crime control in contemporary society', *British Journal of Criminology*, 36(4), pp.445–71

Garland, D. (2001) *Punishment and Control*, Oxford: Oxford University Press

Geis, G. (1967) 'The heavy electrical equipment anti-trust cases of 1961', in M.B. Clinard and R. Quinney (eds) *Criminal Behaviour Systems*, New York: Holt, Rhinehart & Winston

General Household Survey (2001) London: ONS, HMSO

George, V. and Wilding, P. (1994) *Welfare and Ideology*, London: Routledge

Gewirtz, S. (2002) *The Managerial School: Post-welfarism and social justice in education*, London, Routledge

Giddens, A. (1973) *The Class Structure of the Advanced Societies,* London: Hutchinson

Giddens, A. (1984) *The Constitution of Society: Outline of the Theory of Structuration*, Cambridge: Polity Press

Giddens, A. (1991) *Modernity and Self-Identity: Self in Society in the Late Modern Age*, Cambridge: Polity

Giddens, A. (1999*) A Runaway World? The BBC Reith Lectures*, London: BBC Radio 4, BBC Education

Giddens, A. (1999) *The Third Way: the Renewal of Social Democracy*, Cambridge: Polity

Giddens, A. (2001), *Sociology* (4th edn), Cambridge: Polity Press

Giddens, A. and Diamond, P. (2005) *The New Egalitarianism*, Cambridge: Polity

Giddens, A. and Pierson, C. (1998) *Conversations with Anthony Giddens: Making Sense of Modernity*, Cambridge: Polity Press

Gieve, K. (1974) 'i demand', in S. Allen (ed.) *Conditions of Illusion*, London: Feminist Books

Gillborn, D. (1990) *'Race', Ethnicity and Education: Teaching and Learning in Multi-ethnic Schools*, London: Unwin Hyman

Gillborn, D. (2002) *Education and Institutional Reform*, Institute of Education

Gillborn, D. and Gipps, B. (1996) *Recent Research in the Achievement of Ethnic Minority Pupils*, London: HMSO

Gillborn, D. and Mirza, H.S. (2000*) Educational Inequality: Mapping Race and Class*, OFSTED

Gillborn, D. and Youdell, D. (1999) *Rationing Education: Policy, Practice, Reform and Equity*, Milton Keynes: Open University Press

Gilroy, P. (1982a) 'Steppin' out of Babylon: race, class and autonomy, in *The Empire Strikes Back: Race and Racism in Britain*, London: CCCS/Hutchinson

Gilroy, P. (1982b) 'Police and Thieves' in *The Empire Strikes Back: Race and Racism in 70s Britain*, London: CCCS/Hutchinson

Ginn, J., *et al.* (1996) 'Feminist fallacies: a reply to Hakim on women's employment', *British Journal of Sociology*, 47

Ginsburg, N. (1979) *Class, Capital and Social Policy*, Basingstoke, Macmillan

Ginsburg, N. (1998) 'The Socialist Perspective', in P. Alcock, A. Erskine and M. May (eds*) The Student's Companion to Social Policy*, Oxford: Blackwell

Glaser, B.G. and Strauss, A. (1967) *Awareness of Dying*, Chicago: Aldine

Glendinning, C. and Millar, J. (1992) (eds) *Women and Poverty in Britain: The 1990s* (2nd edn), Hemel Hempstead: Harvester Wheatsheaf

Goffman, E. (1961, republished 1984) *Asylums*, Harmondsworth: Penguin

Goffman, E. (1963) *Stigma: Notes on the Management of Spoiled Identity*, New York: Prentice Hall

Goffman, E. (1968) *Asylums*, Harmondsworth: Penguin

Gold, K. (2003) 'Poverty is an excuse', *Times Educational Supplement*, 7 March

Gold, R. (1958) 'Roles in sociological field investigation', *Social Forces*, 36, pp.217–23

Goldthorpe, J. (1980a) *Social Mobility and the Class Structure in Modern Britain*, Oxford: Clarendon Press

Goldthorpe, J. and Lockwood, D. (1969) *The Affluent Worker in the Class Structure* (3 vols), Cambridge: Cambridge University Press

Goodwin, J. and O'Connor, H. (2005) 'Exploring complex transitions: looking back at the golden age of from school to work', *Sociology*, 39(2), pp.201–20

Gordon, P. (1988) 'Black people and the criminal law: rhetoric and reality', *International Journal of the Sociology of Law*, 16

Gough. I. (1979) *The Political Economy of the Welfare State*, Basingstoke: Macmillan

Gouldner, A.W. (1968) 'The sociologist as partisan: sociology and the welfare state', *The American Sociologist*, May

Gove, W.R. (1982) 'The current status of the labeling theory of mental illness', in W.R. Gove (ed.) *Deviance and Mental Illness* (pp.273–300), Beverly Hills, CA: Sage Publications

Graef, R. (1989) *Talking Blues: The Police in Their Own Words,* London: Collins Harvill

Graham, H. (1993) *When Life's A Drag: Women, Smoking and Disadvantage*, London: HMSO

Graham, H. (2002) 'Inequality in men and women's health', in S. Nettleton and U. Gustafsson *The Sociology of Health and Medicine*, Cambridge: Polity

Graham, J. and Bowling, B. (1995) *Young People and Crime*, Home Office Research Study 145, London: Home Office

Gramsci, A. (1971) *Selections from the Prison Notebooks*, London: Lawrence & Wishart

Grant, W. (1999) *Pressure Groups and British Politics*, Basingstoke: Palgrave

Gray, J. (1992) *The Moral Foundations of Market Institutions*, London: IEA

Green, D.G. (1988) *Everyone a Private Patient*, London: Institute of Economic Affairs

Green, H., McGinnity, Á., Meltzer, H., Ford, T. and Goodman, R. (2005) *Mental Health of Children and Young People in Great Britain*, 2004, London: Office for National Statistics

Griffiths, B. (1984) *The Creation of Wealth*, London: Hodder & Stoughton

Grimshaw, D. and Rubery, G. (2001) *The Gender Pay Gap: A Research Review*, Manchester: Equal Opportunities Commission

Gross, E. (1978) 'Organisations as criminal actors', in J. Braithwaite and P. Wilson (eds) *Two Faces of Deviance: Crimes of the Powerless and the Powerful*, Brisbane: University of Queensland Press

Habermas, J. (1979) *Communication and the Evolution of Society*, London: Heinemann

Hagan, J. (1987) *Modern Criminology: Crime, Criminal Behaviour and its Control*, New York: McGraw-Hill

Hagan, J. (1994) *Crime and Disrepute,* Thousand Oaks: Pine Forge Press

Hakim, C. (1979) *Occupational Segregation*, Department of Employment Research Paper no. 9, London: HMSO

Hakim, C. (2000) *Work–Lifestyle Choices in the 21st Century*, Oxford: Oxford University Press

Hall, S. and Jefferson, T. (1976) *Resistance through Rituals*, London: Hutchinson

Hall, S., Critcher, C., Jefferson, T., Clarke J. and Roberts, B. (1978) *Policing the Crisis*, Macmillan: London

Hallam, S. (2002) *Ability Grouping in Schools*, London: Institute of Education

Hallsworth, S. (1994) 'Understanding New Social Movements', *Sociology Review*, 4(1), Oxford: Philip Allen

Ham, C. (1999) *Health Policy in Britain*, Basingstoke: Palgrave

Haque, Z. and Bell, J.F. (2001) 'Evaluating the performances of minority ethnic pupils in secondary schools', *Oxford Review of Education*, 27(3), pp.359–68

Hardey, M. (1998) *The Social Context of Health*, Buckingham: Open University Press

Hardy, C., Phillips, N. and Clegg, S. (2001) 'Reflexivity in organization and management theory: A study of the production of the research "subject"', *Human Relations*, 54, pp.531–60

Hargreaves, D.H. (1967) *Social Relations in a Secondary School*, London: Routledge & Kegan Paul

Harper, D. (1978) 'At home on the rails: ethics in a photographic research project', *Qualitative Sociology*, 1, pp.66–77

Harper, P., Pollak, M., Mooney, J., Whelan, E. and Young, J. (1986) *The Islington Crime Survey,* London Borough of Islington

Harrington, M. (1972) *Socialism*, New York: Bantam Books

Hart, N. (1985) *The Sociology of Health and Medicine*, Ormskirk: Causeway

Hartnett, O. (1990) 'The sex role system', in P. Mayes *Gender*, Longman: London

Harvey, D. (1990) *The Condition of Modernity*, Blackwell: Oxford

Hastings, M. (2005) 'They've never had it so good', *The Guardian*, 6 August, p.19

Hatcher, R. (1996) 'The Limitations of the New Social-Democratic Agendas: Class, Equality and Agency', in R. Hatcher and K. Jones (eds*) Education after the Conservatives,* Stoke-on-Trent: Trentham Books

Hayek, F. (1960) *The Constitution of Liberty*, London: Routledge

Hayek, F. (1976) *Law, Legislation and Liberty; The Mirage of Social Justice*, London: Routledge

Hayek, F.A. (1944/1986/2001) *The Road to Serfdom*, London: Routledge

Healthcare Commission (2005) *State of Healthcare*, Report 2005, London: Healthcare Commission

Hedderman, C. and Hough, M. (1994) *Does the Criminal Justice System Treat Men and Women Differently?*, Home Office Research Findings No. 10, London: Home Office

Heidensohn, F. (1989; 2nd edn 1996) *Women and Crime*, London: Macmillan

Heidensohn, F. (2002) 'Gender and crime', in M. Maguire, R. Morgan and R. Reiner, *The Oxford Handbook of Criminology* (3rd edn), Oxford: Oxford University Press

Held, D. (ed.) (2000) *A Globalising World; Culture, Economics, Politics*, London: Routledge

Held, D. and McGrew, A. (2002) *Globalization and Anti-Globalization*, Cambridge: Polity Press

Henry, S. and Milovanovic, D. (1996) *Constitutive Criminology: Beyond Postmodernism*, London: Sage

Hetherington, K. (1998) *Expressions of Identity: Space, Performance, Politics*, London: Sage

Hills J. (and Gardiner, K.) (1997) *The Future of Welfare: A Guide to the Debate* (revised edn), York: Joseph Rowntree Foundation

Hirschi, T. (1969) *Causes of Delinquency*, Berkeley, CA: University of California Press

Hirst, P.Q. (1975) 'Radical deviancy theory and Marxism: a reply to Taylor, Walton and Young', in E. Taylor, P. Walton and J. Young (eds) *Critical Criminology*, London: Routledge

Hobbs, D. (1998) *Bad Business: Professional Crime in Britain*, Oxford: Oxford University Press

Holdaway, S. (1982/3) *Inside the British Police*, Oxford: Blackwell

Home Office (1998) *British Crime Survey*, Research and Statistics Directorate of the Home Office

Hood, R. and Joyce, K. (1999) 'Three generations: oral testimony of crime and social change in London's East End', *British Journal of Criminology*, 39(1), pp.136–60

Horkheimer, M. (1974) *Eclipse of Reason*, New York: Oxford University Press

Howell, J.M. and Frost, P.J. (1989) 'A Laboratory Study of Charismatic Leadership', *Organizational Behavior and Human Decision Processes,* 43, pp.243–69

Howes, E. and Mullins, D. (1999) *Dwelling on Difference*, London Research Centre

Hutton, W. (1996) *The State We're In*, London: Vantage

Illich, I. (1990) *Limits to Medicine: Medical Nemesis, The Expropriation of Health*, London: Penguin

Illsley, R. (1986) 'Occupational class, selection and the production of inequalities in health', *Quarterly Journal of Social Affairs*, 2(2), pp.151–64

Inland Revenue (2004) Distribution of Personal Wealth – www.hmrc.gov.uk/stats/personal_wealth/menu.htm

Jackson, B. (1978) 'Killing time: life in the Arkansas penitentiary', *Qualitative Sociology*, 1, pp.21–32

Jasper, L. (2002) 'School system failing black children', *Guardian*, 16 March

Jessop, B. (2002) *The Future of the Capitalist State*, Cambridge: Polity Press

Jones, T., Maclean, B. and Young, J. (1995) *The Second Islington Crime Survey*, London Borough of Islington

Joseph Rowntree Foundation (1995) *Income and Wealth: Report of the JRF Inquiry Group*, York: Joseph Rowntree Foundation

Katz, J. (1988) *Seductions of Crime: Moral and Sensual Attractions in Doing Evil*, New York: Basic Books

Keddie, N. (1971) 'Classroom knowledge', in M.F.D. Young (ed.) *Knowledge and Control: New Directions for the Sociology of Education,* London: Collier-Macmillan

Kenway, J. (1997) 'Taking stock of gender reform policies for Australian schools: past, present, future', *British Educational Research Journal*, 23, pp.329–44

Kenyatta, M.L. and Tai, R.H. (1999) *Critical Ethnicity: Countering the Waves of Identity Politics*, Oxford: Rowman and Littlefield

Kitsuse, J. (1962) 'Societal reaction to deviant behaviour', *Social Problems*, (9) Winter

Klein, N. (2001) *No Logo*, London: Flamingo

Krause, I.B. (1989) 'Sinking heart: A Punjabi communication of distress', *Social Science & Medicine,* 29, pp.563–75

Kumar, K. (1978) *Prophecy and Progress*, Harmondsworth: Penguin

Kundnani, A. (2002) *From Oldham to Bradford; The Violence of the Violated*, from www.irr.org.uk

Laqueur, T. (1990) *Making Sex: Body and Gender from the Greeks to Freud*, London: Harvard University Press

Lareau, A. (1997) 'Social class differences in family-school relationships: the importance of cultural capital', in A. Halsey *et al.* (eds) *Education, Culture, Economy and Society*, Oxford: Oxford University Press

Le Grand, J. (1982) *The Strategy of Equality*, London: George Allen & Unwin

Lea, J. and Young, J. (1984, revised 1993) *What is to be Done about Law and Order?,* Harmondsworth: Penguin

Lee-Treweek, G. (2000) 'The insight of emotional danger: research experiences in a home for the elderly', in G. Lee-Treweek and S. Lingogle (eds) *Danger in the Field: Risk and Ethics in Social Research*, London: Routledge

Lemert, E. (1972) *Human Deviance, Social Problems and Social Control,* Englewood Cliffs, NJ: Prentice-Hall

Levi, M. (1987) *Regulating Fraud*, London: Tavistock

Levin, J. and McDevitt, J. (2002) *Hate Crimes Revisited*, Boulder, CO: Westview Press

Lewis, O. (1966) *La Vida*, New York: Random House

Liazos, A. (1972) 'The poverty of the sociology of deviance: nuts, sluts and perverts', *Social Problems* 20

Link, B. and Phelan, J. (1995) 'Social conditions as fundamental cause of disease', *Journal of Health and Social Behaviour*, pp.80–94

Lockwood, D. (1966) 'Sources of variation in working-class images of society', *Sociological Review*, 14

Lovelock, J. (2000, originally 1979) *Gaia: A New Look At Life On Earth*, Oxford: Oxford Paperbacks

Low Pay Unit (2000) press release on October 26

Luhman, N. (1995) *Social Systems*, Stanford: Stanford University Press

Lukes, S. (1974) *Power: A Radical View*, London: Macmillan

Lukes, S. (1986) 'Domination by economic power and authority' in S. Lukes (ed.) *Power*, Oxford: Blackwell

Lupton, D. (1994) *Medicine as Culture: Illness, Disease and the Body in Western Societies*, London: Sage

Lyng, S. (1990) 'Edgework: a social psychological analysis of voluntary risk-taking', *American Journal of Sociology*, 95(4), pp.851–6

Mac an Ghaill, M. (1988) *Young, Gifted and Black*, Milton Keynes: Open University Press

Mac an Ghaill, M. (1992) 'Coming of age in 80s England: reconceptualising black students' educational experience', in D. Gill, B. Mayor and M. Blair (eds) *Racism and Education: Structures and Strategies*, London: Sage

Mac an Ghaill, M. (1994) *The Making of Men*, Buckingham: Open University Press

Mac an Ghaill, M. (ed.) (1996) *Understanding Masculinities: Social Relations and Cultural Arenas*, Buckingham: Open University Press

Macdonald, K. and Tipton, C. (1993) 'Using documents', in N. Gilbert (ed.) *Researching Social Life*, London: Sage

McDowell, L. (1992) 'Gender divisions in a post-Fordist era', in L. McDowell and R. Pringle (eds) *Defining Women*, Cambridge: Polity Press

McIntosh, M. (1968) 'The homosexual role', *Social Problems*, 16(2), pp.182–92

MacIntyre, S. (1993) 'Gender differences in the perceptions of common cold symptoms', *Social Science and Medicine*, 36(1), pp.15–20

McKee, L. and Bell, C. (1985) 'Marital and family relations in times of male unemployment', in B. Roberts, R. Finnegan and D. Gallie (eds) *New Approaches to Economic Life*, Manchester: Manchester University Press

McKeown, T. (1976) *The Modern Rise of Population*, London: Arnold

McKeown, T. (1979) *The Role of Medicine*, Oxford: Blackwell

McKie, L., Bowlby, S. and Gregory, S. (2004) 'Starting well: gender, care and health in the family context', *Sociology*, 38(3), pp.593–611

McNeill, L. (1988) *Contradictions of Control: School Structure and School Knowledge,* New York: Routledge

Macpherson, W. (1999) *The Stephen Lawrence Inquiry: Report of an Inquiry by Sir William Macpherson of Cluny*, London: HMSO

Maffesoli, M. (1996) *The Time of the Tribes*, London: Sage

Maguire, M. (2002) 'Crime statistics: the data explosion and its implications', in M. Maguire, R. Morgan and R. Reiner (eds) *The Oxford Handbook of Criminology* (3rd edn), Oxford: Oxford University Press

Maher, J. and Green, H. (2002) *Carers 2000*, London: The Stationery Office

Malinowski, B. (1982) *Magic, Science and Religion and Other Essays,* London: Souvenir Press

Mann, K. (1992) *The Making of an English Underclass? The Social Divisions of Welfare and Labour*, Milton Keynes: Open University Press

Mann, M. (1986) *The Sources of Social Power*, Vol. 1, Cambridge: Cambridge University Press

Mannheim, K. (1960) *Ideology and Utopia*, London: Routledge

Marcuse, H. (1964/1991) *One Dimensional Man: Studies in the Ideology of Advanced Industrial Societies*, London: Routledge

Marmot, M.G., Smith, G.D., Stansfeld, S., Patel, C., North, F., Head, J., White, I., Brunner, E. and Feeney A. (1991) 'Health inequalities among British civil servants: the Whitehall II study, *The Lancet*, 337, pp.1387-93

Mars, G. (1982) *Cheats at Work: an Anthropology of Workplace Crime*, London: George Allen & Unwin

Marshall, G., Newby. H., Rose, D. and Vogler, C. (1988) *Social Class In Modern Britain*, London, Hutchinson

Marshall, T.H. (1975) *Social Policy* (4th edn), London: Hutchinson

Marsland, D. (1996) *Welfare or Welfare State?*, Basingstoke: Macmillan

Marx, K. and Engels, F. (1848/2002) *Manifesto of the Communist Party*, North Charleston, SC: BookSurge

Marx, K. and Engels, F. (1968) *Selected Works in One Volume*, London: Lawrence & Wishart

Mason, D. (2000) *Race and Ethnicity in Modern Britain*, Oxford: Oxford University Press

Matthews, R. and Young, J. (eds) (1992) *Issues in Realist Criminology*, London: Sage

Matza, D. (1964) *Delinquency and Drift*, New York: Wiley

May, T. (2001) *Social Research: Issues, Methods and Process*, Buckingham: Open University Press

Mayhew, P., Aye Maung, N. and Mirrlees-Black, C. (1993) *The 1992 British Crime Survey*, Home Office Research Study 111, London: Home Office

Mead, G.H. (1934) *Mind, Self and Society* (ed. C. Morris) Chicago: University of Chicago

Meadows, D. and Meadows D. (1977) *The Limits To Growth*, Chicago: New Amer Library

Melucci, A. (1989) *Nomads of the Present*, London: Hutchinson

Merton, R. (1938) 'Social structure and anomie', *American Sociological Review*, 3

Merton, R. (1957) *Social Theory and Social Structure*, New York: The Free Press

Messerschmidt, J. (1993) *Masculinities and Crime*, Lanham, MD: Rowman & Littlefield

Michalowski, R. and Kramer, R. (1987) 'The space between laws: the problem of corporate crime in a transnational context', *Social Problems*, 34

Mies, M (1983) 'Towards a methodology for feminist research', in G. Bowles and R. Duelli Klein (eds) (1983) *Theories of Women's Studies*, London: Routledge Kegan Paul

Miles, R. (1989) *Racism*, London: Routledge

Miliband, R. (1970) *The State in Capitalist Society*, London: Quartet

Miller, W.B. (1962) 'Lower class culture as a generating milieu of gang delinquency', in M.E. Wolfgang, L. Savitz and N. Johnston (eds) *The Sociology of Crime and Delinquency*, New York: Wiley

Millett, K. (1970) *Sexual Politics*, New York: Doubleday

Mirza, H. (1992) *Young, Female and Black*, London: Routledge

Mitsos E. and Browne, K. (1998) 'Gender differences in education: the underachievement of boys', *Sociology Review*, 8(1)

Modood, T. (1992) *Not Easy Being British: Colour, Culture and Citizenship*, Runnymede Trust and Trentham Books

Modood, T., Berthoud, R., *et al.* (1997) *Ethnic Minorities in Britain*, London: PSI

Monaghan, L. (1999) 'Creating "the perfect body": a variable project', *Body and Society*, 5(2–3), pp.267–90

Monaghan, L. (2005) 'Get ready to duck: bouncers and the realities of ethnographic research on violent groups', *British Journal of Criminology*, 41, pp.536–48

Moore, M. (2001) *Stupid White Men*, London: Penguin

Moore, M. (2003) *Dude, Where's My Country?*, London: Penguin

Moore, S. (2002) *Social Welfare Alive!*, Cheltenham: Nelson Thornes

Morgan, I. (1999) *Power and Politics*, London: Hodder & Stoughton

Morley, D. (1980) *The Nationwide Audience*, London: BFI

Morris, L. (1993) *Dangerous Classes: The Underclass and Social Citizenship*, London: Routledge

Mosca, G. (1939) *The Ruling Class*, New York: McGraw Hill

Moser, K., Goldblatt, P., Fox, J. and Jones, D. (1990) 'Unemployment and mortality', in P. Goldblatt (ed.) *Longitudinal Study: Mortality and Social Organisation*, London: HMSO

Mouzelis, N. (1995) *Sociological Theory: What Went Wrong?*, London: Routledge

Murray, C. (1984) *Losing Ground*, New York: Basic Books

Murray, C. (1990) *The Emerging British Underclass*, London: Institute for Economic Affairs

Murray, C. (1994) *Underclass: The Crisis Deepens*, London: IEA

Myers, J. (1975) 'Life events, social integration and psychiatric symptomatology', *Journal of Health and Social Behaviour*, 16, pp.121–7

Myers, K. (2000) *Whatever Happened to Equal Opportunities in Schools?*, Buckingham: Open University Press

Myhill, D. (1999) 'Bad boys and good girls: patterns of interaction and response in whole class teaching', Exeter University School of Education paper

National Foundation for Educational Studies (2002) reported in Kendall, L. (2003) *Evaluation of the Gifted and Talented Strand* (Excellence in Cities Report 10/2003)

Navarro, V. (1977) *Medicine under Capitalism*, London: Martin Robertson

Navarro, V. (1986) *Crisis, Health and Medicine*, London: Tavistock

Nazroo, J.Y. (2001) *Ethnicity, Class and Social Health*, London: PSI

Nelken, D. (2002) 'White collar crime', in M. Maguire, R. Morgan and R. Reiner, *The Oxford Handbook of Criminology* (3rd edn), Oxford: Oxford University Press

Newton, K. (1969) 'A Critique of the Pluralist Model', *Acta Sociologica*, 12

Nightingale, C. (1993) *On the Edge*, New York: Basic Books

Oakley, A. (1974) *Housewife*, London: Allen Lane

Oakley, A. (1986) 'Feminism, motherhood and medicine – Who cares?', in J. Mitchell and A. Oakley (eds) *What is Feminism?*, Oxford: Basil Blackwell

Oakley, A. (1998) 'Gender, methodology and people's ways of knowing: some problems with feminism and the paradigm debate in social science', *Sociology*, 32, pp.707–31

O'Connor, J. (1973) *The Fiscal Crisis of the State*, New York: St Martin's Press

O'Donnell, M. (1991) *Race and Ethnicity*, Harlow: Longman

O'Donnell, M. and Sharpe, S. (2000) *Uncertain Masculinities: Youth, Ethnicity and Class in Contemporary Britain*, London: Routledge

Ofsted (2004) *Quality and Service: Annual Report of Her Majesty's Chief Inspector of Schools 2002/03*, London: The Stationery Office

Oliver, M. (1990) *The Politics of Disablement*, Basingstoke: Macmillan

Olsen, W. and Walby, S. (2004) *Modelling Gender Pay Gaps*, Manchester: Equal Opportunities Commission

O'Malley, P. (1992) 'Risk, power and crime prevention', *Economy and Society*, 21(3), pp.242–75

ONS (2004) *Labour Force Survey Spring 2004*, Office for National Statistics

Oppenheim, C. and Harker, L. (1996) *Poverty: The Facts* (3rd edn) London, CPAG

Owen, D.W. and Green, A.E. (1992) 'Labour market experience and occupational change amongst ethnic groups in Great Britain', *New Community*, 19, pp.7–29

Pakulski, J. and Waters, M. (1996) *The Death of Class*, London: Sage

Pareto, V. (1935) *The Mind and Society*, New York: Dover

Parker, H. (1974 [1st edn], 1992 [2nd edn]) *View from the Boys*, Aldershot: Ashgate

Parker, H., Aldridge, J. and Measham, F. (1998) *Illegal Leisure: the Normalization of Adolescent Recreational Drug Use*, London: Routledge

Parkin, F. (1972) *Class Inequality and Political Order*, St.Albans: Paladin

Parsons, T. (1937) *The Structure of Social Action*, New York: McGraw-Hill

Parsons, T. (1951/2) *The Social System*, Glencoe, IL: The Free Press

Parsons, T. (1963) 'On the concept of political power', *Proceedings of the American Philosophical Society*, 107

Parsons, T. (1964) *Essays in Social Theory*, New York: The Free Press

Parsons, T. (1975) 'The sick role and the role of the physician reconsidered', *Millbank Memorial Fund Quarterly: Health and Society*, 53, pp.257–78

Pascal, G. (1986) Social Policy: *A Feminist Analysis*, London: Tavistock

Patterson, S. (1965) *Dark Strangers*, Harmondsworth: Penguin

Pawson, R. (1989) *A Measure For Measures*, London: Routledge

Pearce, F. (1976) *Crimes of the Powerful*, London: Pluto Press

Pearce, F. and Tombs, S. (1998) *Toxic Capitalism: Corporate Crime and the Chemical Industry*, Aldershot: Ashgate

Penketh, L. and Ali, Y. (1997) 'Racism and social welfare', in M. Lavalette and A. Pratt (eds) *Social Policy: a Conceptual and Theoretical Introduction*, London: Sage

Phillips, C. and Brown, D. (1998) *Entry into the Criminal Justice System: A Survey of Police Arrests and their Outcomes*, Home Office Research Study 185, London: Home Office

Phillips, K. (2004) *American Dynasty; Aristocracy, Fortune and the Politics of Deceit in the House of Bush*, London: Penguin

Phillips, M. (1997) *All Must Have Prizes*, London: Little Brown

Phillips, M. (2001) *America's Social Revolution (Culture Wars)*, Civitas: Institute for the Study of Civil Society

Pilcher, J. and Whelehan, I. (2004) *50 Key Concepts in Gender Studies*, London: Sage

Pilgrim, D. and Rogers, A. (1999) *A Sociology of Mental Health and Illness* (2nd edn), Buckingham: Open University Press

Pirie, M. (2001) 'How exams are fixed in favour of girls', *The Spectator*, 20 January

Platt, T. and Takagi, P. (1977) 'Intellectuals for law and order; a critique of the new realists', *Crime and Social Justice*, 8, pp.1–16

Plummer, K. (2000) *Documents of Life*, Thousand Oaks, CA: Sage

Poulantzas, N. (1973) *Political Power and Social Classes*, London: New Left Books

Power, S. *et al.* (2003) *Education and the Middle Class*, Milton Keynes: Open University Press

Punch, M. (1996) *Dirty Business: Exploring Corporate Misconduct*, London: Sage

Putnam, R. (2000) *Bowling Alone*, New York: Simon and Schuster

Race, D. (ed.) (2003) *Leadership and Change in Human Services: Selected Readings from Wolf Wolfensberger*, London: Routledge

Rathje, W.L. and Murphy, C. (2002, originally 1992) *Rubbish! The Archaeology of Garbage*, Phoenix: University of Arizona Press

Reay, D. (1998) 'Rethinking social class: qualitative perspectives on gender and social class', *Sociology*, 32(2), pp.259–75

Rees, T. (1999) *Mainstreaming Equality in the European Union*, London: Routledge

Reid, I. (1998) *Class in Britain*, Cambridge: Polity Press

Reiman, J. (2003) *The Rich Get Richer and the Poor Get Poorer: Ideology, Class and Criminal Justice*, Harlow: Allyn & Bacon / Pearson Longman

Reiner, R. (1992) *The Politics of the Police*, Hemel Hempstead: Wheatsheaf

Reiner, R. (1997) 'Policy on police', in M. Maguire, R. Morgan, R. Reiner (eds) *The Oxford Handbook of Criminology* (2nd edn), Oxford: Oxford University Press

Reiss, A.J. (1961) 'The social integration of queers and peers', *Social Problems*, 9(2), p.102–20

Rex, J. and Moore, R. (1967) *Race, Community and Conflict*, Oxford: Oxford University Press

Rex, J. and Tomlinson, S. (1979) *Colonial Immigrants in a British City*, London: Routledge & Kegan Paul

Rikowski, G. (2001) *The Battle in Seattle: Its Significance for Education*, London: Tufnell Press

Roberts, K. (2001) *Class in Modern Britain*, Basingstoke: Palgrave

Roberts, K., Cook, F.G., Clark, S.C. and Semeonoff, E. (1977) *The Fragmentary Class Structure*, London: Heinemann

Robinson, P. (2001) 'Choosing justice', in *New Economy*, The Journal of the Institute of Public Policy Research

Rock, P. (1988) 'The present state of British criminology' in *The British Journal of Criminology*, 28(2)

Roker, D. (1994) 'Girls and Private Schools', *Sociology Review*, 4(2), Oxford: Philip Allan

Rosenhan, D.L. (1973/1982) 'On being sane in insane places', *Science*, 179, pp.250–8; also in M. Bulmer (ed.) (1982) *Social Research Ethics*, London: Holmes and Meier

Rosenthal, R. and Jacobson, L. (1968) *Pygmalion in the Classroom*, New York: Holt, Rinehart & Winston

Runciman, W. (1966) *Relative Deprivation and Social Justice*, London: Routledge

Rusche, G. and Kircheimer, O. (1939) *Punishment and Social Structure*, New York: Columbia University Press

Sapiro, V. (2002) *Women in American Society: An Introduction to Women's Studies* (4th edn), Mountain View, CA: Mayfield Publishing

Saraga, E. (1998) *Embodying the Social: Constructions of Difference*, London: Routledge

Saunders, P. (1979) *Urban Politics*, Harmondsworth: Penguin

Saunders, P. (1990) *Social Class and Stratification*, London: Routledge

Saunders, P. (1995) *Capitalism – A Social Audit*, Buckingham: Open University Press

Saunders, P. (1996) *Unequal but Fair? A Study of Class Barriers in Britain*, London: Institute of Economic Affairs

Savage, M. (1995) 'The middle classes in modern Britain', *Sociology Review*, 5(2), Oxford: Philip Allan

Savage, M. (2000) *Class Analysis and Social Transformation*, Buckingham: Open University Press

Savage, M. and Egerton, M. (1997) 'Social mobility, individual ability and the inheritance of class inequality', *Sociology*, 31(4)

Savage, M., Bagnall, G. and Longhurst, B. (2001) 'Ordinary, ambivalent and defensive class identities in the North West of England', *Sociology*, 35(4), pp.875–92

Savage, M., Barlow, J., Dickens, P. and Fielding, I. (1992) *Prosperity, Bureaucracy and Culture: Middle-class Formation in Contemporary Britain*, London: Routledge

Saville, J. (1957) 'The Welfare State: an historical approach', *New Reasoner*, 3

Scambler, G. and Hopkins, A. (1986) 'Being epileptic; coming to terms with stigma', *Sociology of Health and Illness*, 8, pp.26–43

Scarman, Lord (1981) *The Scarman Report*, Harmondsworth: Penguin

Scheff, T. (1966) *Being Mentally Ill: A Sociological Theory*, Chicago: Aldine

Scheff, T.J., Retzinger, S.M. and Ryan, M.T. (1989) 'Crime, violence and self-esteem: review and proposals', in A. Mecca, N.J. Smelser and J. Vaasconcellos (eds) *The Social Importance of Self-Esteem*, Berkeley: University of California

Schumacher, E.F. (1993, originally 1974) *Small Is Beautiful*, New York: Vintage

Schwartz, H. and Jacobs, J. (1979) *Qualitative Sociology: A Method to the Madness*, London: Collier-Macmillan

Scott MacEwen, A. (1994) 'Gender segregation and the SCELI research' in Scott MacEwen, A. (ed.) *Gender Segregation and Social Change*, Oxford: Oxford University Press

Scott, A. (1990) *Ideology and The New Social Movements*, London: Unwin Hyman

Scott, J. (1982) *The Upper Classes: Poverty and Privilege in Britain*, London: Macmillan

Scott, J. (1991) *Who Rules Britain?*, Cambridge: Polity Press

Scraton, P. (1985) *The State of the Police*, London: Pluto

Scraton, P. (1987) *Law, Order and the Authoritarian State: Readings in Critical Criminology*, Milton Keynes: Open University Press

Scraton, P. (1997) 'Whose "childhood"? What "crisis"?', in P. Scraton (ed.) *'Childhood' in 'Crisis'?*, London: UCL Press

Select Committee on Home Affairs (1999) *Examination of Witnesses*, (Questions 1060–1079) Wednesday, March 10 1999, Sir Paul Condon QPM, Mr Denis O'Connor QPM and Commander Richard Cullen

Sewell, T. (1996) *Black Masculinities and Schooling*, Stoke on Trent: Trentham Books

Sewell, T. (2000) 'Identifying the pastoral needs of African-Caribbean students: A case of "critical antiracism"', *Education and Social Justice*, 3(1)

Sharpe, R. and Green A. (1975) *Education and Social Control*, London: Routledge & Kegan Paul

Sharpe, S. (1976) *Just Like a Girl*, Harmondsworth: Penguin (2nd edn 1994)

Sharrock, W., Hughes, J. and Martin, P. (2003) *Understanding Modern Sociology*, London: Sage

Shaw, M., Dorling, D., Gordon, D. and Davey Smith, G. (1999) *The Widening Gap*, Bristol: Policy Press

Siim, B. (1990) 'Women and the welfare state', in C. Ungerson (ed.) *Gender and Caring*, Hemel Hempstead: Harvester Wheatsheaf

Simpson, R. and Cohen, C. (2004) 'Dangerous work: the gendered nature of bullying in the context of higher education', in *Gender Work and Organization*, (11)2, p.163

Skeggs, B. (1997) *Formations of Class and Gender*, London: Sage

Sklair, L. (2004) *Globalization: Capitalism and its Alternatives*, Oxford: Oxford University Press

Skolnick, J. (1966) *Justice without Trial*, New York: Wiley

Slapper, G. and Tombs, S. (1999) *Corporate Crime*, Harlow: Longman

Smart, C. (1990) 'Feminist approaches to criminology; or postmodern woman meets atavistic man', in L. Gelsthorpe and A. Morris (eds) *Feminist Perspectives in Criminology*, Milton Keynes: Open University Press

Smith, D. J. and Gray, J. (1985) *People and Police in London*, London: Gower

Solomos, J. (1993) *Race and Racism In Britain*, Basingstoke: Macmillan

Spicker, P. (1984) *Stigma and Social Welfare*, London: Croom Helm

Stedman Jones, G. (1971) *Outcast London*, Oxford: Oxford University Press

Stephen, C. and Cope, P. (2003) *Moving On to Primary: An Exploratory Study of the Experience of Transition from Pre-School to Primary*, London: Institute of Education

Stone, M. (1981) *The Education of the Black Child in Britain*, Glasgow: Fontana

Storr, M. (2002) 'Sociology and social movements: theories, analyses and ethical dilemmas', in P. Hamilton and K. Thompson (eds) *The Uses of Sociology*, Oxford: The Open University/Blackwell

Sukhnandan, I. and Lee, B. (1998) *Streaming, Setting and Grouping by Ability: A Review of the Literature*, Slough: NFER

Sutherland, E.H. (1940) 'White-collar criminality', *American Sociological Review*, 5, pp.1–12

Sutton, R.I. (1992) 'Feelings about a Disneyland visit: photography and the reconstruction of bygone emotions', Journal *of Management Enquiry*, 1, pp.278–87

Swann Report (1985) *Education for All*, London: HMSO

Swann, J. (1992) *Girls, Boys and Language*, London: Blackwell

Swann, J. and Graddol, D. (1994) 'Gender inequalities in classroom talk', in D. Graddol, J. Maybin and B. Stierer (eds) *Researching Language and Literacy in Social Context*, Clevedon: Multilingual Matters

Swartz, J. (1975) 'Silent killers at work', *Crime and Social Justice*, 3, pp.15–20

Sykes, G.M. and Matza, D. (1962) 'Techniques of neutralization – a theory of delinquency', in M.E. Wolfgang *et al.* (eds) *The Sociology of Crime and Delinquency*, New York: Wiley

Szasz, T. (1973 first published 1962) *The Myth of Mental Illness*, London: Paladin

Tarling, R. (1988) *Police Work and Manpower Allocation*, Paper 47, London: Home Office

Taylor, J., Walton, P. and Young, J. (1973) *The New Criminology*, London: Routledge

Thomas, W.I. and Znaniecki, F. (1918) *The Polish Peasant in Europe and America*, Chicago: University of Chicago Press

Thornton, S. (1995) *Club Cultures: Music, media and subcultural capital*, Cambridge: Polity Press

Thornton, S. (1997) 'General introduction', in K. Gelder and S. Thornton (eds) *The Subcultures Reader*, New York and London: Routledge

Thrasher, F. (1927) *The Gang*, Chicago: University of Chicago Press

Titmuss, R. (1964) *Essays on the Welfare State* (2nd edn), London: Allen and Unwin

Tizard, B. and Hughes, M. (1991) 'Reflections on young people learning', in G. Walford (ed.) *Doing Educational Research*, London: Routledge

Touraine, A. (1982) *The Voice and The Eye*, Cambridge: Cambridge University Press

Trades Union Congress (2005) *Poverty, Exclusion and British People of Pakistani and Bangladeshi Origin*, London: Trades Union Congress

Travis, A. (1999) 'Sex in the 90s: the young take a moral stand', *The Guardian*, 29 December, reprinted on p. 70 of Roberts, K. (2001) *Class in Modern Britain*, London: Palgrave

Troyer, R.J. and Markle, G.E. (1983) *Cigarettes: the Battle over Smoking*, New Brunswick, NJ: Rutgers University Press

Turner, B.S. (1994) 'From regulation to risk', in B.S. Turner (ed.) *Orientalism, Postmodernism and Globalism*, London: Routledge

Turner, B.S. (1995) *Medical Power and Social Knowledge*, London: Sage

Valier, C. (2001) *Theories of Crime and Delinquency*, Harlow: Longman

Virdee, S. (1997) 'Racial harassment', in T. Modood, R. Berthoud, J. Lakey, J. Nazroo, P. Smith, S. Virdee and S. Beishon *Ethnic Minorities in Britain: Diversity and Disadvantage*, London: PSI

Waddington, P.A.J., Stenson, K. and Don, D. (2004) 'In proportion – race, and police stop and search', *British Journal of Criminology*, 44(6)

Wadsworth, M.E.J. (1986) 'Serious illness in childhood associated with later life acheivement', in R.G. Wilkinson (ed.) *Class and Health: Research and Longitudinal Data*, London: Routledge and Keegan Paul

Waitzkin, H. (1979) 'Medicine, superstructure and micropolitics', *Social Science and Medicine*, 13a, pp.601–9

Walby, S. (1986) *Patriarchy at Work*, Cambridge: Polity Press

Walby, S. (1990) *Theorising Patriarchy*, Oxford: Blackwell

Walby, S. (1997) *Gender Transformations*, London: Routledge

Walker, C. (1993) *Managing Poverty: The Limits of Social Assistance*, London, Routledge

Waters, M. (1995) *The Death of Class*, London: Sage

Webb, A. and Wistow, G. (1982) *Whither State Welfare?*, London: Royal Institute of Public Administration

Webb, E.J., Campbell, D.T., Schwartz, R.D. and Sechrest, L. (1966) *Unobtrusive Measures: Nonreactive Measures in the Social Sciences*, Chicago: Rand McNally

Webb, E., Campbell, D., Schwartz, R. and Sechrest, L. (1981) *Nonreactive Measures in the Social Sciences* (2nd edn), Boston: Houghton Mifflin

Weber, M. (1947) *The Theory of Social and Economic Organisation*, New York: Free Press

Wedderburn, D. (1974) *Poverty, Inequality and Class Structure*, Cambridge: Cambridge University Press

Weeks, J. (1992) 'The body and sexuality', in R. Bocock and K. Thompson (eds) *Social and Cultural Forms of Modernity*, Cambridge: Polity Press

Weiner, G. (1995) 'Feminisms and education', in *Feminism and Education*, Buckingham: Open University Press

Weiner, G., Arnot, M. and David, D. (1997) *Is the Future Female? Female success, male disadvantage and changing gender patterns in education*, Cambridge: Polity Press

Wertz, R.W. and Wertz, D.C. (1981) 'Notes on the decline of midwives and the rise of medical obstetricians', in P. Conrad and R. Kerns (eds) *The Sociology of Health and Illness: Critical Perspectives*, New York: St Martin's Press

West, A. and Hind, A. (2003) *Secondary School Admissions In England: Exploring the extent of overt and covert selection*, Centre for Educational Research, Department of Social Policy, London School of Economics and Political Science.

West, C. and Zimmerman, D.H. (1991) 'Doing gender' in J. Larber and S.A. Farrell (eds) *The Social Construction of Gender*, London: Sage, pp.13–37

Westergaard, J. (1995) *Who Gets What: The hardening of class inequality in the late 20th century*, Cambridge: Polity Press

Westergaard, J. (1996) 'Class in Britain since 1979; facts, theories and ideologies', in D. Lee and B. Turner (eds) *Conflicts about Class: Debating Inequality in Later Industrialisation*, Harlow: Longman

Westwood, S. (1999) 'Representing gender', *Sociology Review*, September

Westwood, S. (2002) *Power and the Social*, London: Routledge

White, C. (2004) *The Middle Mind: Why Consumer Culture is Turning Us Into The Living Dead*, London: Penguin

Whyte, W.F. (1943) *Street Corner Society: The Social Structure of an Italian Slum*, Chicago: University of Chicago Press

Wilkins, L. (1964) *Social Deviance: Social Policy, Action and Research*, London: Tavistock

Wilkinson, R. (1996) *Unhealthy Societies: The Afflictions of Inequality*, Routledge: London

Willetts, D. (1992) *Modern Conservatism*, Harmondsworth, Penguin

Williams, F. (1989) *Social Policy: A Critical Introduction*, Cambridge: Polity

Williams, F. (1992) 'Somewhere over the rainbow: universality and diversity in social policy', *Social Policy Review*, 4

Willis, P. (1977) *Learning to Labour: How Working-class Kids get Working-class Jobs*, Farnborough: Saxon House

Willott, S.A. and Griffin, C.E. (1996) 'Men, masculinity and the challenge of long-term unemployment', in M. Mac an Ghaill (ed.) (1996) *Understanding Masculinities: Social Relations and Cultural Arenas*, Buckingham: Open University Press

Wilson, E.O. (1978) *On Human Nature*, London: Harvard

Wilson, J.Q. and Kelling, G. (1982) 'Broken windows', *Atlantic Monthly*, March

Wilson, W.J. (1996) *When Work Disappears*, New York: Random House

Winlow, S. (2004) 'Masculinities and crime', *Criminal Justice Matters*, 55(18)

Witz, A. (1992) *Professions and Patriarchy*, London: Routledge

Woods, P. (1979) *The Divided School*, London: RKP

Working Group on 14–19 Reform (2004) *14–19 Curriculum and Qualifications Reform: Final report of the working group on 14-19 reform*, London: DfES

Wright Mills, C. (1956) *The Power Elite*, Oxford: Oxford University Press

Wright, C. (1992) 'Early education: multi-racial primary classrooms', in D. Gill, B. Mayor and M. Blair (eds) *Racism and Education: Structures and Strategies*, London: Sage

Young, J. (1971) *The Drug Takers*, London: Paladin

Young, J. (1986) 'The failure of criminology: the need for a radical realism', in J. Young and R. Mathews (eds) *Confronting Crime*, London: Sage

Young, J. (1999) *The Exclusive Society: Social Exclusion, Crime and Difference in Late Modernity*, London: Sage

Zweig, E. (1961) *The Worker in an Affluent Society*, London: Heinemann

Sociology A2 for OCR

INDEX